◀ 33RD ANNUAL EDITION ▶

POET'S MARKET

2020

Robert Lee Brewer, Editor

WD
WRITER'S DIGEST
BOOKS

Poet's Market 2020. Copyright © 2019 Penguin Random House LLC. Published by Writer's Digest Books, an imprint of Penguin Random House LLC. Printed and bound in the United States of America. All rights reserved. No part of this book may be reproduced in any form or by any electronic or mechanical means including information storage and retrieval systems without permission in writing from the publisher, except by a reviewer, who may quote brief passages in a review.

www.penguinrandomhouse.com

ISSN: 0883-5470
ISBN-13: 978-1-4403-5495-3
ISBN-10: 1-4403-5495-2

This book contains information gathered at the time of publication from third parties, including telephone numbers, Internet addresses, and other contact information. Neither the publisher nor the author assume any responsibility for errors, or for the changes that occur after publication. Further, the publisher does not have any control over and does not assume any responsibility for author or third-party websites or their content.

Edited by: Robert Lee Brewer
Designed by: Wendy Dunning

CONTENTS

CRAFT OF POETRY

MARKETS

RESOURCES

INDEXES

FROM THE EDITOR

The great thing about *Poet's Market* is that it covers so many facets of the poetic world. First and foremost, it's a directory of publishing opportunities for poets with hundreds of listings for book and chapbook publishers, magazines and journals, contests and awards, and more. In fact, that's the reason most folks buy this book. But there's so much more!

This edition of *Poet's Market* includes advice on the business and promotion of poetry. There are articles on blogging, social media, a 30-day platform challenge, anatomy of a poetry book, how to increase odds of publication, and more.

Plus, there's an excellent craft section, especially the poetic forms article that now boasts more than 75 poetic forms. That's in addition to 101 poetry prompts, how to finish poems, freshen your poetry, and more.

So yeah, it's an incredible resource that's dedicated to helping poets get published. But beyond that, it's dedicated to connecting poets with the world of poetry.

Until next time, keep poeming!

Robert Lee Brewer
Senior Content Editor, *Poet's Market*
twitter.com/robertleebrewer

HOW TO USE POET'S MARKET

Delving into the pages of *Poet's Market* implies a commitment—you've decided to take that big step and begin submitting your poems for publication. How do you really begin, though? Here are eight quick tips to help make sense of the marketing/submission process:

1. BE AN AVID READER. The best way to hone your writing skills (besides writing) is to immerse yourself in poetry of all kinds. It's essential to study the masters; however, from a marketing standpoint, it's equally vital to read what your contemporaries are writing and publishing. Read journals and magazines, chapbooks and collections, anthologies for a variety of voices; scope out the many poetry sites on the Internet. Develop an eye for quality, and then use that eye to assess your own work. Don't try to publish until you know you're writing the best poetry you're capable of producing.

2. KNOW WHAT YOU LIKE TO WRITE—AND WHAT YOU WRITE BEST. Ideally, you should be experimenting with all kinds of poetic forms, from free verse to villanelles. However, there's sure to be a certain style with which you feel most comfortable, that conveys your true "voice." Whether you favor more formal, traditional verse or avant-garde poetry that breaks all the rules, you should identify which markets publish work similar to yours. Those are the magazines and presses you should target to give your submissions the best chance of being read favorably—and accepted.

3. LEARN THE "BUSINESS" OF POETRY PUBLISHING. Poetry may not be a high-paying writing market, but there's still a right way to go about the "business" of submitting and publishing poems. Learn all you can by reading writing-related books and magazines. Read the articles in this book for plenty of helpful advice. Surf the Internet for a wealth of sites filled with writing advice, market news and informative links.

4. RESEARCH THE MARKETS. Study the listings in *Poet's Market* thoroughly; these present submission guidelines, editorial preferences and editors' comments as well as contact information (names, postal and e-mail addresses, and website URLs). In addition, the indexes in the back of this book provide insights into what an editor or publisher may be looking for.

However, studying market listings alone won't cut it. The best way to gauge the kinds of poetry a market publishes is to read several issues of a magazine/journal or several of a press's books to get a feel for the style and content of each. Websites may include poetry samples, reviews, archives of past issues, exclusive content, and especially submission guidelines. (If the market is an online publication, the current issue will be available in its entirety.) Submission guidelines are pure gold for the specific information they provide. However you acquire them—by SASE or e-mail, online, or in a magazine itself—make them an integral part of your market research.

5. START SLOWLY. It may be tempting to send your work directly to *The New Yorker* or *Poetry*, but try sending your work to less competitive markets as well. As you gain confidence and experience (and increased skill in your writing), you can move on to more recognized markets. Although it may tax your patience, slow and steady progress is a proven route to success.

6. BE PROFESSIONAL. Professionalism is not something you should "work up to." Make it show in your first submission, from the way you prepare your manuscript to the attitude you project in your communications with editors.

Follow those guidelines. Submit a polished manuscript. Choose poems carefully with the editor's needs in mind. Such practices show respect for the editor, the publication and the process; and they reflect your self-respect and the fact that you take your work seriously. Editors love that; and even if your work is rejected, you've made a good first impression that could help your chances with your next submission.

7. KEEP TRACK OF YOUR SUBMISSIONS. First, do not send out the only copies of your work. There are no guarantees your submission won't get lost in the mail, misplaced in a busy editorial office, or vanish into a black hole if the publication or press closes down.

KEY TO ICONS & ABBREVIATIONS

⊘ market does not accept unsolicited submissions

✪ Canadian market

⟲ market located outside of the U.S. and Canada

$ market pays

⛌ tips to break into a specific market

◯ market welcomes submissions from beginning poets

◑ market prefers submissions from skilled, experienced poets; will consider work from beginning poets

● market prefers submissions from poets with a high degree of skill and experience

◎ market has a specialized focus

Create a special file folder for poems you're submitting. Even if you use a word processing program and store your manuscripts digitally, keep a hard copy file as well (and be sure to back up your electronic files).

Second, establish a tracking system so you always know which poems are where. This can be extremely simple: index cards, a chart created with word processing or database software, or even a simple notebook used as a log. (You can enlarge and photocopy the Submission Tracker in this book or use it as a model to design your own version.) Note the titles of the poems submitted (or the title of the collection if you're submitting a book/chapbook manuscript); the name of the publication, press, or contest; date sent; estimated response time; and date returned or date accepted. Additional information you may want to log: the name of the editor/contact, date the accepted piece is published and/or issue number of the magazine, type/amount of pay received, rights acquired by the publication or press, and any pertinent comments.

Without a tracking system, you risk forgetting where and when manuscripts were submitted. This is even more problematic if you simultaneously send the same manuscripts to different magazines, presses or contests. And if you learn of an acceptance by one magazine or publisher, you must notify the others that the poem or collection you sent them is no longer available. You run a bigger chance of overlooking someone without an organized approach. This causes hard feelings among editors you may have inconvenienced, hurting your chances with these markets in the future.

8. DON'T FEAR REJECTION. LEARN FROM IT. No one enjoys rejection, but every writer faces it. The best way to turn a negative into a positive is to learn as much as you can from your rejections. Don't let them get you down. A rejection slip isn't a permission slip to doubt yourself, condemn your poetry or give up.

Look over the rejection. Did the editor provide any comments about your work or reasons why your poems were rejected? Probably he or she didn't. Editors are extremely busy and don't necessarily have time to comment on rejections. If that's the case, move on to the next magazine or publisher you've targeted and send your work out again.

If, however, the editor has commented on your work, pay attention. It counts for something that the editor took the time and trouble to say anything, however brief, good or bad. And consider any remark or suggestion with an open mind. You don't have to agree, but you shouldn't automatically disregard the feedback, either. Tell your ego to sit down and be quiet, then use the editor's comments to review your work from a new perspective. You might be surprised by how much you'll learn from a single scribbled word in the margin—or how encouraged you'll feel from a simple "Try again!" written on the rejection slip.

Poem Title	Publication/ Contest	Editor/Contact	Date Sent	Date Returned	Date Acceptec	Date Published	Pay Recieved	Comments

SUBMISSION TRACKER

FREQUENTLY ASKED QUESTIONS

The following FAQ (Frequently Asked Questions) section provides the expert knowledge you need to submit your poetry in a professional manner. Answers to most basic questions, such as "How many poems should I send?," "How long should I wait for a reply?" and "Are simultaneous submissions okay?" can be found by simply reading the listings in the Magazines/Journals and Book/Chapbook Publishers sections. Also, see the Glossary of Listing terms.

Can I submit handwritten poems?

Usually, no. Now and then a publisher or editor makes an exception and accepts handwritten manuscripts. However, check the preferences stated in each listing. If no mention is made, assume your poetry should be typed or computer-printed.

How should I format my poems for online and print publications?

If you're submitting poems by regular mail (also referred to as postal mail or snail mail), follow this format:

Poems should be printed on white 8½×11 paper of at least 20 lb. weight. Left, right and bottom margins should be at least one inch. Starting ½ inch from the top of the page, type your name, address, telephone number, e-mail address and number of lines in the poem in the upper right corner, in individual lines, single-spaced. Space down about six lines and type the poem title, either centered or flush left. The title may appear in all caps or in upper and lower case. Space down another two lines (at least) and begin to type your poem. Poems are usually single-spaced, although some magazines may request double-spaced submissions. (Be alert to each market's preferences.) Double-space between stanzas. Type one poem to a page. For poems longer than one page, type your name in the upper left corner; on the next line, type a key word from the title of your poem, the page number, and indicate whether the stanza begins or is continued on the new page (i.e., MOTHMAN, Page 2, continue stanza or begin new stanza).

If you're submitting poems by e-mail:

In most cases, editors will request that poems be pasted within the body of your e-mail, not sent as attachments. Many editors prefer this format because of the danger of viruses, the possibility of software incompatibility, and other concerns associated with e-mail attachments. Editors who consider e-mail attachments taboo may even delete the message without opening the attachment.

Of course, other editors do accept, and even prefer e-mail submissions as attachments. This information should be clearly stated in the market listing. If it's not, you're probably safer submitting your poems in the body of the e-mail.

Note, too, the number of poems the editor recommends including in the e-mail submission. If no quantity is given specifically for e-mails, go with the number of poems an editor recommends submitting in general. Identify your submission with a notation in the subject line. While some editors simply want the words "Poetry Submission," others want poem titles. Check the market listing for preferences. Note: Because of spam, filters and other concerns, some editors are strict about what must be printed in the subject line and how. If you're uncertain about any aspect of e-mail submission formats, double-check the website (if available) for information or contact the publication for directions.

Some publications may also accept submissions only via online submission forms, such as Submittable or Submishmash. These typically require setting up a log in and then either pasting the poems into a text box or attaching a digital file.

What is a chapbook? How is it different from a regular poetry book?

A chapbook is a booklet, averaging 24-50 pages in length (some are shorter), usually digest-sized (5½×8½, although chapbooks can come in all sizes, even published within the pages of a magazine). Typically, a chapbook is saddle-stapled with a soft cover (card or special paper); chapbooks can also be produced with a plain paper cover the same weight as the pages, especially if the booklet is photocopied.

A chapbook is a much smaller collection of poetry than a full-length book (which runs anywhere from 50 pages to well over 100 pages, longer for "best of" collections and retrospectives). There are probably more poetry chapbooks being published than full-length books, and that's an important point to consider. Don't think of the chapbook as a poor relation to the full-length collection. While it's true a chapbook won't attract big reviews, qualify for major prizes or find national distribution through chain bookstores, it's a terrific way for a poet to build an audience (and reputation) in increments, while developing the kind of publishing history that may attract the attention of a book publisher one day.

Although some presses consider chapbooks through a regular submission process, many choose manuscripts through competitions. Check each publisher's listing for requirements, send for guidelines or visit the website (absolutely vital if a competition is involved), and check out some sample chapbooks the press has already produced (usually available from the press itself). Most chapbook publishers are as choosy as book publishers about the quality of work they accept. Submit your best poems in a professional manner.

How do I format a collection of poems to submit to a book/chapbook publisher?

Before you send a manuscript to a book/chapbook publisher, request guidelines (or consult the publisher's website, if available). Requirements vary regarding formatting, query letters and samples, length, and other considerations. Usually you will use 8½×11, 20 lb. white paper; set left, right and bottom margins of at least one inch; put your name and title of your collection in the top left corner of every page; limit poems to one per page (although poems certainly may run longer than one page); and number pages consecutively. Individual publisher requirements might include a title page, table of contents, credits page (indicating where previously published poems originally appeared) and biographical note.

If you're submitting your poetry book or chapbook manuscript to a competition, you must read and follow the guidelines. Failure to do so could disqualify your manuscript. Guidelines for a competition might call for an official entry form to accompany the submission, a special title page, a minimum and maximum number of pages, and specific formatting instructions (such as paginating the manuscript and not putting the poet's name on any of the manuscript pages).

What is a cover letter?

A cover letter is your introduction to the editor, telling him or her a little about yourself and your work. Most editors indicate their cover letter preferences in their listings. If an editor states a cover letter is "required," absolutely send one! It's also better to send one if a cover letter is "preferred." Experts disagree on the necessity and appropriateness of cover letters, so use your own judgment when preferences aren't clear in the listing.

A cover letter should be professional but also allow you to present your work in a personal manner. Keep your letter brief, no more than one page. Address your letter to the correct contact person. (Use "Poetry Editor" if no contact name appears in the listing.) Include your name, address, phone number and e-mail address (if available). If a biographical note is requested, include two to three lines about your background, interests, why you write poetry, etc. Avoid praising yourself or your poems in your letter (your submission should speak for itself). Include titles (or first lines) of the poems you're submitting. You may list a few of your most recent publishing credits, but no more than five; and keep in mind that some editors find publishing credits tiresome—they're more interested in the quality of the work you're submitting to them.

Show your familiarity with the magazine to which you're submitting: comment on a poem the magazine published, tell the editor why you chose to submit to her magazine, mention poets the magazine has published. Use a business-style format for a professional appearance and proofread carefully; typos, misspellings and other errors make a poor first impression. Remember that editors are people, too. Respect, professionalism and kindness go a long way in poet/editor relationships.

What is an SASE?

An SASE is a self-addressed, stamped envelope—and you should never send a submission by regular mail without one. Also include a SASE if you send an inquiry to an editor. If your submission is too large for an envelope (for instance, a bulky book-length collection of poems), use a box and include a self-addressed mailing label with adequate return postage paper-clipped to it.

What does it mean when an editor says "no previously published" poems?

If your poem appears anywhere in print for a public audience, it's considered "previously published." That includes magazines, anthologies, websites and online journals, and even printed programs (say for a church service, wedding, etc.). See the explanation for rights below, especially second serial (reprint) rights and all rights for additional concerns about previously published material.

One exception to the above guidelines is if your poem appears online in a private poetry forum, critique group, etc. As long as the site is private (i.e., a password is required to view and participate), your poem isn't considered "published." However, if your poem is printed on an online forum or bulletin board that's available for public viewing, even if you must use a password to post the poem or to comment, then your poem is considered "published" as far as rights are concerned.

What rights should I offer for my poems?

Editors usually indicate in their listings what rights they acquire. Most journals and magazines license first rights (a.k.a. first serial rights), which means the poet offers the right to publish the poem for the first time in any periodical. All other rights to the material remain with the poet. (Note that some editors state that rights to poems "revert to poets upon publication" when first rights are acquired.) When poems are excerpted from a book prior to publication and printed in a magazine/journal, this is also called first serial rights. The addition of North American indicates the editor is the first to publish a poem in a U.S. or Canadian periodical. The poem may still be submitted to editors outside of North America or to those who acquire reprint rights.

When a magazine/journal licenses one-time rights to a poem (also known as simultaneous rights), the editor has nonexclusive rights to publish the poem once. The poet may submit that same poem to other publications at the same time (usually markets that don't have overlapping audiences).

Editors/publishers open to submission of work already published elsewhere seek second serial (reprint) rights. The poet is obliged to inform them where and when the poem previously appeared so they can give proper credit to the original publication. In essence, chapbook or book collections license reprint rights, listing the magazines in which poems previously appeared somewhere in the book (usually on the copyright page or separate credits page).

If a publisher or editor requires you to relinquish all rights, be aware that you're giving up ownership of that poem or group of poems. You cannot resubmit the work elsewhere, nor can you include it in a poetry collection without permission or by negotiating for reprint rights to be returned to you. It's highly recommended that poets refuse such an arrangement.

What is a copyright? Should I have my poems copyrighted before I submit them for publication?

Copyright is a proprietary right that gives you the power to control your work's reproduction, distribution and public display or performance, as well as its adaptation to other forms. In other words, you have the legal right to the exclusive publication, sale or distribution of your poetry. What's more, your "original works of authorship" are protected as soon as they are "fixed in a tangible form of expression," i.e., written down or recorded. Since March 1989, copyright notices are no longer required to secure protection, so it's not necessary to include them on your poetry manuscript. Also, in many editors' minds, copyright notices signal the work of amateurs who are distrustful and paranoid about having work stolen.

If you still want to indicate copyright, use the © symbol or the word copyright, your name and the year. If you wish, you can register your copyright with the Copyright Office (directions and form available for download from www.copyright.gov). Since paying per poem is costly and impractical, you may prefer to copyright a group of unpublished poems for that single fee.

HOW TO INCREASE YOUR ODDS OF PUBLICATION

by Sage Cohen

Writing poetry is an art, and so is the process of submitting your poems for publication. If you'd like to increase your odds of getting noticed and getting published, this article can help you align your best work with the right opportunities—so you can give your poems the chance they deserve.

IDENTIFY THE RIGHT PUBLICATIONS FOR YOUR POETRY

You'll have the greatest odds of publication when you submit your poems to journals or contests that are most suited to your work—and therefore most likely to appreciate it. If you're not sure how to identify such possibilities, consider the following:

Read the work of poets you love

A good way to get a feel for publishing possibilities is by reviewing the acknowledgments pages of the poetry collections you admire. If you connect to a particular poet's work, chances are good that your poetry could also be well suited to the journals where s/he has been published.

Do your due diligence

Let's say you've collected a list of possible journals and contests based on the tip above. And let's say you've never sent out work for publication before. You can research here in *Poet's Market* to learn more about how your poetry and these opportunities might line up. For example, you'll want to submit only to journals that say they publish work by emerging as well as established poets. You'll want to confirm that contest submission fees and guidelines are in alignment with what you're willing to send and spend. And you may want to make sure your themes, poetic forms, and approach to language are compatible with the publication's description of what it is seeking. I also suggest learning what you can about the editors or contest judge(s)—and reading their poetry, if possible, so you get a feeling for their personal aesthetic.

Always experience a journal before submitting

Before submitting your work to a publication, purchase its latest issue or view content online to get a sense of the poets and poems it features. Also consider how the publication's front cover, inside art, website design, production, paper quality, and font choice create a particular kind of experience. If you can imagine seeing your poetry in these pages, that's a good indication that the journal or site may be the right fit for you.

Track what you learn to grow your knowledge base

I suggest creating a simple system—a document, binder, or folder—where you track what you've learned about each publication and record your thinking about how your poems align or do not align. This way, you'll have a growing knowledge base about the poetry market—and how various opportunities may be suited to your goals—as you investigate, submit and publish over time.

CHOOSE THE RIGHT POEM/S

When you've chosen a publication or contest to which you'd like to submit, it's time to gather the poems for this opportunity. Consider running the poems you are considering through these filters of inquiry:

Does something significant or resonant happen?

Poems get editors' attention when they introduce a new possibility, provide a palpable experience or revelation, and say something in a way it has never been spoken (or written) before. Ask yourself:

- What happens in this poem? (Or, if the poem is nonnarrative, do the language, sound, and/or imagery create the kind of experience or journey I intended?)
- If this poem is about or addressed to someone I know, does it also reveal something meaningful or relevant to people outside of the dynamic?
- What is discovered or transformed or revealed?

Because it can be tricky to experience your own, highly subjective material objectively, you may want to share your poems with a reader or two you trust and ask these questions of them. If you're not sure you are creating an experience that has impact or resonance, your poem may not yet be ready for publication.

Have I found something fresh to say about a familiar theme?

If you're writing about a historical person or event or one that's been covered in the news in recent years, chances are good that most readers will have a good handle on the facts. To ensure that your poem makes an impact, ask yourself:

- What happens in this poem that is fresh, surprising, and different than the information already available on this topic?
- How is this poem departing from the work of "reporting" and moving into the territory of "illuminating"?
- How is this event or person serving as a leaping-off point for my own inquiry or discovery about myself, history, the natural world, or the human condition?

IS MY WORK AS POLISHED AS POSSIBLE?

These 10 revision tips may help you identify opportunities to nip, tuck, and shine. Ask yourself:

1. Could I trim exposition at the beginning or summary information at the end that is not serving the poem?
2. Could I use a different voice to influence the experience of this poem? (For example, consider changing a third-person voice into the first person and see if this shift in intimacy is of benefit.)
3. Could my similes and metaphors be more distilled or powerful? If I've used an extended metaphor, does it hold up throughout the poem?
4. Where can I bring more energy to the language I've used? Can I use more active language to communicate similar ideas? Can modifiers be cut?
5. What if I changed past-tense verbs to the present tense (or vice versa)?
6. How might I shape the poem (line length, stanza breaks, white space) to more fully enact the emotion and rhythm of its content?
7. Are punctuation and capitalization and verb tense consistent? Would different choices (such as removing punctuation or capitalization) improve the experience?
8. Is there a music of repeating sounds throughout the poem? What words could I replace to create a more cohesive sound experience?
9. Are there opportunities to break lines in ways that give attention to important words or pace the momentum of the narrative more powerfully?
10. How might the title better encapsulate and add dimension to the experience of the poem? Could some of the exposition cut in step one be used to set the context of the poem in its title?

ARRANGE YOUR POEMS INTENTIONALLY

The order of the poems you've submitted can make a difference in an editor's experience and opinion of your work—even if you're just submitting three to five poems. Think about the arrangement as a single composition that provides a coherent reading journey. Where do you want the reader to start—and finish? How do you want them to enter the realm of your poetry, and how are you intending to send them off?

MAKE SUBMISSION GUIDELINES YOUR BIBLE

Every literary publication and contest will offer detailed guidelines about how and when they want to receive poems. Your job is to follow every single detail of those guidelines fanatically to ensure you don't rule yourself out with a simple oversight. Because it's easy to miss a detail when scanning instructions online, I recommend printing out the submission guidelines for any opportunity and then checking off each requirement as you meet it. Specifically:

- Follow simultaneous submission instructions. Some publications accept simultaneous submissions (meaning that you've sent the same poems to more than one publication for consideration at the same time), and others don't. Be careful to understand and honor each journal's parameters.
- Get your timing right. Publications have contest deadlines and specific reading windows. Send your work in advance of the specified deadline.
- Choose poems that fit. Ensure that you have chosen poems that match any specific requirements, such as: theme, form, length (number of lines or pages), number of poems allowed or required.
- Be deliberate about where you include your name. Some publications read and choose poems "blind," others don't. Be sure to understand whether the publication wants identifying information on the poems or not—and follow these guidelines carefully.
- Double-check the mailing address and editor names. No editor wants to see his or her name misspelled or receive mail addressed to his or her predecessor. It's also a good idea to confirm the gender of the person you are addressing if you have any doubt.
- Follow binding requirements. Publications often specify whether they want paper clips, staples or loose pages.
- Provide SASE (self-addressed, stamped envelope) if this is required or requested by the publication. Follow whatever process is requested.
- Include a check if you are submitting to a contest with a required reading fee. Make sure you make it out to the organization as requested in the amount required and specify the name of the contest to which you are submitting.

FORMAT, PROOF, AND POLISH

First impressions are often the last impression. Think of your submission package as a gift that an editor or selection committee will enjoy opening and experiencing—whether you're submitting online or by mail:

- Use a standard font that is easy to read—such as Times New Roman, Garamond, or Calibri—using 12-point font, unless instructed otherwise. Your priority should be legibility and ease for the person(s) who will be considering your poem.
- Unless you are doing so for a very specific reason, think twice about bolding or italicizing fonts. Let your images, word choice, and line breaks do the work of creating emphasis.
- Print your poems on white, unrumpled, and unscented paper.
- Ensure your toner is working or that your photocopies are clear and crisp.

WRITE A COVER LETTER THAT CONNECTS

Your cover letter should first and foremost provide whatever information is requested in the submission guidelines, if any. In the absence of specific instruction, write a concise note that covers the following:

- Explain you are submitting poems for [name of contest, issue, or general consideration].
- Describe in a sentence or two what you admire about the publication and why you chose to submit your work—if you have something authentic to say. Or, if you've had a previous communication with an editor (such as, they sent an encouraging rejection with a note inviting you to submit again in the future) you can mention that here.
- Lists the names of the poems being submitted. If this is a simultaneous submission, it is good form to mention this and confirm you intend to follow whatever process this publication has requested in its submission guidelines.
- Provide a brief biographical paragraph that describes key publishing or education highlights to reflect your literary experience and expertise. If you haven't published yet or don't have anything else relevant to report, no need to say anything here.
- Be polite and gracious.

Remember, this is a business communication. Some mistakes to avoid:

- Do not provide explanations about why you chose these poems for submission, why you wrote them, what they mean to you or your family, or how you have revised them.
- Do not advise editors about when you expect to hear back from them.

- Do not send a follow-up letter with a batch of poems that are edited versions of a previous submission.
- Do send a follow-up letter to withdraw any poems you have submitted as soon as they have been accepted elsewhere.

Over time, you'll get more efficient and adept with this process. Preparing your poems for submission will get faster, easier, and more automatic as you know what steps to take and mistakes to avoid. Your commitment to consistently putting your best work forward—and willingness to learn from the feedback you get along the way—will give you the very best odds of publication.

SAGE COHEN is the author of *Writing the Life Poetic* and *The Productive Writer*, both from Writer's Digest Books, and the poetry collection *Like the Heart, the World*. She holds an MFA in creative writing from New York University and a BA from Brown University. Sage has won first place in the Ghost Road Press poetry contest, been nominated for a Pushcart Prize and published a number of articles in *Writer's Digest* magazine. In 2011, she judged the Writer's Digest contest for non-rhyming poetry. To learn more about Sage, visit pathofpossibility.com.

READY YOUR WORK FOR PUBLICATION

9 Techniques for Perfecting Poems

....

by Lauren Camp

Poetry is a sublime art form, but making it takes time. Breathtaking poems generally emerge from a slow, considered approach and a long gestation period.

Writing technical and magazine articles taught me structure, concision, and reporting strategies. Poetry teaches me to analyze the colors of each thought, and to look for ways to sculpt the statement. If every poem came out perfect right away, the experience would feel too clipped. I want the project to take a while, to "marinate" and evolve into language both exquisite and weirdly unexpected.

To ensure your poems get picked out from the editors' slush pile, take some time to prime your work for publication. Here are nine hands-on, critical techniques to help you assess your poems from different perspectives, and improve your writing.

TIP #1—LISTEN TO MILES DAVIS.

On his 1959 album *Kind of Blue,* trumpeter and composer Miles Davis named a composition "So What." Ask that question of your poem. *So what* if you have a distinctive voice? *So what* if there's melody? Why should others care about your poem?

To create a poem with staying power, you have to be able to answer one tough question: is this worth saying? If you are writing the poem just to share an experience, the poem isn't done yet. Consider what the experience taught you. Would an audience be interested in that? Most experiences are universal in some way. Give readers an insight that they can connect to their lives.

TIP #2—EAT THE BANANA.

Think hard about "the."

"The" means "the one and only." The ultimate. The whole enchilada. The all and every-thing of a subject.

Look at every single place you've used it. Is this what you're trying to infer? Did you really sit on "the" park bench? (I can think of a lot of benches—and a lot of parks). Did you really eat "the" banana? The one and only?

You see what I mean. It's easy to say it and write it, but when you start picking apart what you mean…well, maybe you shouldn't use "the." Try substituting "a"—a park bench, a banana, a trip to Peru—or see if the poem works without any articles at all.

TIP #3—STOP GOING AND DOING.

Another easy fix is to shorten and tighten verbs. Why are you "going" when you could just "go"—or better yet, "fly," "meander," or "trudge"?

Gerunds ("ing" words) are so kind. They whisper over readers with a tinge of apology. They are almost always less effective than a lean verb—one without fat. Be insistent in your writing for a change. Make those verbs muscular. Ask them to really do something, to lift the line. Be more authoritative than you think you can; stop "ing-ing" around.

After you've made these changes, re-read your lines out loud in a big, vigorous, and certain voice. How does the poem sound now?

Clearly, you can't cut all "ing" words all the time. Look for a balance of tensile strength with breathing space.

TIP #4—PULL YOURSELF OUT.

We all write about ourselves in some way, but sometimes poems are just loaded with … well, us.

How many times do you have to say "I" for your readers to know the poem is happening to you? I bet you could safely eliminate some references to self, and readers would still be clued in. Try it. Take one "I" out, and see if it matters. Take out another. Don't forget to read out loud to make sure you haven't lost the flow - or the human quality of the poem.

Remove yourself just enough that you aren't ever-present, but be careful. If you take yourself completely out, the poem will seem choppy and abstract.

TIP #5—LOOK FOR SOFT SPOTS.

My students step into soft spots all the time. So do I, and you will, too, because you must write first for you, and then, revise for someone else.

Where readers sink is the quicksand of the poem. The weight of messy language pulls them down. Sometimes our writing is thick and circular—especially if we are trying to say too much. Because we often write to figure something out for ourselves, rather than writing what we already know, we may be uncertain how to draw the map of what we're exploring. What a writer thinks is solid might not always be so to a reader.

How can you avoid these spots? Let the poem sit for a while. The irony of this technique is that the quick answer to finding your soft spots is time. Let the poem exist on your hard drive, unopened, until it becomes a little unfamiliar to you—one month, three months even, if you can manage that.

Then, when a sufficient amount of time has passed, read it. Anything that is confusing or too abstract will now be evident. You will see where you have taken readers on a side journey, and forgotten to bring them back. Because the poem is again new to you, you will know if you have complicated its map, and if there is a more direct route.

You want readers to get somewhere specific: your revelation. Take out references that send them to the wrong places.

TIP #6—WEAR THE STRONG SUIT OF SPECIFICITY.

Be particular in your writing. Give details without drowning your readers in adjectives. Tell us which street, which store, the hour it happened, the season, the type of insect you heard in the air, the color of buttons on his shirt.

Israeli poet Yehuda Amichai once wrote that you must "put real things in your poems." Ask the poem every possible question you can. Is everything defined precisely? One of my students wrote about how, as a young child, she was instructed to put her small, cold hand inside the pocket of her mother's wool coat as a way for her mother to keep her close on dangerous urban streets. Holding fast to the pocket, the girl felt the nubbly texture. Because she described it, I could also feel the pocket lining, and the sense of security that came with it.

TIP #7—SMASH IT.

Auguste Rodin advised young sculptors to stop gently picking at the clay and plaster of their sculpture when something wasn't going well. Instead, he encouraged them to "drop it on the floor and see what it looks like then."

It's easy to draw an analogy between this and poetry revising. Both creative acts sometimes require drastic changes to find the form your piece needs. Revision is all about seeing new options, but you might not be able to do this when you're trying to stay true to your initial intent.

If you are convinced that a poem isn't working and will never work, you are free to do anything at all to it. Construction workers often relish demolition work. Why not use their approach? Destruction frees the poem of the ghost of its earlier structure. Rather than remedying little parts, rebuild the whole.

Pick a line or phrase that seems strong. Let that chosen line become a new jumping off place, and jump in an unexpected direction.

Of course, if you're an archivist, and the idea of tossing big parts of the poem gives you hives, by all means, save the gems. (I collect the lines that I still like in a separate document.) But eviscerate them if they don't serve the poem you're revising.

TIP #8—INTERLACE.

Have you ever tried splicing two poems together? In a way, it's like braiding hair. You pull a line from here and a line from there, again and again, until you have created a more complex structure, woven with new thoughts.

Take those good lines, and plait them into another poem. If they are on the same subject, aha! an easy fit. If not, well … your job as poet becomes more challenging. How to match them together … ?

In the mid-1960s, John Lennon wrote lyrics inspired by a news headline about a car accident and other events that were current at the time. His musical partner Paul McCartney had written a simple ditty about a man heading out late on a bus, and moving into a hazy dream. These were totally separate stories, neither quite complete in itself. Twined together, the lyrics became "A Day in the Life," an intriguing song on the *Sgt. Pepper's Lonely Hearts Club Band* album.

Lennon said, "I had the bulk of the song and the words, but [Paul] contributed this little lick floating around in his head that he couldn't use for anything."

Isn't that how it is sometimes with a poem—a perfect phrase that needs a new home? Move it to another poem. Encourage it to become a strand in something larger, something with a separate music—maybe even one you didn't realize could exist. Take it from two lyrical masters; poetry interspersed with poetry can double the emotional impact.

TIP #9—CHANGE THE PACING.

Revision is about taking innumerable steps to write the best possible poem. One technique worth trying is to change the speed of the poem—how fast or slow it travels on the page.

If you're writing about something urgent or disturbing, and you want readers to keep moving through the poem—if, in fact, you believe readers should be nearly breathless when reading, try enjambment. In other words, don't let your lines end comfortably with commas or periods. Don't let anyone stop reading. Keep the thought in motion.

Think like a movie director for a thriller. When one of the characters is in danger, you want to design the scene to keep viewers on the edge of their seats, blood racing. How will you do this? Lighting, sound … whatever it takes to keep the suspense constant.

That's what you're after as a poet, too. Make your readers keep hurrying ahead to the next line, and the next. This doesn't mean you can't use punctuation. Instead, place those punctuation marks in the middle of lines, where periods are significantly less weighty and powerful.

For a different way to speed up, you might try incorporating a full line of monosyllables. You'll get a ticker-tape effect from the rapid short words, which will hurtle readers through the line.

What if you want to move more slowly, and let readers revel in your images? Lines that are end-stopped (with periods) allow them to pause deeply. Stanza breaks take this even further—a maximum full stop. A complete resting place.

So, try switching the stride of your poem. As the writer, you know whether it should meander along or hurtle forth; now you just need to make your line decisions fit the mood of the piece, so readers know how to "hear" the poem.

It can take a lot of work to get a poem right, but what seems like discipline can also be a joy. My students call this work "revisioning." Whatever techniques you employ, don't be too controlling. Remember to allow spontaneity to also guide the work.

LAUREN CAMP is the author of the poetry collection *This Business of Wisdom* (West End Press), an interdisciplinary artist, and an educator. Her poems have appeared in *J Journal, Linebreak, Beloit Poetry Journal,* and *you are here,* among other journals. Her work gets accepted almost as frequently as it gets turned down, which she considers good odds. She has also guest edited special sections for *World Literature Today* (on international jazz poetry) and for *Malpaís Review* (on the poetry of Iraq). Lauren blogs about poetry at *Which Silk Shirt.* On Sundays, she hosts "Audio Saucepan," a weekly global music and poetry program on Santa Fe Public Radio. www.laurencamp.com

LAUNCHING A BOOK

Creating and Hosting a Successful Book Launch Party for Your Poetry

by Terri Kirby Erickson

"Nobody puts Baby (i.e. poetry) in a corner," is a line made famous by Patrick Swayze in the movie, *Dirty Dancing*, and also comes to mind as I begin planning the release of a poetry collection, an event typically referred to as a book launch party. When combining the words "poetry" and "launch," however, many people, even poets, tend to think in terms of bottle rockets in the backyard, often choosing a small, free venue like the nether regions of a bookstore or a coffee shop. They might send a few dozen e-mails to friends and family, hoping for the best when it comes to turnout and book sales. Others like myself, fancy a more NASA-style launch.

Hundreds of people have attended my book launch parties to date. In fact, around 250 of them attended the party for my fourth collection, *A Lake of Light and Clouds* (Press 53), and they weren't all blood relatives! There were even some "notables" there, like Ron Powers, the Pulitzer Prize-winning journalist and author who introduced me to the audience, as well as renowned fiction writer John Ehle and his wife, Rosemary Harris, star of stage and screen. My middle school math teacher was there too, would you believe? I'm sure he never recovered from trying to teach me algebra, but there he was as ever, supportive and kind.

How do I do it? How do I convince all these people from so many walks of life to come to what is basically a poetry reading with extra sprinkles? Well, there are millions of people around the world who love poetry, only some of them don't know it yet. That's where we come in—the poets whose work is waiting to be read. After the feelings are felt, the images captured, the poems gathered into a collection, the contract for publication signed and sealed, it's all about marketing unless you want your books to collect dust on bookstore shelves, your party venue empty of guests. And for poetry books published by small presses, the main marketer is you, the writer.

MAKING FRIENDS

Long before my first book was published, I was out in the community, making (and keeping) friends. I love people, always have, always will. I'm interested in their stories and listen intently to what they have to say. I care about others and hope it shows. If they happen to be artists or writers, I do my best to attend their events and buy their books, photographs, or artwork when I can afford to do so. We meet for lunch, talk on the phone, and generally keep up with each other, in some cases for over 50 years. (Two of my buddies were in my first grade class!) These are people who will, as a rule, support your efforts even if all you do is make tiny animals out of Play-doh and have viewing parties in your kitchen.

And after I started writing poetry for publication, I met more and more fellow writers, eventually joining the North Carolina Writers' Network and the North Carolina Poetry Society, both of which advertise members' work and writing accolades. I was also building my writing resume so I could list enough publications and prizes in my author "bio" to convince potential readers my books might be worth the price printed on the cover. Just as important, I talk to people who come to readings, doing my best to be accessible, friendly, upbeat, courteous, and down-to-earth. A sense of humor is helpful, also, and when selling your own books, the correct change!

Forming and nurturing personal and professional relationships is essential to the success of your book launch party. Without social networking, you'll be struggling to persuade people to attend unless Beyoncé is one of the names on your entertainment roster. Good will is a major component of people wanting to support your creative efforts, so sequestering yourself from the public 364 days of the year and expecting them to be there for you when you emerge from your writing cocoon, is unrealistic. Also if, like me, you don't have unlimited funds, you'll need to save your money in order to make your dream celebration come true. You can spend as little or as much as you wish, but as most of us know, even small and intimate gatherings aren't free.

So let's say you have more friends and connections than you know what to do with, have been active in the community, and your work has been widely published. Say your first (or even fifth!) book is coming out and you're thinking about organizing a launch. But you aren't satisfied with a modest gathering and minimal book sales. You want to go large (or at least, not small!) and you've got time and money to do it. In fact, you dream of having so many people vying to purchase copies of your new book, you need an off-duty police officer to direct traffic to the signing table. If you aren't sure how to make it happen or whether such a thing is even possible, let me assure you, (and I know you've heard these words before!), if I can do it, so can you!

PARTNERING WITH CHARITY

One of the best things I've ever done is to partner with a charity for these events, donating ten percent of every book sold during my book launch parties, to people in need. Donating to charity isn't part of my marketing strategy, but I love helping others and it does seem to attract civic-minded folks who've never heard of me or my work, to an event they might not otherwise attend. And if they also come away from my (or your!) book launch as poetry fans when all the poetry they've ever read was The Rime of the Ancient Mariner in their high school English class, so much the better. The more people who fall in love with poetry, the more people who buy and read our books—and being read is what I most desire, followed by a pony! (Well, my cousin had one when we were kids and it didn't seem fair at all...).

After choosing a local charity and meeting with its representatives, I begin, well in advance of my next book release, searching for a suitable venue. Generally speaking, this will be your biggest expense. Figure out how "big" you want to go, what you can afford to pay, and call around town for quotes from various celebration settings that fit your parameters. Art galleries are nice if you want someplace classy, but not necessarily gigantic. And bear in mind, weeknights are usually less costly than weekends when it comes to rental fees. Once you decide on a location, make sure you aren't competing with other major events. Check local calendars to find out what else is happening in your area before picking a date for your party.

ATTENTION TO DETAIL

Also, don't forget you'll need someone to set up chairs and tables. Many places have employees who do this, but if not, you'll have to rely on people you know and can enlist to help. Cleanup is part of the package so find out if you're responsible for tidying up the place after the party. If you need a podium, ask if one is provided. And if the room is fairly large, find out if they have a sound system. If not, you'll have to figure something out. I'm about as technically-minded as Bambi, but if you're like me, you've probably got friends who can help or advise you. Anyway, do address these issues and whatever else you can think of, before signing a contract with any venue.

Next, if you're thinking of providing entertainment besides you reading your work, it's good to book these folks way in advance. Do you want live music? Flamenco dancers? Trapeze artists? If so, who do you (or people in your "circle") know who won't charge three arms and six legs to perform? Maybe there's an "arts" college nearby, with talented students who are looking for performing experience. Call the school. Ask around. And do you know any local celebrities? Ask if he or she would be willing to introduce you to the crowd at your launch party. If you know this individual well (or know someone who does!), he or she might not charge you much or anything at all, particularly if this person is a fan of your work. Or you can ask your publisher, who will no doubt be happy to be your emcee.

We do provide refreshments at my parties because, well, people get hungry and thirsty. Sam's Club is a great resource, and Costco. You can gather copious amounts of food and drink for reasonable prices at these places. And don't forget paper plates, cups, and napkins. One year, a close friend catered one of my parties, providing refreshments for hundreds of people. Another year, a friend funded the entire cost of the venue, while others have simply handed me checks to use for "whatever" when party time rolled around. I refer to the kind souls who have donated money, time, and services as angels, and hope you have an angel or two in your life as well!

Another thing to plan for … If your publisher or his/her assistants are going to sell your books, great, you're covered. If not, you'll need someone you trust to do this. I suggest you keep a table filled with books and have someone sell them throughout the evening. Also, hiring a professional photographer is a great idea if it's in your budget. You can always use these quality photographs for promotional purposes later on. Several of my friends are professionals and for the past few parties, one has taken photos for the price of a signed book. If you don't have a photographer friend handy, however, ask your buddies for copies of any photos they might take during the evening. You'll be glad you did.

GETTING PEOPLE TO ATTEND

So now you have everything you need to throw an awesome party, all except for guests! That's where marketing comes in. Hopefully, you began the party-planning process months in advance so you have plenty of time for advertising. You'll need a professional headshot, a high resolution photo of your book cover, and all the details you want to share about your party within reach. Write and send out press releases to local newspapers. Contact print and online magazines, and inquire about interviews. Call radio stations and ask for air time/interviews to promote your event. Place information about it on every online event calendar you can find.

If you use Facebook or other social media, advertise your party there. Print signs/fliers, even if they're just on copy paper, and put them up in libraries, bookstores, anyplace that has a bulletin board and will let you use it. Send e-mails, invitations, and save-the-date notifications to everyone you ever met since you were born. You have to invite a lot of people to get 100-200 attendees or more! So don't be shy! Invite cashiers at the drugstore, sales clerks at the mall, the guy who installed your cable. You'll be surprised (and grateful for!) whoever shows up.

The most important advice I can give you, however, is to relax and have fun. While there will always be times when most writers find themselves in some dimly lit corner, reading poems to three people (one of whom wandered in by mistake) and a potted plant—tonight is different. Tonight, you and your poetry are center stage because of your hard work and ability to persuade scores of individuals, perhaps some not so keen on poetry but willing to give it a chance, that your book launch party is THE place to be! And if your poems are good, your demeanor genuine, warm, and welcoming, and the party as amazing as you envisioned, just be sure to have extra pens ready at the signing table, because you'll definitely need them!

TERRI KIRBY ERICKSON is the author of five full-length collections of award-winning poetry, including her latest collection, *Becoming the Blue Heron* (Press 53). Her work has appeared in the *2013 Poet's Market*, Ted Kooser's American Life in Poetry, *Asheville Poetry Review, Atlanta Review, Boston Literary Magazine, Connotation Press, Cutthroat, North Carolina Literary Review, storySouth, The Southern Poetry Anthology,* The Writer's Almanac with Garrison Keillor, Verse Daily, and many others. Awards include the Joy Harjo Poetry Prize, Nazim Hikmet Poetry Award, Atlanta Review International Publication Prize, and a Nautilus Book Award. See terrikirbyerickson.com or Press53.com for more information about her poetry.

THE ORGANIZED POET

by Patricia Kennelly

If you're like many poets I've talked with, it's not uncommon to have your poems everywhere. My desktop held overflowing notebooks, file folders and piles of random pieces of paper, scribbled with favorite words, lines, and poem starts. My computer's desktop wasn't any better. Although I knew most of my work was saved, my lack of organization made finding a particular poem time-consuming.

This wasn't too much of a problem until I started submitting my body of work. I struggled with getting my work to the right market. I missed good opportunities and important deadlines and created unnecessary stress by entering my poems at the last minute. Finding contests, markets and journals was the easy part; tracking down a poem or trying to read my illegible note about a "must enter" contest became challenging.

Most organizational experts agree that organizing any part of your life will save you time, money and help to eliminate stress. So why do so many poets have resistance to organizing their work? Some poets think that organization is the opposite of creativity and that being too businesslike will stifle their voices. I found the opposite to be true. Working on organization fueled my desire to write poetry and get my poems published.

When I decided to take ownership of my body of work and organize, I naturally approached the submission process in a professional manner. Doing the hard work ahead of time meant I had more time to find and research markets. The result? More published pieces and a clearer picture of where I wanted to go with my poetry.

Whatever system you choose (pen and paper, computer based, online or a combination of all) make sure it's one that will work for you. And if it doesn't work, consider trying another. The best organizational systems only function if you're ready to get organized and if they fit your personality. If any of these tips seem too daunting, consider asking a fellow poet to work with you in exchange for doing the same for them.

10 WAYS TO GET ORGANIZED

If you don't already have an uncluttered writing space, create one. It's difficult to work on organization if your space causes additional stress or distraction. These tips might help you become a more organized poet:

1. Find all of your publishable poems as well as your incomplete poems. This may take some time. Don't rush this process; finding, reading and organizing your forgotten words may inspire new work. Consider typing up your poem starts into one document so you know where to begin when you're stuck for inspiration.

2. Print hard copies of all work and separate publishable poems and poems that need revision into separate accordion files or three-ring binders. You can choose to file by title, subject/theme or type/form. Other poets include length of poem and tone.

3. Generate a virtual folder on your desktop. I titled mine "All Poetry" and created subfolders entitled "Publishable Poems," "Needs Work," and "Published Poems." Choose subfolder titles that make sense to you—you can use poem title, subject matter, form, or theme. Your goal is to be able to find your poems easily.

4. Create or find a submission tracker. If your goal is publication, having a system that tracks your submissions and that is easy to use and update will help create a sense of order.

5. Write or type up a list of goal markets for the year. I do this by going through *Poet's Market* and my favorite poetry newsletters and websites to find markets that seem to be a good fit. This document will grow every month as you discover more markets, contests and literary journals. Some poets find including the hyperlinks to be helpful.

6. Make an appointment with yourself. At least once every week I set aside some time to follow up with upcoming deadlines and to write a to-do list. More productive writers than myself do a to-do list every day, but with a full-time job I find that this weekly check-in is enough to keep me on task.

7. Subscribe to poetry newsletters and set Google alerts for specific contests you'd like to enter. Here is the challenging part—as soon as you receive the newsletter or alert, fill in your paper or virtual poetry calendar. And then delete the newsletter.

8. Keep office supplies including: envelopes, paper, file folders, printer ink and stamps stocked. While many magazines and journals are set up for e-mail submissions, there are still some journals that require a hard copy submission.

9. Organize your books by genre. I keep chapbooks, craft books, journals, and poetry magazines on one shelf for reference and inspiration. While the Internet makes it easy to access information, having all of your reference materials within easy reach could prevent you from getting distracted online.

10. Do set a date for completion of your new organizational system by choosing a realistic goal date and sticking to it. As Barbara Sher writes in Wishcraft: How to Get What You Really Want, "…your true goal, or target, has to be a concrete action or event, not only so you'll know for sure when you get there, but so that you can make that date with success in advance!"

SET UP A POETRY CALENDAR

At the beginning of every year or starting today, consider purchasing a large spaced desk calendar specifically for poetry. Because I'm sitting at the desk every day it's easy to jot down poetry contests and submission deadlines I don't want to miss, especially the "no-entry fee" contests. If it's on my goal market list, I use different colored highlighters to show when the journal is open to submissions.

Writer Phyllis Kaelin also uses a similar paper-based calendar system but uses colorful sticky notes to chart her progress on a particular project. Her paper calendar system works hand in hand with her computer files. She says, "Within the project folder, I keep a running "notes document" where I put comments, plans, progress, word count etc. When I decide to submit I make a note there too."

If you don't already use an online calendar specifically for poetry set one up. If you're serious about poetry this can be used to track submissions, deadlines and markets but also helps keep you on track with readings, writing groups and poetry events. Popular online calendars include: Google Calendar (www.google.com/calendar), Convenient Calendar (www.convenientcalendar.com), and 30 Boxes (www.30boxes.com). I like using an online calendar that integrates with my smartphone so that I can send reminders to my phone, e-mail and/or virtual desktop.

WHY USE A SUBMISSION TRACKER?

Even if you have a good memory, once you get in the habit of sending out your poems it's very easy to lose track of when and where your poems were sent. And there's nothing more frustrating than finding a good market for a particular poem and not remembering where or if it was sent out.

Poet's Market includes a basic submission tracker that you can enlarge and copy. Or if you're feeling creative, you can design your own paper submission tracker using headlines that make sense to you. Another option many poets use is index cards or a simple journal log. Alternatively you can convert *Poet's Market*'s submission tracker to a computer spreadsheet program such as Excel. If you're not comfortable setting up your own tracking spreadsheet on your computer, there are several free submission trackers available online.

The most popular submission trackers include: Duotrope (www.duotrope.com) and Luminary Writer's Database (www.writersdb.com).

Rooze, an award-winning poet who is currently pursuing her MFA, says about Duotrope, "I like that they have a theme calendar and a deadline calendar. For each journal, they also list the average response time, percentage of submissions accepted, and the last time a response was received. This gives me a better context to know what to expect. Duotrope also specifies additional criteria, such as requirements around simultaneous submissions and previously printed poems."

The benefits of using a submission tracker far outweigh the time it will take to set one up. If you choose to include comments you can easily recognize when a poem needs a second look. If you use an online submission tracker your timely follow-up can also help other poets who use the database. Knowing that we're all in this submission process together, helping fellow poets just feels right.

If spreadsheets and submission trackers seem too left-brain, you might consider poet Jessy Randall's process. She says, "I write, with my hand and a pen, a poem. I mess around with, cross things out, rewrite lines, for a day or two. Then I set it aside for, if possible, at least a month, or even better, three months. Then I take a look at it again. If I think it's any good, I type it into a giant Word document that contains typed versions of all my poems, with the newest ones at the top. I fiddle around with it some more as I type it. I set it aside again for a while, maybe another month. If I still like it after all that, I submit it to a journal, bundling it together with other poems that somehow go with it. I keep track of where I've sent it, and when, in a Word document (to tell the truth, it's the same giant document). I also try to keep track of the general response time so I know when I should send a query. So I'll have something like:

"Name of Journal: Poem Title 1, Poem Title 2, Poem Title 3, sent January 2012, should respond in 6 months."

For the submission process Randall adds that the "submission information is in the top of my Word document, along with a list of the poems that aren't sent out anywhere at the moment. Then come all the typed poems. At the bottom of this giant document is where I keep track of rejections, in alphabetical order by journal name. If I need to, I can do a word search in the document to see if a particular journal has already seen a particular poem."

YOU'RE PUBLISHED!

Unfortunately just being organized doesn't guarantee publication. But if you're committed to poetry and part of that commitment includes being organized and businesslike, with time and persistence, there's a very good chance that your work will be accepted.

When you do receive the letter or e-mail that your work is being accepted make sure to follow through. Update your submission tracker as well as your computer and/or paper files. It's very rewarding to move the poem (physically or virtually) from the publishable folder to the published folder and/or to write where and when your poem will be published. If the poem was a simultaneous submission be professional and notify the other publications that you are withdrawing your work.

Blogger and poet Sonya Fehér of Mama True (www.mamatrue.com) includes a Published Worksheet as part of her organizational system.

"The Published Worksheet includes the following fields:

- **MARKET**—Name of market in which the poem was published
- **DETAILS**—Volume # and other details from publication
- **LINK**—If the poem was published online, this gives me the location."

For poet Jessy Randall, being organized makes poetry more gratifying: "This may sound weird, but I particularly enjoy the housekeeping side of poetry, the keeping-track-of-submissions part. When I open up the file that shows me what's where, what's been rejected, what's forthcoming, I feel a real sense of accomplishment even if I didn't write anything that day. Because look at all the stuff that's percolating along without me doing anything!"

That's the favorite part for me too; once I set my organizational system in place I had more fun with the submission process. I missed fewer deadlines and felt more in control of my poetic career. Whether your body of work consists of five or 50 poems there's no time like today to start organizing. Taking the time to organize your work goes beyond the practical; it's a way to honor your time, work, and commitment to craft. It could very well be the inspiration you need to get published.

PATRICIA KENNELLY is a published poet, business owner and editor in Colorado Springs, Colorado. Her poems have most recently appeared in *Haibun Today*, *Messages from the Hidden Lake* and *The Denver Post*. She gently nags about writing daily and creativity at www.writingnag.com.

THE HABITS OF HIGHLY PRODUCTIVE POETS

by Scott Owens

If they held a convention for all the people who have made a fortune off poetry, I'm not sure anyone would show up. The external rewards of writing poetry are relatively minimal. Writing poetry doesn't produce googobs of money. Any fame generated by the act is rather limited and usually accompanied by equal amounts of misunderstanding, suspicion, and other forms of notoriety. Even moral support is often lacking as family and friends may resent the time that poetry takes away from them, and readers and other poets may not support your particular aesthetic or the subjects you choose to write about.

Still, there are thousands of people who write poetry, some obsessively, some successfully, if productivity and a small following can be construed as success. The questions, then, are *Why do they do it?* and *How do they do it?* Ultimately, of course, the answers to both questions are as diverse as the people who write poetry, but some reasons and ways are common enough to merit general discussion.

W.S. Merwin claims that *poetry reconnects us to the world.* Gerald Stern gets a bit more specific when he writes that *poetry is a kind of religion, a way of seeking redemption, a way of understanding things so that they can be reconciled, explained, justified, redeemed.* Certainly these are wonderful reasons for why people write poetry, and they ring true to my own experience as both a writer and reader of poetry. They also relate to the first answer to the second question.

HABIT #1: BELIEF

The first habit of productive poets is that they **believe** in poetry. They believe that it is more than a game with words, more even than just writing about the world (an admirable enough ambition in itself). They believe that it is, in fact, both an ontological and an epistemological act—both a way of being in the world, and a way of making meaning out of the world. They understand that the act of writing poetry helps them pay attention to, appreciate, and make meaning out of their existence, and they enjoy the way in which poetry deepens their experience of people, moments, and things. They believe poetry, and their poetry more specifically, matters, and they will not be dissuaded from engaging with poetry and engaging with the world through poetry.

HABIT #2: CONFIDENCE

This is, of course, intimately related to the second habit of productive poets in that it necessitates that poets are **confident and courageous**. In other words, they believe in the significance of what they are doing no matter how many times and ways they are told by society, family, friends, even other poets that poetry, especially their poetry, doesn't matter or isn't right. Perhaps the best answer to why people write poetry is simply because they have to or because they like doing it. If, as Merwin suggests, writing poetry makes you feel closer to the world, then you'll probably keep doing it no matter what anyone else says. And if, as Stern suggests, writing poetry helps you make meaning, significance, and value out of your perceptions and experiences, then it's likely you'll seek every opportunity to do it.

HABIT #3: RECEPTIVE

Often, it is less a matter of seeking the opportunity than it is of being ready for it. The third habit of highly productive poets is that they are **ready to receive**. Ideas, images, lines for poetry are everywhere, every minute of every day, but our ability to remember the fine details of any particular event or perception is constantly eroded by the sheer mass of events and perceptions we encounter on a daily basis. Thus, highly productive poets are never without pen and paper so that they can jot down these observations when they occur. My writer's notebook goes with me everywhere. It's on the seat next to me when I drive; it's on my nightstand when I sleep; it's in my bookbag or binder when I go out; and on those rare occasions when I can't have it with me, I'm sure to have a folded up piece of paper in one pocket or another. And I don't use just any notebook either. I use a notebook that I like to spend time with, that I like the feel and heft of, that I want to open even when I don't think I have anything to write, and that I won't get confused with any other notebook. For me it's a Moleskine journal with about 200 unlined pages. Similarly, I keep one of my favorite pens with me at all times. For me that means a heavy, metallic-bodied, gel-type pen. Whatever your favorite is like, having it available enhances the likelihood that you will write with relish rather than discomfort, and thus will do so longer and more frequently.

HABIT #4: ATTENTION

Suitably armed for recording the significant details we encounter throughout every day, the fourth, and perhaps most important, habit of highly productive poets is referenced in Mary Oliver's unforgettable poem, "Summer Day," where she says, "I don't know exactly what a prayer is. / I do know how to **pay attention**." Paying attention consists of learning to notice the finer details, the significance of those details, and the connections between them that most people, caught up in the necessaries of daily existence, miss, or fail to remember for more than a moment. As simple as that sounds, this habit requires more development than any of the others. Perhaps the best method for developing it is to begin by doing it consciously. Set aside 30 minutes every day and pay close attention to something, somewhere. You might sit at a coffee shop and pay attention to people, or take a walk and pay attention to something in nature; you might practice yoga or meditation and learn to pay attention to more internal landscapes. After a while of doing this intentionally, you'll discover that you begin to pay closer attention to such details without having to make yourself do it. You'll notice more; you'll be conscious of the significance of things that most people take for granted; and you'll appreciate the connections between things that too often go unnoticed.

HABIT #5: ATTUNED

Highly productive poets also **stay tuned in** to poetry. I am convinced, in fact, that most successful poets read a great deal more poetry than they ever undertake to write. They read poetry in books and magazines; they attend workshops, classes, and readings; they participate in critique and peer groups; they volunteer to edit journals and anthologies and judge contests; they read and write reviews; and they create opportunities for others to experience poetry, all of which keeps them thinking about poetry and honing their poetic skills and aesthetic. They do this because they love poetry; they do it because they believe that given the opportunity everyone will love and benefit from poetry; and in the process they make themselves better poets. My own hometown lacked a poetry reading series for local poets, so I partnered with a locally-owned coffee shop and created one that has been going on monthly for 7 years and has an average attendance of about 40 people. I also took on writing a semi-weekly poetry column, editing a quarterly online poetry journal, coordinating a quarterly ekphrastic reading series at the local art museum, and serving as an officer of the state poetry society. I think every state has such a society, and joining it is a great way to get tapped into the network of poets and poetry lovers, and to stay on top of opportunities to experience and participate in the world of poetry wherever you might be.

HABIT #6: INIATIVE

Just as highly productive poets dive in to the world of poetry, they also **dive in** to the subjects they choose to write about. As the first habit suggests, whether they write about politics, personal experience, memory, perception, etc., they approach their subjects without letting fear occlude their vision or censor their words. They also dive in in the sense that they immerse themselves in the subject, not rushing to complete the poem, but luxuriating in it, granting it the time it deserves, writing way too much before beginning to whittle down the language and perceptions to the essentials that will form an effective final poem. Examining any act of creation will reveal that creation always involves waste, or "leftovers." Effectiveness comes through a process of sharpening, whittling away what is ineffective. Thus, most poets begin by overwriting, and then eliminate unneeded elements through the process of editing and shaping the poem. This is another one that takes a bit of practice in a world that encourages focusing on the end result and instant gratification rather than relaxing into and fully experiencing the process. Poets will use any number of techniques to help them expand upon the possibilities they venture into: clustering, free association, automatic writing, meditation, focused freewriting, etc. My suggestion is to use them all, sometimes on the same poem, and then make up your own as you discover what works. Driving long distances helps me; another poet friend of mine does his best work while mowing.

HABIT #7: ENJOYMENT

Of course, the correlative habit is just as essential. A highly productive poet will also **enjoy the process**. I've encountered many people who claim to hate revising, but I can't think of a successful poet who has ever said so. Good poets tend to understand that the real craft of writing comes in the rewriting, and as difficult and sometimes painful as that process can be, it is the part of writing that they enjoy the most. It is, in fact, often a form of play for them. They work on a poem for weeks, months, sometimes years, trying out different perspectives, metaphors, arrangements of lines. They seek out criticism from others; they revise after poems are published, or after giving public readings. They see the poem as "finished" perhaps only after their own death has made it so. If Whitman could have at least 8 versions (some say as many as 19) of *Leaves of Grass*, then surely no lesser poet should doubt or fear the process of continual revision.

HABIT #8: THICK-SKINNED

The eighth habit of productive poets, and for some the most difficult, is that they **grow thick skin**. They learn to distinguish between themselves and their work such that they can accept criticism of their work without internalizing it as criticism of themselves. Often poetry is about personal experience, and some writers struggle to separate criticism of the poem from criticism of who they are, what they've been through, or how they view things. Productive poets, however, come to understand that once written and shared, any poem is an artifact, an object, something to be handled and shaped, and not a part of who they are. Thus they are able to consider the poem coldly and critically and ask of it what will make it more effective without taking such questions, regardless of the source, as a personal affront. From that perspective, productive poets strive to listen to criticism objectively. Even if they cannot manage that level of objectivity, however, knowing that ultimately all decisions regarding the poem rest with them, productive poets learn to accept commentary about the poem and move on with the writing they have undertaken.

Good habits are essential to prolonged success in virtually any endeavor. Inspiration is a nice idea, and a wonderful thing when it happens, but I think it unwise to count upon its striking very often without developing certain practices that increase the likelihood of its coming to be. This list of practices for those who wish to be productive poets is far from exhaustive, but it has been useful for me, and I hope that it will prove to be so for other poets as well.

SCOTT OWENS holds degrees from Ohio University, UNC Charlotte, and UNC Greensboro. He currently lives in Hickory, North Carolina, where he teaches at Catawba Valley Community College, edits *Wild Goose Poetry Review* and *234*, writes for the *Outlook Newspaper*, and serves as vice-president of the NC Poetry Society. His 11th book of poetry, *Eye of the Beholder*, was released by Main Street Rag. His work has received awards from the Academy of American Poets, the Pushcart Prize Anthology, the Next Generation/Indie Lit Awards, the NC Writers Network, the NC Poetry Society, and the Poetry Society of SC.

ANATOMY OF A POETRY BOOK

....

by Amy Miller

Congratulations! You just got the proofs for the poetry book you're about to publish with that dream press. You open the package, but all you see is a pile of loose papers—things have been added and moved around, and you're not sure what you're looking at. Or maybe you're self-publishing your book and you're juggling your Word files, trying to figure out what goes where. How much legalese do you need on the copyright page? Acknowledgments in the front or back? And what about the footnote for that poem with the lines in Turkish?

No matter who's publishing your book or what size it is—full-length or chapbook—making it look as professional as possible takes dozens of small decisions that you'll be better equipped to deal with if you know the basic conventions of book layout.

So here, from front to back, are the parts of a poetry book and some tips for polishing them.

FRONT COVER

This one's a no-brainer, right? All it needs is the title and author, and a (hopefully) fabulous design.

But there's another element that appears on most poetry covers: the word "Poems" in small type below the title or above the author's name. While it's not mandatory, this makes it easy for readers and booksellers to distinguish your book from those of other genres, handy in today's crowded literary marketplace.

FRONT MATTER

As the name implies, front matter is everything at the front of the book, before your poems begin. These pages are usually numbered with Roman numerals or have no page numbers.

- **Title page.** This right-hand page, usually the first in the book and always unnumbered, mimics the cover design: title, author, and maybe a black-and-white rendering of the cover graphics. Your publisher may place their logo at the bottom. "Poems" is optional here. The title page serves a crucial function: It's where you'll autograph the book, so make sure there's enough blank space on it to write your signature and an inscription. Some publishers also add a "half-title"—a right-hand page that precedes the title page, with just the book's title and perhaps the publisher's logo, followed by a blank left page.
- **Copyright page.** This is usually the left page following the full title page. It contains these elements: Copyright line, publisher's contact info, ISBN, LCCN, Library of Congress data, printing history, country of origin, design/printing credits and colophon, and contractual language. More on these in Copyright Page sidebar.

COPYRIGHT PAGE

- **Copyright line.** A brief statement legally proclaiming this book as your writing is a publishing convention found in nearly every book. The least you'll need is "Copyright © 2019 by Joe Smith"; the year is when the book is first published, regardless of when the poems were written, and the name is yours. (For an anthology with many authors, it's the publisher's or editor's name; the individual authors retain rights to their poems through a contract with the publisher.) Some publishers spell out copyright protection more explicitly by adding something like, "All rights reserved. Except for brief quotations in critical articles or reviews, no part of this book may be reproduced in any manner without prior written permission from the publisher." There are myriad ways to word this. If you're self-publishing, look at similar books and choose language that's clear but not too complicated; overkill can look amateurish here. **Tip:** Your copyright line (the year the book was originally published) will stay the same no matter which printing it is.
- **Publisher's contact info.** This will be your publisher's address, or, if you're self-publishing, your own website, e-mail address, or P.O. Box (maybe not your street address). If somebody likes your book, make sure they can reach you.
- **ISBN, LCCN, and Library of Congress Data.** If your book has an ISBN (International Standard Book Number, used by retailers to identify and order the book), list it on the copyright page: "ISBN: XXX-X-XXXXXXXX." Similarly, if your publisher decides your book needs an LCCN (Library of Congress Control Number, used by librarians for ordering and cataloging), it goes here too, as does Library of Congress Cataloging-in-Publication Data, the small-print description and cryptic numbers you see in many books. If you're working through a publisher, they will handle all this. If you're

self-publishing, you may decide to get an ISBN; self-publishing platforms like CreateSpace or Blurb can provide one for you. LCCNs and LOC Cataloging Data are usually unnecessary for self-published poetry books.

- **Printing history.** This line states when that individual copy of the book was printed. In the old days of film and plates, it was denoted by a long line of numbers ("1 2 3 4 5 21 20 19 18 17," for example); the outer numbers indicated which printing it was and the year printed. Some publishers still follow this convention, but with digital technology now the norm, this line is often rendered in plain English—"First printing, 2017"—and changed in the digital file with each subsequent printing. But if you're self-publishing through an on-demand service, "first printing" has no real meaning since there is no "first batch" of books—each copy is printed when the buyer orders it. Instead, many print-on-demand authors use a line like "First printed in 2017" on the copyright page; then, on the last page of the book, the printer will automatically insert the date that particular copy was printed.

- **Country of origin.** The country where the book was printed should be listed on the copyright page (e.g., "Printed in the United States of America"). If you're using a print-on-demand service and don't know where it will be printed, you can omit this line; most of these services will automatically print the country of origin on the last page of the book.

- **Design/printing credits and colophon.** If you're using someone else's photos or art in the book, or if you employed a book designer, this is where to acknowledge them. (To credit a longer list of people, see "Acknowledgments page" in "Backmatter.") Some publishers also include a colophon—a note on the fonts used—or mention the printer or paper, especially if it's recycled or otherwise noteworthy.

- **Contractual language.** If the book's writing or publication was supported by a grant, sponsor, or residency, you or the publisher may be obligated to acknowledge that on the copyright page.

- **Table of contents.** Most full-length poetry collections have a table of contents (TOC), if the poems have titles. In a chapbook, it's optional but a nice touch. The TOC should always start on a right-hand page. If it runs an odd number of pages, the left-hand page that follows should be blank; if the TOC is two pages (i.e., it ends on a left page), the following right-hand page should be a half-title (see "Title Page" above), a dedication or book epigraph, or, if your book is divided into sections, a page with the title of your first section. The last page of the frontmatter should be a blank left.

- **Acknowledgments.** If some of the poems appeared previously in literary journals, you're obligated to mention it somewhere in the book. If it's just a few, you can list them on the copyright page: "Grateful acknowledgment is made to *Literary Annual* and *The Big Poetry Review*, in which some of these poems appeared." If the list is longer, put them on their own page. (See "Acknowledgments page" under "Backmatter.")

- **Dedication line.** If you want a short dedication thanking your spouse, your dog, or someone else, you can place this somewhere on the copyright page. Or your publisher may decide to give it a page to itself, usually a right-hand page followed by a blank left just before the table of contents or first poem.

THE POEMS

The first poem should start on a right-hand page. If your book is in sections, each section title should be all by itself on a right-hand page, followed by a blank left, with the first poem of each section starting on the next right page.

Epigraphs and footnotes. An epigraph—a quote, news snippet, etc., that inspired or informs the poem—is printed below the poem's title, often in italics. A footnote, on the other hand, is text separate from the poem that provides something the reader needs to know, such as an explanation of a foreign phrase or unfamiliar term. Footnotes can clutter up a poetry book, so if you have any, consider putting them on a separate Notes page in the back (see "Backmatter").

Tip: In most poetry books, page 1 is either the first poem or the first section-head page. (Again, the frontmatter is either unnumbered or numbered with Roman numerals.) And right-hand pages are always odd-numbered; left pages are always even.

BACK MATTER

Back matter is everything after the poems. While front matter follows very specific industry conventions, back matter is more of a free-for-all; you may have some of the following elements, or none.

- **Acknowledgments page.** If more poems appeared in journals than will fit on the copyright page, list those credits on a page by themselves, alphabetically by poem or journal. You can also use this page to thank people who helped you with the book.
- **Notes page.** Footnotes or any information that would enhance a reader's understanding of a poem—say, a dedication or the inspiration behind it—can be listed by page number and poem title on a Notes page. Notes pages are uncommon but can be illuminating, the kind of insider info that you might hear at a reading.
- **Author bio.** Some books have two bios, one in the back of the book and another on the back cover; some only have one on the back cover. If you have two, make them different; the back-cover one should be brief, while the (inside) bio page can be more expansive.

- **Blank pages.** Some books have a few blank sheets at the back of the book, or even at the front before the title page. Here's an industry secret: Sometimes publishers have to add blank pages because books are printed in signatures, large sheets on which several pages (4, 8, 16, etc.) are printed at once. If the number of pages in the book doesn't come out to a multiple of (4, 8, 16, whatever), the publisher may solve the equation by adding a half-title page and/or putting a few blank sheets at the very back or very front of the book.

Tip: Pages that are blank on both sides should only go at the very front or back, where they serve as decoration, because of a cardinal rule of publishing: "No blank right-hand pages." A blank right anywhere else is considered a design gaffe.

BACK COVER

The back cover has several important elements.

- **Shelving category.** At one time, most books had a shelving category on the back—in our case, "Poetry"—to help bookstore staff know where to put it. Some books still do, usually in the upper or lower left-hand corner, but it's less common now that books are often sold online.
- **Blurbs.** If you have blurbs—testimonials from other writers praising your book—the usual number is three; you rarely see fewer or more than that.
- **Author bio and photo.** Again, your bio can go here and/or on a page of its own at the back of the book. If you're doing two bios, put a photo with only one, preferably the back cover.
- **Barcode.** This electronic rendering of the ISBN number simplifies book handling for stores and online retailers. It should appear in the lower right-hand corner of the back cover, with the ISBN printed above it. Your publisher or print-on-demand service will insert this, but if you're designing your own cover, make sure to leave a space for it.
- **Cover price.** This usually is listed near the barcode, or in an easy-to-spot corner of the back cover. If you're self-publishing, you have the option of not printing a price on it at all, leaving you free to change the price at any time without having to do a reprint.

AMY MILLER'S writing has appeared in journals ranging from *Nimrod*, *Rattle*, and *ZYZZYVA* to *Fine Gardening* and *Asimov's Science Fiction*. She has worked in publishing for more than three decades, including 15 years as a managing editor, during which she has ushered some 80 books from the manuscript stage through the printed product. She blogs at writers-island.blogspot.com.

MISTAKES POETS MAKE

In putting together listings for *Poet's Market*, we ask editors for any words of advice they want to share with our readers. Often the editors' responses include comments about what poets should and shouldn't do when submitting work—the same comments, over and over. That means a lot of poets are repeating similar mistakes when they send out their poems for consideration.

The following list includes the most common of those mistakes—the ones poets should work hardest to avoid.

NOT READING A PUBLICATION BEFORE SUBMITTING WORK

Researching a publication is essential before submitting your poetry. Try to buy a sample copy of a magazine (by mail, if necessary) or at least see if an issue is available at the library. It may not be economically feasible for poets to purchase a copy of every magazine they target, especially if they send out a lot of poems. However, there are additional ways to familiarize yourself with a publication.

Read the market listing thoroughly. If guidelines are available, send for them by e-mail or regular mail, or check for them online. A publication's website often presents valuable information, including sample poems, magazine covers, and guidelines.

SUBMITTING INAPPROPRIATE WORK

Make good use of your research so you're sure you understand what a magazine publishes. Don't rationalize that a journal favoring free verse might jump at the chance to consider your long epic poem in heroic couplets. Don't convince yourself your experimental style will be a good fit for the traditional journal filled with rhyming poetry. Don't go into denial about whether a certain journal and your poetry are made for each other. It's counterproductive and ultimately wastes postage (not to mention time—yours and the editor's).

SUBMITTING AN UNREASONABLE NUMBER OF POEMS

If an editor recommends sending three to five poems (a typical range), don't send six. Don't send a dozen poems and tell the editor to pick the five she wants to consider. If the editor doesn't specify a number (or the listing says "no limit"), don't take that as an invitation to mail off 20 poems. The editors and staff of literary magazines are busy enough as it is, and they may decide they don't have time to cope with you. (When submitting book or chapbook manuscripts to publishers, make sure your page count falls within the range they state.)

Don't go to the other extreme and send only one poem, unless an editor says it's okay (which is rare). One poem doesn't give an editor much of a perspective on your work, and it doesn't give you very good odds on getting the piece accepted.

IGNORING THE EDITOR'S PREFERENCES REGARDING FORMATS

If an editor makes a point of describing a preferred manuscript format, follow it, even if that format seems to contradict the standard. (Standard format includes using 8½ × 11 white paper and conventional typeface and point size; avoid special graphics, colors or type flourishes; put your name and address on every page.) Don't devise your own format to make your submission stand out. Keep everything clean, crisp and easy to read (and professional).

Be alert to e-mail submission formats. Follow directions regarding what the editor wants printed in the subject line, how many poems to include in a single e-mail, whether to use attachments or paste work in the body of the message, and other elements. Editors have good reasons for outlining their preferences; ignoring them could mean having your e-mail deleted before your poems are even read.

OMITTING A SELF-ADDRESSED STAMPED ENVELOPE (SASE)

Why do editors continuously say "include an SASE with your submission?" Because so many poets don't do it. Here's a simple rule: Unless the editor gives alternate instructions, include a #10 SASE, whether submitting poems or sending an inquiry.

WRITING BAD COVER LETTERS (OR OMITTING THEM COMPLETELY)

Cover letters have become an established part of the submission process. There are editors who remain indifferent about the necessity of a cover letter, but many consider it rude to be sent a submission without any other communication from the poet.

Unless the editor says otherwise, send a cover letter. Keep it short and direct, a polite introduction of you and your work. (See "Frequently Asked Questions" for more tips on cover letters, and an example.)

Here are a few important don'ts:

- **DON'T** list all the magazines where your work has appeared; limit yourself to five magazine titles. The work you're submitting has to stand on its own.
- **DON'T** tell the editor what a good poet you are—or how good someone else thinks you are.
- **DON'T** tell the editor how to edit, lay out or print your poem. Some of those decisions are up to the editor, assuming she decides to accept your poem in the first place.
- **DON'T** point out the poem is copyrighted in your name or include the copyright symbol. All poems are automatically copyrighted in the poet's name as soon as they're "fixed" (i.e., written down), and editors know this.

NOT MAINTAINING GOOD EDITOR/POET RELATIONS

Most editors are hard-working poetry lovers dedicated to finding and promoting good work. They aspire to turn submissions around as quickly as possible and to treat all poets with respect. They don't want to steal your work. Often they aren't paid for their labor and may even have to dip into their own pockets just to keep their magazines going.

Poets should finesse their communications with editors regarding problems, especially in initial letters and e-mail. Editors (and their magazines and presses) aren't service-oriented businesses, like the phone company. Getting huffy with an editor as if arguing with your cable provider about an overcharge is inappropriate. Attitude isn't going to get you anywhere; in fact, it could create additional obstacles.

That's not to say poets shouldn't feel exasperated when they're inconvenienced or ill-treated. None of us likes to see our creations vanish, or to pay good money for something we're never going to receive (like a subscription or sample copy). However, exasperated is one thing; outraged is another. Too often poets go on the offensive with editors and make matters worse. Experts on how to complain effectively recommend you keep your cool and stay professional, no matter what kind of problem you're trying to work out.

For additional advice on editor/poet relations, see "Dealing With Problem Editors."

DEALING WITH PROBLEM EDITORS

There *are* problem editors out there. Some rip people off, prey on poets' desires to be published, or treat poets and their work with flagrant disregard. Fortunately, such editors are in the minority.

Now and then you may discover the disorganized editor or the overwhelmed editor; these two cause heartache (and heartburn) by closing up shop without returning manuscripts or failing to honor paid requests for subscriptions and sample copies. More often than not, their transgressions are rooted in chaos and irresponsibility, not malicious intent. Frustrating as such editors are, they're not out to get you.

There are many instances, too, where larger circumstances are beyond an editor's control. For example, a college-oriented journal may be student-staffed, with editors changing each academic year. Funds for the journal may be cut unexpectedly by administration belt-tightening, or a grant could be cancelled. The editorial office may be moved to another part of the university. An exam schedule could impact a publishing schedule. All of these things cause problems and delays.

Then again, a literary journal may be a one-person, home-based operation. The editor may get sick or have an illness in the family. Her regular job may suddenly demand lots of overtime. There may be divorce or death with which the editor has to cope. A computer could crash. Or the editor may need to scramble for money before the magazine can go to the printer. Emergencies happen, and they take their toll on deadlines. The last thing the editor wants is to inconvenience poets and readers, but sometimes life gets in the way.

Usually, difficulties with these kinds of "problem" editors can be resolved satisfactorily through communication and patience. There are always exceptions, though. Here are a few typical situations with problem editors and how to handle them.

AN EDITOR IS RUDE.

If it's a matter of bad attitude, take it with a grain of salt. Maybe he's having a rotten day. If there's abusive language and excessive profanity involved, let us know about it. (See the complaint procedure.)

AN EDITOR HARSHLY CRITICIZES YOUR POEM.

If an editor takes time to comment on your poetry, even if the feedback seems overly critical, consider the suggestions with an open mind and try to find something valid and useful in them. If, after you've given the matter fair consideration, you think the editor was out of line, don't rush to defend your poetry or wave your bruised ego in the editor's face. Allow that the editor has a right to her opinion (which you're not obligated to take as the final word on the quality of your work), forget about it and move on.

AN EDITOR IS SLOW TO RESPOND TO A SUBMISSION.

As explained above, there may be many reasons why an editor's response takes longer than the time stated in the market listing or guidelines. Allow a few more weeks to pass beyond the deadline, then write a polite inquiry to the editor about the status of your manuscript. (Include an SASE if sending by regular mail.) Understand an editor may not be able to read your letter right away if deadlines are pressing or if he's embroiled in a personal crisis. Try to be patient. If you haven't received a reply to your inquiry after a month or so, however, it's time for further action.

AN EDITOR WON'T RETURN YOUR MANUSCRIPT.

Decide whether you want to invest any more time in this journal or publisher. If you conclude you've been patient long enough, write a firm but professional letter to the editor withdrawing your manuscript from consideration. Request that the manuscript be returned; but know, too, a truly indifferent editor probably won't bother to send it back or reply in any way. Keep a copy of your withdrawal letter for your files, make a new copy of your manuscript and look for a better market.

AN EDITOR TAKES YOUR MONEY.

If you sent a check for a subscription or sample copy and you haven't received anything, review your bank statement to see if the check has been cashed. If it has, send the editor a query. Politely point out the editor has cashed your check, but you haven't yet received the material you were expecting. Give the editor the benefit of the doubt: An upcoming issue of a magazine could be running late, your subscription could have been overlooked by mistake, or your copy could have been lost in transit or sent in error to the wrong address.

If your check has *not* been cashed, query the editor to see if your order was ever received. It may have been lost (in the mail or on the editor's desk), the editor may be holding several checks to cash at one time, or the editor may be waiting to cash checks until a tardy issue is finally published.

If you get an unsatisfactory response from the editor (or no response at all), wait a few weeks and try again. Should you continue trying to get your money back from such editors? That's your decision. If your loss is under $10 (say, for a subscription or sample copy), it might cost you less in the long run to let the matter go. And the fee for a "stop payment" order on a check can be hefty—possibly more than the amount you sent the editor in the first place. Yes, it's infuriating to be cheated, but sometimes fighting on principle costs more than it's worth.

If your monetary loss is significant (for instance, you shelled out a couple hundred dollars in a subsidy publishing agreement), consider contacting your state attorney general's office for advice about small claims court, filing a complaint and other actions you can take.

IS IT A CON?

What is a "con?" Con is short for "confidence," an adjective defined by *Webster's* as "of, relating to, or adept at swindling by false promise," as in "confidence man" or "confidence game." While the publishing world is full of legitimate opportunities for poets to gain honor and exposure for their work, there are also plenty of "cons." How can you tell the difference? The following are some of the most common situations that cost poets disappointment, frustration—and cash. Learn to spot them before submitting your work, and don't let your vanity be your guide.

ANTHOLOGIES

Has this happened to you? You see an ad in a perfectly respectable publication announcing a poetry contest with big cash prizes. You enter, and later you receive a glowing letter congratulating you on your exceptional poem, which the contest sponsor wants to include in his deluxe hardbound anthology of the best poetry submitted to the contest. The anthology costs only, say, $65. You don't have to buy it—they'll still publish your poem—but wouldn't you be proud to own one? And wouldn't it be nice to buy additional copies to give to family and friends? And for an extra charge you can include a biographical note. And so on.

Of course, when the anthology arrives, the quality of the poetry may not be what you were expecting, with several poems crammed unattractively onto a page. Apparently everyone who entered the contest was invited to be published; you basically paid cash to see your poem appear in a phone-book-like volume with no literary merit whatsoever.

Were you conned? Depends on how you look at it. If you bought into the flattery and believed you were being published in an exclusive, high-quality publication, no doubt you feel duped. On the other hand, if all you were after was seeing your poem in print, even knowing you'd have to pay for the privilege, then you got what you wanted. (Unless you've deceived yourself into believing you've truly won an honor and now have a worthy publishing credit; you don't.)

If you don't want to add insult to injury, resist additional spiels, like having your poem printed on coffee mugs and T-shirts (you can do this yourself through print shops or online services like www.cafepress.com) or spending large sums on awards banquets and conferences. And, before you submit a single line of poetry, find out what rights the contest sponsor acquires. You may be relinquishing all rights to your poem simply by mailing it in or submitting it through a website. If the poem no longer belongs to you, the publisher can do whatever he wishes with it. Don't let your vanity propel you into a situation you'll always regret.

HELPFUL WEBSITES

The following websites include specific information about questionable poetry publishers and awards. For more websites of value to poets, see Additional Resources.

- An Incomplete Guide to Print On Demand Publishers offers articles on POD publishing, comparisons of POD publishers (contracts, distribution, fees, etc.) and an online forum: http://booksandtales.com/pod/index.php
- Answers to frequently asked questions about poetry awards from the Academy of American Poets: www.poets.org/page.php/prmID/116
- Poets will find warnings and other valuable publishing information on the Preditors & Editors website: www.anotherealm.com/prededitors/
- Writer Beware tracks contests, publishers and literary agents: www.sfwa.org/beware
- Literary Contest Caution at http://windpub.com/literary.scams

---

READING AND CONTEST FEES

Suppose you notice a promising market for your poetry, but the editor requires a set fee just to consider your work. Or you see a contest that interests you, but you have to pay the sponsor a fee just to enter. Are you being conned?

In the case of reading fees, keep these points in mind: Is the market so exceptional that you feel it's worth risking the cost of the reading fee to have your work considered? What makes it so much better than markets that do not charge fees? Has the market been around awhile, with an established publishing schedule? What are you paid if your work is accepted? Are reasonably priced samples available so you can judge the production values and quality of the writing?

Reading fees don't necessarily signal a suspicious market. In fact, they're increasingly popular as editors struggle with the costs of publishing books and magazines, including the man-hours required to read loads of (often bad) submissions. However, fees represent an additional financial burden on poets, who often don't receive any monetary reward for their poems to begin with. It's really up to individual poets to decide whether paying a fee is beneficial to their publishing efforts. Think long and hard about fee-charging markets that are new and untried, don't pay poets for their work (at the very least a print publication should offer a contributor's copy), charge high prices for sample copies or set fees that seem unreasonable.

Entry fees for contests often fund prizes, judges' fees, honorariums and expenses of running and promoting the contest (including publishing a "prize" collection or issue of a magazine). Other kinds of contests charge entry fees, from Irish dancing competitions to bake-offs at a county fair. Why not poetry contests?

That's not to say you shouldn't be cautious. Watch out for contests that charge higher-than-average fees, especially if the fees are out of proportion to the amount of prize money being given. (Look through the Contests & Awards section to get a sense of what most competitions charge.) Find out how long the contest has been around, and verify whether prizes have been awarded each year and to whom. In the case of book and chapbook contests, send for one of the winning publications to confirm that the publisher puts out a quality product. Regard with skepticism any contest that tells you you've won something, then demands payment for an anthology, trophy or other item. (It's okay if a group offers an anthology for a modest price without providing winners with free copies. Most state poetry societies have to do this; but they also present cash awards in each category of the contest, and their entry fees are low.)

SUBSIDY PUBLISHERS, PRINT-ON-DEMAND

Poetry books are a hard sell to the book-buying public. Few of the big publishers handle these books, and those that do feature the "name" poets (i.e., the major prize winners and contemporary masters with breathtaking reputations). Even the small presses publish only so many books per year—far less than the number of poets writing.

No wonder so many poets decide to pay to have their poetry collections published. While some may self-publish (i.e., take full control of their book, working directly with a printer), others turn to subsidy publishers (also called "vanity publishers") and print-on-demand (POD) publishers.

There are many differences between subsidy publishing and POD publishing, as well as similarities (having to pay to get published is a big one). Whether or not you get conned is entirely up to you. You have to take responsibility for asking questions, doing research on presses, and reading the fine print on the contract to make sure you know exactly what you're paying for. There are landmines in dealing with subsidy and POD publishers, and you have to investigate thoroughly and intelligently to avoid damage.

Some questions to keep in mind: Are fees inflated compared to the product and services you'll be receiving? Will you still own the rights to your book? Does the publisher put out a quality product that's attractive and cleanly printed? (Get a sample copy and find out.) How many copies of the book will you receive? How much will you have to pay for additional copies? How will your book be sold and distributed? (Don't count on seeing your volume in bookstores.)

Will you receive royalties? How much? Does the publisher offer any kind of promotional assistance or is it all up to you? Will those promotion efforts be realistic and results-oriented? (Sometimes "promotion" means sending out review copies, which is a waste—such volumes are rarely reviewed.) Don't wait until *after* you've signed a contract (and a check) to raise these issues. Do your homework first.

Obviously, poets who don't stay on their toes may find themselves preyed upon. And a questionable publishing opportunity doesn't have to be an out-and-out rip-off for you to feel cheated. In every situation, you have a choice *not* to participate. Exercise that choice, or at least develop a healthy sense of skepticism before you fling yourself and your poetry at the first smooth talker who compliments your work. Poets get burned because they're much too impatient to see their work in print. Calm your ego, slow down and devote that time, energy and money toward reading other poets and improving your own writing. You'll find that getting published will eventually take care of itself.

BLOGGING BASICS

by Robert Lee Brewer

In these days of publishing and media change, writers have to build platforms and learn how to connect to audiences if they want to improve their chances of publication and overall success. There are many methods of audience connection available to writers, but one of the most important is through blogging.

Since I've spent several years successfully blogging—both personally and professionally—I figure I've got a few nuggets of wisdom to pass on to writers who are curious about blogging or who already are.

Here's my quick list of tips:

1. **START BLOGGING TODAY.** If you don't have a blog, use Blogger, WordPress, or some other blogging software to start your blog today. It's free, and you can start off with your very personal "Here I am, world" post.

2. **START SMALL.** Blogs are essentially simple, but they can get complicated (for people who like complications). However, I advise bloggers start small and evolve over time.

3. **USE YOUR NAME IN YOUR URL.** This will make it easier for search engines to find you when your audience eventually starts seeking you out by name. For instance, my url is http://robertleebrewer.blogspot.com. If you try Googling "Robert Lee Brewer," you'll notice that My Name Is Not Bob is one of the top five search results (behind my other blog: Poetic Asides).

4. **UNLESS YOU HAVE A REASON, USE YOUR NAME AS THE TITLE OF YOUR BLOG.** Again, this helps with search engine results. My Poetic Asides blog includes my name in the title, and it ranks higher than My Name Is Not Bob. However, I felt the play on my name was worth the trade off.

5. **FIGURE OUT YOUR BLOGGING GOALS.** You should return to this step every couple months, because it's natural for your blogging goals to evolve over time. Initially,

your blogging goals may be to make a post a week about what you have written, submitted, etc. Over time, you may incorporate guests posts, contests, tips, etc.

6. **BE YOURSELF.** I'm a big supporter of the idea that your image should match your identity. It gets too confusing trying to maintain a million personas. Know who you are and be that on your blog, whether that means you're sincere, funny, sarcastic, etc.

7. **POST AT LEAST ONCE A WEEK.** This is for starters. Eventually, you may find it better to post once a day or multiple times per day. But remember: Start small and evolve over time.

8. **POST RELEVANT CONTENT.** This means that you post things that your readers might actually care to know.

9. **USEFUL AND HELPFUL POSTS WILL ATTRACT MORE VISITORS.** Talking about yourself is all fine and great. I do it myself. But if you share truly helpful advice, your readers will share it with others, and visitors will find you on search engines.

10. **TITLE YOUR POSTS IN A WAY THAT GETS YOU FOUND IN SEARCH ENGINES.** The more specific you can get the better. For instance, the title "Blogging Tips" will most likely get lost in search results. However, the title "Blogging Tips for Writers" speci-fies which audience I'm targeting and increases the chances of being found on the first page of search results.

11. **LINK TO POSTS IN OTHER MEDIA.** If you have an e-mail newsletter, link to your blog posts in your newsletter. If you have social media accounts, link to your blog posts there. If you have a helpful post, link to it in relevant forums and on message boards.

12. **WRITE WELL, BUT BE CONCISE.** At the end of the day, you're writing blog posts, not literary manifestos. Don't spend a week writing each post. Try to keep it to an hour or two tops and then post. Make sure your spelling and grammar are good, but don't stress yourself out too much.

13. **FIND LIKE-MINDED BLOGGERS.** Comment on their blogs regularly and link to them from yours. Eventually, they may do the same. Keep in mind that blogging is a form of social media, so the more you communicate with your peers the more you'll get out of the process.

14. **RESPOND TO COMMENTS ON YOUR BLOG.** Even if it's just a simple "Thanks," re-spond to your readers if they comment on your blog. After all, you want your read-ers to be engaged with your blog, and you want them to know that you care they took time to comment.

15. **EXPERIMENT.** Start small, but don't get complacent. Every so often, try something new. For instance, the biggest draw to my Poetic Asides blog are the poetry prompts and challenges I issue to poets. Initially, that was an experiment—one that worked very well. I've tried other experiments that haven't panned out, and that's fine. It's all part of a process.

SEO TIPS FOR WRITERS

Most writers may already know what SEO is. If not, SEO stands for *search engine optimization*. Basically, a site or blog that practices good SEO habits should improve its rankings in search engines, such as Google and Bing. Most huge corporations have realized the importance of SEO and spend enormous sums of time, energy and money on perfecting their SEO practices. However, writers can improve their SEO without going to those same extremes.

In this section, I will use the terms of *site pages* and *blog posts* interchangeably. In both cases, you should be practicing the same SEO strategies (when it makes sense).

Here are my top tips on ways to improve your SEO starting today:

1. **USE APPROPRIATE KEYWORDS.** Make sure that your page displays your main keyword(s) in the page title, content, URL, title tags, page header, image names and tags (if you're including images). All of this is easy to do, but if you feel overwhelmed, just remember to use your keyword(s) in your page title and content (especially in the first and last 50 words of your page).

2. **USE KEYWORDS NATURALLY.** Don't kill your content and make yourself look like a spammer to search engines by overloading your page with your keyword(s). You don't get SEO points for quantity but for quality. Plus, one of the main ways to improve your page rankings is when you...

3. **DELIVER QUALITY CONTENT.** The best way to improve your SEO is by providing content that readers want to share with others by linking to your pages. Some of the top results in search engines can be years old, because the content is so good that people keep coming back. So, incorporate your keywords in a smart way, but make sure it works organically with your content.

4. **UPDATE CONTENT REGULARLY.** If your site looks dead to visitors, then it'll appear that way to search engines too. So update your content regularly. This should be very easy for writers who have blogs. For writers who have sites, incorporate your blog into your site. This will make it easier for visitors to find your blog to discover more about you on your site (through your site navigation tools).

5. **LINK BACK TO YOUR OWN CONTENT.** If I have a post on Blogging Tips for Writers, for instance, I'll link back to it if I have a Platform Building post, because the two complement each other. This also helps clicks on my blog, which helps SEO. The one caveat is that you don't go crazy with your linking and that you make sure your links are relevant. Otherwise, you'll kill your traffic, which is not good for your page rankings.

6. **LINK TO OTHERS YOU CONSIDER HELPFUL.** Back in 2000, I remember being ordered by my boss at the time (who didn't last too much longer afterward) to ignore any competitive or complementary websites—no matter how helpful their content—because they were our competitors. You can try basing your online strategy on these

principles, but I'm nearly 100 percent confident you'll fail. It's helpful for other sites and your own to link to other great resources. I shine a light on others to help them out (if I find their content truly helpful) in the hopes that they'll do the same if ever they find my content truly helpful for their audience.

7. **GET SPECIFIC WITH YOUR HEADLINES.** If you interview someone on your blog, don't title your post with an interesting quotation. While that strategy may help get readers in the print world, it doesn't help with SEO at all. Instead, title your post as "Interview With (insert name here)." If you have a way to identify the person further, include that in the title too. For instance, when I interview poets on my Poetic Asides blog, I'll title those posts like this: Interview With Poet Erika Meitner. Erika's name is a keyword, but so are the terms *poet* and *interview*.

8. **USE IMAGES.** Many expert sources state that the use of images can improve SEO, because it shows search engines that the person creating the page is spending a little extra time and effort on the page than a common spammer. However, I'd caution anyone using images to make sure those images are somehow complementary to the content. Don't just throw up a lot of images that have no relevance to anything. At the same time …

9. **OPTIMIZE IMAGES THROUGH STRATEGIC LABELING.** Writers can do this by making sure the image file is labeled using your keyword(s) for the post. Using the Erika Meitner example above (which does include images), I would label the file "Erika Meitner headshot.jpg"—or whatever the image file type happens to be. Writers can also improve image SEO through the use of captions and ALT tagging. Of course, at the same time, writers should always ask themselves if it's worth going through all that trouble for each image or not. Each writer has to answer that question for him (or her) self.

10. **USE YOUR SOCIAL MEDIA PLATFORM TO SPREAD THE WORD.** Whenever you do something new on your site or blog, you should share that information on your other social media sites, such as Twitter, Facebook, LinkedIn, online forums, etc. This lets your social media connections know that something new is on your site/blog. If it's relevant and/or valuable, they'll let others know. And that's a great way to build your SEO.

Programmers and marketers could get even more involved in the dynamics of SEO optimization, but I think these tips will help most writers out immediately and effectively while still allowing plenty of time and energy for the actual work of writing.

BLOG DESIGN TIPS FOR WRITERS

Design is an important element to any blog's success. But how can you improve your blog's design if you're not a designer? I'm just an editor with an English Lit degree and no formal training in design. However, I've worked in media for more than a decade now and can share some very fundamental and easy tricks to improve the design of your blog.

Here are my seven blog design tips for writers:

1. **USE LISTS.** Whether they're numbered or bullet points, use lists when possible. Lists break up the text and make it easy for readers to follow what you're blogging.
2. **BOLD MAIN POINTS IN LISTS.** Again, this helps break up the text while also highlighting the important points of your post.
3. **USE HEADINGS.** If your posts are longer than 300 words and you don't use lists, then please break up the text by using basic headings.
4. **USE A READABLE FONT.** Avoid using fonts that are too large or too small. Avoid using cursive or weird fonts. Times New Roman or Arial works, but if you want to get "creative," use something similar to those.
5. **LEFT ALIGN.** English-speaking readers are trained to read left to right. If you want to make your blog easier to read, avoid centering or right aligning your text (unless you're purposefully calling out the text).
6. **USE SMALL PARAGRAPHS.** A good rule of thumb is to try and avoid paragraphs that drone on longer than five sentences. I usually try to keep paragraphs to around three sentences myself.
7. **ADD RELEVANT IMAGES.** Personally, I shy away from using too many images. My reason is that I only like to use them if they're relevant. However, images are very powerful on blogs, so please use them—just make sure they're relevant to your blog post.

If you're already doing everything on my list, keep it up! If you're not, then you might want to re-think your design strategy on your blog. Simply adding a header here and a list there can easily improve the design of a blog post.

GUEST POSTING TIPS FOR WRITERS

Recently, I've broken into guest posting as both a guest poster and as a host of guest posts (over at my Poetic Asides blog). So far, I'm pretty pleased with both sides of the guest posting process. As a writer, it gives me access to an engaged audience I may not usually reach. As a blogger, it provides me with fresh and valuable content I don't have to create. Guest blogging is a rare win-win scenario.

That said, writers could benefit from a few tips on the process of guest posting:

1. **PITCH GUEST POSTS LIKE ONE WOULD PITCH ARTICLES TO A MAGAZINE.** Include what your hook is for the post, what you plan to cover, and a little about who you are. Remember: Your post should somehow benefit the audience of the blog you'd like to guest post.

2. **OFFER PROMOTIONAL COPY OF YOUR BOOK (OR OTHER GIVEAWAYS) AS PART OF YOUR GUEST POST.** Having a random giveaway for people who comment on a blog post can help spur conversation and interest in your guest post, which is a great way to get the most mileage out of your guest appearance.

3. **CATER POSTS TO AUDIENCE.** As the editor of *Writer's Market* and *Poet's Market*, I have great range in the topics I can cover. However, if I'm writing a guest post for a fiction blog, I'll write about things of interest to a novelist—not a poet.

4. **MAKE IT PERSONAL, BUT PROVIDE NUGGET.** Guest posts are a great opportunity for you to really show your stuff to a new audience. You could write a very helpful and impersonal post, but that won't connect with readers the same way as if you write a very helpful and personal post that makes them want to learn more about you (and your blog, your book, your Twitter account, etc.). Speaking of which...

5. **SHARE LINKS TO YOUR WEBSITE, BLOG, SOCIAL NETWORKS, ETC.** After all, you need to make it easy for readers who enjoyed your guest post to learn more about you and your projects. Start the conversation in your guest post and keep it going on your own sites, profiles, etc. And related to that...

6. **PROMOTE YOUR GUEST POST THROUGH YOUR NORMAL CHANNELS ONCE THE POST GOES LIVE.** Your normal audience will want to know where you've been and what you've been doing. Plus, guest posts lend a little extra "street cred" to your projects. But don't stop there...

7. **CHECK FOR COMMENTS ON YOUR GUEST POST AND RESPOND IN A TIMELY MANNER.** Sometimes the comments are the most interesting part of a guest post (no offense). This is where readers can ask more in-depth or related questions, and it's also where you can show your expertise on the subject by being as helpful as possible. And guiding all seven of these tips is this one:

8. **PUT SOME EFFORT INTO YOUR GUEST POST.** Part of the benefit to guest posting is the opportunity to connect with a new audience. Make sure you bring your A-game, because you need to make a good impression if you want this exposure to actually help grow your audience. Don't stress yourself out, but put a little thought into what you submit.

ONE ADDITIONAL TIP: Have fun with it. Passion is what really drives the popularity of blogs. Share your passion and enthusiasm, and readers are sure to be impressed.

ROBERT LEE BREWER is an editor with the Writer's Digest Writing Community and author of *Solving the World's Problems* (Press 53). Follow him on Twitter @robertleebrewer.

6 WAYS TO PROMOTE YOUR NEW BOOK

by Jeannine Hall Gailey

When your new book arrives, you naturally want to shout the news from the rooftops, run and put a copy in everyone's hand, proudly take a selfie with your box of books and put it on Facebook. But what else can you do to promote your book that won't leave your online reputation in shambles?

In an ideal world, all you'd have to do is write the book, and everyone else—your publisher, your readers, your friends and family—would get word out about your book for you. Sadly, no matter who your publisher is you will be your book's best publicist. You can keep a social media presence with Tumblr, Twitter, Facebook, a blog, etc. But you know those annoying spammy tweets from authors clogging up your feeds with yet another glowing blurb or Amazon rank? You don't want to be that person.

My personal two "golden rules" of promotion—one of which looks a lot like the actual golden rule—are:

1. Do unto others as you would have them do unto you. Whether it's reviews, retweets, or just kind mentions on blogs, remember that you don't live in a vacuum, and you can hardly expect others to enthusiastically support your book if you haven't done much for your peer's books. Show up to your friends' book parties and debut readings, and you'll have a higher likelihood of a full house at your own.
2. Don't do anything online you wouldn't do in real life. If you wouldn't knock on your best friend's doorstep and tell them three days in a row to buy your book, don't do it in e-mail or Facebook messages, either.

Now, here are six ways to create positive buzz about your new title in a seemingly endless sea of new titles, and do it without alienating people. These tips will make the whole process as simple and painless for everyone as possible.

START CLOSE TO HOME

Because you have been working as a positive force for poetry in your immediate community the last few years (right??) you should have some friends and well-wishers who will be happy to help "boost your signal." The greater your involvement in building up your local poetry community and the more people you positively impact, the better.

For instance, I frequently write poetry book reviews for different outlets and write blurbs for writers I like, because I see it as "giving back" to the literary community. I also do it because someone once said to me when I was a young poet: "How can you hope for others to read and review your book if you don't read and review other people's books?" But reviewing isn't the only way to give back. You can run a reading series, edit a literary magazine, or even start your own press. Now that you have a book out, you'll realize that seemingly small gestures such as "liking" a post on Facebook, retweeting a book announcement, or reviewing a great book on Amazon or Goodreads, count more than you thought.

Also remember that it's much easier to sell your book of poetry in your hometown, at a reading full of friends and family, than it will be to sell it to strangers and students you've never met before. Remember, they're already cheering you on.

Similarly, you can reach out to people who have been kind to you in the past—reviewers who liked your previous work, mentors who have offered you help, your writing group—although this can only work if you're keeping either a list of people (with contact information, be it an e-mail address or a physical address) who might be interested in more of your work in the future. So keep up a list that I call it my "literary Christmas card list," and I actually use it to send Christmas cards, not just literary announcements. Again, being genuine friends with a lot of people will only help you in your efforts, so it pays to be generous. Karma, etc.

HELP PROMOTE OTHERS

This ties in with the previous tip. It makes sense that if you are kind and generous to others, helping spread the word about their good news, they are more likely to be kind and generous when you need help. When you think about sharing news about your book, think about the ways that news can help others—your publishers, editors, and others who have supported you along the way.

Award-winning poet Aimee Nezhukumatathil, a Professor of English at SUNY-Fredonia says: "I'm a big fan of using social media to post someone's poem that catches my breath, with a link to his/her recent book, or even better, to share my 'discovery' of an up-and-coming writer. On Twitter, even reading a line or two is enough to prick my curiosity. I've looked up poets and bought books from other people's postings. As for my own work, I share the occasional notice about where a recent poem or essay was published to help spread the word about the editors and magazines who believed in my work in the first place."

Being involved in helping other people succeed is a great way to build your literary community, so give others a boost when you can.

BOOK ANNOUNCEMENTS

A well-written, non-spammy (and spell-checked!) e-mail announcement to send to your friends, family, and colleagues is an easy thing a new author can do to let people know their book is available. Be friendly, respectful, and direct, and be sure to include, perhaps at the end, a direct link to buy your new book. If you want to include a few people who might have sent you kind notes in the past, or indicated interest in hearing about your new work, don't feel bad—do it. Remember that this can be a great way to get back in touch with old friends; I often have childhood friends, teachers, or students who write back after years of being out of contact. But please don't buy one of those prefabricated mailing list or send your news to every business acquaintance.

Marie Gauthier, Director of Sales & Marketing for Tupelo Press, reminds us to "remember to treat friends as allies, not customers. They want to help you spread the word; it's your job to make it as easy for them to help as you can, sending them the cover image of your book or a jpeg of a beautiful publicity release, items with visual appeal that are simple to share." She also advises writers to "include something personal or quirky or extra in your email that can help elevate it in the receiver's mind from 'spam.'"

Jericho Brown, award-winning poet, professor, and editor, has a few pieces of practical advice, warning writers to think hard about when and how they announce their book. "It makes sense to pay attention to the world in which we live and to be a real part of it. Don't post that you've won a big award or send an e-mail about your book the same day Zimmerman is declared not guilty. If you do send an e-mail to a group, make sure it's just once a year and that you include a link to the message or site you're promoting. Finally, if you want 4,000 people to know your good news at once, know also that you want to thank 4,000 people individually for congratulating you."

Be unique, be yourself, and be socially aware of timing when you send out your announcement.

SOCIAL MEDIA

Yes, it's probably a good idea to have a presence on social media—an author page on Facebook that allows people the option of learning news about your work, for instance, or a good basic website, and maybe a Twitter, Instagram, Pinterest, or Tumblr account. The good news about this kind of promotion is that you can do it in your pajamas! The bad news is that it's easy to overdo it and become unintentionally obnoxious. The other downside? Most people aren't constantly reading their Twitter or Facebook feeds, or checking your blog, so it's hard to know when those messages are being missed by a particular audience.

So, be smart about the way you promote your new book on social media.

Catherine Trestini, Digital Marketing and Social Media Strategist, suggests: "One author kept sending me messages on LinkedIn about his book IN ALL CAPS for weeks. It became so irritating that I eventually removed him from my network. So my first rule of thumb is to leave your spam at the front door. Readers need a reason to want your book. Make a good impression. But let him set the example of what not to do on social media. Similarly, remember to post different and new things about your book. Every day, we're zombie-scrolling through our Facebook feeds, subconsciously looking for great things to 'like' or comment on. Use your wit, empathy, and brainy attitude to engage me. My second piece of advice is: Do something awesome that speaks about who 'you' are on your Facebook page, and do it often (at least once a day). It will collect "likes" and comments and woo your readers. Only write what you would want to read, including talking about your book online."

Make your posts authentic, and only talk about your own book part of the time—again, be sure to post other people's news, interesting relevant articles (whether that's on Buffy the Vampire Slayer's impact on pop culture or the latest news on Fukushima) and try to give your followers more than just advertising.

POSTCARDS, BOOKMARKS, AND OTHER "SWAG"

I know it's a new media world, but don't discount the power and pleasure of real mail and the physical object. In my own experience, sending out postcards is one of the best ways to give people a tactile reminder that your book is out—as well as show off a brilliant cover design. You should include a direct link to purchase the book on the postcard somewhere, as well as a way to contact you to get a signed copy, so it will be as easy as possible for them to purchase it. And a personal note on the postcard never hurts.

I've seen fascinating "swag" at readings, from intricate mini-books the size of a business card to elaborate bookmarks, magnets and stickers. The idea is to leave an audience member at a reading or conference-goer a physical memento that will perhaps lead them later to think about your book and purchase it.

READINGS

With a new book coming out, of course you're planning a few readings, maybe around your own town, maybe a more ambitious tour across several states. This one you cannot do in your pajamas, but there are a lot of ways you can make readings more fun for your audience and give your friends a real reason to come out and cheer you on.

Don't just plan a reading—plan a book release party, where you can celebrate and spend time with your friends and family afterward. If your friends are so inclined, they could even host a poetry salon, an informal gathering with cocktails or snacks where you might read a few poems, offer to sell and sign books, but mostly, give writers an excuse to socialize with you and with each other.

For example, when you go to a reading out of town, make sure you're paired up with a popular local writer as well, and try to do something fun to connect—set up a workshop beforehand, or an informal reception afterwards.

Kelly Davio, former editor of *LA Review* and author of *Burn This House*, gives this advice from her recent first book tour: "Anytime I give a reading, I make sure to stay and listen attentively to every other poet, whether that's another featured reader or someone who has just come for the open mic. Listening to others is an important way that we poets can show respect for our readership; if we're asking others to listen to our poems or buy our books, we need to give our attention to their work as well."

In the end, you really want to be able to share your excitement about your book without being pushy or disrespectful, and a lot of that comes down to being genuine and self-aware.

JEANNINE HALL GAILEY served as the second Poet Laureate of Redmond, Washington and is the author of five books of poetry. Her website is www.webbish6.com and you can follow her on Twitter @webbish6.

POETRY ON STAGE

Practical Advice for Live Performance

....

by Daniel Ari

Butterflies. Cottonmouth. Sweaty palms and the sound of your own heart beating. Knowing that these are natural reactions to entering the spotlight—even for seasoned speakers—might make them only slightly easier to endure. But preparation and practice can boost your confidence, so you can enjoy the rewards that come with performing your poetry for an audience.

FACING THE FEAR

If you're not someone who intrinsically loves being on stage, you may decide never to go there. But there are benefits of public reading that can make it worthwhile to work through stage fright.

YOUR POETRY IMPROVES. Going through the process of presenting can help clarify your poetic voice and give you the perspective to catch words or phrases that make you stumble or that cloud your meaning. You might also receive constructive input from friends and supportive audience members.

YOUR AUDIENCE GROWS. Getting on stage can help you build your following. People who like what you do will want to read what you've written and become advocates of your work. Having a venue gives you the opportunity to sell books, plug your blog, add to your mailing list, and so on.

YOUR SPEAKING ABILITY IMPROVES. Becoming a more confident speaker can benefit other areas of your life. If you regularly address groups or run meetings, then café poetry readings are a good place to practice in a situation with lower stakes.

IT CAN BE EXCITING. Connecting with an audience can be truly exhilarating, and the chance to feel proud of your work can be the biggest reward.

AUDIENCES WANT TO HEAR YOU. Audiences at readings have made the decision to be there, and they are ready to receive you. Rise to the occasion with good material that's well prepared, and enjoy their appreciation.

PREPARE TO PERFORM

Attend enough readings, and you're likely to encounter a few brilliant writers—who have no sense of delivery. As you listen, you might notice their richness of language and deft handling of thematic subtleties. But their monotone voice and apparent lack of sensitivity to the audience will have you involuntarily glancing toward the exit.

Though any poet can simply walk up to a microphone and start reading, it's better to think of your reading as a theatrical performance and to devote time and attention to the project. A reading that satisfies both you and your audience takes preparation.

CHOOSE POEMS THAT WORK WELL IN YOUR VOICE. Gather more than enough poetry, too much for the stage time you will be given. Read each piece you are considering out loud a few times, and narrow down your selection to those poems that you can recite most fluidly and sincerely.

PREPARE FOR PRACTICE. Double-check the pronunciation of any difficult or unusual words. Listen carefully to what you are saying in the poem and think how you might emphasize and intone the words appropriately. Would the poem benefit from a brief introduction? If so, consider scripting and practicing that part as well so you can keep it to the point.

THINK LIKE A DIRECTOR. As you start to practice, consider how you want the poem to sound. Formal or conversational? Energetically quick or suspensefully slow? How loud do you want to speak? Will your tone, tempo or volume change? Consider your options, and look for what most naturally supports the poem in your voice.

TAKE NOTES. Many performers mark up practice copies of their poems to remind themselves how they want the reading to sound. You can highlight words you want to emphasize and make notes about when to speed up or slow down. Some poets I know who have studied music use musical notations to indicate crescendos, accents, pauses and so on.

MEMORIZE. The subject of an entire article in its own right, memorization doesn't come naturally to everyone; however, getting off paper can make a huge difference in performance. When you speak from memory, your hands are free to gesture more naturally. Your eyes can engage the audience, and the audience will clearly sense your commitment to the poem when you have committed it to memory.

Here are two techniques I use to memorize poems: 1) Recite the first two lines of your poem until you can speak them from memory; then add lines three and four. Keep adding lines as you recite the whole poem from the beginning, until you've assimilated the whole piece. 2) Record the poem and play it for yourself. Speak along with the recording of your voice. Repeat until you can recite along with yourself without pausing or mistakes.

These techniques can take hours or extend over days. Both are possible to do while you're doing something else like washing dishes, commuting to work, gardening, etc.

Once you have your poems in your memory, be sure to keep them there. Practice at least once a day until your reading date and a couple times a month afterward so the poems stay ready for the next time.

SLOW DOWN AND RELAX. When you're on stage, your tendency will be to speak more quickly than when you rehearse. This will be less of an issue if, when you rehearse, you consciously slow yourself down. Doing so will help offset your natural acceleration in the spotlight.

PRACTICE MORE. It's nearly impossible to over-rehearse. Instead, you're likely to discover new meanings and interpretations in your poems the more your practice them.

VIDEOTAPE YOURSELF. As you critique your performance, seeing yourself as an audience will see you can give you useful insights. Some readers pace as they read; others repeat a gesture or stand unnaturally still. With video, you'll see any unconscious habits you have—and then you can let go of them or consciously change them. Remember to be gentle with yourself. As you watch, focus on what you can improve, but also focus on how cool you are for preparing a performance. Make a point of feeling proud of yourself.

DO A PRE-SHOW. Gather a couple of close friends, a spouse, a supportive sibling or neighbor and recite for them. This is like easing into a hot tub. Reciting for a couple of friendly faces is your warm up to getting on stage in front of strangers. If you'd like feedback from your pre-show audience, ask them direct and specific questions such as:

- Was my voice loud enough?
- Did you understand each word?
- Did you understand and enjoy the poem?

FIND YOUR VENUE

An Internet search for "Poetry Readings" in your area will turn up cafes, bookstores, clubs, bars, theaters, galleries, speakeasies, or other venues. Contact them online or by phone to find out what's going on and how you can participate.

It's a good idea to visit the venue to check out the scene before you go to read, especially if you're new to public reading. By watching other performers and talking to event hosts, you can find out how much time performers get and any other parameters you need to know. You'll also get a sense of what the audience appreciates.

Poetry Slams, for example, usually keep readers to a strict limit of three minutes of high-energy recitation—from memory—before penalties apply in the form of docked points from the volunteer judges. Yes, judges. Delivering a poem significantly different from the usual style at a poetry slam increases the chance of audience heckling, which is not meant to be hurtful, but is a traditional part of some poetry slams. Café open mics, on the other hand, are typically laid back with looser time limits in a wider range of styles. The main thing is to know in advance what you can expect from the venue and its audience.

Many organizers of ongoing events select featured readers whom they've come to know. If you want to be a featured reader at a regular event, a good way to get there is to keep showing up. Introduce yourself to the organizers, and when it seems right, let your interest be known. They'll let you know how you can earn a featured slot.

If performing for strangers worries you, consider arranging your own reading at a private residence. You can decide who to invite, how to decorate, when to start and end, what to charge, what food or beverages to serve, who else will perform, and so on. Though it takes more effort and leadership on your part, setting up your own reading lets you create exactly the event you want.

When you know where and when you're performing, spread the word. If it's your first time and you could use some moral support, invite close friends to be there or to go with you. If you're a seasoned performer doing a featured reading or a one-person show, be sure to advertise. Use Facebook and Evite to get on your desired audiences' calendars. You can also send a quick press release to your local arts weekly, radio station and online calendar sites.

Note that people respond more consistently to personal phone calls, e-mails or texts. If there are people you really want to be there, take the extra time to contact them directly.

BEFORE YOU PERFORM

The poems you choose to recite should be ones that move you and that you're enthusiastic to share. As you practice, you claim the words; they enter your mind and soul. So when it comes time to read, trust the words. Draw confidence from the excellence of the poetry and the time you've put into your performance. On the day or evening of your performance, these steps can support your sense of confidence and help your reading go just right:

DRESS FOR THE VENUE. Attractive, clean and hip are always appropriate. You can do something flashy, but don't let your clothes distract from your words. Dress like Lady Gaga, and your clothing will overshadow your poetry.

EAT LIGHT. If you're feeling nervous, don't eat for a couple of hours before your performance, but stay hydrated.

SET UP YOUR CAMERA. If you're recording or having someone record you, be sure to get connected early and test your equipment before the show starts.

WARM UP. Try to find some time backstage or outside to warm up your voice. It will help you relax and improve your projection, pacing, breathing and enunciation. Here are some easy warm ups:

1. Yawn or sigh deeply a couple of times. Make the natural yawning sounds to relax your throat and vocal chords.
2. Recite a few tongue twisters. Red leather, yellow leather. She sells sea shells by the sea shore. You know New York; you need New York; you know you need unique New York.
3. Recite one or two lines of your poem while grotesquely over-enunciating each word. This will loosen your tongue, lips, jaw and nasal passages.
4. Blow air through your lips with and without engaging your vocal chords.
5. With your fingertips, massage your jaw, lips, cheeks and chin.
6. Make exaggerated chewing motions as though you are chomping twenty pieces of gum at once. Make the sounds that would go with the motions.
7. Finish by taking three slow, deep breaths. This is especially good to do before you go on stage. If an emcee introduces you, take that time to breathe consciously, deeply and slowly. And then...

You're on!

DO IT

Once you're on, you're on. Go with the words of the poem and the performance you prepared. When you practice, it will help to develop these good habits so they come naturally when you're on stage:

- Stand up straight so your lungs and throat are fully open.
- Put your breath behind your voice and project your words to the far end of the room.
- Speak slowly and let the words take their resonance in sound and meaning.
- Let yourself pause between stanzas or thoughts.

Your voice when performing shouldn't sound exactly like your everyday conversational voice, even if you're reciting in a conversational tone. Your words will be somewhat slower, more distinct, more fully enunciated. It may sound funny to you until you're used to it, but an audience depends on the enhanced clarity and resonance to get the full effect of what you're saying.

When you're on stage, strive to make eye contact with the audience. I find it helps to imagine that everyone there is an old friend of mine, even the person dourly glaring up at me from the fourth row.

If there's a microphone, simply project into it with your mouth positioned about a foot away. Many novice performers get distracted trying to adjust the mic stand or cord. The less of that you can do the better—you don't even have to touch the microphone. And if there are any issues with the microphone or sound system, politely ask if you can get some help before you start your recitation.

If you lose your place in the poem or stumble over a word, simply take a breath and start the line or stanza again. It's okay for you to take a moment in quiet to find your place and to look at the audience. You'll see that they are ready for you to continue, and they want you to succeed. Remember: You own the poem. Trust the words and let them come through you.

At the end of your reading, I suggest doing what feels right to you in terms of acknowledging your applause and thanking your emcee or host; but usually a bow of the head is polite and sufficient.

When I get off stage, I try to take a few deep, calming breaths before I talk to anyone. It's good to let your endorphins settle before you start meeting and greeting. But do let yourself receive kudos from your audience.

If you want feedback on your performance, watch the video if you have one and look for ways to inflect words differently or improve your delivery. Don't be overly critical. Focus only on your words and your delivery. Consider asking friends and other performers you trust for honest and constructive input. It's also good to watch other poets perform so you can see what styles and behaviors you want to model and make your own.

For the long term, keep doing it. Keep building your confidence, your repertoire, and your audience. Be sure to practice a few times a month to keep poems ready for opportunities to share. You might find your recitations welcome in your place of worship, among wedding toasts, or at informal social gatherings. When the moment's right, you'll be ready to make the gentle offer, "Would you like to hear a poem?"

DANIEL ARI's book, *One Way to Ask*, pairs poems in an original form called queron with imagery by more than 60 artists. Besides being a professional copywriter, he writes and publishes poetry and organizes poetry performances and events throughout the Pacific Northwest. He blogs at fightswithpoems.blogspot.com.

SOCIAL MEDIA PRIMER FOR POETS

by Robert Lee Brewer

Beyond the actual writing, the most important thing writers can do for their writing careers is to build a writer platform. This writer platform can consist of any number of quantifiable information about your reach to your target audience, and one hot spot is social media.

HERE'S THE THING: It's more important to chase quality connections than quantity connections on social media.

Social media is one way to quantify your reach to your target audience. If you write poetry, your target audience is people who read poetry (often other folks who write poetry). If you write cookbooks, your target audience is people who like to cook.

In both cases, you can drill down into more specifics. Maybe the target audience for the poetry book is actually people who read sonnets. For the cookbook, maybe it's directed at people who like to cook desserts.

4 SOCIAL MEDIA TIPS

Social media is one way to connect with your target audience and influencers (like agents, editors, book reviewers, other writers) who connect to your target audience. Sites like Facebook, Twitter, LinkedIn, YouTube, Pinterest, Goodreads, Red Room, and so many more—they're all sites dedicated to helping people (and in some cases specifically writers) make connections.

Here are my four social media tips for writers:

1. **START SMALL.** The worst thing writers can do with social media is jump on every social media site ever created immediately, post a bunch of stuff, and then quit because they're overwhelmed on the time commitment and underwhelmed by the lack

of response. Instead, pick one site, complete all the information about yourself, and start browsing around in that one neighborhood for a while.

2. **LOOK FOR CONNECTIONS.** Notice that I did not advise looking for leads or followers or whatever. Don't approach strangers online like a used car salesman. Be a potential friend and/or source of information. One meaningful connection is worth more than 5,000 disengaged "followers." Seriously.

3. **COMMUNICATE.** There are two ways to make a mistake here. One, never post or share anything on your social media account. Potential new connections will skip over your ghost town profile assuming your account is no longer active. Plus, you're missing an opportunity to really connect with others. The other mistake is to post a million (hopefully an exaggeration) things a day and never communicate with your connections. It's social media, after all; be social.

4. **GIVE MORE THAN YOU TAKE.** So don't post a million things a day, but be sure to share calls for submissions, helpful information (for your target audience), fun quotes, great updates from your connections (which will endear you to them further). Share updates from your end of the world, but don't treat your social media accounts as a place to sell things nonstop. Remember: Don't be a used car salesman.

ONE FINAL TIP: Focus. Part of effective platform building is knowing your target audience and reaching them. So with every post, every status update, every tweet, every connection, etc., keep focused on how you are bringing value to your target audience.

POPULAR SOCIAL NETWORKING SITES

The social media landscape is constantly shifting, but here are some that are currently popular:

- Bebo (http://bebo.com)
- Digg (http://digg.com)
- Facebook (http://facebook.com)
- Flickr (http://flickr.com)
- Habbo (http://habbo.com)
- Hi5 (http://hi5.com)
- Instagram (http://instagram.com)
- LinkedIn (http://linkedin.com)
- MeetUp (http://meetup.com)
- Ning (http://ning.com)
- Orkut (http://orkut.com)
- Pinterest (http://pinterest.com)
- Reddit (http://reddit.com)

- StumbleUpon (http://stumbleupon.com)
- Twitter (http://twitter.com)
- Yelp (http://yelp.com)
- YouTube (http://youtube.com)
- Zorpia (htttp://zorpia.com)

9 THINGS TO DO ON ANY SOCIAL MEDIA SITE

Not all social media sites are created the same. However, there are some things poets can do on any site to improve the quantity and quality of the connections they make online.

1. **USE YOUR REAL NAME.** If the point of social media is to increase your visibility, then don't make the mistake of cloaking your identity behind some weird handle or nickname. Use your real name—or that is, use your real byline as it appears (or would appear) when published.

2. **USE YOUR HEADSHOT FOR AN AVATAR.** Again, avoid concealing your identity as a cartoon image or picture of a celebrity or pet. The rules of online networking are the same as face-to-face networking. Imagine how silly it would be to see someone holding up a picture of a pet cat while talking to you in person.

3. **COMPLETE YOUR PROFILE.** Each site has different ways to complete this information. You don't have to include religious or political views, but you do want to make your site personal while still communicating your interest and experience in poetry. One tip: Give people a way to contact you that doesn't involve using the social networking site. For instance, an e-mail address.

4. **LINK TO WEBSITES.** If you have a blog and/or author website, link to these in your profile on all social media sites. After all, you want to make it as easy as possible for people to learn more about you. If applicable, link to your previously published books at points of purchase too.

5. **MAKE EVERYTHING PUBLIC.** As a poet, you are a public figure. Embrace that state of mind and make everything you do public on social media. This means you may have to sacrifice some privacy, but there are pre-Facebook ways of communicating private matters with friends and family.

6. **UPDATE REGULARLY.** Whether it's a status update or a tweet, regular updates accomplish two things: One, they keep you in the conversation; and two, they let people you know (and people you don't know) see that you're actively using your account. Activity promotes more connections and conversations, which is what poets want on social media sites.

7. **JOIN AND PARTICIPATE IN RELEVANT GROUPS.** One key to this tip is relevancy.

There are lots of random groups out there, but the ones that will benefit you the most are ones relevant to your interests and goals. Another key is participation. Participate in your group when possible.

8. **BE SELECTIVE.** Piggybacking on the previous tip, be selective about who you friend, who you follow, which groups you join, etc. Don't let people bully you into following them either. Only connect with and follow people or groups you think might bring you value—if not immediately, then eventually.

9. **EVOLVE.** When I started social media, MySpace was the top hangout. Eventually, I moved on to Facebook and Twitter (at the urging of other connections). Who knows which sites I'll prefer in five months, let alone five years, from now. Evolve as the landscape evolves. In fact, even my usage of specific sites has had to evolve as user behavior changes and the sites themselves change.

FINAL THOUGHT

If you have a blog, be sure to use it to feed your social media site profiles. Each new post should be a status update or tweet. This will serve the dual purpose of bringing traffic to your blog and providing value to your social media connections.

ROBERT LEE BREWER is a senior editor with the Writer's Digest Writing Community and author of *Solving the World's Problems* (Press 53). Follow him on Twitter @robertleebrewer.

WHY POETS NEED PLATFORMS

And How to Create One

....

by Sage Cohen

If you want your poetry to be read, people need to know who you are, what you write, and where to find it. A viable platform can take you there. The good news is that anyone who wants to establish a poetry platform can take the necessary steps to build one over time. No matter what your level of writing, publishing and social media savvy, you can have more fun end enjoy more success as you take small steps over time to cultivate your poetry platform. This article will tell you how.

WHAT A PLATFORM IS

Platform is the turf you name and claim as your area of writing expertise, and it's everything you do to make that expertise visible. Just as a thesis is the foundation of a term paper around which its argument is built, a platform is an organizing principle around which a poet's many expressions of work revolve. A platform says to both the poet and the world, "I am an expert in [fill in the blanks with your specialty]!"

Platform is both the destination and the path. Think of your platform as your portfolio of accomplishments (publications, leadership roles, Web presence, public appearances, classes) that demonstrate your authority on a given topic. You build it as you go. It keeps you moving forward, tells you where forward is, and is the measure against which you decide if you're getting there.

HOW A PLATFORM CAN HELP YOU

Every poet can benefit from having a platform—even you. Following are the primary advantages of platform consciousness:

- **POETIC PROWESS.** The more focused you are on taking your poetry forward, the more likely you will stay engaged in honing your craft, polishing drafts, completing poems and identifying organizing principles or themes in your growing collection of work.

- **PUBLISHING.** As you gain experience researching literary journals and sending out your work, your knowledge about the publications best suited (and most receptive) to your work will grow. Over time, you will develop relationships, insight and a publishing track record that may significantly increase your chances of publishing (both individual poems and collections of poems).

- **FUNDRAISING.** Platform gives success an opportunity to snowball. With each publication, award, recognition or other notch on your belt, you'll improve the odds of winning prizes and receiving grants and residencies if this is of interest to you.

- **AUTHORITY.** The more experience you have writing and publishing poetry (and potentially educating/exciting others about their own poetic process), the more you and others will trust in your authority.

- **OPPORTUNITY.** Once you have earned a reputable name among your poetic peers, requests for interviews, articles, speaking engagements, teaching, and more are likely to start rolling in. But more importantly, you will have paved the way to go after exactly what you want to create in your writing life, buoyed by the confidence that comes from proven expertise.

NAMING AND CLAIMING YOUR PLATFORM

Not sure what your platform is or what you want it to be? It may be as simple as "Poetry." Or you could name what you believe your poetry is serving or striving for—if this is relevant to your work. Several years ago I named my platform "Writing the Life Poetic," which quickly led to me authoring a nonfiction book by this name. One thing is certain: naming and claiming your area of expertise is going to give you a new sense of clarity and purpose. And you may be surprised at how quickly this clarity magnetizes new, relevant opportunities to you.

If you'd like to explore some of the possibilities for your poetic platform, the following exercise can help. I encourage you to map out your own Platform at a Glance using the example below as a starting place. It's OK if you don't have all the answers yet. Having a record of what you're aspiring to today can help you learn about where you're headed over time.

PLATFORM AT A GLANCE

PLATFORM BUILDING BLOCKS	INSIGHTS
Theme, topic, genre, or area of expertise	Poetry for the people: with a goal of encouraging writers of all levels to write, read, and enjoy poetry.
Audience(s) you serve	• People who feel afraid, unwelcome, or unsure of how to start writing poetry. • People already writing poetry who want to write more, improve their craft, and have more fun. • Writers of all stripes wanting to invigorate their relationship with language. • People who love poetry and read poems.
Needs, desires, and preferences of your audience(s)	• People who feel afraid: Want to be invited in to poetry and assured that they are welcome/can do it. • People already writing poetry: Seeking tools, techniques, and tips to help improve their craft. • Writers of all stripes: Seeking a poetic lens through which to better appreciate and apply language in anything and everything they write • People who love reading poems: Want to find poems that connect, move them, reveal something new.
Value you bring to each different type of reader	• People who feel afraid: Friendly encouragement and useful information. • People already writing poetry: Vast selection of tips, tools, strategies, and examples. • Writers of all stripes: A way into—and an enjoyable exploration of—the life poetic. • People who love reading poems: Poems I've written that they can embrace and enjoy.

PLATFORM NAME	WRITING THE LIFE POETIC
Why you are the ideal person to develop this platform over time	I have more than 20 years of experience cultivating a poetic way of life. I have an advanced degree in creative writing, a great deal of teaching experience, and a well-established career of writing and publishing poetry.
Why you are passionate about doing so	Poetry matters—not just as a literary form, but as a way of life. I know from my own experience that a relationship with poetry can significantly expand a person's sense of possibility, delight, and camaraderie with one's self, universal human truths, and life itself. I want to make this gift available to anyone who's interested in receiving it—as a teacher, author and poet.

MULTIPLE PATHS TO PLATFORM DEVELOPMENT

Publishing is certainly a significant way to establish and build your platform. But it is one of many. The good news is that while you're waiting for your latest batch of poems to make a safe landing in just the right literary journal(s), there are many ways to grow your visibility as an expert in your field that are available to you right now. Let's consider a few:

- **GO PUBLIC.** Read your work publicly as much as possible—either as a featured reader through a reading series or special event or at an open mic reading. Open mics are far more widely accessible and encourage everyone to participate. They're a good way to establish a community of writers if you attend and share work regularly. Over time, people will start to recognize you and your work. This will help you learn who your audience is and what it is about your poems that appeals to them.

- **TEACH WHAT YOU KNOW.** If you are passionate about poetry and have been schooling yourself in the craft (either through formal education or self-study), chances are good that you have something to offer other poets. From tenured academic positions to workshops you've organized and publicized yourself, you can choose the forum that fits your experience and temperament—then bring people together to learn about what's possible in poetry.

- **GIVE SERVICE.** There are endless ways to give service to poets—both paid and volunteer. You could become active in an online community—or start your own—that writes or contemplates poetry. Depending on your level of expertise, you could offer coaching, consulting, or editing. If you enjoy working with people of certain ages or circumstances (such as students, prisoners, elders), you could find ways to share poetry in your community through religious, educational or civic organizations.

- **PUBLISH.** Most poets are likely to experience multiple types and stages of publishing throughout their career. Because publishing individual poems can be slow and full collections even slower, you may want to explore other ways of sharing your knowledge of poetry along the way by publishing how-to articles, interviews or essays about the life poetic. You can query print and online magazines, share free content with organizations or online communities that serve poets and writers and/or create Squidoo lenses on any number of craft or publishing issues. If self-publishing is of interest to you, you could write and sell instructional e-books or publish print-on-demand collections of your poems (only if you are not seeking "mainstream" publication for this work.)

- **GO SOCIAL.** Social media gives poets instantaneous access to a virtually limitless community that can help your poetry and your platform evolve over time. When you want to exchange ideas, inspiration, poems, encouragement, tips and resources, book reviews, links, or professional recommendations, you can do so using any number of social media outlets. Facebook, Twitter, GoodReads and LinkedIn are just a few of the most popular places to do so. Choose one or two online forums in which to start; spend some time investigating how others are using these; decide what kind of information exchange best reflects your platform; and then pace yourself as you become a relevant contributor to the online conversation.

- **BECOME YOUR OWN MEDIA CHANNEL.** With a wide range of simple and inexpensive interactive media available today, you have numerous options for getting your message out. First, consider your platform aspirations. Then, decide what kind of information you'd like to share—and whether your goal is to inspire, collaborate, teach, build community or some combination of these. Depending on your goals, you might consider employing interactive media such as: webinars, teleclasses, e-zines, podcasts, and specialized online communities such as Ning. Try one and commit to it for at least six months; then evaluate, refine and expand as you go.

COHERENCE AND YOUR POETIC SOUL

These days, readers expect to have a personal connection with the poets they enjoy through their websites, blogs, teaching and live appearances. Plus, with the widespread use of social media bridging the space between writer and reader, anyone who has admired your work can tap into your moment-by-moment publicized thinking through the social media communities you frequent.

Therefore, who you are (or more accurately, how you present yourself publicly) and what you write are often one continuous experience for readers. A writing life that grows out of and reflects who you authentically are is going to be the most grounded and sustainable path to success.

My friend Dan Raphael is an example of someone who has built a writing empire on the foundation of his wildly entertaining and unusual command of language and life. On the back of one of Dan's books is a quote that says:

She: Do you think he's ever taken acid?

He: Taken it? I think he wears a patch.

Dan delivers on this very engaging and entertaining promise. He is a transcendent force of nature and engaging linguistic acrobatics on stage when delivering his poems and behind the scenes, when sending e-mail to friends.

I have another friend who is a widely sought photographer who has recently been recognized in several national magazines. This photographer has a parallel platform as a poet; and a good number of her poems explore the socioeconomic dynamics of being a person providing a service for the elite and the wealthy. This presents a bit of a platform pretzel, as she has no desire to alienate valued clients with her poetry. The expert photographer/poet is very delicately navigating how to hold these two parts of her life with integrity and authenticity as she quickly becomes more visible and respected in both chosen fields.

How is your life in alignment or out of whack with your platform(s) today? Is there anything you need to reconcile to create a greater coherence between what you write and how you live?

HAVE PLATFORM, WILL PROSPER

With a clear platform as the organizing principle in your life poetic, you can take the steps that will make your poems and your life poetic more visible in the communities and publications that matter to you. As you become increasingly effective at creating the writing results you want, over time you will attract more readers, expand your sphere of influence and generate far more opportunities to share your love of poetry.

SAGE COHEN is the author of *Writing the Life Poetic* and *The Productive Writer*, both from Writer's Digest Books, and the poetry collection *Like the Heart, the World*. She holds an MFA in creative writing from New York University and a BA from Brown University. Sage has won first place in the Ghost Road Press poetry contest, been nominated for a Pushcart Prize and published a number of articles in *Writer's Digest* magazine. In 2011, she judged the Writer's Digest contest for non-rhyming poetry. To learn more about Sage, visit pathofpossibility.com.

30-DAY PLATFORM CHALLENGE

Build Your Writing Platform in a Month

by Robert Lee Brewer

Whether writers are looking to find success through traditional publication or the self-publishing route, they'll find a strong writer platform will help them in their efforts. A platform is not marketing; it's the actual and quantifiable reach writers have to their target audience.

Here is a 30-day platform challenge I've developed to help writers get started in their own platform-building activities without getting overwhelmed. By accomplishing one task for one day, writers can feel a sense of accomplishment and still handle their normal daily activities. By the end of the month, writers should have a handle on what they need to do to keep growing their platform into the future.

DAY 1: DEFINE YOURSELF

For Day 1, define yourself. Don't worry about where you'd like to be in the future. Instead, take a look at who you are today, what you've already accomplished, what you're currently doing, etc.

EXAMPLE DEFINE YOURSELF WORKSHEET

Here is a chart I'm using (with my own answers). Your worksheet can ask even more questions. The more specific you can be the better for this exercise.

NAME (AS USED IN BYLINE): Robert Lee Brewer

POSITION(S): Senior Content Editor - Writer's Digest Writing Community; Author; Freelance Writer; Blogger; Event Speaker; Den Leader - Cub Scouts; Curator of Insta-poetry Series

SKILL(S): Editing, creative writing (poetry and fiction), technical writing, copywriting, database management, SEO, blogging, newsletter writing, problem solving, idea generation, public speaking, willingness to try new things, community building.

SOCIAL MEDIA PLATFORMS: Facebook, LinkedIn, Google+, Twitter, Tumblr, Blogger.

URLs: www.writersmarket.com; www.writersdigest.com/editor-blogs/poetic-asides; http://robertleebrewer.blogspot.com/; www.robertleebrewer.com

ACCOMPLISHMENTS: Named 2010 Poet Laureate of Blogosphere; spoken at several events, including Writer's Digest Conference, AWP, Austin International Poetry Festival, Houston Poetry Fest, and more; author of Solving the World's Problems (Press 53); published and sold out of two limited edition poetry chapbooks, *Enter* and *Escape*; edited several editions of *Writer's Market* and *Poet's Market*; former GMVC conference champion in the 800-meter run and MVP of WCHS cross country and track teams; undergraduate award-winner in several writing disciplines at University of Cincinnati, including Journalism, Fiction, and Technical Writing; BA in English Literature from University of Cincinnati with certificates in writing for Creative Writing-Fiction and Professional and Technical Writing.

INTERESTS: Writing (all genres), family (being a good husband and father), faith, fitness (especially running and disc golf), fantasy football, reading.

IN ONE SENTENCE, WHO AM I? Robert Lee Brewer is a married Methodist father of five children (four sons and one daughter) who works as an editor but plays as a writer, specializing in poetry and blogging.

As long as you're being specific and honest, there are no wrong answers when it comes to defining yourself. However, you may realize that you have more to offer than you think. Or you may see an opportunity that you didn't realize even existed.

DAY 2: SET YOUR GOALS

For today's platform-building task, set your goals. Include short-term goals and long-term goals. In fact, make a list of goals you can accomplish by the end of this year; then, make a list of goals you'd like to accomplish before you die.

EXAMPLE GOALS

Here are some of examples from my short-term and long-term goal lists:

SHORT-TERM GOALS:
- Promote new book, *Solving the World's Problems*.
- In April, complete April PAD Challenge on Poetic Asides blog.
- Get *Writer's Market 2016* to printer ahead of schedule.
- Get *Poet's Market 2016* to printer ahead of schedule.
- Lead workshop at Poetry Hickory event in April.
- Etc.

LONG-TERM GOALS:
- Publish book on platform development for small businesses.
- Raise 5 happy and healthy children into 5 happy, healthy, caring, and self-sufficient adults.
- Continue to learn how to be a better husband and human being.
- Become a bestselling novelist.
- Win Poet Laureate of the Universe honors.
- Etc.

Some writers may ask what defining yourself and creating goals has to do with platform development. I maintain that these are two of the most basic and important steps in the platform-building process, because they define who you are and where you want to be.

A successful platform strategy should communicate who you are and help you get where you'd like to be (or provide you with a completely new opportunity). If you can't communicate who you are to strangers, then they won't realize how you might be able to help them or why you're important to them. If you don't have any goals, then you don't have any direction or purpose for your platform.

By defining who you are and what you want to accomplish, you're taking a huge step in establishing a successful writing and publishing career.

DAY 3: JOIN FACEBOOK

For today's task, create a profile on Facebook. Simple as that. If you don't have one, it's as easy as going to www.facebook.com and signing up. It takes maybe 5 or 10 minutes. If that.

10 FACEBOOK TIPS FOR WRITERS

Many readers probably already have a Facebook profile, and that's fine. If you have already created a profile (or are doing so today), here are some tips for handling your profile:

- Complete your profile. The most checked page on most profiles is the About page. The more you share the better.
- Make everything public. Like it or not, writers are public figures. If you try to hide, it will limit the potential platform.
- Think about your audience in everything you do. When your social media profiles are public, anyone can view what you post. Keep this in mind at all times.
- Include a profile pic of yourself. Avoid setting your avatar as anything but a headshot of yourself. Many people don't like befriending a family pet or cartoon image.
- Update your status regularly. If you can update your status once per day, that's perfect. At the very least, update your status weekly. If your profile is a ghost town, people will treat it like one.
- Communicate with friends on Facebook. Facebook is a social networking site, but networking happens when you communicate. So communicate.
- Be selective about friends. Find people who share your interests. Accept friends who share your interests. Other folks may be fake or inappropriate connections trying to build their "friend" totals.
- Be selective about adding apps. If you're not sure, it's probably best to avoid. Many users have wasted days, weeks, and even months playing silly games on Facebook.
- Join relevant groups. The emphasis should be placed on relevancy. For instance, I'm a poet, so I join poetry groups.
- Follow relevant fan pages. As with groups, the emphasis is placed on relevancy. In my case, I'm a fan of several poetry publications.

In addition to the tips above, be sure to always use your name as it appears in your byline. If you're not consistent in how you list your name in your byline, it's time to pick a name and stick with it. For instance, my byline name is Robert Lee Brewer—not Robbie Brewer, Bob Brewer, or even just Robert Brewer.

There are times when I absolutely can't throw the "Lee" in there, but the rest of the time it is Robert Lee Brewer. And the reasoning behind this is that it makes it easier for people who know me elsewhere to find and follow me on Facebook (or whichever social media site). Name recognition is super important when you're building your writer platform.

DAY 4: JOIN TWITTER

For today's task, create a Twitter account. That's right. Go to www.twitter.com and sign up—if you're not already. This task will definitely take less than 5 minutes.

As with Facebook, I would not be surprised to learn that most readers already have a Twitter account. Here are three important things to keep in mind:

- **MAKE YOUR PROFILE BIO RELEVANT.** You might want to use a version of the sentence you wrote for Day 1's task. Look at my profile (twitter.com/robertleebrewer) if you need an example.
- **USE AN IMAGE OF YOURSELF.** One thing about social media (and online networking) is that people love to connect with other people. So use an image of yourself—not of your pet, a cute comic strip, a new age image, flowers, robots, etc.
- **MAKE YOUR TWITTER HANDLE YOUR BYLINE—IF POSSIBLE.** For instance, I am known as @RobertLeeBrewer on Twitter, because I use Robert Lee Brewer as my byline on articles, in interviews, at speaking events, on books, etc. Be as consistent with your byline as humanly possible.

Once you're in Twitter, try finding some worthwhile tweeps to follow. Also, be sure to make a tweet or two. As with Facebook, people will only interact with your profile if it looks like you're actually there and using your account.

SOME BASIC TWITTER TERMINOLOGY

Twitter has a language all its own. Here are some of the basics:

- **TWEET.** This is what folks call the 140-character messages that can be sent on the site. Anyone who follows you can access your tweets.
- **RT.** RT stands for re-tweet. This is what happens when someone shares your tweet, usually character for character. It's usually good form to show attribution for the author of the original tweet.
- **DM.** DM stands for direct message. This is a good way to communicate with someone on Twitter privately. I've actually had a few opportunities come my way through DMs on Twitter.
- **#.** The #-sign stands for hashtag. Hashtags are used to organize group conversations. For instance, Writer's Digest uses the #wdc to coordinate messages for their Writer's Digest Conferences. Anyone can start a hashtag, and they're sometimes used to add humor or emphasis to a tweet.
- **FF.** FF stands for follow Friday—a day typically set asides to highlight follow-worthy tweeps (or folks who use Twitter). There's also a WW that stands for writer Wednesday.

DAY 5: START A BLOG

For today's task, create a blog. You can use Blogger (www.blogger.com), WordPress (www.wordpress.com), or Tumblr (www.tumblr.com). In fact, you can use another blogging platform if you wish. To complete today's challenge, do the following:

- **CREATE A BLOG.** That is, sign up (if you don't already have a blog), pick a design (these can usually be altered later if needed), and complete your profile.
- **WRITE A POST FOR TODAY.** If you're not sure what to cover, you can just introduce yourself and share a brief explanation of how your blog got started. Don't make it too complicated.

If you already have a blog, excellent! You don't need to create a new one, but you might want to check out some ways to optimize what you have.

OPTIMIZE YOUR BLOG

Here are some tips for making your blog rock:

- **USE IMAGES IN YOUR POSTS.** Images are eye candy for readers, help with search engine optimization, and can even improve clicks when shared on social media sites, such as Facebook and Twitter.
- **USE HEADERS IN POSTS.** Creating and bolding little headlines in your posts will go a long way toward making your posts easier to read and scan. Plus, they'll just look more professional.
- **WRITE SHORT.** Short sentences (fewer than 10 words). Short paragraphs (fewer than five sentences). Concision is precision in online composition.
- **ALLOW COMMENTS.** Most bloggers receive very few (or absolutely zero) comments in the beginning, but it pays to allow comments, because this gives your audience a way to interact with you. For my personal blog, I allow anyone to comment on new posts, but those that are more than a week old require my approval.

DAY 6: READ AND COMMENT ON A POST

For today's task, read at least one blog post and comment on it (linking back to your blog). And the comment should not be something along the lines of, "Hey, cool post. Come check out my blog." Instead, you need to find a blog post that really speaks to you and then make a thoughtful comment.

Here are a few possible ways to respond.

- **SHARE YOUR OWN EXPERIENCE.** If you've experienced something similar to what's covered in the post, share your own story. You don't have to write a book or anything, but maybe a paragraph or two.
- **ADD ANOTHER PERSPECTIVE.** Maybe the post was great, but there's another angle that should be considered. Don't be afraid to point that angle out.
- **ASK A QUESTION.** A great post usually will prompt new thoughts and ideas—and questions. Ask them.

As far as linking back to your blog, you could include your blog's URL in the comment, but also, most blogs have a field in their comments that allow you to share your URL. Usually, your name will link to that URL, which should either be your blog or your author website (if it offers regularly updated content).

It might seem like a lot of work to check out other blogs and comment on them, but this is an incredible way to make real connections with super users. These connections can lead to guest post and interview opportunities. In fact, they could even lead to speaking opportunities too.

DAY 7: ADD SHARE BUTTONS TO YOUR BLOG

For today's challenge, add share buttons to your blog and/or website.

The easiest way to do this is to go to www.addthis.com and click on the Get AddThis button. It's big, bright, and orange. You can't miss it.

Basically, the site will give you button options, and you select the one you like best. The AddThis site will then provide you with HTML code that you can place into your site and/or blog posts. Plus, it provides analytics for bloggers who like to see how much the buttons are boosting traffic.

If you want customized buttons, you could enlist the help of a programmer friend or try playing with the code yourself. I recently learned that some really cool buttons on one friend's blog were created by her husband (yes, she married a programmer, though I don't think she had her blog in mind when she did so).

Plus, most blogging platforms are constantly adding new tools. By the time you read this article, there are sure to be plenty of fun new buttons, apps, and widgets available.

Here's the thing about social sharing buttons: They make it very easy for people visiting your site to share your content with their social networks via Facebook, Twitter, LinkedIn, Instagram, Pinterest, and other sites. The more your content is shared the wider your writer platform.

DAY 8: JOIN LINKEDIN

For today's challenge, create a LinkedIn profile. Go to www.linkedin.com and set it up in a matter of minutes. After creating profiles for Facebook and Twitter, this task should be easy.

LINKEDIN TIPS FOR WRITERS

In many ways, LinkedIn looks the same as the other social networks, but it does have its own quirks. Here are a few tips for writers:

- **USE YOUR OWN HEAD SHOT.** You've heard this advice before. People want to connect with people, not family pets and/or inanimate objects.
- **COMPLETE YOUR PROFILE.** The more complete your profile the better. It makes you look more human.
- **GIVE THOUGHTFUL RECOMMENDATIONS TO RECEIVE THEM.** Find people likely to give you recommendations and recommend them first. This will prompt them to return the favor.
- **SEARCH FOR CONNECTIONS YOU ALREADY HAVE.** This is applicable to all social networks. Find people you know to help you connect with those you don't.
- **MAKE MEANINGFUL CONNECTIONS WITH OTHERS.** Remember: It's not about how many connections you make; it's about how many meaningful connections you make.
- **MAKE YOUR PROFILE EASY TO FIND.** You can do this by using your byline name. (For instance, I use linkedin.com/in/robertleebrewer.)
- **TAILOR YOUR PROFILE TO YOUR VISITOR.** Don't fill out your profile thinking only about yourself; instead, think about what your target audience might want to learn about you.

LinkedIn is often considered a more "professional" site than the other social networks like Facebook, Instagram, and Twitter. For one thing, users are prompted to share their work experience and request recommendations from past employers and current co-workers.

However, this site still offers plenty of social networking opportunities for people who can hook up with the right people and groups.

DAY 9: RESPOND TO AT LEAST THREE TWEETS

For today's task, respond to at least three tweets from other tweeps on Twitter.

Since Day 4's assignment was to sign up for Twitter, you should have a Twitter account—and you're hopefully following some other Twitter users. Just respond to at least three tweets today.

As far as your responses, it's not rocket science. You can respond with a "great article" or "cool quote." A great way to spread the wealth on Twitter is to RT (retweet) the original tweet with a little note. This accomplishes two things:

- One, it lets the tweep know that you appreciated their tweet (and helps build a bond with that person); and
- Two, it brings attention to that person for their cool tweet.

Plus, it helps show that you know how to pick great resources on Twitter, which automatically improves your credibility as a resource on Twitter.

DAY 10: DO A GOOGLE SEARCH ON YOURSELF

For today's task, do a search on your name.

First, see what results appear when you search your name on Google (google.com). Then, try searching on Bing (bing.com). Finally, give Yahoo (yahoo.com) a try.

By searching your name, you'll receive insights into what others will find (and are already finding) when they do a search specifically for you. Of course, you'll want to make sure your blog and/or website is number one in the search results. If it isn't, we'll be covering SEO (or search engine optimization) topics later in this challenge.

OTHER SEARCH ENGINES

For those who want extra credit, here are some other search engines to try searching (for yourself):

- DuckDuckGo.com
- Ask.com
- Dogpile.com
- Yippy.com
- YouTube.com

(Note: It's worth checking out which images are related to your name as well. You may be surprised to find which images are connected to you.)

DAY 11: FIND A HELPFUL ARTICLE AND LINK TO IT

For today's task, find a helpful article (or blog post) and share it with your social network—and by social network, I mean that you should share it on Facebook, Twitter, and LinkedIn at a minimum. If you participate on message boards or on other social networks, share in those places as well.

Before linking to an article on fantasy baseball or celebrity news, however, make sure your article (or blog post) aligns with your author platform goals. You should have an idea of who you are and who you want to be as a writer, and your helpful article (or blog post) should line up with those values.

Of course, you may not want to share articles for writers if your platform is based on parenting tips or vampires or whatever. In such cases, you'll want to check out other resources online. Don't be afraid to use a search engine.

For Twitter, you may wish to use a URL shortener to help you keep under the 140-character limit. Here are five popular URL shorteners:

- bit.ly. This is my favorite.
- goo.gl. Google's URL shortener.
- owl.ly. Hootsuite's URL shortener.
- deck.ly. TweetDeck's URL shortener.
- su.pr. StumbleUpon's URL shortener.

By the way, here's an extra Twitter tip. Leave enough room in your tweets to allow space for people to attribute your Twitter handle if they decide to RT you. For instance, I always leave at least 20 characters to allow people space to tweet "RT @robertleebrewer" when retweeting me.

DAY 12: WRITE A BLOG POST AND INCLUDE CALL TO ACTION

For today's task, write a new blog post for your blog. In the blog post, include a call to action at the end of the post.

What's a call to action?

I include calls to action at the end of all my posts. Sometimes, they are links to products and services offered by my employer (F+W Media) or some other entity. Often, I include links to other posts and ways to follow me on other sites. Even the share buttons are a call to action of sorts.

Why include a call to action?

A call to action is good for giving readers direction and a way to engage more with you. Links to previous posts provide readers with more helpful or interesting information. Links to your social media profiles give readers a way to connect with you on those sites. These calls to action are beneficial to you and your readers when they are relevant.

What if I'm just getting started?

Even if you are completely new to everything, you should have an earlier blog post from last week, a Twitter account, a Facebook account, and a LinkedIn account. Link to these at the end of your blog post today. It's a proper starting place.

And that's all you need to do today. Write a new blog post with a call to action at the end. (By the way, if you're at a loss and need something to blog about, you can always comment on that article you shared yesterday.)

DAY 13: LINK TO POST ON SOCIAL MEDIA PROFILES

For today's challenge, link your blog post from yesterday to your social networks.

At a minimum, these social networks should include Facebook, Twitter, and LinkedIn. However, if you frequent message boards related to your blog post or other social networks (like Instagram, Pinterest, etc.), then link your blog post there as well.

I understand many of you may have already completed today's challenge. If so, hooray! It's important to link your blog to your social media accounts and vice versa. When they work together, they grow together.

Is it appropriate to link to my blog post multiple times?

All writers develop their own strategies for linking to their articles and blog posts, but here's my rule. I will usually link to each blog post on every one of my social networks at least once. Since I have a regular profile and a fan page on Facebook, I link to each of those profiles once—and I only link to posts once on LinkedIn. But Twitter is a special case.

The way Twitter works, tweets usually only have a few minutes of visibility for tweeps with an active stream. Even tweeps with at least 100 follows may only have a 30-minute to hour window of opportunity to see your tweet. So for really popular and timely blog posts, I will tweet them more often than once on Twitter.

That said, I'm always aware of how I'm linking and don't want to become that annoying spammer that I typically avoid following in my own social networking efforts.

LINKING TIPS

Some tips on linking to your post:
- Use a URL shortener. These are discussed above.

> - Apply title + link formula. For instance, I might Tweet this post as: Platform Challenge: Day 13: (link). It's simple and to the point. Plus, it's really effective if you have a great blog post title.
> - Frame the link with context. Using this post as an example, I might Tweet: Take advantage of social media by linking to your blog posts: (link). Pretty simple, and it's an easy way to link to the same post without making your Twitter feed look loaded with the same content.
> - Quote from post + link formula. Another tactic is to take a funny or thought-provoking quote from the post and combine that with a link. Example Tweet: "I will usually link to each blog post on every one of my social networks at least once." (link). Again, easy stuff.

DAY 14: JOIN INSTAGRAM

For today's task, create an Instagram (instagram.com) profile.

Many of you may already have Instagram profiles, but this social networking site and app is a little different than Facebook and Twitter. While all three offer opportunities for sharing video and photos, Instagram really emphasizes visual elements.

That might not seem like a good fit for writers, who are often more about text than visual cues. But there are opportunities for writers on this platform. And it's one more venue where the people (or your potential audience) are.

Here are a few getting started tips for Instagram:

- Complete your profile completely. Use your name, concisely describe who you are and what you're about, and make your profile public.
- Use an image of yourself. Not a cartoon. Not an animal. Not a piece of art. Remember that people like to connect with other people.
- Post new content regularly. Let people know you are using your account. A new post every day or three is a good way to achieve this.
- Use unique and relevant hashtags. These provide a way for people with similar interests who aren't already connected to you to find you.

DAY 15: MAKE THREE NEW CONNECTIONS

For today's task, make an attempt to connect with at least three new people on one of your social networks.

Doesn't matter if it's Facebook, Twitter, LinkedIn, or Instagram. The important thing is that you find three new people who appear to share your interests and that you try to friend, follow, or connect to them.

As a person who has limited wiggle room for approving new friends on Facebook, I'd like to share what approach tends to work the best with me for approving new friend requests. Basically, send your request and include a brief message introducing yourself and why you want to connect with me.

That's right. The best way to win me over is to basically introduce yourself. Something along the lines of, "Hello. My name is Robert Lee Brewer, and I write poetry. I read a poem of yours in *XYZ Literary Journal* that I totally loved and have sent you a friend request. I hope you'll accept it." Easy as that.

Notice that I did not mention anything about checking out my blog or reading my poems. How would you like it if someone introduced themselves and then told you to buy their stuff? It sounds a bit telemarketer-ish to me.

While it's important to cultivate the relationships you already have, avoid getting stuck in a rut when it comes to making connections. Always be on the lookout for new connections who can offer new opportunities and spark new ideas. Your writing and your career will benefit.

DAY 16: ADD E-MAIL FEED TO BLOG

For today's challenge, add an e-mail feed to your blog.

There are many ways to increase traffic to your blog, but one that has paid huge dividends for me is adding Feedblitz to my blog. As the subscribers to my e-mail feed have increased, my blog traffic has increased as well. In fact, after great content, I'd say that adding share buttons (mentioned above) and an e-mail feed are the top two ways to build traffic.

Though I have an account on Tumblr, I'm just not sure if it offers some kind of e-mail/RSS feed service.

The reason I think e-mail feeds are so useful is that they pop into my inbox whenever a new post is up, which means I can check it very easily on my phone when I'm waiting somewhere. In fact, this is how I keep up with several of my favorite blogs. It's just one more way to make your blog content accessible to readers in a variety of formats.

If I remember, this task didn't take me long to add, but I've been grateful for finally getting around to adding it ever since.

DAY 17: TAKE PART IN A TWITTER CONVERSATION

For today's task, take part in a Twitter conversation.

Depending upon the time of month or day of week, there are bound to be any number of conversations happening around a hashtag (mentioned above). For instance, various conferences and expos have hashtag conversations that build around their panels and presentations.

Poets will often meet using the #poetparty hashtag. Other writers use #amwriting to communicate about their writing goals. Click on the hashtag to see what others are saying, and then, jump in to join the conversation and make new connection on Twitter.

DAY 18: THINK ABOUT SEO

For today's task, I want you to slow down and think a little about SEO (which is tech-speak for search engine optimization, which is itself an intelligent way of saying "what gets your website to display at or near the top of a search on Google, Bing, Yahoo, etc.").

So this task is actually multi-pronged:

- Make a list of keywords that you want your website or blog to be known for. For instance, I want my blog to be known for terms like "Robert Lee Brewer," "Writing Tips," "Parenting Tips," "Platform Tips," "Living Tips," etc. Think big here and don't limit yourself to what you think you can actually achieve in the short term.
- Compare your website or blog's current content to your keywords. Are you lining up your actual content with how you want your audience to view you and your online presence? If not, it's time to think about how you can start offering content that lines up with your goals. If so, then move on to the next step, which is ...
- Evaluate your current approach to making your content super SEO-friendly. If you need some guidance, check out my SEO Tips for Writers below. There are very simple things you can do with your titles, subheads, and images to really improve SEO. Heck, I get a certain bit of traffic every single day just from my own SEO approach to content—sometimes on surprising posts.
- Research keywords for your next post. When deciding on a title for your post and subheads within the content, try researching keywords. You can do this using Google's free keyword tool (googlekeywordtool.com). When possible, you want to use keywords that are searched a lot but that have low competition. These are the low-hanging fruit that can help you build strong SEO for your website or blog.

A note on SEO: It's easy to fall in love with finding keywords and changing your content to be keyword-loaded and blah-blah-blah. But resist making your website or blog a place that is keyword-loaded and blah-blah-blah. Because readers don't stick around for too much keyword-loaded blah-blah-blah. It's kind of blah. And bleck. Instead, use SEO and keyword research as a way to optimize great content and to take advantage of opportunities as they arise.

SEO TIPS FOR WRITERS

Here are a few SEO tips for writers:

- Use keywords naturally. That is, make sure your keywords match the content of the post. If they don't match up, people will abandon your page fast, which will hurt your search rankings.
- Use keywords appropriately. Include your keywords in the blog post title, opening paragraph, file name for images, headers, etc. Anywhere early and relevant should include your keyword to help place emphasis on that search term, especially if it's relevant to the content.
- Deliver quality content. Of course, search rankings are helped when people click on your content and spend time reading your content. So provide quality content, and people will visit your site frequently and help search engines list you higher in their rankings.
- Update content regularly. Sites that are updated more with relevant content rank higher in search engines. Simple as that.
- Link often to relevant content. Link to your own posts; link to content on other sites. Just make sure the links are relevant and of high interest to your audience.
- Use images. Images help from a design perspective, but they also help with SEO, especially when you use your main keywords in the image file name.
- Link to your content on social media sites. These outside links will help increase your ranking on search engines.
- Guest post on other sites/blogs. Guest posts on other blogs are a great way to provide traffic from other relevant sites that increase the search engine rankings on your site.

DAY 19: WRITE A BLOG POST

For today's task, write a new blog post.

Include a call to action (for instance, encourage readers to sign up for your e-mail feed and to share the post with others using your share buttons) and link to it on your social networks. Also, don't forget toincorporate SEO.

One of the top rules of finding success with online tools is applying consistency. While it's definitely a great thing if you share a blog post more than once a week, I think it's imperative that you post at least once a week.

The main reason? It builds trust with your readers that you'll have something to share regularly and gives them a reason to visit regularly.

So today's task is not about making things complicated; it's just about keeping it real.

DAY 20: CREATE EDITORIAL CALENDAR

For today's task, I want you to create an editorial calendar for your blog (or website). Before you start to panic, read on.

First, here's how I define an editorial calendar: A list of content with dates attached to when the content goes live. For instance, I created an editorial calendar specifically for my Platform Challenge and "Platform Challenge: Day 20" was scheduled to go live on day 20.

It's really simple. In fact, I keep track of my editorial calendar with a paper notebook, which gives me plenty of space for crossing things out, jotting down ideas, and attaching Post-It notes.

EDITORIAL CALENDAR IDEAS

Here are tips for different blogging frequencies:

- Post once per week. If you post once a week, pick a day of the week for that post to happen each week. Then, write down the date for each post. Beside each date, write down ideas for that post ahead of time. There will be times when the ideas are humming and you get ahead on your schedule, but there may also be times when the ideas are slow. So don't wait, write down ideas as they come.
- Post more than once per week. Try identifying which days you'll usually post (for some, that may be daily). Then, for each of those days, think of a theme for that day. For instance, my 2012 schedule offered Life Changing Moments on Wednesdays and Poetic Saturdays on Saturdays.

You can always change plans and move posts to different days, but the editorial calendar is an effective way to set very clear goals with deadlines for accomplishing them. Having that kind of structure will improve your content—even if your blog is personal, fictional, poetic, etc. Believe me, I used to be a skeptic before diving in, and the results on my personal blog speak for themselves.

One more benefit of editorial calendars

There are times when I feel less than inspired. There are times when life throws me several elbows as if trying to prevent me from blogging. That's when I am the most thankful for maintaining an editorial calendar, because I don't have to think of a new idea on the spot; it's already there in my editorial calendar.

Plus, as I said earlier, you can always change plans. I can alter the plan to accommodate changes in my schedule. So I don't want to hear that an editorial calendar limits spontaneity or inspiration; if anything, having an editorial calendar enhances it.

One last thing on today's assignment

Don't stress yourself out that you have to create a complete editorial calendar for the year or even the month. I just want you to take some time out today to think about it, sketch some ideas, and get the ball rolling. I'm 100 percent confident that you'll be glad you did.

DAY 21: SIGN UP FOR SOCIAL MEDIA TOOL

For today's task, try joining one of the social media management tools, such as Tweet-deck, Hootsuite, or Seesmic.

Social media management tools are popular among social media users for one reason: They help save time and effort in managing multiple social media platforms. For instance, they make following specific threads in Twitter a snap.

I know many social media super users who swear by these tools, but I actually have tried them and decided to put in the extra effort to log in to my separate social media accounts manually each day.

Here's my reasoning: I like to feel connected to my profile and understand how it looks and feels on a day-to-day basis. Often, the design and feel of social media sites will change without notice, and I like to know what it feels like at ground zero.

DAY 22: PITCH GUEST BLOG POST

For today's task, pitch a guest blog post to another blogger.

Writing guest posts is an incredible way to improve your exposure and expertise on a subject, while also making a deeper connection with the blogger who is hosting your guest post. It's a win for everyone involved.

In a recent interview with super blogger Jeff Goins, he revealed that most of his blog traffic came as a result of his guest posting on other blogs. Some of these blogs were directly related to his content, but he said many were in completely different fields.

GUEST POST PITCHING TIPS

After you know where you want to guest blog, here are some tips for pitching your guest blog post:

- Let the blogger know you're familiar with the blog. You should do this in one sentence (two sentences max) and be specific. For instance, a MNINB reader could say, "I've been reading your Not Bob blog for months, but I really love this Platform Challenge." Simple as that. It lets me know you're not a spammer, but it doesn't take me a long time to figure out what you're trying to say.

- Propose an idea or two. Each idea should have its own paragraph. This makes it easy for the blogger to know where one idea ends and the next one begins. In a pitch, you don't have to lay out all the details, but you do want to be specific. Try to limit the pitch to 2-4 sentences.
- Share a little about yourself. Emphasis on "a little." If you have previous publications or accomplishments that line up with the blog, share those. If you have expertise that lines up with the post you're pitching, share those. Plus, include any details about your online platform that might show you can help bring traffic to the post. But include all this information in 1-4 sentences.
- Include your information. When you close the pitch, include your name, e-mail, blog (or website) URL, and other contact information you feel comfortable sharing. There's nothing more awkward for me than to have a great pitch that doesn't include the person's name. Or a way to learn more about the person.

What do I do after the pitch is accepted?

First off, congratulations! This is a great opportunity to show off your writing skills. Here's how to take advantage of your guest post assignment:

- **WRITE AN EXCEPTIONAL POST.** Don't hold back your best stuff for your blog. Write a post that will make people want to find more of your writing.
- **TURN IN YOUR POST ON DEADLINE.** If there's a deadline, hit it. If there's not a deadline, try to turn around the well-written post in a timely manner.
- **PROMOTE THE GUEST POST.** Once your guest post has gone live, promote it like crazy by linking to your post on your blog, social networks, message boards, and wherever else makes sense for you. By sending your own connections to this guest post, you're establishing your own expertise—not only through your post but also your connections.

DAY 23: CREATE A TIME MANAGEMENT PLAN

For today's task, create a time management plan.

You may be wondering why I didn't start out the challenge with a time management plan, and here's the reason: I don't think some people would've had any idea how long it takes them to write a blog post, share a link on Twitter and Facebook, respond to social media messages, etc. Now, many of you probably have a basic idea—even if you're still getting the hang of your new-fangled social media tools.

Soooo ... the next step is to create a time management plan that enables you to be "active" socially and connect with other writers and potential readers while also spending a majority of your time writing and publishing.

As with any plan, you can make this as simple or complicated as you wish. For instance, my plan is to do 15 minutes or less of social media after completing each decent-sized task on my daily task list. I use social media time as a break, which I consider more productive than watching TV or playing Angry Birds.

I put my writing first and carve out time in the mornings and evenings to work on poetry and fiction. Plus, I consider my blogging efforts part of my writing too. So there you go.

My plan is simple and flexible, but if you want to get hardcore, break down your time into 15-minute increments. Then, test out your time management plan to see if it works for you. If not, then make minor changes to the plan until it has you feeling somewhat comfortable with the ratio of time you spend writing and time you spend building your platform.

Remember: A platform is a life-long investment in your career. It's not a sprint, so you have to pace yourself. Also, it's not something that happens overnight, so you can't wait until you need a platform to start building one. Begin today and build over time—so that it's there when you need it.

DAY 24: TAKE PART IN A FACEBOOK CONVERSATION

For today's task, take part in a conversation on Facebook.

You should've already participated in a Twitter conversation, so this should be somewhat similar—except you don't have to play with hashtags and 140-character restrictions. In fact, you just need to find a group conversation or status update that speaks to you and chime in with your thoughts.

Don't try to sell or push anything when you join a conversation. If you say interesting things, people will check out your profile, which if filled out will lead them to more information about you (including your website, blog, any books, etc.).

Goal one of social media is making connections. If you have everything else optimized, sales and opportunities will take care of themselves.

DAY 25: CONTACT AN EXPERT FOR AN INTERVIEW POST

For today's task, find an expert in your field and ask if that expert would like to be interviewed.

If you can secure the interview, this will make for a great blog post. Or it may help you secure a freelance assignment with a publication in your field. Or both, and possibly more.

How to Ask for an Interview

Believe it or not, asking for an interview with an expert is easy. I do it all the time, and these are the steps I take.

- **FIND AN EXPERT ON A TOPIC.** This is sometimes the hardest part: figuring out who I want to interview. But I never kill myself trying to think of the perfect person, and here's why: I can always ask for more interviews. Sometimes, it's just more productive to get the ball rolling than come up with excuses to not get started.
- **LOCATE AN E-MAIL FOR THE EXPERT.** This can often be difficult, but a lot of experts have websites that share either e-mail addresses or have online contact forms. Many experts can also be reached via social media sites, such as Facebook, Twitter, LinkedIn, Instagram, etc. Or they can be contacted through company websites. And so on.
- **SEND AN E-MAIL ASKING FOR AN E-MAIL INTERVIEW.** Of course, you can do this via an online contact form too. If the expert says no, that's fine. Respond with a "Thank you for considering and maybe we can make it work sometime in the future." If the expert says yes, then it's time to send along the questions.

How to Handle an E-mail Interview

Once you've secured your expert, it's time to compose and send the questions. Here are some of my tips.

- **ALWAYS START OFF BY ASKING QUESTIONS ABOUT THE EXPERT.** This might seem obvious to some, but you'd be surprised how many people start off asking "big questions" right out of the gate. Always start off by giving the expert a chance to talk about what he or she is doing, has recently done, etc.
- **LIMIT QUESTIONS TO 10 OR FEWER.** The reason for this is that you don't want to overwhelm your expert. In fact, I usually ask around eight questions in my e-mail interviews. If I need to, I'll send along some follow-up questions, though I try to limit those as well. I want the expert to have an enjoyable experience, not a horrible experience. After all, I want the expert to be a connection going forward.
- **TRY NOT TO GET TOO PERSONAL.** If experts want to get personal in their answers, that's great. But try to avoid getting too personal in the questions you ask, because you may offend your expert or make them feel uncomfortable. Remember: You're interviewing the expert, not leading an interrogation.
- **REQUEST ADDITIONAL INFORMATION.** By additional information, I mean that you should request a headshot and a preferred bio—along with any links. To make the interview worth the expert's time, you should afford them an opportunity to promote themselves and their projects in their bios.

Once the Interview Goes Live ...

Link to it on your social networks and let your expert know it is up (and include the specific link to the interview). If you're not already searching for your next expert to interview, be sure to get on it.

DAY 26: WRITE A BLOG POST AND LINK TO SOCIAL PROFILES

For today's task, write a new blog post.

In your blog post, include a call to action and link it on your social networks. Also, don't forget SEO.

Remember: One of the top rules of finding success with online tools is applying consistency. While it's definitely a great thing if you share a blog post more than once a week, I think it's imperative that you post at least once a week.

The main reason? It builds trust with your readers that you'll have something to share regularly and gives them a reason to visit regularly.

If this sounds repetitive, good; it means my message on consistency is starting to take root.

DAY 27: JOIN ANOTHER SOCIAL MEDIA SITE

For today's task, join one new social media site. I will leave it up to you to decide which new social media site it will be.

Maybe you'll join Pinterest. Maybe you'll choose Goodreads. Heck, you might go with RedRoom or some social media site that's not even on my radar at the time of this article. Everything is constantly evolving, which is why it's good to always try new things.

To everyone who doesn't want another site to join ...

I understand your frustration and exhaustion. During a normal month, I'd never suggest someone sign up for so many social media sites in such a short period of time, but this isn't a normal month. We're in the midst of a challenge!

And no, I don't expect you to spend a lot of time on every social media site you join. That's not always the point when you first sign up. No, you sign up to poke around and see if the site interests you at all. See if you have any natural connections. Try mingling a little bit.

If the site doesn't appeal to you, feel free to let it be for a while. Let me share a story with you.

How I Came to Rock Facebook and Twitter

My Facebook and Twitter accounts both boast more than 5,000 followers (or friends/sub-scribers) today. But both accounts were originally created and abandoned, because they just weren't right for me at the time that I signed up.

For Facebook, I just didn't understand why I would abandon a perfectly good MySpace account to play around on a site that didn't feature the same level of music and personal blogging that MySpace did. But then, MySpace turned into Spam-opolis, and the rest is history.

For Twitter, I just didn't get the whole tweet concept, because Facebook already had status updates. Why tweet when I could update my status on Facebook?

But I've gained a lot professionally and personally from Facebook and Twitter—even though they weren't the right sites for me initially. It's not like Facebook is going to be around forever.

The Importance of Experimentation

Or as I prefer to think of it: The importance of play. You should constantly try new things, whether in your writing, your social media networks, or the places you eat food. Not only does it make life more exciting and provide you with new experiences and perspective, but it also helps make you a more well-rounded human being.

So don't complain about joining a new social media site. Instead, embrace the excuse to try something new, especially when there are only three more tasks left this month (and I promise no more new sites after today).

DAY 28: READ POST AND COMMENT ON IT

For today's task, read and comment on a blog post, making sure that your comment links back to your blog or website.

If you remember, this was the same task required way back on Day 6. How far we've come, though it's still a good idea to stay connected and engaged with other bloggers. I know I find that sometimes I start to insulate myself in my own little blogging communities and worlds—when it's good to get out and read what others are doing. In fact, that's what helped inspire my Monday Advice for Writers posts—it gives me motivation to read what others are writing (on writing, of course).

DAY 29: MAKE A TASK LIST

For today's task, make a task list of things you are going to do on each day next month. That's right, I want you to break down 31 days with 31 tasks for each day—similar to what we've done this month.

You see, I don't want you to quit challenging yourself once this challenge is over. Of course, you get to decide what the tasks will be. So if you aren't into new social media sites, don't put them on your list. Instead, focus on blog posts, commenting on other sites, linking to articles, contacting experts, or whatever it is that you are going to do next month to keep momentum building toward an incredible author platform.

Somewhere near the end of the month, you should have a day set aside with one task: Make a task list of things to do on each day of the next month. And so on and so forth. Keep it going, keep it rolling, and your efforts will continue to gain momentum and speed. I promise.

DAY 30: ENGAGE THE WORLD

For today's task, engage the world.

By this, I mean that you should comment on status updates, ask questions, share answers, start debates, continue debates, and listen—that's right, don't be that person who dominates a conversation and makes it completely one-sided.

Engage the world by entering the conversation. Engage the world by having the courage to take risks and share things of consequence. Engage the world by having the courage to make mistakes and fail and learn from those mistakes and failures.

The only people who never fail are those who never try, and those people never succeed at anything except avoiding failure and success. Don't be that person. Engage the world and let the world engage you.

ROBERT LEE BREWER is a senior editor with the Writer's Digest Writing Community and author of *Solving the World's Problems* (Press 53). Follow him on Twitter @robertleebrewer.

POETIC FORMS

....

by Robert Lee Brewer

Not every poet likes the idea of writing in poetic forms, but for many poets—including myself—poetic forms are a sort of fun challenge. Whether playing with a sestina or working haiku, I find that attempting poetic forms often forces me into corners that make me think differently than if I'm just writing in free verse.

If you don't have any—or much—experience with poetic forms, I encourage you to peruse the following list and try them. If you are very familiar with poetic forms, I hope the following list can act as a reference for when you're unsure of the rhyme scheme for a triolet versus a kyrielle—or shadorma.

Have fun poeming!

ABSTRACT POETRY

Apparently, *abstract* was a term used by Dame Edith Sitwell to describe poems in her book *Facade*. Abstract (or sound) poetry is more about how sounds, rhythms, and textures evoke emotions than about the actual meanings of words.

ACROSTIC POETRY

Acrostic poetry is very easy and fun. The most basic form spells words out on the left-hand side of the page using the first letter of each line. For instance,

> I like to write
> Acrostic poems
> Mostly because
> Reading them
> Out loud is
> Bound to be fun.

If you notice, the first letter of every line makes the simple sentence, "I am Rob." It's very simple, and you can make it as difficult as you want—where the fun part begins.

The brave at heart can even try double acrostics—that is, spelling things out using the first and last letter of each line.

ALPHABET POETRY

There are many different ways to write an alphabet poem. You can write a poem in which the first letter of each word is a different letter of the alphabet. A tactic for writing this poem is to write out the alphabet ahead of time so that you can pay attention to which letters have been used and which letters are still up for grabs. Of course, you can also do this consecutively through the alphabet.

Another method for alphabet poems is to go through the alphabet using the first letter of the first word for each line.

Poets can always flip the alphabet, too. That is, instead of going A to Z, write alphabet poems from Z to A. It's all about having fun and stretching your mind, kind of like school.

ANAGRAMMATIC POETRY

In Christian Bok's comments about his poem "Vowels" in *The Best American Poetry 2007*, he writes, "'Vowels' is an anagrammatic text, permuting the fixed array of letters found only in the title. 'Vowels' appears in my book *Eunoia*, a lipogrammatic suite of stories, in which each vowel appears by itself in its own chapter." So an anagrammatic poem uses only the letters used in the title.

For instance, if I titled a poem "Spread," it could use only words like red, dresses, drape, spare, pear, pressed, etc.

The real challenge with this kind of poem is first picking a word that has at least a couple vowels and a good mix of consonants. Then, brainstorm all the words you can think of using only those letters (as many times as you wish, of course).

AWDL GYWYDD

In this case, awdl gywydd is a Welsh form, pronounced "ow-dull gee-youth." Here's how to write one:

- Four lines
- Seven syllables per line
- The final syllable of the first and third lines rhyme with the 3rd-5th syllable of the following lines
- The second and fourth lines rhyme.

Here's a possible version (the a and c rhymes can slide a little):

xxxxxxa

xxaxxxb

xxxxxxc

xxxxcxb

THE BLITZ POEM

The blitz poem was created by Robert Keim and is a 50-line poem of short phrases and images. Here are the rules:

- Line 1 should be one short phrase or image (like "build a boat")
- Line 2 should be another short phrase or image using the same first word as the first word in Line 1 (something like "build a house")
- Lines 3 and 4 should be short phrases or images using the last word of Line 2 as their first words (so Line 3 might be "house for sale" and Line 4 might be "house for rent")
- Lines 5 and 6 should be short phrases or images using the last word of Line 4 as their first words, and so on until you've made it through 48 lines
- Line 49 should be the last word of Line 48
- Line 50 should be the last word of Line 47
- The title of the poem should be three words long and follow this format: (first word of Line 3) (preposition or conjunction) (first word of line 47)
- There should be no punctuation

There are a lot of rules, but it's a pretty simple and fun poem to write once you get the hang of it.

BLACKOUT POEM

A blackout poem is when a poet takes a marker (usually a black marker) to an already established text—like in a newspaper—and starts redacting words until a poem is formed. The key thing with a blackout poem is that the text and redacted text form a sort of visual poem.

THE BOP

The Bop is a poetic form that was developed by poet Afaa Michael Weaver at a Cave Canem summer retreat. Here are the basic rules:

- 3 stanzas
- Each stanza is followed by a refrain
- First stanza is 6 lines long and presents a problem

- Second stanza is 8 lines long and explores or expands the problem
- Third stanza is 6 lines long and either presents a solution or documents the failed attempt to resolve the problem

BREF DOUBLE

A bref double is a quatorzain, which is any stanza or poem of 14 lines that is not a sonnet. Here are the basic rules for a bref double:

- 4 stanzas: 3 quatrains (or 4-line stanzas) and 1 couplet (or 2-line stanza)
- 3 rhymes: an A rhyme, B rhyme, and C rhyme
- The A and B rhymes appear twice in the first 3 stanzas and once in the final couplet
- The C rhyme is the final line in each of the quatrains
- Each poem has a variable line length, but the lines should be a consistent length within each poem

BYR A THODDAID

The byr a thoddaid is a Welsh form. Here are the rules:

- The byr a thoddaid is a quatrain (4-line stanza) or series of quatrains
- The quatrain itself is divided into two combined couplets (2-line stanza)
- One couplet contains 8 syllables for each line with an aa end rhyme
- The other couplet contains 10 syllables in the first line and 6 syllables in the second
- The 10-syllable line of this other couplet has an end rhyme near the end of the line (but not at the end)
- The 6-syllable line of this other couplet has a link (either rhyme, alliteration, etc.) to the end word of the 10-syllable line and then an end rhyme
- The couplets can appear in alternating orders

I realize the explanation might sound complicated, but it's not too bad. Here are the two main options:

X's represent non-rhyming syllables; capital letters represent rhyming syllables; lower-case letters (that aren't x's) represent the linked words/sounds/etc.

Option 1:

    xxxxxxxA
    xxxxxxxA
    xxxxxxxBxc
    xcxxxB

Option2:

xxxxxxxAxb
xbxxxA
xxxxxxxC
xxxxxxxC

Note: The linked sound in the second line of the 10-6 couplet can be the first sound, first syllable, second sound, second syllable, etc.–just as long as it's near the beginning of that second line.

CASCADE POEM

The cascade poem was a form invented by Udit Bhatia. For the cascade poem, a poet takes each line from the first stanza of a poem and makes those the final lines of each stanza afterward. Beyond that, there are no additional rules for rhyming, meter, etc.

So to help this make sense, here's what a cascade poem with a tercet would look like:

A
B
C

a
b
A

c
d
B

e
f
C

A quatrain cascade would look so:

A
B
C
D

a
b
c
A

d
e
f
B

g
h
i
C

j
k
l
D

And, of course, you can make this even more involved if you want.

CATENA RONDO

I found the catena rondo in Robin Skelton's *The Shapes of Our Singing*. In fact, Skelton created the form, and it's a lot of fun. He took the name from *catena*, which means chain, and connected it with *rondo*, which means circle. And the poem is a bit of a "chain circle," because of its intense repetition within stanzas and the poem as a whole

Here's how to write a catena rondo:

- The poem is comprised of a variable number of quatrains
- Each quatrain has a rhyme pattern of AbbA
- The first line of each quatrain is also the final line of the quatrain
- The second line of each quatrain is the first line of the next quatrain
- The final quatrain should repeat the first quatrain word for word

There are no rules for meter, syllables, or subject matter. Just a lot of rhyming refrains.

CHANSO

Chanso poems are adaptable to the needs of the poet. This French form consists of five to six stanzas with an envoy that is roughly half the size of a regular stanza. The main rules are that each line of the poem should have the same number of syllables, and each stanza should be uniform when it comes to line length and rhyme scheme. So a chanso could consist of five tercets written in an *abc* rhyme scheme for each line; or it could be six 12-line stanzas with an intricate rhyme scheme that is halved with the six-line envoy.

CONCRETE POETRY

Concrete poetry is one of the more experimental poetic forms available to poets. Concrete poems use space and sound to communicate the meanings of the words. Words can cover other words; and the poem has trouble standing without the structure. Concrete poetry is more visual than other poetic forms.

Of course, concrete poetry has plenty of detractors because of the weight structure has on the words, but as much thought goes into concrete poetry as any other form.

CONTRAPUNTAL POEM

Contrapuntal poems are influenced by the music world. Contrapuntal music is composed of multiple melodies that are relatively independent sounded together. Contrapuntal poems are poems that intertwine two (or more) separate poems into a single composition. Often, this is accomplished by offering one line of poem A before a corresponding line of poem B from start to finish.

CURTAL SONNET

Gerard Manley Hopkins invented the curtal sonnet in the 19th century. The poem consists of 10 lines written in iambic pentameter and a final line consisting of a single spondee (or foot consisting of two long or stressed syllables). Here's the rhyme scheme:

> Line 1: a
> Line 2: b
> Line 3: c
> Line 4: a
> Line 5: b
> Line 6: c
> Line 7: d
> Line 8: b
> Line 9: c
> Line 10: d
> Line 11: c

CYRCH A CHWTA

The cyrch a chwta is a Welsh poetic form. And like many Welsh forms, this poem involves both end rhymes and internal (or cross) rhymes. Here are the guidelines:

- Octave stanza (8-line stanza)
- 7 syllables per line

- Lines 1-6 and 8 end rhyme together
- Line 7 cross rhymes with line 8 (internally) on either syllable 3, 4, or 5

Note: The "a" rhyme appears at least 7 times per stanza, so it should be a strong one with plenty of rhyming options.

DECIMA

There are various versions of decima, but let's start with the version popular in Puerto Rico. It is a 10-liner with eight syllables per line, invented by Vicente Espinel, in the following rhyme pattern: *ABBAACCDDC*.

In Ecuador, the decima is a 44-line poem comprised of a quatrain and four 10-line stanzas. Each of the lines from the opening quatrain are repeated later in the poem. The lines still retain eight syllables, though the rhyme constraints are loosened.

There is also a *decima Italiana* with 10 eight-syllable lines that rhyme *ababcdedec*.

DESCORT

The descort differentiates itself from other forms by differentiating its lines from other lines within the poem. That is, the main rule of descort poems is that each line needs to be different from every other line in the poem.

A descort poem has different line lengths, meters, avoids rhyming with other lines, no refrains, and that goes for stanzas as well. In other words, no two lines in a descort should look like each other, and the same could be said for each descort.

Note: This is different than free verse, because even free verse may occasionally have similar line lengths and meter. However, descort is very intentional in its variability.

DIMINISHING VERSE

Diminishing verse offers no origin and very few rules, but I enjoyed writing my example below. In fact, the main rule is this: Remove the first letter of end word in previous line. For example:

- Line 1 ends with the word "grad"
- And line 2 ends "rad"
- Then, line 3 ends "ad"

Note: There are no rules for rhymes, syllables, poem length, stanza length, etc. Just a simple removal of a letter. That said, poets can also remove sounds if they wish like "braille" to "rail" to "ale."

DIZAIN

The dizain was a favorite form of 15th and 16th century French poets, but it has also been employed in English by the likes of Philip Sydney and John Keats. Here are the basic rules:

- One 10-line stanza
- 10 syllables per line
- Employs the following rhyme scheme: *ababbccdcd*

DODOITSU

The dodoitsu is a Japanese poetic form developed towards the end of the Edo Period, which came to an end in 1868. This four-line poem has seven syllables in the first three lines and five syllables in the fourth and final line. The dodoitsu often focuses on love or work with a comical twist.

ELEGY

An elegy is a song of sorrow or mourning—often for someone who has died. However, poets being an especially creative and contrary group have also written elegies for the ends of things, whether a life, a love affair, a great era, a football season, etc.

While there are such things as elegiac couplets and elegiac stanzas, form does not rule an elegy; content *is* king (or queen) when writing elegies.

EPITAPHS

The epitaph is a note meant to appear on a tombstone. From the Greek, epitaph means "upon a tomb." Since it has to fit on a tombstone, this note is usually brief and often rhymes. Some epitaphs are funny; most are serious. Most try to get the reader thinking about the subject of the tombstone.

ERASURE POEM

An erasure poem is any poem that sculpts itself out of another larger text without adding any new words. The blackout poem is an example of this.

THE FIB

Fibonacci poetry was founded by Gregory K. Pincus as a 6-line poem that follows the Fibonacci sequence for syllable count per line.

For the 6-line poem that means:

- 1 syllable for first line
- 1 syllable for second line
- 2 syllables for third
- 3 syllables for fourth
- 5 syllables for fifth
- 8 syllables for sixth

There are variations where the Fibonacci expands even further with each line, but to understand how to accomplish this, you need to understand the Fibonacci math sequence of starting with 0 and 1 and then adding the last two numbers together to add to infinity.

$$0+1=1$$
$$1+1=2$$
$$1+2=3$$
$$2+3=5$$
$$3+5=8$$
$$5+8=13$$
$$8+13=21$$
$$13+21=34$$

and so on and so forth...

Anyway, those lines can easily get more and more unwieldy the more you let them expand. So, there's another variation that has taken flight in making Fibonacci poems that ascend and descend in syllables. For poets who also like mathematics, this is definitely an interesting form to get your mind working.

FOUND POEMS

Found poetry is all about taking words not originally meant to be a poem (as they originally appeared) and turning those words into a poem anyway. You can use newspaper articles, bits of conversation, instructions, recipes, letters, e-mails, direct mail and even spam e-mail.

With found poetry, you do not alter the original words, but you can make line breaks and cut out excess before and/or after the poem you've "found." The power of found poetry is how words not intended as poetry can take on new and profound meanings as found poems.

GHAZAL

The ghazal (pronounced "guzzle") is a Persian poetic form. The original form was very simple: five to 15 couplets using the same rhyme with the poet's name in the final couplet. The main themes were usually love or drinking wine.

Contemporary ghazals have abandoned the rhymes and insertion of the poet's name in the final couplet. In fact, even the themes of love and drinking wine are no longer mandatory—as the poem now just needs the couplets which are complete thoughts on their own but also all work together to explore a common theme (whatever that might be).

If you wish to stay traditional though, here's the rhyme scheme you would follow:

a

a

b

a

c

a

and so on to the final stanza (depending upon how many you include).

Many traditional ghazals will also incorporate a refrain at the end of each couplet that could be one word or a phrase.

GOGYOHKA

Gogyohka was a form developed by Enta Kusakabe in Japan and translates literally to "five-line poem." The rules are pretty straightforward: It is a poem comprised of five lines with one phrase per line.

So what constitutes a phrase? A compound or complex sentence would be too long, but I've seen examples as short as one word and others that contain more than five words. So it's a little loose.

GOLDEN SHOVEL

The golden shovel was created by Terrance Hayes. Here are the basic rules:

- Take a line (or lines) from a a poem you admire
- Use each word in the line (or lines) as an end word in your poem
- Keep the end words in order
- Give credit to the poet who originally wrote the line (or lines)
- The new poem does not have to be about the same subject as the poem that offers the end words, but there's obviously opportunity for communication with this form

HAIBUN

Haibun is the combination of two poems: a prose poem and haiku. The form was popularized by the 17th century Japanese poet Matsuo Basho. Both the prose poem and haiku typically communicate with each other, though poets employ different strategies for this communication, with some doing so subtly, while others are more direct.

Also, the prose poem usually describes a scene or moment in an objective manner. In other words, the pronoun "I" isn't often used, if at all.

HAIKU

Haiku is descended from the Japanese *renga* form, which was often a collaborative poem comprised of many short stanzas. The opening stanza of the renga was called *hokku*. Eventually, haiku evolved from the leftover and most interesting hokku that were not used in renga.

Most haiku deal with natural topics. They avoid metaphor and simile. While most poets agree that haiku have three short lines, there is some disagreement on how long those lines are. For instance, some traditional haiku poets insist on 17 syllables in lines of 5/7/5. Other contemporary haiku poets feel that the first and third lines can be any length as long as they're shorter than the middle line.

Haiku do not have to include complete sentences or thoughts. They do not have titles. The best haiku contain some shift in the final line.

HAY(NA)KU

Hay(na)ku is a very simple poetic form created in 2003 by poet Eileen Tabios. Hay(na)ku is a 3-line poem with one word in the first line, two words in the second, and three in the third. There are no restrictions beyond this.

There are already some variations of this new poetic form. For instance, a reverse hay(na)ku has lines of three, two, and one word(s) for lines one, two, and three respectively. Also, multiple hay(na)ku can be chained together to form longer poems.

HIR A THODDAID

Hir a thoddaid is a Welsh form. And this form is like other Welsh forms in regards to a slight variation in line length and some complexity in the rhyme scheme. Here's the structure of this six-line form (with the letters acting as syllables and the a's and b's signifying rhymes:

xxxxxxxxa
xxxxxxxxa
xxxxxxxxa
xxxxxxxxa
xxxxxxxbxx
xxbxxxxxa

So line 5 is 10 syllables in length; the other 5 lines are 9 syllables. Also, the "b" rhyme is somewhere near the end of line 5 and somewhere in the first half of line 6–so those rhymes could move back and forth to suit your needs.

HUITAIN

The huitain is a derivative of the French ballade. In fact, it is a complete eight-line poem composed of one ballade stanza. Here are the basic guidelines:

- eight-line stanza
- *ababbcbc* rhyme scheme
- eight to 10 syllables per line

INSULT POEM

There are no hard and fast rules to the insult poem, but it's usually done in a joking (all in good fun) fashion as opposed to seriously trying to annoy anyone. Many insult poems also have a repetitive form or recurring method of delivering the insults. The insult poem is a good way to show just how clever you are (or think you are). But beware writing them! Once you attack someone (even in jest), you are suddenly fair game to receive an insult poem in retaliation.

INTERLOCKING RUBAIYAT

Interlocking rubaiyat, also referred to as rubai, is often linked to poet Omar Khayyam, but it's also used in Robert Frost's "Stopping by Woods on a Snowy Evening." Here are the rules:

- The poem is comprised of quatrains following an aaba rhyme pattern
- Each successive quatrain picks up the unrhymed line as the rhyme for that stanza. So a three-stanza rubaiyat might rhyme: aaba/bbcb/ccdc
- Lines are usually tetrameter and pentameter

KIMO

Kimo poems are an Israeli version of haiku. Apparently, there was a need for more syllables in Hebrew. That said, most of the rules for writing kimo should be familiar to poets writing in English:

- Three lines
- No rhymes
- 10 syllables in the first line, seven in the second, and six in the third

Also, the kimo is focused on a single frozen image (kind of like a snapshot). So movement is not common in kimo.

KYRIELLE

The kyrielle is a French four-line stanza form—with 8 syllables per line—that has a refrain in the fourth line. Often, there is a rhyme scheme in the poem consisting of the following possibilities:

- aabb
- abab
- aaab
- abcb

The poem can be as long as you wish and as short as two stanzas (otherwise, the refrain is not really a refrain, is it?), and, as with many French forms, it is very nice for stretching your poetic muscles.

LAI

The lai is a nine-line French form that uses an A and B rhyme following this pattern: *aabaabaab*. The lines with an A rhyme use five syllables; the B-rhyme lines have two syllables. It feels kind of like organized skeltonic verse.

LIMERICKS

The origin of the limerick is shrouded in some mystery, but most sources seem to point to the early 18th century—one theory being that soldiers returning from France to the Irish town of Limerick started the form, the other theory pointing to the 1719 publication of *Mother Goose Melodies for Children*. Either way, Edward Lear popularized the form in the mid-19th century.

Basically, the limerick is a five-line poem consisting of a tercet split by a couplet. That is, lines 1, 2, and 5 are a bit longer and rhyme, while the shorter lines of 3 and 4 rhyme. After studying many effective limericks, there is not a precise syllable count per line, but the norm is about 8-10 syllables in the longer lines and around 6 syllables in the shorter lines.

LIST POEMS

A list poem (also known as a catalog poem) is a poem that lists things, whether names, places, actions, thoughts, images, etc. Even a grocery list could turn into a poem with this form.

LUNE

The lune is also known as the American Haiku. It was first created by the poet Robert Kelly and was a result of Kelly's frustration with English haiku. After much experimentation, he settled on a 13-syllable, self-contained poem that has 5 syllables in the first line, 3 syllables in the second line and 5 syllables in the final line.

Unlike haiku, there are no other rules. No need for a cutting word. Rhymes are fine; subject matter is open. While there are fewer syllables to use, this form has a little more freedom.

There is also a variant lune created by the poet Jack Collom. His form is also a self-contained tercet, but it's word-based (not syllable-based) and has the structure of 3 words in the first line, 5 words in the second line and 3 words in the final line.

MADRIGAL

The madrigal originated as an Italian form, actually as a pastoral song. The Italian madrigal is written in lines of either seven or 11 syllables and is comprised of two or three tercets, followed by one or two rhyming couplets. Just as variable as the lines and line lengths is the rhyme scheme. In fact, there's so much variability that I'm going to focus on the "English" madrigal, developed by Geoffrey Chaucer. It is usually written in iambic pentameter with three stanzas (a tercet, quatrain, and sestet) and all the lines in the opening tercet are refrains.

Here's the rhyme scheme:

Line 1: A
Line 2: B1
Line 3: B2

Line 4: a
Line 5: b
Line 6: A
Line 7: B1

Line 8: a
Line 9: b
Line 10: b
Line 11: A
Line 12: B1
Line 13: B2

MAGIC 9

The magic 9 is a newer form that appears to have been inspired by a poet misspelling the word "abracadabra." The nine-line poem has a rhyme scheme of *abacadaba*.

MONOTETRA

The monotetra is a poetic form developed by Michael Walker. Here are the basic rules:

- Comprised of quatrains (four-line stanzas) in tetrameter (four metrical feet) for a total of 8 syllables per line
- Each quatrain consists of mono-rhymed lines (so each line in the first stanza has the same type of rhyme, as does each line in the second stanza, etc.)
- The final line of each stanza repeats the same four syllables
- This poem can be as short as one quatrain and as long as a poet wishes

Personally, I like the rhyme scheme and the repetitive final line of each stanza.

NONET

The nonet is a nine-line form that has nine syllables in the first line, eight syllables in the second, seven syllables in the third, and so on until the ninth and final line, which contains one syllable.

OCCASIONAL POEMS

There are no specific guidelines for occasional poems except that they mark a specific occasion. The poems can be long or short, serious or humorous, good or bad—just as long as they mark the occasion. Good occasions for poems include birthdays, weddings and holidays.

ODES

The ode is a poetic form formed for flattery. There are three types of odes: the Horation; the Pindaric; and the Irregular.

The Horation ode (named for the Latin poet, Horace) contains one stanza pattern that repeats throughout the poem—usually 2 or 4 lines in length.

The Pindaric ode (named for the Greek poet, Pindar) is made up of a pattern of three stanzas called triads. This type of ode can be composed of several triads, but the first (the strophe) and the second (antistrophe) should be identical metrically with the third (epode) wandering off on its own metrical path.

The irregular ode (named for no one in particular) does away with formalities and focuses on the praising aspect of the ode.

OTTAVA RIMA

The earliest known ottava rima were written by Giovanni Boccaccio of Italian descent. In English, Lord Byron used the form to write Don Juan. William Butler Yeats and Kenneth Koch are more contemporary poets to use the form, which is an eight-liner in iambic pentameter with the following rhyme scheme: *ababab cc*.

PALINDROME POETRY

The palindrome seems like a simple enough form—until you actually try to write a good one. The rules are simple enough:

1. You must use the same words in the first half of the poem as the second half, but
2. Reverse the order for the second half, and
3. Use a word in the middle as a bridge from the first half to the second half of the poem.

At first, the simplicity of the rules made me feel like this would be easy enough to do, but I ran into problems almost immediately. For instance, you can't start the poem with the word "the" unless you plan to end the poem on the word "the." And just because something makes sense in the first half doesn't guarantee it'll pass the same test on the way back.

PANTOUM

The pantoum is a poetic form originating in Malay where poets write quatrains (4-line stanzas) with an *abab* rhyme scheme and repeat lines 2 and 4 in the previous stanza as lines 1 and 3 in the next stanza.

Poets differ on how to treat the final quatrain: Some poets repeat lines 1 and 3 of the original quatrain as lines 2 and 4 in the final quatrain; other poets invert lines 1 and 3 so that the beginning line of the poem is also the final line of the poem.

Also, the pantoum can be as long or as short as you wish it to be, though mathematically it does require at least 4 lines.

PARADELLE

The paradelle is a poetic form that Billy Collins originally introduced as "one of the more demanding French forms," though eventually Collins fessed up that he created it as a joke.

However, Collins was not kidding about the demanding rules of the paradelle. Here they are:

- The paradelle is a 4-stanza poem.
- Each stanza consists of 6 lines.

- For the first 3 stanzas, the 1st and 2nd lines should be the same; the 3rd and 4th lines should also be the same; and the 5th and 6th lines should be composed of all the words from the 1st and 3rd lines and only the words from the 1st and 3rd lines.
- The final stanza should be composed of all the words in the 5th and 6th lines of the first three stanzas and only the words from the 5th and 6th lines of the first three stanzas.

PARODY POEMS

A parody poem is one that pokes fun at another poem or poet. The best parodies are those that are easily recognizable—and funny, of course.

PROSE POEMS

Of all poetic forms, prose poetry may be the most controversial. After all, free verse and most experimental forms still contain line breaks. But prose poems "break" free of the line break (sorry, had to do it).

The rules are pretty simple and straightforward: Write a poem and don't break your lines.

QUATERN

The quatern is a 16-line poem broken into four quatrains (or four-line stanzas) with eight syllables per line. The first line is the refrain. In the second stanza, the refrain appears in the second line. In the third stanza, the refrain is in the third line. And yes, the refrain appears in the fourth and final line of the fourth stanza. Beyond that, there are no rules for rhyming, iambics, or subject matter.

RHUPUNT

The rhupunt has some variability to it, but also some rigid rules as well. I've had fun tinkering around with this Welsh form, and I hope you do too.

Here are the guidelines for the rhupunt:

- The form can be broken down into lines or stanzas
- Each line or stanza contains 3 to 5 sections
- Each section has 4 syllables
- All but the final section rhyme with each other
- The final section of each line or stanza rhymes with the final section of the other lines or stanzas

RISPETTO

This is a very old, Italian form. There are many variants, but these are the two most common variations:

Rispetto #1: Poem comprised of two quatrains written in iambic tetrameter.

Rispetto #2: Poem comprised of eight hendecasyllabic lines, usually one stanza.

Both versions appear to the follow the same rhyme scheme: ababccdd, though I also found a mention of one with an abababcc pattern. Plus, I found a few sources that claim rispettos were originally written to pay "respect" to a woman. However, this poem has offered itself up for other subjects and variations over the centuries.

RONDEAU

The rondeau is a form that has a refrain and rhymes. The traditional rondeau is a poem consisting of 3 stanzas, 13 original lines, and 2 refrains (of the first line of the poem) with 8 to 10 syllables per line and an A/B rhyme scheme. The skeleton of the traditional rondeau looks like this:

A(R)
A
B
B
A

A
A
B
A(R)

A
A
B
B
A
A(R)

There are variations of the rondeau, including the rondeau redouble, rondel, rondel double, rondelet, roundel, and roundelay. Of course, poets tend to break the rules on each of these as well, which is what poets like to do.

RONDELET

The rondelet is a typical French form with rhymes and refrains. Here are the basic guidelines for this poetic form:

- 7 lines
- Lines 1, 3, and 7 are refrains
- Refrain lines are 4 syllables long, other lines are 8 syllables
- Rhyme scheme: *AbAabbA*

SEGUIDILLA

Seguidilla is one of those poetic forms that started off as a song (specifically a dance song) before eventually settling on an established poetic form. Here are the basic rules:

- Seven-line poem
- Syllable count for each line is 7-5-7-5-5-7-5
- One assonance rhyme between lines two and four; another one between lines five and seven
- Pause between lines four and five, usually an end stop
- Tone or focus changes between lines four and five as well

SESTINA

The sestina is one of my favorite forms. You pick 6 words, rotate them as the end words in 6 stanzas and then include 2 of the end words per line in your final stanza.

Let's pick 6 random words: bears, carving, dynamite, hunters, mothers, blessing. Here's how the end words would go:

Stanza 1

Line 1-bears (A)
Line 2-carving (B)
Line 3-dynamite (C)
Line 4-hunters (D)
Line 5-mothers (E)
Line 6-blessing (F)

Stanza 2

Line 7-blessing (F)
Line 8-bears (A)
Line 9-mothers (E)
Line 10-carving (B)

Line 11-hunters (D)
Line 12-dynamite (C)

Stanza 3

Line 13-dynamite (C)
Line 14-blessing (F)
Line 15-hunters (D)
Line 16-bears (A)
Line 17-carving (B)
Line 18-mothers (E)

Stanza 4

Line 19-mothers (E)
Line 20-dynamite (C)
Line 21-carving (B)
Line 22-blessing (F)
Line 23-bears (A)
Line 24-hunters (D)

Stanza 5

Line 25-hunters (D)
Line 26-mothers (E)
Line 27-bears (A)
Line 28-dynamite (C)
Line 29-blessing (F)
Line 30-carving (B)

Stanza 6

Line 31-carving (B)
Line 32-hunters (D)
Line 33-blessing (F)
Line 34-mothers (E)
Line 35-dynamite (C)
Line 36-bears (A)

Stanza 7

Line 37-bears (A), carving (B)
Line 38-dynamite (C), hunters (D)
Line 39-mothers (E), blessing (F)

While many poets try to write sestinas in iambic pentameter, that is not a requirement. Also, when choosing your six end words, it does help to choose words that can be altered if needed to help keep the flow of the poem going.

SEVENLING

The sevenling was created by Roddy Lumsden. Here are the rules:

- The sevenling is a 7-line poem (clever, huh?) split into three stanzas.
- The first three lines should contain an element of three. It could be three connected or contrasting statements, a list of three details or names, or something else along these lines. The three things can take up all three lines or be contained anywhere within the stanza.
- The second three lines should also contain an element of three. Same deal as the first stanza, but the two stanzas do not need to relate to each other directly.
- The final line/stanza should act as either narrative summary, punchline, or unusual juxtaposition.
- Titles are not required. But when titles are present, they should be titled Sevenling followed by the first few words in parentheses.
- Tone should be mysterious, offbeat or disturbing.
- Poem should have ambience which invites guesswork from the reader.

SHADORMA

Shadorma is a Spanish 6-line syllabic poem of 3/5/3/3/7/5 syllable lines respectively.

SIJO

The sijo is a Korean poetic form that is only three lines in length, but a lot is packed into those three lines. Here's a quick rundown:

- Three lines in length, averaging 14-16 syllables per line (for a poem total of 44-46 syllables)
- Line one introduces the situation or theme of the poem
- Line two develops the theme with more detail or a "turn" in argument
- Line three presents a "twist" and conclusion

That's a quick overview, but it can get a lot more involved. Here are some more things to consider:

- Sijo are meant to be songs, so this form is more lyrical
- Poems can be profound, humorous, metaphysical, and personal

- Each line should have a pause (or break) somewhere in the middle
- First half of the final line employs a "twist" of meaning, sound, or another poetic device

As mentioned sijo are lyrical and meant to be sung, so even the lines have a traditional syllable break:

- Line 1: 3-4-4-4
- Line 2: 3-4-4-4
- Line 3: 3-5-4-3

SKELTONIC POETRY

Skeltonic verse is named after the poet John Skelton (1460-1529), who wrote short rhyming lines that just sort of go on from one rhyme to the next for however long a poet wishes to take it. Most skeltonic poems average less than six words a line, but keeping the short rhymes moving down the page is the real key to this form.

SONNET

The sonnet is a 14-line poem that usually rhymes and is often written in iambic pentameter, though not always. Over time, this Italian poem has been pushed to its limits and some contemporary sonnets abandon many of the general guidelines.

The two most famous forms of the sonnet are the *Shakespearean Sonnet* (named after William Shakespeare) and the *Petrarcan Sonnet* (named after Francesco Petrarca). The rhyme scheme for a Shakespearean Sonnet is:

a
b
a
b

c
d
c
d

e
f
e
f

g
g

The rhyme scheme for the Petrarcan Sonnet is a little more complicated. The first eight lines (or octave) are always rhymed abbaabba. But the final six lines (or sestet) can be rhymed any number of ways: cdcdcd, cdedce, ccdccd, cdecde, or cddcee. Of course, this offers a little more flexibility near the end of the poem.

But sonnets don't necessarily need to be Shakespearean or Petrarcan to be considered sonnets. In fact, there are any number of other sonnet varieties.

A few extra notes about the sonnet:

- A crown of sonnets is made by seven sonnets. The last line of each sonnet must be used as the first line of the next until the seventh sonnet. The last line of that seventh sonnet must be the first line of the first sonnet.
- A sonnet redouble is a sequence of 15 sonnets. Each line from the first sonnet is used (in order) as the the last line of the following 14 sonnets.

STRAMBOTTO

Some of these forms are older than others, and the strambotto traces back to the 13th century. This Italian form known as ottava siciliana (Sicilian octave) or strambotto popolare was the preferred form in Southern Italy, while strambotto toscano was more popular in Tuscany [hat tip to Edward Hirsch's *A Poet's Glossary*]. Today strambotto toscano is known as ottava rima.

Here are the basic rules for strambotto:

- Octave (8-line) poems or stanzas
- Hendecasyllabic (or 11-syllable) lines
- Rhyme scheme: *abababab*

Alternate version: There's also a six-line variant form (still called strambotto) with hendecasyllabic lines and an *ababab* rhyme scheme.

TANKA

If a haiku is usually (mistakenly) thought of as a 3-line, 5-7-5 syllable poem, then the tanka would be a 5-line, 5-7-5-7-7 syllable poem. However, as with haiku, it's better to think of a tanka as a 5-line poem with 3 short lines (lines 2, 4, 5) and 2 very short lines (lines 1 and 3).

While imagery is still important in tanka, the form is a little more conversational than haiku at times. It also allows for the use of poetic devices such as metaphor and personification (2 big haiku no-no's).

TAUTOGRAM

The tautogram is best explained by its Greek root words of "tauto" meaning "the same" and "gramma" meaning "letter." Basically, all words in the poem begin with the same letter.

Note: A variant form of this poem could employ a unique starting letter for each stanza.

TERZANELLE

What do you get when you mix two super popular forms, specifically the terza rima and villanelle? The terzanelle, of course!

It combines the lyricism of the terza rima with the repitition of the villanelle to make a powerful one-two punch in only 19 lines. The traditional stance on the terzanelle is that the lines should be written in a consistent iambic meter, but there are plenty of contemporary terzanelles that just aspire to keep the lines a consistent length throughout. Here's the rhyme and refrain scheme:

Line 1: A1
Line 2: B
Line 3: A2

Line 4: b
Line 5: C
Line 6: B

Line 7: c
Line 8: D
Line 9: C

Line 10: d
Line 11: E
Line 12: D

Line 13: e
Line 14: F
Line 15: E

Line 16: f
Line 17: A1
Line 18: F
Line 19: A2

THAN-BAUK

The than-bauk is a Burmese form with very simple rules:

- Three lines
- Four syllables per line
- The final syllable of the first line rhymes with the third syllable of the second line and second syllable of the third line.

Here's a visual representation of rhyming and non-rhyming syllables for each line:

xxxa

xxax

xaxx

The poem is conventionally written as an epigram, so it's usually a clever or witty little poem.

TREOCHAIR

The treochair is an Irish form. While there are quite a few mentions online, the only book that appears to mention it is Robin Skelton's *The Shapes of Singing*. Here are the basic rules:

- Variable number of tercets (or three-line stanzas)
- Three syllables in the first line, seven in the second, and seven in the third
- The first line rhymes with the third
- Treochairs employ a lot of alliteration

TRICUBE

The tricube is a mathematical poem introduced by Phillip Larrea. Here are the tricube guidelines:

- Each line contains three syllables
- Each stanza contains three lines
- Each poem contains three stanzas

TRIOLET

The triolet (TREE-o-LAY) has 13th-century French roots linked to the rondeau or "round" poem. Like other French forms, the triolet is great for repetition, because the first line of the poem is used three times and the second line is used twice. If you do the math on this 8-line poem, you'll realize there are only three other lines to write: two of those lines rhyme with the first line, the other rhymes with the second line.

A diagram of the triolet would look like this:

A (first line)
B (second line)
a (rhymes with first line)
A (repeat first line)
a (rhymes with first line)
b (rhymes with second line)
A (repeat first line)
B (repeat second line)

TRIVERSEN

William Carlos Williams developed the triversen, which offers poets a lot of flexibility. Here are the basic rules:

- Each stanza equals one sentence
- Each sentence/stanza breaks into three lines (each line is a separate phrase in the sentence)
- There is a variable foot of two to four beats per line
- The poem as a whole should add up to 18 lines (or six stanzas)

VILLANELLE

The villanelle, like the other French forms, incorporates rhyme and repetition. This French form was actually adapted from Italian folk songs (villanella) about rural life. One of the more famous contemporary villanelles is "Do Not Go Gentle Into That Good Night," by Dylan Thomas.

The villanelle consists of five tercets and a quatrain with line lengths of 8-10 syllables. The first and third lines of the first stanza become refrains that repeat throughout the poem. It looks like this:

A(1)
b
A(2)

a
b
A(1)

a
b
A(2)

a
b
A(1)

a
b
A(2)

a
b
A(1)
A(2)

ROBERT LEE BREWER is a senior editor with the Writer's Digest Writing Community and author of *Solving the World's Problems* (Press 53). Follow him on Twitter @robertleebrewer.

THE ART OF FINISHING A POEM

....

by Sage Cohen

Every poet's process for ideating, generating, and finishing poems is unique. This can be quite liberating—and also tricky. With no Gold Standard against which to measure a poem, it's not always obvious when a poem is complete, or what needs to happen to get it there.

I believe each poem is striving to fulfill its own destiny. And we must attune ourselves to understand when it has arrived. The better you know yourself and the more robust your toolbox, the more practiced you will become at helping each poem reach its potential. So you can cross the finish line with confidence.

THE THREE STAGES OF CREATION

Knowing how to finish a poem depends on knowing how and when to write, incubate, and revise throughout the creation process.

- **Write.** In first draft mode, be as receptive to the poem as possible. Focus on generating only, without editing. Let it all come through without judgment and get it down in all of its messy, unpotentiated glory. Write and keep writing until you have exhausted all possibilities.
- **Incubate.** Many poems are well served by an incubation period after the first or early drafts. When you are at an impasse, try simply letting the poem rest—for as many nights, weeks, or years as necessary. Be intentional about your desire to complete it, but tread lightly. Read the poem before sleep and write down what it reveals to you

the following morning. Keep it folded in your pocket or taped to your bathroom mirror. Consider it a friend you are getting to know. Invite it to reveal itself to you when it is ready.

- **Revise.** There are endless ways to approach revision, and different poems may thrive under different revision conditions. I'm gong to cover a wide swath of possibilities so you can experiment and see what's right for you. The more you practice, the better you'll know which strategies to apply, and when.

Some poems feel cut from whole cloth; they come through us nearly fully formed. Others may go through any number of iterations of incubation and revision. There's no right order for the three steps above, and you can't do it wrong. Just keep exploring until you feel you've made it to the next landmark.

13 WAYS OF LOOKING AT A POEM

A poet and a poem are one. A poet and a poem and the delete key are one. I'm leaning heavily on a Wallace Stevens reference here, from his poem "13 Ways of Looking at a Blackbird." What I love about this poem is that it instructs me in the epic range of seeing, interpreting, and giving voice to what we see. A close study of blackbirds can endlessly inform our human experience. And a close study of your poem can reveal multiple paths to its destiny. When revising, consider these 13 poetic concerns.

1. **Exposition.** Does your poem have introductory information that helped you get started but is not serving the poem now? Trimming unnecessary lines from the beginning and end of a poem can often make a big difference in the poem's energy and impact.
2. **Language.** Does every word in your poem have the nuance you are seeking? Could modifiers be removed, flimsy adjectives be fortified, action verbs made more active, or passive? How would your poem change if "surprised" became "shocked" or "blindsided"?
3. **Imagery.** Are there places where you could increase specificity and even bring in the visceral by showing instead of telling? (Consider the difference between "She was weak" and "She could barely lift the spoon to her mouth.") What do you want the reader to know, see and feel? Could your images be working harder to take them there?
4. **Sound.** When you read it out loud, does your poem's sound augment its gestalt? Is there a music of repeating sounds? Should there be? Could the sounds be more harsh or soft to reflect the emotion and energy of the poem?
5. **Line breaks.** Line breaks control the reader's momentum. Do yours have the energy you're striving for? Is there a quick staccato of short lines, or an unspooling momen-

tum of longer lines? Is the last word of each line the one you want the reader's eye to linger on a moment longer? Could the line break modulate the idea or image in a more engaging way?

6. **Stanzas.** Stanzas give visual shape to a poem, defined by the white space around them. Like lines, stanzas also moderate a poem's pacing by shaping the trajectory of language. Should you change a solid block of even lines to jagged and uneven ones instead to reflect the speaker's struggle? If your poem is a single stanza now, could it benefit from the spaciousness of couplets?

7. **Point of view.** What kind of insights or information could be revealed if you chose a different speaker? Would this serve the poem better? For example, let's say a mother is the speaker and the poem is about her daughter's dead bird. What would happen if the poem were rewritten from the daughter's point of view? Or the bird's?

8. **Titles.** A poem's title is like a moon, absorbing and reflecting back its light. The way it illuminates the journey of the poem is up to you. Is yours working as hard as it could to bring the reader into the poem, and to reveal something fresh about the poem's truth? Is the title that worked well at your first draft still the right fit at draft 15?

9. **Voice and syntax.** The poem's voice and syntax should reflect the person speaking, place, and time period that the reader is entering—or diverge purposefully. The language you use should convey the context and viscerally bring the reader into that moment in time. For example, how would a conflict voiced in a Victorian parlor differ from a conflict at a 1960s protest march, or in a contemporary doctor's office?

10. **Grammar.** Capitalization, punctuation, and grammar choices give important cues to the reader about the speaker, tone, and formality or informality. Are your choices serving the poem best?

11. **Pivot.** Some shift must happen in the poem that leaves the reader somewhere other than where he or she started. How can your poem more effectively pivot to reveal a truth, change the speaker, or land the reader in unexpected terrain?

12. **Emotion.** What is the emotional tone of the poem? Anguished? Content? Tense? Remorseful? How do all of the craft concerns above work in concert to make this tone undeniable?

13. **Shiver factor.** Poems pack a lot of punch when they have a je ne sais quoi resonance that I call "shiver factor". If your poem evokes a physical response (in you, and eventually in your readers), you've arrived. There's no specific way to edit for this; the shiver is more of an outcome of all of your other apt revision choices.

SEEK MEANINGFUL FEEDBACK

Once you've put your poem through your own revision filters, it's a good time to request feedback from others. The input you get will help you better understand the experience others are having of your work—so you can evaluate if you are reaching your intended goal. Here are some ideas for making the feedback you get most useful.

- **Friends and family.** Think of friends and family as a sample of your future readers. When you ask the people you care about to weigh in on your poems, be specific about what you're looking for. If you want to know what's working well, say so. If you're looking for places where they get stuck or confused, make that clear.
- **Writing groups.** Writing groups are a great way to get specific, constructive feedback from people who are practiced in the craft of poetry. You're likely to get a wide range of opinions about the successes and opportunities in your work. Your job is to learn which readers are most useful to you in discovering fresh ways forward.
- **Editors.** If you send out poems for publication and they are not accepted, this suggests that either you haven't found the right home for your work, or your poems could use more refinement. If a poem has been rejected by three or more publications, consider further revision.
- **Audiences.** When reading in front of a live audience, notice where they laugh, gasp, lean forward, make eye contact. Notice also when they seem tuned out and disengaged. These are important clues about how your poems will land with other readers experiencing your work in print. Proceed accordingly.

Remember that you are your best expert. Other people's opinions are a training ground for refining your own opinions and honing of your craft. You get to decide what feedback serves you best, then use it to advance your work.

GET A HANDLE ON PROCRASTINATION AND PERFECTIONISM

Two of the most insidious rivals to finishing poems are procrastination and perfectionism. And I believe both are expressions of fear. Scared that a poem doesn't measure up, we either avoid returning to it at all or we obsessively rewrite it until we've lost the golden thread that led us to the poem in the first place. The best way to relax their grip is to identify procrastination and perfectionism when they come up—then make a game plan for how to work with yourself. Here are two of my best ideas for doing so.

If you find yourself on Facebook for hours when you'd planned to write or revise, I suggest giving yourself a time limit: 10 minutes on Facebook, then 10 minutes at your desk. No pressure to write anything fantastic, just a commitment to sit and write. This gives you an escape valve for your habit of distraction and a simple step to take toward following through on your writing goal.

Or, if you have the tendency to endlessly revise and never finish your poems, try setting a cutoff limit. You could start by allowing only seven drafts per poem, then wean yourself down to three drafts total. Again, you're honoring your tendencies, but also setting a clear limit. This can create a path through your resistance toward your poem's greatest potential.

COMPLETION IS A PRACTICE THROUGH WHICH WE INHERIT OURSELVES

I consider the poems I complete to be "finished for now". This takes the hard-edged finality of "finished" off the table and gives my poems and me more breathing room. (Some I revisit and revise years or decades later. Most simply stay finished.) The distance between drafting a poem and completing a poem is crossed with courage. When we decide to trust our instincts, we discover who we are. When we make choices and stand by them, we refine our craft. Each poem we complete seasons us as people and poets. Nothing is ever lost in the great ache to say something, to reach someone, to bring meaning through the small universe of a poem. Each finished poem takes us closer to the poet we were meant to be.

SAGE COHEN is the author of the poetry collection *Like the Heart, the World* (Queen of Wands Press) and nonfiction books *Writing the Life Poetic*; *The Productive Writer*; and *Fierce on the Page* (all from Writer's Digest Books). Cohen holds an MFA from New York University and a BA from Brown University. She offers strategies and support for writers at pathofpossibility.com and for divorcing parents at radicaldivorce.com.

COMING UNSTUCK

10 Techniques to Break Out of a Poetry Rut

....

by Amy Miller

Sooner or later, it happens to most poets: You've run out of ideas, you're tired of writing in that same old voice, or you feel so pressured to craft a masterpiece that you avoid writing altogether. Maybe you have full-on writer's block, with your mind feeling as dry as a…as a…oh, forget it, you can't think of the word. Or you just feel stale and static every time you try to write. The good news is, that stale, blocked feeling might be a signal that a change is coming: Maybe you're ready to leap to a new level or explore a side of your writing you didn't know existed. If you're stuck in one of these poetry ruts, or just ready to try something new, here are 10 playful, unconventional exercises to help get your creative sparks flying again.

1. WRITE IN A BOX

Sometimes it's daunting just to begin writing on a blank page or screen—all that space demanding to be filled! To sidestep that pressure, think on a smaller scale: Write a poem on a postcard, Post-it note, or nametag. You can't get more than about a 12-line poem on a postcard, and a nametag will hold maybe 6 or 8 lines. Writing in such confinement forces you to narrow your focus; you won't get the whole story of your grandmother's immigration on a Post-it, but you might be able to capture the smell of the ocean or the creaking of the ship. And that kind of detail may make for a more powerful poem than a long epic. (Plus, you can write the epic later, or piece together several small poems to make a larger one.) Writing "small" tricks the brain into thinking poetry is easy, even though any poet knows a good haiku can be as hard to write as a thousand-line narrative. If you'd rather not buy postcards or nametags, just draw boxes in a notebook or set some rulers in your word-processing program: The "letter" part of a postcard is about 3 inches wide by 2½ high; most printer-ready, sheet-style nametags are 4 wide by 2 high.

2. MAKE A BATCH OF PANCAKES

Ever heard the old adage about how you should throw away the first pancake? It has something to do with the griddle not being ready, and this can also apply to poems—sometimes our first "take" on an idea isn't the best one. To get beyond that first impression, go ahead and write a poem on any topic—it doesn't have to be good—then set it aside and write *another* poem on the same subject, perhaps even with the same title. And then another, and if you're feeling like a superpoet, maybe 5 or 10 more. (Keeping them short will prevent burnout.) By the third or fourth poem, you may be surprised by the deeper connections you're making, like tying the wineglass from the first poem to a fight after a party or your aunt's surreally cluttered kitchen. With each subsequent poem, let yourself write whatever comes to mind, no matter how far-fetched—when you're writing a batch of poems, who cares if some things don't work out? If you find a topic especially fertile, extend it over several sittings; you may end up with a set of poems you can later craft into a thematically linked series, or even a chapbook.

3. WRITE A SYMPHONY

That's not daunting at all, right? Actually it isn't, if you consider what a symphony is made of: smaller parts that differ wildly from each other—fast, slow, lilting, bombastic. Set out to write a poem in three, four, or more sections, but make them drastically different from each other in tone, voice, line length, or form. Alternate prose poetry with tanka, first person with third; mix speech patterns, fragments, meter, and rhyme. Build the poem, moving from style to style and keeping it interesting with quick, unexpected cuts. If symphonies aren't your thing, model your poem on an unconventional pop song, like "Band on the Run" or "Suite: Judy Blue Eyes," that's actually a sequence of shorter tunes.

4. STEAL FROM THE GOVERNMENT

One genre that never seems to go out of style is found poetry—poems that take phrases from non-poetic sources like newspapers, ads, and textbooks, and rearrange them into a new work that either comments on the original or veers off into a new subject. One great source for this material is government documents such as voter pamphlets, tax guides, and scientific reports. Driver's manuals, to use one example, are full of evocative phrases—"Others may be daydreaming," "Do not try to beat the train," "Never assume everything will be all right"—that practically beg to be used as metaphors, and not just about motoring safety. Find a source document and start cutting-and-pasting away, moving phrases and deleting connecting tissue to create a poem that's very different than the original source. Note: Many government documents are in the public domain and can be put through your poetry blender without risking copyright violation. But if you're in doubt, do some online research to make sure the material is in fact in the public domain.

5. LET IT FLOOD

If the very thought of sitting down to "write a poem" is turning you off, trick yourself by writing something that's not a poem. Pick a subject—it could be as banal as a diary entry, or maybe an experience fresh in your mind, a memory, or a single word—and start writing about it in an unruly torrent, an unedited freeform monologue without any line breaks. That's crucial: Don't break it into lines or pay any attention to how it's laying out on the page as it spews onto your screen, notebook, or voice-recognition program. Don't stop to edit; leave in every crazy free association and non-sequitur. Then, when the flow has stopped, save or transcribe what you've written, make a copy (set aside the original), and start breaking it into lines, editing things out, and rearranging. This editing process can take it in any number of directions: What words or phrases seem superfluous when you break it into lines? What happens if you keep only the non-sequiturs and wild associations? Or if you edit them all out? Does it really want to be a poem with lines, or does it have more energy as a prose poem, or even as flash-fiction or flash-memoir? Can you extract several small poems from it? This writing prompt is also a revision exercise, giving you raw material that be crafted into any number of poems or prose pieces.

6. DO WHAT COMES UNNATURALLY

As poets, we all have our specialties—our voice, the topics we're known for, our characteristic word choices, sounds, and syntax. There's nothing wrong with having a distinctive style, but these "default" modes can sometimes land us in a poetry rut where we feel like we're writing the same poems over and over. To clear your writing palate, try something that's way out of your comfort zone. If you like full sentences, write a stanza of fragments. If you hate long couplets, write a whole poem of them. If your poems tend to be square-shaped, write a skinny one, or a scattershot one that's all over the page. If your poems tend to unfold in logical narrative, try a surprising twist at each line's start. If you can't stand limericks, write a series of them, making them uniquely your own. The goal here is to attain a sort of "beginner's mind," where being bad at something is fun because you don't expect to be good at it yet. And who knows? It might actually be…good.

7. PAINT YOURSELF OUT OF THE PICTURE

Poetry is, of course, personal writing about our own perceptions of the world. But sometimes writing from the first-person "I" viewpoint can become its own poetry rut, making poems feel repetitive, limited, or tonally flat, even to the poet. To widen the camera's lens, go to a café or park and write about the people and things around you—the barista, the guy absorbed in his laptop, the dog outside the door, the women laughing, the old brick wall, the sign in the bathroom about the cranky plumbing. Use dialog you overhear, or put words in people's mouths. Write only in third person—he, she, they, it—and don't let yourself make an appearance in the poem. Who are those people? What have they seen? What brought them here? Try one person or object, then another. Make each a little story, a character sketch, or even a brash manifesto on how that person thinks and lives. Of course the resulting poems will still be about your own perceptions, memories, biases, and assumptions, but those other people will be the conduit.

8. USE THE NEWS

To reach even farther outside yourself—and then circle back to your own experiences—scan a newspaper or online news site and find a story that strikes a chord with you emotionally. Maybe it's about someone trapped in a sinking ship, triggering your claustrophobia, or a project to help sea turtles that stirs your world-saving compassion, or a hapless criminal who reminds you uncomfortably of your ex. Jot down sensory images that come to mind as you read the story—smells, tastes, sounds, textures—merging the landscape of the news article with an event or person from your own life. Then, incorporating these sensory images, write a poem about that personal experience or memory that this story churns up inside you. This exercise avoids an occasional pitfall of "poems of witness" and news-based poems: appropriating a stranger's story to crassly mine it for emotion. This exercise is about your story, employing the news article as a sensory route back to that experience of your own that you may have forgotten, or haven't been able to write about before.

9. FASHION A FORM

Like writing in small spaces (see #1), writing in forms—sonnets, triolets, ghazals, and the like—can help narrow down your choices, which can be a good thing when a wide-open, blank page is staring you in the face. The beauty of forms is that part of the work is already done for you: With a sonnet, you know you've got to make your point in 14 lines; with a haiku, only three (-ish, depending on whom you talk to). If you're tackling a sestina, after you've set up the first stanza, you already know the end word of every line in the poem. In a pantoum, you've already written half of the lines before you get to them. That's not to say forms are easy; some are notoriously devilish (villanelle, anyone?). But that's part of their beauty too; because writing in form is so difficult to do well, it can help lower your standards a little, tying up your logical, critical mind with the mechanics of the puzzle while freeing your subconscious to make creative leaps, much like those brilliant ideas we get in the shower or while driving to work.

10. APPLY SOME PRESSURE

Many of these suggestions have been about relieving pressure. But pressure isn't always bad; some people do their best work under the force of several G's, with their ears about to pop. To see if you like that ratcheted stress, try challenging yourself to a public writing task, like the April marathon of National Poetry Writing Month (NaPoWriMo). Or try one of the nationwide postcard-poetry projects (google "poetry postcard"), or set up your own poem-a-day writing marathon with friends via an e-mail list or Facebook group. Sometimes there's nothing like accountability—promising you'll be there every day, with a freshly written poem—to pull you out of a rut and get you back on the road and writing.

AMY MILLER's chapbooks include *I Am on a River and Cannot Answer* and *White Noise Lullaby*, and her poetry has appeared in *Crab Orchard Review, Rattle, Willow Springs*, and *ZYZZYVA*. She won the Cultural Center of Cape Cod National Poetry Competition, judged by Tony Hoagland, and the Jack Grapes Poetry Prize from Cultural Weekly. She lives in Oregon and blogs at writers-island.blogspot.com.

POETS AND COLLABORATION

The Benefits and Trials of Collaborating

by Jeannine Hall Gailey

What is collaboration? For a poet, it is the act of working with another artist (or several artists) to create and produce a new piece of art. It could be a collage that incorporates lines of your poems, a piece of music interpreting your work, an interactive art exhibit, even a play.

Many people think of poets as being solitary types, but there are advantages to stepping away from the laptop and into conversation with other types of artists. Interaction and conversation with artists in a variety of media and genres can spark new ideas and build unexpected connections. The rewards of working in multiple art forms include reaching larger (and new) audiences as well as challenging yourself to think about your work in a new mediuam and way.

While poetry often lacks a visual or auditory component, I think including all the senses in an experience helps people connect with a piece more fully. For instance, listening to the Star Wars score by itself is pretty stirring, but the John Williams piece is even more moving when accompanied by the sound effects, imagery, and dialogue of the movie.

Collaboration can be a one-way response, or a conversation where artists respond to each other. You may be familiar with book cover art or ekphrastic poems, which are composed in response to a work of art, such as Auden's "Musée des Beaux Arts" that describes the painting "Landscape with the Fall of Icarus." Those are examples of one-way responses. But collaboration can also be two-way, like a conversation between friends, in which there is an exchange of ideas and art over time. Collaborations can happen between poets and sculptors, neon or glass artists, painters, musicians, and filmmakers.

ADVANTAGES TO COLLABORATIONS

What are the advantages of working with other types of artists? It can be hard for poets to get outside of our little "boxes of words" and be vulnerable enough to share our work with others. The rewards include things like: seeing our work brought to life in a way we never imagined, making friends in our community, building support between different artistic communities, increasing opportunities to be inspired by other works of art and the fascinating conversations to be had with other types of artists (my personal favorite), and also increasing the audiences for your work. One of my bestselling readings was when an artist friend invited me along to one of her gallery openings to read poems to accompany the visuals of her work. Almost everyone there, mostly art patrons, bought a book!

I brought collaboration into much of my work as Redmond, Washington's second Poet Laureate, because I thought it was important to incorporate and introduce multiple points-of-view and media types, and because, in a town known for its techie, rather than literary, population, it would be a way to introduce the unknownwn poetry with the more familiar say, art and music. I wanted to enrich our community's experiences with a wider variety of art forms and show how poetry could be relevant to them. It was also a chance to show the often startling beauty of works emerging from cooperation between artists and art forms.

Similar opportunities can come to you through arts organizations, festivals, and art galleries at any time, so it's good to consider with what type of artist you think you would most like to work.

COLLABORATIONS WITH VISUAL ARTISTS

When you think about poets working with visual artists, you might automatically think about cover art. I had a great time working with the cover artist of my first and third books, Michaela Eaves. She took the time to read early versions of my books and create concepts and hire artist's models to pose for the scenes that eventually became the covers of *Becoming the Villainess* and *Unexplained Fevers*. We went on to collaborate on a series of images and poems interpreting Japanese folk tales for one of my Redmond Poet Laureate projects that were later used inside the second edition of my second book, *She Returns to the Floating World*.

Michaela Eaves talks about her experience with poet-artist collaboration: "The expected rules and boundaries are much looser when it comes collaborating with a poet. If you illustrate a straight-up prose story, the publisher, reader, and author expect a certain level of illustrative representation. Here's a story about a girl that likes to wear glass slippers, so you create a piece about a girl making the best of her bad footwear choices. Poetry allows you to loosen the reins and explore symbolism and intent, not just act out what's on the page. The poet may mention slippers, but you are illustrating the feel of it rather than the facts. Working directly with the poet is great because you can get to the heart of what she's trying to say by asking questions rather than just relying on guesswork."

Visual artist collaborations can include more than just book covers or illustrations; it can include poetry used to accompany a visual art exhibition. Mary Coss of METHOD Gallery in Seattle paired poets with visual artists of different media for the 2015 show, TEXTure. Carol Milne, a talented glass artist recently featured in the *Boston Globe,* worked with my poems for the show, which also featured Northwest poets Sherman Alexie (paired with neon artists Lia Yaranon Hall and Cedar Mannan) and Daemond Arrindell (paired with fabric artist Maura Donegan.) Carol picked out two poems from my book *The Robot Scientist's Daughter* and created a uranium-glass snowman with words like "Cesium" and "Uranium" woven into the pattern of the glass representing radioactive snow, and then I wrote a poem in response to her work.

Carol Milne, when asked to describe how the project came together: "Well, frankly, I've never been too fond of poetry. Most of it is too brooding and esoteric, where I lean towards the ironic, amusing and down-to-earth. However, I think it's good to challenge one's preconceptions, and I thought it sounded like a fun project. I browsed the meager Northwest poetry section of the library, and then, while surfing the Internet for Northwest poets, I ended up on the Jack Straw website where I found Jeannine's poem, 'Cesium Burns Blue.' It struck me with its visual beauty and dark message. I found a kindred spirit working in another medium. It was refreshing to come back to ironic work, making a political/environmental statement, through discovering similar work in written form. Jeannine's work explores innocence and daily life with horrific undertones of environmental hazards. The contrast personalizes and drives home the horror of nuclear contamination. The power of the arts: to get you personally engaged without spewing statistics."

Kelly Davio, the editor of *The Tahoma Literary Review* who collaborated with Redmond, Washington-area visual artists (and me) for the "Voices in the Corridor" project for VALA arts center offers another perspective on collaboration: "Collaborating with the visual artists in the 'Voices in the Corridor' project was a wonderful chance to shake up my own artistic process. While I tend to be measured and exact when I write, the visual artists seemed to work intuitively, feeling the ways in which their pieces fit in and adapted to the gallery space. Riffing off their works and making my own process more flexible allowed me to write work I never would have produced otherwise." And Jessica F. Kravitz Lambert, the founder of VALA and one of the two artists who came up with the idea for our collaborative project, said: "Working with writers allows visual artists another opportunity to share the themes in their work with another set of artists that can interpret and dialogue with the artwork created, allowing the audience to have yet another way of 'seeing' the artwork."

COLLABORATIONS WITH PERFORMANCE ARTISTS—THEATER GROUPS, FILMMAKERS, AND CHOREOGRAPHERS

One of the first collaborations I was even involved with was when I was contacted by a theater group called "The Alley Cat Players." They had a copy of my first book, *Becoming the Villainess*, and wanted to use it as the basis for a series of one-act plays they would perform in Florida. I wish I had lived closer to Florida so I could have seen one of the performances!

Other types of collaborations include "videopoems," in which filmmakers might collaborate with a poet to create a video that choreographs with a poem while it is being read, creating an effect similar to a music video.

Dance teams and choreographers can work to interpret poems as well.

COLLABORATIONS WITH MUSICIANS

Of course, you may have thought of poets working with lyrics (such as Wyn Cooper's poem, "Fun," that became Sheryl Crow's pop hit "All I Wanna Do"), but have you ever thought of writing with a musician and songwriter? Bushwick Book Club is a group of collaborative musicians in Seattle. They interpret writings from Shakespeare, the Bible, and contemporary poetry and turn them into songs that they perform in a spirited venue with much joy and riotous musician-like behavior. (I've been to a few of these performances, and let me say, hanging out with a musician crowd, you can definitely tell which are the poets and which are the musicians—rowdier, more attractive, and better dressed.) Geoff Larson, the executive director of Bushwick Seattle, describes the process of collaboration: "The Bushwick Book Club Seattle process of writing original music inspired by others' writings is a unique exercise that allows songwriters to chase any idea or thread the author's work may spark. Like any writing process, it can be a pretty solitary endeavor, and emerging at the end of it to share the result with an audience is a gratifying and interactive moment. When that audience includes the creator of the 'source material,' that interaction is all the more magical when two creative forces feed off of one another in a moment of mutual appreciation, each having generated something and then let it go into the world for others to receive."

Joy Mills, who collaborated with me on one poem/song ("Sleeping Beauty Loves the Needle") for a Bushwick Book Club project, describes her experience working with poets: "Working with Jeannine and other poets in the past has been such a gratifying experience as a musician because I consider poetry to be a foundation for so many creative forms. Poetry is music. The meter, rhythm, word play, rhyme and structure all lend themselves openly to being placed into song. With Jeannine, I much preferred to put her poem to music, rather than interpret it with my own lyrics. To use an already-existing piece and try to wrap the music around it allowed me to broaden my craft through collaborative approach. Poetry and music come from the same motherland in so many ways, allowing us to distill the vast world around us, if only for a fleeting spell." It was truly surreal and a real treat to get up on stage and read my poem, and then hear Joy perform with her guitar the song she interpreted and created from my poem.

Several famous poets, including Yusef Komunyakaa, Margaret Atwood and Dana Goia, have collaborated with classically trained composers to create operas from their work, in a practice of collaboration that dates back to the seventeenth century.

COLLABORATIONS WITH OTHER WRITERS

This could be the subject of its own article! Collaborating with other poets can result in wonderful work that yields often work that highlights the strong points of both writers. Denise Duhamel, a frequent and generous collaborator with other poets, highlights this: "I love throwing in with another poet and see where the imagination is ignited by the other. The poem becomes less a force of the will of one writer and a magic revelation full of surprises for the collaborators."

For the previously mentioned "Voices in the Corridor" project for the city of Redmond, not only did Kelly Davio and I respond to the projects for four visual artists, but we also wrote haikus responding to both the Redmond landscape and did a kind of "call and response" to each other's work.

REAP THE REWARDS OF REACHING OUT

In any collaboration, the conversation between poet and artist can enlarge and enlighten.

The risks are worth it, because the chance to include, improvise and bring a larger scope to your work is worth the occasional hiccup and increases your chances of reaching a greater and more diverse audience with your work. Branch out and take advantage of opportunities to exchange ideas and to collaborate. Watch a theater group transform your work with their acting abilities, or a musician take your work to a new level with the addition of a score. With inspiration and a little hard work, the results may take you far beyond what you might have achieved alone.

JEANNINE HALL GAILEY served as the second Poet Laureate of Redmond, Washington. She is the author of five books of poetry, including *Becoming the Villainess, She Returns to the Floating World, Unexplained Fevers,* and *The Robot Scientist's Daughter.* Her website is www.webbish6.com.

FRESHEN YOUR POETRY

by Nancy Susanna Breen

During a recent stint of poetry judging, I decided to keep a running list of the words and phrases that turned up again and again in entries. What I discovered is that too many poets, especially new or developing poets, depend on clichés in their writing. Others simply don't stretch enough for originality when crafting their lines. Instead, they invoke wording and images that have become exhausted with use.

You can freshen your poetry and increase your individuality by targeting stale language during the revising process. Like mold on bread, instances of exhausted images and overused words act as alerts once you know what you're looking for.

CLICHÉS

A cliché is any trite phrase or expression; that is, a phrase or expression that has been run into the ground. Avoid clichés like the plague. (See how easy it is to work clichés into your writing? There are two in those two sentences.) Because of their familiarity, clichés are comfortable and seemingly add a conversational touch to a line of poetry. They seem to guarantee clarity as well, because readers know what the clichés mean.

However, when poets turn to the same tired phrases and overused words, their poems all sound alike. Cliché-ridden lines have a cookie cutter effect. They result in poems that seem prefabricated, assembled of standard parts.

Here's a brief list of clichés that turned up more than three times in the batch of poems I was judging:

     lips are/were sealed
     blood, sweat, and tears
     into thin air

heart and soul
thick and thin
bitter end
on a silver platter
life is precious
time stands still
as far as the eye can see
tore like a knife
sands in an hourglass
sun, moon, and stars

If you need help recognizing clichés, the Internet offers some valuable sites. For example, ClicheList.net provides an alphabetized list of clichés, each example linked to an explanation of its meaning. Cliché Finder (www.westegg.com/cliche) allows you to search its 3,000-plus cliché bank by keyword; "cat" turned up over 50 examples, such as "cat has your tongue," "cat's meow," and "raining cats and dogs." There's also a cliché generator that provides 10 random clichés at a time. Make a practice of reading through those 10 random clichés daily for a month and you'll find it much easier to spot clichés in your poems.

OH, NO! NOT ANOTHER [BLANK] POEM

Clichés include dull, stereotypical ideas and situations. Consequently, entire poems can be clichés. Gather a large enough sample of poems, such as entries in a poetry contest or submissions to a magazine, and you'll see several examples of the same clichéd poem, sometimes with surprisingly little variation. Below are types of poems poets can't seem to resist writing. Exercise heightened originality if attempting these poems.

Butterflies

I have nothing against butterflies, and I appreciate how symbolic they are. However, they turn up constantly as poem subjects, accompanied by all the typical verbs: flit, flutter, and so on. Describing or referring to butterflies emerging from cocoons is also popular. Understand how commonplace butterflies are before writing an entire poem about them if you really want to set your work apart. For that matter, restrain yourself from using them as images or symbols without plenty of careful thought.

Sea and sand

Poets simply must write about the ocean. (I certainly have.) They stroll through the tide, meditate on the coming and going of the tide, study what the tide leaves behind, and compare life to the movements of the tide.

There's nothing wrong with writing about strolling on the beach, watching the waves, or examining the shells and driftwood at low tide. However, because they're so popular with poets, the ocean and beach are hard to write about in an original way, especially if the physical descriptions basically make up the poem.

Poets consistently choose the same words to describe the sea and shore, and the ring of familiarity isn't a virtue. Even a touching account of a dying person visiting the seaside for the last time or a broken-hearted lover examining a ruined relationship fades into sameness when the speakers' actions are similar and they seem to be viewing the scene through the same pair of eyes.

Seasonal

The most uninspired, and uninspiring, poetry I see usually focuses on one of the seasons or on all four at once. This is primarily because poets pull out all the standard images, as if putting up those colored cardboard cutouts in a classroom: colored leaves and pumpkins for fall, snowflakes for winter, buds and robins for spring, a big, smiling sun for summer. Such images are beloved and iconic; and because of this, you need to move past them when writing about a season. Read enough poems that cite "the golden leaves drift lazily to ground" and you'll wince at the mere thought of autumn.

I'm going to go a step farther and suggest that freshening the seasonal imagery you use isn't enough—you should avoid the seasons as the sole subjects of poems. Instead, use the season as a background. That way your poem develops into sometime more than a laundry list of the same old spring showers, hot July noons, and shimmering blankets of snow on a rolling landscape.

Love

It's a shame so many love poems come across as time-creased valentines. I've rarely read a clichéd love poem that made me doubt the sincerity of the writer's feelings. When such verse seems cribbed from the most mundane greeting card, though, especially when expressed in *oo-aa* rhymes, the poem appears mass-produced rather than the true expression of an individual. Poems about unrequited love or rejection are especially painful, not because of the sadness involved but because a kind of injured, righteous indignation overrides the poet's artistic common sense. And, of course, the same images are evoked and the same flowery language applied as though squeezed out of a tube of frosting.

When writing a poem that addresses a romantic partner or someone who has cast you aside, consider sending it only to the intended recipient or keeping it strictly to yourself. Otherwise, be sure you can treat the work as a piece of literary art, not a love letter. Even then, make it your own. Don't resort to gooey Valentine verses or resentful poison notes.

A subset of the love poem is the "love is" poem. If you insist on defining love, have something new to say. "Love is" poems range from a list of clichéd comparisons, both positive and negative (a delicate rose, a knife to the heart, a blanket against the cold) to a series of unsurprising adjectives (kind, understanding, forgiving, harsh, demoralizing, etc.). Throw out the cookie-cutter images and the threadbare language or don't bother at all, at least not if you're writing for a general readership. The same goes for "my love is like" poems.

OTHER CLICHÉ PITFALLS

Hearts

In poetry, hearts aren't mere organs that pump blood. Poets have them doing more tricks than a trained poodle in a one-ring circus: pounding, shrieking, weeping, dancing, swelling, bleeding, exploding, freezing, or stopping dead (without killing the poet). Poets assist their hearts in hyperactivity by opening them, shutting them, writing on them, exploring them, hiding things in them, and nursing them. Other people do things to poets' hearts as well: stomp on them, warm them, break them, steal them, stab them, fill them with joy or sadness, play with them, heal them, and reawaken them when they're dead (figuratively speaking).

"Heart" is one of those words you have to handle carefully, if at all. Despite its versatility, in most cases you can leave "heart" out of your poem. It's a cliché that can do more harm than good; and the more animated the heart is in your poem, the more danger of giving the reader a mental image that resembles a Wile E. Coyote cartoon.

Obviously, if you're writing about someone's cardiac event, *heart* is a necessary clinical term, not a cliché. Where emotions are concerned, though, don't go breaking, teasing, or exposing anyone's heart in your poems.

Despair

It's astonishing how many poets "plunge into the abyss" or "descend into oblivion" at some point in their poetry. Sometimes they hurtle their entire beings into the black pit of nothingness; in other instances, their minds or hearts take the dive of despair.

Sadly, it's hard for readers to take you seriously when you're melodramatic. Write with even more finesse when addressing such intense emotional conditions as grief and depression. Imagine an over-the-top actor in 19th-century theater wailing to the balcony, writhing on the stage, or whirling his cape around him like a shroud. This shouldn't be the effect you want your lines to convey.

Read the confessional poetry of Sylvia Plath, Robert Lowell, Anne Sexton, John Berryman, and others to learn how to calibrate your language so you express the most emotion with the least hyperbole.

Tears

Too many poets turn the human face into a Niagara Falls of tears. These tears run, cascade, course, drip, trickle, and flow. Or poets turn to clichés to describe weeping, such as "cried like a baby," "cried a river," or "cried her eyes out."

When you write skillfully, showing rather than telling, you can convey sorrow without using tears at all. Uncontrolled waterworks are just overkill; they don't make the scene more convincing. Think of a movie where an actor cries. It's usually an extreme situation when a character dissolves into heaving sobs; otherwise, the viewers don't buy it. Often a character struggling *not* to cry is more affecting than drenched cheeks. Remember that the next time you're inclined to flood someone's face with tears in your poem.

Colors

Although simply putting "green," "blue," or "red" into your descriptions is pretty mundane, it's almost worse to employ clichéd colors. If you notice "ruby red," "golden yellow," "baby pink," "sky blue," and similar color clichés in your poems, revise them to more specific colors or create original similes—in other words, don't just substitute "red as a ruby" or "blue as a summer sky." Come up with something vivid and new. If your color phrase turns up in the lyrics of pop songs or standards, it's too worn-out to use in your poetry. For inspiration, review some paint company websites for the creative ways they name various colors, then work on original examples of your own.

While I'm discussing colors, I want to mention red, white, and blue. This combination is a favorite of poets writing about the military, patriotism, or the United States in general. Unfortunately, those colors used together have become cliché, detracting from verse that may otherwise make valid statements. There's plenty to say about a soldier's sacrifice, love of one's country, or the esteem for U.S. liberty and democracy without tying everything up in red, white, and blue bunting. Make your poem stirring enough and readers will see the stars and stripes without a specific reference.

ABOUT DEAD METAPHORS

When people repeat a metaphor so often its original imagery gives way to a new, literal meaning, the result is a *dead metaphor*. I once heard the poet Donald Hall cite the use of dead metaphors as one of the most common reasons he rejects poems. One of his examples was *sea of wheat*, which now means an expanse of wheat rather than an ocean-like view of the grain field.

Determining what constitutes a dead metaphor and when to delete it can be confusing. For instance, *eye of the needle* is considered a dead metaphor, yet it's also what we call that opening in the top of a needle. On the other hand, in the phrase *he plowed through the stacks of paper*, "plowed" at first glance seems a vigorous verb choice rather than a dead metaphor. However, consider how many times you hear this metaphor in televised news reports. "The robbery suspect plowed through the festival crowd." "The car plowed into the front porch of the home." *Plow* doesn't conjure up its original imagery of a blade digging through dirt; it's taken on a meaning of its own through heavy repetition as a popular term.

If you're unsure about dead metaphors, apply the yardstick of frequency: If the term in question gets repeated a lot, especially in the media, revise the term whether it's a dead metaphor or not.

BE ALERT, NOT OBSESSIVE

Don't inhibit your writing by being overly conscious about stale language as you're putting the words down. First or even second and third drafts aren't a time for self-editing. When you revise, watch carefully for overused words and tired imagery. They're tricky little devils to catch because we're so used to them. Reread this article and I'm sure you'll target some clichés or dead metaphors that slipped right by me. The point is to be aware of them as you hone your skills. Over time you'll become more astute about when you need to cast them aside to freshen up the lines of your poems.

NANCY SUSANNA BREEN is a poet, freelance writer, and editor. Her poetry is available in e-chapbook form at www.Smashwords.com as is an e-book of writing prompts, *Nudged by Quotes—20 Writing Prompts Inspired by The World's Great Poetry, Volume 10: Poetical Quotations.* She's the former editor of *Poet's Market* and judges poetry contests at the state and national levels.

WRITING POEMS FROM PROMPTS

by Amorak Huey

The prompt is a thoroughly entrenched part of the pedagogy in creative writing courses from kindergarten to college. "Here's a topic," the teacher will say, "here's a challenge, an idea, a form to try." In return, students dutifully respond with a piece of writing that conforms to the instructions as best as they can manage. Perhaps because these kinds of exercises are so associated with "school writing," prompts may for some writers carry a stigma as something "real writers" don't use, as a trick or gimmick, as a crutch for beginners.

It need not be so.

For many poets, the prompt can be an essential component of an active writing life. The first step to using a prompt successfully is not to think of it as a school assignment that must be followed to the letter. A prompt should be a launching pad for your poems, not a leash that ties them down. The best prompt gives you a quick shove off the edge of a cliff you might not have even known was there—and then disappears as you negotiate the fall yourself.

DEFEATING WRITER'S BLOCK

One of the best things a prompt can do for a poet is to eliminate that most difficult of questions: What do I write about? Much of the world has this notion that poems are mystical gifts from the muses, words bestowed from on high to the poet who waits patiently for inspiration. That sounds nice, and while there's certainly something mysterious and intangible in the creative process, sitting around and hoping for some external inspiration is not a recipe for getting much writing done. Perhaps it worked for Wordsworth or Byron, but my guess is that even the poets we study in literature classes got more accomplished by sitting down with quill in hand than by waiting to be granted some divine gift.

Writer's block is usually some blend of anxiety and self-doubt combined with the many things that demand time in our daily lives. An excuse, in other words. A writing prompt can be just the trick to get past that excuse. It frees you up to write without waiting for inspiration; it also removes some of the pressure we all place on ourselves. If the piece of writing doesn't live up to your hopes, you can always blame the prompt.

T.S. Eliot famously said: "When forced to work within a strict framework, the imagination is taxed to its utmost, and will produce its richest ideas. Given total freedom, the work is likely to sprawl." Think of the blank page (or these days, the blank Word document). It's intimidating, that scary expanse of whiteness, all the emptiness, infinite possibilities. Where to start? How does anyone ever write anything? The answer is in the Eliot quote: You need constraint. A framework. Some limitation: steel against which you can strike the flint of your imagination. That's what the prompt is for. Poet and professor Dean Rader says, "Novice poets tend to rely on abstractions and bigness, so I try to give exercises and prompts that force them to be concrete and specific." The prompt, in other words, shrinks the world, narrows the infinite down to the possible.

SETTING CHALLENGES FOR YOURSELF

For student writers, the prompts given by their instructors might feel restrictive, frustrating, a burden weighing down their creativity. Yet once you're writing outside of the classroom context, all that freedom can be a little dizzying: you can write what you want, when you want, *if* you want. One of the most common things former students say to me is that they miss having writing prompts. I've had students e-mail me years after graduation asking for some new prompt to kickstart their writing again. Here's a secret, one of the tricks of the poetry trade: Poets have to invent prompts for themselves. As Diane Thiel says, "All writers learn by reading and by setting themselves exercises."

We all, we writers and poets, set ourselves language challenges every time we sit down with our (metaphorical) quill in hand. Write a five-line poem about X. Use this newspaper headline or that Facebook status in a poem. Write a poem in which the letter *I* does not appear. Write a sonnet. Write a sestina. Write a villanelle. The entire concept of formal poetry is itself a kind of prompt, an artificial constraint in the sense Eliot referred to: Write down your feelings about love, only do it in 14 lines of iambic pentameter following a particular rhyme scheme. Even the very choice to write a poem is a prompt. Why not write a short story, a novel, a journal entry, a blog post? A poem makes a particular kind of demand on your creativity, suggests certain things about form and focus in the same way a prompt suggests things about subject matter or approach. Poet and professor W. Todd Kaneko says, "Often the prompt has less to do with topic and more to do with restraint—do something specific with time or rhyming action or sound—anything to help me get something moving on the page. ... I think writing prompts are most useful when they are based around an element of craft."

Even if you don't have a teacher to spark your writing with a ready-made syllabus full of assignments, you can always come up with them on your own. Invent whatever restrictions you like. Think of it as a game. (And if you want outside assistance, check out the many prompts provided in the sources at the end of this article.)

BEGINNING AND BEGINNING AGAIN

Here's another secret about poetry: Every poet is, in some sense, a beginning poet. Every poem is a fresh start. Sure, some aspects of the craft might grow easier over time, with years of experience in reading and writing, but each new poem offers a new opportunity for discovery, for experimentation—and for failure. Yes, some (much? most?) writing fails. But of course failure is an essential part of writing; as Samuel Beckett said, "Fail again. Fail better." It's easy for a writer to focus too much on product and not enough on process, to see failure as an endpoint instead of a necessary detour on the writing journey.

The best way to think about prompts, then, is to see them as more about process than about product. They are intended to provoke you, to put you into situations that you have to find your way out of, like one of those reality shows where you're dropped on a desert island and have to figure out how to build a hut before it rains. A prompt offers both a challenge and a learning opportunity. Cindy Hunter Morgan says prompts offer a writer "framework and focus." Chris Haven says, "I think poets should think of our writing as responding to an implied assignment. We report on news from worlds that resemble ours or don't, real ones or imagined ones. A prompt allows us to get outside of our own requirements and widen our scope of what readers might require."

MOVING FROM PROMPT TO POEM

But of course, process is not the only thing that matters. In the end, we do want to create meaningful poems—work that appears to have been hand-delivered by the muses even if it wasn't. It might seem that prompts are an artificial way to achieve this kind of writing; that is, writing from a prompt might feel more contrived than natural. And it's probably true that most published poems probably don't come directly from prompts in the sense of the prompts you were given in your writing classes: What did *you* do on your summer vacation?

The key to getting beyond any sort of artificiality goes back to the idea that a prompt should not limit but inspire your work. The prompt is a starting place, not the destination. Robin Behn and Chase Twichell, in the introduction to *The Practice of Poetry*, an excellent book full of exercises and prompts, write:

A good exercise serves as a scaffold—it eventually falls away, leaving behind something new in the language, language that now belongs to the writer. … Exercises can result in a new understanding of the relation of image to meaning, or a way into the unconscious, perhaps a way of marrying autobiography with invention, or a sense of the possibility of different kinds of structures, ways to bring a dead poem to life, a new sense of rhythm, or a slight sharpening of the ear. Exercises can help you think about, articulate, and solve specific creative problems. Or they can undermine certain assumptions you might have, forcing you to think—and write—beyond the old limitations.

A scaffold that eventually falls away—it's the perfect metaphor. Here's another: A writing prompt is not a box that your poem must fit into, but a pot that the poem grows out of. Start in the direction your prompt suggests, but if the poem seems to lead somewhere else, follow. If writing about your most recent summer vacation leads to a memory of some youthful July week spent at your grandmother's lake cabin which in turn leads to a memory of your first crush and you wind up writing more about the crush, so be it. Even if those early lines about last summer disappear entirely from the final piece, they have served a purpose.

Not every prompt will lead you to your favorite poem. Some prompts will be easy. Some will seem hard. Often it's the hard ones you should look at more carefully. Ask yourself: What makes this hard? What in particular am I struggling with here? If you really, really hate a particular prompt, try to figure out why. Try to learn something from the difficulty. One of my goals in every creative writing class I teach and with every prompt I assign is to push students outside their comfort zones and away from their assumptions about themselves and their limitations. Writing should be challenging, every time.

Here are five tips for using prompts effectively:

1. Take the prompt seriously. Work at figuring out what it's asking you do to.
2. Imagine all the different poems that might emerge from a single prompt. Then ask yourself which of those poems you'd like to write.
3. If one prompt is falling flat, combine it with another. The creative process benefits immensely from the friction of two disparate forces.
4. Use the prompt as an excuse to play. Writing poetry should be a playful act most of the time anyway. (That does not mean it's not also serious work. It's both.)
5. Abandon the prompt as soon as it's no longer serving the poem that has emerged on the page.

In the end, to paraphrase Richard Hugo, you owe a prompt nothing and the poem you're writing everything. A poem will never be measured by how well the poet grappled with the prompt that started it. A poem must be measured by its own internal standards, by its music and language and the way it both creates and reflects the world we live in. You won't get to walk around with your poem explaining how the prompt influenced this line or that image. The scaffolding, necessary though it may have been in the composing process, must fall away. Your poem must stand alone.

SIX STELLAR SOURCES OF POETRY PROMPTS

There is no shortage of prompts in the world. A Google search for "poetry writing prompts" yields more than 180,000 hits. If you'd prefer a more curated list, here are six sources of thoughtful, helpful prompts:

- The previously mentioned book *The Practice of Poetry: Writing Exercises from Poets Who Teach* by Robin Behn and Chase Twichell offers a wide range of carefully designed and classroom-tested prompts.
- Natalie Goldberg's classic book *Writing Down the Bones: Freeing the Writer Within* has a Zen approach to writing, with many exercises and activities intended to free you from the self-censor that lurks inside you.
- *Wingbeats: Exercises and Practice in Poetry*, edited by Scott Wiggerman and David Meischen, offers an impressive array of prompts from some of America's preeminent contemporary poets.
- Robert Lee Brewer's "Poetic Asides" blog offers a steady stream of weekly prompts throughout the year and daily prompts for Poem-A-Day challenges in November and April, in addition to poetic form challenges, poet interviews, and more.
- *The Daily Poet: Day-By-Day Prompts for Your Writing Practice* is a fairly new book by Kelli Russell Agodon and Martha Silano designed to lead through a very productive year of writing poems.
- *The Crafty Poet: A Portable Workshop* by Diane Lockward offers model poems and interviews with poets in addition to detailed writing exercises.

AMORAK HUEY, a former newspaper editor and reporter, teaches professional and creative writing at Grand Valley State University, where he assigns all kinds of writing prompts to his students. He is author of the chapbook *The Insomniac Circus* (Hyacinth Girl), and his poems appear in *The Best American Poetry 2012*, *Poet's Market 2014*, *The Southern Review*, *Hayden's Ferry Review*, *Rattle*, and many other journals.

101 POETRY PROMPTS

....

by Robert Lee Brewer

WRITE A POEM ABOUT A FIRST OR SERIES OF FIRSTS. This first could be a first love, first job, first funeral, first marriage, or first poem.

PUT YOURSELF IN SOMEONE (OR SOMETHING) ELSE'S SKIN AND WRITE A POEM ABOUT THE EXPERIENCE. WHO (OR WHAT) EVER YOU BECOME, MAKE THAT THE TITLE OF THE POEM. If you're Buddy Holly, your poem should be titled "Buddy Holly."

WRITE A WORRY POEM. Anything that causes you worry can be used to help you write this poem. Are you worried about paying the bills? Asking a friend on a date? Circus clowns?

RECORD ALL THE DETAILS OF YOUR DAY AND GENERATE A POEM FROM THAT MATERIAL. To make the poem interesting, you probably do NOT want to just list out everything from the beginning of the day to the end. But then again, maybe you could prove me wrong on that assumption.

WRITE A RAMBLE POEM. That is, write a poem in which you just start rambling with-out worrying about where you're headed. Very interesting things can happen in these poems. Then, go back through and revise.

....

Pick a word (any word) and write a poem about it. If you wish, you can make that word the title of your poem. Look up the definition. Think about how the word is used by people and in what situations. Then, write.

....

WRITE A LOCATION POEM. This poem could be about a room, a city, a country or some other specific place. The location you choose could be a place you've actually visited, or just one you'd like to see someday—or that you've created in your imagination.

WRITE AN APOLOGY POEM. If you're not the type of poet who apologizes for anything, then pretend that someone is apologizing to you in the poem.

LISTEN TO A SONG (OR TWO) AND WRITE A POEM IN RESPONSE. Your poem can take the song to another level, or it can level an argument against the lyrics. Or your poem can spring into a completely new direction.

TAKE THE PHRASE "HOW (BLANK) BEHAVES," REPLACE THE BLANK WITH A WORD OR PHRASE, MAKE THE NEW PHRASE THE TITLE OF YOUR POEM, AND THEN, WRITE YOUR POEM. Sample titles might include: "How My Poem Behaves," "How Robert Lee Brewer Behaves," or "How Children Behave." Don't be afraid to misbehave with this prompt.

Take the phrase "I'm so over (blank)," replace the blank with a word or phrase, make the new phrase the title of your poem, and then, write the poem. Example titles: "I'm so over time sheets" or "I'm so over rainy days."

WRITE AN INSULT POEM. If you get along with everyone you meet, this might be a tough one to write. However, if you can find something to criticize in everyone you know, then this prompt alone could give an entire collection worth of material.

GIVE YOUR POEM A TWIST ENDING. The easiest way to accomplish a twist ending

might be to write a narrative poem that takes a left when the reader was expecting a right. But it might also be a twist in rhyme scheme, form, or something else completely unexpected.

WRITE A POEM ABOUT A MEMORY OF YOU THAT YOU DON'T PERSONALLY REMEMBER. Maybe a friend or family member remembers something when you were small or a little too intoxicated or asleep. Write about this memory that you've had to hear through another.

FIND A LINE THAT YOU REALLY ENJOY AND USE IT AS THE FIRST LINE OF YOUR POEM. Be sure to give credit to the source that provided you with the first line.

WRITE A LOVE POEM. That's simple enough, isn't it?

PICK AN IMAGE AND WRITE A POEM ABOUT IT. The image could be a painting, a photograph, graffiti, or something else. If you pick a famous image, you may want to identify it in the title of your poem.

WRITE A SNOOPING (OR EAVESDROPPING) POEM. Pay attention to conversations from the next table or room. Watch people from a balcony or behind a bush. Just don't do anything to get yourself arrested or hit with a restraining order.

WRITE A POEM ABOUT GETTING OLDER. It doesn't matter how old you are, you're aging by the minute. The longer you wait to write this poem the older you'll be when you finally get around to it. So poem.

WRITE A NATURE POEM. This poem can celebrate trees, creeks, birds, and clouds. Or it can dive into the psychological natures of people. Or it can attack the nature of writing poetry.

**TAKE THE PHRASE "I'M SO OVER (BLANK),"
REPLACE THE BLANK WITH A WORD OR
PHRASE, MAKE THE NEW PHRASE THE TITLE OF YOUR POEM, AND THEN, WRITE THE
POEM.** Example titles include: "I'm so over time sheets," "I'm so over bad poetry," or "I'm so over rainy days."

WRITE AN OCCUPATIONAL POEM. Are you a lawyer or paralegal? Write about working in the law field. Do you bus tables or wait on hungry customers? Write about working in a restaurant. Or imagine what it's like to have a job that you don't have.

**WRITE A POEM THAT IS ONLY ONE SIDE OF
A TWO-SIDED CONVERSATION.** Leave the other half of the conversation to the imagination. To help you achieve this poem, you could write both sides of the conversation and then edit out one of the voices.

**PICK AN ANIMAL AND WRITE A POEM
ABOUT IT.** In fact, make the animal the title of your poem so that readers know your subject.

WRITE AN EXERCISE POEM. Either you love it or you hate it, but anyone can write a poem about the act of working out. Plus, there are so many ways to exercise from hitting the gym to stretching or from running around a lake to swimming in a pool.

**VISIT A LANDMARK AND WRITE A POEM
ABOUT IT.** If you're not able to get out of the house, then visit the landmark through a book or the Internet. There are many ways to experience landmarks these days.

WRITE AN ORIGIN POEM. This poem could be about the origin of a superhero or just a regular person. It could be about the origin of a problem or a solution.

**THINK ABOUT SOMETHING THAT'S MISSING
AND WRITE A POEM ABOUT IT.** The missing something might be a physical object (like your keys or a sock) or something more abstract (like an emotion or an idea).

....

Think about a routine you have and write a poem about it. Or write about the routines of other people (or animals). The tricky part is to make the poem anything but routine.

....

WRITE AN OUTSIDER POEM. The outsider in the poem could be yourself or someone else. You could even write a poem about an animal or plant that is considered an outsider.

WRITE A CLEAN POEM. This poem could be about cleaning something or something that's clean. Or it could just be a poem that uses clean language. For extra credit, write a dirty poem.

**TAKE THE PHRASE "THE PROBLEM WITH
(BLANK)," REPLACE THE BLANK WITH
A WORD OR PHRASE, MAKE THE NEW
PHRASE THE TITLE OF YOUR POEM, AND
THEN, WRITE YOUR POEM.** Example titles include: "The Problem With Poets," "The Problem With Money," or "The Problem With Love."

WRITE A POEM WITH AN INTERACTION.
The interaction could be verbal, physical or emotional. For instance, an interaction could be as simple as two people making eye contact and then looking away from each other.

THINK ABOUT A ROUTINE YOU HAVE AND WRITE A POEM ABOUT IT. Or write about the routines of other people (or animals). The tricky part is to make the poem anything but routine.

....

Write an angry poem. Even the most mild-mannered poets surely get upset from time to time. Unleash the fury with a poem.

....

PICK A DAY OF THE WEEK AND WRITE A POEM ABOUT IT. Or write a short seven-poem collection titled Days of the Week. Explore how a Friday poem might be different from a Tuesday or Sunday poem.

WRITE A REBIRTH POEM. This poem could tackle the rebirth of a person's identity or the changing of a season. There are many ways in which animals, people, plants and ideas are reborn.

SELECT AN OBJECT AND WRITE A POEM ABOUT IT. Think of William Carlos Williams' "The Red Wheelbarrow." Of course, pick your own object and do it in your own style.

WRITE A POEM OF REGRET. Think of something you wish you'd done differently. Write about someone else's regrets. This might be a perfect opportunity to write a blues poem, but a hopeful poem with regret may make it even more interesting.

INCORPORATE A HOBBY INTO A POEM. There aren't enough poems about collecting stamps and bird spotting. Write an ode to collecting baseball cards or dolls.

WRITE A POSTCARD POEM. In about the same confined space you would have to scribble a message on a postcard, write a poem. To make it even more realistic, address your poem directly to a reader.

TAKE THE PHRASE "NEVER (BLANK)," REPLACE THE BLANK WITH A WORD OR PHRASE, MAKE THE NEW PHRASE THE TITLE OF YOUR POEM, AND THEN, WRITE THE POEM. Example titles include: "Never Say Never," "Never Leave Home Without a Pen," or "Never Again."

WRITE A MISCOMMUNICATION POEM. Poems are a form of communication between the poet and the reader. However, good poetry can come from the miscommunication between one character and another.

LOOK AT SOMETHING FAMILIAR IN A NEW WAY OR FROM A DIFFERENT ANGLE AND WRITE A POEM ABOUT YOUR NEW PERSPECTIVE. The something familiar could be a physical object (like a statue or building) or it could be something more abstract (like a relationship or daily routine). Just look for something new in the familiar.

WRITE A POEM OF LONGING. IN THIS POEM, HAVE THE NARRATOR OR A CHARACTER PINING AWAY FOR SOMEONE (OR SOMETHING) ELSE. Some might mistake this for a love poem, but people could be longing for a vacation on a tropical island or a bowl of chocolate ice cream.

PICK A COLOR, MAKE THAT THE TITLE OF YOUR POEM, AND WRITE THE POEM. Your color-titled poem can directly investigate the color itself, or the color could suggest a mood that sets the scene for whatever happens in your poem.

WRITE A POSITIVE POEM. Pulling off an effective happy poem may seem difficult for some, but positive poems are often very refreshing for readers. However, if you want an extra challenge, write a negative poem too.

WRITE A SLOW POEM. This is the perfect opportunity to write about turtles and snails or the slow drip of syrup. Or rush hour traffic.

WRITE A GROWTH POEM. This poem could be about physical growth (like growing a few inches or growing hair) or emotional growth. It could even be about a normal-sized person who comes into contact with radiation and turns into the 50-foot Poet. Or something along those lines.

PICK AN INVENTION AND WRITE A POEM ABOUT IT. The invention could be something real, such as an airplane or food processor. The invention could also be something not so real, such as a time travel machine or teleportation device.

WRITE A SLIPPERY POEM. Maybe the subject matter of this poem is on a slippery slope. Or maybe the poem is about slipping on banana peels or black ice.

TAKE THE PHRASE "IF ONLY (BLANK)," REPLACE THE BLANK WITH A WORD OR PHRASE, MAKE THE NEW PHRASE THE TITLE OF YOUR POEM, AND THEN, WRITE THE POEM. Possible titles include: "If Only It Didn't Snow," "If Only We Remembered to Change the Oil," or "If Only This Poem Were Easier to Revise."

WRITE A POEM ABOUT A MEMORY. Sound familiar? Earlier, I had you write about a memory that you did not remember. However, I want you to write about something you do remember for this memory poem.

CHOOSE A SHAPE AND WRITE A POEM ABOUT IT. For instance, you could write a poem about a crescent moon or box kite. There are a lot of simple and complex shapes out there, and some of them can even be used to describe other people or objects.

Write a construction poem. It's your choice whether you want to write about building construction, highway construction or working with construction paper.

PICK A PLANT AND WRITE ABOUT IT. There are so many plant species on this planet that you're bound to find one that's never been tackled before or on which you can put a new spin.

WRITE A POEM INVOLVING LINES. I know, I know, all poems have lines. Well, you could write about poetic lines, sure, but I also encourage you to write about lines drawn in the sand, lines used in architecture, lines used in sports, or lines used in a sports bar.

CONSIDER SOMETHING THAT WILL ALWAYS STICK WITH YOU AND WRITE A POEM ABOUT IT. Maybe it's something that happened to you when you were young. Maybe it's a good thing or a bad thing. Maybe it's just a random thing that someone said that has always stuck with you and even played an important role in decisions you've made afterward.

Write a poem filled with noise. The noise could be loud, but also soft. Noise could be something mechanical or sounds that build in nature. (Note: I do not advise writing a poem about whether trees falling alone in the forest make a sound, but that doesn't mean you can't go that route anyway.)

WRITE A HANGING POEM. There are a lot of things that can hang. Pick one (or more) and write about it.

WRITE AN EMERGENCY POEM. Emergencies can sometimes be a subjective thing, so the possibility for creating tension between two people in a poem is ripe in an emergency poem. Of course, there are other emergencies that put everyone on edge, and those can be engaging too.

WRITE AN ATTACHMENT POEM. People make all manner of attachments—physical, mental and emotional. Pick one (or two) and write about them.

TAKE THE PHRASE "EVERYBODY SAYS (BLANK)," REPLACE THE BLANK WITH A WORD OR PHRASE, MAKE THE NEW PHRASE THE TITLE OF YOUR POEM, AND THEN, WRITE THE POEM. Example titles include: "Everybody Says the Same Thing," "Everybody Says I Should Quit," or "Everybody Says Things in a Foreign Language." For an alternate option, do the same thing with the phrase "Nobody Says (blank)."

WRITE AN EXPLOSION POEM. Write a poem about fireworks or having an explosion of emotion. For extra credit, write an implosion poem.

WRITE A LONELY POEM. The narrator can be lonely or another character, but there should definitely be some loneliness in the poem.

WRITE A POEM FILLED WITH NOISE. The noise could be loud, but also soft. Noise could be something mechanical or sounds that build in nature. (Note: I do not advise writing a poem about whether trees falling along in the forest make a sound, but that doesn't mean you can't go that route anyway.)

THINK ABOUT HISTORY AND WRITE A POEM ABOUT IT. The history could be ancient history, national history or personal history.

The poem could be about big concepts or a very particular snapshot in time.

WRITE A TOO MUCH INFORMATION POEM. This poem could be one in which the narrator shares a little too much personal information, or it could tackle the information overload of the Internet, social media, and smart phones.

WRITE A DEADLINE POEM. Poems and deadlines don't usually go together, which is why this prompt may deliver some good poems. If you want to put some pressure on your poeming, give this poem a deadline to be written, revised and published.

PICK AN EVENT, MAKE THAT THE TITLE OF YOUR POEM, AND THEN, WRITE THE POEM. The event could be a national celebration or a parade. It could be a local festival, an annual gathering, or even something as mundane as a weekly department meeting.

WRITE A FAREWELL POEM. This poem could be about a person leaving a group or situation, or it could be directed to a specific reader or audience.

THINK SCARY AND WRITE A HORROR POEM. Relate an urban legend. Give a new slant on timeless terror.

TAKE THE PHRASE "PARTLY (BLANK)," REPLACE THE BLANK WITH A WORD OR PHRASE, MAKE THE NEW PHRASE THE TITLE OF YOUR POEM, AND THEN, WRITE THE POEM. Example titles include: "Partly Cloudy," "Partly Insane," or "Partly Poetic."

WRITE A WATER POEM. Water can be a main feature of the poem, or it can just factor into the poem in an indirect way, such as a character standing next to a water fountain or a poem that takes place on a yacht.

Write a self-portrait poem. Of course, it's up to every poet whether to airbrush out blemishes or be excessively harsh (or somewhere in between), but I'd really be missing a poetic goldmine if I didn't mention that you can write about yourself.

WRITE A DEATH POEM. You could write about a specific death or consider death in general.

PICK A CITY, MAKE THAT THE TITLE OF YOUR POEM, AND THEN, WRITE THE POEM. Choose your own city, one that you've visited, or one you'd like to visit.

WRITE A SCIENCE POEM. Science encompasses a lot. In fact, science either touches or rubs up against about everything that poetry does.

SELECT A PERSON AND WRITE A POEM ABOUT HIM OR HER. The person could be a famous historical figure, such as Emily Dickinson or Abraham Lincoln, or someone from your own sphere of influence. The person could even be someone you don't personally know, but who you've mythologized over time.

WRITE A LOOKING BACK POEM. There are a couple ways to attack this poem. The narrator could be looking over past events or literally looking over his or her shoulder.

WRITE AN EVENING POEM. Pretty simple—just write a poem that takes place at night.

PICK A TOOL, MAKE THAT THE TITLE OF YOUR POEM, AND THEN, WRITE THE POEM. Tools are everywhere—from writing implements to computers and from hammers to sporks. So while there is plenty of inspiration in the workshop, tools can be found elsewhere too.

Write an agreement poem. In this poem, there could be an agreement made between two parties, or the narrator could agree with a statement. Or the poet could lay out a contractual agreement between him or her self and the reader.

WRITE A SELF-PORTRAIT POEM. Of course, it's up to every poet whether to airbrush out the blemishes or be excessively harsh (or somewhere in between), but I'd really be missing a poetic goldmine if I didn't mention that you can write about yourself.

TAKE THE PHRASE "LOOKING FOR (BLANK)," REPLACE THE BLANK WITH A WORD OR PHRASE, MAKE THE NEW PHRASE THE TITLE OF YOUR POEM, AND THEN, WRITE THE POEM. Example titles include: "Looking for Reasons to Write a Poem," "Looking for the North Pole," or "Looking for the Answer to This Question."

WRITE A HOPEFUL POEM. The poem can present a hopeful vision, or the poem can follow someone who is filled with hope. As an alternative, write a hopeless poem.

LET GO OF SOMETHING AND WRITE A POEM ABOUT IT. Let go of junk. Let go of resentments. Let go of self-loathing. Write a poem (or two) that releases something.

WRITE A CONTAINMENT POEM. The poem could cover containers like plastic baggies and cardboard boxes or containers like jails and prisons. There are also more abstract containers, such as our minds and computers.

WRITE A METAMORPHOSIS POEM. This poem is one in which the original subject changes into something else—maybe even multiple times during the poem.

TAKE A STAND ON AN ISSUE AND WRITE A POEM ABOUT IT. Maybe you can take a stand on form poems or pick a side on the political spectrum. Maybe you support public transportation—write a poem that expresses your position.

WRITE AN AGREEMENT POEM. In this poem, there could be an agreement made between two parties, or the narrator could be agreeing with a statement. Or the poet could lay out a contractual agreement between himself and the reader.

WRITE A CROSSROADS POEM. This could be a poem about a physical, mental or emotional crossroads.

THINK OF A QUESTION, MAKE THAT THE TITLE OF YOUR POEM, AND THEN, WRITE THE POEM. The poem could continue asking more questions, or it could attempt to answer the question that was posed in the title. Or it could describe a scene that is heightened by the question in the title.

WRITE A LOST AND FOUND POEM. You could focus on the actual losing and finding. Or your poem might examine how things change after something is lost—or how things change after something is found.

Pick a type of person and write about him or her. Your person could be a firefighter, police officer, pedestrian, mountain biker, or any number of other people.

TAKE THE PHRASE "BLAME THE (BLANK)," **REPLACE THE BLANK WITH A WORD OR PHRASE, MAKE THE NEW WORD PHRASE THE TITLE OF YOUR POEM, AND THEN, WRITE THE POEM.** Example titles include: "Blame the Prompt," "Blame the Barry White Music," or "Blame the Scientists."

WRITE A SPACES POEM. The spaces could be physical spaces, such as an open field or a confined closet. Or the spaces could be spaces in time or logic.

PICK A NUMBER, MAKE THAT NUMBER THE TITLE OF YOUR POEM, AND THEN, WRITE YOUR POEM. Personally, I like the numbers eight and 23, but there are any number of numbers from which to choose. Sorry, I couldn't resist.

WRITE A LESSONS LEARNED POEM. Usually, you can only learn your lesson after you've made a mistake, so keep that in mind. For an alternate prompt, write a poem in which a character never learns.

IMAGINE THE WORLD WITHOUT YOU AND WRITE A POEM ABOUT IT. If this seems too self-centered to you, then you can always imagine the world without someone else and write a poem about that.

WRITE A GOOFY POEM. Who says poetry always has to be serious? It doesn't. However, if you have trouble getting silly with your verse, write a serious poem. Make it deadly serious even.

WRITE A POEM THAT REMEMBERS AN OLD RELATIONSHIP. The poem could be about a romantic relationship, but also about a long lost friend or an estranged or distant family member.

PICK A TYPE OF PERSON AND WRITE ABOUT HIM OR HER. Your person could be a firefighter, police officer, pedestrian, mountain biker, or any number of other people.

THINK ABOUT THE BIG PICTURE AND WRITE A POEM ABOUT IT. This is your chance to write a poem about what's really important in life—or what's unimportant in the big scheme of things.

WRITE A NEXT STEPS POEM. Think about what you're going to do after you write this poem, after you leave this room, after you wake up tomorrow morning.

TAKE THE PHRASE "THE LAST (BLANK)," REPLACE THE BLANK WITH A WORD OR PHRASE, MAKE THE NEW PHRASE THE TI-TLE OF YOUR POEM, AND THEN, WRITE YOUR POEM. Example titles include: "The Last Poem," "The Last Reader," or "The Last Cupcake."

WRITE A POEM ABOUT ENDINGS OR FIN-ISHES. This poem could be about ending a relationship or finishing a poem. If you've finished this list of prompts, I challenge you to start creating your own

MAGAZINES/ JOURNALS

Literary magazines and journals usually provide a poet's first publishing success. In fact, you shouldn't be thinking about book/chapbook publication until your poems have appeared in a variety of magazines, journals and zines (both print and online). This is the preferred way to develop an audience, build publishing credits and learn the ins and outs of the publishing process.

In this section you'll find hundreds of magazines and journals that publish poetry. They range from small black-and-white booklets produced on home computers to major periodicals with high production values and important reputations. To help you sort through these markets and direct your submissions most effectively, we've organized information in each listing according to a basic format that includes contact information, magazine needs, how to submit, and more.

GETTING STARTED, FINDING MARKETS

If you don't have a certain magazine or journal in mind, read randomly through the listings, making notes as you go. (Don't hesitate to write in the margins, underline, use highlighters; it also helps to flag markets that interest you with Post-It Notes). Browsing the listings is an effective way to familiarize yourself with the kind of information presented and the publishing opportunities that are available at various skill levels.

If you have a specific market in mind, however, begin with the General Index. Here all the book's listings are alphabetized along with additional references that may be buried within a listing (such as a press name or competition title).

2RIVER VIEW

7474 Drexel Dr., University City MO 63130. **E-mail:** 1ong@2river.org. **Website:** www.2river.org. **Contact:** Richard Long. *2River View*, published quarterly online, is a site of poetry, art, and theory. Considers unpublished poetry only. Claims first electronic rights and first North American rights, "meaning that publications here at *2River* must be the first publication to feature the work online and/or in print." Publishes ms 3 months after acceptance. Guidelines available online.

MAGAZINES NEEDS Submit up to 5 poems once per reading period (see website for dates) via online submissions manager. Prefers poems with these qualities: image, subtlety, and point of view; a surface of worldly exactitude, as well as a depth of semantic ambiguity; and a voice that negotiates with its body of predecessors. Publishes 10 poets/issue.

30 N

North Central College, Naperville IL 60540. **E-mail:** 30north@noctrl.edu. **Website:** 30northblog.wordpress.com. **Contact:** Katie Draves, Crystal Ice. *30 N*, published semiannually, considers work in all literary genres, including occasional interviews, from undergraduate writers globally. The journal's goal is for college-level, emerging creative writers to share their work publicly and create a conversation with each other. Acquires first serial rights. Rights revert to author on publication. Publishes ms 1-4 months after acceptance. Responds in 1-4 months. Guidelines online.

Contributors must be currently enrolled as undergraduates at a two- or four-year institution at the time of submission. Reads submissions September-March, with deadlines in February and October.

MAGAZINES NEEDS Submit up to 5 poems via online submissions manager. "You must be a currently enrolled undergraduate at a two- or four-year institution at the time of submission. Please submit using your .edu e-mail address, your institution, and your year." Include brief bio written in third person. No line limit. Pays 2 contributor's copies.

TIPS "Don't send anything you just finished moments ago—rethink, revise, and polish. Avoid sentimentality and abstraction. That said, *30 N* publishes beginners, so don't hesitate to submit and, if rejected, submit again."

34THPARALLEL MAGAZINE

Indie LitMag Digital & Print, Paris , France. **E-mail:** 34thparallel@gmail.com. **Website:** www.34thparallel.net. **Contact:** Martin Chipperfield. *34thParallel Magazine*, monthly in digital and print editions, publishes new and emerging writers. Guidelines on website.

TIPS "It's all about getting your story out there looking good: your reality (creative nonfiction), fiction, journalism, essays, screenplays, poetry (writing that isn't prose), hip-hop, art, photography, photo stories or essays, graphic stories, comics, or cartoons."

A&U

America's AIDS Magazine, Art & Understanding, Inc., 25 Monroe St., Suite 205, Albany NY 12210-2729. (518)426-9010. **Fax:** (518)436-5354. **E-mail:** chaelneedle@mac.com. **Website:** www.aumag.org. Poetry Editor: Noah Stetzer. Fiction Editor: Raymond Luczak.. **Contact:** Chael Needle, managing editor. Buys first North American serial rights, electronic rights. Pays 1-3 months after publication. Publishes ms an average of 1-3 months after acceptance. Responds in 1 month to queries; in 2 months to mss. Editorial lead time 6 months. Sample copy: $5. Guidelines online.

MAGAZINES NEEDS Accepts any length/style (shorter works preferred). Pays $50.

HOW TO CONTACT aumag.poetry@gmail.com

CONTEST/AWARD OFFERINGS Christopher Hewitt Award, annual

TIPS "We're looking for more articles on youth and HIV/AIDS; more international coverage; celebrity interviews; more coverage of how the pandemic is affecting historically underrepresented communities. We are also looking for literary submissions that address the past and present AIDS epidemic in fresh ways. Each year, we sponsor the Christopher Hewitt Award, given to the best poem, short story, creative nonfiction piece, and drama submitted."

ABLE MUSE

Able Muse Press, 467 Saratoga Ave., #602, San Jose CA 95129-1326. **E-mail:** submission@ablemuse.com. **Website:** www.ablemuse.com. **Contact:** Alex Pepple, editor. *Able Muse: A Review of Poetry, Prose & Art*, published twice/year, predominantly publishes metrical poetry complemented by art and photography, fiction, and nonfiction, including essays, book reviews, and interviews with a focus on metrical and formal poetry. Acquires first rights. Time between acceptance and publication is 3 months. Sometimes comments on rejected poems. Responds in 4 months. Sometimes sends prepublication galleys. Subscription: $28 for 1 year.

○ Sponsors 2 annual contests: The Able Muse Write Prize for Poetry & Fiction and The Able Muse Book Award for Poetry (in collaboration with Able Muse Press at www.ablemusepress.com). See website for details.

MAGAZINES NEEDS Has published poetry by Mark Jarman, A.E. Stallings, Annie Finch, Rhina P. Espaillat, Rachel Hadas, and R.S. Gwynn. Receives about 1,500 poems/year, accepts about 5%. Submit 1-5 poems and short bio. Electronic submissions only through the online form at www.ablemuse.com/submit, or by e-mail. "The e-mail submission method is being phased out. We strongly encourage using the online submission method." Reviews books of poetry. Send materials for review consideration.

◑ ACUMEN MAGAZINE

+44(0)1803-851098. **E-mail:** patriciaoxley6@gmail.com. **Website:** www.acumen-poetry.co.uk. **Contact:** Patricia Oxley, general editor. *Acumen*, published 3 times/year in January, May, and September, is "a general literary magazine with emphasis on good poetry." Wants "well-crafted, high-quality, imaginative poems showing a sense of form." Does not want "experimental verse of an obscene type." Has published poetry by Ruth Padel, William Oxley, Hugo Williams, Peter Porter, Danielle Hope, and Leah Fritz. *Acumen* is 120 pages, A5, perfect-bound. Responds in 1-6 weeks. Guidelines online.

MAGAZINES NEEDS Submit up to 4 poems at a time. Mailed submissions should be accompanied by SASE. Include name and address on each separate sheet. Accepts e-mail submissions, but see guidelines on the website. Will send rejections, acceptances, proofs, and other communications via e-mail overseas to dispense with IRCs and other international postage. Any poem that may have chance of publication is shortlisted, and from list final poems are chosen. All other poems returned within 2 months. "If a reply is required, please send IRCs. One IRC for a decision, 3 IRCs if work is to be returned." Willing to reply by e-mail to save IRCs. Unwanted poetry returned if postage or e-mail address attached. Pays "by negotiation" and 1 contributor's copy.

TIPS "Read *Acumen* carefully to see what kind of poetry we publish. Also, read widely in many poetry magazines, and don't forget the poets of the past—they can still teach us a great deal."

THE ADIRONDACK REVIEW

E-mail: editors@theadirondackreview.com. **Website:** www.theadirondackreview.com; www.theadirondackreview.submittable.com. **Contact:** Angela Leroux-Lindsey, editor in chief; Nicholas Samaras, senior poetry editor; Terez Peipins, fiction editor; Sarah Escue, poetry editor; Charles Rammelkamp, reviews editor; Ann Malaspina, copy chief. *The Adirondack Review* is an online quarterly literary magazine featuring contemporary art and photography paired with perspective-shifting poetry, fiction, translations, and essays. Pays $25 stipend for all contributors. Responds to queries in 2-4 months.

MAGAZINES NEEDS Submit 2-5 single-spaced poems via online submissions manager; include brief bio.

TIPS "See more details about our submission cycle and contests online."

THE ADROIT JOURNAL

E-mail: editors@theadroitjournal.org. **Website:** theadroitjournal.org. Garrett Biggs, managing editor. **Contact:** Peter LaBerge, editor-in-chief. At its foundation, the journal has its eyes focused ahead, seeking to showcase what its global staff of emerging writers sees as the future of poetry, prose, and art. The journal currently publishes five online issues per year. Between 5 and 15 days for most, up to 4 months max. Guidelines online: http://www.theadroitjournal.org/general-submissions/.

MAGAZINES NEEDS Submit up to 8 poems at a time, no legth limits.

TIPS "We're ready for your best work. Please note that all submissions should be accompanied by a cover letter and brief third-person biography statement."

AFRICAN VOICES

African Voices Communications, Inc., 270 W. 96th St., New York NY 10025. (212)865-2982. **E-mail:** africanvoicesart@gmail.com. **Website:** www.africanvoices.com. **Contact:** Angela Kinemore, poetry editor. *African Voices*, published quarterly, is an "art and literary magazine that highlights the work of people of color. We publish literature and poetry on any subject. We also consider all themes and styles: avant-garde, free verse, haiku, light verse, and traditional. We do not wish to limit the reader or author." *African Voices* is about 48 pages, magazine-sized, professionally printed, saddle-stapled, with paper cover. Receives about 150 submissions/year, accepts about 30%. Buys first North American serial rights. Pays on publication. Publishes ms an average of 3-6 months after acceptance. Responds in 3 months to queries. Editorial lead time 3 months. Sample copy: $6. Subscription: $20.

MAGAZINES NEEDS Submit no more than 2 poems at a time. Accepts submissions by postal mail. Cover letter and SASE required. Seldom comments on rejected poems. Has published poetry by Sonia Sanchez, Liza Jessie Peterson, Patricia Spears Jones, Jessica Care Moore, Tony Medina and Gabriel Ramirez. Length: 5-100 lines/poem. Pays contributor copies.

ALSO OFFERS Reviews books of poetry in 500-1,000 words. Send materials for review consideration to Ekere Tallie. Considers poetry written by children. Offers periodic poetry contests and readings. Send SASE for details.

TIPS "A manuscript stands out if it is neatly typed with a well-written and interesting storyline or plot. Originality is encouraged. We are interested in more horror, erotic, and drama pieces. *AV* wants to highlight the diversity in our culture. Stories must touch the humanity in us all. We strongly encourage new writers/poets to send in their work. Accepted contributors are encouraged to subscribe."

AFTER HAPPY HOUR REVIEW

136 Conneaut Dr., Pittsburgh PA 15239. **E-mail:** hourafterhappyhour@gmail.com. **Website:** afterhappyhourreview.com. **Contact:** Mike Good. The *After Happy Hour Review* is an independent, online literary journal that publishes poetry, fiction, creative nonfiction, and visual art. Our headquarters are based in Pittsburgh, and we have published writers from around the United States alongside international writers. Curated by the Hour After Happy Hour Writing Workshop, our editors come from varying backgrounds with their own inclinations, tastes, and preferences. Take your time, read an issue, and send us your best work. We aim to respond as quickly as possible to all submissions and nominate work for all major awards, including the Pushcart Prize and Best of Net." Publishes ms 3-6 months after acceptance. Responds in 2-8 weeks.

MAGAZINES NEEDS "Send us something gritty, uninhibited, bewildering, uncouth. Send us work we'll have to mull over, sleep on, and reread over and over. Generally, we look for poems that employ stylistic devices that work against the predictability of form."

AGNI

Boston University, 236 Bay State Rd., Boston MA 02215. **E-mail:** agni@bu.edu. **Website:** www.agnimagazine.org. **Contact:** Sven Birkerts, editor. Eclectic literary magazine publishing first-rate poems, essays, translations, and stories. Buys first serial rights, rights to reprint in *AGNI* anthology (with author's consent). Pays on publication. Publishes ms an average of 6 months after acceptance. Responds in 4 months to mss. No queries please. Sample copy: $12 or online. Guidelines online.

Reading period is September 1-May 31 only. Online magazine carries original content not found in print edition. All submissions are considered for both. Founding editor Askold Melnyczuk won the PEN/Nora Magid Lifetime Achievement Award for Magazine Editing. Work from *AGNI* has been included and cited regularly in the *Pushcart Prize, O. Henry*, and *Best American* anthologies.

MAGAZINES NEEDS Submit online or by regular mail, no more than 5 poems at a time. E-mailed submissions will not be considered. Include a SASE or your e-mail address if sending by mail. Pays $20/page up to $300, plus a one year subscription, and, for print publication, 2 contributor's copies and 4 gift copies.

TIPS "We're also looking for extraordinary translations from little-translated languages. It is important to read work published in *AGNI* before submitting, to see if your own might be compatible."

AGNIESZKA'S DOWRY (AGD)

A Small Garlic Press (ASGP), 5445 N. Sheridan Rd., #3003, Chicago IL 60640. **E-mail:** marek@aspg.com. **Website:** asgp.org. **Contact:** Marek Lugowski and Katrina Grace Craig Valvis, co-editors. *"Agnieszka's Dowry (AgD)* is an innovative installation of mostly contemporary and mostly not-yet-famous literary texts (poems, letters to Agnieszka, occasional short short stories), computer and freehand art, photography, and more. The magazine is published both in print and online. The print version consists of professionally crafted chapbooks. The online version comprises fast-loading pages employing an intuitive, if uncanny, navigation in an interesting space, all conducive to fast and comfortable reading. No restrictions on form or type. We use contextual and juxtapositional tie-ins with other material in making choices, so visiting the online *AgD* or reading a chapbook of an

AgD issue is required of anyone making a submission." Acquires one-time rights where applicable. Responds in 2 months. Single copy: $2 plus $8 s&h. Make checks payable to A Small Garlic Press.

○ *Agnieszka's Dowry* is 5.5x8.5, stapled, 20-60 pages, heavy opaque white laser paper, cardstock cover, saddle-stitched (stapled), with cover art and often with internal art in grayscale.

MAGAZINES NEEDS Submit 5-10 poems at a time. Accepts e-mail submissions only (pasted into body of message in plain text, sent to both editors simultaneously; no attachments). "We ask you to read well into *Agnieszka's Dowry* and to fit your submissions to the partially filled content of its open issues." Pays 1 contributor's copy.

⑤ ALASKA QUARTERLY REVIEW

University of Alaska Anchorage, 3211 Providence Dr., Anchorage AK 99508. **E-mail:** uaa_aqr@uaa.alaska.edu. **Website:** www.uaa.alaska.edu/aqr. **Contact:** Ronald Spatz, editor in chief. "*Alaska Quarterly Review* is a literary journal devoted to contemporary literary art, publishing fiction, short plays, poetry, photo essays, and literary nonfiction in traditional and experimental styles. The editors encourage new and emerging writers, while continuing to publish award-winning and established writers." Buys first North American serial rights. Upon request, rights will be transferred back to author after publication. Publishes ms an average of 6 months after acceptance. Responds in 4 months to queries; in 6 weeks-4 months to mss. Sample copy: $6. Guidelines online.

○ Magazine: 6x9; 232-300 pages; 60 lb. Glatfelter paper; 12 pt. C15 black ink or 4-color; varnish cover stock; photos on cover and photo essays. Reads mss August 15-May 15.

MAGAZINES NEEDS Submit poetry by mail. Include cover letter with contact information and SASE for return of ms. No light verse. Length: up to 20 pages. Pays contributor's copies and honoraria when funding is available.

ALSO OFFERS Guest poetry editors have included Stuart Dybek, Jane Hirshfield, Stuart Dischell, Maxine Kumin, Pattiann Rogers, Dorianne Laux, Peggy Shumaker, Olena Kalytiak Davis, Nancy Eimers, Michael Ryan, and Billy Collins.

TIPS "Although we respond to e-mail queries, we cannot review electronic submissions."

ALBATROSS

The Anabiosis Press, 2 South New St., Haverhill MA 01835. (978)469-7085. **E-mail:** rsmyth@anabiosispress.org. **Website:** www.anabiosispress.org. **Contact:** Richard Smyth, editor. *Albatross*, published "as soon as we have accepted enough quality poems to publish an issue—about once per year," considers the albatross "to be a metaphor for the environment. The journal's title is drawn from Coleridge's *The Rime of the Ancient Mariner* and is intended to invoke the allegorical implications of that poem. This is not to say that we publish only environmental or nature poetry but that we are biased toward such subject matter. We publish mostly free verse, and we prefer a narrative style." Acquires all rights. Returns rights provided that "previous publication in *Albatross* is mentioned in all subsequent reprintings." Time between acceptance and publication is 6 months to a year. Responds in 2-3 months to poems. Sample copy for $5. Subscription: $8 for 2 issues. Guidelines online.

○ *Albatross* is 28 pages, digest-sized, laser-typeset, with linen cover.

MAGAZINES NEEDS Submit 3-5 poems at a time. Accepts e-mail submissions if included in body of message (but is "sometimes quicker at returning mailed submissions"). Name and address must accompany e-mail submissions. Cover letter is not required. "We do, however, need bio notes and SASE for return or response. Poems should be typed, single-spaced, with name, address, and phone number in upper-left corner." Has published poetry by Darren C. Demaree, Beth Suter, Jeremy Yocum, Ann Niedringhaus, and Mark B. Hamilton. Wants "poetry written in a strong, mature voice that conveys a deeply felt experience or makes a powerful statement." Does not want "rhyming poetry, prose poetry, or haiku." Length: up to 100 lines/poem. Pays 1 contributor's copy.

↻ ALBERTA VIEWS

Alberta Views, Ltd., Suite 208, 320 23rd Ave. SW, Calgary AB T2S 0J2, Canada. (403)243-5334; (877)212-5334. **Fax:** (403)243-8599. **E-mail:** queries@albertaviews.ab.ca. **Website:** www.albertaviews.ab.ca. **Contact:** Evan Osenton, editor. "We are a regional magazine providing thoughtful commentary and background information on issues of concern to Albertans. Most of our writers are Albertans." Buys first North American serial rights, electronic rights. Pays on publication. Publishes ms an average of 3 months after acceptance. Responds in 6 weeks to queries; 2 months to mss. Editorial lead time 4 months. Sample copy free. "If you are a writer, illustrator, or photographer interested in contributing to *Alberta Views*, please see our contributor's guidelines online."

🖰 No phone queries.

MAGAZINES NEEDS Accepts unsolicited poetry. Submit complete ms.

THE ALEMBIC

Providence College, English Department, ATTN: The Alembic Editors, 1 Cunningham Square, Providence RI 02918-0001. **Website:** www.providence.edu/english/pages/alembic.aspx. **Contact:** Magazine has revolving editor. Editorial term: 1 year. "*The Alembic* is an international literary journal featuring the work of both established and student writers and photographers. It is published each April by Providence College in Providence, Rhode Island." Acquires first rights. Publication is not copyrighted. Responds in 1 month to queries; in 8 months to mss. Sample: $15. Subscription: $25 for 2 years.

🖰 Magazine: 6x9, 80 pages. Contains illustrations, photographs.

MAGAZINES NEEDS Submit up to 5 poems. Does not accept online submissions. Has published poems by Tara McLaughlin, Melanie Souchet, Jackleen Holton, Peter Mishler, Dennis Rhodes, Donna Pucciani, and Sarah O'Brien.

TIPS "We're looking for stories that are wise, memorable, grammatical, economical, poetic in the right places, and end strongly. Take Heraclitus' claim that 'character is fate' to heart and study the strategies, styles, and craft of such masters as Anton Chekov, J. Cheever, Flannery O'Connor, John Updike, Rick Bass, Phillip Roth, Joyce Carol Oates, William Treavor, Lorrie Moore, and Ethan Canin."

ALIMENTUM

The Literature of Food, P.O. Box 210028, Nashville TN 37221. **E-mail:** editor@alimentumjournal.com. **Website:** www.alimentumjournal.com. **Contact:** Peter Selgin, fiction and nonfiction editor; Esther Cohen, poetry editor. "*Alimentum* celebrates the literature and art of food. We welcome work from like-minded writers, musicians, and artists." Acquires first North American serial rights. Rights revert to authors upon publication. Pays on publication. Manuscript published 1-2 years after acceptance. Responds in 3 months to mss. Sample copy: $10. Guidelines available online.

"We do not read year round. Check website for reading periods."

🖰 Essays appearing in *Alimentium* have appeared in *Best American Essays* and *Best Food Writing*.

MAGAZINES NEEDS Send up to 5 poems by mail. Please include SASE. Has published poetry by Dick Allen, Stephen Gibson, Carly Sachs, Jen Karetnik, and Virginia Chase Sutton. Pays 1 contributor's copy.

ALSO OFFERS Publishes an annual broadside of "menupoems" for restaurants during National Poetry Month in April.

TIPS "No e-mail submissions, only snail mail. Mark outside envelope to the attention of Poetry, Fiction, or Nonfiction Editor."

💲 ALIVE NOW

1908 Grand Ave., P.O. Box 340004, Nashville TN 37203. (615)340-7254. **E-mail:** alivenow@upperroom.org. **Website:** www.alivenow.org; alivenow.upperroom.org. **Contact:** Beth A. Richardson, editor. *Alive Now*, published bimonthly, is a devotional magazine that invites readers to enter an ever-deepening relationship with God. "*Alive Now* seeks to nourish people who are hungry for a sacred way of living. Submissions should invite readers to see God in the midst of daily life by exploring how contemporary issues impact their faith lives. Each word must be vivid and dynamic and contribute to the whole. We make selections based on a list of upcoming themes. Mss which do not fit a theme will be returned." Pays on acceptance. Subscription: $17.95/year (6 issues); $26.95 for 2 years (12 issues). Additional subscription information, including foreign rates, available on website. Guidelines available online.

MAGAZINES NEEDS Prefers electronic submissions attached as Word document. Postal submissions should include SASE. Include name, address, theme on each sheet. Pays $35 minimum.

ALLIGATOR JUNIPER

(928)350-2012. **Website:** alligatorjuniper.org. "*Alligator Juniper* features contemporary poetry, fiction, creative nonfiction, and b&w photography. We encourage submissions from writers and photographers at all levels: emerging, early career, and established." Annual magazine comprised of the winners and finalists of national contests. "All entrants pay an $18 submission fee and receive a complementary copy of that year's issue in the spring. First-place winning writers in each genre receive a $1,000 prize. The first-place winner in photography receives a $500 award. Finalists in writing and images are published and paid in contributor copies. There is currently no avenue for submissions other than the annual contest." Usually responds in January to mss. Always comments on mss. Sample copy: $5. Guidelines online.

MAGAZINES NEEDS Accepts submissions only through annual contest. If submitting by regular mail, include $18 entry fee payable to *Alligator Juniper* for each set of up to 5 poems. Include cover letter with name, address, phone number, and e-mail. Include author's name on first page. "Double-sided submissions are encouraged." No e-mail submissions. Length: open.

⚫⚫💲 AMBIT MAGAZINE

Staithe House, Main Rd., Brancaster Staithe, Norfolk PE31 8PB, United Kingdom. **E-mail:** contact@ambit-magazine.co.uk. **Website:** www.ambitmagazine.co.uk. **Contact:** Briony Bax, editor; André Naffis-Sahely poetry editor; Kate Pemberton, fiction editor; Olivia Bax and Jean Philippe Dordolo, art editors. *Ambit Magazine* is a literary and artwork quarterly published in the UK and read internationally. *Ambit* is put together entirely from previously unpublished poetry and short fiction submissions. "Please read the guidelines on our website carefully concerning submission windows and policies." Publishes fiction up to 6 months after acceptance; publishes poems in 3-6 months after acceptance. Responds in 2-3 months. Sample copy: £9. Guidelines available in magazine or online.

MAGAZINES NEEDS Submit 3-6 poems via Submittable. No previously published poems (including on websites or blogs). Poems should be typed, double-spaced. Never comments on rejected poems. Does not want "indiscriminately center-justified poems, jazzy fonts, or poems all in italics for the sake of it." Payment details on website.

TIPS "Read a copy of the magazine before submitting!"

💲 AMERICA

33 West 60th St., New York NY 10023. **E-mail:** zdavis@americamedia.org. **Website:** www.americamagazine.org. **Contact:** Zac Davis, editorial assistant. "Published weekly for adult, educated, largely Roman Catholic audience. Founded by the Jesuit order and directed today by Jesuits and lay colleagues, *America* is a resource for spiritual renewal and social analysis guided by the spirit of charity. The print and Web editions of *America* feature timely and thought-provoking articles written by prestigious writers and theologians, and incisive book, film, and art reviews." Buys all rights. Pays on acceptance. Guidelines available online.

MAGAZINES NEEDS "Many poems we publish address matters of faith and spirituality, but this is not a requirement for publication. We are looking for authentic, truthful, good poetry." Submit via online submissions manager. Length: up to 30 lines/poem. Pays competitive rate.

THE AMERICAN DISSIDENT

A Journal of Literature, Democracy & Dissidence, 217 Commerce Rd., Barnstable MA 02630. **E-mail:** todslone@hotmail.com. **E-mail:** Only subscribers can e-mail submit.. **Website:** www.theamericandissident.org. **Contact:** G. Tod Slone, editor. *The American Dissident*, published 2 times/year, provides "a forum for, amongst other things, criticism of the academic/literary establishment, which clearly discourages vigorous debate, cornerstone of democracy, and especially vigorous criticism of its icons and institutions, to the evident detriment of American literature. Wants "poetry, reviews, artwork, and short (2-4pp) essays in English, French, or Spanish, written on the edge preferably with a dash of personal risk. and, if possible, stemming from personal experience and/or conflict with power." Submissions should be "iconoclastic and parrhesiastic in nature." Acquires first North American serial rights. Publishes ms 2-6 months after acceptance. Responds in a week or less. Almost always comments on rejected poems and essays. Single copy: $9; subscriptions: $18 for individuals; $20 for institutions. Guidelines available for SASE.

MAGAZINES NEEDS Submit 3 poems at a time. E-mail submissions from subscribers only. "Far too many poets submit without even reading the guidelines. Include SASE and cover letter containing not credits but rather personal dissident information, as well as incidents that provoked you to 'go upright and vital, and speak the rude truth in all ways' (Emerson)." Pays 1 contributor's copy.

TIPS "Every poet knows what he or she should not write about to avoid upsetting those in positions of literary, cultural, and/or academic power. *The American Dissident* seeks to publish those few poets who now and then break that taboo and thus raise truthtelling above getting published, funded, invited, tenured, nominated, and/or anointed. *The American Dissident* is a rare literary journal that not only brooks, but also encourages and publishes in each and every issue hardcore criticism regarding the editor and journal. In fact, I cannot think of another journal that will do that."

AMERICAN LITERARY REVIEW

University of North Texas, 1155 Union Circle #311307, Denton TX 76203. **E-mail:** americanliteraryreview@gmail.com. **Website:** www.americanliteraryreview.com. **Contact:** Bonnie Friedman, editor in chief. "*The American Literary Review* publishes "excellent poetry, fiction, and nonfiction by writers at all stages of their careers." Beginning in fall 2013, *ALR* became an online publication." Publishes ms within 2 years of acceptance. Responds in 3-5 months to mss. Guidelines online.

○ Reading period is from October 1-May 1.

MAGAZINES NEEDS "Poetry selections are made by a widely read group with eclectic tastes who look for the best poems, regardless of form or subject matter." Has published poetry by Kathleen Pierce, Mark Irwin, Stephen Dunn, William Olsen, David St. John, and Cate Marvin. Submit up to 5 poems through online submissions manager for a fee of $3. Does not accept submissions via e-mail or mail.

TIPS "We encourage writers and artists to examine our journal."

⊛ THE AMERICAN POETRY REVIEW

1906 Rittenhouse Square, Philadelphia PA 19103. **E-mail:** escanlon@aprweb.org. **Website:** www.aprweb.org. **Contact:** Elizabeth Scanlon, Editor-in-Chief. "*The American Poetry Review* is dedicated to reaching a worldwide audience with a diverse array of the best contemporary poetry and literary prose. *APR* also aims to expand the audience interested in poetry and literature, and to provide authors, especially poets, with a far-reaching forum in which to present their work." Acquires first serial rights. Responds in 6 months. Sample: $5. Guidelines online.

MAGAZINES NEEDS Submit up to 5 poems via online submissions manager. Has published poetry by John Murillo, Khadijah Queen, Brenda Shaughnessy, Kazim Ali, Gregory Pardlo, Deborah Landau, Sharon Olds, and many more. Pays $1 per line.

THE AMERICAN READER

E-mail: fiction@theamericanreader.com; poetry@theamericanreader.com; criticism@theamericanreader.com. **Website:** theamericanreader.com. **Contact:** Uzoamaka Maduka, editor in chief. *The American Reader* is a bimonthly print literary journal. The

magazine is committed to inspiring literary and critical conversation among a new generation of readers, and restoring literature to its proper place in American cultural discourse. Guidelines online.

MAGAZINES NEEDS Interested in submissions of portfolios only (approximately 4-7 poems). Submit by e-mail: poetry@theamericanreader.com.

⊜ AMPERSAND

Nicholas Building, 915/37 Swanston St., Melbourne VIC 3000, Australia. **E-mail:** alice@ampersandmagazine.com.au. **Website:** ampersandmagazine.com.au. **Contact:** Alice Gage, editor. *Ampersand* is an art and culture journal that explores creativity, societal change, and the human condition through multidisciplines. "We are interested in the discussion of any subject matter, particularly that which is unfashionable, unorthodox, illuminating, or rare." Guidelines online.

MAGAZINES NEEDS *Ampersand* publishes the work of 1 poet in each issue. Submit your work as a Word document, accompanied by an introductory e-mail giving a brief explanation of what you are sending, its word count, and which section you think it would suit.

⊜ ANALOG SCIENCE FICTION & FACT

Dell Magazines, 44 Wall St., Suite 904, New York NY 10005-2401. **E-mail:** analogsf@dellmagazines.com. **Website:** www.analogsf.com. **Contact:** Trevor Quachri, editor. *Analog* seeks "solidly entertaining stories exploring solidly thought-out speculative ideas. But the ideas, and consequently the stories, are always new. Real science and technology have always been important in *ASF*, not only as the foundation of its fiction but as the subject of articles about real research with big implications for the future." Buys first North American serial rights, buys nonexclusive foreign serial rights. Pays on acceptance. Publishes ms an average of 10 months after acceptance. Responds in 2-3 months to mss. Sample copy: $5 and SASE. Guidelines online.

○ Fiction published in *Analog* has won numerous Nebula and Hugo Awards.

MAGAZINES NEEDS Send poems via online submissions manager (preferred) or postal mail. Does not accept e-mail submissions. Length: up to 40 lines/poem. Pays $1/line.

TIPS "I'm looking for irresistibly entertaining stories that make me think about things in ways I've never done before. Read several issues to get a broad feel for our tastes, but don't try to imitate what you read."

ⓢ ANCIENT PATHS

E-mail: skylarburris@yahoo.com. **Website:** www.editorskylar.com/magazine/table.html. **Contact:** Skylar H. Burris, editor. *Ancient Paths* provides "a forum for quality spiritual poetry and short fiction. We consider works from writers of all religions, but poets and authors should be comfortable appearing in a predominantly Christian publication. Works published in *Ancient Paths* explore themes such as redemption, sin, forgiveness, doubt, faith, gratitude for the ordinary blessings of life, spiritual struggle, and spiritual growth. Please, no overly didactic works. Subtlety is preferred." Please send seasonally themed works for Lent and Advent at least 1 month prior to the start of each season. Works on other themes may be sent at any time. Acquires electronic rights. Author is free to republish work elsewhere. Pays on publication. Time between acceptance and publication is 1-4 months. Responds in 8 weeks, usually sooner. Sample copy of printed back issue: $9. Purchase online. Detailed guidelines are available on the website.

MAGAZINES NEEDS E-mail all submissions. Paste poems in e-mail message. Use the subject heading "AP Online Submission (title of your work)." Include your name and e-mail address at the top of your e-mail. Poems may be rhymed, unrhymed, free verse, or formal and should have a spiritual theme, which may be explicit or implicit, but which should not be overly didactic. No "preachy" poetry; avoid inconsistent meter and forced rhyme; no stream-of-consciousness or avant-garde work; no esoteric academic poetry; no concrete (shape) poetry; no use of the lowercase *i* for the personal pronoun; do not center poetry. Length: 8-60 lines. Pays $1.25/poem. Published poets also receive discount code for $3 off 2 printed back issues.

TIPS "Read the great religious poets: John Donne, George Herbert, T.S. Eliot, Lord Tennyson. Remember not to preach. This is a literary magazine, not a pulpit. This does not mean you do not communicate morals or celebrate God. It means you are not overbearing or simplistic when you do so."

ANOTHER CHICAGO MAGAZINE

E-mail: editors@anotherchicagomagazine.net. **Website:** www.anotherchicagomagazine.net. **Contact:** Caroline Eick Kasner, managing editor; Matt Rowan, fiction editor; David Welch, poetry editor; Colleen O'Connor, nonfiction editor. "*Another Chicago Magazine* is a biannual literary magazine that publishes work by both new and established writers. We look for work that goes beyond the artistic and academic to include and address the larger world. The editors read submissions in fiction, poetry, and creative nonfiction year round. The best way to know what we publish is to read what we publish. If you haven't read *ACM* before, order a sample copy to know if your work is appropriate." Sends prepublication galleys. Acquires first serial rights. Responds in 3 months to queries; in 6 months to mss. Guidelines available online.

◖ Work published in *ACM* has been included frequently in *The Best American Poetry* and *The Pushcart Prize* anthologies. **Charges $3 submissions fee.**

MAGAZINES NEEDS Submit poems via online submissions manager in 1 document.

TIPS "Support literary publishing by subscribing to at least 1 literary journal—if not ours, another. Get used to rejection slips, and don't get discouraged. Keep introductory letters short. Make sure ms has name and address on every page, and that it is clean, neat, and proofread. We are looking for stories with freshness and originality in subject angle and style, and work that encounters the world."

◖ⓢ THE ANTIGONISH REVIEW

St. Francis Xavier University, P.O. Box 5000, Immaculata Hall, Room 413, Antigonish NS B2G 2W5, Canada. (902)867-3962. **Fax:** (902)867-5563. **E-mail:** tar@stfx.ca. **Website:** www.antigonishreview.com. **Contact:** Gerald Trites, editor. *The Antigonish Review*, published quarterly, features the writing of new and emerging writers as well as the ideas of established and innovative thinkers through poetry, stories, essays, book reviews and interviews." After publication, rights retained by author. Pays on publication. Publishes ms an average of 8 months after acceptance. Responds in 1 month to queries; 6 months to mss. Editorial lead time 4 months. Guidelines online.

MAGAZINES NEEDS Open to poetry on any subject written from any point of view and in any form. However, writers should expect their work to be considered within the full context of old and new poetry in English and other languages. Has published poetry by Andy Wainwright, W.J. Keith, Michael Hulse, Jean McNeil, M. Travis Lane, and Douglas Lochhead. Submit 6-8 poems at a time. A preferable submission would be 3-4 poems. Lines/poem: not over 80, i.e., 2 pages. Pays $10/page to a maximum of $50 and 2 contributor's copies.

TIPS Contact by e-mail (tar@stfx.ca) and submit through the website using Submittable. There is a submission fee.

🅢 ANTIOCH REVIEW

Antioch College, P.O. Box 148, Yellow Springs OH 45387-0148. (937)769-1365. **E-mail:** review@antiochcollege.edu. **Website:** www.antiochreview.org. **Contact:** Robert S. Fogarty, editor; Judith Hall, poetry editor. Literary and cultural review of contemporary issues and literature for general readership. *The Antioch Review* is an independent quarterly of critical and creative thought. We have a proud 75+ year history of publishing independent writers, exceptional poets, and brilliant thinkers—some only emerging upstarts when originally featured. *The Antioch Review*, founded in 1941, is one of the oldest, continuously publishing literary magazines in America. We publish fiction, essays, and poetry from prominent and promising poets, authors, and critics. Authors published in the *Review* are consistently included in Best American Anthologies and *Pushcart Prizes*. Our writers and poets are routinely recipients of prominent literary awards; and the *Review* has been the recipient of several prominent National Magazine Awards in essays and criticism and fiction. We have an international readership and reputation of publishing the "best words in the best order" for over 75 years. As a result, the competition is keen. We receive thousands of submissions each year from around the world. Form and content are so inseparable and reaction is so personal, it is difficult to state requirements or limitations. Studying prior issues of *The Antioch Review* and reviewing our "Writer's Guidelines" should be helpful. Pays on publication. Publishes ms an average of 10 months after acceptance. Responds varies on our workload. Generally, it is 3 to 6 months; however, could be longer. Sample copies may be purchased online. Guidelines online.

MAGAZINES NEEDS Has published poetry by Sylvia Plath, Mark Strand, Richard Howard, Jacqueline Osherow, Alice Fulton, Richard Kenney, and others. Receives thousands of submissions/year. No previously published poems or simultaneous submissions. Include SASE with all submissions. No light or inspirational verse. Poetry submissions are not accepted between between May 1-September 1. Pays $20/printed page, plus 2 contributor's copies.

HOW TO CONTACT *Antioch Review*, P. O. Box 148, Yellow Springs, OH 45387

APALACHEE REVIEW

Apalachee Press, P.O. Box 10469, Tallahassee FL 32302. (850)644-9114. **E-mail:** chayes@fsu.edu; mtrammell@fsu.edu. **E-mail:** arsubmissions@gmail.com (for queries outside the U.S.). **Website:** apalacheereview.org. **Contact:** Chris Hayes, chief editor; Mary Jane Ryals, fiction editor; Jenn Bronson, poetry editor; Michael Trammell, advisory & managing editor. "At *Apalachee Review*, we are interested in outstanding literary fiction, but we especially like poetry, fiction, and nonfiction that address intercultural issues in a domestic or international setting or context." Acquires one-time rights, electronic rights. Publication is copyrighted. Pays on publication. Publishes mss 1 year after acceptance. Responds to queries in 4-6 weeks; mss in 3-14 months. Sometimes comments on/critiques rejected mss. Sample copy: $8 for current issue; $5 for back issue. Subscription: $15 for 2 issues ($30 foreign). Guidelines online.

🅠 *Apalachee Review*, published annually, is 90 pages, digest-sized, professionally printed, perfect-bound, with card cover. Press run is 300-400. Includes photographs. Member CLMP.

MAGAZINES NEEDS Submit 3-5 poems at a time. Accepts submissions by postal mail only; however, we may be switching to the Submitable online platform soon. Please check the website. "Submit clear copies, with name and address on each." SASE required. Reads submissions year round. Staff reviews books of poetry. Send materials for review consideration. Has published poetry by Rita Mae Reese and Charles Harper Webb. Pays 2 contributor's copies.

APPALACHIAN HERITAGE

CPO 2166, Berea KY 40404. **E-mail:** appalachianheritage@berea.edu. **Website:** appalachianheritage.net. **Contact:** Jason Howard, editor. "We are seeking poetry, short fiction, literary criticism and biography, book reviews, and creative nonfiction, including memoirs, opinion pieces, and historical sketches. Unless you request not to be considered, all poems, stories, and articles published in *Appalachian Heritage* are eligible for our annual Plattner Award. All honorees are rewarded with a sliding bookrack with an attached commemorative plaque from Berea College Crafts, and first-place winners receive an additional stipend of $200." Acquires first print and electronic rights. Responds in 1 month to queries; 3-5 months to mss. Guidelines online.

Submission period: August 15-December 15.

MAGAZINES NEEDS Submit through online submissions manager only. Length: up to 42 lines. "One-page poems cannot exceed 42 lines, and two-page poems cannot exceed 84 lines." Pays 3 contributor's copies.

TIPS "Sure, we are *Appalachian Heritage* and we do appreciate the past, but we are a forward-looking contemporary literary quarterly, and, frankly, we receive too many nostalgic submissions. Please spare us the 'Papaw Was Perfect' poetry and the 'Mamaw Moved Mountains' manuscripts and give us some hard-hitting prose, some innovative poetry, some inventive photography, and some original art. Help us be the ground-breaking, stimulating kind of quarterly we aspire to be."

APPLE VALLEY REVIEW

A Journal of Contemporary Literature, 88 South Third St., Suite 336, San Jose CA 95113. **E-mail:** editor@leahbrowning.net. **Website:** www.applevalley-review.com. **Contact:** Leah Browning, editor. *Apple Valley Review: A Journal of Contemporary Literature*, published semiannually online, features "beautifully crafted poetry, short fiction, and essays." Acquires first rights and first serial rights, and retains the right to archive the work online for an indefinite period of time. "As appropriate, we may also choose to nominate published work for awards or recognition. Author retains all other rights." Time between acceptance and publication is 1-6 months. Sometimes comments on rejected poems and mss. Responds to mss in 1 week-2 months. Guidelines online.

MAGAZINES NEEDS Wants "work that has both mainstream and literary appeal. All work must be original, previously unpublished, and in English. Translations are welcome if permission has been granted. Preference is given to short (under 2 pages), nonrhyming poetry." Has published poetry by Grant Clauser, P. Ivan Young, Amorak Huey, Laura Lee Beasley, Cameron Conaway, Robert Lavett Smith, Sharlene Teo, Donna Vorreyer, Do-hyeon Ahn, and Susan Johnson. Receives about 5,000+ poems/year, accepts less than 1%. Accepts e-mail submissions (pasted into body of message, with "poetry" in subject line). Please do not send via postal mail. Reads submissions year round. Does not want "erotica, work containing explicit language or violence, or work that is scholarly, critical, inspirational, or intended for children." Length: "No line limit, though we prefer shorter poems (under 2 pages)."

CONTEST/AWARD OFFERINGS Offers the annual *Apple Valley Review* Editor's Prize. Award is $100 and a gift of a book. Submit 1-6 poems. **Entry fee:** none. **Deadline:** rolling; all submissions to the *Apple Valley Review* and all work published during a given calendar year will be considered for the prize.

ARC POETRY MAGAZINE

P.O. Box 81060, Ottawa Ontario K1P 1B1, Canada. **E-mail:** managingeditor@arcpoetry.ca. **Website:** www.arcpoetry.ca. **Contact:** Monty Reid, managing editor. *Arc Poetry Magazine* has been publishing the best in contemporary Canadian and international poetry and criticism for over 30 years. *Arc* is published 3 times/year, including an annual themed issue each fall. Canada's poetry magazine publishes poetry, poetry-related articles, interviews, and book reviews, and also publishes on its website; *Arc* also runs a Poet-in-Residence program. Acquires first Canadian serial rights. Responds in 4-6 months. Subscriptions: 1 year: $35 CDN; 2 years: $60 CND (in Canada). U.S. subscriptions: 1 year: $45 CAD; 2 years: $80 CAD. International subscriptions: 1 year: $55 CDN; 2 year: $90 CDN. Online ordering available for subscriptions and single copies (with occasional promotions). Guidelines online.

Arc is 130-160 pages, perfect-bound, printed on matte white stock with a crisp, engaging design and a striking visual art portfolio in each issue. Receives over 2,500 submissions/year; accepts about 40-50 poems. Press run is 1,500.

MAGAZINES NEEDS *Arc* accepts unsolicited submissions of previously unpublished poems from October 15-May 31; maximum of 3 poems, 1 submission per year per person. Use online submissions manager. Has published poetry by Don Coles, Karen Solie, Nicole Brossard, Christian Bok, Elizabeth Bachinsky, George Elliott Clarke, Ken Babstock, Michael Ondaatje, Stephanie Bolster, and Don Domanski. Pays $50 CAD/page, plus 1 contributor's copy.

CONTEST/AWARD OFFERINGS Poem of the Year Contest—**Deadline:** February 1; $5,000 grand prize; entry fee includes one-year subscription. Confederation Poets Prize and Critic's Desk Award for best poem and reviews published in *Arc* in the preceding year. Other awards include the Archibald Lampman Award and the Diana Brebner Prize.

ARC POETRY MAGAZINE

Arc Poetry Society, P.O. Box 81060, Ottawa ON K1P 1B1, Canada. **E-mail:** managingeditor@arcpoetry.ca;

coordinatingeditor@arcpoetry.ca; arc@arcpoetry.ca. **Website:** www.arcpoetry.ca. **Contact:** Monty Reid, managing editor; Chris Johnson, coordinating editor. *Arc*'s focus is poetry, and particularly Canadian poetry, although it also publishes writers from elsewhere. Looking for the best poetry from new and established writers. Often publishes special issues. Send a SASE for upcoming special issues and contests. Buys one-time rights. Pays on publication. Publishes mss an average of 6 months after acceptance. Responds in 4-6 months. Guidelines available online.

○ Only accepts submissions via online submissions manager. Include a brief biographical note with submission. Accepts unsolicited mss each year from October 15, 2016 to May 31, 2017.

MAGAZINES NEEDS For over 30 years, *Arc* has been publishing the best in contemporary poetry. *Arc* invites submissions from emerging and established poets. Poets may only submit once each calendar year. Poetry submissions must not exceed 3 poems total. Submissions must be typed and single-spaced (double spaces will be interpreted as blank lines). Include your name, e-mail address, and mailing address on each page. Submit each poem in a separate document with bio. Your submission will be grouped in submission platform. Biographical statements should be 2-3 sentences or approximately 50 words. *Arc* can't promise to respond to inquiries regarding the status of submissions before the completion of an editorial cycle. Pays $50/printed page (Canadian).

CONTEST/AWARD OFFERINGS Offeres Archibald Lampman Award, Diana Brebner Prize, Poem of the Year Contest, Confederation Poets Prize, Critics' Desk Award.

○ ARENA MAGAZINE

Arena Publishing, P.O. Box 18, North Carlton VIC 3054, Australia. (61)(3)9416-0232. **E-mail:** magazine@arena.org.au. **Website:** www.arena.org.au. John Hinkson. **Contact:** Alison Caddick. Contributors not paid. Responds in 2 weeks. Editorial lead time 2 months. View magazine format before submitting.

MAGAZINES NEEDS Use submission form to submit poetry. Gifts a half-year subscription to contributors.

ARKANSAS REVIEW

A Journal of Delta Studies, Department of English and Philosophy, P.O. Box 1890, Office: Humanities and Social Sciences, State University AR 72467-1890. (870)972-3043; (870)972-2210. **Fax:** (870)972-3045. **E-mail:** mtribbet@astate.edu. **Website:** arkreview.org. **Contact:** Dr. Marcus Tribbett, general editor. "All material, creative and scholarly, published in the *Arkansas Review* must evoke or respond to the natural and/or cultural experience of the Mississippi River Delta region." *Arkansas Review* is 92 pages, magazine-sized, photo offset-printed, saddle-stapled, with 4-color cover. Press run is 400; 50 distributed free to contributors. Buys first North American serial rights. Time between acceptance and publication is about 6-18 months. Occasionally publishes theme issues. Responds in 2 weeks to queries; 6 months to mss. Editorial lead time 4-9 months. Sample copy: $7.50. Subscription: $20. Make checks payable to ASU Foundation. Guidelines online.

MAGAZINES NEEDS Receives about 500 poems/year; accepts about 5%. Accepts e-mail and disk submissions. Cover letter is preferred. Include SASE. Has published poetry by Greg Fraser, Jo McDougall, and Catherine Savage Brosman. Does not want personal or non-Delta-related work. Length: 1-100 lines. Pays 2 contributor's copies.

ALSO OFFERS Staff reviews books/chapbooks of poetry "that are relevant to the Delta" in 500 words, single- and multibook format. Send materials for review consideration to Janelle Collins (inquire in advance).

TIPS "Immerse yourself in the literature of the Delta, but provide us with a fresh and original take on its land, its people, its culture. Surprise us. Amuse us. Recognize what makes this region particular as well as universal, and take risks. Help us shape a new Delta literature."

⑤ THE ARTIST UNLEASHED

E-mail: info@vineleavespress.com. **Website:** www. theartistunleashed.com. **Contact:** Jessica Bell, Publisher. *The Artist Unleashed* is a Vine Leaves Press paying market which publishes articles every Wednesday about living a creative life. Vine Leaves Press publishes memoir/autobiography, creative nonfiction, literary essay collections (single author or multiple authors), novels of all genres with a literary bent, book-length short story collections (single author or multiple author), writing reference books, vignette collections, and poetry collections (single author or multiple author). Buys exclusive rights for 12 months. Then the rights revert back to the author.

Responds in 2 months. Guidelines online. See website for payment rates.

○ Please visit the website for submission guidelines.

$ ARTS & LETTERS JOURNAL OF CONTEMPORARY CULTURE

Georgia College & State University, Milledgeville GA 31061. (478)445-1289. **Website:** al.gcsu.edu. **Contact:** Laura Newbern, editor; Faith Thompson, managing editor. *Arts & Letters Journal of Contemporary Culture*, published semiannually, is devoted to publishing contemporary work from established and emerging writers. Our editors seek work that doesn't try too hard to grab our attention, but rather guides it toward the human voice and its perpetual struggle into language. We're open to both formal and experimental fiction, nonfiction, and poetry; we're also open to work that defies classification. Above all, we look for work in which we can feel writers surprising themselves. Work published in *Arts & Letters Journal* has received the Pushcart Prize. Acquires one-time rights. Pays on publication. Responds in 2-4 months. Guidelines online.

MAGAZINES NEEDS Submit via online submissions manager. Include cover letter. "Poems are screened, discussed by group of readers. If approved by group, poems are submitted to poetry editor for final approval." Has published poetry by Margaret Gibson, Marilyn Nelson, Stuart Lishan, R.T. Smith, Laurie Lamon, and Miller Williams. No light verse. Pays $10/printed page (minimum payment: $50) and 1 contributor's copy.

ALSO OFFERS Offers annual Arts & Letters/Rumi Prize for Poets.

$ ART TIMES

arttimesjournal, P.O. Box 730, Mount Marion NY 12456. (845)246-6944. **Fax:** (845)246-6944. **E-mail:** info@arttimesjournal.com. **Website:** www.arttimesjournal.com. **Contact:** Raymond J. Steiner, editor. "*Art Times*, now an online-only publication, covers the arts fields with essays about music, dance, theater, film, and art, and includes short fiction and poetry as well as editorials. Our readers are creatives looking for resources and people who appreciate good writing." Acquires first North American serial rights, first rights. Pays on publication for short fiction, poetry and essays. Publishes within 4 months Responds in 3 months Guidelines online.

MAGAZINES NEEDS Send poems by mail or e-mail. Wants "poetry that strives to express genuine observation in unique language. All topics, all forms. We prefer well-crafted 'literary' poems. No excessively sentimental poetry." Publishes 2-3 poems each month. Nothing violent, sexist, erotic, juvenile, racist, romantic, political, off-beat, or related to sports or juvenile fiction. Length: up to 20 lines. Pays $5/poem.

ASHEVILLE POETRY REVIEW

P.O. Box 7086, Asheville NC 28802. **E-mail:** kflynn62@hotmail.com. **Website:** www.ashevillepoetryreview.com. **Contact:** Keith Flynn, managing editor. *Asheville Poetry Review*, published annually, prints "the best regional, national, and international poems we can find. We publish translations, interviews, essays, historical perspectives, and book reviews as well." Wants "quality work with well-crafted ideas married to a dynamic style. Any subject matter is fit to be considered so long as the language is vivid with a clear sense of rhythm. We subscribe to the Borges dictum that great poetry is a combination of 'algebra and fire.'" Rights revert back to author upon publication. Publishes poems up to 1 year from acceptance to publishing time. Responds in up to 4 months. Sample: $13. "We prefer poets purchase a sample copy prior to submitting." Guidelines available for SASE or on website.

○ *Asheville Poetry Review* is 160-300 pages, digest-sized, perfect-bound, laminated, with full-color cover. Receives about 8,000 submissions/year, accepts about 5%. Press run is 3,000. Subscription: $22.50 for 2 years, $43.50 for 4 years. Occasionally publishes theme issues. Reviews books/chapbooks of poetry. Send materials for review consideration. Has published poetry by Sherman Alexie, Eavan Boland, Gary Snyder, Colette Inez, Robert Bly, and Fred Chappell.

MAGAZINES NEEDS Submit 3-6 poems at a time. No e-mail submissions. Cover letter is required. Include comprehensive bio, recent publishing credits, and SASE. Reads submissions January 15-July 15. Poems are circulated to an editorial board. Seldom comments on rejected poems. Pays 1 contributor's copy.

CONTEST/AWARD OFFERINGS Sponsors the William Matthews Poetry Prize: $1,000 awarded for a single poem, reads submissions July 15-January 15. See website for complete guidelines.

⚫ ASININE POETRY

E-mail: editor@asininepoetry.com. **Website:** www.asininepoetry.com. **Contact:** Shay Tasaday, editor. Humorous poetry and prose, published quarterly online, "features 8-9 new works each issue. We specialize in poetry that does not take itself seriously." Wants "any form of poetry, but for us the poetry must be in a humorous, parodic, or satirical style. We prefer well-crafted poems that may contain serious elements or cover serious subjects—but which are also amusing, absurd, or hilarious."

MAGAZINES NEEDS Does not want serious, straightforward poems. Has published poetry by Hal Sirowitz, William Trowbridge, Elizabeth Swados, Daniel Thomas Moran, and Colonel Drunky Bob. Receives about 800 poems/year, accepts about 2%. Submit 3-4 poems at a time. Considers previously published poems and simultaneous submissions. Accepts e-mail (pasted into body of message). No mailed submissions. Length: up to 50 lines/poem.

CONTEST/AWARD OFFERINGS Guidelines available on website.

ASSARACUS

Sibling Rivalry Press, P.O. Box 26147, Little Rock AR 72221. **E-mail:** info@siblingrivalrypress.com. **Website:** siblingrivalrypress.com/assaracus. **Contact:** Bryan Borland, publisher; Seth Pennington, editor. *Assaracus* is a literary journal featuring poetry by self-identified gay men. Named for the earth-bound brother of Ganymede, the youth swooped up by Zeus' eagle to serve the god, *Assaracus* is published intermittently. Guidelines online.

MAGAZINES NEEDS Submit up to 10 poems in 1 document along with a 75-max-word bio via online submissions manager. Wants work that "disturbs and enraptures."

TIPS "Poems do not have to be gay-themed or include gay content. We do ask that poets published in *Assaracus* self-identify as gay males, although we do not police identity."

⑤ THE ATLANTIC MONTHLY

The Watergate, 600 New Hampshire Ave., NW, Washington DC 20037. (202)266-6000. **Fax:** (202)266-6001. **E-mail:** submissions@theatlantic.com; pitches@theatlantic.com. **Website:** www.theatlantic.com. **Contact:** Scott Stossel, magazine editor; Ann Hulbert, literary editor. General magazine for an educated readership with broad cultural and public-affairs interests.

"*The Atlantic* considers unsolicited mss, either fiction or nonfiction. A general familiarity with what we have published in the past is the best guide to our needs and preferences." Buys first North American serial rights. Pays on acceptance. Responds in 4-6 weeks to mss. Guidelines online.

MAGAZINES NEEDS "Interest is in the broadest possible range of work: traditional forms and free verse, the meditative lyric and the 'light' or comic poem, the work of the famous and the work of the unknown. We have long been committed to the discovery of new poets. Our 1 limitation is length; we are unable to publish very long poems." *The Atlantic Monthly* publishes some of the most distinguished poetry in American literature. "We read with interest and attention every poem submitted to the magazine and, quite simply, we publish those that seem to us to be the best." Has published poetry by Maxine Kumin, Stanley Plumly, Linda Gregerson, Philip Levine, Ellen Bryant Voigt, and W.S. Merwin. Receives about 60,000 poems/year. Submit 2-6 poems by e-mail or mail.

TIPS "Writers should be aware that this is not a market for beginner's work (nonfiction and fiction), nor is it truly for intermediate work. Study this magazine before sending only your best, most professional work. When making first contact, cover letters are sometimes helpful, particularly if they cite prior publications or involvement in writing programs. Common mistakes: melodrama, inconclusiveness, lack of development, unpersuasive characters and/or dialogue."

AUTUMN SKY POETRY DAILY

E-mail: autumnskypoetryeditor@gmail.com. **E-mail:** autumnskypoetryeditor@gmail.com. **Website:** autumnskypoetrydaily.com. **Contact:** Christine Klocek-Lim, editor. *Autumn Sky Poetry Daily* publishes 1 poem every weekday and occasionally on weekends. The editor reserves the right to skip a day here and there, depending on the poems received, the weather, vacation time, and/or electrical interference with her brain. Acquires first electronic rights upon acceptance. Rights returned to author upon publication. Reserves right to archive poem indefinitely online, but will remove at request of author. Time between acceptance and publication is 1 week. Responds in 1 week. "If your poem isn't published within 1 week, consider it rejected. No formal response (e-mail, owl, aural hallucination) will be sent." Guidelines available at https://autumnskypoetrydaily.com/submission-guidelines/.

MAGAZINES NEEDS Send 1 poem in the body of an e-mail to autumnskypoetryeditor@gmail.com with "SUBMISSION" in subject heading (no cover letter). Include links to your website, Facebook, Twitter, etc. (please, no bio). If submitting a formal poem, please feel free to include the name of the form (sestina, quatina, prose poem, etc.). Does not want "non-thoughtful line breaks, tortured meter, clichés, bad sonics, and all the other things that make poetry unpleasant to read."

THE AVALON LITERARY REVIEW

CCI Publishing, P.O. Box 780696, Orlando FL 32878. **E-mail:** submissions@avalonliteraryreview.com. **Website:** www.avalonliteraryreview.com. **Contact:** Valerie Rubino, managing editor. *"The Avalon Literary Review* welcomes work from both published and unpublished writers and poets. We accept submissions of poetry, short fiction, and personal essays. While we appreciate the genres of fantasy, historical romance, science fiction, and horror, our magazine is not the forum for such work." Quarterly magazine. Buys first time rights Pays on publication. Publishes ms an average of 6 months after acceptance. Editorial lead time is 3-6 months. Sample copy: $10 for hard copy, $2 for PDF on website. Writer's guidelines available online or by e-mail.

MAGAZINES NEEDS Electronic submissions only. No rhyming verse. Length: up to 50 lines. Pays 3 contributor's copies.

TIPS "The author's voice and point of view should be unique and clear. We seek pieces that spring from the author's life and experiences. Fiction submissions that explore both the sweet and bitter of life with a touch of humor, and poetry with vivid imagery, are a good fit for our review."

THE AVOCET

A Journal of Nature Poetry, P.O. Box 19186, Fountain Hills AZ 85269. **E-mail:** cportolano@hotmail.com. **E-mail:** angeldec24@hotmail.com (for The Weekly Avocet). **Website:** www.avocetreview.com. **Contact:** Charles Portolano, editor. *The Avocet, a Journal of Nature Poetry*, published quarterly, is "looking for poetry that moves the reader through the beauty, the peace, and the fury of nature in all its glory. We want poems that have people interacting with nature or with animals in their element, poems that have a message on the importance of Mother Nature and our life on this magical planet. Think of the season when

sending your submission." *The Avocet* is 64 pages, 5.5x8.5, professionally printed, perfect-bound, with glossy cover. Plus, you get 52 weeks of *The Weekly Avocet* every Sunday morning with a subscription. Press run is 350. Time between acceptance and publication is up to 3 months. Responds to submissions in 3 months. Single copy: $7.50. Subscription: $24. Make checks payable to *The Avocet*.

MAGAZINES NEEDS Submit up to 4 poems at a time. Considers previously published poems, if acknowledged. Include cover letter with e-mail. No SASE if you have an e-mail address; mss will not be returned.

TIPS "Read a copy of an issue to get a feel of what we are looking for in nature poetry, please."

THE AWAKENINGS REVIEW

Awakenings Project, The, P.O. Box 177, Wheaton IL 60187. (630)606-8732. **E-mail:** ar@awakeningsproject.org. **Website:** www.awakeningsproject.org. Irene O'Neill, associate editor. **Contact:** Robert Lundin, editor. *The Awakenings Review* is published by the Awakenings Project. Begun in cooperation with the University of Chicago Center for Psychiatric Rehabilitation in 2000, *The Awakenings Review* has been acclaimed internationally and draws writers from all over the United States and from several other countries including Israel, South Africa, Australia, Finland, Switzerland, the United Kingdom, and Canada. Acquires first rights. Publishes ms 8 months after acceptance. Responds in 1 month. Guidelines available in magazine, for SASE, by e-mail, or on website.

MAGAZINES NEEDS Submit 5 poems at a time. No e-mail submissions. Cover letter is preferred. Include SASE and short bio. Poems are read by a board of editors. Often comments on rejected poems. Occasionally publishes theme issue. Length: 61 characters. Pays 1 contributor's copy, plus discount on additional copies.

⊗ BABYBUG

Cricket Media, Inc., 7926 Jones Branch Dr., Suite 870, McLean VA 22102. (703)885-3400. **Website:** www.cricketmedia.com. "*Babybug*, a look-and-listen magazine, presents simple poems, stories, nonfiction, and activities that reflect the natural playfulness and curiosity of babies and toddlers." Rights vary. Pays on publication. Responds in 3-6 months to mss. Guidelines online.

MAGAZINES NEEDS "We are especially interested in rhythmic and rhyming poetry. Poems may explore a baby's day, or they may be more whimsical." Submit via online submissions manager. Pays up to $3/line; $25 minimum.

TIPS "We are particularly interested in mss that explore simple concepts, encourage very young children's imaginative play, and provide opportunities for adult readers and babies to interact. We welcome work that reflects diverse family cultures and traditions."

🟢 THE BALTIMORE REVIEW

E-mail: editor@baltimorereview.org. **Website:** www.baltimorereview.org. **Contact:** Barbara Westwood Diehl, senior editor. *The Baltimore Review* publishes poetry, fiction, and creative nonfiction from Baltimore and beyond. Submission periods are August 1-November 30 and February 1-May 31. Buys first North American serial rights. Pays on publication. Publishes ms 2-6 months after acceptance. Responds in 4 months or less. Guidelines online. Can review work submitted through our website only. No e-mailed submissions.

MAGAZINES NEEDS Submit 1-3 poems. See editor preferences on submission guidelines on website. Pays $40.

CONTEST/AWARD OFFERINGS Sponsors 2 theme contests per year. $500, $200, and $100 prizes; all entries considered for publication. See website for themes and guidelines.

TIPS "See editor preferences on staff page of website."

🔴 THE BANGALORE REVIEW

Website: www.bangalorereview.com. **Contact:** Suhail Rasheed, managing editor; Maitreyee Choudhury and Fehmida Zakeer, co-editors; Mithun Jayaram, arts editor.. *The Bangalore Review* is a monthly online magazine aimed at promoting literature, arts, culture, criticism, and philosophy at a deeper level. Copyrights for articles, artwork, and photographs published in the magazine rest with the authors, with first publication rights to *The Bangalore Review*. Offers honorarium to one selected writer every 3 months. Posts mss between 30 to 60 days after acceptance. Editorial lead time is 2-3 months. http://tbr.submittable.com

MAGAZINES NEEDS Length: Must be at least 5 lines. Does not offer payment.

BARKING SYCAMORES

E-mail: barkingsycamores@gmail.com. **Website:** barkingsycamores.wordpress.com. **Contact:** N.I. Nicholson and V. E. Maday, editors. *Barking Syca-*

mores is a literary journal whose mission is to publish poetry, short fiction (1,000 words or less), creative nonfiction, hybrid genre, and artwork by neurodivergent contributors. "We also seek to add positively to the public discussion about neurodivergence as a whole in the form of essays on literature and the interrelationship between it and the creative process. Additionally, we also publish book reviews (1,000 words or less) of titles either written by or focused on neurodivergent individuals. We pay contributors once their work is included in the yearly print anthology. Payment comes from the Autonomous Press anthology fund." Acquires perpetual electronic rights, and exclusive rights for 60 days from date of publication. Publishes ms 2 weeks after acceptance. Response time no later than 8 weeks to queries and mss. Sample copy online. Guidelines online.

MAGAZINES NEEDS Does not want polemic, preachy, or rant-like poetry. We pay contributors once their work is included in the yearly print anthology. Payment comes from the Autonomous Press anthology fund.

BARN OWL REVIEW

Website: www.barnowlreview.com. **Contact:** Mary Biddinger and Jay Robinson, editors in chief; Sarah Dravec, Susan Grimm, Matthew Guenette, Nathan Kemp, and Amy Bracken Sparks, poetry editors. A handsomely designed print journal looking for work that takes risks while still connecting with readers. Aims to publish the highest-quality poetry from both emerging and established writers.

🔵 Uses online submissions manager for submissions and questions. Open annually for submissions June 1-November 1.

MAGAZINES NEEDS *Barn Owl Review* favors no particular poetic school or style; "however, we look for innovation and risk-taking in the poems we publish." Submit 3-5 poems (in single attachment) via Submittable. Pays 2 contributor's copies.

BARRELHOUSE

E-mail: yobarrelhouse@gmail.com. **Website:** www.barrelhousemag.com. **Contact:** Dave Housley, Joe Killiany, and Matt Perez, fiction editors; Tom McAllister, nonfiction editor; Dan Brady, poetry editor. *Barrelhouse* is a biannual print journal featuring fiction, poetry, interviews, and essays about music, art, and the detritus of popular culture. Responds in 2-3 months to mss.

◯ Stories originally published in *Barrelhouse* have been featured in *The Best American Nonrequired Reading, The Best American Science Fiction and Fantasy*, and the Million Writer's Award.

MAGAZINES NEEDS Submit up to 5 poems via online submissions manager. DOC or RTF files only. Pays $50 and 2 contributor's copies.

BARROW STREET

E-mail: inquiry@barrowstreet.org. **Website:** www.barrowstreet.org. **Contact:** Lorna Knowles Blake, Patricia Carlin, Peter Covino, and Melissa Hotchkiss, editors. *Barrow Street*, published annually, "is dedicated to publishing new and established poets." Wants "poetry of the highest quality; open to all styles and forms." Has published poetry by Molly Peacock, Lyn Hejinian, Carl Phillips, Marie Ponsot, Charles Bernstein, and Stephen Burt. Acquires first rights. Responds in 1 week-4 months. Sample copy: $10. Subscription: $18 for 2 years, $25 for 3 years. Guidelines online.

◯ Poetry published in *Barrow Street* is often selected for *The Best American Poetry. Barrow Street* is 96-120 pages, digest-sized, professionally printed, perfect-bound, with glossy cardstock cover with color or b&w photography. Receives about 3,000 poems/year, accepts about 3%. Press run is 1,000. Reading period: December 1-March 15.

MAGAZINES NEEDS Submit poems via online submissions manager. "Please always check our website to confirm submission guidelines." Does not accept hard copy submissions. Cover letter is preferred. Include brief bio. Must have name, address, e-mail, and phone on each page submitted or submission will not be considered. Length: up to 8 pages/submission. Pays 2 contributor's copies.

BATEAU

105 Eden St., Bar Harbor ME 04609. **E-mail:** dan@bateaupress.org. **Website:** bateaupress.org. **Contact:** Daniel Mahoney, editor in chief. "*Bateau*, published annually, subscribes to no trend but serves to represent as wide a cross-section of contemporary writing as possible. For this reason, readers will most likely love and hate at least something in each issue. We consider this a good thing. To us, it means *Bateau* is eclectic, open-ended, and not mired in a particular strain." Acquires first North American serial rights, electronic rights. Publishes ms 3-8 months after acceptance. Responds in 1-6 months. Single copy: $10.

Make checks payable to Bateau Press. Guidelines for SASE or on website. Submissions closed June-August.

◯ *Bateau* is around 80 pages, digest-sized, offset print, perfect-bound, with a 100% recycled letterpress cover. Press run is 250.

MAGAZINES NEEDS Submit via online submissions manager. Brief bio is encouraged but not required. Has published poetry by Tomaz Salamun, John Olsen, Michael Burkhardt, Joshua Marie Wilkinson, Allison Titus, Allan Peterson, and Dean Young. Receives about 5,000 poems/year, accepts about 60. Length: up to 5 pages. Pays contributor's copies.

TIPS "Send us your best work. Send us funny work, quirky work, outstanding work, work that is well punctuated or lacks punctuation. Fearless work. Work that wants to crash on our sofa."

BEAR CREEK HAIKU

P.O. Box 596, Longmont CO 80502. **E-mail:** darylayaz@me.com. **Website:** bearcreekhaiku.blogspot.com. **Contact:** Ayaz Daryl Nielsen, editor; Frosty and Tama, assistant editors. Time between acceptance and publication varies from 1-3 months. Sample copy via postal mail with SASE. Include note requesting a copy. Guidelines online.

MAGAZINES NEEDS Submit 1-20 lines of poetry by postal mail. Send SASE with submission; SASE is used to mail contributor's copy. If no poetry is accepted, submission is returned; if some poems are accepted, the remainder are shredded (with dignity). E-mail submissions welcomed from countries other than the U.S. (and, if you really must send by e-mail, then go ahead). Length: up to 15 lines. Haiku and related forms are always welcome. Pays 1 contributor's copy.

ADDITIONAL INFORMATION "If requesting a review of your poetry collection, send request to darylayaz@gmail.com. If we're interested (and we often are), we will ask you to mail a print copy, and the review would appear online. We only accept or do positive reviews of poetry collections we really appreciate."

TIPS "We love poetry and poets: without them, there's a distinct possibility our universe wouldn't exist. If you feel you've done well, send it to us—your published poem could, in a subtle (or not so subtle!) manner, make a difference to someone, something, or all of us."

THE BEAR DELUXE MAGAZINE

Orlo, 240 N. Broadway, #112, Portland OR 97227. **E-mail:** beardeluxe@orlo.org. **Website:** www.orlo.org.

Contact: Tom Webb, editor-in-chief; Kristin Rogers Brown, art director. "*The Bear Deluxe Magazine* is a national independent environmental arts magazine publishing significant works of reporting, creative nonfiction, literature, visual art, and design. Based in the Pacific Northwest, it reaches across cultural and political divides to engage readers on vital issues effecting the environment. Published twice per year, *The Bear Deluxe* includes a wider array and a higher percentage of visual artwork and design than many other publications. Artwork is included both as editorial support and as standalone or independent art. It has included nationally recognized artists as well as emerging artists. As with any publication, artists are encouraged to review a sample copy for a clearer understanding of the magazine's approach. Unsolicited submissions and samples are accepted and encouraged." Buys first rights, buys one time rights. Pays on publication. Publishes ms an average of 6 months after acceptance. Responds in 3-6 months to mail queries. Only responds to e-mail queries if interested. Editorial lead time 6 months. Sample copy: $5. Guidelines online.

MAGAZINES NEEDS Submit 3-5 poems at a time. Poems are reviewed by a committee of 3-5 people. Publishes 1 theme issue per year. Length: up to 50 lines/poem. Pays $20, subscription, and contributor's copies.

TIPS "Offer to be a stringer for future ideas. Get a copy of the magazine and guidelines, and query us with specific nonfiction ideas and clips. We're looking for original, magazine-style stories, not fluff or PR. Fiction, essay, and poetry writers should know we have an open and blind review policy and they should keep sending their best work even if rejected once. Be as specific as possible in queries."

BEATDOM

E-mail: editor@beatdom.com. **Website:** www.beatdom.com. **Contact:** David Wills, editor. Beatdom is a Beat Generation-themed literary journal that publishes essays, short stories, and poems related to the Beats. "We publish studies of Beat texts, figures, and legends; we look at writers and movements related to the Beats; we support writers of the present who take their influence from the Beats." Pays on publication. Publishes ms 6 months after acceptance.

THE BEATNIK COWBOY

3410 Corral Dr., Apt. 208, Rapid City SD 57702. **E-mail:** submissions@thebeatnikcowboy.com. **Website:** beatnikcowboy.com. **Contact:** Dr. Randall Rogers and Chris Butler, editors. "*The Beatnik Cowboy* seeks the best poetry from all poets around the world. We do not want poetry that slaps us open-hand across the face, but instead gives us a swift kick in the yarbles." Acquires one-time rights. Responds in 1 month. Sometimes critiques poems. Guidelines available online.

MAGAZINES NEEDS Submit 3 poems by e-mail.

BELLINGHAM REVIEW

Mail Stop 9053, Western Washington University, Bellingham WA 98225. (360)650-4863. **E-mail:** bellingham.review@wwu.edu. **Website:** wwww.bhreview.org. **Contact:** Susanne Paola Antonetta, editor-in-chief; Bailey Cunningham, managing editor. Nonprofit magazine published once/year in the Spring. Seeks "literature of palpable quality: poems, stories, and essays so beguiling they invite us to touch their essence. *Bellingham Review* hungers for a kind of writing that nudges the limits of form or executes traditional forms exquisitely." The editors are actively seeking submissions of creative nonfiction, as well as stories that push the boundaries of the form. Open submission period is from September 15-December 1. Buys first North American serial rights. Pays on publication when funding allows. Publishes ms an average of 6 months after acceptance. Responds in 1-4 months to mss. Editorial lead time 6 months. Sample copy: $12. Guidelines online.

MAGAZINES NEEDS Wants "well crafted poetry, but is open to all styles." Has published poetry by David Shields, Tess Gallagher, Gary Soto, Jane Hirshfield, Albert Goldbarth, and Rebecca McClanahan. Submit up to 3 poems via online submissions manager. Will not use light verse. Pays as funds allow, plus contributor's copies.

TIPS "The *Bellingham Review* holds 3 annual contests: the 49th Parallel Award for poetry, the Annie Dillard Award for Nonfiction, and the Tobias Wolff Award for Fiction. See the individual listings for these contests under Contests & Awards for full details."

BELOIT POETRY JOURNAL

E-mail: bpj@bpj.org. **Website:** www.bpj.org. **Contact:** Rachel Contreni Flynn and Melissa Crowe, editors. *Beloit Poetry Journal*, published biannually, prints "the most outstanding poems we receive, without bias as to length, school, subject, or form. For more than 65 years of continuous publication, we have been distinguished for the extraordinary range of our poetry and our discovery of strong new poets." Wants "poems that investigate the intersection between the political and the personal; language that makes us laugh and weep, recoil, resist—and pay attention. We're drawn to poetry that grabs hold of the whole body, not just the head." Has published poetry by Sherman Alexie, Eduardo Corral, Jenny Johnson, Albert Goldbarth, Sonia Sanchez, A.E. Stallings, Danez Smith, Susan Tichy, and Ocean Vuong. Responds in 4 months to mss. Sample copy: $12. Guidelines online.

MAGAZINES NEEDS Submit via Submittable. Limit submissions to 3-5 poems (or a single long poem). Pays 3 contributor's copies and one-year subscription.

HOW TO CONTACT bpj@bpj.org

bpj@bpj.org

CONTEST/AWARD OFFERINGS We accept submissions for the Adrienne Rich Award for Poetry during the months of March and April.

ALSO OFFERS Publishes one chapbook per year, distributed as part of subscription.

TIPS "We seek only unpublished poems or translations of poems not already available in English. Poems should be submitted electronically via Submittable. Before submitting, please buy a sample issue or browse our website archive."

⑤ BELTWAY POETRY QUARTERLY

626 Quebec Pl. NW, Washington DC 20010. **E-mail:** info@beltwaypoetry.com. **Website:** www.beltwaypoetry.com. **Contact:** Kim Roberts and Venus Thrash, co-editors. *Beltway Poetry Quarterly* is an award-winning online literary journal and resource bank that showcases the literary community in Washington, DC and the surrounding Mid-Atlantic region. As the only journal in the region to focus solely on DC and surrounding jurisdictions, we are able to document a literary community in depth. Since our founding in January 2000, we have showcased the richness and diversity of Washington area authors in every issue, with poets from different backgrounds, races, ethnicities, ages, and sexual orientations represented. We have included Pulitzer Prize winners and those who have never previously published. We have published academic, spoken word, and experimental authors——and also those poets whose work defies categorization. Most issues are curated, but at least one issue per year is open to submissions from regional authors (who live or work in DC, MD, VA, WV and DE). Those issues are themed; submissions must address the announced theme. Reading periods and themes change annually; check website for details. Responds in 2 months to mss.

MAGAZINES NEEDS We seek poems that fit our annual announced theme only. "Other than one annual themed issue, we are a curated journal and consider poems by invitation only. Themed issues and their open reading periods change each year; check website for guidelines. Themed issues have included prose poems, poems about working for the Federal government, and poems celebrating immigrant roots. Two issues per year feature portfolios, a larger group of poems than most journals generally include, up to 8 poems each by 5-7 authors from the greater-DC region, and these issues are open only by invitation. Most featured authors are found through earlier participation in themed issues; featured authors are paid a stipend." We read poems of any length or style. Authors included in themed issues are not paid. We do, however, pay a stipend to poets featured in our Portfolio Issues.

HOW TO CONTACT Please see our online submission form.

⑤ BEYOND CENTAURI

White Cat Publications, LLC, 33080 Industrial Rd., Suite 101, Livonia MI 48150. (734)237-8522. **Fax:** (313)557-5162. **E-mail:** beyondcentauri@whitecatpublications.com. **Website:** www.whitecatpublications.com/guidelines/beyond-centauri. *Beyond Centauri*, published quarterly, contains fantasy, science fiction, sword and sorcery, very mild horror short stories, poetry, and illustrations for readers ages 10 and up. Publishes ms 1-2 months after acceptance. Responds in 2-3 months. Single copy: $7.

○ *Beyond Centauri* is 44 pages, magazine-sized, offset printed, perfect-bound, with paper cover for color art, includes ads. Press run is 100; 5 distributed free to reviewers.

MAGAZINES NEEDS Wants fantasy, science fiction, spooky horror, and speculative poetry for younger readers. Considers poetry by children and teens. Has published poetry by Bruce Boston, Bobbi Sinha-Morey, Debbie Feo, Dorothy Imm, Cythera, and Terrie Leigh Relf. Looks for themes of science fiction and fantasy. Poetry should be submitted in the body of an e-mail, or as an RTF attachment. Does not want horror with excessive blood and gore. Length: up to 50 lines/poem. Pays $2/original poem, $1/reprints, $1/scifaiku and related form, plus 1 contributor's copy.

BIBLE ADVOCATE

Church of God (Seventh Day), P.O. Box 33677, Denver CO 80233. **E-mail:** bibleadvocate@cog7.org. **Website:** baonline.org. **Contact:** Sherri Langton, associate editor. "Our purpose is to advocate the Bible and represent the Church of God (Seventh Day) to a Christian audience." Buys first rights, second serial (reprint) rights, electronic rights. Pays on publication. Publishes ms an average of 3-9 months after acceptance. Responds in 4-10 weeks to queries. Editorial lead time 3 months. Sample copy for SAE with 9x12 envelope and 3 first-class stamps. Guidelines online.

"Though the Church of God (Seventh Day) believes in the virgin birth and resurrection of Christ, we do not publish articles or poetry on celebrating a traditional Christmas or Easter. Please become familiar with our doctrines."

MAGAZINES NEEDS Seldom comments on rejected poems. No avant-garde. Length: 5-20 lines. Pays $20 and 2 contributor's copies.

HOW TO CONTACT Submit to bibleadvocate@cog7.org. Attn: Sherri Langton associate editor

TIPS "Be fresh, not preachy! Articles must be in keeping with the doctrinal understanding of the Church of God (Seventh Day). Therefore, the writer should become familiar with what the Church generally accepts as truth as set forth in its doctrinal beliefs. We reserve the right to edit mss to fit our space requirements, doctrinal stands, and church terminology. Significant changes are referred to writers for approval. Accept email submissions only — no fax or snail mail."

BIG BRIDGE

E-mail: walterblue@bigbridge.org. **Website:** www.bigbridge.org. **Contact:** Michael Rothenberg and Terri Carrion, editors. "*Big Bridge* is one of the oldest and most respected online literary arts magazines. For over 20 years, Big Bridge has published the best in poetry, fiction, nonfiction essays, journalism, and art (photos, line drawings, performance, installations, site-works, comics, graphics)." Guidelines available online.

MAGAZINES NEEDS Only accepts electronic submissions. Submit via e-mail.

TIPS "Big Bridge publishes one very big issue each year. Each issue features an online chapbook. We are interested in anthology concepts and thematic installations as well as individual submissions. Send query to propose installations and anthology ideas for consideration. All individual submissions should include a bio and bio photo."

BIG MUDDY

A Journal of the Mississippi River Valley, Southeast Missouri State University Press, One University Plaza, MS 2650, Cape Girardeau MO 63701. (573)651-2044. **E-mail:** upress@semo.edu. **Website:** bigmuddyjournal.com. James Brubaker.. "*Big Muddy* explores multidisciplinary, multicultural issues, people, and events mainly concerning, but not limited to, the 10-state area that borders the Mississippi River. We publish fiction, poetry, historical essays, creative nonfiction, environmental essays, biography, regional events, photography, art, etc." Acquires first North American serial rights. Usually publishes ms 6-12 months after acceptance. Please allow up to 8 months Sample copy: $6. Guidelines online.

MAGAZINES NEEDS Pays 2 contributor's copies; additional copies $5.

TIPS "We look for clear language, avoidance of clichés, a fresh vision of the theme or issue. Find some excellent and honest readers to comment on your work-in-progress and final draft. Consider their viewpoints carefully. Revise if needed."

BIG PULP

E-mail: editors@bigpulp.com. **Website:** www.bigpulp.com. **Contact:** Bill Olver, editor. *Big Pulp* defines "pulp fiction" very broadly: It's lively, challenging, thought provoking, thrilling, and fun, regardless of how many or how few genre elements are packed in. It doesn't subscribe to the theory that genre fiction is disposable; a great deal of literary fiction could easily fall under one of their general categories. Places a higher value on character and story than genre elements. Acquires first North American serial rights. Pays on publication. Publishes ms 1 year after acceptance. Responds in 2 months to mss. Sample copy: $10; excerpts available online at no cost. Guidelines online.

"Submissions are only accepted during certain reading periods. Our website is updated to reflect when we are and are not reading, and what we are looking for."

MAGAZINES NEEDS All types of poetry are considered, but poems should have a genre connection. Pays $5/poem.

TIPS "We like to be surprised, and we have few boundaries. Fantasy writers may focus on the mundane aspects of a fantastical creature's life or the magic that can happen in everyday life. Romances do not have to be requited or have happy endings, and the object of one's obsession may not be a person. Mysteries need not focus on 'whodunit?' We're always interested in science or speculative fiction focusing on societal issues, but writers should avoid being partisan or shrill. We also like fiction that crosses genre; for example, a science fiction romance or a fantasy crime story. We have an online archive for fiction and poetry and encourage writers to check it out. That said, *Big Pulp* has a strong editorial bias in favor of stories with monkeys. Especially talking monkeys."

BILINGUAL REVIEW

Arizona State University, Hispanic Research Center, P.O. Box 875303, Tempe AZ 85287-5303. (480)965-3867. **Fax:** (480)965-0315. **E-mail:** brp@asu.edu. **Website:** www.asu.edu/brp/submit. **Contact:** Gary Francisco Keller, publisher. *Bilingual Review* is "committed to publishing high-quality writing by both established and emerging writers." Acquires all rights (50% of reprint permission fees given to author as matter of policy). Publishes ms 1 year after acceptance. Responds in 2-3 months. Often comments on rejected mss.

⬤ Magazine: 7x10; 96 pages; 55 lb. acid-free paper; coated cover stock.

MAGAZINES NEEDS Submit via mail. Send 2 copies of poetry with SAE and loose stamps. Does not usually accept e-mail submissions except through special circumstance/prior arrangement.

THE BITTER OLEANDER

4983 Tall Oaks Dr., Fayetteville NY 13066. **E-mail:** info@bitteroleander.com. **Website:** www.bitteroleander.com. **Contact:** Paul B. Roth, editor and publisher. "We're reading to find a language uncommitted to the commonplace and more integrated with the natural world. A language that helps define the same particulars in nature that exist in us and have not been socialized out of us." Biannual magazine covering poetry and short fiction and translations of contemporary poetry and short fiction. Publishes ms an average of 1-6 months after acceptance. Responds in 1 month. Editorial lead time 6 months. Sample copy: $10. Guidelines online.

MAGAZINES NEEDS Seeks "highly imaginative poetry whose language is serious. Particularly interested in translations." Has published poetry by Alberto Blanco (Mexico), José-Flore Tappy (Switzer-

land), Ana Minga (Ecuador), Károly Bari (Hungary), Astrid Cabral (Brazil), and numerous well-known and not-so-well-known U.S. poets. Does not want rhyming, strict metered poetry; confessional or love poetry; profanity. Length: 1-50 lines. Pays 1 contributor's copy.

CONTEST/AWARD OFFERINGS Hosts the Bitter Oleander Press Library of Poetry Award (BOPLOPA). Guidelines online.

TIPS "If you are writing poems or short fiction in the tradition of 98% of all journals publishing in this country, then your work will usually not fit for us. If within the first 400 words our minds start to drift, the rest rarely makes it. Be yourself, and listen to no one but yourself."

BLACKBIRD

Virginia Commonwealth University Department of English, P.O. Box 843082, Richmond VA 23284. (804)827-4729. **E-mail:** blackbird@vcu.edu. **Website:** www.blackbird.vcu.edu. *Blackbird* is published twice a year. Reading period: August 1 to March 15. Responds in 6 months. Guidelines online.

MAGAZINES NEEDS Submit up to 6 poems at a time. "If submitting online, put all poems into 1 document."

TIPS "We like a story that invites us into its world, that engages our senses, soul, and mind. We are able to publish long works in all genres, but query *Blackbird* before you send a prose piece over 8,000 words or a poem exceeding 10 pages."

⬤ BLACKBOX MANIFOLD

University of Cambridge, Faculty of English, 9 West Rd., Cambridge CB3 9DP, United Kingdom. **E-mail:** ah217@cam.ac.uk. **Website:** manifold.group.shef.ac.uk. **Contact:** Dr. Alex Houen and Adam Piette, editors. *Blackbox Manifold* is an online forum with a slant towards innovative poetry that has prose, narrative, or sequences in its sights. "That said, we don't hold allegiance to any one poetry school or group, and we're happy to receive submissions from established and emerging poets alike." Responds in 8-10 weeks. Sample copies online. Guidelines online.

MAGAZINES NEEDS "We welcome submissions of previously unpublished reviews, short essays, and poems (particularly poems with prose, narrative, or sequences in their sights)." Submit up to 4 poems with a brief biographical statement.

❸ BLACK WARRIOR REVIEW

P.O. Box 862936, Tuscaloosa AL 35486. (205)348-4518.
E-mail: interns.bwr@gmail.com. **Website:** www.bwr.
ua.edu. **Contact:** Cat Ingrid Leeches, editor. "We publish contemporary fiction, poetry, reviews, essays, and art for a literary audience. We publish the freshest work we can find." Work that appeared in the *Black Warrior Review* has been included in the *Pushcart Prize* anthology, *Harper's Magazine, Best American Short Stories, Best American Poetry,* and *New Stories from the South.* Buys first rights. Pays on publication. Publishes ms 6 months after acceptance. Responds in 3-6 months. Sample copy: $10. Guidelines online.

MAGAZINES NEEDS "We welcome most styles and forms, and we favor poems that take risks—whether they be quiet or audacious." Submit poems in 1 document. Length: up to 10 pages. Pays one-year subscription and nominal lump-sum fee.

TIPS "We look for attention to language, freshness, honesty, a convincing and sharp voice. Send us a clean, well-printed, proofread ms. Become familiar with the magazine prior to submission."

BLUE COLLAR REVIEW

Partisan Press, P.O. Box 11417, Norfolk VA 23517. **E-mail:** red-ink@earthlink.net. **Website:** www.partisanpress.org. **Contact:** A. Markowitz, editor; Mary Franke, co-editor. *Blue Collar Review (Journal of Progressive Working Class Literature),* published quarterly, contains poetry, short stories, and illustrations "reflecting the working-class experience—a broad range from the personal to the societal. Our purpose is to promote and expand working-class literature and an awareness of the connections between workers of all occupations and the social context in which we live. Also to inspire the creativity and latent talent in 'common' working people." Sample copy: $7. Subscription: $20 for 1 year; $35 for 2 years. Make checks payable to Partisan Press. Guidelines available online. Work not meeting guidelines may be returned or discarded.

MAGAZINES NEEDS Send up to 5 poems. Include name and address on each page. Cover letter is helpful but not required. Size 10 SASE is required for response. Has published poetry by Simon Perchik, Jim Daniels, Mary McAnally, Marge Piercy, Alan Catlin, and Rob Whitbeck. Pays contributor's copies.

ADDITIONAL INFORMATION Partisan Press looks for "poetry of power that reflects a working-class consciousness and moves us forward as a society. Must be good writing reflecting social realism including but not limited to political issues." Publishes about 3 chapbooks/year; not presently open to unsolicited submissions. "Submissions are requested from among the poets published in the *Blue Collar Review.*" Has published *A Possible Explanation* by Peggy Safire and *American Sounds* by Robert Edwards. Chapbooks are usually 20-60 pages, digest-sized, offset-printed, saddle-stapled or flat-spined, with card or glossy covers. Sample chapbooks are $7 and listed on website.

CONTEST/AWARD OFFERINGS Sponsors Working People's Poetry Contest. **Entry fee:** $15/poem. **Deadline:** May 15. Prize: $100, one-year subscription to *Blue Collar Review* and 1 year online posting of poem.

BLUELINE

120 Morey Hall, SUNY Potsdam, Potsdam NY 13676.
E-mail: blueline@potsdam.edu. **Website:** bluelinemagadk.com. **Contact:** Donald J. McNutt, editor and nonfiction editor; Caroline Downing, art editor; Stephanie Coyne-DeGhett, fiction editor; Rebecca Lehmann, poetry editor. "*Blueline* seeks poems, stories, and essays relating to the Adirondacks and regions similar in geography and spirit, or focusing on the shaping influence of nature. Submission period is July-November. *Blueline* welcomes electronic submissions as Word document (DOC or DOCX) attachments. Please identify genre in subject line. Please avoid using compression software." Annual literary magazine publishing fiction, poetry, personal essays, book reviews, and quality visual art for those interested in the Adirondacks or well-crafted nature writing in general. Acquires first North American serial rights. Publishes ms 3-6 months after acceptance. Responds in up to 3 months to mss. "Decisions in early February." Occasionally comments on rejected mss. Sample copy: $9. Guidelines available on website, by SASE, or by e-mail.

○ "Proofread all submissions. It is difficult for our editors to get excited about work containing typographical and syntactic errors."

MAGAZINES NEEDS Submit 3-5 poems at a time. Submit July 1-November 30 only. Include short bio. Poems are circulated to an editorial board. Has published poetry by M.J. Iuppa, Alice Wolf Gilborn, Lyn Lifshin, Todd Davis, Maurice Kenny, Richard Levine, and Lee Slonimsky. Reviews books of poetry in 500-750 words, single- or multibook format. "We are interested in both beginning and established poets whose poems evoke universal themes in nature and show human interaction with the natural world. We look for thoughtful craftsmanship rather than stylistic trickery." Does not want "sentimental or extremely experimental poetry." Length: up to 75 lines/poem. "Occasionally we publish longer poems." Pays 1 contributor's copy.

TIPS "We look for concise, clear, concrete prose that tells a story and touches upon a universal theme or situation. We prefer realism to romanticism but will consider nostalgia if well done. Pay attention to grammar and syntax. Avoid murky language, sentimentality, cuteness, or folksiness. We would like to see more good, creative nonfiction centered on the literature and/or culture of the Adirondacks, Northern New York, New England, or Eastern Canada. If ms has potential, we work with author to improve and reconsider for publication. Our readers prefer fiction to poetry (in general) or reviews. Write from your own experience, be specific and factual (within the bounds of your story), and if you write about universal features such as love, death, change, etc., write about them in a fresh way. You'll catch our attention if your writing is interesting, vigorous, and polished."

BLUE MESA REVIEW

Department of Language and Literature, Humanities Building, Second Floor, MSC03 2170, 1 University of New Mexico, Albuquerque NM 87131. **Website:** bluemesareview.org. **Contact:** Has rotating editorial board; see website for current masthead. "Originally founded by Rudolfo Anaya, Gene Frumkin, David Johnson, Patricia Clark Smith, and Lee Bartlette in 1989, the *Blue Mesa Review* emerged as a source of innovative writing produced in the Southwest. Over the years the magazine's nuance has changed, sometimes shifting towards more craft-oriented work, other times realigning with its original roots." Requests first North American serial rights for print and nonexclusive electronic rights for website. Responds in 2-6 months.

○ Open for submissions from September 30-March 31. Contest: June 1-August 31. Only accepts submissions through online submissions manager.

MAGAZINES NEEDS Submit 3-5 poems via online submissions manager.

TIPS "In general, we are seeking strong voices and lively, compelling narrative with a fine eye for craft. We look forward to reading your best work!"

BLUESTEM

Website: www.bluestemmagazine.com. **Contact:** Olga Abella, editor. *Bluestem*, formerly known as *Karamu*, produces a quarterly online issue (December, March, June, September) and an annual spring print issue. Responds in 2-3 months. "Sample back issues of *Bluestem (Karamu)* are available for $5 for each issue."

○ Only accepts submissions through online submissions manager.

MAGAZINES NEEDS Submit using online submissions manager. Include bio (less than 100 words) with submission. Pays 1 contributor's copy and discount for additional copies.

BLUE UNICORN

A Tri-Quarterly of Poetry, 22 Avon Rd., Kensington CA 94707. **E-mail:** staff@blueunicorn.com. **Website:** www.blueunicorn.org. **Contact:** Ruth G. Iodice, John Hart, and Fred Ostrander, editors. "*Blue Unicorn* wants well-crafted poetry of all kinds, in form or free verse, as well as translations. We shun the trite or inane, the soft-centered, the contrived poem." Publishes in October, February, and June. Publishes poems up to 12 months after acceptance. Responds in 3 months. Sample copy: $8 plus 6x8 SASE. Subscription: $20.

○ Magazine: 40 pages, narrow digest-sized, finely printed, saddle-stapled, with some art.

MAGAZINES NEEDS *Blue Unicorn, A Tri-Quarterly of Poetry*, published in October, February, and June, is "distinguished by its fastidious editing, both with regard to contents and format." Wants "well-crafted poetry of all kinds, in form or free verse, as well as expert translations on any subject matter. We shun the trite or inane, the soft-centered, the contrived poem. Shorter poems have more chance with us because of limited space." Has published poetry by James Applewhite, Kim Cushman, Patrick Worth Gray, Joan LaBombard, James Schevill, and Gail White. *Blue Unicorn* is 56 pages, narrow digest-sized, finely printed, saddle-stapled. Receives more than 2,000 submissions/year, accepts about 150. Single copy: $7 (foreign add $3); subscription: $18 for 3 issues (foreign add $6). Features 35-45 poems in each issue, all styles, with the focus on excellence and accessibility. Receives about 1,500 submissions a year, publishes up to 150. Submit 3-5 poems by mail with SASE on 8.5x11 or A4 paper. Put name and contact information on every page. Cover letter optional. Has published James Applewhite, Kim Cushman, Patrick Worth Gray, Joan LaBombard, James Schevill, and Gail White. "Shorter poems have more chance with us because of layout considerations." Pays 1 contributor's copy.

HOW TO CONTACT Submit 3-5 poems at a time. No previously published poems or simultaneous submissions. Cover letter is "OK, but will not affect our selection." Sometimes comments on rejected poems. Guidelines available for SASE. Responds in up to 3 months (generally within 6 weeks). Pays one contributor's copy.

CONTEST/AWARD OFFERINGS Sponsors an annual (spring) contest with prizes of $150, $75, $50, and sometimes special awards; distinguished poets as judges; publication of top 3 poems and 6 honorable mentions in the magazine. Guidelines available for SASE. Entry fee: $6 for first poem, $3 for each additional poem.

BODY LITERATURE

Website: bodyliterature.com. *BODY* is an international online literary journal. "We publish the highest-quality poetry and prose from emerging and established writers. Sample copies online. Guidelines online.

MAGAZINES NEEDS Submit up to 5 poems in 1 document; each poem should start a new page.

BOMBAY GIN

Naropa University, Creative Writing and Poetics Department, 2130 Arapahoe Ave., Boulder CO 80302. **E-mail:** bgin@naropa.edu. **Website:** www.bombayginjournal.com. **Contact:** Jade Lascelles, editor in chief. *Bombay Gin*, published annually, is the literary journal of the Jack Kerouac School of Disembodied Poetics at Naropa University. Produced and edited by MFA students, *Bombay Gin* publishes established writers alongside unpublished and emerging writers. We have a special interest in works that push conventional literary boundaries. Submissions of poetry, prose, visual art, translation, and works involving hybrid forms and cross-genre exploration are encouraged. Translations are also considered. Guidelines are the same as for original work. Translators are responsible for obtaining any necessary permissions." Subscription: $10 + $3 shipping for 1 year.

⬤ *Bombay Gin* is 150-200 pages, digest-sized, professionally printed, perfect-bound, with color card cover. Has published work by Amiri Baraka, Lisa Robertson, CA Conrad, Sapphire, Fred Moten, Anne Waldman, Diane di Prima and bell hooks, among others.

MAGAZINES NEEDS Submit 3-5 poems through online submissions manager. Include 100-word bio, e-mail, and mailing address. Pays 1 contributor's copies.

🟢 BOMB MAGAZINE

80 Hanson Place, Ste. 703, Brooklyn NY 11217. (718)636-9100. **Fax:** (718)636-9200. **E-mail:** saul@bombsite.com. **Website:** www.bombmagazine.com. **Contact:** Saul Anton, senior editor. "Written, edited, and produced by industry professionals and funded by those interested in the arts, *BOMB Magazine* publishes work which is unconventional and contains an edge, whether it be in style or subject matter." Buys first rights, one-time rights. Pays on publication. Publishes ms an average of 3-6 months after acceptance. Responds in 3-5 months to mss. Editorial lead time 3-4 months. Sample copy: $10. Guidelines by e-mail.

MAGAZINES NEEDS *BOMB Magazine* accepts unsolicited poetry and prose submissions for our literary supplement *First Proof* by online submission manager in January and August. Submissions sent outside these months will not be read. Submit 4-6 poems via online submission manager. E-mailed submissions will not be considered. Pays $100 and contributor's copies.

TIPS "Mss should be typed, double-spaced, and proofread, and should be final drafts. Purchase a sample issue before submitting work."

BORDERLANDS: TEXAS POETRY REVIEW

P.O. Box 40876, Austin TX 78704. **E-mail:** borderlandspoetry@gmail.com. **Website:** www.borderlands.org. **Contact:** Ryan Sharp, editor. *Borderlands: Texas Poetry Review*, published semiannually, prints high-quality, outward-looking poetry by new and established poets, as well as brief reviews of poetry books and critical essays. Cosmopolitan in content, but particularly welcomes Texas and Southwest writers. Wants poems that exhibit social, political, geographical, historical, feminist, or spiritual awareness coupled with concise artistry. Does not want introspective work about the speaker's psyche, childhood, or intimate relationships. Has published poetry by Walter McDonald, Naomi Shihab Nye, Mario Susko, Wendy Barker, Larry D. Thomas, Reza Shirazi, and Scott Hightower. Sample copy: $12. Guidelines available online.

⬤ *Borderlands* is 100-150 pages, digest-sized, offset-printed, perfect-bound, with 4-color cover. Receives about 2,000 poems/year, accepts about 120. Press run is 1,000.

MAGAZINES NEEDS Submit 5 typed poems at a time. Include cover letter and SASE with sufficient return postage. Open to traditional and experimental forms. Pays 1 contributor's copy.

TIPS "Editors read year round in 2 cycles. Submissions postmarked March 15-June 15 will be considered for the Fall/Winter issue, and submissions postmarked September 15-December 15 will be considered for the Spring/Summer issue. Occasionally, work may be held for publication in the following issue. Note that response times may be slower for work received immediately after a deadline. Do not submit work while we are considering a previous submission."

⑤ BOULEVARD

Opojaz, Inc., 6614 Clayton Rd., Box 325, Richmond Heights MO 63117. **E-mail:** editors@boulevardmagazine.org. **Website:** www.boulevardmagazine.org; boulevard.submittable/submit. Managing Editor: Dusty Freund.. **Contact:** Jessica Rogen, editor. "*Boulevard* is a diverse literary magazine presenting original creative work by well-known authors as well as by writers of exciting promise." Triannual magazine featuring fiction, poetry, and essays. Sometimes comments on rejected mss. *Boulevard* has been called "one of the half-dozen best literary journals" by Poet Laureate Daniel Hoffman in *The Philadelphia Inquirer*. "We strive to publish the finest in poetry, fiction, and nonfiction. We frequently publish writers with previous credits, and we are very interested in publishing less experienced or unpublished writers with exceptional promise. We've published everything from John Ashbery to Donald Hall to a wide variety of styles from new or lesser known poets. We're eclectic. We are interested in original, moving poetry written from the head as well as the heart. It can be about any topic." *Boulevard* is 175-250 pages, digest-sized, flat-spined, with glossy card cover. Receives over 600 unsolicited mss/month. Accepts about 10 mss/issue. Publishes 10 new writers/year. Recently published work by Joyce Carol Oates, Floyd Skloot, John Barth, Stephen Dixon, David Guterson, Albert Goldbarth, Molly Peacock, Bob Hicok, Alice Friman, Dick Allen, and Tom Disch. Buys first North American serial rights. Rights revert to author upon publication. Pays on publication. Publishes ms an average of 9 months after acceptance. Responds in 2 weeks to queries; 4-5 months to mss. Sample copy: $10. Subscription: $16 for 3 issues, $29 for 6 issues, $42 for 9 issues. Foreign subscribers, please add $10. Make checks payable to Opojaz, Inc. Subscriptions are available online at www.boulevardmagazine.org/subscribe.html. Guidelines online.

MAGAZINES NEEDS Submit by mail or Submittable. Accepts multiple submissions. Does not accept poems May 1-October 1. SASE for reply. Does not consider book reviews. "Do not send us light verse." Does not want "poetry that is uninspired, formulaic, self-conscious, unoriginal, insipid." Length: up to 200 lines/poem. Pays $25-250.

ALSO OFFERS Also offers the Poetry Contest for Emerging Writers: $1,000 and publication in *Boulevard*, awarded to the winning group of 3 poems. Postmark deadline is June 1. Entry fee is $15 for each group of 3 poems, with no limit per author. It includes a one-year subscription to *Boulevard*. For contests, make check payable to *Boulevard* or submit online at boulevard.submittable.com/submit.

TIPS "Read the magazine first. The work *Boulevard* publishes is generally recognized as among the finest in the country. We continue to seek more good literary or cultural essays. Send only your best work."

THE BREAKTHROUGH INTERCESSOR

Breakthrough, Inc., P.O. Box 121, Lincoln VA 20160. (540)338-4131. **Fax:** (540)338-1934. **E-mail:** breakthrough@intercessors.org. **E-mail:** editor@intercessors.org. **Website:** intercessors.org. *The Breakthrough Intercessor*, published quarterly, focuses on "encouraging people in prayer and faith; preparing and equipping those who pray." Accepts multiple articles per issue: 300- to 1,000-word true stories on prayer, or poems on prayer. Time between acceptance and publication varies. Magazine is Free to All visit intercessors.org to review and share with friends on social media. Guidelines available on website.

○ *The Breakthrough Intercessor* is 32-36 pages, magazine-sized, professionally printed, saddle-stapled with self-cover, includes art/graphics. Electronic magazine posted on website and limited hard copy prints.

MAGAZINES NEEDS Send poem, along with title, author's name, address, phone number, and e-mail. Accepts fax, e-mail (pasted into body of message or attachment), and mailed hard copy. Length: 12 lines/poem minimum.

THE BRIAR CLIFF REVIEW

3303 Rebecca St., Sioux City IA 51104. (712)279-1651. **E-mail:** tricia.currans-sheehan@briarcliff.edu. **Web-**

site: bcreview.org. **Contact:** Tricia Currans-Sheehan, editor; Jeanne Emmons, poetry editor; Phil Hey, fiction editor; Paul Weber, Siouxland and nonfiction editor. *The Briar Cliff Review*, published annually in April, is "an attractive, eclectic literary/art magazine." It focuses on, but is not limited to, "Siouxland writers and subjects. We are happy to proclaim ourselves a regional publication. It doesn't diminish us; it enhances us." Acquires first serial rights. Time between acceptance and publication is up to 6 months. Responds in 4-5 months to mss; in 6-8 months to poems. Sample copy: $15, plus 9x12 SAE. Guidelines available on website or for #10 SASE.

○ Member: CLMP, Humanities International Complete.

MAGAZINES NEEDS Wants quality poetry with strong imagery and tight, well-wrought language. Especially interested in, but not limited to, regional, Midwestern content. Receives about 1,000 poems/year; accepts about 30. Considers simultaneous submissions but expects prompt notification of acceptance elsewhere. Submit by mail (send SASE for return of ms) or online submissions manager. No e-mail submissions, unless from overseas. Cover letter is required. "Include short bio. Submissions should be typewritten or letter quality, with author's name and address on each page. No mss returned without SASE." Seldom comments on rejected poems. Pays 2 contributor's copies; additional copies available for $12.

TIPS "So many stories are just telling. We want some action. It has to move. We prefer stories in which there is no gimmick, no mechanical turn of events, no moral except the one we would draw privately."

BRILLIANT CORNERS: A JOURNAL OF JAZZ & LITERATURE

Lycoming College, 700 College Place, Williamsport PA 17701. **Website:** www.lycoming.edu/brilliantcorners. **Contact:** Sascha Feinstein, editor. "We publish jazz-related literature—fiction, poetry, and nonfiction. We are open as to length and form." Semiannual. Acquires first North American serial rights. Publishes ms 4-12 months after acceptance. Responds in 2 weeks to queries; in 1-2 months to mss. Rarely comments on rejected mss. Sample copy: $7. Guidelines online.

○ Reading period: September 1-May 15.

MAGAZINES NEEDS Submit 3-5 poems at a time. No e-mail or fax submissions. Cover letter is preferred. Staff reviews books of poetry. Send materials for review consideration. Wants "work that is both passionate and well crafted—work worthy of our recent contributors." Has published poetry by Amiri Baraka, Jayne Cortez, Yusef Komunyakaa, Philip Levine, Sonia Sanchez, and Al Young. Does not want "sloppy hipster jargon or improvisatory nonsense."

TIPS "We look for clear, moving prose that demostrates a love of both writing and jazz. We primarily publish established writers, but we read all submissions carefully and welcome work by outstanding young writers."

THE BROADKILL REVIEW

c/o John Milton & Company, 104 Federal St., Milton DE 19968. **E-mail:** broadkillreview@gmail.com. **Website:** broadkillreview.com, www.thebroadkillreview.blogspot.com; sites.google.com/site/thebroadkillreview. **Contact:** James C.L. Brown, founding editor; Stephen Scott Whitaker, managing editor; Linda Blaskey, poetry and interview editor, HA Maxson, fiction editor. Responds in 4 weeks to queries; in 3 months to mss. Editorial lead time is 2-3 months. Sample copy available online and by e-mail. Guidelines available by e-mail and online.

○ "*The Broadkill Review* accepts the best fiction, poetry, and nonfiction by new and established writers. We have published Pushcart-nominated fiction and poetry." *TBR* publishes many writers from the Mid-Atlantic region, but does not limit itself to work from this region, as they are an internationally read publication that publishes a wide variety of work from around the globe, including Canada, U.S., Western and Eastern Europe, China, Vietnam, Australia, and Pakistan.

MAGAZINES NEEDS Send poetry with cover letter by e-mail or online submissions manager. Pays contributor's copy.

TIPS "Query the editor first. Visit our website to familiarize yourself with the type of material we publish. Request and read a copy of the magazine first!"

BUENOS AIRES REVIEW

E-mail: editors@buenosairesreview.org. **Website:** buenosairesreview.org. *The Buenos Aires Review* presents the best and latest work by emerging and established writers from the Americas, in both Spanish and English. "We value translation and conversation. We're bilingual. And we're passionate about the art and craft that allows us to be, so we provide a dedicated space for translators to discuss their recent projects." Guidelines online.

MAGAZINES NEEDS Submit 3-6 poems through online portal.

⑤ BURNSIDE REVIEW

Website: www.burnsidereview.org. **Contact:** Sid Miller, founder and editor; Dan Kaplan, managing editor. *Burnside Review*, published every 9 months, prints "the best poetry and short fiction we can get our hands on. We tend to publish writing that finds beauty in truly unexpected places; that combines urban and natural imagery; that breaks the heart." Acquires first rights. Pays on publication. Publishes ms 9 months after acceptance. Responds in 1-6 months. Submit seasonal material 3-6 months in advance. Single copy: $8; subscription: $13.

 Burnside Review is 80 pages, 6x6, professionally printed, perfect-bound. Charges a $3 submission fee to cover printing costs.

MAGAZINES NEEDS "We like lyric. We like narrative. We like when the two merge. We like whiskey. We like hourglass figures. We like to be surprised. Surprise us." Has published poetry by Linda Bierds, Dorianne Laux, Ed Skoog, Campbell McGrath, Paul Guest, and Larissa Szporluk. Reads submissions year round. "Editors read all work submitted." Seldom comments on rejected work. Submit 3-5 poems via online submissions manager. Pays $25 and 1 contributor's copy.

BY&BY POETRY

Website: byandbylit.org. **Contact:** Jason Sears, editor. *By&By Poetry* aims to provide an eclectic online showcase for both established and up-and-coming poets. "We aspire to shape *By&By* into a celebration of poetry, a place where poets can congregate, read, and be heard. Join us." Responds in 1 month. Sample copies online. Guidelines online.

MAGAZINES NEEDS Submit up to 5 poems with a cover letter and short bio through online submissions manager.

TIPS "We welcome poems of any form, length, or style. Quite simply, we want your best."

CALIFORNIA QUARTERLY

California State Poetry Society, P.O. Box 7126, Orange CA 92863. **Website:** www.californiastatepoetrysociety.org. **Contact:** John Forrest Harrell, president. The California State Poetry Society is dedicated to the advancement of poetry and its dissemination. Although located in California, its members are from all over the U.S. and abroad. Levels of membership/dues: $35/year for an individual, $39/year for a family or library, $51/year foreign. Benefits include membership in the National Federation of State Poetry Societies (NFSPS); 4 issues of *California Quarterly*, *Newsbriefs*, and *The Poetry Letter*. Sponsors monthly and annual contests. Additional information available for SASE or on the website. Acquires first rights. Rights revert to poet after publication. Sample copy: $10. See *CQ Submissions*'s tab of website or mail request with $10 to CSPS VP/Membership, 2560 Calabria Court, Dublin, California 94568.

MAGAZINES NEEDS Submit no more than six poems by mail with SASE (or e-mail address) or via the website. Submit original poems only; no previously published poems. Foreign poems with translations welcome. Pays 1 contributor's copy.

CALLALOO

A Journal of African Diaspora Arts & Letters, Texas A&M University, 249 Blocker Hall, College Station TX 77843-4212, United States. (979)458-3108. **Fax:** (979)458-3275. **E-mail:** callaloo@tamu.edu. **Website:** callaloo.tamu.edu. *Callaloo: A Journal of African Diaspora Arts & Letters*, published quarterly, is devoted to poetry dealing with the African Diaspora, including North America, Europe, Africa, Latin and Central America, South America, and the Caribbean. Features about 15-20 poems (all forms and styles) in each issue along with short fiction, interviews, literary criticism, and concise critical book reviews. Responds in 6 months to mss. Sample available online: muse.jhu.edu/journals/callaloo/toc/cal.36.1.html. Submission guidelines available online. All manuscripts should be double spaced and submitted as a Word document (.doc or docx). Identifying information, including names of authors, addresses, phone numbers, and e-mail addresses, should be removed from manuscript submission. Manuscripts must follow *MLA Style Manual and Guide to Scholarly Publishing* and include a works cited and endnotes, not footnotes. All submissions made to the journal are considered final drafts.

MAGAZINES NEEDS Submit no more than 5 poems at a time; no more than 10 per calendar year. Submit using online submissions manager only: callaloo.expressacademic.org/login.php. Has published poetry by Aimeé Ceésaire, Lucille Clifton, Rita Dove, Yusef Komunyakaa, Natasha Trethewey, and Carl Phillips.

TIPS "We look for freshness of both writing and plot, strength of characterization, plausibility of plot. Read what's being written and published, especially in journals such as *Callaloo*."

CALYX

P.O. Box B, Corvallis OR 97339. (541)753-9384. **E-mail:** info@calyxpress.org; editor@calyxpress.org. **Website:** www.calyxpress.org. **Contact:** Brenna Crotty, senior editor. *"CALYX* exists to publish fine literature and art by women and is dedicated to publishing the work of all women, including women of color, older women, working-class women and other voices that need to be heard. We are committed to discovering and nurturing developing writers." Publishes ms an average of 6-12 months after acceptance. Responds in 4-8 months to mss. Sample copy: $10 plus $4 postage and handling.

○ Annual open submission (poetry and prose) period is October 1 - December 31. Lois Cranston Memorial Poetry Prize ($300 cash prize) is open March 1 - June 30. Margarita Donnelly Prize for Prose Writing ($500 cash prize) is open July 1 - September 30.

MAGAZINES NEEDS "When submitting through our online submissions manager, please put all poems in the same document." Wants "excellently crafted poetry that also has excellent content." Pays in contributor's copies and one-volume subscription.

TIPS "A forum for women's creative work—including work by women of color, lesbian and queer women, young women, old women—*CALYX* breaks new ground. Each issue is packed with new poetry, short stories, full-color artwork, photography, essays, and reviews."

THE CAPILANO REVIEW

102-281 Industrial Ave., Vancouver BC V6A 2P2, Canada. **E-mail:** contact@thecapilanoreview.ca. **E-mail:** online through submittable. **Website:** www.thecapilanoreview.com. **Contact:** Matea Kulic, managing editor. Triannual visual and literary arts magazine that "publishes only what the editors consider to be the very best fiction, poetry, drama, or visual art being produced. *TCR* editors are interested in fresh, original work that stimulates and challenges readers. Over the years, the magazine has developed a reputation for pushing beyond the boundaries of traditional art and writing. We are interested in work that is new in concept and in execution. We no longer accept submissions by mail. Please review our submission guidelines on our website and submit online through submittable." Buys first North American serial rights. Pays on publication. Publishes work within 1 year after acceptance. Responds in 4-6 months. Sample copy: $10 (outside of Canada, USD). Guidelines online.

MAGAZINES NEEDS Submit up to 8 pages of poetry. Pays $50-150.

THE CARIBBEAN WRITER

University of the Virgin Islands, RR 1, P.O. Box 10,000, Kingshill, St. Croix USVI 00850. (340)692-4152. **E-mail:** info@thecaribbeanwriter.org. **Website:** www.thecaribbeanwriter.org. **Contact:** Alscess Lewis-Brown, editor in chief. *The Caribbean Writer* features new and exciting voices from the region and beyond that explore the diverse and multi-ethnic culture in poetry, short fiction, personal essays, creative nonfiction, and plays. Social, cultural, economic, and sometimes controversial issues are also explored, employing a wide array of literary devices. Acquires first North American serial rights. Responds in 2-3 months. Single copy: $20; subscription: $25 for 2 years. Guidelines available by e-mail or on website.

○ Poetry published in *The Caribbean Writer* has appeared in *The Pushcart Prize. The Caribbean Writer* is 300+ pages, digest-sized, handsomely printed on heavy stock, perfect-bound, with glossy card cover. Press run is 1,200.

MAGAZINES NEEDS Reviews books of poetry and fiction in 1,000 words. Send materials for review consideration. Submit up to 5 poems through online submissions manager. Name, address, phone number, e-mail address, and title of ms should appear in cover letter along with brief bio. Title only on ms. Has published poetry by Edwidge Danticat, Geoffrey Philp, and Thomas Reiter. Pays 1 contributor's copy.

THE CAROLINA QUARTERLY

CB #3520 Greenlaw Hall, University of North Carolina, Chapel Hill NC 27599-3520. (919)408-7786. **E-mail:** carolina.quarterly@gmail.com. **Website:** www.thecarolinaquarterly.com; thecarolinaquarterly.submittable.com/submit. **Contact:** Sarah George-Waterfield, editor-in-chief; Travis Alexander, nonfiction editor; Laura Broom, fiction editor; Calvin Olsen, poetry editor. *The Carolina Quarterly*, published 2 times/year, prints fiction, poetry, reviews, nonfiction, and visual art. No specifications regarding form, length, subject matter, or style. Considers translations of work originally written in languages other than English. *The Carolina Quarterly* is about 100 pages, digest-sized, professionally printed, perfect-bound, with glossy cover; includes ads. Press run is 1,000. Accepts submissions September through May. Acquires first rights. Responds in 4-6 months. Sample copy: $9.

MAGAZINES NEEDS Submit up to 6 poems via online submissions manager or postal mail (address submissions to Poetry Editor). Has published poetry by Denise Levertov, Richard Wilbur, Robert Morgan, Ha Jin, and Charles Wright. Receives about 6,000 poems/year, accepts about 1%.

CAVEAT LECTOR

400 Hyde St., #606, San Francisco CA 94109. **E-mail:** caveatlectormagazine@gmail.com. **Website:** www.caveat-lector.org. **Contact:** Christopher Bernard, co-editor. *Caveat Lector*, published 2 times/year, is devoted to the arts and cultural and philosophical commentary. As well as literary work, it publishes art, photography, music, streaming audio of selected literary pieces, and short films. "Don't let those examples limit your submissions. Send what you feel is your strongest work, in any style and on any subject." All submissions should be sent with a brief bio and SASE, or submitted electronically at caveatlectormagazine@gmail.com. (Poetry submissions are only accepted through postal mail.) Reads poetry submissions February 1-June 30; reads all other submissions year round. Acquires first rights.

MAGAZINES NEEDS Wants poetry on any subject, in any style, as long as the work is authentic in feeling and appropriately crafted. Looking for accomplished poems, something that resonates in the mind long after the reader has laid the poem aside. Wants work that has authenticity of emotion and high craft; poems that, whether raw or polished, ring true; and if humorous, are actually funny, or at least witty. Classical to experimental. Note: Will sometimes request authors for audio of work to post on website. Has published poetry by Joanne Lowery, Simon Perchik, Les Murray, Alfred Robinson, and Ernest Hilbert. **Submit poetry through postal mail only.** Send brief bio and SASE with submission. Pays contributor's copies.

CAVE WALL

Cave Wall Press, LLC, P.O. Box 29546, Greensboro NC 27429-9546. **E-mail:** editor@cavewallpress.com. **Website:** www.cavewallpress.com. "*Cave Wall,* published twice a year, is a national literary magazine dedicated to publishing the best in contemporary poetry. We are interested in poems of any length and style from both established and emerging poets. Each issue includes b&w art. Poems first published in *Cave Wall* have been featured on *Poetry Daily, Verse Daily, The Writer's Almanac*, and in the *Best New Poets* awards anthology." Buys first North American serial rights. Responds in 1-5 months to mss. Guidelines on website.

MAGAZINES NEEDS Submit poems by mail with SASE. *Cave Wall* reads unsolicited poetry submissions twice a year. Check the website for reading periods. Pays 2 contributor's copies.

TIPS "We encourage you to read an issue of *Cave Wall* before you submit. Find out what kind of poetry we like. Please note that we read blind. Your name should not appear on your poems."

CC&D: CHILDREN, CHURCHES & DADDIES

The Unreligious, Non-Family-Oriented Literary and Art Magazine, Scars Publications and Design, 1316 Porterfield Dr., Austin TX 78753. **E-mail:** ccandd96@scars.tv. **Website:** scars.tv/ccd. **Contact:** Janet Kuypers. 99% of our submissions are vias email and we prefer email submissions to snail mail submissions. Our biases are works that relate to issues such as politics, sexism, society, and the like, but are definitely not limited to such. We publish good work that makes you think, that makes you feel like you've lived through a scene instead of merely reading it. If it relates to how the world fits into a person's life (political story, a day in the life, coping with issues people face), it will probably win us over faster. We have received comments from readers and other editors saying that they thought some of our stories really happened. They didn't, but it was nice to know they were so concrete, so believable that people thought they were nonfiction. Do that to our readers. Publishes every other month online and in print (though sometimes it may vary and we will publish monthly); issues sold via Amazon.com throughout the U.S., U.K., and continental Europe (online web page issues are available for free to view any time). Publishes short shorts, essays, and stories, as well as artwork. Also publishes poetry. Always comments on/critiques rejected mss if asked. Has published Patrick Fealey, Linda M. Crate, Kenneth DiMaggio, Linda Webb Aceto, Brian Looney, Joseph Hart, Fritz Hamilton, G.A. Scheinoha, Ken Dean and many more (see the writings section of http://scars.tv directly at http://scars.tv/cgi-bin/framesmain.pl?writers for a listing of writers published through Scars Publications' "cc&d" magazine and "Down in the Dirt" magazine over the years. By submitting writing or artwork to Scars Publications (and cc&d magazine) you are giving us the right, if accepted, to broadcast your work. The rights otherwise always remain with the author.artist. Publishes ms max 1 year after acceptance. Responds in 2 weeks to queries and mss. "Responds much faster to e-mail submissions and queries (since 99% of our submissions are vias email and we prefer email submissions)." Samples are online to look through. Many oast issues are available for sale through Amazon (and older issues through lulu press). Guidelines online.

MAGAZINES NEEDS If you do not have e-mail and want to snail-mail a poetry submission, we do not accept poetry snail-mail submissions longer than 10 lines.

CELLPOEMS

E-mail: submissions@cellpoems.org. **E-mail:** submissions@cellpoems.org. **Website:** cellpoems.org. Saara Raappanna; Stephen Priest. **Contact:** Christopher Shannon, Editor. *Cellpoems* is a poetry journal distributed via text message. In the tradition of great, short poems, we hope to present work that has undergone the duress of revision and come out hard-boiled and striking. Guidelines online.

MAGAZINES NEEDS Submit strange, profound, weird, and memorable language condensed in 140 characters or less (including title and author's first initial + last name; previously unpublished work only, please). 140 characters, including name of poet and title of poem. Spaces are included in the character count. No poetry payment.

THE CHAFFIN JOURNAL

E-mail: nancy.jensen@eku.edu. **Website:** www.english.eku.edu/chaffin_journal. **Contact:** Nancy Jensen, editor. *The Chaffin Journal* is a print journal for literary fiction, poetry, and creative nonfiction, published annually through the English Department at Eastern Kentucky University. "We seek diverse and original poetry, fiction, and creative nonfiction rooted in literary tradition. We value strong voices, freshness of vision, precision in language, and a sense of urgency in the literary fiction, poetry, and creative nonfiction we publish." Online submission period: April 1-July 15. Use the Submittable link on website. No postal mail or e-mailed submissions will be considered. Acquires first rights. Pays in 1 contributor's copy on publication. Publishes 6-12 months after acceptance. Responds in 3-5 months. Sample copy: $6.

MAGAZINES NEEDS Submit up to 5 poems in a single document per reading period. No light verse, children's verse, or greeting card poetry. Pays 1 contributor's copy.

CHANTARELLE'S NOTEBOOK

E-mail: chantarellesnotebook@yahoo.com. **Website:** chantarellesnotebook.com. **Contact:** Kendall A. Bell and Christinia Bell, editors. *Chantarelle's Notebook*, published online, seeks "quality work from seasoned and undiscovered poets. We enjoy poems that speak to us—poems with great sonics and visuals." Acquires one-time rights. Rights revert to poet upon publication. Responds in 1-4 weeks. Never comments on rejected poems. Sample copy online. Guidelines available on website. "Please follow the guidelines—all the information is there!"

MAGAZINES NEEDS Receives about 500 poems/year, accepts about 15%. Submit 3-5 poems at a time. Accepts e-mail submissions (pasted into body of message; "we will not open any attachments—they will be deleted"). Cover letter is required. "Please include a short bio of no more than 75 words, should we decide to accept your work." Reads submissions year round. "The editors will review all submissions and make a decision within 1-4 weeks." Has published poetry by Shaindel Beers, Meggie Royer, Taylor Emily Copeland, Amber Decker, Raina Masters, and Donna Vorreyer. Does not want "infantile rants, juvenile confessionals, greeting card-styled verse, political posturing, or religious outpourings." Considers poetry by children and teens. "There are no age restrictions, but submissions from younger people will be held to the same guidelines and standards as those from adults." Length: "shorter poems have a better chance, but long poems are fine."

THE CHARITON REVIEW

Truman State University Press, 100 E. Normal Ave., Kirksville MO 63501. (660)785-7336. **Fax:** (660)785-4480. **E-mail:** chariton@truman.edu. **Website:** tsup.truman.edu/product/chariton-review/. *The Chariton Review* is an international literary journal publishing the best in short fiction, essays, poetry, and translations in 2 issues each year. Responds in 3 months. Guidelines available on website.

MAGAZINES NEEDS Submit 3-6 poems through online submissions manager. Include all poems in 1 file; start a new page for each poem. English only.

CHAUTAUQUA

Chautauqua Institution and University of North Carolina at Wilmington, Department of Creative Writing, 601 S. College Rd., Wilmington NC 28403. **E-mail:** chautauquajournal@gmail.com. **Website:** ciweb.org. **Contact:** Jill Gerard and Philip Gerard, editors. *Chautauqua*, published annually in June, prints poetry, short fiction, and creative nonfiction. The editors actively solicit writing that expresses the values of Chautauqua Institution broadly construed: a sense of inquiry into questions of personal, social, political, spiritual, and aesthetic importance, regardless of genre. Considers the work of any writer, whether or not affiliated with Chautauqua Institution. Looking for a mastery of craft, attention to vivid and accurate language, a true lyric "ear," an original and compelling vision, and strong narrative instinct. Above all, it values work that is intensely personal, yet somehow implicitly comments on larger public concerns, like work that answers every reader's most urgent question: Why are you telling me this? Reads submissions February 15-April 15 and August 15-November 15. Work published in *Chautauqua* has been included in *The Pushcart Prize* anthology; notable work in Best American Series; notable issues Best American Series. Acquires first rights and one-time nonexclusive rights to reprint accepted work in an anniversary issue. Publishes ms 1 year after acceptance. Responds in 3-6 months. Guidelines online.

MAGAZINES NEEDS "A *Chautauqua* poem is not just a pretty exercise in language. It exhibits the writer's craft and attention to language, employs striking images and metaphors, and engages the mind. It emerges from the poet's deep reading and knowledge of poetic tradition, reacts to that tradition to reveal a definite aesthetic approach, opening insights into the larger world of human concerns. This may include traditional or experimental work, but each poem should be meaningful to a serious reader beyond the writer's private code of expression." Submit up to 3 poems through online submissions manager. Pays 2 contributor's copies.

TIPS "*Chautauqua* has added a new section, which celebrates young writers, ages 12-18. Work should be submitted by a teacher, mentor, or parent. Please confirm on the entry that the piece can be classified as a Young Voices entry. We ask that young writers consider the theme. Essays and stories should remain under 1,500 words. For poetry, please submit no more than 3 poems and/or no more than 6 pages."

CHEST

CHEST Global Headquarters, 2595 Patriot Blvd., Glenview IL 60026. (800)343-2222. **E-mail:** poetrychest@aol.com. **Website:** www.chestjournal.org. **Contact:** Michael Zack, M.D., Poetry Editor. *CHEST*, published monthly, "is the official medical journal of the American College of Chest Physicians, the world's largest medical journal for pulmonologists, sleep, and critical care specialists, with over 30,000 subscribers." Wants "poetry with themes of medical relevance." Retains all rights. Responds in 2 months; always sends prepublication galleys. Subscription: $276. Make checks payable to American College Chest Physicians.

○ *CHEST* is approximately 300 pages, magazine-sized, perfect-bound, with a glossy cover, and includes ads. Press run is 22,000. Number of unique visitors: 400,000 to website.

MAGAZINES NEEDS Only accepts e-mail submissions (as attachment or in body of e-mail); no fax or disk submissions. Brief cover letter preferred. Reads submissions year round. Poems are circulated to an editorial board. Sometimes comments on rejected poems. Never publishes theme issues. Guidelines available in magazine and on website. Submit no more than two poems. Length: up to 350 words.

CHICAGO QUARTERLY REVIEW

E-mail: cqr@icogitate.com. **Website:** www.chicagoquarterlyreview.com. **Contact:** S. Afzal Haider and Elizabeth McKenzie, senior editors. "The *Chicago Quarterly Review* is a nonprofit, independent literary journal publishing the finest short stories, poems, translations, and essays by both emerging and established writers. We hope to stimulate, entertain, and inspire." Acquires one-time rights. Publishes ms 6 months-1 year after acceptance. Responds in 6-8 months to mss. Sometimes comments on rejected mss. Sample copy: $15. Guidelines available online.

○ The *Chicago Quarterly Review* is 6x9; 225 pages; illustrations; photos. Receives 250 unsolicited mss/month. Accepts 10-15 mss/issue; 20-30 mss/year. Agented fiction 5%. **Publishes 8-10 new writers/year.**

MAGAZINES NEEDS Submit 3-5 poems through online submissions manager only. Pays 2 contributor's copies.

TIPS "The writer's voice ought to be clear and unique and should explain something of what it means to be human. We want well-written stories that reflect an appreciation for the rhythm and music of language, work that shows passion and commitment to the art of writing."

CHICAGO REVIEW

Taft House, 935 E. 60th St., Chicago IL 60637. **E-mail:** editors@chicagoreview.org. **Website:** chicagoreview.org. **Contact:** Gerónimo Sarmiento Cruz, managing editor. "Since 1946, *Chicago Review* has published a range of contemporary poetry, fiction, and criticism. Each year typically includes two single issues and a double issue with a special feature section." Guidelines available on website.

MAGAZINES NEEDS Submit via online submission form, Submittable. Include cover letter. Length: no strict length requirements, but the poetry editors prefer to read at least 3 pages of work. Pays contributor's copies.

TIPS "We strongly recommend that authors familiarize themselves with recent issues of *Chicago Review* before submitting. Submissions that demonstrate familiarity with the journal tend to receive more attention than those that appear to be part of a carpet-bombing campaign."

CHICKEN SOUP FOR THE SOUL PUBLISHING, LLC

Chicken Soup for the Soul Publishing, LLC, P.O. Box 700, Cos Cob CT 06807. **E-mail:** webmaster@chickensoupforthesoul.com (for all inquires). **Website:** www.chickensoup.com. Buys one-time rights. Pays on publication. Responds upon consideration. Guidelines available online.

"Stories must be written in the first person."

MAGAZINES NEEDS No controversial poetry.

TIPS "We no longer accept submissions by mail or fax. Stories and poems can only be submitted on our website. Select the 'Submit Your Story' tab on the left toolbar. The submission form can be found there."

CHIRON REVIEW

Chiron, Inc., 522 E. South Ave., St. John KS 67576-2212. **E-mail:** editor@chironreview.com. **Website:** www.chironreview.com. **Contact:** Michael Hathaway, publisher. *Chiron Review*, published quarterly, presents the widest possible range of contemporary creative writing—fiction and nonfiction, traditional and off-beat—in an attractive, perfect-bound digest, including artwork and photographs. No taboos. Acquires first-time rights. Pays on publication. Publishes ms 3-12 months after acceptance. Responds in

2-8 weeks. Subscription: $60, ppd/year (4 issues) and $100 ppd overseas. Single issue: $20 ppd and $34 ppd overseas. Guidelines available for SASE, or on website.

MAGAZINES NEEDS Submit up to 3 poems by mail with SASE, or by e-mail as DOC attachment. Has published poetry by Charles Bukowski, Charles Harper Webb, Edward Field, Wanda Coleman, Thich Nhat Hanh, and Marge Piercy. Pays 1 contributor's copy.

TIPS "Please check our website to see if we are open to submissions. When you do send submissions, please have mercy on the editors and follow the guidelines noted here and on our website."

THE CHRISTIAN CENTURY

104 S. Michigan Ave., Suite 1100, Chicago IL 60603-5901. (312)263-7510. **Fax:** (312)263-7540. **E-mail:** main@christiancentury.org. **E-mail:** submissions@christiancentury.org; poetry@christiancentury.org. **Website:** www.christiancentury.org. **Contact:** Jill Peláez Baumgaertner, poetry editor. "We seek mss that articulate the public meaning of faith, bringing the resources of religious tradition to bear on such topics as poverty, human rights, economic justice, international relations, national priorities, and popular culture. We are also interested in pieces that examine or critique the theology and ethos of individual religious communities. We welcome articles that find fresh meaning in old traditions and that adapt or apply religious traditions to new circumstances. Authors should assume that readers are familiar with main themes in Christian history and theology, are accustomed to the historical-critical study of the Bible and are already engaged in relating faith to social and political issues. Many of our readers are ministers or teachers of religion at the college level. Book reviews are solicited by our books editor. Please note that submissions via e-mail will not be considered. If you are interested in becoming a reviewer for *The Christian Century*, please send your résumé and a list of subjects of interest to "Attn: Book reviews." Authors must have a critical and analytical perspective on the church and be familiar with contemporary theological discussion." Buys all rights. Pays on publication. Responds in 4-6 weeks to queries; in 2 months to mss. Editorial lead time 1 month. Sample copy: $3.50. Guidelines available online.

MAGAZINES NEEDS Wants "poems that are not statements but experiences, that do not talk about the world but show it. We want to publish poems that are grounded in images and that reveal an awareness of the sounds of language and the forms of poetry even when the poems are written in free verse." Submissions without SASE (or SAE and IRCs) will not be returned. Submit poems typed, double-spaced, 1 poem/page. Include name, address, and phone number on each page. Please submit poetry to poetry@christiancentury.org. Has published poetry by Jeanne Murray Walker, Ida Fasel, Kathleen Norris, Luci Shaw, J. Barrie Shepherd, and Wendell Berry. Prefers shorter poems. Inquire about reprint permission. Does not want "pietistic or sentimental doggerel." Length: up to 20 lines/poem. Usually pays $50/poem plus 1 contributor's copy and discount on additional copies. Acquires all rights.

ALSO OFFERS Reviews books of poetry in 300-400 words for single-book format; 400-500 words for multibook format.

TIPS "We suggest reading the poems in the past several issues to gain a clearer idea of the kinds of poetry we are seeking. We publish shorter poems that are grounded in images and that reveal an awareness of the sounds of language and the forms of poetry even when the poems are written in free verse."

⑤ CHRISTIAN COMMUNICATOR

American Christian Writers, 9118 W. Elmwood Dr., Suite 1G, Niles IL 60714-5820. (847)296-3964. **E-mail:** ljohnson@wordprocommunications.com. **E-mail:** submissions@wordprocommunications.com. **Website:** acwriters.com. **Contact:** Lin Johnson, managing editor; Sally Miller, poetry editor (sallymiller@ameritech.net). Buys first rights, buys second serial (reprint) rights. Pays on publication. Publishes ms an average of 6-12 months after acceptance. Responds in 2-8 weeks to queries; in 3-12 weeks to mss. Editorial lead time 3 months. Sample copy online. Writers guidelines by e-mail or on website.

MAGAZINES NEEDS Length: 4-20 lines. Pays $5.

TIPS "Everything, including poetry, must be related to writing, publishing, or speaking. We primarily use how-to articles but are willing to look at other types of manuscripts."

CHRISTIANITY AND LITERATURE

Pepperdine University, Humanities Division, 24255 Pacific Coast Hwy., Malibu CA 90263-7232. **E-mail:** cal@apu.edu. **Website:** christianityandliterature.com/journal. Poetry submissions: Tulane University, Department of English, Norman Mayer 122, New Orleans, LA 70118.. **Contact:** Mark Eaton, editor; Peter Cooley,

poetry editor. "*Christianity & Literature* is devoted to the scholarly exploration of how literature engages Christian thought, experience, and practice. The journal presupposes no particular theological orientation but respects an orthodox understanding of Christianity as a historically defined faith. Contributions appropriate for submission should demonstrate a keen awareness of the author's own critical assumptions in addressing significant issues of literary history, interpretation, and theory." Rights to republish revert to poets upon written request. Time between acceptance and publication is 6-12 months. "Poems are chosen by our poetry editor." Responds within 4 months. Sample copy: $10 (back issue). Subscription: $25 for 1 year; $45 for 2 years. Guidelines available on website.

MAGAZINES NEEDS "The poetry editor looks for poems that are clear and surprising. They should have a compelling sense of voice, formal sophistication (though not necessarily rhyme and meter), and the ability to reveal the spiritual through concrete images." Submit up to 6 poems. Accepts submissions by mail only. Cover letter is required. Submissions must be accompanied by SASE. Pays 1 contributor's copy and 5 offprints of poem.

⑤ CHRISTIAN LIVING IN THE MATURE YEARS

The United Methodist Publishing House, 2222 Rosa L. Parks Blvd., Nashville TN 37228. **E-mail:** matureyears@umpublishing.org. **Website:** matureyears.submittable.com. Purchases non-exclusive and unlimited rights. Pays on acceptance. Publishes ms an average of 1 year after acceptance. Responds in 2-3 months to mss. Guidelines online.

⑤ THE CHRISTIAN SCIENCE MONITOR

210 Massachussetts Ave., Boston MA 02115. **E-mail:** homeforum@csmonitor.com. **Website:** www.csmonitor.com. **Contact:** Editor, The Home Forum. *The Christian Science Monitor Weekly* is the print product of *The Christian Science Monitor,* which also publishes a daily digital product. The Weekly publishes personal nonfiction essays and, occasionally, poetry in its Home Forum section. "We're looking for upbeat essays of 600-800 words and short (20 lines maximum) poems that explore and celebrate daily life." Buys 90 days' exclusive rights, nonexclusive thereafter. Pays on publication. Publishes MSS 1-8 months after acceptance. Responds in 4 weeks to mss; only responds to accepted mss. Editorial lead time 6-8 weeks. Sample

copy available online. Guidelines available online or by e-mail (send e-mail with "Submission" in "Subject" field to receive autoreply with link).

MAGAZINES NEEDS Accepts submissions via email or Word attachment Does not want "work that presents people in helpless or hopeless states; poetry about death, aging, or illness; or dark, violent, sensual poems. No poems that are overtly religious or falsely sweet." Length: up to 20 lines/poem. Pays $25/haiku; $75/poem.

CIDER PRESS REVIEW

P.O. Box 33384, San Diego CA 92163. **Website:** ciderpressreview.com. **Contact:** Caron Andregg, publisher/editor in chief; Ruth Foley, managing editor. *Cider Press Review*, published quarterly online and annually in print, features "the best new work from contemporary poets." It was founded by co-publishers/editors Caron Andregg and Robert Wynne. Since its inception, *CPR* has published thousands of poems by over 500 authors. "Our reading period is from January 1-May 31 each year, and full mss (in conjunction with the *CPR* Annual Book Award) between September 1-November 30 and again between April 1 and June 30 each calendar year." Acquires first North American serial rights. Publishes ms 3-12 months after acceptance. Responds in 1-6 months. Single copy: $14.95; subscription: $24 for 2 issues (1 journal, 1 book from the *Cider Press Review* Book Award). Sample: $12 (journal). Guidelines online.

○ *Cider Press Review* is 128 pages, digest-sized, offset-printed, perfect-bound, with 4-color coated card cover. Receives about 2,500 poems/year, accepts about 3%. Press run for print edition is 500.

MAGAZINES NEEDS Wants "thoughtful, well-crafted poems with vivid language and strong images. We prefer poems that have something to say. We would like to see more well-written humor. We also encourage translations." Does not want "didactic, inspirational, greeting card verse, empty word play, therapy, or religious doggerel." Always sends prepublication galleys. Has published poetry by Robert Arroyo, Jr., Virgil Suárez, Linda Pastan, Kathleen Flenniken, Tim Seibles, Joanne Lowery, Thomas Lux, and Mark Cox. Submit up to 5 poems at a time. Strongly prefers submissions through online submissions manager, but accepts mailed submissions. Cover letter is preferred. Include short bio (25 words maximum). SASE or valid e-mail address required for reply. Poems are circulated to an editorial board. Pays 1 contributor's copy.

ALSO OFFERS Also welcomes reviews under 500 words of current full-length books of poetry.

TIPS Each year, Cider Press publishes an annual journal of poetry and the winning mss from the *Cider Press Review* Book Award and the Editors' Prize for a first or second book. Mss entries must be accompanied by a required entry fee. Prize is $1,000 or $1,500 and publication for a full-length book of poetry and 25 copies.

CIMARRON REVIEW

205 Morrill Hall, English Department, Oklahoma State University, Stillwater OK 74078. **E-mail:** cimarronreview@okstate.edu. **Website:** cimarronreview.okstate.edu. **Contact:** Toni Graham, editor and fiction editor; Lisa Lewis, poetry editor; Sarah Beth Childers, nonfiction editor. "One of the oldest quarterlies in the nation, *Cimarron Review* publishes work by writers at all stages of their careers, including Pulitzer Prize winners, writers appearing in the Best American Series and the Pushcart anthologies, and winners of national book contests. Since 1967, *Cimarron* has showcased poetry, fiction, and nonfiction with a wide-ranging aesthetic. Our editors seek the bold and the ruminative, the sensitive and the shocking, but above all they seek imagination and truth-telling, the finest stories, poems, and essays from working writers across the country and around the world." Buys first North American serial rights. Publishes ms 2-6 months after acceptance. Responds in 3-6 months to mss. Sample copy: $9. Guidelines available on website.

○ *Cimarron Review* is 6.5x8.5; 110 pages. Accepts 3-5 mss/issue; 12-15 mss/year. Publishes 2-4 new writers/year. Eager to receive mss from both established and less experienced writers "who intrigue us with their unusual perspective, language, imagery, and character." Has published work by Molly Giles, Gary Fincke, David Galef, Nona Caspers, Robin Beeman, Edward J. Delaney, William Stafford, John Ashbery, Grace Schulman, Barbara Hamby, Patricia Fargnoli, Phillip Dacey, Holly Prado, and Kim Addonizio.

MAGAZINES NEEDS Submit 3-6 poems at a time with SASE, or submit online through submission manager; include cover letter. No restrictions as to subject matter. Wants "poems whose surfaces and structures risk uncertainty and which display energy, texture, intelligence, and intense investment." Pays 2 contributor's copies.

TIPS "All electronic and postal submissions should include a cover letter. Postal submissions must include a SASE. We do not accept submissions by e-mail. Please follow our guidelines as they appear on our website. In order to get a feel for the kind of work we publish, please read several issues before submitting."

⑤ THE CINCINNATI REVIEW

P.O. Box 210069, Cincinnati OH 45221-0069. **E-mail:** editors@cincinnatireview.com. **Website:** www.cincinnatireview.com. **Contact:** Michael Griffith, fiction editor; Rebecca Lindenberg, poetry editor; Kristen Iversen, literary nonfiction editor; Brant Russell, drama editor. A journal devoted to publishing the best new literary fiction, creative nonfiction, and poetry, as well as a short play, book reviews, essays, and occasional interviews. Buys first North American serial rights, electronic rights. All rights revert to author/poet upon publication. Pays on publication. Publishes ms an average of 6 months after acceptance. Responds in 4-10 months to mss. Always sends prepublication galleys. Sample copy: $7 (back issue). Single copy: $9 (current issue). Subscription: $15. Guidelines available on website.

○ *The Cincinnati Review* is 200-360 pages, digest-sized, perfect-bound, with matte paperback cover with full-color art. Press run is 1,500. Reads submissions September 1-March 1.

MAGAZINES NEEDS Submit up to 5 poems (10 pages maximum) of poetry at a time via submission manager only. Pays $30/page.

✪ THE CLAREMONT REVIEW

1581-H Hillside Ave., Suite 101, Victoria BC V8T 2C1, Canada. **E-mail:** claremontreview@gmail.com. **Website:** www.theclaremontreview.ca. **Contact:** Ali Blythe, Editor-in-chief. The editors of *The Claremont Review* publish the best poetry, short stories, visual art and photography by youth ages 13-19, from anywhere in the English-speaking world. "We publish work in many styles that range from traditional to modern. We prefer edgy pieces that take chances, show your commitment to craft, explore real characters, and reveal authentic emotion. Read the samples in our resources or in past issues for a clearer understanding of what we accept. We strongly encourage readers to subscribe to our magazine, to read, connect with and support youth writing from all over the world." Ac-

quires first publication rights. Pays on publication. Responds in 3-6 months. Guidelines available.

MAGAZINES NEEDS Rarely publishes rhyming poetry. Only accepts submissions from writers ages 13-19. Pays $10.

TIPS "We love: Wild minds like yours..don't be afraid to try something new with form or thinking. Images, metaphor, leaps, research, specificity, images, sensory details, images. Writing that reveals YOUR artistic spirit..are you formal? Tricky? Elusive? Allusive? Quiet? Bold? Clean writing: read your piece word by word, then line by line, and fix spelling or grammatical errors. Entries that meet all our guidelines, read them."

CLOUDBANK

Journal of Contemporary Writing, P.O. Box 610, Corvallis OR 97339. (541)752-0075 or (877)782-6762. **E-mail:** cloudbank@cloudbankbooks.com. **Website:** www.cloudbankbooks.com. **Contact:** Michael Malan, editor. *Cloudbank* publishes poetry, short prose, and book reviews. Acquires one-time rights. Rights revert to writer upon publication. Responds in 4 months. Single copy: $8. Subscription: $15. Make checks payable to *Cloudbank*. Guidelines available in magazine, for SASE, by e-mail, or on website.

○ *Cloudbank* is digest-sized, 96 pages of print, perfect-bound; color artwork on cover, includes ads. Press run is 400. Subscribers: 300; shelf sales: 100 distributed free. Prefers submissions from skilled, experienced poets; will consider work from beginning poets. Reviews books of poetry in 500 words.

MAGAZINES NEEDS Submit up to 5 poems by mail with SASE. Cover letter is preferred. Does not accept fax, e-mail, or disk submissions from U.S.; overseas e-mail submissions accepted. Reads year round. Rarely sends pre-publication galleys. Receives 1,600 poems/year; accepts about 8%. Has published poetry by Dennis Schmitz, Christopher Buckley, Stuart Friebert, Dore Kiesselbach, Karen Holmberg, and Vern Rutsala. Length: up to 150 lines/submission. Pays $200 prize for 1 poem or flash fiction piece per issue.

CONTEST/AWARD OFFERINGS Offers Vern Rutsala Poetry Prize for full-length ms, which awards $1,000 plus publication. Offers *Cloudbank* Contest, which awards $200. **Entry fee:** $15. See website for guidelines.

TIPS "Please consider reading a copy of *Cloudbank* before submitting."

CLOUD RODEO

E-mail: jakesyersak@gmail.com. **E-mail:** submit@cloudrodeo.org. **Website:** cloudrodeo.org. **Contact:** Jake Syersak, editor. "*Cloud Rodeo* is an irregularly published journal of the irregular. So let's get weird." Acquires first electronic publishing rights. Guidelines available online.

MAGAZINES NEEDS Submit up to 5 poems via e-mail as a DOC or PDF attachment.

COAL CITY REVIEW

Coal City Press, English Department, University of Kansas, Lawrence KS 66045. **Website:** coalcitypress.wordpress.com. **Contact:** Brian Daldorph, editor. *Coal City Review*, published annually, usually late in the year, publishes poetry, short stories, reviews: "the best material I can find." Publishes ms 6 months after acceptance. Responds in 3 months. Guidelines on website.

MAGAZINES NEEDS "Check out a copy to see what we like." Pays contributor copies.

COLD MOUNTAIN REVIEW

Department of English, Appalachian State University, ASU Box 32052, Boone NC 28608. (828)262-7687. **E-mail:** coldmountain@appstate.edu. **Website:** www.coldmountainreview.org. **Contact:** Mark Powell, editor; Katherine Abrams, managing editor; Rachel Sasser, assistant editor. *Cold Mountain Review*, published twice/year (in spring and fall), features fiction, nonfiction, poetry, and b&w art. "Themed fall issues rotate with general spring issues, but all work is considered beneath our broad social- and eco-justice umbrella." *Cold Mountain Review* is about 130 pages, digest-sized, perfect-bound, with light cardstock cover. Reading period is August and January. Responds in 1-2 months.

MAGAZINES NEEDS Publishes only 15-20 poems/issue. "We are extremely competitive: Send only your best." Submit up to 5 poems through online submissions manager or by mail. Poems should be single-spaced on one side of the page. When submitting online, submit a Word document rather than a PDF. Pays contributor's copies.

THE COLLAGIST

Dzanc Books, **E-mail:** editor@thecollagist.com; poetry@thecollagist.com; bookreviews@thecollagist.com. **Website:** thecollagist.com. **Contact:** Gabriel Blackwell, editor in chief; Marielle Prince, poetry editor; Michael Jauchen, book review editor. *The Collagist* is a monthly journal published on the 15th of each month, containing short fiction, poetry, essays, book reviews, and one of more excerpts from novels forthcoming from (mostly) independent presses. Guidelines online.

MAGAZINES NEEDS Submit through online submission manager. Check site for reading periods.

🚯 COLORADO REVIEW

Center for Literary Publishing, Colorado State University, 9105 Campus Delivery, Fort Collins CO 80523. (970)491-5449. **E-mail:** creview@colostate.edu. **Website:** coloradoreview.colostate.edu. **Contact:** Stephanie G'Schwind, editor-in-chief and nonfiction editor; Steven Schwartz, fiction editor; Don Revell, Sasha Steensen, and Matthew Cooperman, poetry editors; Harrison Candelaria Fletcher, nonfiction editor; Dan Beachy-Quick, poetry book review editor; Jennifer Wisner Kelly, fiction and nonfiction book review editor. Literary magazine published 3 times/year. Work published in *Colorado Review* has been included in *Best American Essays*, *Best American Short Stories*, *Best American Poetry*, *Best New American Voices*, *Best Travel Writing*, *Best Food Writing*, and the *Pushcart Prize Anthology*. Buys first North American serial rights. Rights revert to author upon publication. Pays on publication. Publishes ms an average of 6 months after acceptance. Responds in 2 months to mss. Editorial lead time 1 year. Sample copy: $10. Guidelines online.

MAGAZINES NEEDS Considers poetry of any style. Poetry mss are read August 1-April 30. Mss received May 1-July 31 will be returned unread. Has published poetry by Sherman Alexie, Laynie Browne, John Gallaher, Mathias Svalina, Craig Morgan Teicher, Pam Rehm, Elizabeth Robinson, Elizabeth Willis, and Rosmarie Waldrop. Pays $30 minimum or $10/page for poetry.

COLUMBIA

A Journal of Literature and Art, Columbia University, New York NY 10027. **E-mail:** info@columbiajournal.org. **Website:** columbiajournal.org. **Contact:** Staff rotates each year. "*Columbia: A Journal of Literature and Art* is an annual publication that features the very best in poetry, fiction, nonfiction, and art. We were founded in 1977 and continue to be one of the few national literary journals entirely edited, designed, and produced by students. You'll find that our minds are open, our interests diverse. We solicit mss from writers we love and select the most exciting finds from our virtual submission box. Above all, our commitment is to our readers—to producing a collection that informs, surprises, challenges, and inspires."

○ Reads submissions March 1-September 15.

MAGAZINES NEEDS Submit poetry via online submissions manager. Include short bio. Length: up to 5 pages.

COMMON GROUND REVIEW

Western New England University, H-5132, Western New England University, 1215 Wilbraham Rd., Springfield MA 01119. **E-mail:** editors@cgreview.org. **Website:** cgreview.org. **Contact:** Janet Bowdan, editor. *Common Ground Review*, published twice yearly (Spring/Summer, Fall/Winter), prints poetry and 1 short nonfiction piece in the Fall issue and 1 short fiction piece in the Spring issue. Holds annual poetry contest. Acquires one-time rights. Publishes ms 4-6 months after acceptance. Tries to respond in 2-3 months to mss. Sample copy: $5 on request. Guidelines and Submittable link online.

MAGAZINES NEEDS Cover letter and biography are required. Submit via mail or online submissions manager. "Poems should be single-spaced indicating stanza breaks; include name, address, phone number, e-mail address, brief bio, and, for postal mail submissions, SASE (submissions without SASE will not be notified)." Reads submissions year round, but deadlines for noncontest submissions are August 31 and March 1. "Editor reads and culls submissions. Final decisions made by editorial board." Seldom comments on rejected poems. Has published poetry by Matthew Spireng, Sean Prentiss, Carol Frith, B.Z. Niditch, Ann Lauinger, Sjohnna McCray, Kathryn Howd Machan, and Karen Skolfield. Does not want "greeting card verse, overly sentimental, unrelievedly gloomy, or stridently political poetry." Length: up to 60 lines/poem. Pays 1 contributor's copy.

ALSO OFFERS Sponsors an annual poetry contest, open January 1-March 15. Offers 1st Prize ($500), 2nd Prize ($200), 3rd Prize ($100), honorable mentions. **Entry fee:** $15 for 1-3 unpublished poems. **Deadline:** March 1 for contest submissions only. All contest submissions are considered for publication in *Common Ground Review*.

TIPS "For poems, use a few good images to ground and convey ideas; take ideas further than the initial thought. Poems should be condensed and concise, free from words that do not contribute. The subject matter should be worthy of the reader's time and should appeal to a wide range of readers. Form should be an extension of content. Sometimes the editors may suggest possible revisions."

COMMON THREADS

Ohio Poetry Association, 12886 Coventry Ave., Pickerington OH 43147. **E-mail:** team@ohiopoetryassn.org. **E-mail:** editor@ohiopoetryassn.org. **Website:** www.ohiopoetryassn.org. Common Threads Editor: Steve Abbott.. **Contact:** Chuck Salmons, OPA president. *Common Threads*, published annually in autumn, is the Ohio Poetry Association's member journal. Submissions limited to OPA members and student and other contest winners. "We accept poems from both beginners and accomplished writers. We like poems to make us think as well as feel. We are uninterested in work that is highly sentimental, overly morbid, religiously coercive, or pornographic. Poetry by students will also be considered and prioritized if student is an OPA high school contest winner." While devoted primarily to members' poetry, *Common Threads* can include book reviews, essays on craft, interviews, and other articles related to poetry as an art. All rights revert to poet upon publication. Single copy: $10 back issues; $12 current issue. Subscription ($20; $15 for seniors 65+) in the form of annual OPA membership dues, which includes annual issue of *Common Threads*. Visit www.ohiopoetryassn.org for membership form and additional information on submissions.

MAGAZINES NEEDS Previously published poems are considered if first publisher is noted on submission. Submit up to 3 poems at a time to editor@ohiopoetryassociation.org (preferred) or as hard copies c/o 91 E. Duncan St., Columbus OH 43202 (with SASE or e-mail address) throughout the year, with August 31 deadline for consideration. Length: up to 50 lines/poem.

COMMONWEAL

Commonweal Foundation, 475 Riverside Dr., Room 405, New York NY 10115. (212)662-4200. **Fax:** (212)662-4183. **E-mail:** editors@commonwealmagazine.org. **Website:** www.commonwealmagazine.org. **Contact:** Paul Baumann, editor; Tiina Aleman, production editor. Buys all rights. Pays on publication. Responds in 2 months to queries. Sample copy free. Guidelines available online.

MAGAZINES NEEDS *Commonweal*, published every 2 weeks, is a Catholic general interest magazine for college-educated readers. Does not publish inspirational poems. Length: no more than 75 lines. Pays 75¢/line plus 2 contributor's copies. Acquires all rights. Returns rights when requested by the author.

TIPS "Articles should be written for a general but well-educated audience. While religious articles are always topical, we are less interested in devotional and churchy pieces than in articles which examine the links between 'worldly' concerns and religious beliefs."

THE COMSTOCK REVIEW

4956 St. John Dr., Syracuse NY 13215. **E-mail:** poetry@comstockreview.org. **Website:** www.comstockreview.org. **Contact:** Betsy Anderson, managing editor. *The Comstock Review* accepts "poetry strictly on the basis of quality, not reputation. We publish both noted and mid-career poets as well as those who are new to publishing. It is the quality of the poem that is the decisive factor. We do not accept overly sexual material, sentimental or 'greeting card' verse, and very few haiku." First North American publication credits. Pays 1 copy except for contest winners. Responds in 2-3 months. Submit 4-5 poems, typed, by mail or on-line January 1-March 31 with SASE for mail. See website for details or Submittable link.

MAGAZINES NEEDS "We look for well-crafted poetry, either free or formal verse, with attention paid to the beauty of language, exceptional metaphor, unique voice, and fresh, vivid imagery. Poems may reflect any subject, although we have a slight bias toward poems dealing with the human condition in all its poignancy and humor." Accepts submissions of 4-5 poems by mail (include SASE) or online submissions manager during the Open Reading Period postmarked from January 1-March 31. Length: up to 38 lines/poem.

CONCEIT MAGAZINE

Perry Terrell Publishing, P.O. Box 884223, San Francisco CA 94188-4223. **E-mail:** conceitmagazine2007@yahoo.com and conceitmagazine@yahoo.com. **Website:** https://sites.google.com/site/conceitmagazine/; http://conceitmagazine.weebly.com. **Contact:** Perry Terrell, editor. crochet "We are a literary sharing organization. Magazine publishes poetry, short stories, articles, cartoons and essays. Very few guidelines—let me see your creative work. We will decide after reading." Acquires one-time rights. Publication is copyrighted. Responds in 3 weeks or less to queries; in 6 months or less to mss. Send either SASE (or IRC) for return of ms or disposable copy of ms and #10 SASE for reply only. Please be patient. Sample copy free with 4 first-class stamps. Guidelines available for SASE, via e-mail, or on website.

MAGAZINES NEEDS Query first or send poems with cover letter. Accepts submissions by e-mail and snail mail. Include estimated word count, brief bio, list of publications. Pays 1 contributor's copy. Additional copies $3.00. Pay via PayPal to conceitmagazine@yahoo.com or checks and money orders payable to: PERRY TERRELL. Also accepts payment through VENMO payable to: perryterrell@perryterrell and CASH APP payable to: $epterrell. Pays writers through contests. Send SASE or check blog on websites for details.

HOW TO CONTACT Contact Perry Terrell - editor.

TIPS "We are a 'literary sharing' organization. Uniqueness and creativity makes a manuscript stand out. Be brave and confident. Let me see what you created. Also, patience is ultimately required."

CONCHO RIVER REVIEW

Angelo State University, ASU Station #10894, San Angelo TX 76909. **E-mail:** ageyer@usca.edu; haleya@acu.edu; jerry.bradley@lamar.edu; roger.jackson@angelo.edu. **Website:** conchoriverreview.org. **Contact:** R. Mark Jackson, general editor and book review editor; Andrew Geyer, fiction editor; Albert Haley, nonfiction editor; Jerry Bradley, poetry editor. "*CRR* aims to provide its readers with escape, insight, laughter, and inspiration for many years to come. We urge authors to submit to the journal and readers to subscribe to our publication." Requests first print and electronic rights. Responds in 1-2 months for poetry and in 2-6 months for fiction and nonfiction. Guidelines online.

MAGAZINES NEEDS Welcomes original poetry submissions from all poets, established or emerging. Submit 3-5 poems at a time. Electronic submissions preferred. See website for appropriate section editor. "Length and form are open, but shorter poems (1 page or less) are preferred."

Ⓢ CONFRONTATION

English Department, LIU Post, Brookville NY 11548. **E-mail:** confrontationmag@gmail.com. **Website:** www.confrontationmagazine.org. **Contact:** Jonna G. Semeiks, editor in chief; Belinda Kremer, poetry editor; Terry Kattleman, publicity director/production editor. "*Confrontation* has been in continuous publication since 1968. Our taste and our magazine is eclectic, but we always look for excellence in style, an important theme, a memorable voice. We enjoy discovering and fostering new talent. Each issue contains work by both well-established and new writers. We read August 16-April 15. Do not send mss or e-mail submissions between April 16 and August 15." Buys first North American serial rights, electronic rights, first rights, one-time rights, all rights. Pays on publication. Publishes work in the first or second issue after acceptance. Responds in 10 weeks to mss. "We prefer single submissions. Clear copy. **No e-mail submissions unless writer resides outside the U.S.** Mail submissions with a SASE."

○ *Confrontation* has garnered a long list of awards and honors, including the Editor's Award for Distinguished Achievement from CLMP (given to Martin Tucker, the founding editor of the magazine) and NEA grants. Work from the magazine has appeared in numerous anthologies, including the *Pushcart Prize*, *Best Short Stories*, and *The O. Henry Prize Stories*. "We also publish the work of 1 visual artist per issue, selected by the editors."

MAGAZINES NEEDS *"Confrontation* is interested in all poetic forms. Our only criterion is high literary merit. We think of our audience as an educated, lay group of intelligent readers." Has published poetry by David Ray, T. Alan Broughton, David Ignatow, Philip Appleman, Jane Mayhall, and Joseph Brodsky. Submit no more than 12 pages at a time (up to 6 poems). *Confrontation* also offers the annual Confrontation Poetry Prize. No sentimental verse. No previously published poems. Length: up to 2 pages. Pays $75-100; more for commissioned work.

CONTEST/AWARD OFFERINGS Offers Confrontation Poetry Prize. See website for details.

TIPS "We look for literary merit. Keep honing your skills, and keep trying."

CONJUNCTIONS

Bard College, 21 E. 10th St., #3E, New York NY 10003. (845)758-7054. **E-mail:** conjunctions@bard.edu. **Website:** www.conjunctions.com. "We provide a forum for writers and artists whose work challenges accepted forms and modes of expression, experiments with language and thought, and is fully realized art." Unsolicited mss cannot be returned unless accompanied by SASE. Electronic and simultaneous submissions will not be considered.

TIPS "Final selection of the material is made based on the literary excellence, originality, and vision of the writing. We have maintained a consistently high editorial and production quality with the intention of attracting a large and varied audience."

THE CONNECTICUT RIVER REVIEW

E-mail: ctriverreview1@gmail.com. **Website:** www. ctpoetry.net. **Contact:** Ginny Connors, editor. *Connecticut River Review*, published annually each summer by the Connecticut Poetry Society, prints original, honest, diverse, vital, well-crafted poetry. Wants any form, any subject. Has published poetry by Marge Piercy, Rhina P. Espaillat, Wally Swist, Charles Rafferty, Maria Mazziotti Gillan, and Vivian Shipley. Accepts submissions from January 1-April 15. Electronic submission only, through Sumittable. *Connecticut River Review* is digest-sized, attractively printed, perfect-bound. Receives about 2,000 submissions/year, accepts about 65. Membership in the Connecticut Poetry Society is $30 per year and includes *Connecticut River Review*. You need not be a CPS member to submit or to enter *CPS* contests. Poet retains copyright. Typical response time 1-3 months. Guidelines available on the Connecticut Poetry Society website and through Submittable.

MAGAZINES NEEDS Submit up to 5 original poems on one document, one poem/page, with name and email on each page. Considers simultaneous submissions if notified of acceptance elsewhere; no previously published poems. Pays 1 contributor's copy.

CONNOTATION PRESS

Website: www.connotationpress.com. **Contact:** Ken Robidoux, publisher. *Connotation Press* accepts submissions in poetry, fiction, creative nonfiction, playwriting, screenplay, interview, book review, music review, etc. "Basically, we're looking at virtually every genre or crossover genre you can create." Acquires first serial rights. Responds in 6 weeks. Guidelines online.

MAGAZINES NEEDS Submit 3-5 poems through online submissions manager.

⊕ CONTEMPORARY HAIBUN

E-mail: boblucky01@yahoo.com; ray@raysweb.net. **Website:** www.contemporaryhaibunonline.com; www.redmoonpress.com. **Contact:** Bob Lucky, editor/publisher; Ray Rasmussen, technical editor. *Contemporary Haibun Online* is a quarterly journal published in January, April, July, and October. It publishes haibun and tanka prose only. Acquires first rights. Time between acceptance and publication varies according to time of submission. Sample available for SASE or by e-mail. Subscription: $17 plus $5 p&h.

○ Receives several hundred submissions/year, accepts about 5%. Print run is 1,000. Has published poetry by J. Zimmerman, Chen-ou Liu, Renée Owen, and Matthew Caretti.

MAGAZINES NEEDS Submit up to 3 poems at a time. Accepts e-mail submissions.

CONTEMPORARY VERSE 2

Contemporary Verse 2, Inc., 502-100 Arthur St., Winnipeg MB R3B 1H3, Canada. (204)949-1365. **Fax:** (204)942-5754. **E-mail:** submissions@contemporaryverse2.ca. **Website:** www.contemporaryverse2.ca. *CV2* publishes poetry of demonstrable quality as well as critical writing in the form of interviews, essays, articles, and reviews. With the critical writing we tend to create a discussion of poetry which will interest a broad range of readers, including those who might be skeptical about the value of poetry. Reading period: September 1-May 31. Buys first North American serial rights, buys second serial (reprint) rights. Pays on publication. Responds in 2-3 weeks to queries; 3-8 months to mss. Editorial lead time 3-6 months. Guidelines online.

MAGAZINES NEEDS No rhyming verse, traditionally inspirational. Pays $20/poem.

CONTRARY

E-mail: chicago@contrarymagazine.com. **Website:** www.contrarymagazine.com. **Contact:** Jeff McMahon, editor; Frances Badgett, fiction editor; Shaindel Beers, poetry editor. *Contrary* publishes fiction, poetry, and literary commentary, and prefers work that combines the virtues of all those categories. Founded at the University of Chicago, it now operates independently and not-for-profit on the South Side of Chicago. Quarterly. Member CLMP. "We like work that is not only contrary in content but contrary in its evasion of the expectations established by its genre. Our fiction defies traditional story form. For example, a story may bring us to closure without ever delivering an ending. We don't insist on the ending, but we do insist on the closure. And we value fiction as poetic as any poem." Acquires first rights and perpetual archive and anthology rights. Publication is copyrighted. Pays on publication and receipt of invoice. Publishes ms 90 days after acceptance. Responds in 2 weeks to queries; 3 months to mss. Rarely comments on/critiques

rejected mss. Editorial lead time 3 months. Guidelines available online.

MAGAZINES NEEDS Accepts submissions through website only. Include estimated word count, brief bio, list of publications. Often comments on rejected poems. Pays $20 per byline, $60 for featured work.

TIPS "Beautiful writing catches our eye first. If we realize we're in the presence of unanticipated meaning, that's what clinches the deal. Also, we're not fond of expository fiction. We prefer to be seduced by beauty, profundity, and mystery than to be presented with the obvious. We look for fiction that entrances, that stays the reader's finger above the mouse button. That is, in part, why we favor microfiction, flash fiction, and short shorts. Also, we hope writers will remember that most editors are looking for very particular species of work. We try to describe our particular species in our mission statement and our submission guidelines, but those descriptions don't always convey nuance. That's why many editors urge writers to read the publication itself, in the hope that they will intuit an understanding of its particularities. If you happen to write that particular species of work we favor, your submission may find a happy home with us. If you don't, it does not necessarily reflect on your quality or your ability. It usually just means that your work has a happier home somewhere else."

THE COPPERFIELD REVIEW

E-mail: copperfieldreview@gmail.com. **Website:** www.copperfieldreview.com. **Contact:** Meredith Allard, executive editor. "We are an online literary journal that publishes historical fiction, reviews, and interviews related to historical fiction. We believe that by understanding the lessons of the past through historical fiction, we can gain better insight into the nature of our society today, as well as a better understanding of ourselves." Acquires one-time rights. Accepts one submission per author per month. Responds to mss 12-16 weeks after submission, sometimes sooner. Never comments on rejected mss. Sample copy online. Guidelines available online only.

○ "Remember that we are a journal for readers and writers of historical fiction. We only consider submissions that are historical in nature."

MAGAZINES NEEDS Accepts submissions pasted into an e-mail only. Anything not related to historical fiction. Pays $15.

ADDITIONAL INFORMATION Poetry submissions must be historical in nature.

TIPS "We wish to showcase the very best in historical fiction. Stories that use historical periods to illuminate universal truths will immediately stand out. We are thrilled to receive thoughtful work that is polished, poised, and written from the heart. Be professional, and only submit your very best work. Be certain to adhere to a publication's submission guidelines, and always treat your e-mail submissions with the same care you would use with a traditional publisher."

⑤ COPPER NICKEL

English Department, Campus Box 175, CU Denver, P.O. Box 173364, Denver CO 80217. (303)315-7358. **E-mail:** wayne.miller@ucdenver.edu. **Website:** copper-nickel.org. **Contact:** Wayne Miller, editor/managing editor; Brian Barker and Nicky Beer, poetry editors; Joanna Luloff, fiction and nonfiction editor; Teague Bohlen, fiction editor. *Copper Nickel*—the national literary journal housed at the University of Colorado Denver—was founded by poet Jake Adam York in 2002. Work published in *Copper Nickel* has appeared in *Best American Poetry*, *Best American Short Stories*, and *Pushcart Prize* anthologies. Contributors to *Copper Nickel* have received numerous honors for their work, including the National Book Critics Circle Award; the Kingsley Tufts Poetry Award; the American, California, Colorado, Minnesota, and Washington State Book Awards; the Georg Büchner Prize; the T.S. Eliot and Forward Poetry Prizes; the Anisfield-Wolf Book Award; the Whiting Writers Award; the Alice Fay Di Castagnola Award; the Lambda Literary Award; and fellowships from the National Endowment for the Arts; the MacArthur, Guggenheim, Ingram Merrill, Witter Bynner, Soros, Rona Jaffe, Bush, and Jerome Foundations; the Bunting Institute; Cave Canem; and the American Academy in Rome. Submission period: September 1 to December 15; January 15 to March 1. First North American Serial Rights, which revert back to the author upon publication. Pays on publication. Publishes ms 6 months-1 year. Tries to respond in 2 months. Guidelines online.

MAGAZINES NEEDS Submit 4-6 poems through submittable. Pays $30/printed page, 2 contributor's copies, and a one-year subscription.

CRAB CREEK REVIEW

7315 34th Ave. NW, Seattle WA 98117. **E-mail:** crabcreekreview@gmail.com. **Website:** www.crabcreekreview.org. **Contact:** Jenifer Lawrence, editor-in-chief; Laura Read, poetry editor. *Crab Creek Review* is a 100-page, perfect-bound paperback. "We are a literary journal based in the Pacific Northwest that is looking for poems, stories, and essays that pay attention to craft. We appreciate risk-taking, wild originality, and consummate craftsmanship. We publish established and emerging writers." Nominates for the Pushcart Prize. Annual *Crab Creek Review* poetry prize: $500. Buys first North American rights. Pays in contributor copies only. Publishes ms 6 months or less after acceptance. Responds in 2-4 months to mss. Sample copy: $6. Subscription: $15/year, $28/2 year. Accepts submissions via Submittable only. Guidelines online.

MAGAZINES NEEDS Submit via online submission form. Has published poetry by Diane Seuss, Oliver de la Paz, Dorianne Laux, Denise Duhamel, and translations by Ilya Kaminsky and Matthew Zapruder. Length: no limit. Pays 1 contributor's copy.

CONTEST/AWARD OFFERINGS Crab Creek Review Poetry Prize

⑤ CRAB ORCHARD REVIEW

Southern Illinois University Carbondale, Department of English, Faner Hall 2380, Mail Code 4503, 1000 Faner Dr., Carbondale IL 62901. (618)453-6833. **Fax:** (618)453-8224. **E-mail:** jtribble@siu.edu. **Website:** www.craborchardreview.siu.edu. **Contact:** Allison Joseph, editor-in-chief and poetry editor; Carolyn Alessio, prose editor; Jon Tribble, managing editor. "We are a general-interest literary journal published twice/year. We strive to be a journal that writers admire and readers enjoy. We publish fiction, poetry, creative nonfiction, fiction translations, interviews, and reviews." Buys first North American serial rights. Publishes ms an average of 9-12 months after acceptance. Responds in 3 weeks to queries; 9 months to mss. Sample copy online. Guidelines online.

MAGAZINES NEEDS Wants all styles and forms from traditional to experimental. Does not want greeting card verse; literary poetry only. Has published poetry by Luisa A. Igloria, Erinn Batykefer, Jim Daniels, and Bryan Tso Jones. Submit through online submissions manager. Cover letter is preferred. "Indicate stanza breaks on poems of more than 1 page. Poems under serious consideration are discussed and decided on by the managing editor and poetry editor." Pays $25/published magazine page ($100 minimum), 2 contributor's copies, and one-year subscription.

CRAZYHORSE

College of Charleston, Department of English, 66 George St., Charleston SC 29424. (843)953-4470. **E-mail:** crazyhorse@cofc.edu. **Website:** crazyhorse.cofc.

edu. **Contact:** Jonathan Bohr Heinen, managing editor; Emily Rosko, poetry editor; Anthony Varallo, fiction editor; Bret Lott, nonfiction editor. "We like to print a mix of writing regardless of its form, genre, school, or politics. We're especially on the lookout for original writing that doesn't fit the categories and that engages in the work of honest communication." Buys first North American serial rights. Publishes ms an average of 6-12 months after acceptance. Responds in 1 week to queries; 3-4 months to mss. Sample copy: $5. Guidelines online.

○ Reads submissions September 1-May 31.

MAGAZINES NEEDS "*Crazyhorse* aims to publish work that reflects the multiple poetries of the 21st century. While our taste represents a wide range of aesthetics, from poets at all stages of their writing careers, we read with a discerning eye for poems that demonstrate a rhetorical and formal intelligence—that is, poems that know why they are written in the manner that they are. We seek poems that exhibit how content works symbiotically with form, evidenced in an intentional art of the poetic line or in poems that employ or stretch lyric modes. Along with this, poems that capture our attention enact the lyric utterance through musical textures, tone of voice, vivid language, reticence, and skillful syntax. For us, overall, the best poems do not idly tell the reader how to feel or think, they engender feeling and thought in the reader. " Submit 3-5 poems at a time through online submissions manager. Pays $20/page ($200 maximum) and 2 contributor's copies.

TIPS "Write to explore subjects you care about. The subject should be one in which something is at stake. Before sending, ask, 'What's reckoned with that's important for other people to read?'"

CREAM CITY REVIEW

University of Wisconsin-Milwaukee, Department of English, P.O. Box 413, Milwaukee WI 53201. **E-mail:** info@creamcityreview.org. **Website:** uwm.edu/creamcityreview. **Contact:** Caleb Nelson, editor-in-chief; Su Cho, managing editor. *Cream City Review* publishes "memorable and energetic fiction, poetry, and creative nonfiction. Features reviews of contemporary literature and criticism as well as author interviews and artwork. We are particularly interested in camera-ready art depicting themes appropriate to each issue." Responds in 8 months to mss. Sample back issue: $7. Guidelines online.

○ Reading periods: August 1-November 1 for fall/winter issue; January 1-April 1 for spring/summer issue.

MAGAZINES NEEDS "We have a wide range of aesthetic tastes, so we highly recommend you read our recent issues to get a sense of what kind of work we are interested in." Submit up to 5 poems via online submissions manager. Pays one-year subscription beginning with the issue in which the author's work appears.

CREATIVE WITH WORDS PUBLICATIONS

P.O. Box 223226, Carmel CA 93922. **E-mail:** geltrich@mbay.net. **Website:** creativewithwords.tripod.com. **Contact:** Brigitta Gisella Geltrich-Ludgate, publisher and editor. *Creative with Words* publishes "poetry, prose, illustrations, photos by all ages." Publishes ms 1-2 months after acceptance. Responds in 2-4 weeks. Guideline online.

MAGAZINES NEEDS Submit up to 5 poems by mail or e-mail. Always include SASE and legitimate address with postal submissions. Cover letter preferred. Length: up to 20 lines/poem.

TIPS "We offer a great variety of themes. We look for clean family-type fiction and poetry. Also, we ask the writer to look at the world from a different perspective, research the topic thoroughly, be creative, apply brevity, tell the story from a character's viewpoint, tighten dialogue, be less descriptive, proofread before submitting, and be patient. We will not publish every ms we receive. It has to be in standard English, well written, and proofread. We do not appreciate receiving mss where we have to do the proofreading and correct the grammar."

CRICKET MEDIA, INC.

f/k/a Carus Publishing, Cricket Media Services, 70 East Lake St., Suite 800, Chicago IL 60601. **Website:** www.cricketmedia.com. Cricket Media® is a global education company creating high-quality print and multi-media products for children, families, mentors, teachers, and partners that improve learning opportunities for everyone. Led by our 10 award-winning children's magazines and our customizable research-tested collaborative learning platform, we are committed to creating and supporting innovative learning experiences that help children safely explore and engage with their expanding world.

CRUCIBLE

Barton College, P.O. Box 5000, Wilson NC 27893. **E-mail:** crucible@barton.edu. **Website:** www.barton.edu/crucible. *Crucible*, published annually in the fall, publishes poetry and fiction as part of its Poetry and Fiction Contest run each year. Deadline for submissions is May 1. Acquires first rights. Notifies winners by October each year. Sample: $8. Guidelines online.

○   *Crucible* is under 100 pages, digest-sized, professionally printed on high-quality paper, with matte card cover. Press run is 500.

MAGAZINES NEEDS Submit "poetry that demonstrates originality and integrity of craftsmanship as well as thought. Traditional metrical and rhyming poems are difficult to bring off in modern poetry. The best poetry is written out of deeply felt experience which has been crafted into pleasing form." Wants "free verse with attention paid particularly to image, line, stanza, and voice." Does not want "very long narratives, poetry that is forced." Has published poetry by Robert Grey, R.T. Smith, and Anthony S. Abbott. Submit up to 5 poems by e-mail. Do not include name on poems. Include separate bio. Pays $150 for first prize, $100 for second prize, contributor's copies.

CUMBERLAND RIVER REVIEW

Trevecca Nazarene University, Department of English, 333 Murfreesboro Rd., Nashville TN 37210. E-mail: crr@trevecca.edu. **Website:** crr.trevecca.edu. **Contact:** Graham Hillard, editor; Torri Frye, managing editor. *The Cumberland River Review* is a quarterly online publication of new poetry, fiction, essays, and art. The journal is produced by the department of English at Trevecca Nazarene University and welcomes submissions from both national and international writers and artists. Reading period: September through April. Acquires first North American serial rights. Responds in 3 months. Guidelines online.

MAGAZINES NEEDS Submit 3-5 poems in a single document through online submissions manager or mail (include SASE).

CURA

E-mail: curamag@fordham.edu. **Website:** www.curamag.com. **Contact:** Sarah Gambito, editor. *CURA: A Literary Magazine of Art and Action* is a multimedia initiative based at Fordham University committed to integrating the arts and social justice. Featuring creative writing, visual art, new media, and video in response to current news, we seek to enable an artistic process that is rigorously engaged with the world at the present moment. *CURA* is taken from the Ignatian educational principle of "cura personalis," care for the whole person. On its own, the word *cura* is defined as guardianship, solicitude, and significantly, written work. Acquires first rights. Publishes ms 5 months

after acceptance. Editorial lead time is 5 months. Sample copy online. Guidelines online.

○   Reading period: October 15-March 15.

MAGAZINES NEEDS Submit up to 6 poems through online submissions manager. Pays 1 contributor's copy.

CURRENT ACCOUNTS

Current Accounts, Apt. 2D, Bradshaw Hall, Hardcastle Gardens, Bolton BL2 4NZ, United Kingdom. **E-mail:** fjameshartnell@aol.com. **Website:** www.bankstreet-writers.uk. **Contact:** James Hartnell, editor. *Current Accounts*, an online publication, prints poetry, drama, fiction, and nonfiction by members of Bank Street Writers, and other contributors. E-mail submissions please. Receives about 200 poems and stories/plays per year; accepts about 5%. Acquires first rights. Uploads ms 3-6 months after acceptance. Responds ASAP. Guidelines available by e-mail or online.

MAGAZINES NEEDS Open to all types of poetry. No requirements, although some space is reserved for members. Considers poetry by children and teens. Has published poetry by Pat Winslow, M.R. Peacocke, and Gerald England. E-mail submissions only. Doesn't mind rhyming poetry. Travel or tourist poetry needs to be more than just exotic names and places. Titles need care. Poetry should be poetic in some form. Experimental work is welcome. Length: up to 40 lines/poem. Pays 1 contributor's copy.

TIPS Bank Street Writers meets once/month and offers workshops, guest speakers, and other activities. E-mail for details. "We like originality of ideas, images, and use of language. No inspirational or religious verse unless it's also good in poetic terms."

CUTTHROAT

A Journal of the Arts, P.O. Box 2414, Durango CO 81302. (970)903-7914. **E-mail:** cutthroatmag@gmail.com. **Website:** www.cutthroatmag.com. **Contact:** Pamela Uschuk, editor in chief; Beth Alvarado, fiction editor; William Luvaas, online fiction editor; William Pitt Root, poetry editor. "We publish only high-quality fiction, creative nonfiction, and poetry. We are looking for the cutting edge, the endangered word, fiction with wit, heart, soul, and meaning." *CUTTHROAT* is a literary magazine/journal and "one separate online edition of poetry, translations, short fiction, essays, and book reviews yearly." Acquires first North American serial rights. Sends galleys to author. Publication is copyrighted. Responds in 1-2 weeks to queries; in 6-8 months to mss. Sometimes comments on/critiques rejected mss. Sample copy: $10. Guidelines available for SASE or on website.

○ Member CLMP.

MAGAZINES NEEDS Submit 3-5 poems through online submissions manager (preferred) or mail (include SASE). Reading periods for online editions are March 15-June 1; for print editions, July 15-October 10. Has published Joy Harjo, Linda Hogan, Patricia Smith, Wendell Berry, Naomi Shihab Nye, Marvin Bell, Richard Jackson, Sean Thomas Dougherty, Doug Anderson, Dan Vera, Martin Espada, TR Hummer, Daniel Nathan Terry, and many more. Pays contributor's copies.

TIPS "Read our magazine, and see what types of work we've published. The piece must have heart and soul, excellence in craft. "

○ THE DALHOUSIE REVIEW

Dalhousie University, 6420 Coburg Road, Halifax NS B3H 4R2, Canada. **E-mail:** dalhousie.review@dal.ca. **Website:** dalhousiereview.dal.ca. **Contact:** Lynne Evans, production manager. *Dalhousie Review*, published 3 times/year, is a journal of criticism publishing poetry and fiction. Considers works from both new and established writers. Responds in 3-9 months. Subscription: $30 U.S. for 1 year.

○ *Dalhousie Review* is 144 pages, digest-sized. Press run is 500.

MAGAZINES NEEDS Submit up to 5 poems by e-mail. Include cover letter. Length: up to 6 pages total. Pays 2 contributor's copies.

DARKLING MAGAZINE

Darkling Publications, 28780 318th Ave., Colome SD 57528. **E-mail:** darkling@mitchelltelecom.net; jvanoort@darklingpublications.com. **Website:** darklingpublications.com. **Contact:** James C. Van Oort, editor in chief. *Darkling Magazine*, published annually in late summer, is "primarily interested in poetry. All submissions should be dark in nature and should help expose the darker side of man. Dark nature does not mean whiny or overly murderous, and being depressed does not make an artist's work dark." Has published poems by Robert Cooperman, Kenneth DiMaggio, Arthur Gottlieb, Simon Perchik, Cathy Porter, and Susanna Rich, among others.

○ Reading period: October 1-May 15.

MAGAZINES NEEDS Submit by postal mail (with SASE) or e-mail (pasted into the body of message or as attachment). "Profanity should be used with extreme caution, and should be inherently necessary to the piece in order to be considered. Pornography of any sort will not be considered and will merit no response whatsoever." Length: any length is acceptable, but epic-length poetry must be of exceptional quality and content to be considered.

TIPS "Darkling Publications considers serious work from serious artists, and publishes only the best of the best alongside work from artists we feel show great promise but are early in their writing careers. Please submit only what you feel is your best work; darkness has many veins, sinews, and bloodlines, so show us the best of your dark art."

THE DEAD MULE SCHOOL OF SOUTHERN LITERATURE

E-mail: deadmule@gmail.com. **Website:** www.deadmule.com. Technical and Design: Robert MacEwan.. **Contact:** Valerie MacEwan, publisher and editor. "No good southern fiction is complete without a dead mule." *The Dead Mule* is one of the oldest, if not *the* oldest, continuously published online literary journals alive today. Publisher and editor Valerie MacEwan welcomes submissions. *The Dead Mule School of Southern Literature* wants flash fiction, visual poetry, essays, and creative nonfiction. Twenty-three Years Online, 1996-2019, Celebrate With a Dead Mule. 2019 means 23 years online that's a century in cyber-time. "*The Dead Mule School of Southern Literature* Institutional Alumni Association recruits year round. We love reading what you wrote." Acquires first electronic rights and indefinite archival rights. All other rights revert to author upon publication. Publishes ms less than 9 months after acceptance. Responds in 6 weeks. "Submissions handled through the website, not via e-mail. We use Submittable. Go to deadmule.com/submissions for the link. Please do not query the editor directly." deadmule.submittable.com for submission direct link.

MAGAZINES NEEDS Check the *Mule* for poetry samples. No limits. We have a poetry contest each year with a prize. Check the site for dates.

TIPS "Read the site to get a feel for what we're looking to publish. Read the guidelines. We look forward to hearing from you. We are nothing if not for our writers. *The Dead Mule* strives to deliver quality writing in every issue. It is in this way that we pay tribute to our authors. Send us something original."

⑤ DECEMBER

A Literary Legacy Since 1958, December Publishing, P.O. Box 16130, St. Louis MO 63105-0830. (314)301-9980. **E-mail:** editor@decembermag.org. **Website:** decembermag.org. **Contact:** Gianna Jacobson, editor; Jennifer Goldring, managing editor. Committed to distributing the work of emerging writers and artists, and celebrating more seasoned voices through a semi-annual nonprofit literary magazine featuring fiction, poetry, creative nonfiction, and visual art. Buys first North American serial rights. Pays on publication. Responds in 2 months to mss. Editorial lead time 5 months. Sample copy: $12. Guidelines online.

MAGAZINES NEEDS No length requirements. Pays $10/page (minimum $40; maximum $200).

CONTEST/AWARD OFFERINGS Holds annual poetry contest. See website for details.

⑤ DELAWARE BEACH LIFE

Endeavours LLC, P.O. Box 417, Rehoboth Beach DE 19971. (302)227-9499. **E-mail:** info@delaware-beachlife.com. **Website:** www.delawarebeachlife.com. **Contact:** Terry Plowman, publisher/editor. "*Delaware Beach Life* focuses on coastal Delaware: Fenwick to Lewes. You can go slightly inland as long as there's water and a natural connection to the coast, e.g., Angola or Long Neck." Buys first North American serial rights. Pays on acceptance. Publishes ms 4 months after acceptance. Responds in 2 months to queries; in 6 months to mss. Editorial lead time 6 months. Sample copy available online at website. Guidelines free and by e-mail.

> "*Delaware Beach Life* is the only full-color glossy magazine focused on coastal Delaware's culture and lifestyle. Created by a team of the best freelance writers, the magazine takes a deeper look at the wealth of topics that interest coastal residents. *Delaware Beach Life* features such top-notch writing and photography that it inspires 95% of its readers to save it as a 'coffee-table' magazine."

MAGAZINES NEEDS Does not want anything not coastal. No erotic poetry. Length: 6-15 lines/poem. Pays up to $50.

⑤ THE DERONDA REVIEW

P.O. Box 6709, Efrat , Israel. **E-mail:** derondareview@gmail.com; maber4kids@yahoo.com. **Website:** www.derondareview.org; www.pointandcircumference.com. **Contact:** Esther Cameron, editor-in-chief; Mindy Aber Barad, co-editor. Annual literary journal publishing poetry of formal integrity, beauty, and dignity. Short prose (up to 500 words) is also considered. Acquires first rights. Publishes ms 1 year after

acceptance. Responds in 4 months; "if longer, please query by e-mail." "Please read an online issue before submitting."

> Now mainly a digital publication, with print copies available for libraries and subscribers.

MAGAZINES NEEDS Cover letter is unnecessary. E-mail submissions preferred. "If submitting by mail, include SASE with sufficient postage to return all mss or clearly indicate 'Reply Only' on submission. Poets whose work is accepted will be asked for URLs and titles of books available to be published in the online Contributors Exchange." Please mark simultaneous submissions as such. Does not want vulgarity, bad language, or sensationalism.

DESCANT

Fort Worth's Journal of Poetry and Fiction, TCU Department of English, Box 297270, Ft. Worth TX 76129. **E-mail:** descant@tcu.edu. **Website:** www.descant.tcu.edu. **Contact:** Matthew Pitt, editor in chief and fiction editor; Alex Lemon, poetry editor. "*descant* seeks high-quality poems and stories in both traditional and innovative form." Acquires one-time rights. Pays on publication. Responds in 4-6 months to mss. Sample copy: $15. Guidelines online.

> Member CLMP. Magazine: 6x9; 120-150 pages; acid-free paper; paper cover. Reading period: September 1-April 1. Offers 4 annual cash awards for work already accepted for publication in the journal: The $500 Frank O'Connor Award for the best story in an issue, the $250 Gary Wilson Award for an outstanding story in an issue, the $500 Betsy Colquitt Award for the best poem in an issue, and the $250 Baskerville Publishers Award for outstanding poem in an issue. Several stories first published by *descant* have appeared in *Best American Short Stories*.

MAGAZINES NEEDS Submit up to 5 poems through online submissions manager or mail. Length: up to 60 lines/poem. Pays 2 contributor's copies; additional copies $6.

TIPS "We look for character and quality of prose. Send your best short work."

DEVIL'S LAKE

600 N. Park St., Suite 6195, Madison WI 53706. **E-mail:** devilslake.editor@gmail.com. **Website:** english.wisc.edu/devilslake. Responds in 5 months. Guidelines online.

MAGAZINES NEEDS Submit 3-5 poems in a single document.

💲 DEVOZINE

1908 Grand Ave., P.O. Box 340004, Nashville TN 37203-0004. **E-mail:** devozine@upperroom.org. **Website:** www.devozine.org. **Contact:** Sandy Miller, editor. *devozine,* published bimonthly, is a 64-page devotional magazine for youth (ages 14-19) and adults who care about youth. Offers meditations, scripture, prayers, poems, stories, songs, and feature articles to "aid youth in their prayer life, introduce them to spiritual disciplines, help them shape their concept of God, and encourage them in the life of discipleship."

MAGAZINES NEEDS Considers poetry by teens. Submit by postal mail with SASE, or by e-mail. Include name, age/birth date (if younger than 25), mailing address, e-mail address, phone number, and fax number (if available). Always publishes theme issues (available for SASE or online). Indicate theme you are writing for. Length: 10-20 lines/poem. Pays $25.

DIAGRAM

Department of English, University of Arizona, P.O. Box 210067, ML 445, Tucson AZ 85721-0067. **E-mail:** editor@thediagram.com. **Website:** www.thediagram.com. **Contact:** Ander Monson, editor; T. Fleischmann and Nicole Walker, nonfiction editors; Sarah Blackman and Thomas Mira y Lopez, fiction editors; Heidi Gotz, Rafael Gonzalez, and Katie Jean Shinkle, poetry editors. "*DIAGRAM* is an electronic journal of text and art, found and created. We're interested in representations, naming, indicating, schematics, labeling and taxonomy of things; in poems that masquerade as stories; in stories that disguise themselves as indices or obituaries. We specialize in work that pushes the boundaries of traditional genre or work that is in some way schematic. We do publish traditional fiction and poetry, too, but hybrid forms (short stories, prose poems, indexes, tables of contents, etc.) are particularly welcome! We also publish diagrams and schematics (original and found)." Publishes 15 new writers/year. Bimonthly. Member CLMP. "We cosponsor a yearly chapbook contest for prose, poetry, or hybrid work with New Michigan Press with a Spring deadline. Guidelines on website." Buys first North American serial rights & electronic rights. Publishes ms 6-9 months after acceptance. Responds in 2 weeks to queries; in 2 months to mss. Sometimes comments on rejected mss. Sample copy: $12. Writer's guidelines online. Submit most work via submissions manager.

MAGAZINES NEEDS Submit 3-6 poems. Electronic submissions accepted through submissions manager only; or send print. Electronic submissions much preferred; print submissions must include SASE if response is expected. Cover letter is preferred. Reads submissions year round. Poems are circulated to an editorial board. Sometimes comments on rejected poems. Sometimes publishes theme issues. Receives about 4,000 poems/year, accepts about 5%. Does not want light verse. No length limit.

ADDITIONAL INFORMATION *DIAGRAM* also publishes periodic, perfect-bound print anthologies.

TIPS "Submit interesting text, images, sound, and new media. We value the insides of things, vivisection, urgency, risk, elegance, flamboyance, work that moves us, language that does something new, or does something old—well. We like iteration and reiteration. Ruins and ghosts. Mechanical, moving parts, balloons, and frenzy. We want art and writing that demonstrates interaction; the processes of things; how functions are accomplished; how things become or expire, move or stand. We'll consider anything."

💿 DIODE POETRY JOURNAL

E-mail: submit@diodepoetry.com. **Website:** www.diodepoetry.com. **Contact:** Patty Paine, editor. "We welcome all types of poetry (including, but not limited to, narrative experimental, visual, found and erasure poetry). We also accept poetry in translation, and collaborative poems. We accept submissions of book reviews, interviews, and essays on poetics. Submissions are accepted year-round, and we do not charge a reading fee. We publish three times a year, and we respond to submissions in 30 days, and often within 5 days. We do not accept work that has been previously published, in print or online. We accept simultaneous submissions, but please let us know immediately if your work is accepted elsewhere. Please submit 3–5 poems with a cover letter and contributor's bio. There are no length restrictions for submissions of reviews, interviews, or essays. Please submit a cover letter and bio, and send the review, interview or essay as a Word document." Acquires one-time rights. Rights revert to poet upon publication. Time between acceptance and publication varies. Responds in 1-2 months. Always sends prepublication galleys. Guidelines available on website.

Does not want "light verse, erotic." Receives about 12,000 poems/year; accepts about 2%.

MAGAZINES NEEDS Submit 3-5 poems at a time. Accepts submissions by e-mail. Cover letter is required. Reads submissions year round. Sometimes comments on rejected poems. Has published poetry by Bob Hicok, Beckian Fritz Golberg, G.C. Waldrep, sam sax, Kaveh Akbar, Dorianne Laux, David Wojahn, Tarfia Faizullah, and Rae Armantrout.

DMQ REVIEW

E-mail: editors@dmqreview.com. **Website:** www.dmqreview.com. **Contact:** Sally Ashton, editor in chief. *DMQ Review* seeks work that represents the diversity of contemporary poetry and demonstrates literary excellence, whether it be lyric, free verse, prose, or experimental form. Buys first North American serial rights. Publishes ms 1-3 months after acceptance. Responds in 3 months. Guidelines online.

MAGAZINES NEEDS Submit up to 5 poems via online submissions manager. Has published poetry by David Lehman, Ellen Bass, Amy Gerstler, Bob Hicok, Ilya Kaminsky, and Jane Hirshfield. Receives about 3,000-5,000 poems/year, accepts about 1%.

ALSO OFFERS Nominates for the Pushcart Prize. Also considers submissions of visual art, which is published with the poems in the magazine with links to the artists' websites.

TIPS "Check our current and past issues, and read and follow submission guidelines closely."

THE DOS PASSOS REVIEW

Briery Creek Press, Longwood University, Department of English and Modern Languages, 201 High St., Farmville VA 23909. **E-mail:** brierycreek@gmail.com. **E-mail:** dospassosreview@gmail.com. **Website:** brierycreekpress.wordpress.com/the-dos-passos-review. **Contact:** Managing Editor. "We are looking for writing that demonstrates characteristics found in the work of John Dos Passos, such as an intense and original exploration of specifically American themes, an innovative quality, and a range of literary forms, especially in the genres of fiction and creative nonfiction. We are not interested in genre fiction or prose that is experiment for the sake of experiment. We are also not interested in nonfiction that is scholarly or critical in nature. Send us your best unpublished literary prose or poetry." Responds in 2 weeks-4 months. Guidelines available by e-mail or on the website.

⬤　Reading periods: April 1-July 31 for Fall issue; February 1-May 31 for Spring issue.

MAGAZINES NEEDS Submit 3-5 poems by e-mail as attachment. Include cover letter and brief bio. Pays 2 contributor's copies.

DOWN IN THE DIRT

E-mail: dirt@scars.tv. **Website:** www.scars.tv/dirt. **Contact:** Janet Kuypers, editor. 99% of our submissions are vias email and we prefer email submissions to snail mail submissions. *Down in the Dirt*, published every other month online and in print issues sold via Amazon.com throughout the U.S., U.K., and continental Europe, prints "good work that makes you think, that makes you feel like you've lived through a scene instead of merely read it." Also considers poems. *Down in the Dirt* is published "electronically as well as in print, either as printed magazines sold through our printer over the Internet, on the Web, or sold through our printer. And for prose, because we get so much of it, all we can suggest is, the shorter the better." Has published work by Mel Waldman, Ken Dean, Jon Brunette, John Ragusa, and Liam Spencer. By submitting writing or artwork to Down in the dirt at Scars Publications, you are giving us the right to broadcast your work - but the right to the work are always obtained by the author. Publishes ms within 1 year after acceptance. Responds in 1 month to queries; in 1 month to mss. If asked, will comment on rejected mss. Guidelines for SASE, e-mail, or on website.

MAGAZINES NEEDS Accepts e-mail submissions (vastly preferred to snail mail; pasted into body of message or as Microsoft Word DOC file attachment) and disk submissions (formatted for Macintosh). "If you do not have e-mail and want to snail-mail a poetry submission, we do not accept poetry snail-mail submissions longer than 10 lines. Currently, accepted writings get their own Web page in the 'writings' section at scars.tv/dirt, and samples of accepted writings are placed into an annual collection book that Scars Publications produces." Has published work by I.B. Rad, Pat Dixon, Mel Waldman, and Brian Looney. Does not want smut, rhyming poetry, or religious writing. Any length is appreciated.

ALSO OFFERS Scars Publications sponsors a contest where accepted writing appears in a collection book. Write or e-mail (dirt@scars.tv) for information. Also able to publish electronic chapbooks. Write for more information.

DRESSING ROOM POETRY JOURNAL

E-mail: dressingroompoetryjournal@gmail.com. **Website:** dressingroompoetryjournal.com. **Contact:** Meg Johnson, editor. *Dressing Room Poetry Journal* publishes original poetry and interviews with poets. Guidelines online.

MAGAZINES NEEDS Send 3-7 poems in an attachment by e-mail. Include contact info and a brief bio.

DUCTS

E-mail: vents@ducts.org. **Website:** www.ducts.org. **Contact:** Mary Cool, editor in chief; Tim Tomlinson, fiction editor; Lisa Kirchner, memoir editor; Amy Lemmon, poetry editor; Jacqueline Bishop, art editor. *Ducts* is a semiannual webzine of personal stories, fiction, essays, memoirs, poetry, humor, profiles, reviews, and art. "*Ducts* was founded in 1999 with the intent of giving emerging writers a venue to regularly publish their compelling, personal stories. The site has been expanded to include art and creative works of all genres. We believe that these genres must and do overlap. *Ducts* publishes the best, most compelling stories, and we hope to attract readers who are drawn to work that rises above." Pays on publication. Responds in 1-6 months. Guidelines available on website.

MAGAZINES NEEDS Submit 3-5 poems to poetry@ducts.org. Reads poetry January 1-August 31. Pays $20.

TIPS "We prefer writing that tells a compelling story with a strong narrative drive."

EARTHSHINE

P.O. Box 245, Hummelstown PA 17036. **E-mail:** poetry@earthshinepoetry.org. **Website:** www.earthshinepoetry.org. **Contact:** Sally Zaino and Julie Moffitt, editors. *Earthshine*, published irregularly in print and constantly online, features poetry and 1-2 pieces of cover art per printed volume. "When the online journal is full, a printed volume is produced and offered for sale. Subscriptions will be available as the publication becomes regular. The voice of *Earthshine* is one of illumination, compassion, humanity, and reason. Please see the submission guidelines webpage for updated information. Poems are the ultimate rumination, and if the world is to be saved, the poets will be needed; they are who see the connections between all things, and the patterns shared. We seek poetry of high literary quality, which will generate its own light for our readers." Has published poetry by Richard Schiffman, Anne Pierson Wiese, Steven Keletar, Mario Susko, and Daniel J. Langton. Acquires first rights and requests ongoing electronic rights. Accepted poets receive 2 copies of the printed journal. Time between acceptance and publication is "almost immediate" for online publication and "TBD" for printed publication. Electronic publication is often immediate. Tries to respond in 2 months; query if longer. Sample: $8. Guidelines available.

MAGAZINES NEEDS Pays 2 contributor's copies.

ECLECTICA MAGAZINE

E-mail: editors@eclectica.org. **Website:** www.eclectica.org. **Contact:** Tom Dooley, managing editor. "*Eclectica* is a sterling-quality quarterly electronic literary magazine on the World Wide Web, not bound by formula or genre, harnessing technology to further the reading experience without distracting from its dynamic, global content. Founded in 1996, *Eclectica* has been devoted to showcasing the best writing on the Web regardless of genre for over two decades, and it remains one of a handful of still active publications from the earliest days of the Internet. 'Literary' and 'genre' work appear side-by-side in each issue, along with pieces blurring the distinctions between such categories. Pushcart Prize, National Poetry Series, and Pulitzer Prize winners, as well as Nebula Award nominees, have shared issues with previously unpublished authors. On the fiction front, *Eclectica* has been recognized for more Million Writers Award notable and top ten stories than any other site." Submission deadlines: December 1 for January/February issue, March 1 for April/May issue, June 1 for July/August issue, September 1 for October/November issue. Buys first world electronic (online/Internet) rights. All rights revert to author upon publication, except for anthology rights. Guidelines online.

MAGAZINES NEEDS Seeks "outstanding poetry." Submit using online submissions manager.

TIPS "We pride ourselves on giving everyone (high schoolers, convicts, movie executives, etc.) an equal shot at publication, based solely on the quality of their work. Because we like eclecticism, we tend to favor the varied perspectives that often characterize the work of international authors, people of color, women, alternative lifestylists—but others who don't fit into these categories often surprise us."

EKPHRASIS

Frith Press, P.O. Box 161236, Sacramento CA 95816-1236. **E-mail:** frithpress@aol.com. **Website:** ekphrasisjournal.com. **Contact:** Laverne Frith and Carol Frith, editors. *Ekphrasis*, published semiannually in March and September, is an "outlet for the growing body of poetry focusing on individual works from any artistic genre. Poetry should transcend mere description. Open to all forms." *Ekphrasis* is 32-50 pages, digest-sized, photocopied, saddle-stapled. Poems from *Ekphrasis* have been featured on *Poetry Daily*. Nominates for the Pushcart Prize. Acquires first North American serial rights, one-time rights. Publishes ms 1 year after acceptance. Responds in 4 months. Seldom comments on rejected poems. Sample: $6. Subscription: $12/year. Make checks payable, in U.S. funds, to Laverne Frith. Guidelines available for SASE or on website.

MAGAZINES NEEDS Submit 3-5 poems at a time. Considers previously published poems "infrequently; must be credited." Cover letter is required, including short bio with representative credits and phone number. Include SASE. Until further notice, Frith Press will publish **occasional chapbooks by invitation only**. Has published poetry by Jeffrey Levine, Peter Meinke, David Hamilton, Barbara Lefcowitz, Molly McQuade, Alice Friman, and Annie Boutelle. Does not want "poetry without ekphrastic focus. No poorly crafted work. No archaic language." Pays 1 contributor's copy.

ELLIPSIS

Westminster College, 1840 S. 1300 E., Salt Lake City UT 84105. (801)832-2321. **E-mail:** ellipsis@westminstercollege.edu. **Website:** ellipsis.westminstercollege.edu. *Ellipsis*, published annually in April, needs good literary poetry, fiction, essays, plays, and visual art. Buys first North American serial rights. Pays on publication. Publishes ms an average of 3 months after acceptance. Responds in 6 months to mss. Sample copy: $7.50. Guidelines available online.

Reads submissions August 1-November 1. Staff changes each year; check website for an updated list of editors. *Ellipsis* is 120 pages, digest-sized, perfect-bound, with color cover. Accepts about 5% of submissions received. Press run is 2,000; most distributed free through college.

MAGAZINES NEEDS Submit poems via online submissions manager. Include cover letter. Has published poetry by Allison Joseph, Molly McQuade, Virgil Suaárez, Maurice Kilwein-Guevara, Richard Cecil, and Ron Carlson. Pays $10/poem and 2 contributor's copies.

EPOCH

251 Goldwin Smith Hall, Cornell University, Ithaca NY 14853-3201. (607)255-3385. **Website:** www.epoch.cornell.edu. **Contact:** Michael Koch, editor; Heidi E. Marschner, managing editor. Looking for well-written literary fiction, poetry, personal essays. Newcomers welcome. Open to mainstream and avant-garde writing. Buys first North American serial rights. Pays on publication. Publishes ms an average of 6 months after acceptance. Responds in 2 weeks to queries; in 6 weeks to mss. Sometimes comments on rejected mss. Editorial lead time 6 months. Sample copy: $5. Guidelines online and for #10 SASE.

Magazine: 6×9; 128 pages; good quality paper; good cover stock. Receives 500 unsolicited mss/month. Accepts 15-20 mss/issue. Reads unsolicited submissions September 15-April 15. Publishes 3-4 new writers/year. Has published work by Antonya Nelson, Doris Betts, Heidi Jon Schmidt.

MAGAZINES NEEDS Mss not accompanied by SASE will be discarded unread. Occasionally provides criticism on poems. Considers poetry in all forms. Pay varies; pays $50 minimum/poem.

TIPS "Tell your story, speak your poem, straight from the heart. We are attracted to language and to good writing, but we are most interested in what the good writing leads us to, or where."

EUROPEAN JUDAISM

Leo Baeck College, The Sternberg Centre for Judaism, 80 East End Rd., London N3 2SY, England. **E-mail:** european.judaism@lbc.ac.uk. **Website:** www.journals.berghahnbooks.com/ej. **Contact:** Managing Editor. "For over 40 years, *European Judaism* has provided a voice for the postwar Jewish world in Europe. It has reflected the different realities of each country and helped rebuild Jewish consciousness after the Holocaust. It is a peer-reviewed journal with emphasis on European Jewish theology, philosophy, literature, and history. Each issue includes a poetry and book reviews section." *European Judaism* is available online. Individual Rate (Online Only): $34.95/£21.95/€24.95. Student Rate (Online Only): $19.95/ £12.95/ €14.95. Please visit the website for institutional pricing. Guidelines available online.

MAGAZINES NEEDS Submit by e-mail, accompanied by 1 double-spaced copy and a brief biographical note on the author. Please visit the website for further details.

EVANSVILLE REVIEW

University of Evansville Creative Writing Department, 1800 Lincoln Ave., Evansville IN 47722. (812)488-1042. **E-mail:** evansvillereview@evansville.edu. **Website:** https://theevansvillereview.submittable.com/submit. **Contact:** Amanda Alexander, editor in chief; Sari Baum, editor in chief; Brittney Kaleri, nonfiction editor; William Capella, fiction editor; Beth Brunmeier, poetry editor. "*The Evansville Review* is an annual literary journal published at the University of Evansville. Our award-winning journal includes poetry, fiction, nonfiction, plays, and interviews by a wide range of authors, from emerging writers to Nobel Prize recipients. Past issues have included work by Joyce Carol Oates, Arthur Miller, John Updike, Joseph Brodsky, Elia Kazan, Edward Albee, Willis Barnstone, Shirley Ann Grau, and X.J. Kennedy." Acquires one-time rights. Pays on publication. Responds in 3 months. Sample: $5. Guidelines available online.

Reading period: September 1-October 31.

MAGAZINES NEEDS No fax or e-mail submissions; postal and submittable submissions only. Cover letter is required. Include brief bio. Pays contributor's copies.

EVENING STREET REVIEW

Evening Street Press, Inc., 2881 Wright St, Sacramento CA 95821. (614)937-2124. **E-mail:** editor@eveningstreetpress.com. **Website:** www.eveningstreetpress.com. **Contact:** Barbara Bergmann, managing editor. "Intended for a general audience, *Evening Street Press* is centered on Elizabeth Cady Stanton's 1848 revision of the Declaration of Independence: 'that all men and women are created equal,' with equal rights to 'life, liberty, and the pursuit of happiness.' It focuses on the realities of experience, personal and historical, from the most gritty to the most dreamlike, including awareness of the personal and social forces that block or develop the possibilities of this new culture." Rights revert to author upon publication. Publishes ms an average of 8 months after acceptance. Responds in 2-6 months to mss. Editorial lead time 6 months. Sample copy: $12. Guidelines online or for #10 SASE.

MAGAZINES NEEDS Submit 3-6 poems. E-mail submissions preferred. Does not want "the incoherent kind" of poetry. Pays 1 contributor's copy.

CONTEST/AWARD OFFERINGS Helen Kay Chapbook submissions accepted year round. Sinclair Poetry Book May 1-December 1 in odd numbered years.

TIPS "Does not want to see male chauvinism. Mss are read year round. See website for chapbook and book competitions."

EXIT 13 MAGAZINE

P.O. Box 423, Fanwood NJ 07023-1162. (908)889-5298. **E-mail:** exit13magazine@yahoo.com. **Website:** www.facebook.com/exit13magazine. **Contact:** Tom Plante, editor. "*Exit 13*, published annually, uses poetry that is short, to the point, with a sense of geography. It features poets of all ages, writing styles, and degrees of experience, focusing on where and how we live and what's going on around us. The emphasis is on geography, travel, adventure, and the fertile ground of the imagination. It's a travelogue in poetry, a reflection of the world we see, and a chronicle of the people we meet along the way." *Exit 13* is about 76 pages. Press run is 300. Acquires one-time and possible anthology rights. Responds in 4 months. Sample copy: $10. Guidelines available on Facebook page, in magazine or for SASE.

MAGAZINES NEEDS Submit up to 5 poems through postal mail or e-mail. Paste in body of e-mail. Has published poetry by Carole Stone, Wanda Praisner, Laura Boss, A.D. Winans, Paul Sohar, and Charles Rammelkamp. Pays one contributor's copy.

FEMINIST STUDIES

4137 Susquehanna Hall, University of Maryland, College Park MD 20742. (301)405-7415. **Fax:** (301)405-8395. **E-mail:** info@feministstudies.org; brittany@feministstudies.org. **E-mail:** kmantilla@feministstudies.org. **Website:** www.feministstudies.org. **Contact:** Ashwini Tambe, editorial director; Karla Mantilla, managing editor. Over the years, *Feminist Studies* has been a reliable source of significant writings on issues that are important to all classes and races of women. Those familiar with the literature on women's studies are well aware of the importance and vitality of the journal and the frequency with which articles first published in *Feminist Studies* are cited and/or reprinted elsewhere. Indeed, no less than 4 anthologies have been created from articles originally published in *Feminist Studies*: *Clio's Consciousness Raised: New Perspectives on the History of Women*; *Sex and Class in Women's History*; *U.S. Women in Struggle: A Feminist Studies Anthology*; and *Lesbian Subjects: A Feminist Studies Reader*. *Feminist Studies* is committed to publishing an interdisciplinary body of feminist knowledge that sees intersections of gender with racial identity, sexual orientation, economic means, geographical location, and physical ability as the touchstone for our politics and our intellectual analysis. Whether work is drawn from the complex past or the shifting present, the articles and essays that appear in *Feminist Studies* address social and political issues that intimately and significantly affect women and men in the United States and around the world." Guidelines available online.

MAGAZINES NEEDS Submit complete ms by mail and e-mail (creative@feministstudies.org).

THE FIDDLEHEAD

Campus House, 11 Garland Crt, PO Box 4400, University of New Brunswick, Fredericton NB E3B 5A3, Canada. (506)453-3501. **E-mail:** fiddlehd@unb.ca. **Website:** www.thefiddlehead.ca. Sue Sinclair, editor. **Contact:** Kathryn Taglia, managing editor or Ian LeTourneau, design & layout. *The Fiddlehead* is open to good writing in English or translations into English from all over the world and in a variety of styles, including experimental genres. Our editors are always happy to see new unsolicited works in fiction (including novel excerpts), creative nonfiction, and poetry. We also publish reviews, and occasionally other selected creative work such as excerpts from plays. Work is read on an ongoing basis; the acceptance rate is around 1-2% (we are, however, famous for our rejection notes!). We particularly welcome submissions from Indigenous writers, writers of colour, writers with disabilities, LGBTQQIA+ writers, and writers from other intersectional and under-represented communities. If you are comfortable identifying yourself as one or more of the above, please feel free to mention this in your cover letter. *The Fiddlehead*'s mandate is to publish accomplished poetry, short fiction, and Canadian literature reviews; to discover and promote new writing talent; to represent the Atlantic Canada's lively cultural and literary diversity; and to place the best of new and established Canadian writing in an international context. *The Fiddlehead* has published works from a long list of Canadian authors including Margaret Atwood, George Elliott Clarke, Kayla Czaga, Eden Robinson, Gregory Scofield, and Clea Young alongside international authors such as Jorie Graham, Jaki McCarrick, Thylias Moss, Les Murray, and Daniel Woodrell. *The Fiddlehead* also sponsors annual writing contests for creative nonfiction, poetry, and short fiction. Purchases first serial rights for unsolicited stories, poems, and creative nonfiction. All other rights remain with the author. Pays on publication. Every attempt is made to publish work with 1-2 issues (3-8 months) of acceptance. If longer wait, editors will

usually try to indicate this before final acceptance. Responds in 3-9 months to mss. Occasionally comments on rejected mss. Sample copy: $15 U.S. Writer's guidelines online. Writers may only submit once per calendar year per genre. (This does not include submissions to *The Fiddlehead*'s contests. For that you may submit multiple times, so long as the work is not under consideration elsewhere.) For unsolicited submissions we only consider unpublished work. Please do not submit work that has been previously published or accepted for publication, including in anthologies, chapbooks, blogs, Facebook pages, or online journals.

MAGAZINES NEEDS Send SASE with Canadian postage for response or self-addressed envelope with cheque/money to cover postage (US or CA dollars). May request e-mail response if you do not want ms. returned. No e-mail or faxed submissions. Simultaneous submissions only if stated on cover letter; must contact immediately if accepted elsewhere. *The Fiddlehead* is now accepts online submissions via Submittable.com, please check website for details. No poetry aimed at children; no limericks, doggerel. Pays up to $60 (Canadian)/published page and 2 contributor's copies.

CONTEST/AWARD OFFERINGS Sponsors an annual poetry contest.

TIPS "If you are serious about submitting to *The Fiddlehead*, you should subscribe or read several issues to get a sense of the journal. Contact us if you would like to order sample back issues."

FIELD

Contemporary Poetry & Poetics, Oberlin College Press, 50 N. Professor St., Oberlin OH 44074. (440)775-8408. **Fax:** (440)775-8124. **E-mail:** oc.press@oberlin.edu. **Website:** www.oberlin.edu/ocpress. **Contact:** Marco Wilkinson, managing editor. *FIELD: Contemporary Poetry and Poetics*, published semiannually in April and October, is a literary journal with "emphasis on poetry, translations, and essays by poets. See electronic submission guidelines." Buys first rights. Pays on publication. Responds in 6-8 weeks to mss. Editorial lead time 4 months. Sample copy: $8. Subscription: $16/year, $28 for 2 years. Guidelines available online and for #10 SASE.

FIELD is 100 pages, digest-sized, printed on rag stock, flat-spined, with glossy color card cover.

MAGAZINES NEEDS Submissions are read August 1 through May 31. Submit 2-6 of your best poems through online submissions manager. No e-mail submissions. Has published poetry by Michelle Glazer, Tom Lux, Carl Phillips, Betsy Sholl, Charles Simic, Jean Valentine, and translations by Marilyn Hacker and Stuart Friebert. Pays $15/page and 2 contributor's copies.

TIPS "Keep trying!"

⊗⊜ FILLING STATION

P.O. Box 22135, Bankers Hall RPO, Calgary AB T2P 4J5, Canada. **E-mail:** mgmt@fillingstation.ca. **Website:** www.fillingstation.ca. **Contact:** Kyle Flemmer, managing editor. *filling Station*, published 3 times/year, prints contemporary poetry, fiction, visual art, interviews, reviews, and articles. "We are looking for all forms of contemporary writing, but especially that which is innovative and/or experimental." Acquires first North American serial rights. Publishes ms 3-4 months after acceptance. Responds in 3-6 months. "After your work is reviewed by our Collective, you will receive an e-mail from an editor to let you know if your work has been selected for publication. If selected, you will later receive a second e-mail to let you know which issue your piece has been selected to appear in. Note that during the design phase, we sometimes discover the need to shuffle a piece to a future issue instead. In the event your piece is pushed back, we will inform you." Sample copy: $12. Subscription: $25 for 3 issues, $8 for 6. Guidelines online.

○ *filling Station* is 60 - 80 pages, 8.5x11, perfect-bound, with card cover, includes photos and artwork. Receives about 100 submissions for each issue, accepts approximately 10%. Press run is 500.

MAGAZINES NEEDS Submit up to 6 pages of poetry via Submittable. "If your poem is spaced in a particular way, please make sure to use spaces, never tabs, so we can accurately replicate your layout." Has published poetry by Fred Wah, Larissa Lai, Margaret Christakos, Robert Kroetsch, Ron Silliman, Susan Holbrook, and many more. Pays $25 honorarium and three-issue subscription.

TIPS "*filling Station* accepts singular or simultaneous submissions of previously unpublished poetry, fiction, creative nonfiction, nonfiction, or art. We are always on the hunt for great writing!"

FIVE POINTS

Georgia State University, P.O. Box 3999, Atlanta GA 30302-3999. **Website:** www.fivepoints.gsu.edu. **Contact:** David Bottoms, co-editor. *Five Points*, published 3 times/year, is committed to publishing work that compels the imagination through the use of fresh and convincing language. Buys first North American serial rights. Sends galleys to author. Publishes ms an average of 6 months after acceptance. Responds in 2 months. Sample copy: $10. Guidelines available on website.

○ Magazine: 6x9; 200 pages; cotton paper; glossy cover; photos. Has published Alice Hoffman, Natasha Tretheway, Pamela Painter, Billy Collins, Philip Levine, George Singleton, Hugh Sheehy, and others. All submissions received outside of our reading periods are returned unread.

MAGAZINES NEEDS Reads poetry August 15-December 1 and January 3-March 31. Submit through online submissions manager. Include cover letter. Length: up to 50 lines/poem.

TIPS "We place no limitations on style or content. Our only criteria is excellence. If your writing has an original voice, substance, and significance, send it to us. We will publish distinctive, intelligent writing that has something to say and says it in a way that captures and maintains our attention."

FLINT HILLS REVIEW

Department of English, Modern Languages, and Journalist, Emporia State University, 1 Kellogg Circle, Emporia KS 66801. **E-mail:** awebb@emporia.edu. **E-mail:** bluestem@emporia.edu. **Website:** www.emporia.edu/fhr. **Contact:** Amy Sage Webb and Kevin Rabas, editors. *Flint Hills Review*, published annually, is "a regionally focused journal presenting writers of national distinction alongside new authors. *FHR* seeks work informed by a strong sense of place or region, especially Kansas and the Great Plains region. We seek to provide a publishing venue for writers of the Great Plains and Kansas while also publishing authors whose work evidences a strong sense of place, writing of literary quality, and accomplished use of language and depth of character development." Magazine: 6x9; 75-200 pages; perfect-bound; 60 lb. paper; glossy cover; illustrations; photos. Has published work by Julene Bair, Elizabeth Dodd, Dennis Etzel Jr., Patricia Lawson, and Amanda Frost. Reads mss November to mid-March. Acquires one-time rights. Publishes ms 4-12 months after acceptance. Responds in 3-9 months to mss. Sample: $7. Guidelines online.

MAGAZINES NEEDS Nearly all forms of poetry. Has published poetry by E. Ethelbert Miller, Elizabeth

Dodd, Walt McDonald, and Gwendolyn Brooks. Include short bio (150 words or less). Reads submissions November-March. Does not want excessive rhyming, sentimental or gratuitous verse. Pays 1 contributor's copy; additional copies at discounted price.

TIPS "Submit writing that has strong imagery and voice, writing that is informed by place or region, writing of literary quality with depth of character development. Hone the language to the most literary depiction possible in the shortest space that still provides depth of development without excess length."

THE FLORIDA REVIEW

Department of English, University of Central Florida, P.O. Box 161346, Orlando FL 32816-1346. **E-mail:** fl-review@ucf.edu. **Website:** floridareview.cah.ucf.edu. **Contact:** Lisa Roney, editor. "*The Florida Review* publishes exciting new work from around the world from writers both emerging and well known. We are not Florida-exclusive, though we acknowledge having a jungle mentality and a preference for grit, and we have provided and continue to offer a home for many Florida writers." We ask for first publication rights only. Like most small literary magazines, we cannot pay all of our authors. We pay $1,000 to four prize-winners each year. In addition, we have a small $50 award for one author/artist per year in each genre that submits to us through our general submissions process. Publishes ms usually 3 months to 1 year after acceptance. Responds in 2-4 weeks to queries; in 3-8 months to mss. Sample copy: $10. Writer's guidelines online.

○ Has published work by Gerald Vizenor, Billy Collins, Sherwin Bitsui, Kelly Clancy, Denise Duhamel, Tony Hoagland, Baron Wormser, Marcia Aldrich, and Patricia Foster. Accepts mailed submissions only if author does not have regular access to the Internet.

MAGAZINES NEEDS "We look for clear, strong poems, filled with real people, emotions, and objects. Any style will be considered." Submit via online submissions manager.

HOW TO CONTACT Submit complete ms via online submissions manager.

TIPS "We're looking for writers with fresh voices and original stories. We like risk. Please visit our website and/or read a back issue of our magazine to understand what we seek."

FLOYD COUNTY MOONSHINE

720 Christiansburg Pike, Floyd VA 24091. (540)745-5150. **E-mail:** floydshine@gmail.com. **Website:** www.floydcountymoonshine.com. **Contact:** Aaron Lee Moore, editor-in-chief. *Floyd County Moonshine*, published biannually, is a "literary and arts magazine in Floyd, Virginia, and the New River Valley. We accept poetry, short stories, and essays addressing all manner of themes; however, preference is given to those works of a rural or Appalachian nature. *Floyd County Moonshine* publishes a variety of home-grown Appalachian writers in addition to writers from across the country. The mission of *Floyd County Moonshine* is to publish thought-provoking, well-crafted, free-thinking, uncensored prose and poetry. Our literature explores the dark and Gothic as well as the bright and pleasant in order to give an honest portrayal of the human condition. We aspire to publish quality literature in the local color genre, specifically writing that relates to Floyd, Virginia, and the New River Valley. Floyd and local Appalachian authors are given priority consideration; however, to stay versatile we also aspire to publish some writers from all around the country in every issue. We publish both well-established and beginning writers." Wants literature addressing rural or Appalachian themes. Has published poetry by Steve Kistulentz, Louis Gallo, Ernie Wormwood, R.T. Smith, Chelsea Adams, and Justin Askins. Acquires one-time print rights and indefinite archival rights. Pays contributor copy. Publication after 6-12 months. Responds in 6 months. Single copy: $10. Subscription: $20 for 1 year, $38 for 2 years. Guidelines online.

MAGAZINES NEEDS Accepts e-mail (preferred). Submit a Word document as attachment. Accepts previously published works and simultaneous submissions on occasion. Cover letter is unnecessary. Include brief bio. Reads submissions year round. Does not want religious devotional. Pays 1 contributor's copy.

FLUENT MAGAZINE

245 Timber Lane, Harpers Ferry WV 25425. **E-mail:** info@fluent-magazine.com. **E-mail:** poetry@fluent-magazine.com; fiction@fluent-magazine.com; nonfiction@fluent-magazine.com. **Website:** www.fluent-magazine.com. **Contact:** Nancy McKeithen. *FLUENT Magazine*, headquartered in West Virginia's Eastern Panhandle, is a free-subscription quarterly online magazine covering arts and culture in West Virginia, Pennsylvania, Maryland, Virginia, and the Washington DC area. "We reach an audience in four states plus other subscribers around the world. Each issue features a two-page spread by an individual poet. *FLUENT*'s broader arts and culture coverage emphasizes visual

arts, and includes fiction, music, personal essays, humor and interviews drawn from the four-state region."

MAGAZINES NEEDS "We prefer material that has never been published. We will consider poems excerpted from previously published books and chapbooks. Explicitly sexual or violent material will likely not work for us. We feature four poets a year, devoting a two-page spread to each. We'll need your home address and phone. Brief biographical material if you care to provide it."

FLYWAY

Journal of Writing and Environment, Department of English, 206 Ross Hall, Iowa State University, Ames IA 50011-1201. (515)294-8273. **Fax:** (515)294-6814. **E-mail:** flywayjournal@gmail.com. **Website:** www.flywayjournal.org. **Contact:** Zachary Lisabeth, managing editor. Based out of Iowa State University, *Flyway: Journal of Writing and Environment* publishes poetry, fiction, nonfiction, and visual art exploring the many complicated facets of the word environment—at once rural, urban, and suburban—and its social and political implications. Also open to all different interpretations of environment.Reading period is August 15-May 15. Has published work by Rick Bass, Jacob M. Appel, Madison Smartt Bell, Jane Smiley. Also sponsors the annual fall Notes from the Field contest in creative nonfiction, the spring Sweet Corn Prize in Fiction and Poetry contest and a themed winter contest. Details on website. "We look for stories that bring in environment as a character or central element. Does this mean we only take stories about ecology/nature/treehuggers? Nope. We want stories that wouldn't be remarkable or couldn't happen in another place than where they happen. We want writing that shows tension between character and surroundings, that shows how changes in living space affect actions and interactions in that living space. This environment could be an abandoned school, a strip mall comic bookstore, a thinning forest or a hiking trail—if it shapes the characters, affects events, and if it's of interest to us. We are open to work of all genres and subjects if it fits our aesthetic, and we are always happy to be surprised." Acquires first North American serial rights, electronic rights, First digital and future anthology rights. Publishes ms 2-4 months after acceptance. Often comments on rejected mss. Sample copy and guidelines on website.

MAGAZINES NEEDS Submit up to 5 poems (combined in 1 document) only via online submission manager. Pays one-year subscription to *Flyway*.

TIPS "For *Flyway*, there should be tension between the environment or setting of the story and the characters in it. A well-known place should appear new, even alien and strange through the eyes and actions of the characters. We want to see an active environment, too—a setting that influences actions, triggers its own events."

FOGGED CLARITY

(231)670-7033. **E-mail:** editor@foggedclarity.com; submissions@foggedclarity.com. **Website:** www.foggedclarity.com. **Contact:** Editors. "*Fogged Clarity* is an arts review that accepts submissions of poetry, fiction, nonfiction, music, visual art, and reviews of work in all mediums. We seek art that is stabbingly eloquent. Our print edition is released once every year, while new issues of our online journal come out at the beginning of every month. Artists maintain the copyrights to their work until they are monetarily compensated for said work. If your work is selected for our print edition and you consent to its publication, you will be compensated." Acquires first North American serial rights. Rights revert to author upon publication. Averages 1-2 months from acceptance to publishing. Responds in 3 months to mss. Accepts queries by e-mail only. Sample copy online. Guidelines available at www.foggedclarity.com/submissions.

"By incorporating music and the visual arts and releasing a new issue monthly, *Fogged Clarity* aims to transcend the conventions of a typical literary journal. Our network is extensive, and our scope is as broad as thought itself; we are, you are, unconstrained. With that spirit in mind, *Fogged Clarity* examines the work of authors, artists, scholars, and musicians, providing a home for exceptional art and thought that warrants exposure."

MAGAZINES NEEDS Submit up to 5 poems by e-mail (submissions@foggedclarity.com) as attached .DOC or .DOCX file. Subject line should be formatted as: "Last Name: Medium of Submission." For example, "Evans: Poetry." Include brief cover letter, complete contact information, and a third-person bio.

TIPS "The editors appreciate artists communicating the intention of their submitted work and the influences behind it in a brief cover letter. Any artists with proposals for features or special projects should feel free to contact Ben Evans directly at editor@foggedclarity.com."

FOLIATE OAK LITERARY MAGAZINE

University of Arkansas-Monticello, Arts & Humanities, 562 University Dr., Monticello AR 71656. (870)460-1247. **E-mail:** foliateoak@gmail.com. **Website:** www.foliateoak.com. **Contact:** Diane Payne, faculty advisor. The *Foliate Oak Literary Magazine* is an online student-run magazine accepting hybrid prose, poetry, fiction, flash, creative nonfiction, and artwork. "After you receive a rejection/acceptance notice, please wait 1 month before submitting new work. **Submission Period: August 1-April 24**. We do not read submissions during summer break. If you need to contact us for anything other than submitting your work, please write to foliateoak@gmail.com." No e-mail submissions. Acquires one-time, nonexclusive rights. Publishes ms an average of 1 month after acceptance. Responds in 1 week to queries; in 2 month to mss. Editorial lead time: 1 month. Guidelines online.

MAGAZINES NEEDS Submit poems via online submission manager. "We enjoy poems that we understand, preferably not rhyming poems, unless you make the rhyme so fascinating we'll wonder why we ever said anything about avoiding rhymes. Give us something fresh, unexpected, and that will make us say, 'Wow!'" "No homophobic, religious rants, or pornographic, violent poems. Please avoid using offensive language. We tend to shy away from poems that rhyme."

TIPS "Please submit all material via our online submission manager. Read our guidelines before submitting. We are eager to include multimedia submissions of videos, music, and collages. Submit your best work."

FOOTHILL

A Journal of Poetry, 165 E. 10th St., Claremont CA 91711. **E-mail:** foothill@cgu.edu. **Website:** www.cgu.edu/foothill. **Contact:** Brock Rustin and Emily Schuck, co-editors-in-chief. Directed by students at Claremont Graduate University, *Foothill: A Journal of Poetry* is an annual journal devoted exclusively to poetry written by graduate students from around the world. *Foothill* acquires electronic rights as well as right to print poem in print journal. Rights revert to poets upon publication. Responds in 5 weeks. Sometimes comments on rejected poems. Subscription: $25. Make checks payable to CGU. Guidelines available in magazine, by e-mail, and on website.

⚪ Published online and in print annually. Digest-sized, 72 pages, digital press, perfect bound. Press run is 500. No ads. Never publishes theme issues.

MAGAZINES NEEDS Currently or recently enrolled in a graduate studies program. Accepts any poetry by graduate students (currently enrolled or recently graduated) from anywhere in the world. Students do not need to be enrolled in an MFA or writing program. Welcomes poetry submissions from those in other disciplines. Submit via e-mail. Include document as attachment in e-mail. Cover letter preferred. Poems are circulated to an editorial board. Accepts submissions year round. Welcomes submissions from beginning poets. Does not consider poetry by children or teens. No limit for poem length.

FOURTEEN HILLS

Department of Creative Writing, San Francisco State University, 1600 Holloway Ave., San Francisco CA 94137. **E-mail:** hills@sfsu.edu. **Website:** www.14hills. net. "*Fourteen Hills* publishes the highest-quality innovative fiction and poetry for a literary audience." Acquires one-time rights. Always sends prepublication galleys. Response time varies; upwards of 10 mo. Sometimes comments on rejected mss. SASE for return of ms. Sample copy: $10. Guidelines online.

⚪ Annual magazine: 6x9; 200 pages; 60 lb. paper; 10-point C15 cover. Reading periods: March 1-June 1 for following year spring magazine release.

MAGAZINES NEEDS Submit up to 3 poems via online submissions manager. Length: up to 7 pages for entire submission. Pays 2 contributor's copies and offers discount on additional copies.

TIPS "Please read an issue of *Fourteen Hills* before submitting."

THE FOURTH RIVER

Chatham University, Woodland Rd., Pittsburgh PA 15232. **E-mail:** 4thriver@gmail.com. **Website:** thefourthriver.com. *The Fourth River*, an annual publication of Chatham University's MFA in Creative Writing Programs, features literature that engages and explores the relationship between humans and their environments. Wants writings that are richly situated at the confluence of place, space, and identity, or that reflect upon or make use of landscape and place in new ways. Buys first North American serial rights. Pays with contributor's copies only. Publishes mss in 5-8 months after acceptance. Responds in 3-5 months to mss. Sample copy: $5 (back issue). Single copy: $10; subscription: $16 for 2 years. Guidelines available online.

The Fourth River is digest-sized, perfect-bound, with full-color cover by various artists. *The Fourth River*'s contributors have been published in *Glimmer Train*, *Alaska Quarterly Review*, *The Missouri Review*, *The Best American Short Stories*, *The O. Henry Prize Stories*, and *The Best American Travel Writing*. Reading periods: November 1-January 1 (fall online issue) and July 1-September 1 (spring print issue).

MAGAZINES NEEDS Submit 3-5 poems via online submissions manager.

◐⑤ FREEFALL MAGAZINE

FreeFall Literary Society of Calgary, 460, 1720 29th Ave. SW, Calgary AB T2T 6T7, Canada. **E-mail:** editors@freefallmagazine.ca. **Website:** www.freefallmagazine.ca. **Contact:** Ryan Stromquist, managing editor. Magazine published triannually containing fiction, poetry, creative nonfiction, essays on writing, interviews, and reviews. "We are looking for exquisite writing with a strong narrative." Buys first North American serial rights (ownership reverts to author after one-time publication). Pays on publication. Guidelines and submission forms on website.

MAGAZINES NEEDS Submit 2-5 poems via online submissions manager. Accepts any style of poetry. Length: up to 6 pages. Pays $25/poem and 1 contributor's copy.

TIPS "Our mission is to encourage the voices of new, emerging, and experienced Canadian writers and provide a platform for their quality work."

⑤ FREEXPRESSION

Peter F Pike T/As FreeXpresSion, 44 Hambledon Circuit, Harrington Park NSW 2567, Australia. 0425-273-703. **E-mail:** editor@freexpression.com.au. **Website:** www.freexpression.com.au. **Contact:** Peter F. Pike, managing editor. *FreeXpresSion*, published monthly, contains creative writing, how-to articles, short stories, and poetry, including cinquain, haiku, etc., and bush verse. Open to all forms. "Christian themes OK. Humorous material welcome. No gratuitous sex; bad language OK. We don't want to see anything degrading." *FreeXpresSion* also publishes books up to 200 pages **through subsidy arrangements with authors**. Some poems published throughout the year are used in *Yearbooks* (annual anthologies). *FreeXpresSion* is 32 pages, magazine-sized, offset-printed, saddle-stapled, full color. Receives about 3,500 poems/year, accepts about 30%. Purchases first Australian rights. Publishes ms 2

months after acceptance. Responds in 1 month. Subscription: $25 AUS for 3 months, $50 AUS for 6 months, $100 AUS for 1 year. Guidelines available in magazine, for SAE and IRC, or by fax or e-mail.

MAGAZINES NEEDS Submit 3-4 poems at a time. Accepts e-mail (pasted into body of message) and disk submissions. Cover letter is preferred. Has published poetry by many prize-winning poets like Ron Stevens, Ellis Campbell, Brenda Joy, David Campbell, and Max and Jacqui Merckenschlager. Length: Very long poems are not desired but would be considered.

ALSO OFFERS Sponsors an annual contest with 3 categories for poetry: blank verse (up to 120 lines), traditional verse (up to 120 lines), and haiku. 1st Prize in blank verse: $250 AUS; 2nd Prize: $100 AUS; 1st Prize in traditional rhyming poetry: $250 AUS; 2nd Prize: $100 AUS. Haiku, 1st Prize $120 AUS; 2nd Prize $80 AUS; 3rd Prize $50 AUS. Guidelines and entry form available by e-mail or download from website.

⑤ THE FRIEND

The Friend Publications Ltd, 173 Euston Rd., London England NW1 2BJ, United Kingdom. (44)(207)663-1010. **Fax:** (44)(207)663-1182. **E-mail:** editorial@thefriend.org. **Website:** www.thefriend.org. **Contact:** Elinor Smallman (Production and office manager). Completely independent, *The Friend* brings readers news and views from a Quaker perspective, as well as from a wide range of authors whose writings are of interest to Quakers and non-Quakers alike. There are articles on issues such as peace, spirituality, Quaker belief, and ecumenism, as well as news of Friends from Britain and abroad. Prefers queries, but sometimes accepts unsolicited mss. Guidelines online.

MAGAZINES NEEDS There are no rules regarding poetry, but doesn't want particularly long poems.

⑤ THE FRIEND MAGAZINE

The Church of Jesus Christ of Latter-day Saints, 50 E. North Temple St., Salt Lake City UT 84150. (801)240-2210. **Fax:** (801)240-2270. **E-mail:** friend@ldschurch.org. **Website:** www.lds.org/friend. **Contact:** Paul B. Pieper, editor; Mark W. Robison, art director. "The *Friend* is published by The Church of Jesus Christ of Latter-day Saints for boys and girls up to 3-12 years of age." Available online.

MAGAZINES NEEDS Pays $30 for poems.

⑤ THE FROGMORE PAPERS

The Frogmore Press, 21 Mildmay Rd., Lewes, East Sussex BN7 1PJ, England. **E-mail:** frogmorepress@

gmail.com (accepted from outside UK only). **Website:** www.frogmorepress.co.uk. Managing Editor, The Frogmore Press: Dr Alexandra Loske.. **Contact:** Jeremy Page, editor. *The Frogmore Papers*, published semiannually, is a literary magazine with emphasis on new poetry, short stories and flash fiction. *The Frogmore Papers* is 42 pages, photocopied in photo-reduced typescript, saddle-stapled, with matte card cover. Accepts 2% of poetry received. Press run is 500. Reading periods: October 1-31 for March issue and April 1-30 for September issue. Publishes ms up to 5 months after acceptance. Responds in 3 months. Subscription: £10 for 1 year (2 issues); £15 for 2 years (4 issues). Guidelines online.

MAGAZINES NEEDS "Poems where the form drives the meaning are unlikely to find favour. Poems written by people who clearly haven't read any poetry since Wordsworth will not find favour. Prose may be experimental or traditional, but is unlikely to be accepted if it's either very experimental or very traditional." Has published poetry by Clare Pollard, Carole Satyamurti, Linda France and Jonathan Edwards. Submit 4-6 poems by e-mail or mail (e-mail submissions only accepted from outside the UK). Length: 20-80 lines/poem. Pays 1 contributor's copy.

ALSO OFFERS Sponsors the annual Frogmore Poetry Prize. Write for information.

💲 FUGUE LITERARY JOURNAL

E-mail: fugue@uidaho.edu. **Website:** www.fugue-journal.com. **Contact:** Alexandra Teague, faculty advisor. "Begun in 1990 by the faculty in the Department of English at University of Idaho, *Fugue* has continuously published poetry, plays, fiction, essays, and interviews from established and emerging writers biannually. We take pride in the work we print, the writers we publish, and the presentation of each and every issue. Working in collaboration with local and national artists, our covers display some of the finest art from photography and digital art to ink drawings and oil paintings. We believe that each issue is a print and digital artifact of the deepest engagement with our culture, and we make it our personal goal that the writing we select and presentation of each issue reflect the reverence we have for art and letters." Work published in *Fugue* has won the Pushcart Prize and has been cited in *Best American Essays*. Submissions are accepted online only. Poetry, fiction, and nonfiction submissions are accepted September 1-May 1. All material received outside of this period will not be read. $3 submission fee per entry. See website for submission instructions. Responds in 3-6 months to mss. Sample copy: $10. Guidelines online.

MAGAZINES NEEDS Submit up to 5 poems using online submissions manager. Pays 1 contributor's copy and $15 per published piece.

ALSO OFFERS "For information regarding our annual prose and poetry contest, please visit our website."

TIPS "The best way, of course, to determine what we're looking for is to read the journal. As the name *Fugue* indicates, our goal is to present a wide range of literary perspectives. We like stories that satisfy us both intellectually and emotionally, with fresh language and characters so captivating that they stick with us and invite a second reading. We are also seeking creative literary criticism which illuminates a piece of literature or a specific writer by examining that writer's personal experience."

GARGOYLE

Paycock Press, 3819 13th St. N, Arlington VA 22201. (703) 380-4893. **E-mail:** rchrdpeabody9@gmail.com. **Website:** www.gargoylemagazine.com. **Contact:** Richard Peabody, editor/publisher. "*Gargoyle* has always been a scallywag magazine, a maverick magazine, a bit too academic for the underground and way too underground for the academics. We are a writer's magazine in that we are read by other writers and have never worried about reaching the masses." Annual. The submission window opens each year in August and remains open until full. Recently published works by: Jill Adams, Roberta Allen, Cathy Alter, Jacob Appel, Donna Baier Stein, Stacy Barton, C.L. Bledsoe, Caroline Bock, Jamie Brown, Grace Cavalieri, Laura Cesarco Eglin, Patrick Chapman, Juliet Cook, Rachel Dacus, Michael Dailey, Kristina Marie Darling, William Virgil Davis, Glenn Deutsch, Andrew Gifford, Sid Gold, Suzanne Feldman, Heather Fowler, Susan Gubernat, Myronn Hardy, Abhay K. George Kalamaras, Jesse Lee Kercheval, Leonard Kress, W. F. Lantry, Lyn Lifshin, Susan Neville, Kevin O'Cuinn, Donaji Olmedo, Frances Park, Pedro Ponce, Glen Pouricau, Melissa Reddish, Aria Riding, Bruce Sager, John Saul, Marija Stajic, Liza Nash Taylor, Susan Tepper, Sally Toner, Gretchen A. Van Lente, Idea Vilarino, Jesse Waters, Kathleen Wheaton, Andrea Wyatt, Katherine E. Young, and Bonnie ZoBell. Acquires first North American rights, which revert to the authors upon publication. "We do retain the right to load work onto our website or to collect in a 'best of' anthology down the road." Publishes ms 1 year after acceptance. Responds in 1 month. Sample copy: $12.95. Catalog available online at FAQ link. "We don't have guidelines; we have never believed in them." Query in an e-mail. "We prefer electronic submissions. Please use submission engine online." For snail mail, send SASE for reply and return of ms, or send a disposable copy of ms.

MAGAZINES NEEDS Pays 1 contributor's copy and offers 50% discount on additional copies.

TIPS "We have to fall in love with a particular fiction."

A GATHERING OF THE TRIBES

P.O. Box 20693, Tompkins Square Station, New York NY 10009. (212)777-2038. **E-mail:** gatheringofthetribes@gmail.com. **Website:** www.tribes.org. **Contact:** Steve Cannon. *A Gathering of the Tribes* is a multicultural and multigenerational publication featuring poetry, fiction, interviews, essays, visual art, and musical scores. The audience is anyone interested in the arts from a diverse perspective. Publishes ms 3-6 months after acceptance. "Due to the massive number of submissions we receive, we do not guarantee responses or return work that is not accepted for publication." Sample copy: $15. Guidelines online.

Magazine: 8.5x10; 130 pages; glossy paper and cover; illustrations; photos. Receives 20 unsolicited mss/month. Publishes 40% new writers/year. Has published work by Carl Watson, Ishle Park, Wang Pang, and Hanif Kureishi.

MAGAZINES NEEDS Submit up to 5 poems by postal mail or e-mail. No metrical or rhyming poetry, "unless it is exceedingly contemporary/experimental." Pays 1 contributor's copy.

TIPS "Make sure your work has substance."

THE GEORGIA REVIEW

The University of Georgia, Main Library, Room 706A, 320 S. Jackson St., Athens GA 30602. (706)542-3481. **Fax:** (706)542-0047. **E-mail:** garev@uga.edu. **Website:** thegeorgiareview.com. **Contact:** Stephen Corey, editor. "*The Georgia Review* is a literary quarterly committed to the art of editorial practice. We collaborate equally with established and emerging authors of essays, stories, poems, and reviews in the pursuit of extraordinary works that engage with the evolving concerns and interests of intellectually curious readers from around the world. Our aim in curating content is not only to elevate literature, publishing, and the arts, but also to help facilitate socially conscious

partnerships in our surrounding communities." $3 online submission fee waived for subscribers. No fees for manuscripts submitted by post. Reading period: August 15-May 15. Buys first North American serial rights. Pays on publication. Publishes ms an average of 6 months after acceptance. Responds in 2 weeks to queries; in 2-3 months to mss. Sample copy: $15. Guidelines online.

MAGAZINES NEEDS We seek original, excellent poetry. Submit 3-5 poems at a time. Pays $4/line.

GERTRUDE

Queer Literary Journal and Book Club, 4857 NE 13th Ave., Portland OR 97211. **E-mail:** editorgertrudepress@gmail.com. **Website:** www.gertrudepress.org. **Contact:** Tammy Lynne Stoner. *Gertrude* is a "literary journal featuring the voices and visions of LGBTQA writers and artists" whose editors also make selections from the best of new and notable queer, literary novels for GERTIE - their 'quarterly, queer book club.'" Cover art $50; bigger prize purse for annual chapbook contests. Publishes ms 6 months after acceptance. Responds in 3-9 months, typically. Sample copy online. Guidelines online.

MAGAZINES NEEDS Has published poetry by Judith Barrington, Deanna Kern Ludwin, Casey Charles, Michael Montlack, Megan Kruse, and Noah Tysick. Submit via online submissions manager. Length: open, but "poems less than 60 lines are preferable."

TIPS "We look for strong characterization and imagery, and new, unique ways of writing about universal experiences. Or anything bizarre."

THE GETTYSBURG REVIEW

Gettysburg College, Gettysburg College, 300 N. Washington St., Gettysburg PA 17325. (717)337-6770. **E-mail:** mdrew@gettysburg.edu. **Website:** www.gettysburgreview.com. **Contact:** Mark Drew, editor; Jess L. Bryant, managing editor. Published quarterly, *The Gettysburg Review* considers unsolicited submissions of poetry, fiction, and essays. "Our concern is quality. Mss submitted here should be extremely well written." Reading period September 1-May 31. Buys first North American serial rights. Pays on publication. Publishes ms an average of 6 months after acceptance. Responds in 1 month to queries; in 3-6 months to mss. Editorial lead time 1 year. Sample: $15. Guidelines online.

MAGAZINES NEEDS Considers "well-written poems of all kinds on all subjects." Has published poetry by Rita Dove, Alice Friman, Philip Schultz, Michelle

Boisseau, Bob Hicok, Linda Pastan, and G. C. Waldrep. Does not want sentimental, clichéd verse. Pays $2.50/line, a one-year subscription, and 1 contributor's copy.

GINOSKO LITERARY JOURNAL

Ginosko, P.O. Box 246, Fairfax CA 94978. (415)785-3160. **E-mail:** editorginosko@aol.com. **Website:** www.ginoskoliteraryjournal.com. **Contact:** Robert Paul Cesaretti, editor. "*Ginosko* (ghin-océ-koe): To perceive, understand, realize, come to know; knowledge that has an inception, a progress, an attainment. The recognition of truth by experience." Accepting short fiction and poetry, creative nonfiction, interviews, social justice concerns, and literary insights for www.ginoskoliteraryjournal.com. Reads year round. Length of articles flexible; accepts excerpts. Publishing as semiannual e-zine. Print anthology every 2 years. Check downloadable issues on website for tone and style. Downloads free; accepts donations. Member CLMP. Copyright reverts to author. No payment. Publishes ms 0-6 months after acceptance. Editorial lead time 1-2 months. Sample copy free online. Guidelines online.

MAGAZINES NEEDS Online submissions manager (ginosko.submittable.com/submit), see website http://GinoskoLiteraryJournal.com.

HOW TO CONTACT Check website.

TIPS "Read several issues for tone and style."

💲 GRASSLIMB

P.O. Box 420816, San Diego CA 92142-0816. **E-mail:** editor@grasslimb.com. **Website:** www.grasslimb.com. **Contact:** Valerie Polichar, editor. *Grasslimb* publishes literary prose, poetry, and art. Fiction is best when it is short and avant-garde or otherwise experimental. Acquires first print publication serial rights (or one-time reprint rights, if appropriate). Pays on acceptance. Publishes ms 1-6 months after acceptance. Responds in 4-6 months to mss. Rarely comments on rejected mss. Sample copy: $3. Guidelines for SASE, e-mail, or on website.

⬤ Submit full mss—no queries. Although general topics are welcome, we're less likely to select work regarding romance, sex, aging, and children. Fiction in an experimental, avant-garde or surreal mode is often more interesting to us than a traditional story. When submitting poetry, 4-6 pieces are preferred; line count is not necessary. For artwork, please submit photocopies or electronic versions (if electronic, 600 dpi preferred) only. Prose must include a word count and should not exceed 2,500 words; 1,000-2,000 is best for us. Submissions over 3,000 words will be returned unread. Reviews of 500-1,000 words are preferred. Please do not submit work to us more often than once every six months unless you have had work accepted previously to our publication, in which case you are not subject to a limit.

MAGAZINES NEEDS Submit poems via e-mail or postal mail with SASE. Pays $5-20/poem.

TIPS "We publish brief fiction work that can be read in a single sitting over a cup of coffee. Work is generally 'literary' in nature rather than mainstream. Experimental work welcome. Remember to have your work proofread and to send short work. We cannot read over 3,000 words and prefer under 2,000 words. Include word count."

THE GREAT AMERICAN POETRY SHOW

Eavesdropping on the Cosmos, LLC, **E-mail:** larry@tgaps.com. **Website:** tgaps.net. **Contact:** Larry Ziman, editor/publisher. *The Great American Poetry Show* is a hardcover, serial poetry anthology. "Volume 1, published in 2005 with 150 pages, featured 113 poems from 83 poets. Volume 2, published in 2010 with 176 pages, featured 134 poems from 92 poets. And Volume 3, published in 2015 with 181 pages, featured 135 poems from 73 poets." Press run for each volume was 1,000. Print and reprint rights specified by contract; poets keep copyrights to their poems. Responds within 1-4 weeks ("depends on how busy we are"). Single copy: $35 (print), $0.99 (PDF download only).

⬤ *The Great American Poetry Show* is sheet-fed offset-printed, perfect-bound, with cloth cover and art/graphics.

MAGAZINES NEEDS Submit any number and length of poems at a time. Accepts e-mail submissions in body of e-mail or as 1 attachment. Cover letter is optional. No stamped-mail submissions. "If we reject a submission of your work, please send us another group to go through." Has published poetry by Brad Johnson, Carol Carpenter, Philip Wexler, Fredrick Zydek, Patricia Polak, Steve De France, Lois Swann, Alan Catlin, Sarah Brown Weitzman, Kevin Pilkington, Susan Sonde, Doug Ramspeck, Leonard Orr, and Julie M. Tate. Wants poems on any subject, in any style, of any length. Pays 2 contributor's copies.

TIPS "Please visit our website, which has over 10,000 links to articles, essays, interviews, reviews, magazines, publishers, and blogs."

GREEN HILLS LITERARY LANTERN

Truman State University, Department of English, Truman State University, Kirksville MO 63501. E-mail: adavis@truman.edu. Website: ghll.truman.edu. Contact: Adam Brooke Davis, prose editor/managing editor; Joe Benevento, poetry editor. *Green Hills Literary Lantern* is published annually, in June, by Truman State University. Historically, the print publication ran between 200-300 pages, consisting of poetry, fiction, reviews, and interviews. The digital magazine is of similar proportions and artistic standards. Open to the work of new writers, as well as more established writers. Holds all rights, but returns rights to author on request. Does not provide payment. Publishes ms an average of 6 months after acceptance. Responds in 2 months to mss and queries. Sample copies online. Guidelines online.

MAGAZINES NEEDS "We prefer poetry written by poets who are more interested in communicating something that seems important, beautiful, funny, or interesting to them than they are in making themselves seem erudite, clever, or in the know. We pay attention to all the usual things—command of line; attention to the sound, rhythm, and imagery; arresting figurative language—but we also seek poetry that has some investment of real feeling rather than bloodless exhibitions of technical talent." Length: up to 60 lines/poem.

GREEN MOUNTAINS REVIEW

Northern Vermont University- Johnson, 337 College Hill, Johnson VT 05656. (802)635-1350. E-mail: gmr@northernvermont.edu. Website: greenmountainsreview.com. Contact: Elizabeth Powell, editor; Darcie Abbene, nonfiction and managing editor; Jensen Beach, fiction editor; Didi Jackson, assistant poetry editor. Semiannual magazine covering poems, stories, and creative nonfiction by both well-known authors and promising newcomers. Acquires first North American serial rights. Rights revert to author upon request. Publishes ms 6-12 months after acceptance. Responds in 1 month to queries; in 6 months to mss. Sample copy: $7. Guidelines available free.

○ The editors are open to a wide range of styles and subject matter. Open reading period: September 1-March 1.

MAGAZINES NEEDS Submit poems via online submissions manager. Has published poetry by Carol Frost, Sharon Olds, Carl Phillips, David St. John, and David Wojahn.

TIPS "We encourage you to order some of our back issues to acquaint yourself with what has been accepted in the past."

GREENPRINTS

P.O. Box 1355, Fairview NC 28730. (828)628-1902. E-mail: pat@greenprints.com. Website: www.greenprints.com. Contact: Pat Stone, managing editor. "*GreenPrints* is the 'Weeder's Digest.' We share the human—*not* how-to—side of gardening. We publish true personal gardening stories and essays: humorous, heartfelt, insightful, inspiring. We love good, true, well-told personal *stories*—all must be about gardening!" Buys first North American serial rights. Responds in 3 months to mss. No editorial lead time. Sample: $5. Guidelines available online (look under About Us).

MAGAZINES NEEDS "If it's not hands-on and gardening based, please don't send it." Pays $25.

TIPS Wants "a great, true, *unique* personal *story* with dialogue, a narrative, and something special that happens to make it truly stand out."

THE GREENSBORO REVIEW

MFA Writing Program, 3302 MHRA Building, UNC-Greensboro, Greensboro NC 27402. E-mail: jlclark@uncg.edu. Website: tgronline.net. Contact: Jim Clark, editor. "A local lit mag with an international reputation. We've been 'old school' since 1965." Acquires first North American serial rights. Responds in about 4 months. Sample copy: $8. Guidelines online.

○ Stories for *The Greensboro Review* have been included in *Best American Short Stories, The O. Henry Awards Prize Stories, New Stories from the South* and *Pushcart Prize*. Does not accept e-mail submissions.

MAGAZINES NEEDS Submit via online submission form or postal mail. Include cover letter. Length: no limit. Pays contributor's copies.

TIPS "We want to see the best being written regardless of theme, subject, or style."

⑤ GRIST: A JOURNAL OF THE LITERARY ARTS

English Dept., 301 McClung Tower, Univ. of Tennessee, Knoxville TN 37996-0430. E-mail: gristeditors@gmail.com. Website: www.gristjournal.com. Editor-in-Chief: Jeremy Michael Reed.. *Grist* is a nationally distributed journal of fiction, nonfiction, poetry, interviews, and craft essays. We seek work of high literary quality from both emerging and established writers, and we welcome all styles and aesthetic approaches. Each issue is accompanied by Grist Online, which features some of the best work we receive during our reading period. In addition to general submissions, *Grist* holds the ProForma Contest every spring, recognizing unpublished creative work that explores the relationship between content and form, whether in fiction, nonfiction, poetry, or a hybrid genre. Throughout the year, we publish interviews, craft essays, and reviews on our blog, The Writing Life. Pays on publication. See website for details.

MAGAZINES NEEDS Pays $10/page.

TIPS "*Grist* seeks work from both emerging and established writers, whose work is of high literary quality."

GULF STREAM MAGAZINE

English Department, FIU, Biscayne Bay Campus, 3000 NE 151 St., AC1-335, North Miami FL 33181. **E-mail:** gulfstreamlitmag@gmail.com. **Website:** www.gulfstreamlitmag.com. **Contact:** T.C. Jones, editor in chief. "*Gulf Stream Magazine* has been publishing emerging and established writers of exceptional fiction, nonfiction, and poetry since 1989. We also publish interviews and book reviews. Past contributors include Sherman Alexie, Steve Almond, Jan Beatty, Lee Martin, Robert Wrigley, Dennis Lehane, Liz Robbins, Stuart Dybek, David Kirby, Ann Hood, Ha Jin, B.H. Fairchild, Naomi Shihab Nye, F. Daniel Rzicznek, and Connie May Fowler. *Gulf Stream Magazine* is supported by the Creative Writing Program at Florida International University in Miami, Florida." Acquires first serial rights. Responds in 6 months. Guidelines online.

MAGAZINES NEEDS "Submit online only. Please read guidelines on website in full. Submissions that do not conform to our guidelines will be discarded. We do not accept e-mailed or mailed submissions. We read from September 1-November 1 and January 15-April 1." Cover letter is required. Wants "poetry of any style and subject matter as long as it's of high literary quality."

TIPS "We look for fresh, original writing: well-plotted stories with unforgettable characters, fresh poetry, and experimental writing."

HAIGHT ASHBURY LITERARY JOURNAL

558 Joost Ave., San Francisco CA 94127. (415)584-8264. **E-mail:** haljeditor@gmail.com. **Website:** haightashburyliteraryjournal.wordpress.com. **Contact:** Alice Rogoff and Cesar Love, editors. *Haight*

Ashbury Literary Journal, publishes well-written poetry and fiction. *HALJ*'s voices are often of people who have been marginalized, oppressed, or abused. *HALJ* strives to bring literary arts to the general public, to the San Francisco community of writers, to the Haight Ashbury neighborhood, and to people of varying ages, genders, ethnic groups, and sexual preferences. The Journal is produced as a tabloid to maintain an accessible price for low-income people. Rights revert to author. Publishes ms 6 months-a year after acceptance. Responds in 4 months. Sample: $6. Subscription: $14 for 2 issues, $28 for 4 issues; $75 for back issues and future issues. Only send up to 6 poems once a year or up to 3 short pieces of fiction or one longer piece. Send a SASE. Only by mail unless overseas.

MAGAZINES NEEDS Submit up to 6 poems at a time. Submit only once every 6 months. No e-mail submissions (unless overseas); postal submissions only. Please type 1 poem to a page, put name and address on every page, and include SASE. No bio. Sometimes publishes theme issues (each issue changes its theme and emphasis). Has published poetry by Dan O'Connell, Diane Frank, Dancing Bear, Lee Herrick, Elaine Gerard and Al Young. Length: prefer under 2 pages.

⑤ HANGING LOOSE

Hanging Loose Press, 231 Wyckoff St., Brooklyn NY 11217. (347)529-4738. **Fax:** (347)227-8215. **E-mail:** print225@aol.com. **Website:** www.hangingloosepress.com. **Contact:** Robert Hershon and Mark Pawlak, editors. *Hanging Loose*, published in April and October, concentrates on the work of new writers. Wants excellent, energetic poems and short stories. Responds in 3 months. Sample copy: $14. Guidelines available online.

○ *Hanging Loose* is 120 pages, offset-printed on heavy stock, flat-spined, with 4-color glossy card cover.

MAGAZINES NEEDS Submit up to 6 poems at a time by postal mail with SASE. "Would-be contributors should read the magazine first." Has published poetry by Sherman Alexie, Paul Violi, Donna Brook, Kimiko Hahn, Harvey Shapiro, and Ha Jin. Considers poetry by teens (1 section contains poems by high-school-age poets). Pays small fee and 2 contributor's copies.

ALSO OFFERS Hanging Loose Press does not consider unsolicited book mss or artwork.

HARTWORKS

D.C. Creative Writing Workshop, 601 Mississippi Ave. SE, Washington DC 20032. (202)297-1957. **Fax:** (202)645-3426. **E-mail:** info@dccww.org. **Website:** www.dccww.org. **Contact:** Nancy Schwalb, artistic director. *hArtworks* appears 3 times/year. "We publish the poetry of Hart Middle School students (as far as we know, Hart may be the only public middle school in the U.S. with its own poetry magazine) and the writing of guest writers such as Nikki Giovanni, Alan Cheuse, Arnost Lustig, Henry Taylor, Mark Craver, and Cornelius Eady, along with interviews between the kids and the grown-up pros. We also publish work by our writers-in-residence, who teach workshops at Hart, and provide trips to readings, slams, museums, and plays." Wants "vivid, precise, imaginative language that communicates from the heart as well as the head." Does not want "poetry that only 'sounds' good; it also needs to say something meaningful." Has published poetry by Maryum Abdullah, Myron Jones, Nichell Kee, Kiana Murphy, James Tindle, and Sequan Wilson. Single copy: $12; subscription: $30. Make checks payable to D.C. Creative Writing Workshop.

Although this journal doesn't accept submissions from the general public, it's included here as an outstanding example of what a literary journal can be (for anyone of any age). *hArtworks* is 92 pages, magazine-sized, professionally printed, perfect bound, with card cover. Receives about 1,000 poems/year, accepts about 20%. Press run is 500; 100 distributed free to writers, teachers.

MAGAZINES NEEDS "Writers-in-residence solicit most submissions from their classes, and then a committee of student editors makes the final selections. Each year, our second issue is devoted to responses to the Holocaust."

HARVARD REVIEW

Harvard University, Lamont Library, Harvard University, Cambridge MA 02138. **E-mail:** info@harvardreview.org. **Website:** harvardreview.fas.harvard.edu. Chloe Garcia Roberts. **Contact:** Christina Thompson, editor; Suzanne Berne, fiction editor; Major Jackson, poetry editor; Chloe Garcia Roberts, managing editor. Semiannual magazine covering poetry, fiction, essays, drama, graphics, and reviews in the spring and fall by an eclectic range of international writers. "Previous contributors include John Updike, Alice Hoffman, Joyce Carol Oates, Miranda July, and Jim Crace. We also publish the work of emerging and previously unpublished writers." Does not accept e-mail submissions. Responds in 6 months to mss. Guidelines online.

MAGAZINES NEEDS Submit up to 5 poems via online submissions manager or postal mail.

TIPS "Writers at all stages of their careers are invited to apply; however, we can only publish a very small fraction of the material we receive. We recommend that you familiarize yourself with *Harvard Review* before you submit your work."

HAWAI'I PACIFIC REVIEW

Website: hawaiipacificreview.org. **Contact:** Tyler McMahon, editor; Christa Cushon, managing editor. *"Hawai'i Pacific Review* is the online literary magazine of Hawai'i Pacific University. It features poetry and prose by authors from Hawai'i, the mainland, and around the world. *HPR* was started as a print annual in 1987. In 2013, it began to publish exclusively online. *HPR* publishes work on a rolling basis. Poems, stories, and essays are posted 1 piece at a time, several times a month. All contents are archived on the site." Acquires online rights. All other rights remain with the author.

MAGAZINES NEEDS Submit up to 3 poems at a time via online submissions manager (each poem should be a separate submission). "Because we try to be readable on all sorts of screens and devices, we can't do justice to poems with unorthodox spacing. For this reason, we strongly prefer poetry that sticks to the left margin."

TIPS "We look for the unusual or original plot, and prose with the texture and nuance of poetry. Character development or portrayal must be unusual/original; humanity shown in an original, insightful way (or characters); sense of humor where applicable. Be sure it's a draft that has gone through substantial changes, with supervision from a more experienced writer, if you're a beginner. Write about intense emotion and feeling, not just about someone's divorce or shaky relationship. No soap-opera-like fiction."

HAWAI'I REVIEW

University of Hawaii Board of Publications, 2445 Campus Rd., Hemenway Hall 107, Honolulu HI 96822. (808)956-3030. **Fax:** (808)956-3083. **E-mail:** hawaiireview@gmail.com. **Website:** http://hawaiireview.org/. *Hawai'i Review* is a student-run biannual literary and visual arts print journal featuring national and international writing and visual art, as well as regional literature and visual art of Hawai'i and the Pacific. Buys first North American serial rights, archive rights. Publishes ms an average of 3 months after acceptance. Responds in 3 months to mss. Sample copy: free, plus $5 shipping (back issue). Single copy: $12.50. Guidelines available online.

○ Accepts submissions online through Submittable only. Offers yearly award with $500 prizes in poetry and fiction.

MAGAZINES NEEDS Submit up to 6 poems via online submission manager. Length: up to 500 lines/poem (though space limitations are taken into account for longer poems).

TIPS "Make it new."

HAYDEN'S FERRY REVIEW

E-mail: hfr@asu.edu. **Website:** haydensferryreview. com. **Contact:** Katie Berta. "*Hayden's Ferry Review* publishes the best-quality fiction, poetry, and creative nonfiction from new, emerging, and established writers." Work from *Hayden's Ferry Review* has been selected for inclusion in *Pushcart Prize* anthologies and the *Best American* series. No longer accepts postal mail or e-mail submissions (except in the case of the incarcerated and the visually impaired). Acquires first North American serial rights. Publishes ms an average of 6 months after acceptance. Responds in 6-7 months. Editorial lead time 5 months. Sample copy: $13. Back issues: $9. Guidelines online.

MAGAZINES NEEDS Submit up to 5 poems via online submissions manager. Pays 1 contributor's copy.

HELIOTROPE

E-mail: heliotropeditor@gmail.com. **Website:** www. heliotropemag.com. *Heliotrope* is a quarterly e-zine that publishes fiction, articles, and poetry. Buys first world electronic rights with 120-day exclusivity, first print rights for series of chapbooks, nonexclusive anthology rights. Pays on publication. Responds in 1 month to mss. Guidelines available online.

MAGAZINES NEEDS Submit via e-mail. Pays $50.

◑ THE HELIX

E-mail: helixmagazine@gmail.com. **Website:** helix-magazine.org. **Contact:** See website for current editorial staff.. "The *Helix* is a Central Connecticut State University undergraduate publication that puts out an issue every semester. The magazine features writing from CCSU students, writing from the Hartford

County community, and an array of submissions from all over the world. The magazine publishes multiple genres of literature and art, including poetry, fiction, drama, nonfiction, paintings, photography, watercolor, collage, stencil, and computer-generated artwork. It is a student-run publication and is funded by the university." Acquires first North American serial rights. All rights revert to author upon publication. Wait time will vary from a few weeks to six months. Guidelines online.

MAGAZINES NEEDS Submit by online submissions manager.

TIPS "Please see our website for specific deadlines, as it changes every semester based on a variety of factors, but we typically leave the submission manager open sometime starting in the summer to around the end of October for the Fall issue, and during the winter to late February or mid-March for the Spring issue. Contributions are invited from all members of the campus community, as well as the literary community at large."

HELLOHORROR

Houston TX (512)537-0504. **E-mail:** info@hellohorror. com. **E-mail:** submissions@hellohorror.com. **Website:** www.hellohorror.com. **Contact:** Brent Armour, editor-in-chief. "*HelloHorror* is an online literary magazine. We are currently in search of literary pieces, photography, and visual art, including film from writers and artists that have a special knack for inducing goose bumps and raised hairs. This genre has become, especially in film, noticeably saturated in gore and high shock-value aspects as a crutch to avoid the true challenge of bringing about real psychological fear to an audience that's persistently more and more numb to its tactics. While we are not opposed to the extreme, blood and guts need bones and cartilage. Otherwise it's just a sloppy mess. Specifically, we are looking for pieces grounded in psychological fear induced by surreal situations unusual to horror rather than gore. We will not automatically pass on a gore-drenched story, but it needs to have its foundations in psychological horror." Buys first serial rights. Publishes ms 3-12 months after acceptance. Responds in 1-6 months to queries and mss. Sample copy online. Guidelines online.

MAGAZINES NEEDS Submit poems via e-mail. "All types are accepted so long as they are of the horror genre."

TIPS "We like authors that show consideration for their readers. A great horror story leaves an impression on the reader long after it is finished. Consider your reader and consider yourself. What really scares you as opposed to what's stereotypically supposed to scare you? Bring us and our readers into that place of fear with you."

HIGHLIGHTS FOR CHILDREN

803 Church St., Honesdale PA 18431. (570)253-1080. **Fax:** (570)251-7847. **E-mail:** eds@highlights.com (Do not send submissions to this address.). **E-mail:** Highlights.submittable.com. **Website:** www.highlights.com. **Contact:** Christine French Cully, editor-in-chief. "This book of wholesome fun is dedicated to helping children grow in basic skills and knowledge, in creativeness, in ability to think and reason, in sensitivity to others, in high ideals, and worthy ways of living—for children are the world's most important people." We publish stories and articles for beginning and advanced readers. Up to 400 words for beginning readers, up to 750 words for advanced readers. Guidelines updated regularly at Highlights.submittable.com. Buys all rights. Pays on acceptance. Responds in 2 months. Guidelines online.

MAGAZINES NEEDS See Highlights.submittable.com. No previously published poetry. Buys all rights. 16 lines maximum. Pays $50 and up.

TIPS "We update our guidelines and current needs regularly at Highlights.submittable.com. Read several recent issues of the magazine before submitting. In addition to fiction, nonfiction, and poetry, we purchase crafts, puzzles, and activities that will stimulate children mentally and creatively. We judge each submission on its own merits. Expert reviews and complete bibliography are required for nonfiction. Include special qualifications, if any, of author. Speak to today's kids. Avoid didactic, overt messages. Even though our general principles haven't changed over the years, we are contemporary in our approach to issues."

HIRAM POETRY REVIEW

P.O. Box 162, Hiram OH 44234. **E-mail:** poetryreview@hiram.edu. **Website:** hirampoetryreview.wordpress.com. **Contact:** Willard Greenwood, poetry editor. *Hiram Poetry Review*, published annually in spring, features distinctive, beautiful, and heroic poetry. Wants works of high and low art. Tends to favor poems that are pockets of resistance in the undeclared war against plain speech, but interested in any work of high quality. Acquires first North American serial rights. Rights return to poets upon publication. Responds in 6 months. Subscription: $9/year; $23 for 3 years.

Press run is 400 (300 subscribers, 150 libraries). **MAGAZINES NEEDS** Send 3-5 poems at a time. Considers simultaneous submissions. No e-mail submissions unless international. Cover letter is required. Include brief bio. Reads submissions year round. Length: up to 50 lines/poem. Pays 2 contributor's copies.

THE HOLLINS CRITIC

P.O. Box 9538, Hollins University, Roanoke VA 24020-1538. **Website:** www.hollins.edu/who-we-are/news-media/hollins-critic. *The Hollins Critic*, published 5 times/year, presents the first serious surveys of the whole bodies of contemporary writers' work, with complete checklists. In past issues, you'll find essays on such writers as Claudia Emerson (by Allison Seay), Wilma Dykeman (by Casey Clabough), Jerry Mirskin (by Howard Nelson), Sally Mann (by Martha Park), James Alan McPherson (by James Robert Saunders), Elise Partridge (by Nicholas Birns), and Ron Rash (by Jerry Wayne Wells). Buys first North American serial rights. Pays on publication. Publishes ms an average of 1 year after acceptance. Responds in 2 months to mss. Sample copy: $3. Guidelines for #10 SASE or online.

Uses a few short poems in each issue, interesting in form, content, or both. *The Hollins Critic* is 24 pages, magazine-sized. Press run is 500. Subscription: $12/year ($17 outside US). No postal or e-mail submissions. Has published poetry by Natasha Trethewey, Carol Moldaw, David Huddle, Margaret Gibson, and Julia Johnson.

MAGAZINES NEEDS Submit up to 5 poems at a time using the online submission form at www.hollinscriticsubmissions.com, available September 15-December 1. Submissions received at other times will be returned unread. Publishes 16-20 poems/year. Pays $25/poem plus 5 contributor's copies.

TIPS "We accept unsolicited poetry submissions; all other content is by prearrangement."

HOME PLANET NEWS ONLINE

E-mail: homeplanetnewsol@gmail.com. **Website:** homeplanetnews.org/AOnLine.html. **Contact:** Frank Murphy, chief editor. *Home Planet News* publishes mainly poetry along with some fiction, as well as reviews (books, theater, and art) and articles of literary interest. Home Planet News Online was created when the print edition could no longer be published. Donald Lev ask Frank Murphy (who had been doing an online version of some of the magazine) to continue the magazine online. We have just finished our 5th Issue. Acquires one-time rights. Publishes 6-8 months after acceptance. Responds in 6 months to e-mail submission. Guidelines online.

MAGAZINES NEEDS Submit 3-6 poems at a time. Length: no limit, but shorter poems (under 30 lines) stand a better chance. Pays one-year gift subscription plus 3 contributor's copies.

TIPS "Read an Issue before sending in to us. It will give you an idea of what we are looking for."

⑤ HOOT

A Postcard Review of (Mini) Poetry and Prose, 4234 Chestnut St., Apt. 1 R, Philadelphia PA 19104. **E-mail:** info@hootreview.com. **Website:** www.hootreview.com. **Contact:** Jane-Rebecca Cannarella, editor in chief; Amanda Vacharat and Dorian Geisler, editors/co-founders. *HOOT* publishes 1 piece of writing, designed with original art and/or photographs, on the front of a postcard every month, as well as 2-3 pieces online. The postcards are intended for sharing, to be hung on the wall, etc. Therefore, *HOOT* looks for very brief, surprising-yet-gimmick-free writing that can stand on its own, that also follows "The Refrigerator Rule"—something that you would hang on your refrigerator and would want to read and look at for a whole month. This rule applies to online content as well. Buys first North American serial rights and electronic rights. Pays on publication. Publishes ms 2 months after acceptance. Sample copy: $2. Guidelines available online.

○   Costs $2 to submit up to 2 pieces of work. Submit through online submissions manager or postal mail.

MAGAZINES NEEDS Length: up to 10 lines. Pays $10-100 for print publication.

TIPS "We look for writing with audacity and zest from authors who are not afraid to take risks. We appreciate work that is able to go beyond mere description in its 150 words. We offer free online workshops every other Wednesday for authors who would like feedback on their work from the *HOOT* editors. We also often give feedback with our rejections. We publish roughly 6-10 new writers each year."

HOTEL AMERIKA

Columbia College Chicago, The Department of Creative Writing, 600 S. Michigan Ave., Chicago IL 60605. (312)369-8175. **Website:** www.hotelamerika.net. **Con-**

tact: David Lazar, editor; Jenn Tatum, managing editor. *Hotel Amerika* is a venue for both well-known and emerging writers. Publishes exceptional writing in all forms. Strives to house the most unique and provocative poetry, fiction, and nonfiction available. Guidelines online.

○   Mss will be considered between September 1 and May 1. Materials received after May 1 and before September 1 will be returned unread. Work published in *Hotel Amerika* has been included in *The Pushcart Prize* and *The Best American Poetry*, and featured on *Poetry Daily*.

MAGAZINES NEEDS Welcomes submissions in all genres.

⑤ HUBBUB

5344 SE 38th Ave., Portland OR 97202. **Website:** www.reed.edu/hubbub. **Contact:** J. Shugrue and Lisa M. Steinman, co-editors. *Hubbub*, published once/year, is designed "to feature a multitude of voices from interesting, contemporary American poets." Wants "poems that are well crafted, with something to say. We have no single style, subject, or length requirement and in particular will consider long poems." Acquires first North American serial rights. Pays on publication. Publishes poems 1-12 months (usually) after acceptance. Responds in 4 months. Sample: $3.35 (back issues), $7 (current issue). Subscription: $7/year. Guidelines for SASE or online.

○   *Hubbub* is 50-70 pages, digest-sized, offset-printed, perfect-bound, with cover art. Receives about 1,200 submissions/year, accepts up to 2%. Press run is 350.

MAGAZINES NEEDS Submit 3-6 typed poems at a time. Include SASE. "We review 2-4 poetry books/year in short (three-page) reviews; all reviews are solicited. We do, however, list books received/recommended." Send materials for review consideration. Has published poetry by Madeline DeFrees, Cecil Giscombe, Carolyn Kizer, Primus St. John, Shara McCallum, and Alice Fulton. Does not want light verse. No length requirements. Pays $20/poem.

CONTEST/AWARD OFFERINGS Offers 4 prizes/issue: the Vern Rutsala Award ($1,000), the Vi Gale Award ($500), the Kenneth O. Hanson Award ($200), and the Stout Award ($175). No applications; no submission fees.

⑤ THE HUDSON REVIEW

33 W. 67th St., New York NY 10023. (212)650-0020. **E-mail:** info@hudsonreview.com. **Website:** hudsonre-

view.com. **Contact:** Paula Deitz, editor. Since its beginning, the magazine has dealt with the area where literature bears on the intellectual life of the time and on diverse aspects of American culture. It has no university affiliation and is not committed to any narrow academic aim or to any particular political perspective. The magazine serves as a major forum for the work of new writers and for the exploration of new developments in literature and the arts. It has a distinguished record of publishing little-known or undiscovered writers, many of whom have become major literary figures. Each issue contains a wide range of material including poetry, fiction, essays on literary and cultural topics, book reviews, reports from abroad, and chronicles covering film, theater, dance, music, and art. *The Hudson Review* is distributed in 25 countries. Unsolicited mss are read according to the following schedule: April 1 through June 30 for poetry, September 1 through November 30 for fiction, and January 1 through March 31 for nonfiction. Pays on publication. Publishes ms an average of 6 months after acceptance. Responds in 6 months to mss. Editorial lead time 3 months. Sample copy: $11. Guidelines online.

MAGAZINES NEEDS Submit up to 7 poems by mail from **April 1 through June 30** only.

TIPS "We do not specialize in publishing any particular 'type' of writing; our sole criterion for accepting unsolicited work is literary quality. The best way for you to get an idea of the range of work we publish is to read a current issue. Unsolicited mss submitted outside of specified reading times will be returned unread. Do not send submissions via e-mail."

⑤ HUNGER MOUNTAIN

Vermont College of Fine Arts, 36 College St., Montpelier VT 05602. (802)828-8517. **E-mail:** hungermtn@vcfa.edu. **Website:** www.hungermtn.org. Editor: Erin Stalcup.. **Contact:** Cameron Finch, managing editor. Accepts high-quality work from unknown, emerging, or successful writers. Publishing fiction, creative nonfiction, poetry, and young adult & children's writing. Four writing contests annually. *Hunger Mountain* is a print and online journal of the arts. The print journal is about 200 pages, 7x9, professionally printed, perfect-bound, with full-bleed color artwork on cover. Press run is 1,000. Over 10,000 visits online monthly. Uses online submissions manager (Submittable). Member: CLMP. Buys first worldwide serial rights. Pays on publication. Publishes ms an average of 1 year after acceptance. Responds in 4-6 months to mss. Single issue: $12; subscription: $18 for 2 issues/2 years; back issue: $8. Checks payable to Vermont College of Fine Arts, or purchase online. Guidelines online.

MAGAZINES NEEDS Submit 1-5 poems at a time. "We are looking for truly original poems that run the aesthetic gamut: lively engagement with language in the act of pursuit. Some poems remind us in a fresh way of our own best thoughts; some poems bring us to a place beyond language for which there aren't quite words; some poems take us on a complicated language ride that is, itself, its own aim. Complex poem-architectures thrill us and still-points in the turning world do, too. Send us the best of what you have." Submit using online submissions manager. No light verse, humor/quirky/catchy verse, greeting card verse. Pays $25 for poetry up to 2 poems (plus $5/poem for additional poems).

ALSO OFFERS Annual contests: Ruth Stone Poetry Prize; The Howard Frank Mosher Short Fiction Prize; the Katherine Paterson Prize for Young Adult and Children's Writing; The Hunger Mountain Creative Nonfiction Prize. Visit www.hungermtn.org for information about prizes.

TIPS "Mss must be typed, prose double-spaced. Poets submit poems as one document. No multiple genre submissions. Fresh viewpoints and human interest are very important, as is originality and diversity. We are committed to publishing an outstanding journal of the arts. Do not send entire novels, mss, or short story collections. Do not send previously published work."

HYDE PARK LIVING

Community Publications, Inc., 179 Fairfield Ave., Bellevue KY 41073. (859)291-1412. **E-mail:** hydepark@livingmagazines.com. **Website:** www.livingmagazines.com. **Contact:** Grace DeGregorio. Buys all rights. Pays on publication. Editorial lead time 2 months. Guidelines by e-mail.

MAGAZINES NEEDS Please query.

I-70 REVIEW

Writing from the Middle and Beyond, 913 Joseph Dr., Lawrence KS 66049. **E-mail:** i70review@gmail.com. **Website:** www.fieldinfoserv.com. **Contact:** Gary Lechliter, Maryfrances Wagner, Greg Field, Gay Dust, editors; Jan Duncan-O'Neal editor emeritus. *I-70 Review* is an annual literary magazine. "Our interests lie in writing grounded in fresh language, imagery, and metaphor. We prefer free verse in which the writer pays attention to the sound and rhythm of the language. We appreciate poetry with individual voice and a good lyric or a strong narrative. In fiction, we like short pieces that are surprising and uncommon. We want writing that captures the human spirit with unusual topics or familiar topics with a different perspective or approach. We reject stereotypical and clichéd writing, as well as sentimental work or writing that summarizes and tells instead of shows. We look for writing that pays attention to words, sentences, and style. We publish literary writing. We do not publish anything erotic, religious, or political." Open submission period is July 1-December 31. Buys one-time, first North American serial rights. Pays with contributor copies only. Publishes annually in September. "We publish once a year in September." Responds in 4-6 weeks, often sooner. Sample poetry available online. Sample copy available for SASE and $13.00 +$4.00 for postage. Submission guidelines are also online. View our website for featured writers to get an idea of what we like.

MAGAZINES NEEDS "We publish a variety of literary styles but prefer lyric and narrative. We want nothing sentimental, nothing with sing-songy rhyme, nothing abstract or clichéd or predictable. Nothing political, religious, didactic, or erotic. We accept some experimental as long as it is well-crafted and accessible. We reject writing that makes no sense or provides no meaning for the reader, and we rarely publish work difficult to format." Length: 3-40 lines/poem unless solicited. Pays contributor copies.

TIPS "Read a copy of the issue or check our website to see writers we've featured to get a good idea of what we publish."

IBBETSON ST. PRESS

25 School St., Somerville MA 02143-1721. (617)628-2313. **E-mail:** tapestryofvoices@yahoo.com. **Website:** ibbetsonpress.com. **Contact:** Doug Holder, Dianne Robitaille, and Richard Wilhelm, editors; Lawrence Kessenich and Rene Schwiesow, co-managing editors; Harris Gardner, poetry editor. *Ibbetson St. Press*, published semiannually in June and November, prints "down-to-earth" poetry that is well written and has clean, crisp images with a sense of irony and humor. Wants mostly free verse but is open to rhyme. Does not want maudlin, trite, overly political, vulgar-for-vulgar's-sake work. Acquires one-time rights. Time between acceptance and publication is up to 8 months. Responds in 2 months. Single copy: $10. Subscription: $19. Make checks payable to *Ibbetson St. Press*. Guidelines available online or for SASE.

Ibbetson St. Press is 50 pages, magazine-sized, desktop-published, with glossy white cover; includes ads. Receives about 1,000 poems/year, accepts up to 10%. Press run is 200. Also archived at Harvard, Brown, University of Wisconsin, Poets House-NYC, Endicott College, and Buffalo University Libraries.

MAGAZINES NEEDS Submit 3-5 poems at a time. E-mail submissions only. Cover letter is required. Three editors comment on submissions. Has published poetry by Marge Piercy, X.J. Kennedy, Ted Kooser, Elizabeth Swados, Teisha Twomey, Gloria Mindock, Harris Gardner, Diana-der Hovanessian, Michael Todd Steffan, and Gary Metras. Does not accept unsolicited chapbook mss. Has published *Dead Beats* by Sam Cornish, *On the Wings of Song* by Molly Lynn Watt, *Fairytales and Misdemeanors* by Jennifer Matthews, *Steerage* by Bert Stern, *From the Paris of New England* by Doug Holder, *Blood Soaked Dresses* by Gloria Mindock; *East of the Moon* by Ruth Kramer Baden, and *Lousia Solano: The Grolier Poetry Book Shop* edited by Steve Glines and Doug Holder. Pays 1 contributor's copy.

ALSO OFFERS Reviews books/chapbooks of poetry and other magazines in 250-500 words. Send materials for review consideration.

ICONOCLAST

1675 Amazon Rd., Mohegan Lake NY 10547-1804. **Website:** www.iconoclastliterarymagazine.com. **Contact:** Phil Wagner, editor and publisher. *Iconoclast* seeks and chooses the best new writing and poetry available—of all genres and styles and entertainment levels. Its mission is to provide a serious publishing opportunity for unheralded, unknown, but deserving creators, whose work is often overlooked or trampled in the commercial, university, or Internet marketplace. Buys first North American serial rights. Pays on publication. Responds in 6 weeks to mss. Sample copy: $4. Subscription: $20 for 6 issues.

MAGAZINES NEEDS "Try for originality; if not in thought than expression. No greeting card verse or noble religious sentiments. Look for the unusual in the usual, parallels in opposites, the capturing of what is unique or often unnoticed in an ordinary or extraordinary moment. What makes us human—and the resultant glories and agonies. The universal usually wins out over the personal. Rhyme isn't as easy as it looks—especially for those unversed in its study."

Submit by mail; include SASE. Cover letter not necessary. Length: up to 2 pages. Pays $2-6/poem and 1 contributor's copy per page or work. Contributors get 40% discount on extra copies.

TIPS "Please don't send preliminary drafts—rewriting is half the job. If you're not sure about the story, don't truly believe in it, or are unenthusiastic about the subject (we will not recycle your term papers or thesis), then don't send it. This is not a lottery (luck has nothing to do with it)."

⑤ THE IDAHO REVIEW

Boise State University, 1910 University Dr., Boise ID 83725. **E-mail:** mwieland@boisestate.edu. **Website:** idahoreview.org. **Contact:** Mitch Wieland, editor. *The Idaho Review* is the literary journal of Boise State University. Recent stories appearing in *The Idaho Review* have been reprinted in *The Best American Short Stories*, *The O. Henry Prize Stories*, *The Pushcart Prize*, and *New Stories from the South*. Recent contributors include Joyce Carol Oates, Rick Moody, Ann Beattie, T.C. Boyle, and Joy Williams. Reading period: September 15-March 15. Acquires one-time rights. Pays on publication. Publishes ms 1 year after acceptance. Responds in 3-5 months. Guidelines online.

MAGAZINES NEEDS Submit up to 5 poems using online submissions manager.

TIPS "We look for strongly crafted work that tells a story that needs to be told. We demand vision and intelligence and mystery in the fiction we publish."

● IDIOM 23

Central Queensland University, P.O. Box 172, 554-700 Yaamba Rd., Rockhampton QLD 4702, Australia. **E-mail:** idiom@cqu.edu.au; n.anae@cqu.edu.au. **Website:** www.cqu.edu.au/idiom23. **Contact:** Dr. Nicole Anae, editor. *Idiom 23*, published annually, is "named for the Tropic of Capricorn and is dedicated to developing the literary arts throughout the Central Queensland region. Submissions of original short stories, poems, articles, and b&w drawings and photographs are welcomed by the editorial collective. *Idiom 23* is not limited to a particular viewpoint but, on the contrary, hopes to encourage and publish a broad spectrum of writing. The collective seeks out creative work from community groups with as varied backgrounds as possible." Single copy: $20. Guidelines online.

MAGAZINES NEEDS Submit poetry via online submissions manager. Length: 1 page/poem.

ILLUMINATIONS

Department of English, College of Charleston, 66 George St., Charleston SC 29424-0001. (843)953-1920. **E-mail:** illuminations@cofc.edu. **Website:** illuminations.cofc.edu. **Contact:** Simon Lewis, editor. "Over these many years, *Illuminations* has remained consistently true to its mission statement to publish new writers alongside some of the world's finest, including Nadine Gordimer, James Merrill, Carol Ann Duffy, Dennis Brutus, Allen Tate, interviews with Tim O'Brien, and letters from Flannery O'Connor and Ezra Pound. A number of new poets whose early work appeared in *Illuminations* have gone on to win prizes and accolades, and we at *Illuminations* sincerely value the chance to promote the work of emerging writers." Returns rights on request. Sample copy: $10.

○   "As a magazine devoted primarily to poetry, we publish only 1-2 pieces of short fiction and/or nonfiction in any given year, and sometimes publish none at all. "

MAGAZINES NEEDS Open to any form and style, and to translations. Does not want to see anything "bland or formally clunky." Has published poetry by Brenda Marie Osbey, Geri Doran, Dennis Brutus, and Carole Satyamurti. Submit up to 6 poems by mail, or online submissions manager. Length: open. Pays 2 contributor's copies of current issue and 1 copy of subsequent issue.

⑤ IMAGE

3307 Third Ave. W., Seattle WA 98119. (206)281-2988. **Fax:** (206)281-2979. **E-mail:** image@imagejournal. org. **Website:** www.imagejournal.org. **Contact:** Gregory Wolfe, publisher and editor. "*Image* is a unique forum for the best writing and artwork that is informed by—or grapples with—religious faith. We have never been interested in art that merely regurgitates dogma or falls back on easy answers or didacticism. Instead, our focus has been on writing and visual artwork that embody a spiritual struggle, that seek to strike a balance between tradition and a profound openness to the world. Each issue explores this relationship through outstanding fiction, poetry, painting, sculpture, architecture, film, music, interviews, and dance. *Image* also features 4-color reproductions of visual art." Magazine: 7×10; 136 pages; glossy cover stock; illustrations; photos. Buys first North American serial rights. Pays on acceptance. Publishes ms an average of 8 months after acceptance. Responds in 1 month to queries; in 5 months to mss. Sample copy: $16 or available online. Guidelines online.

MAGAZINES NEEDS Wants poems that grapple with religious faith, usually Judeo-Christian. Send up to 5 poems by postal mail (with SASE for reply or return of ms) or online submissions manager. Does not accept e-mail submissions. Length: up to 10 pages. Pays $2/line ($150 maximum) and 4 contributor's copies.

TIPS "Fiction must grapple with religious faith, though subjects need not be overtly religious."

INDEFINITE SPACE

P.O. Box 40101, Pasadena CA 91114. **E-mail:** indefinitespace@yahoo.com. **Website:** www.indefinitespace.net. "Published annually. From minimalist to avant garde, *Indefinite Space* is open to innovative, imagistic, philosophical, experimental creations: poetry, drawings, collage, photography. Reads year round." Poet retains all rights. Responds in 3 months. Seldom comments on rejected poems. Single copy: $12; subscription: $20 for 2 issues. Make checks payable to Marcia Arrieta or pay on website.

○   *Indefinite Space* is 48 pages, digest-sized.

MAGAZINES NEEDS No rhyming poetry. Has published poetry by Andrea Moorhead, Rob Cook, Linda King, Bob Heman, Khat Xiong, and Guy R. Beining. Pays 1 contributor's copy.

⑨ INDIANA REVIEW

Ballantine Hall 529, 1020 E. Kirkwood Ave., Indiana University, Bloomington IN 47405. **E-mail:** inreview@indiana.edu. **Website:** indianareview.org. **Contact:** See masthead for current editorial staff.. "*Indiana Review*, a nonprofit organization run by IU graduate students, is a journal of innovative fiction, nonfiction, and poetry. We're interested in energy, originality, and careful attention to craft. While we publish many well-known authors, we also welcome new and emerging poets and fiction writers." See website for open reading periods. Buys first North American serial rights. Pays on publication. Publishes ms an average of 6-8 months after acceptance. We make every effort to respond to work in four months. Back issues available for $10. Guidelines available online. We no longer accept hard-copy submissions. All submissions must be made online.

MAGAZINES NEEDS "We look for poems that are skillful and bold, exhibiting an inventiveness of language with attention to voice and sonics." Wants experimental, free verse, prose poem, traditional form,

lyrical, narrative. Submit poetry via online submissions manager. Pays $5/page ($10 minimum), plus 2 contributor's copies.

CONTEST/AWARD OFFERINGS Holds yearly poetry and prose poem contests.

TIPS "We're always looking for more nonfiction. We enjoy essays that go beyond merely autobiographical revelation and utilize sophisticated organization and slightly radical narrative strategies. We want essays that are both lyrical and analytical, where confession does not mean nostalgia. Read us before you submit. Back issues are available for $10. Our most recent issues have online previews available for free and accessible through the "Shop" page on our website. Often reading is slower in summer and holiday months. Submit work that 'stacks up' with the work we've published."

INDIA-USA PUNJABI ENGLISH MAGAZINE

www.indiausamagazine.com, 22619 97th Ave. S., Kent WA 98031. **E-mail:** aasra@q.com. **Website:** www.indiausamagazine.com. **Contact:** Sarab Singh, editor. general craft *India-USA Punjabi English Magazine*, published bimonthly, features current events, mainly Indian, but has featured others, too, of interest. Also features interviews, nature photographs, yoga and other articles, and poetry. Acquires one-time rights. Rights revert to poet upon publication. Time between acceptance and publication is 2 months. Sometimes comments on rejected poems. Single copy: $3 (postage); subscription: $20/year. We charge $3/copy for p&h or $2/copy if you purchase more than 10 copies. Back issue: $2." We encourage new budding poets and writers. Submit 2-3 small poems at a time. Cover letter is required. Include SASE, name, address, telephone number, and e-mail address with age and gender on cover letter. Include a short bio. "If interested, we can print 'About the Poet' along with the poem." Reads submissions year round. "We will print 1 poem per issue. We usually charge $4 to print a small poem and more for long poems. The money usually goes to cover p&h. After the poem is published in the Magazine we will publish it on our website also. The Poems will be shuffled on the website every few weeks. Those in the back will have an opportunity to come to the front.

MAGAZINES NEEDS We encourage budding poets and writers. *We can print poems written by children also. Their parents/guardian name and address should be sent to us. You can also send us the age of the child.* Submit 2-3 small poems at a time. Cover letter is required. Include SASE, **name, address, telephone number, and e-mail address** with age and gender on cover letter. Include a short bio. "If interested, we can print 'About the Poet' along with the poem." Reads submissions year round. Sometimes publishes theme issues. Has published poetry by Michael Dylan Welch, Nancy Dahl, J.T. Whitehead and Maura Gage Cavell. Please visit our website: www.indiausamagazine.com. After the Poem is printed in the magazine it will be published on the website. The Poems will be shuffled on the website every few weeks. Those in the back will have an opportunity to come to the front.

CONTEST/AWARD OFFERINGS Best Poem of the Year is awarded one-year free subscription.

INNISFREE POETRY JOURNAL

E-mail: editor@innisfreepoetry.org. **Website:** www.innisfreepoetry.org. **Contact:** Greg McBride, editor. *Innisfree Poetry Journal* "welcomes original, previously unpublished poems year round. We accept poems only via e-mail from both established and new writers whose work is excellent. We publish well-crafted poems, poems grounded in the specific, which speak in fresh language and telling images. And we admire musicality. We welcome those who, like the late Lorenzo Thomas, 'write poems because I can't sing.'" Acquires first North American serial rights. "Acquires first publication rights, including the right to publish it online and maintain it there as part of the issue in which it appears, to make it available in a printer-friendly format, to make the issue of *Innisfree* in which it appears downloadable as a PDF document and available as a printed volume. All other rights revert to the poet after online publication of the poem in *The Innisfree Poetry Journal*." Guidelines available on website.

MAGAZINES NEEDS Submit up to 5 poems by e-mail; single Word attachment. "Include your name as you would like it to appear in *Innisfree* in the subject line of your submission. Format all poems flush with the left margin—no indents other than any within the poem itself. Simultaneous submissions are welcome. If a poem is accepted elsewhere, however, please be sure to notify us immediately."

INTERPRETER'S HOUSE

'Scrimshaw', 63 Strait Path, Gardenstown Aberdeenshire AB45 3ZQ, Scotland. **E-mail:** theinterpretershouse@aol.com. **Website:** www.theinterpretershouse.com. **Contact:** Martin Malone, editor. *The Interpret-er's House*, published 3 times/year spring, summer, and autumn, prints short stories and poetry. Submission windows: October for the Spring issue, February for the Summer issue, June for the Autumn issue. Responds in 3 months. Sample copy: £5 plus £1.20 postage. Guidelines online.

MAGAZINES NEEDS Submit up to 5 poems by mail (with SASE) or e-mail. Wants "good poetry, not too long." Has published poetry by Dannie Abse, Tony Curtis, Pauline Stainer, Alan Brownjohn, Peter Redgrove, and R.S. Thomas. "All work is dealt with swiftly. Usually no more than 1 poem is accepted, and writers who have already appeared in the magazine are asked to wait for at least 3 issues before submitting again." Does not want "Christmas-card verse or incomprehensible poetry." Pays in contributor's copies.

THE IOWA REVIEW

308 EPB, The University of Iowa, Iowa City IA 52242. (319)335-0462. **E-mail:** iowa-review@uiowa.edu. **Website:** www.iowareview.org. Lynne Nugent, managing editor. **Contact:** Harilaos Stecopoulos. *The Iowa Review*, published 3 times/year, prints fiction, poetry, essays, reviews, and, occasionally, interviews. Receives about 5,000 submissions/year, accepts up to 100. Press run is 2,900; 1,500 distributed to stores. Buys first North American serial rights; buys nonexclusive anthology, classroom, and online serial rights. Pays on publication. Publishes ms an average of 12-18 months after acceptance. Responds to mss in 4 months. Sample: $8.95 and online. Subscription: $20. Guidelines online.

This magazine uses the help of colleagues and graduate assistants. Its reading period for unsolicited work is September 1-December 1. From January through April, the editors read entries to the annual Iowa Review Awards competition. Check the website for further information.

MAGAZINES NEEDS Submit up to 8 pages at a time. Online submissions accepted, but no e-mail submissions. Cover letter (with title of work and genre) is encouraged. SASE required. Reads submissions only during the fall semester, September through November, and then contest entries in the spring. Occasionally comments on rejected poems or offers suggestions on accepted poems. "We simply look for poems that, at the time we read and choose, we find we admire. No specifications as to form, length, style, subject matter, or purpose. Though we print work from established writers, we're always delighted when we discover new talent." Pays $1.50/line, $40 minimum.

TIPS "We publish essays, reviews, novel excerpts, stories, poems, and photography. We have no set guidelines regarding content but strongly recommend that writers read a sample issue before submitting."

IRIS

E-mail: submissions@creatingiris.org. **E-mail:** editorial@creatingiris.org. **Website:** www.creatingiris.org. "*Iris* seeks works of fiction and poetry that speak to LGBT young adults and their allies. We are interested in creative, thoughtful, original work that engages our young readers. We seek writing that challenges them and makes them think. We're looking for stories that capture their imaginations and characters that are relatable. We think there's a need in the young adult literary market for writing that speaks to the everyday experiences of LGBT adolescents: Themes of identity, friendship, coming out, families, etc., are especially welcome. The protagonist need not identify as LGBT, but we do ask that there be some kind of LGBT angle to your story. We welcome all genres of fiction and poetry!" Acquires first digital rights. Sample copy online. Guidelines available online.

○ "Because we publish for a young demographic, work submitted to *Iris* may not include depictions of sex, drug use, and violence. They can certainly be discussed and referenced, but not directly portrayed."

MAGAZINES NEEDS Submit poems via e-mail as attachment. Include cover letter in text of e-mail.

◐ ISLAND

Island Magazine, P.O. Box 4703, Hobart Tasmania 7000, Australia. (+61)(03)6234-1462. **E-mail:** admin@islandmag.com. **Website:** www.islandmag.com. **Contact:** Kate Harrison, general manager. *Island* seeks quality fiction, poetry, and essays. It is "one of Australia's leading literary magazines, tracing the contours of our national, and international, culture while still retaining a uniquely Tasmanian perspective." Only publishes the work of subscribers; you can submit if you are not currently a subscriber, but if your piece is chosen, the subscription will be taken from the fee paid for the piece. Buys one-time rights. Subscriptions and sample copies available for purchase online. Guidelines online.

MAGAZINES NEEDS Submit via online submissions manager. Pay varies.

JABBERWOCK REVIEW

Department of English, PO Box E, Mississippi State MS 39762. **E-mail:** jabberwockreview@english.msstate.edu. **Website:** www.jabberwock.org.msstate.edu. **Contact:** Michael Kardos, editor. *Jabberwock Review* is a literary journal published semi-annually by students and faculty of Mississippi State University. Each issue features an eclectic mix of poetry, fiction, and creative nonfiction. Submissions accepted August 15-October 20 and January 15-March 15. Rights revert to author upon publication. Our typical response time is 2-3 months. If you have not heard from us in 5 months, feel free to contact us about the status of your submission. Guidelines online.

○ Send us your best work! We're open to everything from traditional to experimental. We look forward to reading.

MAGAZINES NEEDS Poems of multiple pages should indicate whether or not stanza breaks accompany page breaks. Pays contributor's copies.

CONTEST/AWARD OFFERINGS Submissions to the Nancy D. Hargrove Editors' Prizes in Fiction and Poetry accepted January 15-March 15.

TIPS "It might take a few months to get a response from us, but your work will be read with care. Our editors enjoy reading submissions (really!) and will remember writers who are persistent and committed to getting a story 'right' through revision."

⑤ JACK AND JILL

U.S. Kids, P.O. Box 88928, Indianapolis IN 46208. (317)634-1100. **E-mail:** jackandjill@uskidsmags.com. **Website:** www.uskidsmags.com. *Jack and Jill* is an award-winning magazine for children ages 6-12. It promotes the healthy educational and creative growth of children through interactive activities and articles. The pages are designed to spark a child's curiosity in a wide range of topics through articles, games, and activities. Inside you will find: current real-world topics in articles in stories; challenging puzzles and games; and interactive entertainment through experimental crafts and recipes. Please do not send artwork. "We prefer to work with professional illustrators of our own choosing. Write entertaining and imaginative stories for kids, not just about them. Writers should understand what is funny to kids, what's important to them, what excites them. Don't write from an adult 'kids are so cute' perspective. We're also looking for health and healthful lifestyle stories and articles, but don't be preachy." Buys all rights. Pays on publication. Publishes ms an average of 8 months after acceptance. Responds to mss in 3 months. Guidelines online.

MAGAZINES NEEDS Submit via postal mail; no e-mail submissions. Wants light-hearted poetry appropriate for the age group. Mss must be typewritten with poet's contact information in upper-right corner of each poem's page. SASE required. Length: up to 30 lines/poem. Pays $25-50.

TIPS "We are constantly looking for new writers who can tell good stories with interesting slants—stories that are not full of outdated and time-worn expressions. We like to see stories about kids who are smart and capable but not sarcastic or smug. Problem-solving skills, personal responsibility, and integrity are good topics for us. Obtain current issues of the magazine and study them to determine our present needs and editorial style."

JEWISH CURRENTS

P.O. Box 111, Accord NY 12404. (845)626-2427. E-mail: editor@jewishcurrents.org. **Website:** jewishcurrents.org. **Contact:** Lawrence Bush, editor; Jacob Plitman, associate editor. *Jewish Currents*, published 4 times/year, is a progressive Jewish quarterly magazine that carries on the insurgent tradition of the Jewish left through independent journalism, political commentary, and a 'countercultural' approach to Jewish arts and literature. Our website is an active magazine in its own right, with new material published daily. *Jewish Currents* is 88 pages, magazine-sized, offset-printed, saddle-stapled with a full-color arts section, "JCultcha & Funny Pages." The Winter issue is a 12-month arts calendar. Publishes mss 1-4 months after acceptance. Responds in 1 month or less. Subscription: $30/year. First-year subscription: $18.

MAGAZINES NEEDS Submit 3 poems at a time with a cover letter. "Writers should include brief biographical information." Poems should be typed, double-spaced; include SASE. Pays contributor's copies.

ALSO OFFERS "We also run a national poetry contest November 1-January 15."

J JOURNAL: NEW WRITING ON JUSTICE

524 W. 59th St., Seventh Floor, New York NY 10019. (212)237-8697. **E-mail:** jjournal@jjay.cuny.edu. **E-mail:** submissionsjjournal@gmail.com. **Website:** www.jjournal.org. **Contact:** Adam Berlin and Jeffrey Heiman, editors. *"J Journal* publishes literary fiction, creative nonfiction, and poetry on the justice theme—

social, political, criminal, gender, racial, religious, economic. While the justice theme is specific, it need not dominate the work. We're interested in innovative writing that examines justice from all creative perspectives. Tangential connections to justice are often better than direct." Several works from *J Journal* have been recognized in *Pushcart Prize* anthologies. Acquires first rights. Publication is copyrighted. Pays on publication. Publishes ms 6 months after acceptance. Responds in 1 month to queries; 3 months to mss. Sometimes comments on/critiques rejected mss. Sample: $10. Guidelines online.

MAGAZINES NEEDS Submit up to 3 poems. Include brief bio and list of publications. Pays 2 contributor's copies. Additional copies $10.

TIPS "We're looking for literary fiction, memoir, personal narrative, or poetry with a connection, direct or tangential, to the theme of justice."

JOSEPHINE QUARTERLY

Website: www.josephinequarterly.com. **Contact:** Jenny Sadre-Orafai and Komal Patel Mathew, co-founders/editors. *Josephine Quarterly* is a quarterly online literary journal accepting only unpublished poetry and art. "Our tastes tend to run wild, from Mary Ruefle to Anne Sexton to Bob Hicok to Olena Kalytiak Davis to Zachary Schomburg to Lucille Clifton to Louise Gluck. A good poem is a good poem. We know what we want when we see it." The editors are interested in work from both established and new voices. Acquires one-time and nonexclusive journal rights to publish an author's work online. Responds in 7-10 weeks. Guidelines online.

MAGAZINES NEEDS Submit up to 5 poems of any length via online submissions manager.

✪ THE JOURNAL

The Ohio State University, 164 Annie and John Glenn Ave., Columbus OH 43210. **E-mail:** managingeditor@thejournalmag.org. **Website:** thejournalmag.org. "We are interested in quality fiction, poetry, nonfiction, art, and reviews of new books of poetry, fiction, and nonfiction. We impose no restrictions on category, type, or length of submission for fiction, poetry, and nonfiction. We are happy to consider long stories and self-contained excerpts of novels. Please double-space all prose submissions. Please send 3-5 poems in 1 submission. We only accept online submissions and will not respond to mailed submissions." Buys first North American serial rights. Publishes ms an average of 1 year after acceptance. Responds in 4-6 months to mss. Sample copy: $8 on Submittable, or free online. Guidelines available online.

> "We're open to all forms; we tend to favor work that gives evidence of a mature and sophisticated sense of the language."

MAGAZINES NEEDS "However else poets train or educate themselves, they must do what they can to know our language. Too much of the writing we see indicates poets do not, in many cases, develop a feel for the possibilities of language and do not pay attention to craft. Poets should not be in a rush to publish—until they are ready." Submit 3-5 poems via online submissions manager. Pays 2 contributor's copies and one-year subscription.

THE JOURNAL

Original Plus Press, 38 Pwllcarn Terrace, Blaengarw Wales CF32 8AS, United Kingdom. 01656 857483. E-mail: asamsmith@hotmail.com. **Website:** http://sites. google.com/site/samsmiththejournal/. **Contact:** Sam Smith. *The Journal*, published 3 times/year, features English poetry/translations, reviews, and articles. Wants "new poetry howsoever it comes; translations and original English-language poems." Does not want "staid, generalized, all form/no content." Since 1997, Original Plus Press has been publishing collections of poetry. Has recently published books by Grahaeme Barrasford Young, Dina Kafiris, Alfred Todd, Fiona Sinclair, Neil Leadbeater, Janette Ayachi, Paul Lee, Kate Ruse, Chris Deakins, Rupert Loydell, Joan Michelson, F.J. Williams, and Brian Daldorph. "From now on we will be publishing mainly chapbooks. Send SASE (or SAE and IRC) or e-mail for details." Buys all rights. Pays on publication. Publishes ms an average of 6 months after acceptance. Responds in 4 weeks to queries. Often comments on rejected poems. Editorial lead time 6 months.

MAGAZINES NEEDS Submit up to 6 poems at a time. Accepts e-mail submissions. Cover letter is preferred. Hard copy submissions with SASE. Pays 1 contributor's copy "only to U.K. contributors. Contributors outside the U.K. receive PDF copy of that issue."

TIPS "Send 6 poems; I'll soon let you know if it's not *Journal* or Original Plus material."

JOURNAL OF NEW JERSEY POETS

County College of Morris CH 300, 214 Center Grove Rd., Randolph NJ 07869-2086. **E-mail:** journalofnjpoets@ccm.edu. **Website:** www.journalofnjpoets.org.

Contact: Emily Birx, editor. *Journal of New Jersey Poets*, published annually in April, is "not necessarily about New Jersey—but of, by, and for poets from New Jersey." Wants "serious work that conveys the essential, real, whole emotional moment of the poem to the reader without sentimentality." Acquires first North American serial rights. Publishes ms 1 year after acceptance. Responds in up to 1 year. Sample: $10 (includes p&h). Subscription: $16 for 2 issues ($16/issue for institutions). Guidelines available for SASE or by e-mail.

> *Journal of New Jersey Poets* is about 90 pages, perfect-bound, offset-printed on recycled stock. Press run is 500.

MAGAZINES NEEDS All reviews are solicited. Send 2 copies of books for review consideration. Poets who live or work in New Jersey (or who formerly lived or worked here) are invited to submit up to 3 poems with their New Jersey bio data mentioned in the cover letter. Accepts e-mail submissions. For mailed submissions, include SASE with sufficient postage for return of ms, or provide instructions to recycle. Annual deadline for submissions: November 1. Has published poetry by X.J. Kennedy, Allen Ginsberg, Amiri Baraka, Gerald Stern, Kenneth Burke, Stephen Dobyns, Thomas Edison, Ruth Moon Kempher, Joe Weil, Joe Salerno, and Catherine Doty. Pays 2 contributor's copies and one-year subscription.

ALSO OFFERS Offers New Jersey Poets Prize. Deadline: November 1.

JOURNAL OF THE AMERICAN MEDICAL ASSOCIATION (JAMA)

330 N. Wabash Ave., Chicago IL 60611-5885. (312)464-4444 or (312)464-2402. **E-mail:** jamams@ jamanetwork.org. **Website:** www.jama.com. **Contact:** Howard Bauchner, editor-in-chief; Phil B. Fontanarosa, executive editor. *JAMA* is an international peer-reviewed general medical journal published 48 times/ year. It is the most widely circulated journal in the world. *JAMA* publishes Original Investigations, Reviews, Brief Reports, Special Communications, Viewpoints, and other categories of articles. Publishes mss 1 month after acceptance. Guidelines available online.

> Receives about 6,000 mss annually. Publishes 9% of mss.

MAGAZINES NEEDS *JAMA* includes a poetry and medicine column, and publishes poetry in some way related to a medical experience, whether from the point of view of a health care worker or patient, or simply an observer. Has published poetry by Jack

Coulehan, Floyd Skloot, and Walt McDonald. Length: up to 50 lines/poem.

KAIMANA

Literary Arts Hawai'i, Hawai'i Literary Arts Council, P.O. Box 11213, Honolulu HI 96828. **E-mail:** reimersa001@hawaii.rr.com. **Website:** www.hawaii.edu/hlac. *Kaimana: Literary Arts Hawai'i*, published annually, is the magazine of the Hawai'i Literary Arts Council. Wants submissions with "some Pacific reference—Asia, Polynesia, Hawai'i—but not exclusively." Responds with "reasonable dispatch." Subscription: $15, includes membership in HLAC. Sample: $10.

◎ *Kaimana* is 64-76 pages, 7.5x10, saddle-stapled, with high-quality printing. Press run is 1,000. "Poets published in *Kaimana* have received the Pushcart Prize, the Hawaii Award for Literature, the Stefan Baciu Award, the Cades Award, and the John Unterecker Award."

MAGAZINES NEEDS Submit poems with SASE. No e-mail submissions. Cover letter is preferred. Sometimes comments on rejected poems. Has published poetry by Kathryn Takara, Howard Nemerov, Anne Waldman, Reuel Denney, Haunani-Kay Trask, and Simon Perchik. Pays 2 contributor's copies.

TIPS "Hawai'i gets a lot of 'travelling regionalists,' visiting writers with inevitably superficial observations. We also get superb visiting observers who are careful craftsmen anywhere. *Kaimana* is interested in the latter, to complement our own best Hawai'i writers."

Ⓛ KALEIDOSCOPE

United Disability Services, 701 S. Main St., Akron OH 44311-1019. (330)762-9755. **Fax:** (330)762-0912. **E-mail:** kaleidoscope@udsakron.org. **Website:** www.kaleidoscopeonline.org. **Contact:** Editor. Kaleidoscope magazine creatively focuses on the experiences of disability through literature and the fine arts. As a pioneering literary resource for the field of disability studies, this award-winning publication expresses the diversity of the disability experience from a variety of perspectives including: individuals, families, friends, caregivers, educators, and healthcare professionals, among others." Buys first rights. Rights revert to author upon publication. Pays on publication. Publishes ms 1-3 years after acceptance. Responds in 6-9 months. 3 months prior to publication Guidelines available online. Submissions and queries electronically via website and e-mail.

◯ Kaleidoscope has received awards from the Great Lakes Awards Competition and Ohio Public Images; received the Ohioana Award of Editorial Excellence.

MAGAZINES NEEDS Wants poems that have strong imagery, evocative language. Submit up to 5 poems by website or e-mail. Include cover letter. Do not get caught up in rhyme scheme. Reviews any style. $10 per poem

TIPS "The material chosen for Kaleidoscope challenges and overcomes stereotypical, patronizing, and sentimental attitudes about disability. We accept the work of writers with and without disabilities; however the work of a writer without a disability must focus on some aspect of disability. The criteria for good writing apply: effective technique, thought-provoking subject matter, and, in general, a mature grasp of the art of storytelling. Writers should avoid using offensive language and always put the person before the disability."

KANSAS CITY VOICES

Whispering Prairie Press, P.O. Box 410661, Kansas City MO 64141. **E-mail:** info@wppress.org. **Website:** www.wppress.org. **Contact:** Tom Sullivan, managing editor. *Kansas City Voices*, published annually, features an eclectic mix of fiction, poetry, and art. "We seek exceptional written and visual creations from established and emerging voices." Submission period: December 15 through March 15. Note: We will not be publishing KCV in 2018. Our next submission period begins December 15, 2018, for publication in 2019. Buys first North American serial rights. Pays on publication. Publishes ms an average of 6 months after acceptance. Sample copy online. Guidelines online.

MAGAZINES NEEDS Length: up to 35 lines/poem. Pays small honorarium and 1 contributor's copy.

TIPS "There is no 'type' of work we are looking for, and while we would love for you to read through our previous issues, it is not an indicator of what kind of work we actively seek. Our editors rotate, our tastes evolve, and good work is just *good work*. We want to feel something when we encounter a piece. We want to be excited, surprised, thoughtful, and interested. We want to have a reaction. We want to share the best voices we find. Send us that one."

THE KELSEY REVIEW

E-mail: kelsey.review@mccc.edu. **Website:** www.mccc.edu/community_kelsey-review.shtml; kelsey-review.com. **Contact:** Jacqueline Vogtman, editor.

The Kelsey Review, published annually in print and online formats by Mercer County Community College, serves as an outlet for literary talent of people living and working in the larger Mercer County, New Jersey, area. Submissions are open between January 15-May 15 via our Submittable site. Rights revert to author on publication. Responds no later than August 15. Sample copy online. Guidelines online.

MAGAZINES NEEDS Submit up to 6 pages of poetry via online submissions manager. Submissions are limited to people who live, work, or give literary readings in the Mercer County, New Jersey, area. Has published poetry by Vida Chu, Dan O'Brien, and Carolina Morales.

TIPS "See *The Kelsey Review* website for current guidelines. Note: We only accept submissions from the Mercer County, New Jersey, area."

⑤ THE KENYON REVIEW

Finn House, 102 W. Wiggin, Gambier OH 43022. (740)427-5208. **Fax:** (740)427-5417. **E-mail:** kenyonreview@kenyon.edu. **Website:** www.kenyonreview.org. **Contact:** Alicia Misarti. "An international journal of literature, culture, and the arts, dedicated to an inclusive representation of the best in new writing (fiction, poetry, essays, interviews, criticism) from established and emerging writers." The *Kenyon Review* receives about 8,000 submissions/year. Also publishes KROnline, a separate and complementary online literary magazine. Buys first rights. Pays on publication. Publishes ms an average of 1 year after acceptance. Responds in 6 months to mss. Editorial lead time 1 year. Sample: $10; includes s&h. Call or e-mail to order. Guidelines online.

MAGAZINES NEEDS Features all styles, forms, lengths, and subject matters. Considers translations. Submit up to 6 poems at a time. No previously published poems. Only accepts mss via online submissions program; visit website for instructions. Do not submit via e-mail or snail mail. Accepts submissions September 15-November 1. Has recently published work by Rae Armantrout, Stephen Burt, Meghan O'Rourke, Carl Phillips, Solmaz Sharif, and Arthur Sze. Pays 16¢/published word of poetry (minimum payment $40; maximum payment $200); word count does not include title, notes, or citations.

TIPS "We no longer accept mailed or e-mailed submissions. Work will only be read if it is submitted through our online program on our website. Reading period is September 15 through November 1. We look for strong voice, unusual perspective, and power in the writing."

⑤ LADY CHURCHILL'S ROSEBUD WRISTLET

Small Beer Press, 150 Pleasant St., #306, Easthampton MA 01027. **E-mail:** info@smallbeerpress.com. **Website:** www.smallbeerpress.com/lcrw. **Contact:** Gavin Grant, editor. *Lady Churchill's Rosebud Wristlet* accepts fiction, nonfiction, poetry, and b&w art. "The fiction we publish tends toward, but is not limited to, the speculative. This does not mean only quietly desperate stories. We will consider items that fall out with regular categories. We do not accept multiple submissions." Semiannual. Acquires first serial, nonexclusive anthology, and nonexclusive electronic rights. Pays on publication. Publishes ms 6-12 months after acceptance. Responds in 6 months to mss. Sometimes comments on rejected mss. Sample copy: $5. Guidelines online.

MAGAZINES NEEDS Send submission with a cover letter. Include estimated word count. Send SASE (or IRC) for return of submission, or send a disposable copy of submission and #10 SASE for reply only. Pays $10/poem.

TIPS "We recommend you read *Lady Churchill's Rosebud Wristlet* before submitting. You can pick up a copy from our website or from assorted book shops."

LAKE EFFECT

An International Literary Journal, School of Humanities & Social Sciences, Penn State Erie, The Behrend College, Erie PA 16563-1501. **E-mail:** gol1@psu.edu; alp248@psu.edu. **Website:** psbehrend.psu.edu/school-of-humanities-social-sciences/academic-programs-1/creative-writing/cw-student-organizations/lake-effect. **Contact:** George Looney, editor in chief. *Lake Effect* is a publication of the School of Humanities and Social Sciences at Penn State Erie, The Behrend College. Responds in 4 months. Sample copy: $6. Guidelines online at website.

MAGAZINES NEEDS "*Lake Effect* is looking for poems that demonstrate an original voice and that use multilayered, evocative images presented in a language shaped by an awareness of how words sound and what they mean. Each line should help to carry the poem. *Lake Effect* seeks poems from both established poets and from new and emerging voices." Submit up to 4 poems via online submissions manager. Length: open.

LANDFALL: NEW ZEALAND ARTS AND LETTERS

Otago University Press, P.O. Box 56, Dunedin 9054, New Zealand. (64)(3)479-4155. **E-mail:** landfall.press@otago.ac.nz. **Website:** www.otago.ac.nz/press/landfall. **Contact:** Editor. *Landfall: New Zealand Arts and Letters* contains literary fiction and essays, poetry, extracts from works-in-progress, commentary on New Zealand arts and culture, work by visual artists including photographers and reviews of local books. (*Landfall* does not accept unsolicited reviews.) Guidelines for SASE or on website.

○ Deadlines for submissions: January 10 for the May issue, July 10 for the November issue. "*Landfall* is open to work by New Zealand and Pacific writers or by writers whose work has a connection to the region in subject matter or location. Work from Australian writers is occasionally included as a special feature."

MAGAZINES NEEDS Prefers e-mail submissions. Accepts postal mail submissions, but must include SASE. Include contact information and brief bio.

LEADING EDGE MAGAZINE

Brigham Young University, 4087 JKB, Provo UT 84602. **E-mail:** editor@leadingedgemagazine.com; fiction@leadingedgemagazine.com; art@leadingedgemagazine.com; poetry@leadingedgemagazine.com; nonfiction@leadingedgemagazine.com. **Website:** www.leadingedgemagazine.com. **Contact:** Abigail Miner, editor-in-chief. "*Leading Edge* is a magazine dedicated to new and upcoming talent in the fields of science fiction, fantasy, and horror. We strive to encourage developing and established talent and provide high-quality speculative fiction to our readers." Does not accept mss with sex, excessive violence, or profanity. Accepts unsolicited submissions. Buys first North American serial rights. Pays on publication. Publishes ms an average of 2-4 months after acceptance. Responds within 12 months to mss. Single copy: $6.99. "We no longer provide subscriptions, but *Leading Edge* is now available on Amazon Kindle, as well as print-on-demand." Guidelines online.

MAGAZINES NEEDS Publishes 2-4 poems per issue. Poetry should reflect both literary value and popular appeal and should deal with science fiction- or fantasy-related themes. Cover letter is preferred. Include name, address, phone number, length of poem, title, and type of poem at the top of each page. Please include SASE with every submission. Pays $10 for first 4 pages; $1.50/each subsequent page.

HOW TO CONTACT poetry@leadingedgemagazine.com

TIPS "Buy a sample issue to know what is currently selling in our magazine. Also, make sure to follow the writer's guidelines when submitting."

LILITH MAGAZINE: INDEPENDENT, JEWISH & FRANKLY FEMINIST

119 West 57th St., Suite 1210, New York NY 10019. (212)757-0818. **Fax:** (212)757-5705. **E-mail:** info@lilith.org. **Website:** www.lilith.org. **Contact:** Susan Weidman Schneider, editor in chief; Naomi Danis, managing editor. *Lilith Magazine: Independent, Jewish & Frankly Feminist*, published quarterly, welcomes submissions of high-quality, lively writing: reportage, opinion pieces, memoirs, fiction, and poetry on subjects of interest to Jewish women. Responds in 3 months. Sample copy: $7. Guidelines online.

○ *Lilith Magazine* is 48 pages, magazine-sized, with glossy color cover. Press run is about 10,000 (about 6,000 subscribers). Subscription: $26/year. For all submissions: Make sure name and contact information appear on each page of mss. Include a short bio (1-2 sentences), written in third person. Accepts submissions year round.

MAGAZINES NEEDS Has published poetry by Irena Klepfisz, Lyn Lifshin, Marcia Falk, Adrienne Rich, and Muriel Rukeyser. Send up to 3 poems at a time via online submissions form or mail; no e-mail submissions. Copy should be neatly typed and proofread for typos and spelling errors.

TIPS "Read a copy of the publication before you submit your work. Please be patient."

LILLIPUT REVIEW

282 Main St., Pittsburgh PA 15201-2807. **E-mail:** lilliputreview@gmail.com. **Website:** sites.google.com/site/lilliputreview/home. *Lilliput Review*, is published and shipped irregularly, 2 issues at a time, every fourth issue being a broadside that features the work of a single poet." Wants poems in any style or form, no longer than 10 lines. Has published poetry by Roberta Beary, Albert Huffstickler, Charlie Mehrhoff, and John Martone. *Lilliput Review* is 12-16 pages, 4.25x3.5, laser-printed on colored paper, stapled. Press run is 400. Acquires first rights. Usually publishes poems 1 year after acceptance. Responds in 12

months. Sample: $1 or SASE. Subscription: $5 for 6 issues, $10 for 15 issues; $12 for institutions (12 issues). Make checks payable to Don Wentworth, or make a payment to Paypal on the blog. Guidelines available for SASE or on website.

MAGAZINES NEEDS Submit up to 3 poems at a time, 10 lines or less. SASE required. Considers previously published poems if noted as such. Editor comments on submissions "occasionally; I always try to establish human contact." Does not want any poetry over 10 lines. Length: up to 10 lines/poem. Pays 2 contributor's copies/poem.

ALSO OFFERS The Modest Proposal Chapbook Series began in 1994, publishing 1 chapbook/year, 18-24 pages in length. Has published *Now Now* by Cid Corman. **Chapbook submissions are by invitation only.** Query with standard SASE. Sample chapbook: $3.

☼ LINE

6079 Academic Quadrangle, 8888 University Dr., Simon Fraser University, Burnaby BC V5A 1S6, Canada. **E-mail:** wcl@sfu.ca. **Website:** linejournal.tumblr.com/about. "*Line* (formerly *West Coast Line*) is a journal of poetry and critique." Buys one-time rights. Pays on publication. Responds in 6 months to queries and mss. Editorial lead time 4 months. Sample copy for $15 CAD, $20 U.S. Guidelines for SASE (U.S. must include IRC).

MAGAZINES NEEDS No light verse, traditional. Pays $8/page.

TIPS Submissions must be either scholarly or formally innovative. Contributors should be familiar with current literary trends in Canada and the U.S. Scholars should be aware of current schools of theory. All submissions should be accompanied by a brief cover letter; essays should be formatted according to the MLA guide. The publication is not divided into departments. We accept innovative poetry, experimental prose, and scholarly essays.

LINEBREAK

333 Kimpel Hall, University of Arkansas, Fayetteville AR 72701. **E-mail:** editors@linebreak.org. **Website:** linebreak.org. **Contact:** Johnathon Williams, founding editor; Ash Bowen. "*Linebreak* is a weekly online magazine of original poetry. Each poem we publish is read and recorded by another working poet selected by the editors." Has published Dorianne Laux, Bob Hicok, D.A. Powell, C. Dale Young, Richard Siken, Sandra Beasley. Publishes ms 4 months after acceptance. Responds in 6 weeks. Guidelines available on website.

○ Poems published on *Linebreak* have been selected for the Best New Poets anthology and nominated for the Pushcart Prize.

MAGAZINES NEEDS Submit up to 5 poems at a time through upload form on website. Considers simultaneous submissions. Reads submissions year round. Poems are circulated to an editorial board. Sometimes comments on rejected poems. Guidelines available on website. Sometimes sends prepublication galleys. Acquires electronic rights: "We require the rights to publish and archive the work indefinitely on our website, and the right to create an audio recording of each poem, which is also archived indefinitely. Copyright remains with the author."

LIPS

P.O. Box 616, Florham Park NJ 07932. (201)724-8500. **E-mail:** lboss79270@aol.com. **Website:** laurabosspoet. wordpress.com. **Contact:** Laura Boss, poetry editor. *Lips*, published twice/year, takes pleasure "in publishing previously unpublished poets as well as the most established voices in contemporary poetry. We look for quality work: the strongest work of a poet; work that moves the reader; poems that take risks that work. We prefer clarity in the work rather than the abstract. Poems longer than 6 pages present a space problem." *Lips* is about 150 pages, digest-sized, flat-spined. Has published poetry by Robert Bly, Allen Ginsberg, Michael Benedikt, Marge Piercy, Maria Mazziotti Gillan, Stanley Barkan, Lyn Lifshin, and Ishmael Reed. Acquires first rights. Responds in 2 months (but has gotten backlogged at times). Sometimes sends prepublication galleys. Sample: $10, plus $2.50 for postage. Guidelines available for SASE.

MAGAZINES NEEDS Submit 6 pages maximum at a time. Poems should be typed. Reads submissions September through March only. Receives about 16,000 submissions/year, accepts about 1%. Pays 1 contributor's copy.

THE LISTENING EYE

Kent State University Geauga Campus, 14111 Claridon-Troy Rd., Burton OH 44021. (440)286-3840. **E-mail:** grace_butcher@msn.com. **E-mail:** Only from other countries. **Contact:** Grace Butcher, editor. "We look for powerful, unusual imagery, content, and plot in our short stories. In poetry, we look for tight lines that don't sound like prose, unexpected images or juxtapositions, the unusual use of language, noticeable relationships of sounds, a twist in viewpoint, an ordinary idea in extraordinary language, an amazing and complex idea simply stated, play on words and with words, an obvious love of language. Poets need to read the 'Big Three'—Cummings, Thomas, Hopkins—to see the limits to which language can be taken. Then read the 'Big Two'—Dickinson to see how simultaneously tight, terse, and universal a poem can be, and Whitman to see how sprawling, cosmic, and personal. Then read everything you can find that's being published in literary magazines today, and see how your work compares to all of the above." Acquires first or one-time rights. Time between acceptance and publication is up to 6 months. Responds in 4 weeks to queries; 4 months to mss. Sample copy: $5 plus $1 postage. Writer's guidelines for SASE.

⚲ Magazine: 5.5×8.5; 60 pages; photographs. "We publish the occasional very short stories (750 words/3 pages double-spaced) in any subject and any style, but the language must be strong, unusual, free from cliché and vagueness. We are a shoestring operation from a small campus, but we publish high-quality work." Reads submissions January 1-April 15 only.

MAGAZINES NEEDS Submit up to 4 poems at a time. Accepts previously published poems "occasionally"; no simultaneous submissions. No e-mail submissions "unless from overseas." Cover letter is required. Poems should be typed, single-spaced, with 1 poem/page—name, address, phone number, and e-mail address on each page with SASE for return of work. Poems are circulated to the editor and 2 assistant editors who read and evaluate work separately, then meet for final decisions. Length: Prefers shorter poems (less than 2 pages), but will consider longer if space allows. Pays 2 contributor's copies.

ALSO OFFERS Awards $30 to the best sports poem in each issue.

LITERAL LATTÉ

200 E. 10th St., Ste. 240, New York NY 10003. (212)260-5532. **E-mail:** litlatte@aol.com. **Website:** www.literal-latte.com. **Contact:** Jenine Gordon Bockman and Jeffrey Michael Bockman, editors and publishers. Bimonthly online publication. Print anthologies featuring the best of the website. "We want great writing in all styles and subjects. A feast is made of a variety of flavors." Buys first rights and requests permission for use in anthology. Publishes an average of 6 months after acceptance. Responds in 6 months to mss. Editorial lead time 3 months. Guidelines online.

MAGAZINES NEEDS "We want any poem that captures the magic of the form." Length: up to 4,000 words.

ADDITIONAL INFORMATION "We will publish an anthology in book form featuring the best of our Web magazine."

CONTEST/AWARD OFFERINGS Also offers the Literal Latté Poetry Award: $1,000 first prize.

TIPS "Keeping free thought free and challenging entertainment are not mutually exclusive. Words make a ms stand out, words beautifully woven together in striking and memorable patterns."

LITERARY MAMA

E-mail: lminfo@literarymama.com. **E-mail:** Specific to departments; see website. **Website:** www.literary-mama.com. **Contact:** Karna Converse, editor-in-chief. Online monthly magazine that features writing about the complexities and many faces of motherhood. Departments include columns, creative nonfiction, fiction, literary reflections, poetry, profiles, and book reviews. "We prefer previously unpublished work and are interested in work that offers a fresh perspective." Responds in 3 weeks-3 months to mss. "We correspond via e-mail only." Guidelines online.

⚲ "*Literary Mama* is not currently a paying market. We are all volunteers here: editors, writers, and editorial assistants. With the publication of each issue, we make a concerted effort to promote the work of our contributors via Facebook, Twitter, and our newsletter."

MAGAZINES NEEDS "We are looking for poems extraordinary for their vision, craft, integrity, and originality. Poems of any length and form are welcome. Maximum of 2 poems per submission, please."

THE LITERARY REVIEW

285 Madison Ave., Madison NJ 07940. (973)443-8564. **E-mail:** info@theliteraryreview.org. **Website:** www.theliteraryreview.org. **Contact:** Minna Proctor, editor. *The Literary Review* is published by Fairleigh Dickinson University. Work published in *The Literary Review* has been included in *Editor's Choice*, *Best American Short Stories*, and *Pushcart Prize* anthologies. Uses online submissions manager. Acquires first rights. Responds in 8-12 months. Sample copy: $15. Guidelines online.

MAGAZINES NEEDS Submit electronically only. Does not accept paper submissions. Pays 2 contributor's copies and one-year subscription.

TIPS "We want original dramatic situations with complex moral and intellectual resonance and vivid prose. We don't want versions of familiar plots and relationships. Too much of what we are seeing today is openly derivative in subject, plot, and prose style. We pride ourselves on spotting new writers with fresh insight and approach."

THE LITERARY REVIEW

An International Journal of Contemporary Writing, Fairleigh Dickinson University, 285 Madison Ave., Madison NJ 07940. (973)443-8564. **E-mail:** info@theliteraryreview.org. **Website:** www.theliteraryreview.org. **Contact:** Minna Proctor, editor. *The Literary Review*, published quarterly, is "interested in innovative writing, engaging stories, and work that feels as if it had to be written. In other words, we like writing that has the courage of its convictions." *TLR Online*, available on the website, features original work not published in the print edition. *The Literary Review* is about 200 pages, digest-sized, professionally printed, flat-spined, with glossy color cover. Receives about 1,200 submissions/year, accepts 100-150. Press run is 2,000 (800 subscribers, one-third are overseas). Acquires first rights. Responds in 8-12 months. Sample copy: $15 domestic, $15 + $5 shipping outside U.S.; request a "general issue."

MAGAZINES NEEDS Submit via online submissions manager. Has published poetry by Albert Goldbarth, Mary Jo Bang, David Citino, Lois Marie Harrod, Alex Lemon, Brandon Davis Jennings, and Virgil Suárez. Pays 2 contributor's copies and one-year subscription.

LITTLE PATUXENT REVIEW

P.O. Box 6084, Columbia MD 21045. **E-mail:** editor@littlepatuxentreview.org. **Website:** www.littlepatuxentreview.org. **Contact:** Steven Leyva, editor. "*Little Patuxent Review* (*LPR*) is a community-based, biannual print journal devoted to literature and the arts, primarily in the Mid-Atlantic region. We profile the work of a major poet or fiction writer and a visual artist in each issue. We celebrate the launch of each issue with a series of readings and broadcast highlights on *LPR*'s YouTube channel. All forms and styles considered. Please see our website for the current theme." *LPR* is about 120 pages; digest-sized; 100# finch cover; artwork (varies depending on featured artist). Has published poetry by Lucille Clifton, Martín Espada, Donald Hall, Joy Harjo, Marie Howe, Myra Sklarew, Clarinda Harriss, and Alan King. Buys first rights.

Responds in 3-5 months to mss. Sample copy: $10. Guidelines available in magazine and on website.

MAGAZINES NEEDS Submit up to 3 poems by online submissions manager; no mail or e-mail submissions. Include word count and 75-word bio. Length: up to 100 lines/poem. Pays 1 contributor's copy.

ALSO OFFERS "*LPR* co-sponsors monthly arts Salon Series events in conjunction with the Columbia Art Center, featuring literary readings, art presentations, and musical performances. Events are free and open to the public. Contributors are invited to participate in reading series and literary festivals, such as the Baltimore Book Festival. As part of our outreach effort, the *LPR* in the Classroom Program provides *LPR* issues to high schools and colleges at a discounted rate."

TIPS "Please see our website for the current theme. Poetry and prose must exhibit the highest quality to be considered. Please read a sample issue before submitting."

🌑🛇 THE LONDON MAGAZINE

11 Queen's Gate, London SW7 5EL, United Kingdom. (44)(0)20 7584 5977. **E-mail:** info@thelondonmagazine.org. **Website:** www.thelondonmagazine.org. **Contact:** Steven O'Brien, editor. "The Oldest Literary Magazine, established 1732. We publish literary writing of the highest quality. We look for poetry and short fiction that startles and entertains us. Reviews, essays, memoir pieces, and features should be erudite, lucid, and incisive. We are obviously interested in writing that has a London focus, but not exclusively so, since London is a world city with international concerns." Buys first rights. Pays on publication. Published ms an average of 4 months after acceptance. Responds in 1 month to queries; 3 months to mss. Editorial lead time 3 months. Sample copy: £6.95. Guidelines online.

MAGAZINES NEEDS "Abstraction is the enemy of good poetry. Poetry should display a commitment to the ultra specificities of language and show a refined sense of simile and metaphor. The structure should be tight and exact." Submit up to 6 poems via online submissions manager, e-mail (as an attachment), or postal mail (enclose SASE). "We do not publish long, loose poems." Length: up to 40 lines/poem.

TIPS "Please look at *The London Magazine* before you submit work so that you can see the type of material we publish."

LONE STARS MAGAZINE

4219 Flinthill St., San Antonio TX 78230-1619. E-mail: lonestarsmagazine@yahoo.com. Website: www.lonestarsmagazine.net. Contact: Milo Rosebud, editor/publisher. *Lone Stars*, published 3 times/year, features contemporary poetry and artwork. *Lone Stars* is 25+ pages, magazine-sized, photocopied, saddle-stapled, bound with tape. Press run is 300+. Acquires one-time publication rights. Authors retain all rights. Time between acceptance and publication is 3-6 months. Responds within 3 months. Sample (past issues): $5.50. Single copy: $7. Subscription: $20 for 3 issues. Guidelines available for SASE.

MAGAZINES NEEDS Wants poetry that holds a continuous line of thought. Does not want porn or profanity. Considers poetry by children and teens. Submit 3-5 poems at a time. Cover letter is preferred. Submit poems on any subject, formatted and typed the way you want them in print. **Charges reading fee of $1 per poem**. Has published poetry by Terry Lee, Eve J. Blohm, John Brummel, Linda Amos, and many more.

ALSO OFFERS Sponsors Annual Songbook Lyric Poetry Contest, Annual Light of the Stars Poetry Contest, The Write Idea Interactive Poetry Contests, and Great "One Liner" Contributions. Details available with e-mail or SASE.

TIPS "Submit poetry that expresses a reasonable train of thought."

LONG LIFE

Longevity through Technology, The Immortalist Society, 24355 Sorrentino Ct., Clinton Township MI 48035. **E-mail:** info@cryonics.org. **Website:** www.cryonics.org/resources/long-life-magazine. "*Long Life* magazine is a publication for people who are particularly interested in cryonic suspension: the theory, practice, legal problems, etc. associated with being frozen when you die in the hope of eventual restoration to life and health. Many people who receive the publication have relatives who have undergone cryonic preparation or have made such arrangements for themselves or are seriously considering this option. Readers are also interested in other aspects of life extension such as anti-aging research and food supplements that may slow aging. Articles we publish include speculation on what the future will be like; problems of living in a future world, and science in general, particularly as it may apply to cryonics and life extension." Publication is copyrighted. Responds in 1 month to queries and mss. Sample copy is free for SASE.

MAGAZINES NEEDS "Poems are welcomed, especially short, humorous poems with a cryonics or life-extension theme." Pays 1 contributor's copy.

TIPS "We are a small magazine but with a highly intelligent and educated readership which is socially and economically diverse. We currently don't pay for material but are seeking new authors and provide contributors with copies of the magazine with the contributor's published works. Look over a copy of *Long Life*, or talk with the editor to get the tone of the publication. There is an excellent chance that your ms will be accepted if it is well written and 'on theme.' Pictures to accompany the article are always welcome, and we like to publish photos of the authors with their first ms."

LONG STORY SHORT, AN E-ZINE FOR WRITERS

P.O. Box 475, Lewistown MT 59457. **E-mail:** alongstory_short@aol.com. **Website:** www.alongstoryshort.net. **Contact:** Anisa Claire, Kim Bussey, editors. *Long Story Short, An E-zine for Writers* publishes "the best fiction and poetry from both emerging and established writers. Acquires nonexclusive world electronic and print rights, nonexclusive archival Web rights. Publishes ms up to 6 months after acceptance, depending on theme. Guidelines available on website. "Read them!"

○ Free newsletter with poetry of the month chosen by poetry editor; includes author's bio and web page listed in the e-zine. Offers light critique of submissions upon request and a free writing forum.

MAGAZINES NEEDS Submit by e-mail; no attachments. Considers poetry by children (ages 10 and up) and teens. Has published poetry by Michael Lee Johnson, Maria Ercilla, Shonda Buchanan, Patricia Wellingham-Jones, Floriana Hall, and Russell Bittner. Length: up to 32 lines/poem. Pays 1 contributor's copy.

THE LOS ANGELES REVIEW

P.O. Box 2458, Redmond WA 98073. (626)356-4760. **Fax:** (626)356-9974. **E-mail:** lareview.trager.editor@gmail.com. **Website:** losangelesreview.org. **Contact:** Alisa Trager, managing editor. Acquires one-time rights. Pays on publication. Publishes ms 2-5 months after acceptance. Responds in 1-2 months to mss. Sample copy: $15. Guidelines available on website.

MAGAZINES NEEDS Submit 3-4 poems at a time. Wants poems that "will surprise us, wow us, and make us wish we'd written them ourselves. We are open to form, free verse, prose poems, and experimental styles. Our only criterion is quality."

TIPS "Read a few recent issues to see what we're about. Pay close attention to the submission guidelines. We like cover letters, but please keep them brief."

LOST LAKE FOLK OPERA

Shipwreckt Books Publishing Company, 309 W. Stevens Ave., Rushford MN 55971. **E-mail:** contact@shipwrecktbooks.com. **Website:** www.shipwrecktbooks.press. **Contact:** Tom Driscoll, managing editor. *Lost Lake Folk Opera* magazine, published twice annually, accepts submissions of critical journalism, short fiction and plays, poetry, B&W photography and graphic art. Seeks high-quality submissions. For journalistic pieces, please query first. Retains one-time rights. First North American rights. Pays on publication, one contributor copy. Publishes ms 6-12 months after acceptance. Responds in 6 weeks to queries; 3-6 months to mss. Editorial lead time 3 months minimum. Sample copy available for cover price with SASE. Use submissions portal at www.shipwrecktbooks.press; follow guidelines. Paper submissions are no longer accepted.

MAGAZINES NEEDS Length: 1-250 lines. Pays contributor copy.

TIPS "When in doubt, edit and cut. Please remember to read your submission. Don't expect *LLFO* to wash your car and detail it. Send clean copies of your work."

LOUISIANA LITERATURE

SLU Box 10792, Hammond LA 70402. **E-mail:** lalit@selu.edu. **Website:** www.louisianaliterature.org. **Contact:** Jack B. Bedell, editor. "Since 1984, *Louisiana Literature* has featured some of the finest writing published in America. The journal has always striven to spotlight local talent alongside nationally recognized authors. Whether it's work from established writers or from first-time publishers, *Louisiana Literature* is always looking to print the finest poetry and fiction available." Acquires one-time rights. Publishes ms 6-12 after acceptance. Responds in 1-3 months to mss. Sometimes comments on rejected mss. Sample copy: $8. Guidelines for SASE or online.

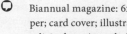 Biannual magazine: 6x9; 150 pages; 70 lb. paper; card cover; illustrations. Receives 100 unsolicited mss/month. May not read mss June-

July. Publishes 4 new writers/year. Publishes theme issues. Has published work by Anthony Bukowski, Aaron Gwyn, Robert Phillips, and R.T. Smith. Work first published in *Louisiana Literature* is regularly reprinted in collections and is nominated for prizes from the National Book Awards for both genres and the Pulitzer. Recently, stories by Aaron Gwyn and Robert Olen Butler were selected for inclusion in *New Stories from the South*.

MAGAZINES NEEDS Submit 3-5 poems as a single document via online submissions manager. Reads submissions year round, "although we work more slowly in summer." Sometimes sends prepublication galleys. Send materials for review consideration; include cover letter. Pays 2 contributor's copies.

TIPS "Cut out everything that is not a functioning part of the story. Make sure your ms is professionally presented. Use relevant, specific detail in every scene. We love detail, local color, voice, and craft. Any professional ms stands out."

THE LOUISIANA REVIEW

Louisiana State University Eunice, Division of Liberal Arts, P.O. Box 1129, Eunice LA 70535. (337)550-1315. **E-mail:** bfonteno@lsue.edu. **Website:** web.lsue.edu/la-review. **Contact:** Dr. Billy Fontenot, editor and fiction editor; Dr. Jude Meche, poetry editor; Dr. Diane Langlois, art editor. *The Louisiana Review*, published annually during the fall or spring semesters, offers "Louisiana poets, writers, and artists a place to showcase their most beautiful pieces. Others may submit Louisiana- or Southern-related poetry, stories, and art. Publishes photographs. Sometimes publishes nonfiction." Wants "strong imagery, metaphor, and evidence of craft." Acquires one-time rights. Not copyrighted, but has an ISSN number. Publishes ms 6-12 months after acceptance. Single copy: $5.

The Louisiana Review is 100 pages, digest-sized, professionally printed, perfect-bound. Press run is 300-600.

MAGAZINES NEEDS Submit up to 5 poems at a time. No previously published poems. No fax or e-mail submissions. "Include cover letter indicating your association with Louisiana, if any." Has published poetry by Gary Snyder, Antler, and David Cope. Receives up to 2,000 poems/year, accepts 30-50. Does not want "sing-song rhymes, abstract, religious, or overly sentimental work." Pays 1 contributor's copy.

TIPS "We do like to have fiction play out visually as a film would rather than be static and undramatized. Louisiana or Gulf Coast settings and themes preferred."

THE LOUISVILLE REVIEW

Spalding University, 851 S. Fourth St., Louisville KY 40203. (502)873-4398. **E-mail:** louisvillereview@spalding.edu. **Website:** www.louisvillereview.org. **Contact:** Ellyn Lichvar, managing editor. *The Louisville Review*, published twice/year, prints poetry, fiction, nonfiction, and drama. Has a section devoted to poetry by writers under age 18 (grades K-12) called "The Children's Corner." *The Louisville Review* is 150 pages, digest-sized, flat-spined. Receives about 700 submissions/year, accepts about 10%. Responds in 3-6 months to mss. Sample copy: $5. Single copy: $8. Subscription: $14/year, $27/2 years, $40/3 years (foreign subscribers add $6/year for s&h). Guidelines online.

MAGAZINES NEEDS Accepts submissions via online manager; please see website for more information. "Poetry by children must include permission of parent to publish if accepted. Address those submissions to 'The Children's Corner.'" Reads submissions year round. Has published poetry by Wendy Bishop, Gary Fincke, Michael Burkard, and Sandra Kohler. Pays contributor's copies.

LULLWATER REVIEW

Emory University, P.O. Box 122036, Atlanta GA 30322. **E-mail:** emorylullwaterreview@gmail.com. **Website:** emorylullwaterreview.com. **Contact:** Aneyn M. O'Grady, editor in chief. "We're a small, student-run literary magazine published out of Emory University in Atlanta, Georgia, with 2 issues yearly—once in the fall and once in the spring. You can find us in the *Index of American Periodical Verse*, the *American Humanities Index* and as a member of the Council of Literary Magazines and Presses. We welcome work that brings a fresh perspective, whether through language or the visual arts." Acquires first world serial rights. Publishes ms an average of 3-4 months after acceptance. Responds in 1-3 months to queries; 3-6 months to mss. Sample copy: $8 Guidelines online at emorylullwaterreview.com/submissions.

MAGAZINES NEEDS Has published poetry by Amy Greenfield, Peter Serchuk, Katherine McCord, and Ha Jin. Submit up to 6 poems at a time. Cover letter is preferred. Prefers poems single-spaced with name and contact info on each page. "Poems longer than 1 page should include page numbers. We must

have a SASE with which to reply." Reads submissions September 1-May 15 only. Poems are circulated to an editorial board. Seldom comments on rejected poems. No profanity or pornographic material. Pays 3 contributor's copies.

TIPS "We at the *Lullwater Review* look for clear, cogent writing, strong character development, and an engaging approach to the story in our fiction submissions. Stories with particularly strong voices and well-developed central themes are especially encouraged. Be sure that your ms is ready before mailing it to us. Revise, revise, revise! Be original, honest, and, of course, keep trying."

LUMINA JOURNAL

Sarah Lawrence College, 1 Mead Way, Bronxville NY 10708. **E-mail:** lumina@gm.slc.edu. **Website:** luminajournal.com. **Contact:** Victoria Johnson, editor-in-chief. "*LUMINA*'s mission is to provide a journal where emerging and established writers and visual artists come together in exploration of the new and appreciation of the traditional. We want to see sonnets sharing space with experimental prose; we want art that pushes boundaries and bends rules with eloquence." All rights revert to author upon publication. Responds in 3-6 months. Sample copy for $12. Guidelines online.

MAGAZINES NEEDS Submit via online submissions manager. All submissions are read blind; do not include personal information on submission documents. Length: up to 60 lines/poem.

LUNGFULL!MAGAZINE

316 23rd St., Brooklyn NY 11215. **E-mail:** customerservice@lungfull.org. **Website:** lungfull.org. **Contact:** Brendan Lorber, editor/publisher. "*LUNGFULL!* Magazine World Headquarters in Brooklyn is home to a team of daredevils who make it their job to bring you only the finest in typos, misspellings, and awkward phrases. That's because *LUNGFULL!magazine* is the only literary and art journal in America that prints the rough drafts of people's work so you can see the creative process as it happens." Responds in 1 year to mss. Submit by postal mail. Include SASE. If sending by e-mail (not preferred) do NOT send attachments and put "Submission by [Your Name]" in the subject line.

○ *LUNGFULL!* was the recipient of a grant from the New York State Council for the Arts.

MAGAZINES NEEDS Submit up to 8 poems. Include cover letter.

THE LUTHERAN DIGEST

The Lutheran Digest, Inc., P.O. Box 100, Princeton MN 55371. **E-mail:** editor@lutherandigest.com. **Website:** www.lutherandigest.com. **Contact:** Nick Skapyak, editor. Articles frequently reflect a Lutheran Christian perspective but are not intended to be sermonettes. Popular stories show how God has intervened in a person's life to help solve a problem. Buys first rights, second serial (reprint) rights. Pays on publication. Publishes ms an average of 6 months after acceptance. Responds in 4 months to mss. No response to e-mailed mss unless selected for publication. Editorial lead time 9 months. Sample copy: $3.50. Subscription: $16/year, $22 for 2 years. Guidelines online.

◯ *The Lutheran Digest* is 64 pages, digest-sized, offset-printed, saddle-stapled, with 4-color paper cover, includes local ads. Press run is 20,000-30,000; most distributed free to Lutheran churches.

MAGAZINES NEEDS Submit up to 3 poems at a time. Prefers e-mail submissions but also accepts mailed submissions. Cover letter is preferred. Include SASE only if return is desired. Poems are selected by editor and reviewed by publication panel. Length: up to 25 lines/poem. Pays 1 contributor's copy.

TIPS "Reading our writers' guidelines and sample articles online is encouraged and is the best way to get a feel for the type of material we publish."

💲 LYRICAL PASSION POETRY E-ZINE

Arlington VA **E-mail:** lpezinesubmissions@gmail.com. **Website:** lyricalpassionpoetry.yolasite.com. **Contact:** Raquel D. Bailey, founder & editor-in-chief. Founded by award-winning poet Raquel D. Bailey, *Lyrical Passion Poetry E-Zine* is an attractive monthly online literary magazine specializing in Japanese short-form poetry. Publishes quality artwork, well-crafted short fiction, and poetry in English by emerging and established writers. Literature of lasting literary value will be considered. Welcomes the traditional to the experimental. Poetry works written in German will be considered if accompanied by translations. Offers annual short fiction and poetry contests. Acquires first rights, electronic rights (must be the first literary venue to publish online or in any electronic format). Rights revert to poets upon publication. Publishes ms 1 month after acceptance. Responds in 1-5 months. Guidelines and upcoming themes available on website.

MAGAZINES NEEDS Multiple submissions are permitted, but no more than 3 submissions in a six-month period. Does not want dark, cliché, limerick, erotica, extremely explicit, violent, or depressing literature. Length: 1-40 lines (free verse).

THE LYRIC

The Lyric Literary Arts, Inc., P.O. Box 110, Jericho Corners VT 05465. (802)899-3993. **Fax:** (802)899-3993. **E-mail:** themuse@thelyricmagazine.com. **Website:** www.thelyricmagazine.com. *The Lyric*, published quarterly, is the oldest magazine in North America in continuous publication devoted to traditional poetry. *The Lyric* is 32 pages, digest-sized, professionally printed with varied typography, with matte card cover. Receives about 3,000 submissions/year, accepts 5%. Acceptances will be published within a year. Typically responds in 3 months; inquire after that time. Sample: $5. Subscription: $18/year, $32/2 years, $42//3 years (U.S.), $20//year for Canada and other countries . Guidelines online and available by mail.

◯ We welcome most traditional forms and publish a sprinkling of short free verse. We do not publish haikus or translations, and, in most cases, avoid previously published work.

MAGAZINES NEEDS Submit by postal mail; out-of-country poems may be submitted by e-mail. Cover letter is often helpful, but not required. Has published poetry by Michael Burch, Gail White, Constance Rowell Mastores, Ruth Harrison, Barbara Loots, Tom Riley, Catherine Chandler, and Glenna Holloway. "Our themes are varied, ranging from religious ecstasy to humor to raw grief, but we feel no compulsion to shock, embitter, or confound our readers. We also avoid poems about contemporary political or social problems—'grief but not grievances,' as Frost put it. Frost is helpful in other ways: If yours is more than a lover's quarrel with life, we are not your best market. And most of our poems are accessible on first or second reading." Length: up to 40 lines. Pays 1 contributor's copy, and quarterly and yearly prizes, judged by fellow respected poets.

CONTEST/AWARD OFFERINGS Offers The Lyric Memorial Prize ($100), The Leslie Mellichamp Prize ($100), The Roberts Memorial Prize ($100), The New England Prize ($50), The Fluvanna Prize ($50), Quarterly Prize ($50), and the College Poetry Contest (1st Prize: $500, 2nd Prize $150, 3rd Prize, $100). Information on website.

💲 MĀNOA

A Pacific Journal of International Writing, University of Hawaii at Mānoa, English Department, Honolulu HI 96822. **E-mail:** mjournal-l@lists.hawaii.edu. **Website:** manoajournal.hawaii.edu. **Contact:** Frank Stewart, editor. *Mānoa* is seeking high-quality literary fiction, poetry, essays, and translations for an international audience. In general, each issue is devoted to new work from an area of the Asia-Pacific region. Because we feature different places and have guest editors, please contact us to see if your submission is appropriate for what we're working on. *Mānoa* has received numerous awards, and work published in the magazine has been selected for prize anthologies. Please see our website for recently published issues. Buys first North American serial rights and non-exclusive, one-time print rights. Pays on publication. Responds in 3 weeks to queries. Editorial lead time 9 months. Sample: $20. Guidelines online.

MAGAZINES NEEDS No light verse. Pays $25/poem.

TIPS "Not accepting unsolicited mss at this time because of commitments to special projects. Please query before sending mss as e-mail attachments. If you would like to view a copy of the journal, you may do so at Project Muse or JSTOR, online archives available through universities, community libraries, and other institutions."

THE MACGUFFIN

Schoolcraft College, 18600 Haggerty Rd., Livonia MI 48152. (734)462-4400, ext. 5327. **E-mail:** macguffin@schoolcraft.edu. **Website:** www.schoolcraft.edu/macguffin. **Contact:** Steven A. Dolgin, editor; Gordon Krupsky, managing editor;. "Our purpose is to encourage, support, and enhance the literary arts in the Schoolcraft College community, the region, the state, and the nation. We also sponsor annual literary events and give voice to deserving new writers as well as established writers." Acquires first rights. Once published, rights revert back to author. Publishes ms 3-4 months after acceptance. Responds to submissions in 2-4 months. Sample copy: $6. "Use the order form on our website." Guidelines available online.

MAGAZINES NEEDS Wants "poetry that shows rather than tells." Submit via e-mail or postal mail. Poetry should be typed, single-spaced, with only 1 poem per page. Length: up to 400 lines/poem. Pays 2 contributor's copies.

THE MADISON REVIEW

University of Wisconsin, 600 N. Park St., 6193 Helen C. White Hall, Madison WI 53706. **E-mail:** madisonrevw@gmail.com. **Website:** www.english.wisc.edu/madisonreview. **Contact:** Abigail Zemach and John McCracken, fiction editors; Fiona Sands and Kiyoko Reidy, poetry editors. *The Madison Review* is a student-run literary magazine that looks to publish the best available fiction and poetry. Buys one-time rights. Publishes ms an average of 9 months after acceptance. Responds in 4 weeks to queries; in 6 months to mss. Editorial lead time 6 months. Sample copy: $3. Guidelines available online.

💬 Does not publish unsolicited interviews or genre fiction. Send all submissions through online submissions manager.

MAGAZINES NEEDS Cover letter is preferred. Does not want religious or patriotic dogma and light verse. Pays 2 contributor's copies.

TIPS "Our editors have very eclectic tastes, so don't specifically try to cater to us. Above all, we look for original, high-quality work."

THE MAGNOLIA QUARTERLY

Returns rights to author upon publication. Time between acceptance and publication varies. Single copy: $3; subscription: included in $30 GCWA annual dues. Make checks payable to Gulf Coast Writers Association. Guidelines available in magazine.

MAGAZINES NEEDS Length: up to 40 lines/poem. No payment.

ALSO OFFERS Holds the "Let's Write" contest, with cash prizes for poetry and prose. Additional information available on website.

THE MAIN STREET RAG

Douglass-Rausch, Ent. LLC, P.O. Box 690100, Charlotte NC 28227-7001. (704)573-2516. **E-mail:** editor@mainstreetrag.com. **Website:** www.mainstreetrag.com. **Contact:** M. Scott Douglass, publisher/managing editor. *The Main Street Rag*, published quarterly, prints "poetry, short fiction, essays, interviews, reviews, photos, and art. We like publishing good material from people who are interested in more than notching another publishing credit, people who support small independent publishers like ourselves." Will consider "almost anything," but prefers "writing with an edge—either gritty or bitingly humorous. Contributors are advised to visit our website prior to submission to confirm current needs." *The Main*

Street Rag receives about 5,000 submissions/year; publishes 50+ poems and 3-5 stories per issue, a featured interview, photos, and an occasional nonfiction piece. Press run is about 500 (250 subscribers, 15 libraries). Acquires first North American print rights. Time between acceptance and publication is usually 6 months to 1 year. Responds in 8-12 weeks, query after 12 weeks if you have not heard from us. Single copy: $8. Subscription: $24/year, $45 for 2 years. No hard copy submissions. We use Submittable. Details on our website.

MAGAZINES NEEDS Submit 6 pages of poetry at a time; no more than 1 poem per page. No hard copy submissions—all electronic. See website for details. No bios or credits—let the work speak for itself. Pays 1 contributor's copy.

⚙️💲 THE MALAHAT REVIEW

The University of Victoria, P.O. Box 1700, STN CSC, Victoria BC V8W 2Y2, Canada. (250)721-8524. **E-mail:** malahat@uvic.ca (for queries only). **Website:** www.malahatreview.ca. Rhonda Batchelor, assistant editor. **Contact:** Iain Higgins, editor. Quarterly magazine covering poetry, fiction, creative nonfiction, and reviews. "We try to achieve a balance of views and styles in each issue. We strive for a mix of the best writing by both established and new writers." Buys first world rights. Pays on acceptance. Publishes an average of 6 months after acceptance. Responds in approximately 2 weeks to queries; 3-10 months to mss. Sample: $16.95 (U.S.). Guidelines online.

MAGAZINES NEEDS Submit 3-6 poems via Submittable link on Submissions page. Length: up to 6 pages. Pays $60/magazine page.

CONTEST/AWARD OFFERINGS The P.K. Page Founders' Award for Poetry, a $1,000 prize to the author of the best poem or sequence of poems to be published in *The Malahat Review*'s quarterly issues during the previous calendar year. Also offers the Open Season Awards, biennial Long Poem Prize, biennial Novella Prize, Constance Rooke Creative Nonfiction Prize, the biennial Far Horizons Award for Short Fiction, and the biennial Far Horizons Award for Poetry.

TIPS "Please do not send more than 1 submission at a time: 3-6 poems, 1 piece of creative nonfiction, or 1 short story (do not mix poetry and prose in the same submission). See *The Malahat Review*'s Contests section of our website for more info on our annual contests involving poetry, short fiction, creative nonfiction, long poems, and novellas."

THE MANHATTAN REVIEW

440 Riverside Dr., #38, New York NY 10027. **E-mail:** phfried@gmail.com. **Website:** themanhattanreview. com. **Contact:** Philip Fried. *The Manhattan Review* publishes only poetry, reviews of poetry books, and poetry-related essays. The editor reads unsolicited submissions year round but requests that you observe the guidelines. Acquires first North American serial rights. Responds in 3-6 months if possible. Guidelines available online.

MAGAZINES NEEDS Send 3-5 poems with SASE and brief bio. Read magazine before submitting. Pays contributor's copies.

💲 THE MASSACHUSETTS REVIEW

University of Massachusetts, Photo Lab 309, 211 Hicks Way, Amherst MA 01003. (413)545-2689. **E-mail:** massrev@external.umass.edu. **Website:** www. massreview.org. **Contact:** Emily Wojcik, managing editor. Seeks a balance between established writers and promising new ones. Interested in material of variety and vitality relevant to the intellectual and aesthetic questions of our time. Aspire to have a broad appeal. Buys first North American serial rights. Pays on publication. Publishes ms an average of 18 months after acceptance. Responds in 2-6 months to mss. Sample copy: $8 for back issue, $10 for current issue. Guidelines available online.

💭 Does not respond to mss without SASE.

MAGAZINES NEEDS Has published poetry by Catherine Barnett, Billy Collins, and Dara Wier. Include your name and contact on every page. Length: There are no restrictions for length, but generally poems are less than 100 lines. Pays $50/publication and 2 contributor's copies.

TIPS "No manuscripts are considered May-September. Electronic submission process can be found on website. No fax or e-mail submissions. Shorter rather than longer stories preferred (up to 28-30 pages)." Looks for works that "stop us in our tracks." Manuscripts that stand out use "unexpected language, idiosyncrasy of outlook, and are the opposite of ordinary."

MEASURE: A REVIEW OF FORMAL POETRY

526 S. Lincoln Park Dr., Evansville IN 47714. (812)488-2963. **E-mail:** editors@measurepress.com. **Website:** www.measurepress.com/measure. *Measure*, an international journal of formal poetry, began in 2005 in conjunction with the University of Evansville. Measure Press is a new enterprise by editors Rob Griffith and

Paul Bone. The goal is to continue bringing readers the best new poetry from both established and emerging writers through the biannual journal. *Measure* has a mission not only to publish the best new poetry from both established and emerging writers but also to reprint a small sampling of poems from books of metrical poetry published the previous year. Likewise, each issue includes interviews with some of the most important contemporary poets and also offers short critical essays on the poetry that has helped to shape the craft. Responds in 3 months. Guidelines online at website.

MAGAZINES NEEDS Send no more than 3 to 5 poems at a time. Poems must be metrical. Include poet's name and phone number. Submit electronically on website.

MERIDIAN

University of Virginia, P.O. Box 400145, Charlottesville VA 22904-4145. **E-mail:** meridianuva@gmail.com; meridianpoetry@gmail.com; meridianfiction@gmail.com. **Website:** www.readmeridian.org. *Meridian*, published semiannually, prints poetry, fiction, nonfiction, interviews, and reviews. "*Meridian* is interested in writing that is vibrant, moving, and alive, and welcomes contributions from a variety of aesthetic approaches. Has published such poets as Alexandra Teague, Gregory Pardlo, Sandra Meek, and Bob Hicok, and such fiction writers as Matt Bell, Kate Milliken, and Ron Carlson. Has recently interviewed C. Michael Curtis, Ann Beatty, and Claire Messud, among other luminaries. Also publishes a recurring feature called 'Lost Classic,' which resurrects previously unpublished work by celebrated writers and which has included illustrations from the mss of Jorge Luis Borges, letters written by Elizabeth Bishop, Stephen Crane's deleted chapter from *The Red Badge of Courage*, and a letter written by Flannery O'Connor about her novel *Wise Blood*." Publishes ms 1-2 months after acceptance. Seldom comments on rejected poems and mss. Responds in 1-4 months. Always sends prepublication galleys and author contracts. Sample copy: $6 (back issue). Single print copy: $7. Print subscription: $12 for 1 year; $22 for 2 years. Single digital copy: $3. Digital subscription: $4 for 1 year; $7 for 2 years. Buy subscriptions online via credit card, or mail an order form with a check made out to *Meridian*. Guidelines online.

- *Meridian* is 130 pages, digest-sized, offset-printed, perfect-bound, with color cover. Receives about 2,500 poems/year, accepts about 40 (less than 1%). Press run is 1,000 (750 subscribers, 15 libraries, 200 shelf sales); 150 distributed free to writing programs. Work published in *Meridian* has appeared in *The Best American Poetry* and *The Pushcart Prize Anthology*.

MAGAZINES NEEDS Submit up to 5 poems via online submissions manager. Length: up to 10 pages total. Pays 2 contributor's copies (additional copies available at discount).

ALSO OFFERS *Meridian* Editors' Prize Contest offers annual $1,000 award. Submit online only; see website for formatting details. **Entry fee:** $8.50, includes one-year subscription to *Meridian* for all U.S. entries or 1 copy of the prize issue for all international entries. **Deadline:** December or January; see website for current deadline.

🟢 MICHIGAN QUARTERLY REVIEW

0576 Rackham Bldg., 915 E. Washington, Ann Arbor MI 48109-1070. (734)764-9265. **E-mail:** mqr@umich.edu. **Website:** www.michiganquarterlyreview.com. **Contact:** Jonathan Freedman, editor; Vicki Lawrence, managing editor. *Michigan Quarterly Review* is an eclectic interdisciplinary journal of arts and culture that seeks to combine the best of poetry, fiction, and creative nonfiction with outstanding critical essays on literary, cultural, social, and political matters. The flagship journal of the University of Michigan, *MQR* draws on lively minds here and elsewhere, seeking to present accessible work of all varieties for sophisticated readers from within and without the academy. Buys first serial rights. Pays on publication. Publishes ms an average of 1 year after acceptance. Responds in 2 months to queries and mss. Sample: $4. Guidelines available online.

- The Laurence Goldstein Award is a $500 annual award to the best poem published in *MQR* during the previous year. The Lawrence Foundation Award is a $1,000 annual award to the best short story published in *MQR* during the previous year. The Page Davidson Clayton Award for Emerging Poets is a $500 annual award given to the best poet appearing in *MQR* during the previous year who has not yet published a book.

MAGAZINES NEEDS No previously published poems. No e-mail submissions. Cover letter is preferred. "It puts a human face on the ms. A few sentences of biography is all I want, nothing lengthy or defensive." Prefers typed mss. Reviews books of poetry. "All reviews are commissioned." Length: should not exceed 8-12 pages. Pays $8-12/published page.

TIPS "Read the journal and assess the range of contents and the level of writing. We have no guidelines to offer or set expectations; every ms is judged on its unique qualities. On essays, query with a very thorough description of the argument and a copy of the first page. Watch for announcements of special issues, which are usually expanded issues and draw upon a lot of freelance writing. Be aware that this is a university quarterly that publishes a limited amount of fiction and poetry and that it is directed at an educated audience, one that has done a great deal of reading in all types of literature."

MID-AMERICAN REVIEW

Bowling Green State University, Department of English, Bowling Green OH 43403. (419)372-2725. **E-mail:** mar@bgsu.edu. **E-mail:** marsubmissions.bgsu.edu. **Website:** www.bgsu.edu/midamericanreview. **Contact:** Abigail Cloud, editor-in-chief; Bridget Adams, fiction editor. "We aim to put the best possible work in front of the biggest possible audience. We publish contemporary fiction, poetry, creative nonfiction, translations, and book reviews." Contests: The Fineline Competition for Prose Poems, Short Shorts, and Everything In Between (June 1 deadline, $10 per 3 pieces, limit 500 words each); The Sherwood Anderson Fiction Award (November 1 deadline, $10 per piece); and the James Wright Poetry Award (November 1 deadline, $10 per 3 pieces). Buys first North American serial rights. Publishes mss an average of 6 months after acceptance. Responds in 5 months to mss. Sample copy: $9 (current issue), $5 (back issue), $10 (rare back issues). Guidelines online.

MAGAZINES NEEDS Submit by mail with SASE, or through online submission manager. Publishes poems with "textured, evocative images, an awareness of how words sound and mean, and a definite sense of voice. Each line should help carry the poem, and an individual vision must be evident." Recently published work by Mary Ann Samyn, G.C. Waldrep, and Daniel Bourne.

TIPS "We are seeking translations of contemporary authors from all languages into English; submissions must include the original and proof of permission to translate. We would also like to see more creative nonfiction."

MIDWAY JOURNAL

216 Banks St. #2, Cambridge MA 02138. (763)516-7463. **E-mail:** editors@midwayjournal.com. **Website:** www.midwayjournal.com. See website for specific genre contacts and e-mails.. **Contact:** Christopher Lowe, nonfiction editor; Ralph Pennel, fiction editor; Paige Riehl, poetry editor. "Just off of I-94 and on the border between St. Paul and Minneapolis, the Midway, like any other state fairgrounds, is alive with a mix of energies and people. Its position as mid-way, as a place of boundary crossing, also reflects our vision for this journal. The work here complicates and questions the boundaries of genre, binary, and aesthetic. It offers surprises and ways of re-seeing, re-thinking, and re-feeling: a veritable banquet of literary fare. Which is why, in each new issue, we are honored to present work by both new and established writers alike." Member CLMP. Responds in 6-9 months. Sample copy online. Guidelines online.

MAGAZINES NEEDS Submit 3-5 poems, no more than 10 pages in a single document, via online submissions manager. No line-length limits.

TIPS "An interesting story with engaging writing, both in terms of style and voice, make a ms stand out. Round characters are a must. Writers who take chances either with content or with form grab an editor's immediate attention. Spend time with the words on the page. Spend time with the language. The language and voice are not vehicles; they, too, are tools."

THE MIDWEST QUARTERLY

Pittsburg State University, 1701 S. Broadway, Pittsburg KS 66762. **E-mail:** chermansson@pittstate.edu; lkmartin@pittstate.edu. **Website:** www.pittstate.edu/department/english/midwest-quarterly. **Contact:** Dr. Casie Hermansson, editor in chief; Lori Martin, poetry editor. *The Midwest Quarterly* publishes "articles on any subject of contemporary interest, particularly literary criticism, political science, philosophy, education, biography, and sociology. Each issue contains a section of poetry usually 12 poems in length. We seek discussions of an analytical and speculative nature and well-crafted poems." For publication in *MQ* and eligibility for the annual Emmett Memorial Prize competition, the editors invite submission of articles on any literary topic but preferably on Victorian or Modern British Literature, Literary Criticism, or the Teaching of Literature. The winner receives an honorarium and invitation to deliver the annual Emmett Memorial Lecture. Acquires first serial rights. Responds in 2 months to mss. Sample: $5. Subscription: $15 US; $25 foreign. Guidelines available on website.

○ *The Midwest Quarterly* is 130 pages, digest-sized, professionally printed, flat-spined, with matte cover. Press run is 650 (600 subscribers, 500 are libraries).

MAGAZINES NEEDS Submit up to 10 poems at a time via e-mail or postal mail. "Mss should be typed with poet's name on each page. Include e-mail address for notification of decision. SASE only for return of poem." Comments on rejected poems "if the poet or poem seems particularly promising." Occasionally publishes theme issues or issues devoted to the work of a single poet. Receives about 3,500-4,000 poems/year; accepts about 60. Has published poetry by Peter Cooley, Lyn Lifshin, Judith Skillman, Naomi Shihab Nye, Jonathan Holden, and Ted Kooser. "Both traditional forms and free verse are accepted. Whatever the form, however, we want poems that are fresh, that move us, have strong imagery, and which use language in a surprising, musical, and interesting way." Length: up to 80 lines/poem ("occasionally longer if exceptional"). Pays 2 contributor's copies.

MILLER'S POND

E-mail: submissions@millerspondpoetry.com (Julie Damerell); mail@handhpress.com (C.J. Houghtaling). **Website:** www. millerspondpoetry.com. **Contact:** C.J. Houghtaling, publisher; Julie Damerell, editor. *miller's pond* is exclusively an e-zine and does not publish in hard-copy format. Web version is published 3 times/year. Submissions accepted year round but read in late December, late April, and in late August. Submissions that do not indicate the poet has read the guidelines are deleted without comment. Writers are encouraged to submit near the reading dates to avoid long waits. Responses usually sent only in late December or early January, April, and late August. "Current guidelines, updates, and changes are always available on our website. Check there first before submitting anything."

MAGAZINES NEEDS Submit poems to Julie Damerell, editor. Mail sent through the post office will be discarded. No payment for accepted poems or reviews.

TIPS "Read the pages on the website to see the range of poetry I like."

MINAS TIRITH EVENING-STAR

Journal of the American Tolkien Society, American Tolkien Society, P.O. Box 97, Highland MI 48357-

0097. **E-mail:** americantolkiensociety@yahoo.com. **E-mail:** editor@americantolkiensociety.org. **Website:** www.americantolkiensociety.org. **Contact:** Amalie A. Helms, editor. *Minas Tirith Evening-Star: Journal of the American Tolkien Society*, published occasionally, publishes poetry, book reviews, essays, and fan fiction. *Minas Tirith Evening-Star* is now online at www.americantolkiensociety.org. There is no charge to website users, Society membership is $5 US per year. Responds in 2 weeks. Guidelines online.

MAGAZINES NEEDS Uses poetry of fantasy about Middle-earth and Tolkien. Considers poetry by children and teens. Has published poetry by Thomas M. Egan, Anne Etkin, Nancy Pope, and Martha Benedict. Submit by mail or e-mail. Reviews related books of poetry; length depends on the volume (a sentence to several pages). Send materials for review consideration. Does not pay for contributions.

ALSO OFFERS Membership in the American Tolkien Society is open to all, regardless of country of residence, and entitles one to receive the quarterly journal. Dues are $12.50/year to addresses in U.S., Canada, and Mexico, and $15 elsewhere. Sometimes sponsors contests.

THE MINNESOTA REVIEW

E-mail: editors@theminnesotareview.org. **E-mail:** submissions@theminnesotareview.org. **Website:** minnesotareview.wordpress.com. **Contact:** Janell Watson, editor. *The Minnesota Review*, published bi-annually, is a journal featuring creative and critical work from writers on the rise or who are already established. Each issue is about 200 pages, digest-sized, flat-spined, with glossy card cover. Press run is 1,000 (400 subscribers). Also available online. Subscription: $30 for 2 years for individuals, $60/year for institutions. Sample: $15. Guidelines available online.

○ Open to submissions August 1-November 1 and January 1-April 1.

MAGAZINES NEEDS Submit 3-5 poems per reading period as 1 document via online submissions manager Pays 2 contributor's copies.

◐ M.I.P. COMPANY

P.O. Box 27484, Minneapolis MN 55427. **Website:** www.mipco.com. **Contact:** Michael Peltsman, editor. The publisher of controversial Russian literature (erotic prose and poetry). Responds in 1 month to queries. Seldom comments on rejected poems.

MAGAZINES NEEDS Considers simultaneous submissions; no previously published poems.

🟢 THE MISSOURI REVIEW

357 McReynolds Hall, University of Missouri, Columbia MO 65211. (573)882-4474. **E-mail:** question@moreview.com. **Website:** www.missourireview.com. **Contact:** Kate McIntyre. Publishes contemporary fiction, poetry, interviews, personal essays, and special features—such as History as Literature series, Found Text series, and Curio Cabinet art features—for the literary and the general reader interested in a wide range of subjects. Acquires first serial rights. Pays on publication Responds in 2 weeks to queries; in 10-12 weeks to mss. Editorial lead time 4-6 months. Sample copy: $10 or online. Guidelines online.

MAGAZINES NEEDS *TMR* publishes poetry features only—6-14 pages of poems by each of 3-5 poets per issue. Keep in mind the length of features when submitting poems. Typically, successful submissions include 8-20 pages of unpublished poetry. (Note: Do not send complete mss—published or unpublished—for consideration.) No inspirational verse. Pays $40/printed page and 3 contributor's copies.

ADDITIONAL INFORMATION The Gerald T. Perkoff Prize in Poetry is an ongoing series, awarded at least once a year at the discretion of the editors. This prize is given to a poet published in the most recent volume year whose poetry addresses some aspect of the experience or meaning of illness, healing, death and dying, or the practice of medicine. No application is required.

TIPS "Send your best work."

MOBIUS

The Journal of Social Change, 149 Talmadge St., Madison WI 53704. **E-mail:** fmschep@charter.net (fiction); demiurge@fibitz.com (poetry). **Website:** www.mobiusmagazine.com. **Contact:** Fred Schepartz, publisher and executive editor. *Mobius: The Journal of Social Change* is an online-only journal, published quarterly in March, June, September, and December. "At *Mobius* we believe that writing is power and good writing empowers both the reader and the writer. We feel strongly that alternatives are needed to an increasingly corporate literary scene. *Mobius* strives to provide an outlet for writers disenfranchised by a bottom-line marketplace and challenging writing for those who feel that today's literary standards are killing us in a slow, mind-numbing fashion." Acquires one-time electronic publishing rights. Publishes ms 3-6 months after acceptance. Responds in 1 month. Guidelines online.

MAGAZINES NEEDS Submit poetry dealing with themes of social change. Accepts e-mailed poetry submissions only. "We have a marked distate for prosaic didacticism (but a weakness for prose poems)." Do not submit poems by postal mail.

TIPS "We like high impact. We like plot- and character-driven stories that function like theater of the mind. We look first and foremost for good writing. Prose must be crisp and polished; the story must pique my interest and make me care due to a certain intellectual, emotional aspect. *Mobius* is about social change. We want stories that make some statement about the society we live in, either on a macro or micro level. Not that your story needs to preach from a soapbox (actually, we prefer that it doesn't), but it needs to have something to say."

THE MOCCASIN

The League of Minnesota Poets, 427 N. Gorman St., Blue Earth MN 56013. (507)526-5321. **Website:** www.mnpoets.com. **Contact:** Meredith R. Cook, editor. *The Moccasin*, published annually in October, is the literary magazine of The League of Minnesota Poets. Membership is required to submit work.

🎧 *The Moccasin* is 40 pages, digest-sized, offset-printed, stapled, with 80 lb. linen-finish text cover with drawing and poem. Receives about 190 poems/year, accepts about 170. Press run is 200. Single copy: $6.25; subscription is free with LOMP membership.

MAGAZINES NEEDS Send submissions by mail by mid-July each year. (Check website for exact deadline.) Looking for all forms of poetry. Prefer strong, short poems. Considers poetry by children and teens who are student members of The League of Minnesota Poets (write grade level on poems submitted). Has published poetry by Diane Glancy, Laurel Winter, Susan Stevens Chambers, Doris Stengel, Jeanette Hinds, and Charmaine Donovan. Does not want profanity or obscenity. Do not use inversions or archaic language. Length: up to 24 lines/poem.

TIPS To become a member of The League of Minnesota Poets, send $20 ($10 if high school student or younger) to Angela Foster, LOMP Treasurer, 30036 St. Croix Rd, Pine City MN 55063. Make checks payable to LOMP. You do not have to live in Minnesota to become a member of LOMP. "Membership in LOMP automatically makes you a member of the National Federation of State Poetry Societies, which makes you eligible to enter its contests at a cheaper (members') rate."

THE MOCHILA REVIEW

Missouri Western State University, Department of English & Modern Languages, 4525 Downs Dr., St. Joseph MO 64507. **E-mail:** mochila@missouriwestern.edu. **Website:** www.missouriwestern.edu/orgs/mochila/homepage.htm. **Contact:** Dr. Marianne Kunkel, editor in chief. "*The Mochila Review* is an annual international undergraduate journal published with support from the English and Modern Languages department at Missouri Western State University. Our goal is to publish the best short stories, poems, and essays from the next generation of important authors: student writers. Our staff, comprised primarily of undergraduate students, understands the publishing challenges that emerging writers face and is committed to helping talented students gain wider audiences in the pages of *The Mochila Review* and on our website." Responds in 3-4 months to mss. Guidelines available online.

MAGAZINES NEEDS Submit up to 5 poems via online submissions manager. Include cover letter, contact information, SASE. Pays contributor's copies.

TIPS "Mss with fresh language, energy, passion, and intelligence stand out. Study the craft, and be entertaining and engaging."

⑤ MODERN HAIKU

P.O. Box 930, Portsmouth RI 02871. **E-mail:** modernhaiku@gmail.com. **Website:** modernhaiku.org. **Contact:** Paul Miller, editor. *Modern Haiku* is the foremost international journal of English-language haiku and criticism and publishes high-quality material only. Haiku and related genres, articles on haiku, haiku book reviews, and translations comprise its contents. It has an international circulation; subscribers include many university, school, and public libraries. *Modern Haiku* is 140 pages (average), digest-sized, printed on heavy-quality stock, with full-color cover illustrations, 4-page full-color art sections. Receives about 15,000 submissions/year, accepts about 1,000. Acquires first North American serial rights, first international serial rights. Publishes ms an average of 6 months after acceptance. Responds in 1 week to queries; in 6-8 weeks to mss. Editorial lead time 4 months. Sample copy: $15 in North America, $16 in Canada, $20 in Mexico, $22 overseas. Subscription: $35 ppd by regular mail in the U.S. Payment possible by PayPal on the *Modern Haiku* website. Guidelines available for SASE or on website.

MAGAZINES NEEDS Postal submissions: "Send 5-15 haiku on 1 or 2 letter-sized sheets. Put name and address at the top of each sheet. Include SASE." E-mail submissions: "May be attachments (recommended) or pasted in body of message. Subject line must read: MH Submission. Adhere to guidelines on the website." Publishes 1000 poems/year. Has published haiku by Roberta Beary, Billy Collins, Lawrence Ferlinghetti, Carolyn Hall, Sharon Olds, Gary Snyder, John Stevenson, George Swede, and Cor van den Heuvel. Does not want "general poetry, tanka, renku, linked-verse forms. No special consideration given to work by children and teens." Offers no payment.

ALSO OFFERS Reviews of books of haiku by staff and freelancers by invitation in 350-1,000 words, usually single-book format. Send materials for review consideration with complete ordering information. Sponsors the annual Robert Spiess Memorial Haiku Competition. Guidelines available for SASE or on website.

TIPS "Study the history of haiku, read books about haiku, learn the aesthetics of haiku and methods of composition. Write about your sense perceptions of the suchness of entities; avoid ego-centered interpretations. Be sure the work you send us conforms to the definitions on our website."

●⑤ MSLEXIA

Mslexia Publications Ltd, P.O. Box 656, Newcastle upon Tyne NE99 1PZ, United Kingdom. (+44) (191)204-8860. **E-mail:** postbag@mslexia.co.uk. **E-mail:** submissions@mslexia.co.uk. **Website:** www.mslexia.co.uk. **Contact:** Debbie Taylor, editorial director. "*Mslexia* tells you all you need to know about exploring your creativity and getting into print. No other magazine provides *Mslexia*'s unique mix of advice and inspiration; news, reviews, interviews; competitions, events, grants; all served up with a challenging selection of new poetry and prose. *Mslexia* is read by authors and absolute beginners. A quarterly master class in the business and psychology of writing, it's the essential magazine for women who write. We accept submissions from any woman from any country writing in English. There are 14 ways of submitting to the magazine, for every kind of writing, and we pay for everything we publish. Submissions guidelines are on our website. We also run a series of women's fiction competitions with top cash prizes and career development opportunities for finalists."

Buys one-time rights. Pays on publication. Publishes ms an average of 1 month after acceptance. Responds in 12 weeks. Editorial lead time 12 weeks. Purchase of single issues via office or website. Writer's guidelines online or by e-mail.

MAGAZINES NEEDS Pays £25 per poem plus contributor's copies.

TIPS "Read the magazine; subscribe if you can afford it. *Mslexia* has a particular style and relationship with its readers which is hard to assess at a quick glance. The majority of our readers live in the UK, so feature pitches should be aware of this. We never commission work without seeing a written sample first. We rarely accept unsolicited manuscripts, but prefer a short letter suggesting a feature, plus a brief bio and writing sample."

MUDFISH

Box Turtle Press, 184 Franklin St., Ground Floor, New York NY 10013. (212)219-9278. **Website:** www.mudfish.org. **Contact:** Jill Hoffman, editor. *Mudfish*, a journal of art and poetry (and some fiction), takes its title from the storyteller's stool in Nigerian art. The poems each tell a story. They are resonant and visceral, encapsulating the unique human experience. There is a wide range to the subject matter and style, but the poems all have breath and life, a living voice. *Mudfish* has featured work from the best established and emerging artists and poets—including John Ashbery, Charles Simic, and Frank Stella—since it burst onto the poetry scene. Responds in 3 months, or ASAP.

MAGAZINES NEEDS Wants free verse with energy, intensity, and originality of voice, mastery of style, the presence of passion. Submit 5-6 poems at a time. No e-mail submissions; postal submissions only. Pays 1 contributor's copy.

CONTEST/AWARD OFFERINGS Sponsors the Mudfish Poetry Prize Award of $1,000. **Entry fee:** $15 for up to 3 poems, $3 for each additional poem. **Deadline:** varies. Guidelines available for SASE.

MUDLARK

An Electronic Journal of Poetry & Poetics, Department of English, University of North Florida, Jacksonville FL 32224. **E-mail:** mudlark@unf.edu. **Website:** www.unf.edu/mudlark. **Contact:** William Slaughter, editor and publisher. *Mudlark: An Electronic Journal of Poetry & Poetics*, published online "irregularly, but frequently," offers 3 formats: Issues of *Mudlark* are the electronic equivalent of print chapbooks; posters are the electronic equivalent of print broadsides; and flashes are poems with "news that stays news" in them, poems that feel like current events. The poem is the thing at *Mudlark*, and the essay about it. "As our full name suggests, we will consider accomplished work that locates itself anywhere on the spectrum of contemporary practice. We want poems, of course, but we want essays, too, that make us read poems (and write them?) differently somehow. Although we are not innocent, we do imagine ourselves capable of surprise. The work of hobbyists is not for *Mudlark*. As for representative authors: No naming names here. If we are, as we imagine ourselves, capable of surprise, then there is no such thing as a 'representative author' in the *Mudlark* archive, which is 'never in and never out of print.' The *Mudlark* archive, going back to 1995, is as wide as it is deep, as rich and various as it is full." *Mudlark* is archived and permanently on view at www.unf.edu/mudlark. Acquires one-time rights. Offers no payment; however, "one of the things we can do at *Mudlark* to 'pay' our authors for their work is point to it here and there. We can tell our readers how to find it, how to subscribe to it, and how to buy it—if it is for sale. Toward that end, we maintain A-Notes on the authors we publish. We call attention to their work." Publishes ms no more than 3 months after acceptance. Responds in "1 day-1 month, depending." Guidelines online.

MAGAZINES NEEDS Submit any number of poems at a time. Prefers not to receive simultaneous submissions but will consider them if informed of the fact, up front, and if notified immediately when poems are accepted elsewhere. Considers previously published work only as part of a *Mudlark* issue, the electronic equivalent of a print chapbook, and only if the previous publication is acknowledged in a note that covers the submission. Only poems that have not been previously published will be considered for *Mudlark* posters or flashes. Accepts e-mail or USPS submissions with SASE; no fax submissions. Cover letter is optional. Seldom comments on rejected poems. Always sends prepublication galleys in the form of inviting the author to proof the work on a private website that *Mudlark* maintains for that purpose.

NARRATIVE MAGAZINE

E-mail: contact@narrativemagazine.com. **Website:** www.narrativemagazine.com. **Contact:** Michael Croft, senior editor; Mimi Kusch, managing editor; Michael Wiegers, poetry editor. "*Narrative* publishes high-quality contemporary literature in a full range of styles, forms, and lengths. Submit poetry, fiction, and nonfiction, including stories, short shorts, novels, novel excerpts, novellas, personal essays, humor, sketches, memoirs, literary biographies, commentary, reportage, interviews, and short audio recordings of short-short stories and poems. We welcome submissions of previously unpublished mss of all lengths, ranging from short-short stories to complete book-length works for serialization. In addition to submissions for issues of *Narrative* itself, we also encourage submissions for our Story of the Week, Poem of the Week, literary contests, and Readers' Narratives. Please read our Submission Guidelines for all information on mss formatting, word lengths, author payment, and other policies. We accept submissions only through our electronic submission system. We do not accept submissions through postal services or e-mail. You may send us mss for the following submission categories: General Submissions, Narrative Prize, Story of the Week, Poem of the Week, Readers' Narrative, iPoem, iStory, Six-Word Story, or a specific Contest. Your mss must be in one of the following file forms: DOC, RTF, PDF, DOCX, TXT, WPD, ODF, MP3, MP4, MOV, or FLV." Buys exclusive first serial rights in English for 90 days, and nonexclusive rights thereafter "to maintain the work in our online library." Responds in 1 month-14 weeks to queries. Guidelines online. **Charges $25 reading fee except for 2 weeks in April.**

○ *Narrative* has received recognitions in *New Stories from the South*, *Best American Mystery Stories*, *O. Henry Prize Stories*, *Best American Short Stories*, *Best American Essays*, and the *Pushcart Prize Collection*. In an article on the business of books, the National Endowment for the Arts featured *Narrative* as the model for the evolution of both print and digital publishing.

TIPS "Log on and study our magazine online. Narrative fiction, graphic art, and multimedia are selected, first and foremost, for quality."

THE NATIONAL POETRY REVIEW

Website: www.nationalpoetryreview.com. **Contact:** Angela Vogel, editor in chief. *The National Poetry Review* seeks "distinction, innovation, and *joie de vivre*. We agree with Frost about delight and wisdom. We believe in rich sound. We believe in the beautiful—even if that beauty is not in the situation of the poem but simply the sounds of the poem, the images, or (ide-

ally) the way the poem stays in the reader's mind long after it's been read." *TNPR* considers both experimental and 'mainstream' work." Does not want "overly self-centered or confessional poetry." Acquires first rights. Time between acceptance and publication is no more than 1 year. "The editor makes all publishing decisions." Sometimes comments on rejected poems. Usually responds in 3-4 months. Guidelines available on website.

○ *The National Poetry Review* is an annual online journal that accepts less than 1% of submissions received. Poetry appearing in *The National Poetry Review* has also appeared in *The Pushcart Prize*. Has published poetry by Bob Hicok, Jennifer Michael Hecht, Larissa Szplorluk, Martha Zweig, Nance Van Winkel, William Waltz, and Ted Kooser.

MAGAZINES NEEDS "Our reading period is January 1-April 1 annually. Please submit all poems in 1 file. Include a brief bio with previous publications."

ALSO OFFERS Review copies of new poetry books may be sent for consideration to Douglas Basford, TNPR Reviews Editor: 306 Clemens Hall, Department of English, The University at Buffalo, Buffalo, NY 14260. Please do NOT send poetry submissions to this address! ALL poetry submissions must be sent via the Submittable link. Poems sent through other means will be discarded.

🛈 THE NATION

520 Eighth Avenue, 8th Flo, New York NY 10018. **E-mail:** submissions@thenation.com. **Website:** www.thenation.com. Steven Brower, art director. **Contact:** Roane Carey, managing editor; Ange Mlinko, poetry editor. *The Nation*, published weekly, is a journal of left/liberal opinion, with arts coverage that includes poetry. The only requirement for poetry is excellence. Guidelines available online.

○ Poetry published by *The Nation* has been included in *The Best American Poetry*. Has published poetry by W.S. Merwin, Maxine Kumin, James Merrill, May Swenson, Edward Hirsch, and Charles Simic.

MAGAZINES NEEDS "Please email poems in a single PDF attachment to PoemNationSubmit@gmail.com. Submissions are not accepted from June 1-September 15."

NATURAL BRIDGE

Department of English, University of Missouri-St. Louis, 1 University Blvd., St. Louis MO 63121. **E-mail:**

natural@umsl.edu. **Website:** www.umsl.edu/~natural. *Natural Bridge*, published biannually in April and December, invites submissions of poetry, fiction, personal essays, and translations. Acquires first North American rights. Publishes ms 9 months after acceptance. Responds in 4-8 months. Guidelines available online at website.

○ No longer accepts submissions via e-mail. Accepts submissions through online submission manager and postal mail only.

MAGAZINES NEEDS Seeks "fresh, innovative poetry, both free and formal, on any subject. We want poems that work on first and subsequent readings—poems that entertain and resonate, and challenge our readers." Submit 4-6 poems at a time. Submit year round; however, "we do not read May 1-August 1. Work is read and selected by the guest-editor and editor, along with editorial assistants made up of graduate students in our MFA program. We publish work by both established and new writers." Length: no limit. Pays 2 contributor's copies and one-year subscription.

NAUGATUCK RIVER REVIEW

P.O. Box 368, Westfield MA 01085. **E-mail:** naugatuckriver@aol.com. **Website:** http://naugatuckriverreview.com. **Contact:** Lori Desrosiers, managing editor and publisher. *Naugatuck River Review*, published semiannually, "is a print literary journal looking for narrative poetry of high caliber, where the narrative is compressed with a strong emotional core." Acquires first North American serial rights. Publishes ms 1-3 months after acceptance. Responds in 2-5 months. Always sends prepublication galleys. Guidelines available in magazine and on website.

○ Accepts submissions through online submission form only.

MAGAZINES NEEDS Submit up to 3 poems. Prefers unpublished poems. Accepts online submissions through submission manager only; no e-mail, fax, or disk submissions. Include a brief bio and mailing information. Reads submissions January 1-March 1 and July 1-September 1 for contest (fee). Length: up to 50 lines/poem. Pays 1 contributor's copy.

HOW TO CONTACT Write us at naugatuckriver@aol.com with questions, not submissions.

CONTEST/AWARD OFFERINGS Submissions made July 1-September 1 are entered into annual contest, which offers $1,350 total in prizes.

TIPS "What is narrative poetry? What *NRR* is looking for are poems that tell a story or have a strong

sense of story. They can be stories of a moment or an experience, and can be personal or historical. A good narrative poem that would work for our journal has a compressed narrative, and we prefer poems that take up 2 pages or less of the journal. Any style of poem is considered, including prose poems. Poems with very long lines don't fit well in the 6x9 format."

NEBO

Arkansas Tech University, Department of English, Russellville AR 72801. **E-mail:** nebo@atu.edu. **E-mail:** nebo@atu.edu. **Website:** www.atu.edu/world-languages/Nebo.php. **Contact:** Editor. *Nebo*, published in the spring and fall, publishes fiction, poetry, creative nonfiction, drama, comics, and art from Arkansas Tech students and unpublished writers as well as nationally known writers. Acquires one-time rights. Publishes mss 3-6 months after acceptance. Responds in 2 weeks-4 months to mss. Occasionally comments on rejected mss. Sample copy: $6. Subscriptions: $10. Guidelines available on website.

○ Reads submissions August 15-May 1.

MAGAZINES NEEDS Accepts all forms of poetry. Submit up to 5 poems by e-mail or postal mail.

TIPS "Avoid pretentiousness. Write something you genuinely care about. Please edit your work for spelling, grammar, cohesiveness, and overall purpose. Many of the mss we receive should be publishable with a little polishing. Mss should never be submitted handwritten or on 'onion skin' or colored paper."

○ ⑤ NEON MAGAZINE

E-mail: info@neonmagazine.co.uk. **E-mail:** subs@neonmagazine.co.uk. **Website:** www.neonmagazine.co.uk. **Contact:** Krishan Coupland. Twice-yearly online and print magazine featuring alternative work of any form of poetry and prose, short stories, flash fiction, artwork, and reviews. "*Neon* sits on the edge of horror and science-fiction, but with strong literary leanings. If you have a taste for the magical realist or uncanny, *Neon* is the magazine for you." Buys one-time rights. "After publication all rights revert back to you." Responds in 6 months. Query if you have not received a reply after 6 months. Guidelines online.

MAGAZINES NEEDS "No nonsense poetry. Rhyming poetry is discouraged." No word limit. Pays royalties.

TIPS "Send several poems, 1-2 pieces of prose, or several images via e-mail. Include the word 'submission' in your subject line. Include a short biographical note (up to 100 words). Read submission guidelines before submitting your work."

NEW AMERICAN WRITING

369 Molino Ave., Mill Valley CA 94941. **Website:** www. newamericanwriting.com. **Contact:** Maxine Chernoff and Paul Hoover, editors. *New American Writing* is a literary magazine emphasizing contemporary American poetry. It appears once a year in early June. The magazine is distinctive for publishing a range of innovative writing. Responds in 2 weeks-6 months. Sample copy: $15. Guidelines available online.

MAGAZINES NEEDS Reading period: September 1-January 15. Submit via postal mail.

⑤ THE NEW CRITERION

900 Broadway, Ste. 602, New York NY 10003. **Website:** www.newcriterion.com. **Contact:** Roger Kimball, editor and publisher; David Yezzi, poetry editor. "A monthly review of the arts and intellectual life, *The New Criterion* began as an experiment in critical audacity—a publication devoted to engaging, in Matthew Arnold's famous phrase, with 'the best that has been thought and said.' This also meant engaging with those forces dedicated to traducing genuine cultural and intellectual achievement, whether through obfuscation, politicization, or a commitment to nihilistic absurdity. We are proud that *The New Criterion* has been in the forefront both of championing what is best and most humanely vital in our cultural inheritance and in exposing what is mendacious, corrosive, and spurious. Published monthly from September through June, *The New Criterion* brings together a wide range of young and established critics whose common aim is to bring you the most incisive criticism being written today."

○   *The New Criterion* is 90 pages, 7x10, flat-spined. Single copy: $12.

MAGAZINES NEEDS Has published poetry by Donald Justice, Andrew Hudgins, Elizabeth Spires, and Herbert Morris.

⑤ NEW ENGLAND REVIEW

Middlebury College, Middlebury VT 05753. (802)443-5075. **E-mail:** nereview@middlebury.edu. **Website:** www.nereview.com. **Contact:** Marcia Pomerance, managing editor. *New England Review* is a prestigious, nationally distributed literary journal. Reads September 1-May 31 (postmarked dates). *New England Review* is 200+ pages, 7x10, printed on heavy stock, flat-spined, with glossy cover with art. Re-

ceives 3,000-4,000 poetry submissions/year, accepts about 70-80 poems/year. Receives 550 unsolicited mss/month, accepts 6 mss/issue, 24 fiction mss/year. Does not accept mss June-August, December-January. Agented fiction less than 5%. Buys first North American serial rights, first rights, second serial (reprint) rights. Sends galleys to author. Pays on publication. Publishes ms an average of 6 months after acceptance. Responds in 2 weeks to queries; in 3 months to mss. Sometimes comments on rejected mss. Sample copy: $10 (add $5 for overseas). Subscription: $35. Overseas shipping fees add $25 for subscription, $12 for Canada. Guidelines online.

MAGAZINES NEEDS Submit up to 6 poems at a time. No previously published or simultaneous submissions for poetry. Accepts submissions by online submission manager only; accepts questions by e-mail. "Cover letters are useful." Address submissions to "Poetry Editor." Pays $20/page ($20 minimum), and 2 contributor's copies.

ALSO OFFERS *NER* pays $50 per published online essay in their digital series "Confluences," works of 500-1,000 words. Submission details appear online.

TIPS "We consider short fiction, including short shorts, novellas, and self-contained extracts from novels in both traditional and experimental forms. In nonfiction, we consider a variety of general and literary but not narrowly scholarly essays; we also publish long and short poems, screenplays, graphics, translations, critical reassessments, statements by artists working in various media, testimonies, and letters from abroad. We are committed to exploration of all forms of contemporary cultural expression in the U.S. and abroad. With few exceptions, we print only work not published previously elsewhere."

⑤ NEW LETTERS

University of Missouri-Kansas City, 5101 Rockhill Rd., Kansas City MO 64110. (816)235-1168. **Fax:** (816)235-2611. **E-mail:** newletters@umkc.edu. **Website:** www. newletters.org. **Contact:** Robert Stewart, editor-in-chief. "*New Letters*, published quarterly, continues to seek the best new writing, whether from established writers or those ready and waiting to be discovered. In addition, it supports those writers, readers, and listeners who want to experience the joy of writing that can both surprise and inspire us all." Submissions are not read June 1st through July 30th. Buys first North American serial rights. Pays on publication. Publishes ms an average of 6 months after acceptance. Responds in 1 month to queries; 5 months to mss. Editorial lead time 6 months. Sample copy: $10; sample articles online. Guidelines online.

MAGAZINES NEEDS No light verse. Length: open. Pays $10-25.

TIPS "We aren't interested in essays that are footnoted or essays usually described as scholarly or critical. Our preference is for creative nonfiction or personal essays. We prefer shorter stories and essays to longer ones (an average length is 3,500-4,000 words). We have no rigid preferences as to subject, style, or genre, although commercial efforts tend to put us off. Even so, our only fixed requirement is good writing."

NEW MADRID

Journal of Contemporary Literature, Murray State University, Department of English and Philosophy, 7C Faculty Hall, Murray KY 42071-3341. (270)809-4730. **E-mail:** msu.newmadrid@murraystate.edu. **Website:** newmadridjournal.org. **Contact:** Ann Neelon, editor; Jacque E. Day, managing editor. "*New Madrid* is the national journal of the low-residency MFA program at Murray State University. It takes its name from the New Madrid seismic zone, which falls within the central Mississippi Valley and extends through western Kentucky." Acquires first North American serial rights. Publication is copyrighted. Responds within three months of close of reading period. Guidelines available on website.

○ See website for guidelines and upcoming themes. "We have 2 reading periods, August 15-October 15 and January 15-March 15." Also publishes poetry and creative nonfiction. Rarely comments on/critiques rejected mss.

MAGAZINES NEEDS Accepts submissions by online submissions manager only. Include brief bio, list of publications. Considers multiple submissions.

TIPS "Quality is the determining factor for breaking into *New Madrid*. We are looking for well-crafted, compelling writing in a range of genres, forms, and styles."

⑤ NEW OHIO REVIEW

English Department, 201 Ellis Hall; 45 University Terrace, Ohio University, Athens OH 45701. **E-mail:** noreditors@ohio.edu. **Website:** www.ohiou.edu/nor. **Contact:** David Wanczyk, editor. *New Ohio Review*, published biannually in spring and fall, publishes fiction, nonfiction, and poetry. Member CLMP. Reading period is September 15-December 15 and January 15-April 15. Annual contests, Jan 15th-Apr 15th

($1,000 prizes). Responds in 2-4 months. Single copy: $9. Subscription: $16. Guidelines online.

MAGAZINES NEEDS Please do not submit more than once every 6 months unless requested to do so.

⑤ NEW ORLEANS REVIEW

Box 195, Loyola University, New Orleans LA 70118. (504)865-2295. **E-mail:** noreview@loyno.edu. **Website:** neworleansreview.org. **Contact:** Heidi Braden, managing editor; Mark Yakich, Editor. *New Orleans Review* is an annual journal of contemporary literature and culture, publishing new poetry, fiction, nonfiction, art, photography, film, and book reviews. Buys first North American serial rights. Pays on publication. Responds in 4 months to mss. Sample copy: $5.

○ The journal has published an eclectic variety of work by established and emerging writers, including Walker Percy, Pablo Neruda, Ellen Gilchrist, Nelson Algren, Hunter S. Thompson, John Kennedy Toole, Richard Brautigan, Barry Spacks, James Sallis, Jack Gilbert, Paul Hoover, Rodney Jones, Annie Dillard, Everette Maddox, Julio Cortazar, Gordon Lish, Robert Walser, Mark Halliday, Jack Butler, Robert Olen Butler, Michael Harper, Angela Ball, Joyce Carol Oates, Diane Wakoski, Dermot Bolger, Roddy Doyle, William Kotzwinkle, Alain Robbe-Grillet, Arnost Lustig, Raymond Queneau, Yusef Komunyakaa, Michael Martone, Tess Gallagher, Matthea Harvey, D. A. Powell, Rikki Ducornet, and Ed Skoog.

MAGAZINES NEEDS Submit using online submissions manager ($3 fee).

TIPS "We're looking for dynamic writing that demonstrates attention to the language and a sense of the medium, writing that engages, surprises, moves us. We're not looking for genre fiction or academic articles. We subscribe to the belief that in order to truly write well, one must first master the rudiments: grammar and syntax, punctuation, the sentence, the paragraph, the line, the stanza. We receive about 3,000 mss a year and publish about 3% of them. Check out a recent issue, send us your best, proofread your work, be patient, be persistent."

◑⑤ THE NEW QUARTERLY

St. Jerome's University, 290 Westmount Rd. N., Waterloo ON N2L 3G3, Canada. (519)884-8111, ext. 28290. **E-mail:** editor@tnq.ca; info@tnq.ca. **Website:** www.tnq.ca. Sophie Blom. "Emphasis on emerging writers and genres, but we publish more traditional work as well if the language and narrative structure are fresh." Open to Canadian writers only. Reading periods: March 1-August 31; September 1-February 28. Buys first Canadian rights. Pays on publication. Responds in early January to submissions received March 1-August 31; in early June to submissions received September 1-February 28. Editorial lead time 6 months. Sample copy: $16.95 (cover price, plus mailing). Guidelines online.

MAGAZINES NEEDS *Canadian work only.* Send with submission cover sheet and bio. Does not accept submissions by e-mail. Accepts simultaneoues submissions if indicated in cover letter. Pays $40/poem

TIPS "Reading us is the best way to get our measure. We don't have preconceived ideas about what we're looking for other than that it must be Canadian work (Canadian writers, not necessarily Canadian content). We want something that's fresh, something that will repay a second reading, something in which the language soars and the feeling is complexly rendered."

NEW SOUTH

Georgia State University, Campus Box 1894, MSC 8R0322 Unit 8, Atlanta GA 30303-3083. **E-mail:** newsoutheditors@gmail.com. **Website:** www.newsouth journal.com. Semiannual magazine dedicated to finding and publishing the best work from artists around the world. Wants original voices searching to rise above the ordinary. Seeks to publish high-quality work, regardless of genre, form, or regional ties. *New South* is 160+ pages. Press run is 1,500, and free to GSU students. The *New South* Annual Writing Contest offers $1,000 for the best poem and $1,000 for the best story or essay; one-year subscription to all who submit. Submissions must be unpublished. Submit up to 3 poems, 1 story, or 1 essay on any subject or in any form. Guidelines available online. Competition receives 300 entries. Past judges include Sharon Olds, Jane Hirschfield, Anthony Hecht, Phillip Levine, Mark Doty, and Jake Adam York. Winners will be published in the Fall issue. Acquires first North American serial rights. Time between acceptance and publication is 3-5 months. Responds in 3-5 months. Sample: $4 (back issue). Single copy: $6; subscription: $9/year. Guidelines online.

MAGAZINES NEEDS Submit up to 5 poems at a time through Submittable. Pays 2 contributor's copies.

TIPS "We want what's new, what's fresh, and what's different—whether it comes from the Southern United States, the South of India, or the North, East or West of Anywhere."

THE NEW VERSE NEWS

Tangerang Selatan , Indonesia. **E-mail:** nvneditor@gmail.com. **Website:** www.newversenews.com. **Contact:** James Penha, editor. *The New Verse News*, published online and updated every day, has a clear liberal bias but will consider various visions and views. Acquires first rights. Rights revert to poet upon publication. Normally, poems are published immediately upon acceptance. Responds in 1-2 weeks. Does not comment on rejected poems. Timely poems may be published immediately. Guidelines online.

MAGAZINES NEEDS Wants previously unpublished poems, both serious and satirical, on current events and topical issues; will also consider prose poems. Accepts only non-simultaneous e-mail submissions (pasted into body of message); use "Verse News Submission" as the subject line; no postal submissions. Send brief bio. Reads submissions year round. Poems are circulated to an editorial board. Receives about 3,000 poems/year; accepts about 365. Does not want work unrelated to the news. No length restrictions. No financial remuneration.

TIPS "Take a look at the website to get to know the kind of poetry published."

NEW WELSH REVIEW

P.O. Box 170, Aberystwyth, Ceredigion SY23 1 WZ, United Kingdom. 01970-628410. **E-mail:** editor@newwelshreview.com. **E-mail:** submissions@new-welshreview.com. **Website:** www.newwelshreview.com. **Contact:** Gwen Davies, editor. "*New Welsh Review*, a literary magazine published 3 times/year and ranked in the top 5 British literary magazines, publishes stories, poems, and critical essays. The best of Welsh writing in English, past and present, is celebrated, discussed, and debated. We seek poems, short stories, reviews, special features/articles, and commentary."

MAGAZINES NEEDS Submit by e-mail. Pays direct to account or sends check on publication and 1 copy at discounted contributor's rate of £5 inc p&p."

NIMROD INTERNATIONAL JOURNAL

International Journal of Prose and Poetry, University of Tulsa, 800 S. Tucker Dr., Tulsa OK 74104-3189. (918)631-3080. **E-mail:** nimrod@utulsa.edu. **Website:** https://nimrod.utulsa.edu. **Contact:** Eilis O'Neal, editor-in-chief; Cassidy McCants, associate editor. Since its founding in 1956 at The University of Tulsa, *Nimrod International Journal of Prose and Poetry*'s mission has been the discovery, development, and promotion of new writing. On a national and international scale, *Nimrod* helps new writers find their audiences through publication in our semiannual journal. We offer new and promising work that may be unfamiliar to readers, such as writing from countries not well represented in the American mainstream, writing in translation, and writing from people of under-represented ages, races, and sexual identities. *Nimrod* supports and defends the literary tradition of small magazines, spotlighting lesser-known poets and writers and providing foundations for their literary careers. We promote a living literature, believing that it is possible to search for, recognize, and reward contemporary writing of imagination, substance, and skill. Semiannual magazine: 200 pages; perfect-bound; 4-color cover. Receives 300 unsolicited mss/month. **Publishes 50-120 new writers/year.** Reading period: January 1 through November 30. Online submissions accepted at nimrodjournal.submittable.com/submit. Does not accept submissions by email unless the writer is living outside the U.S. and cannot submit using the submissions manager. Buys first North American rights. Pays on publication. Responds in 3-5 months to mss. Sample copy: $11. Subscription: $18.50/year U.S., $25.00/year outside U.S. Guidelines online or for SASE.

MAGAZINES NEEDS Submit poems by mail or through the online submissions manager. Include SASE for work submitted by mail. Length: up to 7 pages. Pays $10/page and 2 contributor's copies.

$ NINTH LETTER

Department of English, University of Illinois, 608 S. Wright St., Urbana IL 61801. **E-mail:** info@ninthletter.com; editor@ninthletter.com; fiction@ninthletter.com; poetry@ninthletter.com; nonfiction@ninthletter.com. **Website:** www.ninthletter.com. **Contact:** Editorial staff rotates; contact genre-specific e-mail address with inquiries. "*Ninth Letter* accepts submissions of fiction, poetry, and essays from September 1-February 28 (postmark dates). *Ninth Letter* is published semiannually at the University of Illinois, Urbana-Champaign. We are interested in prose and poetry that experiment with form, narrative, and nontraditional subject matter, as well as more traditional literary work." Buys first North American serial rights. Pays on publication.

🖵 *Ninth Letter* won Best New Literary Journal 2005 from the Council of Editors of Learned Journals (CELJ) and has had poetry selected

for *Best American Poetry, The Pushcart Prize, Best New Poets*, and *The Year's Best Fantasy and Horror.*

MAGAZINES NEEDS Submit 3-6 poems (no more than 10 pages) at a time. "All mailed submissions must include an SASE for reply." Pays $25/printed page and 2 contributor's copies.

ALSO OFFERS Member: CLMP; CELJ.

NITE-WRITER'S INTERNATIONAL LITERARY ARTS JOURNAL

E-mail: nitewritersliteraryarts@gmail.com. **Website:** https://sites.google.com/site/nitewriterinternational/home. **Contact:** John Thompson. *Nite-Writer's International Literary Arts Journal* is "dedicated to the emotional intellectual with a creative perception of life." Retains first North American serial rights. Copyright reverts to author upon publication. Guidelines available on website. Does not pay authors but offers international exposure to the individual artist.

🖵 Journal is open to beginners as well as professionals.

MAGAZINES NEEDS Wants strong imagery. Considers previously published poems and simultaneous submissions (note when and where your work has been published). Cover letter is preferred. "Give brief bio, state where you heard of us, state if material has been previously published and where." Receives about 1,000 poems/year, accepts about 10-15%. Has published poetry by Lyn Lifshin, Rose Marie Hunold, Peter Vetrano, Carol Frances Brown, and Richard King Perkins II. Does not want porn or violence. Length: open.

TIPS "Read a lot of what you write—study the market. Don't fear rejection, but use it as a learning tool to strengthen your work before resubmitting."

THE NORMAL SCHOOL

E-mail: editors@thenormalschool.com. **Website:** thenormalschool.com. **Contact:** Sophie Beck, managing editor. Semiannual magazine that accepts outstanding work by beginning and established writers. Acquires first North American serial rights. Publication is copyrighted. Publishes ms 3-6 months after acceptance. Responds in 2 months. Sample copy: $7. Guidelines available online.

🖵 Mss are read September 1-December 1 and January 15-April 15. Address submissions to the appropriate editor. Charges $3 fee for each online submission, due to operational costs.

MAGAZINES NEEDS Considers poetry of any style. "Limit the number of cat poems (unless, of course, they are really, really good cat poems)." Pays 2 contributor's copies and one-year subscription.

💲 NORTH AMERICAN REVIEW

University of Northern Iowa, 1200 W. 23th St., Cedar Falls IA 50614. (319)273-6455. **E-mail:** nar@uni.edu. **Website:** northamericanreview.org. "The *North American Review* is the oldest literary magazine in America and one of the most respected; though we have no prejudices about the subject matter of material sent to us, our first concern is quality." Buys first North American serial rights, first rights. Publishes ms an average of 1 year after acceptance. Responds in 3 months to queries; 4 months to mss. Sample copy: $7. Guidelines online.

○ This is the oldest literary magazine in the country and one of the most prestigious. Also one of the most entertaining—and a tough market for the young writer.

MAGAZINES NEEDS Submit up to 5 poems via online submissions manager.

TIPS "We like stories that start quickly and have a strong narrative arc. Poems that are passionate about subject, language, and image are welcome, whether they are traditional or experimental, whether in formal or free verse (closed or open form). Nonfiction should combine art and fact with the finest writing."

💲 NORTH CAROLINA LITERARY REVIEW

East Carolina University, Mailstop 555 English, Greenville NC 27858-4353. (252)328-1537. **Fax:** (252)328-4889. **E-mail:** bauerm@ecu.edu; nclruser@ecu.edu. **E-mail:** nclrsubmissions@ecu.edu. **Website:** www.nclr.ecu.edu. **Contact:** Margaret Bauer. "Articles should have a North Carolina slant. Fiction, creative nonfiction, and poetry accepted through yearly contests. First consideration is always for quality of work. Although we treat academic and scholarly subjects, we do not wish to see jargon-laden prose; our readers, we hope, are found as often in bookstores and libraries as in academia. We seek to combine the best elements of a magazine for serious readers with the best of a scholarly journal." Accepts submissions through Submittable. Acquires first North American serial rights. Rights returned to writer after publication. Publishes ms an average of 1 year after acceptance. Responds in 1 month to queries; in 3-6 months to mss. Editorial lead time 6 months. Sample copy: $5-25. Guidelines online.

MAGAZINES NEEDS Submit poetry for the James Applewhite Poetry Prize competition via Submittable. Only subscribers can submit, and all poets must have a North Carolina connection. Submit up to 3 poems with a one-year subscription ($15), or up to 5 poems with a two-year subscription ($25). First-place winners of contests receive a prize of $250. Other poets whose poems are selected for publication receive contributor's copies.

TIPS "By far the easiest way to break in is with special issue sections. We are especially interested in reports on conferences, readings, meetings that involve North Carolina writers, and personal essays or short narratives with a strong sense of place. See back issues for other departments. Interviews are probably the other easiest place to break in; no discussions of poetics/theory, etc., except in reader-friendly (accessible) language. Interviews should be personal, more like conversations, and extensive, exploring connections between a writer's life and his or her work."

NORTH DAKOTA QUARTERLY

University of North Dakota, 276 Centennial Dr. Stop 7209, Merrifield Hall Room 15, Grand Forks ND 58202. (701)777-3322. **E-mail:** ndq@und.edu. **Website:** www.ndquarterly.org. **Contact:** William Caraher, editor; Gilad Elbom, fiction editor; Heidi Czerwiec, poetry editor; Sharon Carson, book reviews editor. *North Dakota Quarterly* strives to publish the best fiction, poetry, and essays that in our estimation we can. Our tastes and interests are best reflected in what we have been recently publishing, and we suggest that you look at some current issues for guidance. Buys first North American serial rights and rights to publish electronically on website. Pays only in contributors' copies. Guidelines online: https://ndquarterly.submittable.com/submit

○ Work published in *North Dakota Quarterly* was selected for inclusion in *The O. Henry Prize Stories*, *The Pushcart Prize Series*, and *Best American Essays*.

MAGAZINES NEEDS Send 3-5 pages of your best work. No preference with regard to form, style, as long as the content isn't lame and the language works. Published and unpublished poets are welcome, as are translations from across the globe. We are digitally capable for the performance oriented, so send video if the body is your best medium. Editors enjoy everything from Sappho to Mayakovsky, from Dante to Anzaldúa. No simultaneous submissions. No length restrictions.

💲 NOTRE DAME REVIEW

University of Notre Dame, B009C McKenna Hall, Notre Dame IN 46556. **Website:** ndreview.nd.edu. "The *Notre Dame Review* is an independent, noncommercial magazine of contemporary American and international fiction, poetry, criticism, and art. Especially interested in work that takes on big issues by making the invisible seen, that gives voice to the voiceless. In addition to showcasing celebrated authors like Seamus Heaney and Czelaw Milosz, the *Notre Dame Review* introduces readers to authors they may have never encountered before but who are doing innovative and important work. In conjunction with the *Notre Dame Review*, the online companion to the printed magazine, the *nd[re]view*, engages readers as a community centered in literary rather than commercial concerns, a community we reach out to through critique and commentary as well as aesthetic experience." Buys first North American serial rights. Pays on publication. Publishes ms an average of 6 months after acceptance. Responds in 4 or more months to mss. Sample copy: $6. Guidelines online.

🚫 Does not accept e-mail submissions. Only reads hardcopy submissions September through November and January through March.

MAGAZINES NEEDS Submit 3-5 poems via online submissions manager.

TIPS "Excellence is our sole criteria for selection, although we are especially interested in fiction and poetry that take on big issues."

NOW & THEN

The Appalachian Magazine, East Tennessee State University, Box 70556, Johnson City TN 37614-1707. (423)439-5348. **Fax:** (423)439-7074. **E-mail:** nowandthen@etsu.edu; sandersr@etsu.edu. **Website:** www.etsu.edu/cas/cass/nowandthen. **Contact:** Randy Sanders, managing editor. *Now & Then* accepts a variety of writing genres: fiction, poetry, nonfiction, essays, interviews, memoirs, and book reviews. All submissions must relate to Appalachia and to the issue's specific theme. Readership is educated and interested in the region. Sample copy: $8 plus $3 shipping.

🚫 "At this time, the magazine is in the process of transitioning to an online-only publication. Therefore, we are currently not accepting submissions. Follow our progress by visiting the *Now & Then* website at www.etsu.edu/cas/cass/nowandthen."

NTH DEGREE

E-mail: submissions@nthzine.com. **Website:** www.nthzine.com. **Contact:** Michael D. Pederson. Free online fanzine to promote up-and-coming new science fiction and fantasy authors and artists. Also supports the world of fandom and conventions. No longer accepts hard copy submissions. Acquires one-time rights. Responds in 2 weeks to queries; 3 months to mss. Online e-zine; copies available upon request. Guidelines online.

MAGAZINES NEEDS Submit through e-mail. Looking for poetry about science fiction, fantasy, horror, alternate history, well-crafted mystery, and humor. Pays in contributor's copies.

TIPS "Don't submit anything that you may be ashamed of 10 years later."

NUTHOUSE

Website: www.nuthousemagazine.com. *Nuthouse*, published every 3 months, uses humor of all kinds, including homespun and political. Acquires one-time rights. Publishes ms 6-12 months after acceptance. Responds in 1 month. Sample: $1.50. Make checks payable to Twin Rivers Press. Guidelines for #10 SASE.

🚫 *Nuthouse* is 12 pages, digest-sized, photocopied from desktop-published originals. Receives about 500 poems/year, accepts about 100. Press run is 100. Subscription: $5 for 4 issues.

MAGAZINES NEEDS Wants "humorous verse; virtually all genres considered." Has published poetry by Holly Day, Daveed Garstenstein-Ross, and Don Webb. Send complete ms with SASE and cover letter. Include bio (paragraph) and list of publications. No e-mail submissions. Pays 1 contributor's copy per poem.

OBSIDIAN

E-mail: obsidianatbrown@gmail.com. **Website:** obsidian-magazine.tumblr.com. **Contact:** Staff rotates each year; see website for current masthead. *Obsidian* is a "literary and visual space to showcase the creativity and experiences of black people, specifically at Brown University, formed out of the need for a platform made for us, by us." It is "actively intersectional, safe, and open: a space especially for the stories and voices of black women, black queer and trans people, and black people with disabilities." Acquires one-time rights. Guidelines available online.

MAGAZINES NEEDS Submit by e-mail as attachment. Include brief bio up to 3 sentences long.

TIPS "Following proper format is essential. Your title must be intriguing and text clean. Never give up. Some of the writers we publish were rejected many times before we published them."

OFF THE COAST

Resolute Bear Press, P.O. Box 266, E Machias ME 04630. **E-mail:** offthecoastcontact@gmail.com. **Website:** www.offthecoastmag.com. **Contact:** A.E. Talbot, editor/publisher. "The mission of *Off the Coast* is to become recognized around the world as Maine's international poetry journal, a publication that prizes quality, diversity, and honesty in its publications and in its dealings with poets. *Off the Coast*, a biannual online journal, publishes poetry and artwork. Arranged much like an anthology, each issue bears a title drawn from a line or phrase from one of its poems." Poet retains all rights. Publishes poems 3-4 months after acceptance. Responds in 1-4 months. Editorial decisions are made on a rolling basis. For samples of poetry and art, visit website. Sample print issue for $10 (the journal has since moved online). Guidelines available.

MAGAZINES NEEDS Submit 1-3 poems via online submissions manager or postal mail.

OHIO TEACHERS WRITE

Department of English, University of Dayton, 300 College Park, Dayton OH 45469. (937)229-3463. **E-mail:** pthomas1@udayton.edu. **Website:** octela.org/publications/ohio-teachers-write. **Contact:** Patrick Thomas. "*Ohio Teachers Write* is a literary magazine published annually by the Ohio Council of Teachers of English Language Arts. This publication seeks to promote both poetry and prose of Ohio teachers and to provide an engaging collection of writing for our readership of educators and other like-minded adults. Invites electronic submissions from both active and retired Ohio educators for our annual literary print magazine." Guidelines available online.

MAGAZINES NEEDS Submit up to 4 poems by e-mail. Pays 2 contributor's copies.

TIPS Check website for yearly theme.

OLD RED KIMONO

Georgia Highlands College, 3175 Cedartown Hwy. SE, Rome GA 30161. **E-mail:** napplega@highlands.edu. **Website:** www.highlands.edu/site/ork. Literary Editor: Jasmine Holley. **Contact:** Dr. Nancy Applegate. *Old Red Kimono*, published annually, prints original, high-quality poetry and fiction. *Old Red Kimono* is 72

pages, magazine-sized, professionally printed, color cover and 16 color pages. Receives about 250 submissions/year, accepts about 60-70. Sample: $3. Contributors receive two copies. Acquires one-time rights. Responds in 2 months. Sample Copy $3. Accepts e-mail submissions. Reads submissions September 1-February 15; publishes in April. Guidelines available for SASE or on website for more submission information.

MAGAZINES NEEDS Has published poetry by Raymond Atkins, Walter McDonald, Peter Huggins, Ruth Moon Kempher, John Cantey Knight, Kirsten Fox, and Al Braselton. Submit 3-5 poems at a time. Pays 2 contributor's copies.

ON SPEC

P.O. Box 4727, Station South, Edmonton AB T6E 5G6, Canada. (780)628-7121. **E-mail:** onspec@onspec.ca. **Website:** www.onspec.ca. "We publish speculative fiction and poetry by new and established writers, with a strong preference for Canadian-authored works." Buys first North American serial rights. Pays on acceptance. Publishes ms an average of 6-18 months after acceptance. Responds in 2 weeks to queries; in 6 months after deadline to mss. Editorial lead time 6 months. Sample copy: $8. Guidelines on website.

See website guidelines for submission announcements. "Please refer to website for information regarding submissions, as we are not open year round."

MAGAZINES NEEDS No rhyming or religious material. Length: 4-100 lines. Pays $50 and 1 contributor's copy.

TIPS "We want to see stories with plausible characters, a well-constructed, consistent, and vividly described setting, a strong plot, and believable emotions; characters must show us (not tell us) their emotional responses to each other and to the situation and/or challenge they face. Also: Don't send us stories written for television. We don't like media tie-ins, so don't watch TV for inspiration! Read instead! Strong preference given to submissions by Canadians."

OPEN MINDS QUARTERLY

36 Elgin St., 2nd Floor, Sudbury ON P3C 5B4, Canada. (705)222-6472, ext. 303. **E-mail:** openminds@nisa.on.ca. **Website:** www.openmindsquarterly.com. **Contact:** Sarah Mann, editor. *Open Minds Quarterly* provides a venue for individuals who have experienced mental illness to express themselves via poetry, short fiction, essays, first-person accounts of living

with mental illness, and book/movie reviews. Wants unique, well-written, provocative work. Does not want overly graphic or sexual violence. Time between acceptance and publication is 1-2 years. Responds in up to 20 weeks. Single copy: $7 CAD, $7 USD; subscription: $24.95 CAD and USD (special rates also available). Make checks payable to NISA/Northern Initiative for Social Action. Guidelines available for SASE, by e-mail, or on website.

○ *Open Minds Quarterly* is 24 pages, magazine-sized, saddle-stapled, with 100 lb. stock cover with original artwork, includes ads. Press run is 550; 150 distributed free to potential subscribers, published writers, NISA member, advertisers, and conferences and events.

MAGAZINES NEEDS Submit 1-4 poems at a time. Submit through website. Cover letter is required. Information in cover letter: indicate your lived experience with mental illness. Reads submissions year round. Poems are first reviewed by poetry editor, then accepted/rejected by the editor. Sometimes, submissions are passed on to a third party for input or a third opinion. Seldom comments on rejected poems. Rarely sends pre-publication galleys. Considers poetry by teens. Has published poetry by Beth Brown Preston, Sophie Soil, Ky Perraun, and Kurt Sass. Length: up to 30 lines, including stanza breaks. Pays contributor's copies.

ALSO OFFERS The Brainstorm Poetry Contest runs in first 2 months of each year (1st prize: $250; 2nd prize: $150, 3rd prize: $75). Details on website.

ORBIS

17 Greenhow Ave., West Kirby Wirral CH48 5EL, United Kingdom. **E-mail:** carolebaldock@hotmail.com. **Website:** www.orbisjournal.com. **Contact:** Carole Baldock, editor; Noel Williams, reviews editor. "*Orbis* has long been considered one of the top 20 small-press magazines in the U.K. We are interested in social inclusion projects and encouraging access to the arts, young people, under 20s, and 20-somethings. Subjects for discussion: 'day in the life,' technical, topical." Responds in 3 months.

○ Please see guidelines on website before submitting.

MAGAZINES NEEDS Submit by postal mail or e-mail (overseas submissions only). Include cover letter.

TIPS "Any publication should be read cover to cover because it's the best way to improve your chances of getting published. Enclose SAE with all correspondence. Overseas: 2 IRCs, 3 if work is to be returned."

OSIRIS

E-mail: osirispoetry@gmail.com. **Website:** www.facebook.com/osiris.poetry. **Contact:** Andrea Moorhead, editor. *Osiris*, published semiannually, prints contemporary poetry in English, French, and Italian without translation, and in other languages with translation, including Danish, Spanish, Portuguese, and German. Responds in 2 months. Sends prepublication galleys. Sample copy: $15.

MAGAZINES NEEDS Wants poetry that is "lyrical, non-narrative, post-modern. Also looking for translations from non-Indo-European languages." Has published poetry by Hanne Bramness (Norway); Alan Britt, Rob Cook, Patty Dickson Pieczka (US); Flavio Ermini (Italy); Fabrice Farre, Marie-Christine Masset (France); and Frances Presley, Giles Goodland, Peter King (UK). Submit 4-6 poems at a time. "Poems with short biblio-bio should be sent to osirispoetry@gmail.com. Translators should include a letter of permission from the poet or publisher as well as copies of the original text." Pays 2 contributor's copies.

OTOLITHS

P.O. Box 531, Home Hill QLD 4806, Australia. **E-mail:** otolitheditor@gmail.com. **Website:** the-otolith.blogspot.com.au. **Contact:** Mark Young, editor. The intention is for *Otoliths* to appear quarterly, to contain a variety of what can be loosely described as e-things, that is, anything that can be translated (visually at this stage) to an electronic platform. "If it moves, we won't shoot at it." Sample copy online. Guidelines online.

MAGAZINES NEEDS Submit poems by e-mail as attachment, and include brief bio.

OXFORD MAGAZINE

Miami University, Oxford OH 45056. **E-mail:** oxmag@miamioh.edu. **Website:** www.oxfordmagazine.org. *Oxford Magazine*, published annually online in May, is open in terms of form, content, and subject matter. "Since our premiere in 1984, our magazine has received Pushcart Prizes for both fiction and poetry and has published authors such as Charles Baxter, William Stafford, Robert Pinsky, Stephen Dixon, Helena Maria Viramontes, Andre Dubus, and Stuart Dybek." Acquires first North American serial rights, one-time anthology rights, online serial rights. Responds in 6 months, starting in September.

○ Work published in *Oxford Magazine* has been included in the *Pushcart Prize* anthology. Does not read submissions July through August.

MAGAZINES NEEDS Submit 3-5 poems via online submissions manager.

OYEZ REVIEW

Roosevelt University, Dept. of Literature & Languages, 430 S. Michigan Ave., Chicago IL 60605. **E-mail:** oyezreview@roosevelt.edu. **Website:** oyezreview.wordpress.com. Annual magazine of the Creative Writing Program at Roosevelt University, publishing fiction, creative nonfiction, poetry, and art. There are no restrictions on style, theme, or subject matter. Buys first North American serial rights. Publishes ms an average of 2-3 months after acceptance. Responds by mid-December each year. Sample copies available by request, or using e-book retailers. Guidelines online.

Ⓞ Reading period is August 1-October 1. Each issue has 104 pages: 92 pages of text and an 8-page spread of 1 artist's work (in color or b&w). Work by the issue's featured artist also appears on the front and back cover, totaling 10 pieces. The journal has featured work from such writers as Charles Bukowski, James McManus, Carla Panciera, Michael Onofrey, Tim Foley, John N. Miller, Gary Fincke, and Barry Silesky, and visual artists Vivian Nunley, C. Taylor, Jennifer Troyer, and Frank Spidale. Accepts queries by e-mail.

MAGAZINES NEEDS Send up to 5 poems via online submissions manager or postal mail. Length: up to 10 pages total.

OYSTER BOY REVIEW

P.O. Box 550060, South Lake Tahoe CA 96155. **E-mail:** email@oysterboyreview.com. **Website:** www.oysterboyreview.com. **Contact:** Damon Sauve, editor/publisher. Electronic and print magazine. *Oyster Boy Review*, published annually, is interested in "the underrated, the ignored, the misunderstood, and the varietal. We'll make some mistakes." Publishes ms 12 months after acceptance. Responds in 6 months. Guidelines by e-mail or online at website.

MAGAZINES NEEDS Submit by post or e-mail. Pays two contributor's copies.

TIPS "Keep writing, keep submitting, keep revising."

PACIFICA LITERARY REVIEW

E-mail: pacificalitreview@gmail.com. **Website:** www.pacificareview.com. **Contact:** Matt Muth, editor-in-chief; Sarina Sheth and Paul Vega, managing editors. "*Pacifica Literary Review* is a small literary arts magazine based in Seattle. *Pacifica* publishes three web is-

sues annually in September, January, and May, and one print editon. *PLR* is now accepting submissions of poetry, fiction, creative nonfiction, and art/photography. Submission period: year-round." Acquires first North American rights. Rights revert to author upon publication, but we ask that *Pacifica Literary Review* is credited in any subsequent collections or anthologies in which the work appears. Responds in 1-3 months. Guidelines online.

MAGAZINES NEEDS Submit poems via onlline submission form. Pays copy of issue in which author was published and copy of next issue.

PACKINGTOWN REVIEW

E-mail: packingtownreview@gmail.com. **Website:** www.packingtownreview.com. *Packingtown Review* publishes imaginative and critical prose and poetry by emerging and established writers. Welcomes submissions of poetry, scholarly articles, drama, creative nonfiction, fiction, and literary translation, as well as genre-bending pieces. Acquires first North American serial rights. Sends galleys to author. Publication is copyrighted. Pays on publication. Publishes ms up to 1 year after acceptance. Responds in 3 weeks to queries; in 3 months to mss. Single copy: $10 (back issue). Guidelines available on website.

Ⓞ Literary magazine/journal: 8.5 x 11, 250 pages. Press run: 500.

MAGAZINES NEEDS Wants well-crafted poetry. Open to most styles and forms. Looking for poetry that takes risks and does so successfully. Send 3-5 poems as attachment. Include cover letter in body of e-mail. Length: up to 10 pages of single-spaced verse. Pays 2 contributor's copies.

TIPS "We are looking for well-crafted prose. We are open to most styles and forms. We are also looking for prose that takes risks and does so successfully. We will consider articles about prose."

Ⓢ PAINTED BRIDE QUARTERLY

E-mail: info@pbqmag.org. **Website:** pbqmag.org. **Contact:** Kathleen Volk Miller and Marion Wrenn, editors. *Painted Bride Quarterly* seeks literary fiction (experimental and traditional), poetry, and artwork and photographs. Buys first North American serial rights. Responds in 6 months to mss. Guidelines available online and by e-mail.

MAGAZINES NEEDS Submit up to 3 poems through online submissions manager. "We have no specifications or restrictions. We'll look at anything." Pays $20/poem.

ALSO OFFERS Sponsors annual poetry contest and chapbook competition. Guidelines available for SASE or on website.

TIPS "We look for freshness of idea incorporated with high-quality writing. We receive an awful lot of nicely written work with worn-out plots. We want quality in whatever—we hold experimental work to as strict standards as anything else. Many of our readers write fiction; most of them enjoy a good reading. We hope to be an outlet for quality. A good story gives, first, enjoyment to the reader. We've seen a good many of them lately, and we've published the best of them."

PANK

Website: www.pankmagazine.com. "*PANK* Magazine fosters access to emerging and experimental poetry and prose, publishing the brightest and most promising writers for the most adventurous readers. To the end of the road, up country, a far shore, the edge of things, to a place of amalgamation and unplumbed depths, where the known is made and unmade, and where unimagined futures are born, a place inhabited by contradictions, a place of quirk and startling anomaly. *PANK*, no soft pink hands allowed." Buys first North American serial rights and electronic rights. Publishes ms an average of 3-12 months after acceptance. Guidelines available on website.

MAGAZINES NEEDS Submit through online submissions manager. Pays $20, a one-year subscription, and a *PANK* t-shirt.

TIPS "To read *PANK* is to know *PANK*. Or, read a lot within the literary magazine and small-press universe—there's plenty to choose from. Unfortunately, we see a lot of submissions from writers who have clearly read neither *PANK* nor much else. Serious writers are serious readers. Read. Seriously."

☻ PAPERPLATES

19 Kenwood Ave., Toronto ON M6C 2R8, Canada. **E-mail:** magazine@paperplates.org. **Website:** www.paperplates.org. **Contact:** Bernard Kelly, publisher. *paperplates* is a literary journal published once a year. "We make no distinction between veterans and beginners. Some of our contributors have published several books; some have never before published a single line." No longer accepts IRCs. Acquires first North American serial rights. Responds in 6-9 months. Guidelines online.

MAGAZINES NEEDS Submit no more than 5 poems via surface mail or e-mail with short bio. Length: no more than 1,500 words.

THE PARIS REVIEW

544 West 27th St., New York NY 10001. (212)343-1333. **E-mail:** queries@theparisreview.org. **Website:** www.theparisreview.org. **Contact:** Lorin Stein, editor; Robyn Creswell, poetry editor. *The Paris Review* publishes "fiction and poetry of superlative quality, whatever the genre, style, or mode. Our contributors include prominent, as well as less well-known and previously unpublished writers. The Writers at Work interview series includes important contemporary writers discussing their own work and the craft of writing." Buys all rights, buys first English-language rights. Pays on publication. Responds in 4 months to mss. Guidelines available online.

☻ Address submissions to proper department. Do not make submissions via e-mail.

MAGAZINES NEEDS Submit no more than 6 poems at a time. Poetry can be sent to the poetry editor (please include a self-addressed, stamped envelope). Poets receive $100/poem.

PARNASSUS

Poetry in Review, Poetry in Review Foundation, 205 W. 89th St., #8F, New York NY 10024. (212)787-3569. **E-mail:** info@parnassus.com. **Website:** www.parnassusreview.com. **Contact:** Herbert Leibowitz, editor and publisher. *Parnassus: Poetry in Review* provides "a forum where poets, novelists, and critics of all persuasions can gather to review new books of poetry, including translations—international poetries have occupied center stage from our very first issue—with an amplitude and reflectiveness that Sunday book supplements and even the literary quarterlies could not afford. Our editorial philosophy is based on the assumption that reviewing is a complex art. Like a poem or a short story, a review essay requires imagination; scrupulous attention to rhythm, pacing, and supple syntax; space in which to build a persuasive, detailed argument; analytical precision and intuitive gambits; verbal play, wit, and metaphor. We welcome and vigorously seek out voices that break aesthetic molds and disturb xenophobic habits." Buys one-time rights. Pays on publication. Publishes ms an average of 12-14 months after acceptance. Responds in 2 months to mss. Sample copy: $15.

MAGAZINES NEEDS Accepts most types of poetry.

TIPS "Be certain you have read the magazine and are aware of the editor's taste. Blind submissions are a waste of everybody's time. We'd like to see more poems that display intellectual acumen and curiosity about history, science, music, etc., and fewer trivial lyrical poems about the self, or critical prose that's academic and dull. Prose should sing."

PASSAGER

Passager, 1420 N. Charles St., Baltimore MD 21201. **E-mail:** editors@passagerbooks.com. **Website:** www.passagerbooks.com. **Contact:** Kendra Kopelke, Mary Azrael, Christine Drawl. *"Passager* has a special focus on older writers. Its mission is to encourage, engage, and strengthen the imagination well into old age and to give mature readers opportunities that are sometimes closed off to them in our youth-oriented culture. We are dedicated to honoring the creativity that takes hold in later years and to making public the talents of those over the age of 50." *Passager* publishes 2 issues/year, an Open issue (winter) and a Poetry Contest issue (summer). Open to writers over 50. Acquires first North American serial rights. Publication is copyrighted. Publishes ms 3-6 months after acceptance. Responds in 3 months to mss. Sample copy: $15. Guidelines online.

MAGAZINES NEEDS Publishes poetry as part of annual poetry contest. **Deadline:** April 15. Send up to 5 poems with cover letter. Include estimated word count, brief bio, list of publications. Send either SASE or email for reply only. **Reading fee:** $20 (includes one-year subscription). Length: up to 40 lines/poem.

CONTEST/AWARD OFFERINGS $500 Poetry Contest prize; winner interview and multiple poems published.

TIPS "Stereotyped images of old age will be rejected. Read the publication, or at least visit the website."

PASSAGES NORTH

English Department, Northern Michigan University, 1401 Presque Isle Ave., Marquette MI 49855. (906)227-1203. **E-mail:** passages@nmu.edu. **Website:** www.passagesnorth.com. **Contact:** Jennifer A. Howard, editor-in-chief; Ethan Brightbill & Willow Grosz, managing editors; Matthew Gavin Frank & Rachel May, nonfiction and hybrids editors; Patricia Killelea, poetry editor; Monica McFawn, fiction editor. *Passages North*, published annually in spring, prints poetry, short fiction, creative nonfiction, essays, hybrids, and interviews. Current issue: $13; Back issues: $7. Guidelines available for SASE, by e-mail, or on website.

Magazine: 7×10; 200-350 pgs; 60 lb. paper. Publishes work by established and emerging writers.

MAGAZINES NEEDS "We're looking for poems that give us pause, poems that surprise us, poems that keep us warm during long northern nights. We want them to sing and vibrate with energy. We're open to all forms and aesthetics." Submit up to 5 poems together in 1 document. Has published poetry by Moira Egan, Frannie Lindsay, Ben Lerner, Bob Hicok, Gabe Gudding, John McNally, Steve Almond, Tracy Winn, and Midege Raymond.

TIPS "We look for voice, energetic prose, writers who take risks. We look for an engaging story in which the author evokes an emotional response from the reader through carefully rendered scenes, complex characters, and a smart, narrative design. Revise, revise. Read what we publish."

THE PATERSON LITERARY REVIEW

Passaic County Community College, 1 College Blvd., Paterson NJ 07505. (973)684-6555. **Website:** www.patersonliteraryreview.com. **Contact:** Maria Mazziotti Gillan, editor/executive director. *Paterson Literary Review*, published annually, is produced by the The Poetry Center at Passaic County Community College. Acquires first North American serial rights. Publishes ms 6-12 months after acceptance. Reads submissions June 1-September 30. Responds within 1 year. Sample copy: $13 plus $1.50 postage.

Work for *PLR* has been included in the *Pushcart Prize* anthology and *Best American Poetry*.

MAGAZINES NEEDS Wants poetry of "high quality; clear, direct, powerful work." Submit up to 5 poems at a time. Has published poetry and work by Diane di Prima, Ruth Stone, Marge Piercy, Laura Boss, Robert Mooney, and Abigail Stone. Length: up to 2 pages/poem. Pays contributor's copies.

ALSO OFFERS Publishes *The New Jersey Poetry Resource Book* ($5 plus $1.50 p&h) and *The New Jersey Poetry Calendar*. The Distinguished Poets Series offers readings by poets of international, national, and regional reputation. Poetryworks/USA is a series of programs produced for UA Columbia-Cablevision. See website for details about these additional resources.

PEACE & FREEDOM

Peace & Freedom Press, 6 Trinity Ct., Albion St., Crowland, Lincs PE6 0EA, England. **Website:** pandf.booksmusicfilmstv.com/index.htm. Published annually; emphasizes social, humanitarian, and environmental issues. Not currently accepting new submissions until 2019. Usual poetry guidelines - maximum,

32 lines. Has published poetry by Dorothy Bell-Hall, Freda Moffatt, Andrew Bruce, Bernard Shough, Mona Miller, and Andrew Savage. *Peace & Freedom* has a varied format. Sample copies: $7 U.S., £4 UK. Sample copies can be purchased from the above address. Banks charge the equivalent of $5 to cash foreign checks in the UK, so please only send bills, preferably by registered post. Responds to submissions in less than a month usually, with SAE/IRC.

MAGAZINES NEEDS No simultaneous submissions. Please include bio. Reads submissions year round. "Work without correct postage will not be responded to or returned until proper postage is sent." Pays one contributor's copy. Reviews books of poetry. Lines/poem: 32 max.

TIPS "Too many writers have lost the personal touch that editors generally appreciate. It can make a difference when selecting work of equal merit."

ⓢ THE PEDESTAL MAGAZINE

E-mail: pedmagazine@carolina.rr.com. **Website:** www.thepedestalmagazine.com. **Contact:** John Amen, editor in chief. Committed to promoting diversity and celebrating the voice of the individual. Buys first rights. All rights revert back to the author/artist upon publication. Retains the right to publish the piece in any subsequent issue or anthology without additional payment. Responds in 1-2 months to mss. Guidelines available online.

💬 See website for reading periods for different forms. Member: CLMP.

MAGAZINES NEEDS Open to a wide variety of poetry, ranging from the highly experimental to the traditionally formal. Submit all poems in 1 form. No need to query before submitting. No length restriction.

TIPS "If you send us your work, please wait for a response to your first submission before you submit again."

ⓢ PENNINE INK MAGAZINE

1 Neptune St., Burnley BB11 1SF, England. **E-mail:** piwwmag40@gmail.com. **Website:** www.pennine-ink. weebly.com. **Contact:** Alex Marsh, compiling editor. *Pennine Ink*, published annually in November, prints poems and short prose pieces. *Pennine Ink* is 48 pages, A5, with b&w illustrated cover. Receives about 400 poems/year, accepts about 40. Press run is 200. "Contributors wishing to purchase a copy of *Pennine Ink* should go to the Amazon website and search for

Pennine Ink. More information on our website." Responds to submissions in 3 months. Submit between February 1-September 1 each year. Poetry should be no longer than 40 lines, prose no longer than around 800 words. Please include your e-mail address so we can contact you, or failing that, a small SAE for our reply. Work will not be returned, so please keep a copy of everything you send.

MAGAZINES NEEDS Submit up to 6 poems at a time. Accepts e-mail submissions. Seldom comments on rejected poems. Length: up to 40 lines/poem; up to 1,000 words for prose. Pays 1 contributor's copy.

CONTEST/AWARD OFFERINGS Annual Competition - pays £50 for First Prize + publication in Pennine Ink and on website.

PENNSYLVANIA ENGLISH

Indiana University of Pennsylvania, Department of English, Indiana University of Pennsylvania, HSS 506A, 981 Grant St., Indiana PA 15705. (724)357-5913. **E-mail:** mtwill@iup.edu. **Website:** paenglish. submittable.com/submit. **Contact:** Dr. Michael T. Williamson, editor (mtwill@iup.edu); Dr. Michael Cox, creative prose editor (mwcox@pitt.edu); Tony Vallone, MFA, poetry editor (avallone@psu.edu); Dr. Ann Rea (anr@pitt.edu) and Dr. Michael T. Williamson, literary criticism editors. *Pennsylvania English*, published annually, is "sponsored by the Pennsylvania College English Association. Our philosophy is quality. We publish literary fiction (and poetry and nonfiction) and essays about literature. Our intended audience includes people who love literature and writing, university professors, college professors, Community College professors, temporary faculty, K-12 teachers, and literate readers from around the world." *Pennsylvania English* is 6x9 up to 175 pages, perfect-bound, full-color cover featuring the artwork of a Pennsylvania artist. Reads mss during the summer. Publishes 4-6 new writers/year. Has published work by Marcia Loughran, Benjamin Goluboff, Evalyn Lee, Gary Grieve Carlson, Glen Adelson, Simon Perchik, Len Lawson, Dave Kress, Dan Leone, Paul West, Liz Rosenberg, Walt MacDonald, Amy Pence, Jennifer Richter, and Jeff Schiff. Acquires first North American serial rights. Pays upon publication. Publishes ms up to 1 year after acceptance. Responds in 1-3 months to mss. Sometimes comments on rejected mss. Sample copy: $10. Guidelines online.

MAGAZINES NEEDS Submit 3 or more poems at a time via the online submissions manager. "For all submissions, please include a brief bio for the contributors' page. Be sure to include your name, address, phone number, e-mail address, institutional affiliation (if you have one), the title of your poem(s), and any other relevant information. We will edit if necessary for space." Wants poetry of "any length, any style." Pays 1 contributor's copy.

TIPS "Quality of the writing is our only measure. We're not impressed by long-winded cover letters detailing awards and publications we've never heard of. Beginners and professionals have the same chance with us. We receive stacks of competently written but boring fiction. For a story to rise from the rejection pile, it takes more than the basic competence."

PENNSYLVANIA LITERARY JOURNAL

Anaphora Literary Press, 1108 W 3rd St., Quanah TX 79252. (470)289-6395. **E-mail:** director@anaphoraliterary.com. **Website:** anaphoraliterary.com. **Contact:** Anna Faktorovich, editor/director. *Pennsylvania Literary Journal* is a printed, peer-reviewed journal that publishes critical essays, book reviews, short stories, interviews, photographs, art, and poetry. Published triannually, it features special issues on a wide variety of different fields from film studies to literary criticism to interviews with bestsellers. Submissions in all genres from emerging and established writers are warmly welcomed. A free pdf or print copy of the issue. A monetary payment might be offered to an A-list major award-winning author. Publishes ms an average of 2 months after acceptance. Responds on the same day to queries and mss. Sample copy: $15. Guidelines available online. Accepts queries and ms submissions by e-mail at director@anaphoraliterary.com.

MAGAZINES NEEDS No line limit. Does not provide payment.

TIPS "We are just looking for great writing. Send your materials; if they are good and you don't mind working for free, we'll take it."

PENNY DREADFUL

Tales & Poems of Fantastic Terror, P.O. Box 719, Radio City Station, Hell's Kitchen NY 10101-0719. **E-mail:** mmpendragon@aol.com. **Website:** www.mpendragon.com/pennydreadful.html. *Penny Dreadful: Tales & Poems of Fanastic Terror*, published irregularly (about once a year), features goth-romantic poetry and prose. Publishes poetry, short stories, essays, letters, listings, reviews, and b&w artwork "which celebrate the darker aspects of Man, the World, and their Creator." Wants "literary horror in the tradition of Poe, M.R. James, Shelley, M.P. Shiel, and LeFanu—dark, disquieting tales and verses designed to challenge the reader's perception of human nature, morality, and man's place within the Darkness. Stories and poems should be set prior to 1910 and/or possess a timeless quality." Does not want "references to 20th- and 21st-century personages/events, graphic sex, strong language, excessive gore and shock elements." Acquires one-time rights. Sample: $10. Subscription: $25/3 issues. Make checks payable to Michael Pendragon. Guidelines online.

"Works appearing in *Penny Dreadful* have been reprinted in *The Year's Best Fantasy and Horror*." *Penny Dreadful* nominates best tales and poems for Pushcart Prizes. *Penny Dreadful* is over 100 pages, digest-sized, desktop-published, perfect-bound. Press run is 200.

MAGAZINES NEEDS Submit by mail or e-mail. Rhymed, metered verse preferred. Has published poetry by Nancy Bennett, Michael R. Burch, Lee Clark, Louise Webster, K.S. Hardy, and Kevin N. Roberts. Length: up to 5 pages. Pays 1 contributor's copy.

ALSO OFFERS *Penny Dreadful* "includes market listings for, and reviews of, kindred magazines." Pendragon Publications also publishes *Songs of Innocence & Experience*.

PEREGRINE

Amherst Writers & Artists Press, P.O. Box 1076, Amherst MA 01004. (413)253-3307. **E-mail:** peregrinejournal@gmail.com. **E-mail:** peregrine@amherstwriters.com. **Website:** amherstwriters.info/peregrine. **Contact:** Kate Eliza Frank, managing editor; Milo Muise, fiction editor, Rachelle Parker, poetry editor. *Peregrine*, published annually, features poetry and fiction. "*Peregrine* has provided a forum for national and international writers since 1983 and is committed to finding excellent work by emerging as well as established writers. We welcome work reflecting diversity of voice. We like to be surprised. We look for writing that is honest, unpretentious, and memorable. All decisions are made by the editors." Acquires first rights. Sample copy: $12. Guidelines online.

Magazine: 6x9; 100+ pages; 60 lb. white offset paper; glossy cover. Member: CLMP. Reading period: March 15-May 15.

MAGAZINES NEEDS Submit 3 single-spaced, one-page poems. "We seek poems that inform and surprise us. We appreciate fresh and specific imagery and layered metaphors, but not excessive verbiage, abstractions, or clichés. We will not consider inspirational poetry, greeting-card verse, religious tirades, or nostalgia." Length: up to 40 lines and spaces/poem. Pays 2 contributor's copies.

TIPS "Check guidelines before submitting your work. Familiarize yourself with *Peregrine*. We look for heart and soul as well as technical expertise. Trust your own voice."

PERMAFROST: A LITERARY JOURNAL

E-mail: editor@permafrostmag.com. **Website:** permafrostmag.uaf.edu. *Permafrost Magazine*, a literary journal, contains poems, short stories, hybrid pieces, creative nonfiction, b&w drawings, photographs, and prints. We print both new and established writers, hoping and expecting to see the best work out there. We have published work by E. Ethelbert Miller, W. Loran Smith, Peter Orlovsky, Jim Wayne Miller, Allen Ginsberg, and Andy Warhol. *Permafrost* is about 200 pages, digest-sized, professionally printed, flat-spined. Also publishes summer online edition. Responds in 3-6 months. Back issues: $5. Subscription: $10 for 1 year, $18 for 2 years. Guidelines online. Reads submissions May 1-October 31 for print edition, November 1-April 30 for summer online edition.

MAGAZINES NEEDS We publish any style of poetry provided it is conceived, written, and revised with care. We also welcome poems about anywhere, from anywhere. Submit up to 5 poems via online submissions manager at permafrostmag.submittable.com; "e-mail submissions will not be read." Sometimes comments on poems. Pays 1 contributor's copy. Reduced contributor rate of $5 on additional copies.

PERSPECTIVES

P.O. BOX 441130 #94102, DETROIT MI 48244-1130. **E-mail:** editors@perspectivesjournal.org. **E-mail:** submissions@perspectivesjournal.org. **Website:** perspectivesjournal.org. Malcolm McBryde. **Contact:** Jason Lief, Sara Tolsma. "*Perspectives* is a journal of theology in the broad Reformed tradition. We seek to express the Reformed faith theologically; to engage issues that Reformed Christians meet in personal, ecclesiastical, and societal life; and thus to contribute to the mission of the church of Jesus Christ.The editors are interested in submissions that contribute to a contemporary Reformed theological discussion. Our readers tend to be affiliated with the Presbyterian Church (USA), the Reformed Church in America, and the Christian Reformed Church. Some of our subscribers are academics or pastors, but we also gear our articles to thoughtful, literate laypeople who want to engage in Reformed theological reflection on faith and culture." Acquires first rights. Time between acceptance and publication is 3-12 months. Responds in 3-6 months. Editorial lead time 6 months. Sample: $3.50. Subscription: $20.

Perspectives is 24 pages, magazine-sized, Web offset-printed, saddle-stapled, with paper cover containing b&w illustration. Receives about 300 poems/year, accepts 6-20. Press run is 1,575.

MAGAZINES NEEDS Wants "poems excellent in craft and significant in subject, both traditional and free in form. We publish 1-2 poems every other issue." Has published poetry by Ann Hostetler, Paul Willis, and Priscilla Atkins. Submit poems via e-mail. Pays 5 contributor's copies.

PHILADELPHIA STORIES

Fiction/Nonfiction/Art/Poetry of the Delaware Valley, 93 Old York Rd., Suite 1/#1-753, Jenkintown PA 19046. **E-mail:** info@philadelphiastories.org. **Website:** www.philadelphiastories.org. Editorial Director/Co-Publisher: Carla Spataro.. **Contact:** Christine Weiser, executive director/co-publisher. *Philadelphia Stories*, published quarterly, publishes "fiction, poetry, creative nonfiction, and art written by authors living in, or originally from, Pennsylvania, Delaware, or New Jersey. *Philadelphia Stories* also hosts 2 national writing contests: The Marguerite McGlinn Short Story Contest ($2,500 first-place prize; $750 second-place prize; $500 third-place prize) and the Sandy Crimmins National Poetry Contest ($1,000 first-place prize, 3 $100 runner-up prizes). Visit our website for details." Literary magazine/journal: 8.5x11; 32 pages; 70# matte text, all 4-color paper; 70# matte text cover. Contains illustrations, photographs. Subscription: "We offer $20 memberships that include home delivery." Make checks payable to *Philadelphia Stories*. Member: CLMP. Acquires one-time rights. Publication is copyrighted. Publishes ms 1-2 months after acceptance. Responds in 6 months. Rarely comments on/critiques rejected mss. Sample copy: $5 and on website. Guidelines online.

MAGAZINES NEEDS Submit 3 poems at a time. No previously published poems. Cover letter is preferred. Reads submissions year round. "Each poem is reviewed by a preliminary board that decides on a final list; the entire board discusses this list and chooses the mutual favorites for print and Web. We send a layout proof to check for print poems." Receives about 600 poems/year, accepts about 15%. Considers poetry by teens. Wants "polished, well-crafted poems." Does not want "first drafts." Length: 36 lines/poem.

TIPS "We look for exceptional, polished prose, a controlled voice, strong characters and place, and interesting subjects. Follow guidelines. We cannot stress this enough. Read every guideline carefully and thoroughly before sending anything out. Send out only polished material. We reject many quality pieces for various reasons; try not to take rejection personally. Just because your piece isn't right for one publication doesn't mean it's bad. Selection is an extremely subjective process."

PHOEBE

A Journal of Literature and Art, MSN 2C5, George Mason University, 400 University Dr., Fairfax VA 22030. **Website:** www.phoebejournal.com. **Contact:** Kate Branca, editor-in-chief; Rachel Purdy, assistant editor. Publishes poetry, fiction, nonfiction, and visual art. "*Phoebe* prides itself on supporting up-and-coming writers, whose style, form, voice, and subject matter demonstrate a vigorous appeal to the senses, intellect, and emotions of our readers." Responds in 4-6 months. Guidelines online.

MAGAZINES NEEDS Submit 3-5 poems via online submission manager. Pays 2 contributor's copies and $400 for winner.

PILGRIMAGE MAGAZINE

Colorado State University-Pueblo, Dept. of English, 2200 Bonforte Blvd., Pueblo CO 81001. **E-mail:** info@pilgrimagepress.org. **Website:** www.pilgrimagepress.org. **Contact:** Juan Morales, editor. Serves an eclectic fellowship of readers, writers, artists, naturalists, contemplatives, activists, seekers, adventurers, and other kindred spirits. Guidelines available online. Submit via online submissions manager (https://pilgrimagemagazine.submittable.com/submit) or snail mail (with SASE for reply only).

MAGAZINES NEEDS Fit poetry on 1 page.

TIPS "Our interests include wildness in all its forms; inward and outward explorations; home ground, the open road, service, witness, peace, and justice; symbols, story, and myth in contemporary culture; struggle and resilience; insight and transformation; wisdom wherever it is found; and the great mystery of it all. We like good storytellers and a good sense of humor. No e-mail submissions, please."

THE PINCH

English Department, University of Memphis, Memphis TN 38152. **E-mail:** editor@pinchjournal.com. **Website:** www.pinchjournal.com. Semiannual literary magazine. "We publish fiction, creative nonfiction, poetry, and art of literary quality by both established and emerging artists." Acquires first North American serial rights. Publication is copyrighted. Responds in 3 months to mss. Sample copy: $5. Guidelines online.

○ "The Pinch Literary Awards in Fiction, Poetry, and Nonfiction offer a $1,000 prize and publication. Check our website for details."

MAGAZINES NEEDS Submit up to 5 poems via online submissions manager. Pays 2 contributor's copies. "One work from each genre will be awarded a $200 Featured Writer award, as determined by the editors."

TIPS "We have a new look and a new edge. We're soliciting work from writers with a national or international reputation as well as strong, interesting work from emerging writers."

THE PINK CHAMELEON

E-mail: dpfreda@juno.com. **Website:** www.thepinkchameleon.com. **Contact:** Dorothy Paula Freda, editor/publisher. general craft, knitting, cross stitch, scrapbooking, mixed media art *The Pink Chameleon*, published annually online, contains family-oriented, upbeat poetry, stories, essays, and articles, any genre in good taste that gives hope for the future. Reading period is February 1-March 31 and September 1-October 31. Acquires one-time rights for 1 year. Time between acceptance and publication is up to 1 year, depending on date of acceptance. Responds in 1 month to ms. Sometimes comments on rejected mss. Guidelines available.

MAGAZINES NEEDS Also considers poetry by children and teens. Submit 1-4 poems at a time. Accepts e-mail submissions only (pasted into body of message; no attachments.) Use plain text and include a brief bio. Often comments on rejected poems. Receives about 50 poems/year, accepts about 50%. **PLEASE, NO ATTACHMENTS.** Does not want pornography, cursing, swearing; nothing violent; nothing evoking despair. Length: 6-24 lines. No payment.

TIPS Wants "simple, honest, evocative emotion; upbeat fiction and nonfiction submissions that give hope for the future; well-paced plots; stories, poetry, articles, essays that speak from the heart. Read guidelines carefully. Use a good, but not ostentatious, opening hook. Stories should have a beginning, middle, and end that make the reader feel the story was worth his or her time. This also applies to articles and essays. In the latter 2, wrap your comments and conclusions in a neatly packaged final paragraph. Turnoffs include violence and bad language. Simple, genuine, and sensitive work does not need to shock with vulgarity to be interesting and enjoyable."

PINYON POETRY

Mesa State College, Languages, Literature, and Mass Communications, Mesa State College, Grand Junction CO 81502. **E-mail:** rphillis@mesa5.mesa.colorado.edu. **Website:** org.coloradomesa.edu/~rphillis. **Contact:** Randy Phillis, editor. *Pinyon Poetry*, published annually in June, prints "the best available contemporary American poetry. No restrictions other than excellence. We appreciate a strong voice." Sample copy: $5. Subscription: $8/year. Make checks payable to Pinyon Poetry. Guidelines for SASE or online.

Literary magazine/journal: 8.5x5.5, 120 pages, heavy paper. Contains illustrations and photographs. Press run is 300; 100 distributed free to contributors, friends, etc.

MAGAZINES NEEDS Does not want "inspirational, light verse, or sing-song poetry." Has published poetry by Mark Cox, Barry Spacks, Wendy Bishop, and Anne Ohman Youngs. Receives about 4,000 poems/year, accepts 2%. Submit 3-5 poems at a time. Cover letter is preferred. "Name, address, e-mail, and phone number on each page. SASE required." Reads submissions year round. Seldom comments on rejected poems. Pays 2 contributor's copies.

TIPS "Ask yourself if the work is something you would like to read in a publication."

PIRENE'S FOUNTAIN

E-mail: pirenesfountain@gmail.com; pfjournal@glasslyrepress.com. **Website:** pirenesfountain.com. *Pirene's Fountain* is published annually. Reading period: May 1-August 1. Receives about 400 poems/year, accepts about 10%. Poets retain copyright to their work; rights revert to poets upon publication. Publishes the following year after acceptance. Responds in 1-4 months. Guidelines online.

MAGAZINES NEEDS Submit 3-8 poems at a time. Poems are circulated to an editorial board. No comments on rejected poems. Sometimes publishes theme issues. A 50- to 100-word bio note is required with submissions. Has published work by Lisel Mueller, Linda Pastan, J.P. Dancing Bear, Dorianne Laux, Rebecca Seiferle, Joseph Millar, Kim Addonizio, Jane Hirshfeld, and Jim Moore, among others. Does not want "anything obscene, pornographic, or discriminatory in nature."

ALSO OFFERS "Poets whose work has been selected for publication in our journal during the past calendar year (with the exception of staff/featured poets) are automatically entered for the annual Liakoura Poetry award. Our editors will each choose 1 poem from all of the selections. The 5 nominated poems will be sent blind to an outside editor/publisher for the final decision. The winning poet will be awarded a certificate and a $100 Amazon gift card via e-mail. Pushcart and Best of the Net nominations: Editors select the best work published by *PF* during the year. This is open to all submitting and featured poets. Nominated poets are notified after selections have been sent in."

TIPS "Please read submission guidelines carefully and send in at least 3 poems. We offer a poetry discussion group on Facebook, titled Pirene's Fountain Poetry."

PISGAH REVIEW

Division of Humanities, Brevard College, 1 Brevard College Dr., Brevard NC 28712. (828)577-8324. **E-mail:** tinerjj@brevard.edu. **Website:** www.pisgahreview.com. **Contact:** Jubal Tiner, editor. "*Pisgah Review* publishes primarily literary short fiction, creative nonfiction, and poetry. Our only criteria is quality of work; we look for the best." Has published Ron Rash, Thomas Rain Crowe, Joan Conner, Gary Fincke, Steve Almond, and Fred Bahnson. Also published Rick Bass, Marjorie Hudson, Ron Rash, Jane Smiley, Robert Morgan, Sy Montgomey and others in our Looking Glass Rock Writer's Conference special issues. Pays on publication. Sends galleys to author. Publishes mss 6-9 months after acceptance. Responds to mss in 4-6 months. Sometimes comments on/critiques rejected mss. Sample copy: $7. Guidelines online.

MAGAZINES NEEDS "Send complete ms to our submission manager on our website."

TIPS "We select work of only the highest quality. Grab us from the beginning and follow through. Engage us with your language and characters. A clean ms goes a long way toward acceptance. Stay true to the vision of your work, revise tirelessly, and submit persistently."

PLAINSONGS

Hastings College Press, 710 Turner Ave., Hastings NE 68901. **E-mail:** plainsongs@hastings.edu. **Website:** https://sites.google.com/hastings.edu/hastings-college-press/plainsongs. Associate Editor: Dr. Ali Beheler. **Contact:** Eric R. Tucker, editor. *Plainsongs*, published 2 times/year, considers poems on any subject, in any style, but free verse predominates. *Plainsongs'* title suggests not only its location on the Great Plains, but its preference for the living language, whether in free or formal verse. Featuring poetry that runs the gamut from traditional to experimental, from realist to surrealist, *Plainsongs* strives to capture the multiplicity of voices—including those of feminist, non-white, immigrant, and LGBTQ writers—that make up this vibrant and wonderfully diverse Midwestern soundscape. Acquires first rights. 2-3 months between acceptance and publication. Responds 3-4 months after deadline. Sample: $5. Subscription: $20 for one-year sub; $35 for two-year sub; $50 for three-year sub. Guidelines online.

MAGAZINES NEEDS Submit up to 6 poems at a time. Please use online submission form. Reads submissions according to the following deadlines: June 15 for winter issue; December 15 for summer issue. Pays 1 contributor's copy.

CONTEST/AWARD OFFERINGS Three poems in each issue receive a $50 prize. A short essay in appreciation accompanies each award poem.

PLANET: THE WELSH INTERNATIONALIST

Berw Ltd., P.O. Box 44, Aberystwyth Ceredigion SY23 3ZZ, United Kingdom. 01970 622408. **E-mail:** admin@planetmagazine.org.uk. **E-mail:** submissions@planetmagazine.org.uk. **Website:** www.planetmagazine.org.uk. Administrative and Marketing Assistant: Lowri Angharad Pearson.. **Contact:** Emily Trahair, editor. A literary/cultural/political journal centered on Welsh affairs but with a strong interest in minority cultures in Europe and elsewhere. *Planet: The Welsh Internationalist*, published quarterly, is a cultural magazine centered on Wales, but with broader interests in arts, sociology, politics, history, and science. *Planet* is 96 pages, A5, professionally printed, perfect-bound, with glossy colour card cover. Receives about 500 submissions/year, accepts about 5%. Press run is 1,000 (800 subscribers, about 10% libraries, 200 shelf sales). Publishes ms 4-6 months after acceptance. Responds in 3 months. Single copy: £6.75; subscription: £22 (£40 overseas). Sample copy: £5. Guidelines online.

MAGAZINES NEEDS Wants good poetry in a wide variety of styles. No limitations as to subject matter; length can be a problem. Has published poetry by Nigel Jenkins, Anne Stevenson, and Les Murray. Submit 4-6 poems via mail or e-mail (with attachment). For postal submissions, no submissions returned unless accompanied by an SASE. Writers submitting from abroad should send at least 3 IRCs for return of typescript; 1 IRC for reply only. Pays £30/poem.

TIPS "We do not look for fiction that necessarily has a 'Welsh' connection, which some writers assume from our title. We try to publish a broad range of fiction, and our main criterion is quality. Try to read copies of any magazine you submit to. Don't write out of the blue to a magazine which might be completely inappropriate for your work. Recognize that you are likely to have a high rejection rate, as magazines tend to favor writers from their own countries."

PLEIADES

Literature in Context, University of Central Missouri, Department of English, Martin 336, 415 E. Clark St., Warrensburg MO 64093. (660)543-4268. **E-mail:** clintoncrockettp@gmail.com (nonfiction inquiries); pnguyen@ucmo.edu (fiction inquiries); pleiadespoetryeditor@gmail.com (poetry inquiries). **Website:** www.pleiadesmag.com. **Contact:** Clinton Crockett Peters, nonfiction editor; Phong Nguyen, fiction editor; and Jenny Molberg, poetry editor. "We publish contemporary fiction, poetry, interviews, literary essays, special-interest personal essays, and reviews for a general and literary audience from authors from around the world." Reads in the months of July for the summer issue and December for the winter issue. Acquires first North American serial rights, second serial (reprint) rights. Occasionally requests rights for TV, radio reading, website. Pays on publication. Publishes ms an average of 9 months after acceptance. Responds in 2 months to queries; in 1-4 months to mss. Editorial lead time 9 months. Sample copy for $5 (back issue); $6 (current issue). Guidelines online.

MAGAZINES NEEDS Submit 3-5 poems via online submission manager. "Nothing didactic, pretentious, or overly sentimental." Pays $3/poem and contributor copies.

ALSO OFFERS "Also sponsors the Lena-Miles Wever Todd Poetry Series competition, a contest for the best book ms by an American poet. The winner receives $2,000, publication by Pleiades Press (1,000 copies), and distribution by Louisiana State University Press. Check website for deadline and details."

TIPS "Submit only 1 genre at a time to appropriate editors. Show care for your material and your readers—submit quality work in a professional format. Cover art is solicited directly from artists. We accept queries for book reviews."

⑤ PLOUGHSHARES

Emerson College, 120 Boylston St., Boston MA 02116. (617)824-3757. **E-mail:** pshares@pshares.org. **Website:** www.pshares.org. **Contact:** Ladette Randolph, editor-in-chief/executive director; Ellen Duffer, managing editor. *Ploughshares* publishes issues four times a year. 2 of these issues are guest-edited by different, prominent authors. A third issue, a mix of both prose and poetry, is edited by our staff editors. The fourth issue is a collection of longform work edited by our Editor-in-chief, Ladette Randolph; these stories and essays are first published as e-books known as Ploughshares Solos. Translations are welcome if permission has been granted. We accept electronic submissions—there is a $3 fee per submission, which is waived if you are a subscriber. Ploughshares is 200 pages, digest-sized. Receives about 11,000 poetry, fiction, and essay submissions/year. Reads submissions June 1-January 15 (postmark); hosts the Emerging Writer's Contest, for writers who have yet to publish a book-length work, March 1-May 15; mss submitted at all other times will be returned unread. A competitive and highly prestigious market. Rotating and guest editors make cracking the line-up even tougher, since it's difficult to know what is appropriate to send. Buys first North American serial rights. Pays on publication. Publishes ms an average of 6 months after acceptance. Responds in 3-5 months to mss. Sample copy: $14 for current issue, $7 for back issue; please inquire for shipping rates. Subscription: $30 domestic, $30 plus shipping (see website) foreign. Guidelines online.

MAGAZINES NEEDS Submit up to 5 poems via online submissions form or by mail. Has published poetry by Donald Hall, Li-Young Lee, Robert Pinsky, Brenda Hillman, and Thylias Moss. Pays $45/printed page ($90 minimum, $450 maximum); 2 contributor's copies; and one-year subscription.

PMS

University of Alabama at Birmingham, HB 217, 1530 Third Ave. S., Birmingham AL 35294. (205)934-2641.

Fax: (205)975-8125. **E-mail:** poemmemoirstory@gmail.com. **Website:** www.uab.edu/cas/englishpublications/pms-poemmemoirstory. **Contact:** Kerry Madden, editor in chief. "*PMS poemmemoirstory* appears once a year. We accept unpublished, original submissions of poetry, memoir, and short fiction during our January 1-March 31 reading period. We accept simultaneous submissions; however, we ask that you please contact us immediately if your piece is published elsewhere so we may free up space for other authors. While *PMS* is a journal of exclusively women's writing, the subject field is wide open." Copyright returns to author after publication, but work published elsewhere should acknowledge first publication in *PMS poemmemoirstory*. Sample copy: $10. Subscription: $10 for 1 year, $15 for 2 years, $18 for 3 years. Guidelines online.

💬 "*PMS* has gone all-digital on Submittable. There is now a $3 fee, which covers costs associated with our online submissions system. Please send all submissions to poemmemoirstory.submittable.com/submit."

MAGAZINES NEEDS Submit up to 5 poems through online submissions manager. Pays 2 contributor's copies.

TIPS "We strongly encourage you to familiarize yourself with *PMS* before submitting. You can find links to some examples of what we publish in the pages of *PMS* 8 and *PMS* 9. We look forward to reading your work."

⑤ POCKETS

The Upper Room, P.O. Box 340004, Nashville TN 37203. (615)340-7333. **E-mail:** pockets@upperroom.org. **Website:** pockets.upperroom.org. **Contact:** Lynn W. Gilliam, editor. Magazine published 11 times/year. "*Pockets* is a Christian devotional magazine for children ages 6-12. All submissions should address the broad theme of the magazine. Each issue is built around a theme with material which can be used by children in a variety of ways. Scripture stories, fiction, poetry, prayers, art, graphics, puzzles and activities are included. Submissions do not need to be overtly religious. They should help children experience a Christian lifestyle that is not always a neatly wrapped moral package but is open to the continuing revelation of God's will. Seasonal material, both secular and liturgical, is desired." Buys first North American serial rights. Pays on acceptance. Publishes ms an average of 1 year after acceptance. Responds in 8 weeks to mss. Each issue reflects a specific theme. Guidelines online.

○ Does not accept e-mail or fax submissions.

MAGAZINES NEEDS Both seasonal and theme poems needed. Considers poetry by children. Length: up to 20 lines. Pays $25 minimum.

TIPS "Theme stories, role models, and retold scripture stories are most open to freelancers. Poetry is also open. It is very helpful if writers read our writers' guidelines and themes on our website."

POEM

Huntsville Literary Association, P.O. Box 2006, Huntsville AL 35804. **E-mail:** poem@hlahsv.org. **Website:** www.hlahsv.org/poem. **Contact:** Rebecca Harbor, editor; Harry V. Moore and James Miller Robinson, assistant editors. *Poem*, published twice/ year in the spring and fall, consists entirely of poetry. Welcomes submissions from established poets as well as from lesser-known and beginning poets. *Poem* is 90 pages, digest-sized, flat-spined, printed on good stock paper, with a clean design and a matte cover. Prints more than 60 poems/issue, generally features 1 per page. Press run is 500. Acquires first serial rights. Responds in 1-3 months. Sample copy: $7 (back issue). Single copy: $10. Subscription: $20. Submit 3-5 poems, cover letter preferred, include SASE for response.

MAGAZINES NEEDS Wants poems characterized by compression, rich vocabulary, significant content, and evidence of a tuned ear and a practiced pen. Wants coherent work that moves through the particulars of the poem to make a point. Submit poems with a cover letter. Include name, address, telephone number, and e-mail address on cover letter and on each poem. Include SASE with sufficient postage. Submissions are read year round. Has published poetry by Ronald Wallace, Bill Brown, and Margaret Holley. Does not want translations, greeting card verse, or "proselytizing or didactic poems." Pays 2 contributor's copies.

◐ POEMELEON

Website: www.poemeleon.org. **Contact:** Cati Porter, founder and editor in chief. Each issue of *Poemeleon* is devoted to a specific kind of poetry. Previous emphases include poetry of place, ekphrastic poetry, poems in form, prose poems, persona poems, humor, gender, and collaboration. Acquires one-time, nonexclusive rights. Responds in 1-3 months after close of submissions. Guidelines available online.

MAGAZINES NEEDS Submit 1-5 poems using online submission manager. Include a brief third-person bio in cover letter.

POESY MAGAZINE

P.O. Box 2573, Santa Cruz CA 95063. **E-mail:** info@ poesy.org; submissions@poesy.org. **Website:** www. poesy.org. **Contact:** Brian Morrisey, editor in chief. *POESY Magazine*, published biannually, is "an anthology of American poetry. *POESY*'s main concentrations are Boston, Massachusetts, and Santa Cruz, California, 2 thriving homesteads for poets, beats, and artists of nature. Our goal is to unite the 2 scenes, updating poets on what's happening across the country." Wants to see "original poems that express observational impacts with clear and concise imagery. Acceptance is based on creativity, composition, and relation to the format of *POESY*." Does not want "poetry with excessive profanity. We would like to endorse creativity beyond the likes of everyday babble." Has published poetry by Lawrence Ferlinghetti, Jack Hirschman, Edward Sanders, Todd Moore, Diane Di Prima, and Julia Vinograd. Acquires first rights. Publishes ms 1 month after acceptance. Responds in 4-6 weeks. Guidelines available online.

○ *POESY* is 16 pages, magazine-sized, newsprint, glued/folded, includes ads. Receives about 1,000 poems/year, accepts about 10%. Press run is 1,000; most distributed free to local venues.

MAGAZINES NEEDS Submit up to 5 poems by e-mail or postal mail. Cover letter is preferred. Reads submissions year round. Indicate if you want your poems returned, and include SASE. "We encourage poems .. that create an image, stop moments in time, and leave your reader with a lasting impression. Please no poems about dogs, cats, angels, or the food you ate recently." Length: up to 32 lines/poem. Pays 3 contributor's copies.

TIPS "Our main focus is on Santa Cruz and Boston poetry, but we also accept submissions across the country. We see the poem as something to immerse the reader into a welcomed world of arresting images that jerks the eyes onto the page and leaves the reels of the mind turning long after the poem is finished. We see the poem as a work of art; save the narrative voice for the enlightenment of prose. We see the poem as a camera documenting a moment in time seen before the lens rather than from the eyes of its beholder behind the lens. To accomplish this goal, we have to be very precise that everything we publish falls within our portrayal of the poem."

POETALK

Bay Area Poets Coalition, 1791 Solano Ave. #A11, Berkeley CA 94707-2209. **E-mail:** bapc.poetalk@

gmail.com. **Website:** www.bayareapoetscoalition. org. **Contact:** John Rowe, acquisitions. *POETALK*, currently published annually, is the poetry journal of the Bay Area Poets Coalition (BAPC) and publishes 60-plus poets in each issue. "*POETALK* is open to all. No particular genre. Rhyme must be well done." All rights revert to author upon publication. Usually responds in up to 6 months. Guidelines available by e-mail, or see posting on website.

○ *POETALK* is 36 pages, digest-sized, photocopied, saddle-stapled, with heavy card cover. Press run is 400. Subscription: $6/2 issues. Sample copy: $2. Submissions are read year-round.

MAGAZINES NEEDS In general, poets may submit 3-5 poems at a time. Cover letter is preferred. Include SASE. Mss should be clearly typed, single-spaced, and include author's name and mailing address on every page. Provide an e-mail address. Length: up to 35 lines/poem; longer poems of "outstanding quality" considered. Pays 1 contributor's copy.

CONTEST/AWARD OFFERINGS Sponsors yearly contest.

TIPS "If you don't want suggested revisions, you need to say so clearly in your cover letter or indicate on each poem submitted." Bay Area Poets Coalition holds monthly readings in Berkeley, CA. BAPC has approx. 100 members; basic membership is $15/year (includes subscription to *POETALK* and other privileges); extra outside U.S.

POETICA MAGAZINE

Contemporary Jewish Writing, Mizmor L'David Anthology, 5215 Colley Ave. #138, Norfolk VA 23508. (757)617-0821. **E-mail:** poeticapublishing@aol.com. **Website:** www.poeticamagazine.com. **Contact:** Michal Mahgerefteh, publisher. *Poetica Magazine, Contemporary Jewish Writing*, is the publisher of the annual Mizmor L'David Anthology, offers "an outlet for the many writers who draw from their Jewish background and experiences to create poetry/prose/short stories, giving both emerging and recognized writers the opportunity to share their work with the larger community." *Poetica* is 80 pages, perfect-bound, full-color cover. Receives about 300 poems/year, accepts about 80%. Press run is 350. Poets retain all rights. Publishes 4 months after acceptance. Responds in 1 month. Contact the editor if reply not received. Single copy: $10. subject to change Please visit the website for the latest projects.

MAGAZINES NEEDS Submit ms through online submissions manager Submittable form. Include e-mail, bio, and mailing address. Does not want political.

CONTEST/AWARD OFFERINGS Anna Davidson Rosenberg Annual Poetry Awards for Individual Works.

TIPS "We publish original, unpublished works by Jewish and non-Jewish writers alike. We are interested in works that have the courage to acknowledge, challenge, and celebrate modern Jewish life beyond distinctions of secular and sacred. We like accessible works that find fresh meaning in old traditions that recognize the challenges of our generation. We evaluate works on several levels, including its skillful use of craft, its ability to hold interest, and layers of meaning."

POET LORE

The Writer's Center, 4508 Walsh St., Bethesda MD 20815. (301)654-8664. **E-mail:** poetlore@writer.org. **Website:** poetlore.com; www.writer.org. **Contact:** Emily Holland, managing editor; Jody Bolz and E. Ethelbert Miller, editors. *Poet Lore*, published semi-annually, is dedicated to the best in American and world poetry as well as timely reviews and commentary. Wants fresh uses of traditional forms and devices. Has published poetry by Ai, Denise Duhamel, Jefferey Harrison, Eve Jones, Carl Phillips, and Ronald Wallace. *Poet Lore* is 144 pages, digest-sized, professionally printed, perfect-bound, with glossy card cover. Receives about 4,200 poems/year, accepts 125. Press run is at least 800. Responds in 3 months. Single copy: $10; subscription: $18 for 1 year, $28 for 2 years. Guidelines for SASE or online.

MAGAZINES NEEDS Considers simultaneous submissions with notification in cover letter. No e-mail or disk submissions. Submit typed poems, with author's name and address on each page; SASE is required. Pays 2 contributor's copies and a one-year subscription.

ⓢ POETRY

The Poetry Foundation, 61 W. Superior St., Chicago IL 60654. (312)787-7070. **Fax:** (312)787-6650. **E-mail:** editors@poetrymagazine.org. **Website:** www.poetrymagazine.org. **Contact:** Don Share, editor. *Poetry*, published monthly by The Poetry Foundation, "has no special ms needs and no special requirements as to form: We examine in turn all work received and accept that which seems best." Has published poetry by the major voices of our time as well as new talent.

Poetry's website offers featured poems, letters, reviews, interviews, essays, and web-exclusive features. *Poetry* is elegantly printed, flat-spined. Receives 150,000 submissions/year, accepts about 300-350. Press run is 16,000. Buys first serial rights. Pays on publication. Publishes ms an average of 9 months after acceptance. Responds within 8 months to mss and queries. Guidelines online.

MAGAZINES NEEDS Publishes poetry all styles and subject matter. Submit up to 4 poems via Submittable. Reviews books of poetry, most solicited. Length: up to 10 pages total. Pays $10 line (minimum payment of $300).

ALSO OFFERS Offers 8 prizes (Bess Hokin Prize, Levinson Prize, Frederick Bock Prize, J. Howard and Barbara M.J. Wood Prize, John Frederick Nims Memorial Prize for Translation, Friends of Literature Prize, Editors Prize for Feature Article, Editors Prize for Reviewing) ranging from $500-5,000 are awarded annually to poets whose work has appeared in the magazine that year. Only work already published in *Poetry* is eligible for consideration; no formal application is necessary.

POETRYBAY

P.O. Box 114, Northport NY 11768. **E-mail:** poetrybay@aol.com. **E-mail:** info@poetrybay.com. **Website:** www.poetrybay.com. **Contact:** George Wallace, editor and publisher. *Poetrybay*, published semiannually online, seeks "to add to the body of great contemporary American poetry by presenting the work of established and emerging writers. Also, we consider essays and reviews." Has published poetry by Robert Bly, Yevgeny Yevtushenko, Marvin Bell, Diane Wakoski, Cornelius Eady, and William Heyen. Guidelines available online.

MAGAZINES NEEDS Open to format, length, and style. Works previously published in magazine or online publications will not be considered. Submit 3-5 poems in the body of an e-mail, with name, a brief bio, and address, or submit poems via snail mail with a cover letter and SASE for reply.

POETRY INTERNATIONAL

San Diego State University, 5500 Campanile Dr., San Diego CA 92182-6020. (619)594-1522. **Fax:** (619)594-4998. **E-mail:** poetryintl@gmail.com. **Website:** poetryinternational.sdsu.edu. **Contact:** Jenny Minniti-Shippey, Managing Editor. *Poetry International*, published annually, is "an eclectic poetry magazine intended to reflect a wide range of poetry being written today" and wants "a wide range of styles and subject matter. We're particularly interested in translations." Does not want "cliché-ridden, derivative, or obscure poetry." Has published poetry by Kim Addonizio, Robert Bly, Jericho Brown, Hayden Carruth, Maxine Kumin, Li-Young Lee, Adrienne Rich, Tracy K. Smith, and Gary Soto. "We intend to continue to publish poetry that makes a difference in people's lives, and startles us anew with the endless capacity of language to awaken our senses and expand our awareness." Responds in 6-8 months to mss. Subscription: $19.95/1 year. Sample: $15.

○ *Poetry International* is 400-600 pages, perfect-bound, with coated cardstock cover. Features the The C.P. Cavafy Poetry Prize and the Poetry International Prize (both for $1,000) for best original poem. Submit up to 3 poems with a $15 entry fee via Submittable.

MAGAZINES NEEDS Features the poetry of a different nation of the world as a special section in each issue. Submit via online submissions manager only. Pays in contributor's copies.

TIPS "Seeks a wide range of styles and subject matter."

● ⑤ POETRY IRELAND REVIEW

Poetry Ireland, 11 Parnell Square E., Dublin 1 , Ireland. +353(0)16789815. **E-mail:** publications@poetryireland.ie. **Website:** www.poetryireland.ie. Pays on publication. Responds in 1 week to queries; 3 months to mss. Guidelines online.

MAGAZINES NEEDS Pays €40-75/submission.

● POETRY NEW ZEALAND

Poetry New Zealand Yearbook, Massey University Press, School of English and Media Studies, Massey Albany Pvt Bag 102 904, North Shore Mail Centre Auckland 0745, New Zealand. **E-mail:** editor@poetrynz.net. **Website:** www.poetrynz.net. **Contact:** Dr. Jack Ross. Each annual issue has 20-30 pages of poetry from a developing or established poet, together with an interview. The rest of the issue is devoted to a selection of poetry from New Zealand and abroad, plus essays, reviews, and general criticism to a total of 250+ pages. Responds in 3 months to mss. Sample copy online. Guidelines online.

MAGAZINES NEEDS Poetry NZ accepts any theme/style of poetry. Send complete ms, bio, and up-to-date postal address either (preferably) by e-mail or by post (with SAE) to the address above.

POETRY SALZBURG REVIEW

Poetry Salzburg, University of Salzburg, Department of English and American Studies, Unipark Nonntal, Erzabt-Klotz-Strasse 1, Salzburg A-5020, Austria. (43)(662)8044-4424. **Fax:** (43)(662)8044-167. **E-mail:** editor@poetrysalzburg.com. **E-mail:** psr@poetrysalzburg.com. **Website:** www.poetrysalzburg.com. Prof. Dr. Robert Dassanowsky, rvondass@uccs.edu; Keith Hutson, keith.j.hutson@gmail.com.. **Contact:** Dr. Wolfgang Goertschacher, editor. *Poetry Salzburg Review*, published twice/year, contains "articles on poetry, mainly contemporary, and 70% poetry. Also includes long poems, sequences of poems, essays on poetics, review essays, interviews, artwork, and translations. We tend to publish selections by authors who have not been taken up by the big poetry publishers. Nothing of poor quality." *Poetry Salzburg Review* is about 200 pages per issue, A5, professionally printed, perfect-bound, with illustrated card cover (artwork). Receives about 10,000 poems/year; accepts 3%. Print run is 500. Acquires first rights. Payment for review essays that are commissioned and cover artwork. Time between acceptance and publication is 2-3 months, but depends on issue publication (spring, fall/winter). Responds in 6-8 weeks. Single copy: $16; subscription: $28 (only cash; subscribers can also pay with PayPal). Published on our website.

MAGAZINES NEEDS Accepts e-mail submissions (as attachment). Seldom comments on rejected poems. Has published poetry by Brian W. Aldiss, Rae Armantrout, Paul Muldoon, Alice Notley, Samuel Menashe, Jerome Rothenberg, Michael Heller, and Nathaniel Tarn. No length restriction. Pays 1 contributor's copy.

ALSO OFFERS Reviews books/chapbooks of poetry as well as books on poetics. Send materials for review consideration.

TIPS "No requirements, but it is a good idea to subscribe to *Poetry Salzburg Review* and to read issues first before submitting new poems."

POETS AND ARTISTS (O&S)

Website: www.poetsandartists.com. **Contact:** Didi Menendez, publisher. Reviews books of poetry, chapbooks of poetry, and other magazines/journals. Reads poetry submissions year round. Sometimes upcoming themes are available online at website. Authors published include Denise Duhamel, Bob Hicok, Billy Collins, Ron Androla, Blake Butler, and Matthew Hittinger. "We are a multi-interactive publication focusing on art: figurative, representational, portraits, and poetry. We interview art collectors, poets, artists, gallery owners, and art dealers to keep our readers in the know." Rights revert to poets upon publication. Time between acceptance and publication is 1 month. Sample copy: $25.

Prefers submissions from skilled, experienced poets; will consider work from beginning poets.

MAGAZINES NEEDS Paste submissions into body of e-mail message. Cover letter is unnecessary. Does not like "weird" formats.

TIPS Publisher also publishes *MiPOesias Magazine*, which has been featured in *Best American Poetry*, and *OCHO*, which has received Pushcart Prize nominations and has been featured in *Best American Poetry*.

THE POET'S HAVEN

Website: www.poetshaven.com. **Contact:** Vertigo Xi'an Xavier, publisher/editor. *The Poet's Haven* publishes poetry, artwork, stories, essays, and more. Online galleries, podcasts, and print books and anthologies. Work published in *The Poet's Haven* online galleries is left on the website permanently. Receives about 500 poems/year, accepts about 20%. Acquires rights to publish on the website permanently. Author retains rights to have works published elsewhere, provided the other publishers do not require first-time or exclusive rights. Time between acceptance and online publication is immediate. Never comments on rejected poems. Guidelines online.

MAGAZINES NEEDS Accepts submissions through online form only. Wants work that is emotional, personal, and intimate with the author or subject. Topics can cover just about anything. Has published poetry by Lucy Chau Lai-Tuen, Marc Jampole, Mala Hoffman, Herb Kauderer, Jennifer Polhemus, and AKeemjamal Rollins. Does not publish religious material. No payment for online publication. Book authors receive 25% of each print-run.

ALSO OFFERS Also publishes books, anthologies, and audio podcasts. Check website for themed calls and submission information.

POINTED CIRCLE

Portland Community College, Cascade Campus, SC 206, 705 N. Killingsworth St., Portland OR 97217. **Website:** www.pcc.edu/about/literary-magazines/pointed-circle. **Contact:** Wendy Bourgeois, faculty advisor. Publishes "anything of interest to educationally/culturally mixed audience. We will read whatever is sent, but we encourage writers to remember we are a quality literary/arts magazine intended to promote the arts in the community. No pornography, nothing trite. Be mindful of deadlines and length limits." Accepts submissions by e-mail, mail; artwork in high-resolution digital form. Acquires one-time rights.

○ Reading period: October 1-February 7. Magazine: 80 pages; b&w illustrations; photos.

MAGAZINES NEEDS Submit up to 6 pages of poetry. Submitted materials will not be returned; include SASE for notification only. Accepts multiple submissions. No pornography, nothing trite. Pays 2 contributor's copies.

THE PORTLAND REVIEW

Portland State University, P.O. Box 751, Portland OR 97207. **E-mail:** editor@portlandreview.org. **Website:** portlandreview.org. **Contact:** Alex Dannemiller, editor-in-chief. Portland Review has been publishing exceptional writing and artwork by local and international artists since 1956. Buys first North American serial rights. Publishes ms an average of 3-6 months after acceptance. Responds in 2-4 months to mss. Guidelines available online: portlandreview.submittable.com/submit.

TIPS "Please visit portlandreview.org for access to our submission manager and for more information."

○❸ THE PRAIRIE JOURNAL

A Magazine of Canadian Literature, P.O. Box 68073, 28 Crowfoot Terrace NW, Calgary AB T3G 3N8, Canada. **E-mail:** editor@prairiejournal.org (queries only); prairiejournal@yahoo.com. **Website:** www.prairiejournal.org. **Contact:** Anne Burke, literary editor. "The audience is literary, university, library, scholarly, and creative readers/writers. We welcome newcomers and unsolicited submission of writing and artwork. In addition to the print issues, we publish online long poems, fiction, interviews, drama, and reviews." Buys first North American serial rights or buys electronic rights. In Canada, author retains copyright and owns permission to republish (with acknowledgement appreciated). Pays on publication. Publishes ms an average of 4-6 months after acceptance. Responds in 2 weeks to queries; 2-6 months to mss. Editorial lead time 2-6 months. Sample copy: $5. Guidelines online.

MAGAZINES NEEDS Seeks poetry "of any length; free verse, contemporary themes (feminist, nature, urban, nonpolitical), aesthetic value, a poet's poetry." Does not want to see "most rhymed verse, sentimentality, egotistical ravings. No cowboys or sage brush." Has published poetry by Liliane Welch, Cornelia Hoogland, Sheila Hyland, Zoe Lendale, and Chad Norman. Receives about 1,000 poems/year, accepts 10%. No heroic couplets or greeting-card verse. Length: 3-50 lines. Pays $5-50.

TIPS "We publish many, many new writers and are always open to unsolicited submissions because we are 100% freelance. Do not send U.S. stamps; always use IRCs. We have poems, interviews, stories, and reviews online (query first)."

PRAIRIE SCHOONER

University of Nebraska–Lincoln, 123 Andrews Hall, Lincoln NE 68588. (402)472-0911. **Fax:** (402)472-1817. **E-mail:** prairieschooner@unl.edu. **Website:** prairieschooner.unl.edu. **Contact:** Ashley Strosnider, managing editor. "We look for the best fiction, poetry, and nonfiction available to publish, and our readers expect to read stories, poems, and essays of extremely high quality. We try to publish a variety of styles, topics, themes, points of view, and writers with a variety of backgrounds in all stages of their careers. We like work that is compelling—intellectually or emotionally—either in form, language, or content." Buys all rights, which are returned to the author upon request after publication. Pays on publication. Publishes ms an average of 1 year after acceptance. Responds in 1 week to queries; in 3-4 months to mss. Editorial lead time 6 months. Sample copy: $6. Guidelines online.

○ Submissions must be received between September 1 and May 1. Poetry published in *Prairie Schooner* has been selected for inclusion in *The Best American Poetry* and the *Pushcart Prize* anthologies. "All mss published in *Prairie Schooner* will automatically be considered for our annual prizes." These include The Strousse Award for Poetry ($500), the Bernice Slote Prize for Beginning Writers ($500), the Hugh J. Luke Award ($250), the Edward Stanley Award for Poetry ($1,000), the Virginia Faulkner Award for Excellence in Writing ($1,000), the Glenna Luschei Prize for Excellence ($1,500), and the Jane Geske Award ($250). Also, each year 10 Glenna Luschei Awards ($250 each) are given for poetry, fiction, and nonfiction. All contests are open only to those writers whose work was published in the magazine the previous year. Editors serve as judges. Also sponsors The *Prairie Schooner* Book Prize.

MAGAZINES NEEDS Wants "poems that fulfill the expectations they set up." No specifications as to form, length, style, subject matter, or purpose. Has published poetry by Alicia Ostriker, Marilyn Hacker, D.A. Powell, Stephen Dunn, and David Ignatow. Pays 3 copies of the issue in which the writer's work is published.

TIPS "Send us your best, most carefully crafted work, and be persistent. Submit again and again. Constantly work on improving your writing. Read widely in literary fiction, nonfiction, and poetry. Read *Prairie Schooner* to know what we publish."

⟁⑤ PRISM INTERNATIONAL

Dept. of Creative Writing, Buch E462, 1866 Main Mall, University of British Columbia, Vancouver BC V6T 1Z1, Canada. (604)822-2514. **Fax:** (604)822-3616. **E-mail:** prismcirculation@gmail.com. **Website:** www. prismmagazine.ca. A quarterly international journal of contemporary writing—fiction, poetry, drama, creative nonfiction and translation. *PRISM international* is digest-sized, elegantly printed, flat-spined, with original colour artwork on a nylon card cover. Readership: public and university libraries, individual subscriptions, bookstores—a world-wide audience concerned with the contemporary in literature. "We have no thematic or stylistic allegiances: Excellence is our main criterion for acceptance of manuscripts." Receives 1,000 submissions/year, accepts about 80. Circulation is for 1,200 subscribers. Subscription: $35/year for Canadian subscriptions, $40/year for US subscriptions, $45/year for international. Sample: $13. Buys first North American serial rights. Pays on publication. Publishes ms an average of 4 months after acceptance. Responds in 4 months to queries; 3-6 months to mss. Sample copy for $13, more info online. Guidelines online.

MAGAZINES NEEDS Wants "fresh, distinctive poetry that shows an awareness of traditions old and new. We read everything." Considers poetry by children and teens. "Excellence is the only criterion." Has published poetry by Margaret Avison, Elizabeth Bachinsky, John Pass, Warren Heiti, Don McKay, Bill Bissett, and Stephanie Bolster. Pays $40/printed page, and 2 copies of issue.

HOW TO CONTACT Submit up to 6 poems at a time. No previously published poems simultaneous submissions. No e-mail submissions. Cover letter is required. Include brief introduction and list of previous publications. Poems must be typed or computer-generated (font and point size open). Include SASE

(or SAE with IRCs). "Note: American stamps are not valid postage in Canada. No SASEs with U.S. postage will be returned. Translations must be accompanied by a copy of the original." Guidelines available for SASE (or SAE with IRCs), by e-mail, or on website. Responds in up to 6 months. Editors sometimes comment on rejected poems. Acquires first North American serial rights.

ADDITIONAL INFORMATION Sponsors annual Earle Birney Prize for Poetry. Prize awarded by the outgoing poetry editor to an outstanding poetry contributor published in *PRISM international*. Enter by regular submission only: no fee required. $500 prize.

CONTEST/AWARD OFFERINGS The Inaugural Pacific Spirit Poetry Prize First prize: $1,500; Runner Up: $600; 2nd Runner up $400. Entry fee: $35 for 3 poems; $5 per additional poem. Entry fee includes one-year subscription. Deadline: see website.

TIPS "We are looking for new and exciting fiction. Excellence is still our No. 1 criterion. As well as poetry, imaginative nonfiction and fiction, we are especially open to translations of all kinds, very short fiction pieces and drama which work well on the page. Translations must come with a copy of the original language work."

⑤ THE PROGRESSIVE

30 W. Mifflin St., Suite 703, Madison WI 53703. (608)257-4626. **E-mail:** normstoc@progressive.org. **E-mail:** editorial@progressive.org. **Website:** www. progressive.org. **Contact:** Norman Stockwell, publisher. A voice for peace, justice, and the common good. Pays on publication. Publishes ms an average of 6 weeks after acceptance. Responds in 1 month to queries. Sample copy for 9x12 SASE with 4 first-class stamps or sample articles online. Guidelines online.

MAGAZINES NEEDS Publishes 1 original poem a month. "We prefer poems that connect up—in 1 fashion or another, however obliquely—with political concerns." Pays $150.

TIPS Sought-after topics include electoral coverage, social movements, foreign policy, activism, and book reviews.

A PUBLIC SPACE

323 Dean St., Brooklyn NY 11217. (718)858-8067. **E-mail:** general@apublicspace.org. **Website:** www. apublicspace.org. **Contact:** Brigid Hughes, founding editor; Anne McPeak, managing editor. *A Public Space*, published quarterly, is an independent magazine of literature and culture. "In an era that has rel-

egated literature to the margins, we plan to make fiction and poetry the stars of a new conversation. We believe that stories are how we make sense of our lives and how we learn about other lives. We believe that stories matter." Single copy: $15; subscription: $36/year or $60/2 years.

◐ Accepts unsolicited submissions from September 15-April 15. Submissions accepted through Submittable or by mail (with SASE).

MAGAZINES NEEDS Submit via online submissions manager. No limit on line length.

PUERTO DEL SOL

E-mail: puertodelsoljournal@gmail.com. **Website:** www.puertodelsol.org. **Contact:** Richard Greenfield, editor-in-chief; Marissa Bond, prose editor; Caroline Chavatel, poetry editor; Jill Mceldowney, managing editor. Publishes innovative work from emerging and established writers and artists. Wants poetry, fiction, nonfiction, drama, theory, artwork, interviews, reviews, and interesting combinations thereof. *Puerto del Sol* is 150 pages, digest-sized, professionally printed, flat-spined, with matte card cover with art. Press run is 1,250 (300 subscribers, 25-30 libraries). Reading period for the print issue is June-October 15. General submissions reading period is variable. Acquires one-time print and electronic rights and anthology rights. Rights revert to author after publication. Publishes ms 4 months after acceptance. Responds in 3-6 months to mss. Free copies. Guidelines online.

MAGAZINES NEEDS Wants top-quality poetry, any style, from anywhere; excellent poetry of any kind, any form. Submit 3-5 poems at a time through online submissions manager. Brief cover letter is welcome. Do not send publication vitae. One poem/page. Sometimes sends prepublication galleys. Has published poetry by Richard Blanco, Maria Ercilla, Pamela Gemin, John Repp, and Lee Ann Roripaugh. Pays 1 contributor copy.

TIPS "We are especially pleased to publish emerging writers who work to push their art form or field of study in new directions."

◐ PULSAR POETRY WEBZINE

Ligden Publishers, 34 Lineacre, Grange Park, Swindon, Wiltshire SN5 6DA, United Kingdom. **E-mail:** pulsar.ed@btinternet.com. **Website:** www.pulsarpoetry.com. **Contact:** David Pike, editor. Acquires first rights. Originators retain copyright of their poems. Publishes ms 6 months after acceptance. Responds in 1 month. Send unpublished, hard-hitting poems, in the body of an email. Concentrate on message and meaning. Don't seek to rhyme above all else. Not keen on religious poems. Don't send simultaneous submissions. Suggest read the FAQ page of www.pulsarpoetry.com before sending.

◐ Send unpublished, hard-hitting poems, in the body of an email. Concentrate on message and meaning. Don't seek to rhyme above all else. Not keen on religious poems. Don't send simultaneous submissions. Suggest read the FAQ page of www.pulsarpoetry.com before sending.

MAGAZINES NEEDS "We will publish poems on the *Pulsar* web on a quarterly basis, i.e. March, June, September, and December. The selection process for poems will not alter, and we will continue to publish on a merit basis only; be warned, the editor is very picky! See poem submission guidelines online. We encourage the writing of poetry from all walks of life." Wants "hard-hitting, thought-provoking work; interesting and stimulating poetry." Does not want "racist material. Not keen on religious poetry." Has published poetry by Ann Egan, Mark Rutter, David Sapp, Julia Stothard, Stephen Komarnyckyi, Donna Pucciani, Sam Silva, Ian C. Smith, B. Diehl, Richard Dinges Jr., and Michael Jannings.

TIPS "Give explanatory notes if poems are open to interpretation. Be patient, and enjoy what you are doing. Check grammar, spelling, etc. (should be obvious). Note: We are a nonprofit society."

⑤ PURPOSE

MennoMedia, P.O. Box 866, 100 S. Mason St., Suite B, Harrisonburg VA 22801. **E-mail:** purposeeditor@mennomedia.org. **Website:** www.mennomedia.org/purpose. Publisher: Amy Gingerich.. **Contact:** Melodie M. Davis. *Purpose* is published monthly by Mennomedia, the publisher for Mennonite Church Canada and Mennonite Church USA. It is a faith-based adult monthly magazine that focuses on every day inspiration, discipleship-living, simplicity, and the Christian faith. Check the theme list on the website. Buys one-time rights. Pays upon publication. Publishes ms 6-9 months after acceptance. Responds in 1-3 months. Editorial lead time: 9 months. Sample articles can be viewed on the website. Guidelines online.

MAGAZINES NEEDS Poetry must address monthly themes. and be of a spiritual nature. Length: 12 lines maximum. Pays $10-20/poem.

TIPS "We seek true stories that follow monthly themes. Be sure to look at the website for the theme list and deadlines, as we only consider stories that are tied to the themes. Follow the writer guidelines on the website for the latest submission information."

QUARTER AFTER EIGHT

Ohio University, 306 Ellis Hall, Athens OH 45701. **E-mail:** editor@quarteraftereight.org. **Website:** www.quarteraftereight.org. **Contact:** Derek Robbins, editor; Justin Mundhenk, editor; Kristin Distel, assistant editor. "*Quarter After Eight* is an annual literary journal devoted to the exploration of innovative writing. We celebrate work that directly challenges the conventions of language, style, voice, or idea in literary forms. In its aesthetic commitment to diverse forms, *QAE* remains a unique publication among contemporary literary magazines." Reading period: October 15-April 15. Holds annual short prose (any genre) contest with grand prize of $1,008.15. Deadline is November 30. Acquires first North American serial rights. Rights revert to author upon publication. Publishes ms 6-12 months after acceptance. Responds in 6 months. Current Issue: $10. Back Issues: $5. Subscriptions: one-year subscription (1 volume): $10; two-year subscription (2 volumes): $18; three-year subscription (3 volumes): $25. Guidelines online.

MAGAZINES NEEDS Submit through online submissions manager.

TIPS "We look for prose and poetry that is innovative, exploratory, and—most importantly—well written. Please subscribe to our journal and read what is published to get acquainted with the *QAE* aesthetic."

⑤ QUARTERLY WEST

E-mail: quarterlywest@gmail.com. **Website:** www.quarterlywest.com. **Contact:** Sara Eliza Johnson and J.P. Grasser, editors. "We publish fiction, poetry, nonfiction, and new media in long and short formats, and will consider experimental as well as traditional works." Acquires first North American serial rights. All rights revert back to the author upon publication. Publishes ms an average of 6 months after acceptance. Responds in 3-4 months to mss. Guidelines available online.

○ *Quarterly West* was awarded first place for Editorial Content from the American Literary Magazine Awards. Work published in the magazine has been selected for inclusion in the *Pushcart Prize* anthology, the *Best of the Net* anthology, and *The Best American Short Stories* anthology.

MAGAZINES NEEDS Submit 3-5 poems at a time using online submissions manager only.

TIPS "We publish a special section of short shorts every issue, and we also sponsor an annual novella contest. We are open to experimental work—potential contributors should read the magazine! Don't send more than 1 story per submission. Novella competition guidelines available online. We prefer work with interesting language and detail—plot or narrative are less important. We don't do religious work."

○⑤ QUEEN'S QUARTERLY

402D - Douglas Library, 93 University Ave., Queen's University, Kingston ON K7L 5v4, Canada. (613)533-2667. **E-mail:** queens.quarterly@queensu.ca. **Website:** www.queensu.ca/quarterly. **Contact:** Dr. Boris Castel, editor; Joan Harcourt, literary editor. *Queen's Quarterly* is "a general-interest intellectual review featuring articles on science, politics, humanities, arts and letters, extensive book reviews, and some poetry and fiction." Has published work by Gail Anderson-Dargatz, Tim Bowling, Emma Donohue, Viktor Carr, Mark Jarman, Rick Bowers, and Dennis Bock. Acquires first North American serial rights. Pays on publication. Sends galleys to author. Publishes ms on average 6-12 months after acceptance. Responds in 2-3 months to queries; 1-2 months to mss. Sample copy: $6.50. U.S. Subscription: $20 for Canada, $25 for U.S./Int'l Guidelines online.

MAGAZINES NEEDS Receives about 400 submissions of poetry/year; accepts 40. Submissions can be sent on hard copy with SASE (no replies/returns for foreign submissions unless accompanied by an IRC) or by e-mail, and will be responded to by same. "We are especially interested in poetry by Canadian writers. Shorter poems preferred." Has published poetry by Evelyn Lau, Sue Nevill, and Raymond Souster. Each issue contains about 12 pages of poetry. Usually pays $50 (Canadian)/poem (but it varies), plus 2 contributor's copies.

RADIX MAGAZINE

Radix Magazine, Inc., P.O. Box 4307, Berkeley CA 94704. (510)548-5329. **E-mail:** radixmag@aol.com. **Website:** www.radixmagazine.com. **Contact:** Sharon Gallagher, editor. *Radix Magazine*, published quarterly, is named for the Latin word for "root" and "has its roots both in the 'real world' and in the truth of Christ's teachings." Wants poems that reflect a Christian world-view, but aren't preachy. Has published poetry by John Leax, Czeslaw Milosz, Madeleine L'Engle, and Luci Shaw. Interested in first North American serial rights. Publishes ms 3 months to 3 years after acceptance. Responds in 2 months to queries and to mss. Editorial lead time 6 months. Sample copy for $5. Guidelines available by e-mail.

○ *Radix* is 32 pages, magazine-sized, offset-printed, saddle-stapled, with 60-lb. self cover. Receives about 120 poems/year, accepts about 10%. Press run varies. Subscription: $15. Sample: $5. Make checks payable to *Radix Magazine*."

MAGAZINES NEEDS Submit 1-4 poems at a time. Length: 4-20 lines. Pays 2 contributor's copies.

TIPS "We accept very few unsolicited manuscripts. We do not accept fiction. All articles and poems should be based on a Christian world view. Freelancers should have some sense of the magazine's tone and purpose."

THE RAINTOWN REVIEW

Central Ave. Press, 5390 Fallriver Row Court, Columbia MD 21044. **E-mail:** theraintownreview@gmail.com. **Website:** www.theraintownreview.com. **Contact:** Anna Evans, editor. *The Raintown Review*, published 2 times/year in winter and summer, contains poetry, reviews, and belletristic critical prose. Wants well-crafted poems. Primarily a venue for formal/metrical poetry. Has published poetry by Julie Kane, Alexandra Oliver, Rick Mullin, Annie Finch, Kevin Higgins, David Mason, A.E. Stallings, Richard Wilbur, and many others. Acquires first rights. Responds in 10-12 weeks. One can also subscribe online via our website preferred method. Guidelines available online.

○ *The Raintown Review* is 120 pages, perfect-bound. Receives about 2,500 poems/year, accepts roughly 5%. Press run is approximately 500. Subscription: $24/year, $45 for 2 years, $65 for 3 years. Sample: $12. Make checks/money orders payable to Central Ave Press.

MAGAZINES NEEDS Submit 3-5 poems at a time. Accepts e-mail submissions only (pasted into body of message); no postal submissions. Guidelines available on website. Strong bias toward formal/metrical poetry. No restrictions on length. Pays 1 contributor's copy.

⑤ RALEIGH REVIEW LITERARY & ARTS MAGAZINE

Box 6725, Raleigh NC 27628-6725. **E-mail:** info@raleighreview.org. **Website:** www.raleighreview.org. **Contact:** Rob Greene, editor; Landon Houle, fiction editor; Bryce Emley, poetry editor. "*Raleigh Review* is a national nonprofit magazine of poetry, short fiction (including flash), and art. We believe that great literature inspires empathy by allowing us to see the world through the eyes of our neighbors, whether across the street or across the globe. Our mission is to foster the creation and availability of accessible yet provocative contemporary literature. We look for work that is emotionally and intellectually complex." Buys first North American serial rights. Publication is copyrighted. Pays on publication. Publishes ms 3-6 months after acceptance. Responds typically in 1-3 months, though sometimes up to 3-6 months. "Poetry and fiction submissions through Submittable; no prior query required." Sample copy: $15 hardcopy or $4.95 on Kindle. "Sample work also online at website." Guidelines online.

MAGAZINES NEEDS Submit up to 5 poems. "If you think your poems will make a perfect stranger's toes tingle, heart leap, or brain sizzle, then send them our way. We typically do not publish avant garde, experimental, or language poetry. We *do* like a poem that causes—for a wide audience—a visceral reaction to intellectually and emotionally rich material." Length: open. Pays $15 per accepted title.

TIPS "Please be sure to read the guidelines and look at sample work on our website. Every piece is read for its intrinsic value, so new/emerging voices are often published alongside nationally recognized, award-winning authors."

⑤ RATTAPALLAX

Rattapallax Press, 217 Thompson St., Suite 353, New York NY 10012. **E-mail:** devineni@rattapallax.com. **Website:** www.rattapallax.com. **Contact:** Ram Devineni, founder & president; Flávia Rocha, editor in chief. *Rattapallax*, published semiannually, is named for "Wallace Stevens's word for the sound of thunder. The magazine includes a DVD featuring poetry films and audio files. *Rattapallax* is looking for the extraordinary in modern poetry and prose that reflect the diversity of world cultures. Our goals are to create international dialogue using literature and focus on what is relevant to our society." Buys first North American serial rights, South American rights. Pays on publication. Publishes ms an average of 6 months after acceptance. Responds in 3 months to queries; in 3 months to mss. Editorial lead time 6 months. Sample copy: $7.95. Make checks payable to *Rattapallax*. Guidelines online.

○ *Rattapallax* is 112 pages, magazine-sized, offset-printed, perfect-bound, with 12-pt. CS1 cover; some illustrations; photos. Press run is 2,000 (100 subscribers, 50 libraries, 1,200 shelf sales); 200 distributed free to contributors, reviews, and promos.

MAGAZINES NEEDS Submit via online submission manager at rattapallax.submittable.com/submit. Often comments on rejected poems. Length: 1 page per poem. Pays 2 contributor's copies.

⑤ RATTLE

Rattle Foundation, 12411 Ventura Blvd., Studio City CA 91604. (818)505-6777. **E-mail:** tim@rattle.com. **Website:** www.rattle.com. **Contact:** Timothy Green, editor. *Rattle* publishes unsolicited poetry and translations of poetry, quarterly in print and daily online. Acquires first rights and electronic permissions. Publication Responds in 1-6 months. Guidelines online.

⬯ At Rattle, anything always goes. If a poem is accessible, interesting, moving, and memorable, if it makes you laugh or cry, then it's the kind of poem that rattles around inside you for years, and it's our kind of poem.

MAGAZINES NEEDS "We're looking for poems that move us, that might make us laugh or cry, or teach us something new. We like both free verse and traditional forms—we try to publish a representative mix of what we receive. We read a lot of poems, and only those that are unique, insightful, and musical stand out—regardless of style." Submit up to 4 poems via online submissions manager or postal mail. Pays $100/poem and a one-year subscription for print contributors; $50/poem for online contributors.

ALSO OFFERS "All submissions are automatically considered for the Neil Postman Award for Metaphor, an annual $1,000 prize for the best use of metaphor as judged by the editors. No entry fee or special formatting is required; simply follow the regular guidelines." Also holds the *Rattle* Poetry Prize (see separate listing in Contests & Awards). Also considers poetry by children and teens under the age of 16 for a separate annual anthology, *Rattle Young Poets Anthology*. Parents must submit through an online portal. See www.rattle.com/poetry/children for more information.

RATTLING WALL

c/o PEN USA, 269 S. Beverly Dr. #1163, Beverly Hills CA 90212. **E-mail:** therattlingwall@penusa.org. **Website:** therattlingwall.com. **Contact:** Michelle Meyering, editor. Acquires first rights. Rights revert to author upon publication. Pays on publication. Publishes

ms 2 months after acceptance. Responds in 6 months. Sample copy: $18.95. Guidelines online.

⬯ Magazine: 6x9, square bound.

MAGAZINES NEEDS Submit 3-5 poems at a time. Does not want sentimental love poetry or religious verse. Does not consider poetry by children or teens. Pays 2 contributor's copies.

⑤ THE RAVEN CHRONICLES

A Journal of Art, Literature, & the Spoken Word, 15528 12th Ave. NE, Shoreline WA 98155. (206)941-2955. **E-mail:** editors@ravenchronicles.org. **E-mail:** https://ravenchronicles.submittable.com/submit. **Website:** www.ravenchronicles.org. **Contact:** Phoebe Bosché, managing editor; Priscilla Long, nonfiction editor; Kathleen Alcalá, fiction editor; Gary Lilley, poetry editor. "*The Raven Chronicles* publishes work which reflects the cultural diversity of the Pacific Northwest, Canada, and other areas of North America. We promote art, literature, and the spoken word for an audience that is hip, literate, funny, informed, and lives in a society that has a multicultural sensibility. We publish fiction, talk art/spoken word, poetry, essays, reflective articles, reviews, interviews, and contemporary art. We look for work that reflects the author's experiences, perceptions, and insights." First North American Serial Rights. Pays on publication. Publishes ms 3 months after acceptance. Responds in 1-3 months. Sample copy online. Guidelines online.

MAGAZINES NEEDS Send up to 3 poems at a time via online submissions manager. Focus is on content that melds with form—whether traditional or experimental. Needs to fit 4x7 book formatted page.

⬮ THE READER

The Reader Organisation, Calderstones Mansion, Calderstones Park, Liverpool L18 3JB, United Kingdom. **E-mail:** magazine@thereader.org.uk; info@thereader.org.uk. **Website:** www.thereader.org.uk. **Contact:** Grace Frame. "*The Reader* is a quarterly literary magazine aimed at the intelligent 'common reader'—from those just beginning to explore serious literary reading to professional teachers, academics, and writers. As well as publishing short fiction and poetry by new writers and established names, the magazine features articles on all aspects of literature, language, and reading; regular features, including a literary quiz and a section on the Reading Revolution, reporting on The Reader Organisation's outreach work; reviews; and readers' recommendations of books that have made a difference to them. *The Reader* is unique among literary magazines in its focus on reading as a creative, important, and pleasurable activity, and in its combination of high-quality material and presentation with a genuine commitment to ordinary but dedicated readers." Also publishes literary essays, literary criticism, poetry. Pays on publication. Publishes ms 16 months after acceptance. Responds to queries and mss in 2 months. Guidelines for SASE and available online.

MAGAZINES NEEDS Submit up to 6 poems with cover letter. No e-mail submissions. Include estimated word count, brief bio, list of publications.

TIPS "The style or polish of the writing is less important than the deep structure of the story (though, of course, it matters that it's well written). The main persuasive element is whether the story moves us—and that's quite hard to quantify. It's something to do with the force of the idea and the genuine nature of enquiry within the story. When fiction is the writer's natural means of thinking things through, that'll get us. "

REAL

Regarding Arts & Letters, Stephen F. Austin State University, Nacogdoches TX 75962 3007. **Website:** regardingartsandletters.wordpress.com. **Contact:** Mark Sanders, editor. *"REAL: Regarding Arts & Letters* was founded in 1968 as an academic journal which occasionally published poetry. Now, it is an international creative magazine dedicated to publishing the best contemporary fiction, poetry, and nonfiction." Features both established and emerging writers. Magazine: semiannual, 120 pages, perfect-bound. Responds in 3 months, though response time is slower in summer months.

MAGAZINES NEEDS Submit up to 5 poems at a time via online submissions manager. Pays contributor's copies.

TIPS "We are looking for the best work, whether you are established or not."

REALPOETIK

E-mail: realpoetikblog@gmail.com. **Website:** www.realpoetik.club. **Contact:** Thibault Raoult, editor. *RealPoetik* publishes innovative work. Poems are published online and also sent to subscribers via e-mail. "We provide a club/poem atmosphere." Publishes poetry 2-4 months after acceptance. Responds in 1 month to queries. Sometimes comments on rejected mss. Sample copy online.

O   Publishes 20-30 new poets/year.

MAGAZINES NEEDS Query first via e-mail with short bio, project description (if applicable), and any assertions/questions you might have.

REDACTIONS

Poetry & Poetics, 604 N. 31st Ave., Apt. D-2, Hattiesburg MS 39401. **E-mail:** redactionspoetry@yahoo.com. **Website:** www.redactions.com. **Contact:** Tom Holmes. *Redactions,* released every 12 months, covers poems, reviews of new books of poems, translations, manifestos, interviews, essays concerning poetry, poetics, poetry movements, or concerning a specific poet or a group of poets; and anything dealing with poetry. "We no longer publish fiction or creative nonfiction." All rights revert back to the author. Responds in 3 months. Guidelines online.

MAGAZINES NEEDS Anything dealing with poetry. Pays contributor's copy.

TIPS "We only accept submissions by e-mail. We read submissions throughout the year. E-mail submission as an attachment in one Word, RTF, or PDF document, or paste in the body of an e-mail. Include brief bio and your snail mail address. E-mails that have no subject line or have nothing written in the body of the e-mail will be deleted. We do not accept blank e-mails with only an attachment. Query after 90 days if you haven't heard from us. See website for full guidelines, including for cover artwork."

REDHEADED STEPCHILD

E-mail: redheadedstepchildmag@gmail.com. **Website:** www.redheadedmag.com/poetry. **Contact:** Malaika King Albrecht. *"Redheaded Stepchild* only accepts poems that have been rejected by other magazines. We publish biannually, and we accept submissions in the months of August and February only. We do not accept previously published work. We do, however, accept simultaneous submissions, but please inform us immediately if your work is accepted somewhere else. We are open to a wide variety of poetry and hold no allegiance to any particular style or school. If your poem is currently displayed online on your blog or website or wherever, please do not send it to us before taking it down, at least temporarily." Acquires first rights. Rights revert to poet upon publication. Time between acceptance and publication is 3 months. Poems are circulated to an editorial board. Sometimes comments on rejected poems. Responds in 3 months. Guidelines on website.

O   Wants a wide variety of poetic styles.

MAGAZINES NEEDS "Submit 3-5 poems that have been rejected elsewhere with the names of the magazines that rejected the poems. We do not want multiple submissions, so please wait for a response to your first submission before you submit again. As is standard after publication, rights revert back to the author, but we request that you credit *Redheaded Stepchild* in subsequent republications. We do not accept e-mail attachments; therefore, in the body of your e-mail, please include the following: a brief bio, 3-5 poems, and the publication(s) that rejected the poems." Has published poetry by Kathryn Stripling Byer, Alex Grant, Amy King, Diane Lockward, Susan Yount, and Howie Good.

REDIVIDER

Department of Writing, Literature, and Publishing, Emerson College, 120 Boylston St., Boston MA 02116. **E-mail:** editor@redividerjournal.org. **Website:** www.redividerjournal.org. *Redivider*, a journal of literature and art, is published twice a year by graduate students in the Writing, Literature, and Publishing Department of Emerson College. Prints new art, fiction, nonfiction, and poetry from new, emerging, and established artists and writers. Every spring, *Redivider* hosts the Beacon Street Prize Writing Contest, awarding a cash prize and publication to the winning submission in fiction, poetry, and nonfiction categories. Hosts the Blurred Genre Contest each fall, awarding cash prizes and publication for flash fiction, flash nonfiction, and prose poetry. See website for details. Responds in 3-6 months. Sample copy: $8. Subscription: $15 for 1 year; $25 for 2 years. Make checks payable to *Redivider* at Emerson College. Guidelines online.

MAGAZINES NEEDS Submit up to 4 poems via online submissions manager. Pays 2 contributor's copies.

TIPS "To get a sense of what we publish, pick up an issue!"

🟢 THE RED MOON ANTHOLOGY OF ENGLISH LANGUAGE HAIKU

P.O. Box 2461, Winchester VA 22604-1661. **E-mail:** jim.kacian@redmoonpress.com. **Website:** www.redmoonpress.com. **Contact:** Jim Kacian, editor/publisher. *The Red Moon Anthology of English Language Haiku*, published annually in February, is "a collection of the best haiku published in English around the world." *The Red Moon Anthology of English Language Haiku* is 160-210 pages, digest-sized, offset-printed on quality paper, with 4-color heavy-stock cover. Receives several thousand submissions/year; accepts less than 2%. Print run is 1,000 for subscribers and commercial distribution. Considers poetry by children and teens. Acquires North American serial rights. Sample available for SASE or by e-mail. Subscription: $17 plus $6 p&h. Guidelines available for SASE or by e-mail.

MAGAZINES NEEDS "We do not accept direct submissions to the *Red Moon Anthology*. Rather, we employ an editorial board who are assigned journals and books from which they cull and nominate. Nominated poems are placed on a roster and judged anonymously by the entire editorial board twice a year." Has published haiku and related forms by Susan Antolin, Terry Ann Carter, Alan Summers and Julie Warther.

RED RIVER REVIEW

E-mail: info@redriverreview.com. **Website:** www.redriverreview.com. **Contact:** Michelle Hartman, editor. "Our editorial philosophy is simple: It is the duty of the writer to accurately chronicle our times and to reflect honestly on how these events affect us. Poetry which strikes a truth, which artfully conveys the human condition, is most likely to be selected. Vulgarity and coarseness are part of our daily life and are thus valid. Life isn't always pretty. However, vulgarity and coarseness just for the sake of the exercise doesn't generally benefit anyone. *Red River Review* is open to all styles of writing. Abstract, beat, confessional, free verse, synthetic, formal—we will publish just about anything that has the authenticity and realism we're seeking. With this said, however, rhymed poetry of any nature is rarely accepted." Acquires first North American electronic rights and possible future anthology electronic rights. Rights revert to poets upon publication. Time between acceptance and publication is tops, 2 months. Responds in 2 weeks to poems. Sometimes comments on rejected poems. **Charges criticism fee. Handled on individual basis.** Guidelines online.

MAGAZINES NEEDS Submit 1 poem per page, up to 5 poems at a time via online submissions manager; no e-mail submissions. Receives about 2,000 poems/year. Does not consider previously published poems (poetry posted on a public website, blog, or forum). "Please be very sure you have entered your e-mail address correctly. If an acceptance comes back as bad mail, we pull the poem. Please include a serious bio. If you do not respect your work, why should we?" Has published poetry by Naomi Shihab Nye, Larry Thomas, Rob Walker, Alan Gann, Loretta Walker, David Ades, Steve Kleptar, Jerry Bradley, and Ann Howells.

Rarely takes rhyming or form poems, "although we love a good sonnet every now and then."

RED ROCK REVIEW

College of Southern Nevada, CSN Department of English, J2A, 3200 E. Cheyenne Ave., North Las Vegas NV 89030. (702)651-4094. **Fax:** (702)651-4455. **E-mail:** redrockreview@csn.edu. **Website:** sites.csn.edu/english/redrockreview. **Contact:** Todd Moffett, senior editor; Erica Vital-Lazare, associate editor. Dedicated to the publication of fine contemporary literature. Accepts fine poetry and short fiction year round. Buys first North American serial rights. All other rights revert to the authors and artists upon publication. Occasionally comments on rejected submissions. Sample copy: $6.50. Subscription: $9.50/year. Guidelines available online.

○ *Red Rock Review* is about 130 pages, magazine-sized, professionally printed, perfect-bound, with 10-pt. CS1 cover.

MAGAZINES NEEDS Looking for the very best literature. Poems need to be tightly crafted, characterized by expert use of language. Submit 2-3 poems at a time via e-mail as Word, RTF, or PDF file attachment. Length: up to 80 lines/poem. Pays 2 contributor's copies.

RED WHEELBARROW

De Anza College, 21250 Stevens Creek Blvd., Cupertino CA 95014. **Website:** www.deanza.edu/redwheelbarrow. Buys first North American serial rights. Publishes ms an average of 2-4 months after acceptance. Responds in 2 weeks to queries; in 2-4 months to mss. Sample copy: $10 ($2.50 for back issues). Guidelines available online.

○ "We seek to publish a diverse range of styles and voices from around the country and the world." Publishes a student edition and a national edition.

MAGAZINES NEEDS Send up to 5 poems by mail (include SASE) or e-mail with brief bio. Does not want excessively abstract or excessively sentimental poetry.

TIPS "Write freely, rewrite carefully. Resist clichés and stereotypes. We are not affiliated with Red Wheelbarrow Press or any similarly named publication."

REED MAGAZINE

San Jose State University, Dept. of English, One Washington Square, San Jose CA 95192. **E-mail:** mail@reedmag.org; cathleen.miller@sjsu.edu. **Website:** www.reedmag.org. **Contact:** Cathleen Miller, editor-in-chief.

Reed Magazine is California's oldest literary journal. "We publish works of short fiction, nonfiction, poetry, and art, and offer cash prizes in each category." Accepts electronic submissions only. Buys first North American rights. Pays award winners, over $4,000 in cash prizes. Publishes ms an average of 5 months after acceptance. Responds annually in December. Guidelines available on website and through Submittable.

MAGAZINES NEEDS Submit up to 5 poems per attachment via online submissions manager. Contest contributors receive 1 free copy; additional copies: $15.

CONTEST/AWARD OFFERINGS Edwin Markham Prize for $1,000. Submission fee $15, accepted June 1-November 1.

TIPS "Well-written, original, clean grammatical prose is essential. We are interested in established authors as well as fresh new voices. Keep submitting!"

RENDITIONS

A Chinese-English Translation Magazine, Research Centre for Translation, Chinese University of Hong Kong, Shatin, N.T. , Hong Kong. (852)3943-7399. **Fax:** (852)2603-5110. **E-mail:** renditions@cuhk.edu.hk; rct@cuhk.edu.hk. **Website:** www.cuhk.edu.hk/rct/renditions/index.html. *Renditions: A Chinese-English Translation Magazine*, published 2 times/year in May and November, uses "exclusively translations from Chinese, ancient and modern." Poems are printed with Chinese and English texts side by side. Has published translations of the poetry of Yang Lian, Gu Cheng, Shu Ting, Mang Ke, and Bei Dao. Responds in 2 months. Single copy: $21.90; subscription: $33.90/year, $59.90 for 2 years, $79.90 for 3 years. Guidelines on website.

○ *Renditions* is about 132 pages, magazine-sized, elegantly printed, perfect-bound, with glossy card cover.

MAGAZINES NEEDS Submissions should be accompanied by Chinese originals. Accepts e-mail and fax submissions. "Submissions by postal mail should include 2 copies. Use British spelling." Sometimes comments on rejected translations. Publishes theme issues.

ADDITIONAL INFORMATION Also publishes a hardback series (Renditions Books) and a paperback series (Renditions Paperbacks) of Chinese literature in English translation. Will consider book mss; query with sample translations.

RHINO

The Poetry Forum, Inc., P.O. Box 591, Evanston IL 60204. **E-mail:** editors@rhinopoetry.org. **Website:**

rhinopoetry.org. **Contact:** Ralph Hamilton, editor-in-chief. "This independent, eclectic annual journal of 40 plus years accepts poetry, flash fiction (up to 500 words), and poetry-in-translation that experiments, provokes, compels. Emerging and established poets are showcased." Accepts general submissions April 1-July 31 and Founders' Prize submissions September 1-October 31. Buys first North American serial rights. Response time: 3-6 months. Single copy: $16 plus $3.50 s/h. Back issues: $6 plus $3 s/h. Guidelines online.

MAGAZINES NEEDS Wants "work that reflects passion, originality, engagement with contemporary culture, and a love affair with language. We welcome free verse, formal poetry, innovation, humor, and risk-taking. All entries considered for the Editors' Prize." Submit up to 5 poems (1 poem per page) or 5 pages maximum via online submissions manager (preferred) or postal mail. Include cover letter. Accepted poems are published in our annual print journal and online within a year of publication. Accepted poems may include audio component on our website. Pays 1 contributor's copy and offers contributor discounts for additional copies.

TIPS "Our diverse group of editors looks for the very best in contemporary writing, and we have created a dynamic process of soliciting and reading new work by local, national, and international writers. We are open to all styles and look for idiosyncratic, rigorous, well-crafted, lively, and passionate work."

●⊜ THE RIALTO

P.O. Box 309, Aylsham, Norwich NR11 6LN, England. **E-mail:** info@therialto.co.uk. **Website:** www.therialto.co.uk. **Contact:** Michael Mackmin, editor. *The Rialto*, published 3 times/year, seeks to publish the best new poems by established and beginning poets. Seeks excellence and originality. Has published poetry by Alice Fulton, Jenny Joseph, Les Murray, George Szirtes, Philip Gross, and Ruth Padel. Copyright remains with poets. Pays on publication. Publishes ms 5 months after acceptance. Responds in 3-4 months. Guidelines available online.

○ *The Rialto* is 64 pages, A4, with full-color cover. Receives about 12,000 poems/year; accepts about 1%. Press run is 1,500. Single copy: £8.50; subscription: £24 (prices listed are U.K.: for U.S. and Canada add £12 shipping charge). Make checks payable to *The Rialto*. Checks in sterling only. Online payment also available on website.

MAGAZINES NEEDS Submit up to 6 poems at a time via postal mail (with SASE) or online submissions manager. Pays £20/poem.

TIPS *The Rialto* also publishes occasional books and pamphlets. Please do not send book-length mss. Query first. Details available in magazine and on website. Before submitting, "you will probably have read many poems by many poets, both living and dead. You will probably have put aside each poem you write for at least 3 weeks before considering it afresh. You will have asked yourself, 'Does it work technically?'; checked the rhythm, the rhymes (if used), and checked that each word is fresh and meaningful in its context, not jaded and tired. You will hopefully have read *The Rialto*."

RIBBONS

Tanka Society of America Journal, 1470 Keoncrest Dr., Berkeley CA 94702. **E-mail:** drice2@comcast.net. **Website:** sites.google.com/site/tankasocietyofamerica/home. **Contact:** David Rice, editor; Susan Weaver, tanka prose editor. Published 3 times/year, *Ribbons* seeks and regularly prints the best tanka poetry being written in English, together with reviews, critical and historical essays, commentaries, and translations. Wants poetry that exemplifies the very best in English-language tanka, having a significant contribution to make to the short poem in English. All schools and approaches are welcome. Tanka should reflect contemporary life, issues, values, and experience, in descriptive, narrative, and lyrical modes. Does not want work that merely imitates the Japanese masters. Considers poetry by teens. Publishes ms 2 months after acceptance. Respond in 1-3 months. Guidelines online.

○ *Ribbons* is 90-120 pages, 6x9 perfect-bound, with color cover and art. Receives about 2,000 poems/year, accepts about 20%. Press run is 300; 15 distributed free. Single copy: $10; subscription: $30. Make checks payable to Tanka Society of America, and contact Kathabela Wilson, secretary (e-mail: poetsonsite@gmail.com; 439 S. Catalina Avenue, #306, Pasadena, CA 91106.

MAGAZINES NEEDS "*Ribbons* seeks fresh material of the highest standard to present to our readers. Any tanka with a sensibility that distinguishes the form will be considered. Therefore, we welcome different syllable counts, varying individual styles and techniques, and we're open to diverse yet appropriate subject material." Submit up to 10 tanka or 2 tanka prose piece by e-mail or postal mail. Deadlines: April 30 (spring/summer issue), August 31 (fall issue), and December 31 (winter issue). Length: 5 lines. Sequences of up to 30 total lines considered.

TIPS "Work by beginning as well as established English-language tanka poets is welcome; first-time contributors are encouraged to study the tanka form and contemporary examples before submitting. No particular school or style of tanka is preferred over another; our publications seek to showcase the full range of English-language tanka expression and subject matter through the work of new and established poets in the genre from around the world."

THE ROAD NOT TAKEN

E-mail: kathryn.jacobs@tamuc.edu. **E-mail:** jacobskathryn2@gmail.com. **Website:** www.journalformalpoetry.com. **Contact:** Dr. Kathryn Jacobs, editor; Rachel Jacobs, associate editor. *The Road Not Taken: A Journal of Formal Poetry*, published 3 times/year online. *The Road Not Taken* aims for a modern metrical style written in contemporary idiom on contemporary subjects. Please make only sparing use of end-stopped lines and strive for flexible rhymes, this is the 21st century, not the 18th. In short, explore tradition but make it new. Responds in up to 4 months, please wait until the next issue appears before querying. Sometimes comments on rejected poems.

MAGAZINES NEEDS Submit 3-5 poems by e-mail only. Simultaneous submissions are acceptable, but contact promptly if a poem is accepted elsewhere.

💲 ROANOKE REVIEW

221 College Lane, Miller Hall, Salem VA 24153. E-mail: review@roanoke.edu. **Website:** roanokereview.org. "The *Roanoke Review* is an online literary journal that is dedicated to publishing new and established voices in fiction, nonfiction, visual poetry, and poetry." Recent work by Henry Taylor, Adrian Blevins, Sharbari Ahmed, John Sibley Williams, and Karl Harshbarger. Publishes ms 6-9 months after acceptance. Responds in 3-6 months to submissions. Guidelines online.

MAGAZINES NEEDS Submit via Submittable, e-mail, or send SASE for reply only.

TIPS "Send us something you love."

THE ROCKFORD REVIEW

Rockford Writers' Guild, P.O. Box 858, Rockford IL 61105. **E-mail:** sally@rockfordwritersguild.org. **Website:** www.rockfordwritersguild.org. **Contact:** Sally

Hewitt. Since 1947, the Rockford Writers' Guild has published The Rockford Review twice a year. Anyone may submit to the winter-spring edition of The Rockford Review from July 15-October 15. If published, payment is one contributor copy of journal and $5 per published piece. We also publish a "Members Only" edition in the summer which is open to members of Rockford Writers' Guild. Anyone may be a member of RWG and we have over 100 members from the United States, England, Canada, and Mexico. Members are guaranteed publication at least once a year. Check website for frequent updates at www.rockfordwritersguild.org. Follow us Facebook under Rockford Writers' Guild or Twitter and Instagram @ guildypleasures. Poetry 50 lines or less, prose 1,300 words or less. No racist, supremacist, pornographic or sexist content. If published in the winter-spring edition of *The Rockford Review*, writer receives one copy of journal and $5 per published piece. Pays on publication. Credit line given. Buys first North American serial rights. Buys first North American serial rights. Pays on publication. Sample copy available for $12.

MAGAZINES NEEDS Send us your eclectic, courageous, provacative, lovely, new poetry. No racist, supremacist, or sexist content. Length: up to 50 lines. If published in the winter-spring edition of the *Rockford Review*, payment is one copy of journal and $5 per published piece. Pays on publication. Writers published in the summer-fall "Members Only" edition are not paid, but will receive a copy of the journal.

TIPS "We're wide open to new and established writers alike."

♻️💲 ROOM

West Coast Feminist Literary Magazine Society, P.O. Box 46160, Station D, Vancouver BC V6J 5G5, Canada. **E-mail:** contactus@roommagazine.com. **Website:** www.roommagazine.com. "*Room* is Canada's oldest feminist literary journal. Published quarterly by a collective based in Vancouver, *Room* showcases fiction, poetry, reviews, artwork, interviews, and profiles by writers and artists who identify as women or genderqueer. Many of our contributors are at the beginning of their writing careers, looking for an opportunity to get published for the first time. Some later go on to great acclaim. *Room* is a space where women can speak, connect, and showcase their creativity. Each quarter we publish original, thought-provoking works that reflect women's strength, sensuality, vulnerability, and wit." Buys first rights. Pays on publication. Responds in 6 months. Sample copy: $12 or online at website.

○ *Room* is digest-sized; contains illustrations, photos. Press run is 1,600 (900 subscribers, 50-100 libraries, 100-350 shelf sales).

MAGAZINES NEEDS *Room* uses "poetry by women, including trans and genderqueer writers, written from a feminist perspective. Nothing simplistic, cliché. We prefer to receive up to 5 poems at a time, so we can select a pair or group." Submit via online submissions manager. Pays $50-120 CAD, 2 contributor's copies, and a one-year subscription.

ROSEBUD

N3310 Asje Rd., Cambridge WI 53523. (608)423-9780. **Website:** www.rsbd.net. Poetry Editor Emeritus & Senior Advisor: John Smelcer. Founder and Advisor: John Lehman.. **Contact:** Rod Clark, managing editor & publisher. *Rosebud*, published 2-3 times/year has presented many of the most prominent voices in the nation and has been listed as among the very best markets for writers. Publishes fiction, poetry, and art. Since 2018, Rosebud includes a full-color section featuring art, including graphic art. Rosebud administers a number of literary prizes each year. Responds in 45 days. Sample copy: $7.95. Subscription: $20 for 3 issues, $35 for 6 issues. Guidelines online.

○ *Rosebud* is elegantly printed with full-color cover. Press run is 5,000.

MAGAZINES NEEDS Wants poetry that avoids "excessive or well-worn abstractions, not to mention clichés. Present a unique and convincing world (you can do this in a few words!) by means of fresh and exact imagery, and by interesting use of syntax. Explore the deep reaches of metaphor. But don't forget to be playful and have fun with words." E-mail up to 5 poetry submissions to poetry editor John Smelcer at jesmelcer@aol.com.

ALSO OFFERS Sponsors The William Stafford Poetry Award and the X.J. Kennedy Award for Creative Nonfiction. Guidelines for both available on website.

TIPS "Each issue has 6 or 7 flexible departments (selected from a total of 16 departments that rotate). We are seeking stories; articles; profiles; and poems of love, alienation, travel, humor, nostalgia, and unexpected revelation. Something has to 'happen' in the pieces we choose, but what happens inside characters is much more interesting to us than plot manipulation. We like good storytelling, real emotion, and authentic voice."

⑤ THE SAINT ANN'S REVIEW

Saint Ann's School, 129 Pierrepont St., Brooklyn NY 11201. Best to email. **Fax:** (718)522-2599. **E-mail:** sareview@saintannsny.org. **Website:** www.saintannsreview.com. "*The Saint Ann's Review* publishes short fiction, poetry, essays, drama, novel excerpts, reviews, translations, interviews, and experimental works." Buys first North American serial rights. Pays on publication. Publishes ms an average of 4 months after acceptance. Responds up to 4-6 months to mss. Sample copy: $8. Guidelines online.

○ We seek honed work that conveys a sense of its necessity.

MAGAZINES NEEDS Guidelines available online. Length: up to 10 pages. Pays $50/contributor and 2 contributor copies.

⑤ ST. ANTHONY MESSENGER

Franciscan Media, 28 W. Liberty St., Cincinnati OH 45202-6498. (513)241-5615. **Fax:** (513)241-0399. **E-mail:** magazineeditors@franciscanmedia.org. **Website:** www.stanthonymessenger.org. **Contact:** Pat McCloskey, OFM, Franciscan Editor. *St. Anthony Messenger* is a Catholic family magazine which aims to help its readers lead more fully human and Christian lives. "We publish articles that report on a changing church and world, opinion pieces written from the perspective of Christian faith and values, personality profiles, and fiction which entertains and informs. Take our writer's guidelines very seriously. We do!" Buys first North American serial rights, buys electronic rights, buys first worldwide serial rights. Pays on acceptance. Publishes ms within an average of 1 year after acceptance. Responds in 3 weeks to queries; 2 months to mss. Sample copy for 9x12 SAE with 4 first-class stamps. Please study writer's guidelines at StAnthonyMessenger.org.

MAGAZINES NEEDS Submit a few poems at a time. "Please include your phone number and a SASE with your submission. Do not send us your entire collection of poetry. Poems must be original." Submit seasonal poems several months in advance. "Our poetry needs are very limited." Length: up to 20-25 lines; "the shorter, the better." Pays $2/line; $20 minimum.

TIPS "The freelancer should consider why his or her proposed article would be appropriate for us, rather than for *Redbook* or *Saturday Review*. We treat human problems of all kinds, but from a religious perspective. Articles should reflect Catholic theology, spirituality, and employ a Catholic terminology and vocabulary. We need more articles on prayer, scripture, Catholic worship. Get authoritative information (not merely library research); we want interviews with experts. Write in popular style; use lots of examples, stories, and personal quotes. Word length is an important consideration."

SALMAGUNDI

Skidmore College, 815 N. Broadway, Saratoga Springs NY 12866. **Fax:** (518)580-5188. **E-mail:** salmagun@skidmore.edu. **Website:** https://salmagundi.skidmore.edu. Circulation Manager: Kara Sage. Editor: Robert Boyers. Executive Editor: Peg Boyers.. **Contact:** Marc Woodworth, associate editor. "*Salmagundi* publishes an eclectic variety of materials, ranging from short-short fiction to novellas from the surreal to the realistic, as well as poems, essays, symposia and interviews. Authors include Allan Gurganus, Phillip Lopate, Lincoln Perry, Max Nelson, David Bromwich, J.M. Coetzee, Russell Banks, Rick Moody, Binnie Kirschenbaum, Akeel Bilgrami, Carolyn Forché, Chase Twichell, Linda Pastan, Debora Greger, William Logan, Bina Gogenini, Thomas Chatterton Williams, Marilynne Robinson, Orlando Patterson, Gordon Lish, Anthony Appiah, Clark Blaise, Henri Cole, Mary Gordon, Frank Bidart, Louise Glück, George Steiner, Robert Pinsky, Joyce Carol Oates, Mary Gaitskill, Amy Hempel, Nadine Gordimer, George Scialabba, Rochelle Gurstein, Catherine Pond, Richard Howard, Jennifer Delton and Cynthia Ozick. Our audience is a generally literate population of people who read for pleasure and enjoy the occasional bracing argument." Magazine: 8x5; illustrations; photos. *Salmagundi* authors are regularly represented in *Pushcart* collections and *Best American Short Story* collections. Reading period: November 1-December 1. Acquires first rights, electronic rights. Publishes ms up to 2 years after acceptance. Responds in 1 year to mss. "If you do not hear back from us within 1 year, it means we did not find a space for your work in our magazine." Sample copy: $5. only for U.S. addresses Guidelines on website.

MAGAZINES NEEDS Submit up to 6 poems in hard copy via snail mail only with SASE. Pays 6-10 contributor's copies and one-year subscription.

TIPS "I look for excellence and a very unpredictable ability to appeal to the interests and tastes of the editors. Be brave. Don't be discouraged by rejection. Keep stories in circulation. Of course, it goes without saying: Work hard on the writing. Revise tirelessly. Study other magazines as well as this one, and send only to those whose sensibility matches yours."

SALT HILL JOURNAL

Creative Writing Program, Syracuse University, English Department, 401 Hall of Languages, Syracuse University, Syracuse NY 13244. **E-mail:** salthilljournal@gmail.com. **E-mail:** salthill.submittable.com. **Website:** salthilljournal.net. Ariel Chu, social media editor. **Contact:** Ariel Chu, Myriam Lacroix, Rainie Oet, Ally Young, editors-in-chief. *Salt Hill* is a biannual literary journal publishing outstanding new fiction, poetry, creative nonfiction, and art by people at various stages in their literary and artistic careers. We publish new and emerging writers alongside those with long, illustrious careers in the literary arts. Previous contributors include Terrance Hayes, Patricia Smith, Eduardo C. Corral, Laura Kasischke, W. S. Merwin, Aimee Nezhukumatathil, Mary Ruefle, Sam Sax, Charles Simic, James Tate, Jean Valentine, Dean Young, and even Stephen King, among so many brilliant others. *Salt Hill* is produced by writers in and affiliated with the Graduate Creative Writing Program at Syracuse University and is funded in part by the College of Arts & Sciences and the Graduate Student Organization of Syracuse University. Guidelines online.

○ We are interested in work that shines, work that represents a broad spectrum of experience, and work that makes us feel in new and exciting ways. In order to put out the best magazine we can, full of all that is glimmering, we believe it is critical to lift up the voices of writers and artists who have been traditionally underrepresented in the literary arts. As such, we feel a strong urgency to read and consider work by people of color, women, queer/trans people, non-binary folks, and anyone else who has been marginalized by the institutions which have, for so long, dominated the publishing scene.

MAGAZINES NEEDS Submit up to 5 poems via online submissions manager; contact poetry editor via e-mail for retractions and queries only.

THE SAME

P.O. Box 494, Mount Union PA 17066. **E-mail:** editors@thesamepress.com. **E-mail:** submissions@thesamepress.com. **Website:** www.thesamepress.com. **Contact:** Nancy Eldredge, managing editor. *The Same*, published biannually, prints nonfiction (essays, reviews, literary criticism), poetry, and short fiction. Acquires first North American serial rights and on-line rights for up to 9 months; returns rights to author. Publishes ms 11 months after acceptance. Responds within 6 months. Single copy: $8; subscription: $16 for 2 issues, $30 for 4 issues.

○ *The Same* is 50-100 pages, desktop-published, perfect-bound.

MAGAZINES NEEDS "We want eclectic poetry (formal to free verse, 'mainstream' to experimental, all subject matter.)" Submit 3-5 poems at a time. No previously published poems or simultaneous submissions without query. Prefers e-mail submissions as attachments. Cover letter is optional. Include SASE if you want a snail-mail response. "If you don't want your ms returned, you may omit the SASE if we can respond by e-mail. Please query before submitting fiction and non-fiction. Submissions are read year round. Length: up to 120 lines/poem. Pays 1 contributor's copy.

THE SANDY RIVER REVIEW

University of Maine at Farmington, 114 Prescott St., Farmington ME 04938. **E-mail:** thesandyriverreview@gmail.com. **E-mail:** sandyriversubmissions@gmail.com. **Website:** sandyriverreview.com. **Contact:** Alexandra Dupuis and Elayna Chamberlin, print editors; Richard Southard and Meagan Jones, the River editors. "*The Sandy River Review* seeks prose, poetry, and art submissions once a year for our annual print issue. *The River*, our regularly flowing stream of high-quality digital content, accepts these as well, along with podcasts and music. Deadline for the print issue is in December, while *The River* has rolling submissions. Prose submissions may be either fiction or creative nonfiction and should be a maximum of 3,500 words in length, 12-point, Times New Roman font, and double-spaced. Most of our art is published in b&w and must be submitted as 300-dpi quality, CMYK color mode, and saved as a TIFF file. We publish a wide variety of work from students as well as professional, established writers. Your submission should be polished and imaginative with strongly drawn characters and an interesting, original narrative. The review is the face of the University of Maine at Farmington's venerable BFA Creative Writing program, and we strive for the highest quality prose and poetry standard." Rights for the work return to the writer once published. Pays on publication. Publishes 2-3 months after acceptance. Guidelines online.

MAGAZINES NEEDS Submit via e-mail.

TIPS "We recommend that you take time with your piece. As with all submissions to a literary journal, submissions should be fully completed, polished final drafts that require minimal to no revision once accepted. Double-check your prose pieces for basic grammatical errors before submitting."

SANSKRIT LITERARY ARTS MAGAZINE

UNC Charlotte, Student Union 045, 9201 University City Blvd., Charlotte NC 28223. (704)687-7141. **E-mail:** editor@sanskritmagazine.com. **Website:** sanskritmagazine.com. **Contact:** Melissa Martin, editor in chief. *Sanskrit* is a collection of poems, short stories, and art from people all around the world, including students. All of the work goes through a selection process that includes staff and university professors. Finally, each year, the magazine has a theme. This theme is completely independent from the work and is chosen by the editor as a design element to unify the magazine. The theme is kept secret until the return of the magazine in April. Responds to mss and poems by January. Guidelines online.

○ *Sanskrit* is UNC Charlotte's nationally recognized, award-winning literary arts magazine. It is published once a year in April. Submissions deadline: first Friday in November.

MAGAZINES NEEDS Submit up to 15 poems by mail or through online submissions manager. Cover letter is required. Include 30- to 70-word third-person bio. Do not list previous publications as a bio. Pays 1 contributor's copy.

⑤ THE SARANAC REVIEW

Dept. of English, SUNY Plattsburgh, 101 Broad St., Plattsburgh NY 12901. (518)564-2241. **Fax:** (518)564-2140. **E-mail:** saranacreview@plattsburgh.edu. **Website:** www.saranacreview.com. **Contact:** Aimee Baker, executive editor. "*The Saranac Review* is committed to dissolving boundaries of all kinds, seeking to publish a diverse array of emerging and established writers from Canada and the U.S. *The Saranac Review* aims to be a textual clearing in which a space is opened for cross-pollination between American and Canadian writers. In this way the magazine reflects the expansive, bright spirit of the etymology of its name, Saranac, meaning 'cluster of stars.' *The Saranac Review* is digest-sized, with color photo or painting on cover. Publishes both digital and print-on-demand versions. Has published Lawrence Raab, Jacob M. Appel, Marilyn Nelson, Tom Wayman, Colette Inez, Louise Warren, Brian Campbell, Gregory Pardlo, Myfanwy Collins, William Giraldi, Xu Xi, Julia Alvarez, and other fine emerging and established writers." Published annually. Purchases first North American serial rights. Pays on publication. Publishes ms 8 months-1 year after acceptance. Responds in 4-6 months to mss. Sample copy: $4.95. Guidelines online.

MAGAZINES NEEDS "We're open to most forms and styles. We want poetry that, to paragraph Dickinson, blows the top of your head off, and that, in Williams's view, prevents us from dying miserably every day." Submit 3-5 poems via online submissions manager. Length: up to 4 pages but typically 20-25 lines. Pays $10/published page.

⑤ SCIFAIKUEST

Alban Lake Publishing, P.O. Box 782, Cedar Rapids IA 52406. **E-mail:** gatrix65@yahoo.com. **Website:** https://www.albanlakepublishing.com/. **Contact:** Tyree Campbell, managing editor; Teri Santitoro, editor. *Scifaikuest*, published quarterly both online and in print, features "science fiction/fantasy/horror minimalist poetry, especially scifaiku, and related forms. We also publish articles about various poetic forms and reviews of poetry collections. The online and print versions of *Scifaikuest* are different." *Scifaikuest* (print edition) is 32 pages, digest-sized, offset-printed, perfect-bound, with color cardstock cover, includes ads. Receives about 500 poems/year, accepts about 160 (32%). Press run is 100/issue; 5 distributed free to reviewers. Member: The Speculative Literature Foundation. Acquires first North American serial rights. Time between acceptance and publication is 1-2 months. Responds in 6-8 weeks. Single copy: $7; subscription: $20/year, $37 for 2 years. Make checks payable to Tyree Campbell/Alban Lake Publishing. Guidelines online.

MAGAZINES NEEDS Wants artwork, scifaiku, and speculative minimalist forms such as tanka, haibun, ghazals, senryu. Submit no more than 10 poems at a time. Accepts e-mail submissions (pasted into body of message). No disk submissions; artwork as e-mail attachment or inserted body of e-mail. Submission should include snail-mail address, email address, PayPal address and a short (1-2 lines) bio. Reads submissions year round. Editor Teri Santitoro makes all decisions regarding acceptances. Often comments on rejected poems. Has published poetry by Tom Brinck, Oino Sakai, Deborah P. Kolodji, Aurelio Rico Lopez III, Joanne Morcom, and John Dunphy. No 'traditional'

poetry. Length: varies, depending on poem type. Pays $1/poem, $6/review or article, and 1 contributor's copy.

SCREAMINMAMAS

Harmoni Productions, LLC, 1911 Cleveland St., Hollywood FL 33020. **E-mail:** screaminmamas@gmail.com. **Website:** www.screaminmamas.com. **Contact:** Darlene Pistocchi, editor; Lena, submissions coordinator. "We are the voice of everyday moms. We share their stories, revelations, humorous rants, photos, talent, children, ventures, etc." Acquires one-time rights. Publishes ms 1-3 months after acceptance. Responds in 3-6 weeks to queries; 1-3 months on mss. Editorial lead time: 3 months. Available for purchase by request. Sample submissions available online. Guidelines online.

MAGAZINES NEEDS Length: 2-20 lines.

TIPS "Visit our submissions page and themes page on our website."

THE SEATTLE REVIEW

Box 354330, University of Washington, Seattle WA 98195. (206)543-2302. **E-mail:** seattlereview@gmail.com. **Website:** www.seattlereview.org. **Contact:** Andrew Feld, editor in chief. *The Seattle Review* includes poetry, fiction, and creative nonfiction. Buys first North American serial rights. Pays on publication. Responds in 2-4 months to mss. Subscriptions: $20 for 3 issues, $32 for 5 issues. Back issue: $6. Guidelines available online.

○ *The Seattle Review* will only publish long works. Poetry must be 10 pages or longer, and prose must be 40 pages or longer. *The Seattle Review* is 8x10; 175-250 pages. Receives 200 unsolicited mss/month. Accepts 10-15 mss/issue; 20-30 mss/year. Publishes ms 6 months-1 year after acceptance.

MAGAZINES NEEDS "We are looking for exceptional, risk-taking, intellectual, and imaginative poems between 10 and 30 pages in length." *The Seattle Review* will publish, and will only publish, long poems and novellas. The long poem can be a single long poem in its entirety, a self-contained excerpt from a book-length poem, or a unified sequence or series of poems. Accepts electronic submissions only. Pays 2 contributor's copies and 1-year subscription.

TIPS "Know what we publish; no genre fiction. Look at our magazine and decide if your work might be appreciated. Beginners do well in our magazine if they send clean, well-written manuscripts. We've published a lot of 'first stories' from all over the country and take pleasure in discovery."

💲 THE SECRET PLACE

P.O. Box 851, Valley Forge PA 19482. (610)768-2434. **Fax:** (610)768-2441. **E-mail:** thesecretplace@abc-usa. org. **Website:** www.judsonpress.com/catalog_secret-place.cfm. Buys first rights. Pays on acceptance. Editorial lead time 1 to 2 years. Guidelines online.

MAGAZINES NEEDS Submit up to 6 poems by mail or e-mail. E-mail preferred. Length: 4-30 lines/poem. Pays $20.

TIPS "Prefers submissions via e-mail."

SEEMS

Lakeland University, W 3718 South Dr., Plymouth WI 53073-4878. (920)565-1000 x2295 or (920)565-3871. **Fax:** (920)565-1206. **E-mail:** seems@lakeland. edu. **Website:** seemsmagazine.wixsite.com/seems. *SEEMS*, published irregularly, prints poetry, fiction, and essays. Focuses on work that integrates economy of language, "the musical phrase," forms of resemblance, and the sentient. Will consider unpublished poetry, fiction, and creative nonfiction. See the editor's website at www.karlelder.com. "Links to my work and an interview may provide insight for the potential contributor." Acquires first North American serial rights and permission to publish online. Returns rights upon publication. Responds in 4 months (slower in the summer). Guidelines online.

MAGAZINES NEEDS Submit by mail or e-mail. Cover letter is optional. Include biographical information, SASE. Reads submissions year round. "People may call or fax with virtually any question, understanding that the editor may have no answer." Guidelines available on website. Length: open. Pays 1 contributor's copy.

SENECA REVIEW

Hobart and William Smith Colleges, 300 Pulteney St., Geneva NY 14456. (315)781-3392. **Website:** www. hws.edu/senecareview/index.aspx. The editors have special interest in translations of contemporary poetry from around the world. Publisher of numerous laureates and award-winning poets, *Seneca Review* also publishes emerging writers and is always open to new, innovative work. Poems from *SR* are regularly honored by inclusion in *The Best American Poetry* and *Pushcart Prize* anthologies. Distributed internationally. Responds in 6-9 months. Guidelines available online.

💬 Reading period is March 1-May 1.

MAGAZINES NEEDS Submit 3-5 poems through online submissions manager or postal mail. Pays 2 contributor's copies and two-year subscription.

💲 SEQUESTRUM

E-mail: sequr.info@gmail.com. **Website:** www.sequestrum.org. **Contact:** R.M. Cooper, managing editor. All publications are paired with a unique visual component. Regularly holds contests and features well-known authors, as well as promising new and emerging voices. Buys first North American serial rights and electronic rights. Pays on acceptance. Publishes ms 2-6 months after acceptance. Editorial lead time: 3 months. Sample copy available for free online. Guidelines online.

MAGAZINES NEEDS Length: 40 lines. Pays $10/set of poems.

TIPS "Reading a past issue goes a long way; there's little excuse not to. Our entire archive is available online to preview, and subscription rates are variable. Send your best, most interesting work. General submissions are always open, and we regularly hold contests and offer awards which are themed."

💲 THE SEWANEE REVIEW

735 University Ave, Sewanee TN 37383. (931)598-1185. **E-mail:** sewaneereview@sewanee.edu. **Website:** thesewaneereview.com. **Contact:** Adam Ross, editor. *The Sewanee Review* is America's oldest continuously published literary quarterly. Publishes original fiction, poetry, essays, and interviews. Does not accept submissions June 1-Aug 31. Buys first North American print and online rights, second serial (reprint) rights. Pays on publication. Responds in 10 weeks Sample copy: $12. Guidelines online.

MAGAZINES NEEDS Submit up to 6 poems via online submissions manager. Pays $3.33/line, $100 minimum.

🐚 SHEARSMAN

Shearsman Books Ltd., 50 Westons Hill Dr., Emersons Green, Bristol BS16 7DF, United Kingdom. **E-mail:** editor@shearsman.com. **Website:** www.shearsman.com. **Contact:** Tony Frazer, editor. "We are inclined toward the more exploratory end of the current spectrum. Notwithstanding this, however, quality work of a more conservative kind will always be considered seriously, provided that the work is well written. I always look for some rigor in the work, though I will be more forgiving of failure in this regard if the writer is trying to push out the boundaries." Publishes ms an average of 3 months after acceptance. Responds in 3 months. Guidelines online.

MAGAZINES NEEDS Avoid sending attachments with e-mails unless they are in PDF format. For mailed submissions, include SASE; no IRCs. If submitting from outside the U.K., try to permit replies by e-mail. No poetry for children. No religious or devotional poetry. No length restrictions. Pays 2 contributor's copies.

TIPS "We no longer read through the year. Our reading window for magazines is March 1 through March 31 for the October issue and September 1 through September 30 for the April issue; this window is for magazine submissions only. See guidelines online."

SHEMOM

2486 Montgomery Ave., Cardiff CA 92007. **E-mail:** peggydfrench@gmail.com. **Website:** peggydugan-french.com. **Contact:** Peggy French, editor. *Shemom*, published 3 times/year, is a zine that showcases a wide variety of writers reflecting on life's varied experiences. Includes poetry, haiku, and occasional essays. Open to any style, but prefers free verse. "We like to hear from anyone who has a story to tell and will read anything you care to send our way." *Shemom* is 20-30 pages. Receives about 200 poems/year, accepts 50%. Press run is 60 (30 subscribers). Acquires one-time rights. Publishes ms 3 months after acceptance. Responds in 1 month. Single copy: $4; subscription: $12/3 issues. Make checks payable to Peggy French. Guidelines for SASE.

MAGAZINES NEEDS Submit 3-10 poems at a time. Accepts e-mail submissions (as attachment or pasted into body of message). "Prefer e-mail submission, but not required; if material is to be returned, please include an SASE." Pays 1 contributor's copy.

SHENANDOAH

Washington and Lee University, Lexington VA 24450. (540)458-8908. **E-mail:** shenandoah@wlu.edu. **Website:** shenandoahliterary.org. **Contact:** Beth Staples, editor. For nearly 70 years, *Shenandoah* has been publishing poems, stories, essays, and reviews which display passionate understanding, formal accomplishment, and serious mischief. As of 2018, under new editor Beth Staples, *Shenandoah* aims to to showcase a wide variety of voices and perspectives in terms of gender identity, race, ethnicity, class, age, ability, nationality, regionality, sexuality, and educational background. We're excited to consider short stories,

essays, excerpts of novels in progress, poems, comics, and translations of all the above. Buys first North American serial rights, one-time rights. Pays on publication. Publishes ms an average of 10 months after acceptance. Responds in 8 weeks to mss. Sample copy online. Guidelines online.

MAGAZINES NEEDS Submit 3-7 poems via online submissions manager. Pays $100/poem.

SIERRA NEVADA REVIEW

999 Tahoe Blvd., Incline Village NV 89451. **E-mail:** sncreview@sierranevada.edu. **Website:** blog.sierranevada.edu/sierranevadareview. "*Sierra Nevada Review*, published annually in May, features poetry, short fiction, and literary nonfiction by new and established writers. Wants "writing that leans toward the unconventional, surprising, and risky." Reads submissions September 1-February 15 only. Responds in 3 months. Guidelines online.

MAGAZINES NEEDS Submit up to 5 poems at a time or 5 pages, whichever comes first. Pays 2 contributor's copies.

SINISTER WISDOM

2333 McIntosh Rd., Dover FL 33527. (813)502-5549. **E-mail:** julie@sinisterwisdom.org. **Website:** www.sinisterwisdom.org. *Sinister Wisdom* is a quarterly lesbian-feminist journal providing fiction, poetry, drama, essays, journals, and artwork. Past issues include "Lesbians of Color," "Old Lesbians/Dykes," and "The Lesbian Body." *Sinister Wisdom* is 5.5x8.5; 128-144 pages; 55 lb. stock; 10 pt. C1S cover; with illustrations, photos. Acquires one-time rights. Publishes ms 1 year after acceptance. Responds in 6 months to mss. Sample copy: $12. Guidelines online.

MAGAZINES NEEDS Submit up to 5 poems. Strongly prefers submissions through online submissions manager. Pays 1 contributor's copy and one-year subscription.

TIPS *Sinister Wisdom* is "a multicultural lesbian journal reflecting the art, writing, and politics of our communities."

SKIPPING STONES

A Multicultural Literary Magazine, Skipping Stones. Inc., P.O. Box 3939, Eugene OR 97403-0939. (541)342-4956. **E-mail:** editor@skippingstones.org. **Website:** www.skippingstones.org. **Contact:** Arun Toké, editor. "*Skipping Stones* is an award-winning multicultural, nonprofit magazine designed to promote cooperation, creativity and celebration of cultural and ecological richness. We encourage submissions by children of color, minorities and under-represented populations. We want material meant for children and young adults/teenagers with multicultural or ecological awareness themes. Think, live and write as if you were a child, tween or teen. We want material that gives insight to cultural celebrations, lifestyle, customs and traditions, glimpse of daily life in other countries and cultures. Photos, songs, artwork are most welcome if they illustrate/highlight the points. Translations are invited if your submission is in a language other than English." Themes may include cultural celebrations, living abroad, challenging disability, hospitality customs of various cultures, cross-cultural understanding, African, Asian and Latin American cultures, humor, international understanding, turning points and magical moments in life, caring for the earth, spirituality, and multicultural awareness. *Skipping Stones* is magazine-sized, saddle-stapled, printed on recycled paper. Published quarterly during the school year (4 issues). Buys first North American serial rights, nonexclusive reprint, and electronic rights. Publishes ms an average of 4-8 months after acceptance. Responds only if interested. Send nonreturnable samples. Editorial lead time 3-4 months. Sample: $7. Subscription: $25. Guidelines available online or for SASE.

MAGAZINES NEEDS Submit up to 5 poems at a time. Considers simultaneous submissions; no previously published poems. Accepts e-mail submissions. Cover letter is preferred. "Include your cultural background, experiences, and the inspiration behind your creation." Time between acceptance and publication is 6-9 months. "A piece is chosen for publication when most of the editorial staff feel good about it." Seldom comments on rejected poems. Publishes multi-theme issues. Responds in up to 4 months. Poems by youth under the age of 19 only. Length: 30 lines maximum. Pays 2 contributor's copies, offers 40% discount for more copies and subscription, if desired.

CONTEST/AWARD OFFERINGS Sponsors annual youth honor awards for 7- to 17-year-olds. Theme is "multicultural, social, international, and nature awareness." Guidelines available for SASE or on website. Entry fee: $5 (entitles entrant to a free issue featuring the 10 winners). Deadline: June 25.

TIPS "Be original and innovative. Use multicultural, nature, or cross-cultural themes. Multilingual submissions are welcome."

SLANT

A Journal of Poetry, University of Central Arkansas, P.O. Box 5063, Conway AR 72035-5000. (501)450-5107. E-mail: jamesf@uca.edu. **Website:** uca.edu/english/slant-a-journal-of-poetry. **Contact:** James Fowler, editor. *Slant: A Journal of Poetry*, published annually in May, aims "to publish a journal of fine poetry from all regions of the U.S. and beyond." *Slant* is 112 pages, professionally printed on quality linen stock, flat-spined, with matte card cover. Receives about 925 poems/year, accepts 70-75. Press run is 170 (65-70 subscribers). Accepts submissions September 1-November 15. Rights revert to poet after publication. Publishes ms 6 months after acceptance. Responds in 3 months from November 15 deadline. Sample: $10. Guidelines available in magazine, for SASE, or on website.

MAGAZINES NEEDS Wants traditional and 'modern' poetry, even experimental; moderate length, any subject on approval of Board of Readers. Doesn't want previously published poems, single haiku, translations. Submit up to 5 poems at a time. Submissions should be typed; include SASE. Put name, address (including e-mail if available), and phone number at the top of each page. Comments on rejected poems on occasion. Has published poetry by Mark Brazaitis, Holly Day, Marc Jampole, Sandra Kohler, Mary Makofske, and Charles Harper Webb. Poems should be of moderate length (up to 100 lines). Pays 1 contributor's copy (print for US poets, digital for international).

SLIPSTREAM

P.O. Box 2071, Dept. W-1, Niagara Falls NY 14301. **E-mail:** editors@slipstreampress.org. **Website:** www.slipstreampress.org. **Contact:** Dan Sicoli, co-editor. All rights revert to author/artist on publication. Sample copy $10. Guidelines online.

Does not accept e-mail submissions.

MAGAZINES NEEDS Submit poetry via mail or online submissions manager. Prefers contemporary urban themes—writing from the grit that is not afraid to bark or bite. Shies away from pastoral, religious, and rhyming verse. Pays 1 contributor's copy.

CONTEST/AWARD OFFERINGS Also offers Chapbook Contest prize: $1,000 plus 50 professionally printed copies of your chapbook. Submit up to 40 pages of poetry: any style, format, or theme. Deadline: December 1.

SNREVIEW

E-mail: editor@snreview.org. **Website:** www.snreview.org. **Contact:** Joseph Conlin, editor. *SNReview* is a quarterly literary e-zine created for writers of non-genre fiction, nonfiction, and poetry. Quarterly. Acquires first electronic and print rights. Publishes ms 3 months after acceptance. Responds in 1 year to mss. Sample copy and guidelines online.

MAGAZINES NEEDS Submit via e-mail; label the e-mail "SUB: Poetry." Copy and paste work into the body of the e-mail. Don't send attachments. Include 100-word bio and list of publications. Length: up to 200 words/poem.

THE SOCIETY OF CLASSICAL POETS JOURNAL

The Society of Classical Poets, 11 Heather Ln., Mount Hope NY 10940. **E-mail:** submissions@classicalpoets.org. **Website:** www.classicalpoets.org. **Contact:** Evan Mantyk, president. Annual literary magazine, published in book format, that features poetry, essays, and artwork. Interested in poetry with rhyme and meter. Believes in reviving classical poetry and classical arts. Acquires electronic and reprint rights. Publishes ms an average of 6 months after acceptance. Responds in 1 weeks to queries; 1 month to mss. Editorial lead time is 2 months. Guidelines available for SASE.

MAGAZINES NEEDS Some type of meter, such as iambic pentameter, is preferred but not absolutely required. If you want feedback on your submission, indicate it on the submission. Accepts poetry only on 5 themes (generally): beauty (in human nature, culture, the natural world, classical art forms, and the divine), great culture (good figures, stories, and other elements from classical history and literature), persecution of Falun Dafa practitioners in China (and plight of the world under communism in general), humor (clean humor only, including riddles), and translations. Also will consider short stories, essays, art, news, and videos on the above themes. Does not want free verse. Does not offer payment.

SONORA REVIEW

University of Arizona, Dept. of English, Tucson AZ 85721. **Website:** sonorareview.com/. "We look for the highest-quality poetry, fiction, and nonfiction, with an emphasis on emerging writers. Our magazine has a long-standing tradition of publishing the best new literature and writers. Check out our website for a sample of what we publish and our submission guidelines." Acquires first North American serial rights, one-time rights, electronic rights. Publishes ms an average of 3-4 months after acceptance. Responds in 3-6 months to mss. Sample copy: $6. Guidelines online.

MAGAZINES NEEDS Submit up to 5 poems in 1 document via online submissions manager. Pays 2 contributor's copies.

SO TO SPEAK

George Mason University, 4400 University Dr., MSN 2C5, Fairfax VA 22030. **E-mail:** sotospeak@sotospeakjournal.org. **Website:** sotospeakjournal.org. **Contact:** Kristen Brida, editor in chief. *So to Speak*, published semiannually, prints "high-quality work relating to feminism, including poetry, fiction, nonfiction (including book reviews and interviews), photography, artwork, collaborations, lyrical essays, and other genre-questioning texts." Wants "work that addresses issues of significance to women's lives and movements for women's equality. Especially interested in pieces that explore issues of race, class, and sexuality in relation to gender." Acquires first electronic, anthology, and archival rights. Publishes ms 6-8 months after acceptance. Responds in 6 months to mss. Sample copy: $7; subscription: $12.

○ *So to Speak* is 100-128 pages, digest-sized, photo-offset-printed, perfect-bound, with glossy cover; includes ads. Press run is 1,000 (75 subscribers, 100 shelf sales); 500 distributed free to students/contributors. Reads submissions September 15-November 15 for spring issue and January 1-April 15 for fall issue.

MAGAZINES NEEDS Submit up to 5 poems via online submissions manager. Pays 2 contributor's copies.

TIPS "Every writer has something they do exceptionally well; do that and it will shine through in the work. We look for quality prose with a definite appeal to a feminist audience. We are trying to move away from strict genre lines. We want high-quality fiction, nonfiction, poetry, art, innovative and risk-taking work."

SOUL FOUNTAIN

E-mail: soulfountain@antarcticajournal.com. **Website:** www.antarcticajournal.com/soul-fountain/. **Contact:** Tone Bellizzi, editor. *Soul Fountain* is produced by The Antarctica Journal, a not-for-profit arts project of the Hope for the Children Foundation, committed to empowering young and emerging artists of all disciplines at all levels to develop and share their talents through performance, collaboration, and networking. Digitally publishes poetry, art, photography, short fiction, and essays on the antarcticajournal.com website. Open to all. Publishes quality submitted work, and specializes in emerging voices. Favors visionary, challenging, and consciousness-expanding material. Guidelines online.

MAGAZINES NEEDS Submit 2-3 poems by e-mail. No cover letters, please. Does not want poems about pets, nature, romantic love, or the occult. Sex and violence themes not welcome. Welcomes poetry by teens.

SOUNDINGS EAST

Salem State University, English Department, MH249, 352 Lafayette St., Salem MA 01970. **E-mail:** soundingseast@salemstate.edu. **Website:** www.salemstate.edu/soundingseast. **Contact:** Kevin Carey (kcarey@salemstate.edu). *Soundings East* is the literary journal of Salem State University, published annually with support from the Center for Creative and Performing Arts. Responds in 3 months to mss. Guidelines available online.

Reading period: September 1-Feburary 15.

MAGAZINES NEEDS Submit up to 5 poems via online submissions manager or by postal mail.

THE SOUTH CAROLINA REVIEW

Center for Electronic and Digital Publishing, 801 Strode Tower, Clemson SC 29634-0522. **Fax:** (864)656-1345. **E-mail:** screv@clemson.edu. **Website:** http://www.clemson.edu/caah/sites/south-carolina-review/index.html. **Contact:** Elizabeth Stansell, managing editor (eander3@clemson.edu). Since 1968, *The South Carolina Review* has published fiction, poetry, interviews, unpublished letters and mss, essays, and reviews from well-known and aspiring scholars and writers. *The South Carolina Review* is 7.5 x 9.25; 150-200 pages. Semiannual. Does not read mss June-August or December. Responds in 2 months. Please send PDF manuscripts to screv@clemson.edu.

MAGAZINES NEEDS Submit 3-10 poems at a time in PDF or Word file. Cover letter is preferred. Do not submit during June, July, August, or December. Occasionally publishes theme issues.

THE SOUTHEAST REVIEW

Department of English, Florida State University, Tallahassee FL 32306. **E-mail:** southeastreview@gmail.com. **Website:** southeastreview.org. **Contact:** Alex Quinlan, editor in chief. "The mission of *The Southeast Review* is to present emerging writers on the same stage as well-established ones. In each semiannual issue, we publish literary fiction, creative nonfiction, poetry, interviews, book reviews, and art. With nearly 60 members on our editorial staff who come from throughout the country and the world, we strive to publish work that is representative of our diverse interests and aesthetics, and we celebrate the eclectic mix this produces. We receive approximately 400 submissions per month, and we accept less than 1-2% of them." Acquires first North America serial rights, which then revert to the author. Publishes ms 2-6 months after acceptance. Responds in 2-6 months.

Publishes 4-6 new (not previously published) writers/year. Accepts submissions year round, "though please be advised that the response time is slower during the summer months." Has published work by A.A. Balaskovits, Hannah Gamble, Michael Homolka, Brandon Lingle, and Colleen Morrissey.

MAGAZINES NEEDS Submit 3-5 poems at a time through online submissions manager. Reviews books and chapbooks of poetry. Please query the book review editor before submitting a book review. Pays 2 contributor's copies.

ALSO OFFERS Sponsors an annual poetry, nonfiction, and short fiction contest. Winner receives $1,000 and publication; 2-5 finalists will also be published in each category. **Entry fee:** $16 for 3 poems, 3 short stories, or 1 piece of narrative nonfiction. **Deadline:** March. Guidelines available on website.

TIPS "Avoid trendy experimentation for its own sake (present-tense narration, observation that isn't also revelation). Fresh stories, moving and interesting characters, and a sensitivity to language are still fiction mainstays. We also publish the winner and runners-up of the World's Best Short Story Contest, Poetry Contest, and Creative Nonfiction Contest."

SOUTHERN HUMANITIES REVIEW

Auburn University, 9088 Haley Center, Auburn University AL 36849. (334)844-9088. **Fax:** (334)844-9027. **E-mail:** shr@auburn.edu. **Website:** www.southernhumanitiesreview.com. **Contact:** Aaron Alford, managing editor. *Southern Humanities Review* publishes fiction, essays, and poetry. Acquires first American serial rights. Copyright reverts to author after publication. Sample copy: $8. Guidelines online.

ALSO OFFERS Sponsors the Theodore Christian Hoepfner Award, a $50 prize for the best poem published in a given volume of *Southern Humanities Review*.

SOUTHERN POETRY REVIEW

Department of Languages, Literature and Philosophy, Armstrong Atlantic State University, 11935 Abercorn St., Savannah GA 31419. **E-mail:** editor@southernpoetryreview.org. **Website:** www.southernpoetryreview.org. **Contact:** James Smith, editor. *Southern Poetry Review*, published twice a year, is one of the oldest poetry journals in America. Work appearing in *Southern Poetry Review* received 2005 and 2013 Pushcart Prizes. Often has poems selected for Poetry Daily (poems.com) and versedaily.org. Member: CLMP. *Southern Poetry Review* is 65-75 pages, digest-sized, perfect-bound, with 80 lb. matte card stock cover and b&w photography. Includes ads. Acquires one-time rights. Publishes ms 6 months after acceptance. Responds within 3 months. Single copy: $8. Guidelines available in journal, by SASE, by e-mail, or on website.

MAGAZINES NEEDS Wants "poetry eclectically representative of the genre; no restrictions on form, style, or content." Has published poetry by Claudia Emerson, Carl Dennis, Robert Morgan, Linda Pastan, A.E. Stallings, R.T. Smith, and David Wagoner. Submit through online submissions manager or by postal mail ("Include SASE for reply; ms returned only if sufficient postage is included. No international mail coupons. U.S. stamps only"). No e-mail submissions. Cover letter is preferred. Reads submissions year round. Sometimes comments on rejected poems. Sends prepublication galleys. Does not want fiction, essays, reviews, or interviews. Pays 1-2 contributor's copies.

CONTEST/AWARD OFFERINGS Sponsors annual Guy Owen Prize. Winner receives $1,000. Entry fee: $20. Deadline: May 31. See website for guidelines.

⊗ THE SOUTHERN REVIEW

338 Johnston Hall, Louisiana State University, Baton Rouge LA 70803. (225)578-6453. **Fax:** (225)578-6461. **E-mail:** southernreview@lsu.edu. **Website:** thesouthernreview.org. **Contact:** Jessica Faust, coeditor and poetry editor; Sacha Idell, coeditor and prose editor. "*The Southern Review* is one of the nation's premiere literary journals. Hailed by *Time* as 'superior to any other journal in the English language,' we have made literary history since our founding in 1935. We publish a diverse array of fiction, nonfiction, poetry, and translation by the country's—and the world's—most respected contemporary writers." Unsolicited submissions period: September 1 through December 1 (prose); September 1 through January 1 (poetry and translation). All mss submitted outside the reading period will be recycled. Buys first worldwide English-language serial rights. Pays on publication. Publishes ms an average of 7 months after acceptance. Responds in 6-11 months. Sample copy: $12. Guidelines online.

MAGAZINES NEEDS Has published poetry by Marilyn Nelson, Wendy Barker, David Hernandez, Piotr Florczyk, Charles Simic, Jill Osier, Charles Rafferty, and Maggie Smith. Submit poems through online submission form. Pays $50 for first page and $25 for each subsequent printed page (max $200); 2 contributor's copies, and 1-year subscription.

TIPS "Careful attention to craftsmanship and technique combined with a developed sense of the creation of story will always make us pay attention."

⊕ SOUTH POETRY MAGAZINE

P.O. Box 4228, Bracknell RG42 9PX, United Kingdom. **E-mail:** south@southpoetry.org. **Website:** www.southpoetry.org. *SOUTH Poetry Magazine*, published biannually in spring and autumn, is based in the southern counties of England. Poets from or about the South region are particularly welcome, but poets from all over the world are encouraged to submit work on all subjects. Has published poetry by Ian Caws, Stella Davis, Lyn Moir, Elsa Corbluth, Paul Hyland, and Sean Street. *SOUTH* is 68 pages, digest-sized, litho-printed, saddle-stapled, with gloss-laminated duotone cover. Receives about 1,500 poems/year; accepts about 120. Press run is 350 (250 subscribers). Publishes ms 2 months after acceptance. Single copy: £7; subscription: £12/year, £22 years. Make cheques (in sterling) payable to *SOUTH Poetry Magazine*. Guidelines online.

MAGAZINES NEEDS Submit up to 3 poems at a time by postal mail with submission form on website; send 2 copies of each poem submitted. Selection does not begin prior to the deadline and may take up to 8 weeks or more from that date. Deadlines are May 31 for the autumn issue and November 30 for the spring issue.

TIPS "Buy the magazine and read it. That way you will see the sort of work we publish and whether your work is likely to fit in. You'll also be contributing to its continued success."

SOUTHWESTERN AMERICAN LITERATURE

Center for the Study of the Southwest, Texas State University, Brazos Hall, 601 University Dr., San Marcos TX 78666-4616. (512)245-2224. **Fax:** (512)245-7462. **E-mail:** wj13@txstate.edu. **Website:** www.txstate.edu/cssw/publications/sal.html. **Contact:** William Jensen, editor. *Southwestern American Literature* is a biannual scholarly journal that includes literary criticism, fiction, poetry, and book & film reviews concerning the Greater Southwest. "We are interested only in material dealing with the **Southwest**." Responds in 3-6 months. "Please feel free to e-mail the editors after 6 months to check on the status of your work." Sample copy: $11. Guidelines online.

MAGAZINES NEEDS Generally speaking, we seek material covering the Greater Southwest. Length: no more than 100 lines. Pays 2 contributor's copies.

TIPS "**Fiction and poetry must deal with the greater Southwest.** We look for crisp language, an interesting approach to material. Read widely, write often, revise carefully. We seek stories that, as William Faulkner noted in his Nobel Prize acceptance speech, treat subjects central to good literature—the old verities of the human heart, such as honor and courage and pity and suffering, fear and humor, love and sorrow."

SOU'WESTER

Website: souwester.org. **Contact:** Joshua Kryah, poetry editor; Valerie Vogrin, prose editor. *Sou'wester* appears biannually in spring and fall. All rights revert to author on publication. Responds in 3 months. Sample copy: $8.

Sou'wester is professionally printed, flat-spined, with textured matte card cover, press run is 300 for 500 subscribers of which 50 are libraries. Open to submissions in mid-August for fall and spring issues.

MAGAZINES NEEDS Leans toward poetry with strong imagery, successful association of images, and skillful use of figurative language. Has published poetry by Robert Wrigley, Beckian Fritz Goldberg, Eric Pankey, Betsy Sholl, and Angie Estes. Submit up to 5 poems. Editor comments on rejected poems "usually, in the case of those that we almost accept." Pays 2 contributor's copies and a one-year subscription.

THE SOW'S EAR POETRY REVIEW

308 Greenfield Ave., Winchester VA 22602. **E-mail:** sepoetryreview@gmail.com. **Website:** sowsearpoetry. org. **Contact:** Kristin Camitta Zimet, editor; Sarah Kohrs, managing editor. *The Sow's Ear* prints fine poetry of all styles and lengths, complemented by b&w art. Also welcomes reviews, interviews, and essays related to poetry. Open to group submissions. "Crossover" section features poetry married to any other art form, including prose, music, and visual media. Acquires first publication rights. Publishes ms an average of 1-6 months after acceptance. Responds in 2 weeks to queries; 3 months to mss. Editorial lead time 1-6 months. Sample copy for $8. Guidelines available for SASE, by e-mail, or on website.

MAGAZINES NEEDS Considers simultaneous submissions "if you tell us promptly when work is accepted elsewhere"; no previously published poems, although will consider poems from chapbooks if they were never published in a magazine. Previously published poems may be included in Crossover if rights are cleared. No e-mail submissions, except for poets outside the US; postal submissions only. Include brief bio and SASE. Pays 2 contributor's copies. Inquire about reviews, interviews, and essays. Contest/Award offerings: *The Sow's Ear* Poetry Competition and *The Sow's Ear* Chapbook Contest. Open to any style or length. No limits on line length.

TIPS "We like work that is carefully crafted, keenly felt, and freshly perceived. We respond to poems with voice, a sense of place, delight in language, and a meaning that unfolds. We look for prose that opens new dimensions to appreciating poetry."

🚫 SPACE AND TIME

Website: www.spaceandtimemagazine.com. **Contact:** Hildy Silverman, publisher. *Space and Time* is the longest continually published small-press genre fiction magazine still in print. "We pride ourselves in having published the first stories of some of the great writers in science fiction, fantasy, and horror." Acquires first North American serial rights and one-time rights; includes electronic rights. All rights revert to author after publication. Pays on publication. Publishes stories/poems 6-12 months after acceptance. Sample copy: $6. Guidelines online. Only opens periodically—announcements of open reading periods appear on Facebook page and website. No fiction or poetry considered outside of open reading periods.

"We love stories that blend elements—horror and science fiction, fantasy with science fiction elements, etc. We challenge writers to try something new and send us their hard to classify works-—what other publications reject because the work doesn't fit in their 'pigeonholes.'"

MAGAZINES NEEDS "Multiple submissions are okay within reason (no more than 3 at a time). Submit embedded in an e-mail, a Word doc, or .rtf attachment. Only submit during open poetry reading periods, which are announced via the Facebook page and on the website. All other poetry submitted outside these reading periods will be rejected out of hand." Poetry without any sort of genre or speculative element. No longer than a single standard page. Pays $5/poem.

SPILLWAY

E-mail: spillway1@spillway.org. **E-mail:** spillway2@spillway.org; spillway3@spillway.org. **Website:** www.spillway.org. **Contact:** Marsha de la O and Phil Taggart, editors; Lynne Thompson, essay and book review editor. Published annually in June, *Spillway* celebrates "writing's diversity and power to affect our lives." Open to all voices, schools, and tendencies. *Spillway* is about 125 pages, digest-sized, attractively printed, perfect-bound, with full-color card cover. Press run is 2,000. "We recommend ordering a sample copy before you submit, though acceptance does not depend on purchasing a sample copy." Submissions open February 1-March 31 only. Acquires one-time rights. Responds in up to 6 months. Single copy: $13.50, including s&h. Subscription: $23 for 1 year, including s&h $40 for 2 years, including s&h. To order, visit the website and use PayPal. Guidelines online.

MAGAZINES NEEDS Submit 3-5 poems in a single document (DOC or PDF) via e-mail (spillway2@spillway.org). Cover letter is required. Include brief bio. Pays 1 contributor's copy.

SPINNING JENNY

E-mail: editor@spinning-jenny.com. **Website:** www.spinning-jenny.com. **Contact:** C.E. Harrison, editor. *Spinning Jenny* has published poetry by Abraham Smith, Cynthia Cruz, Michael Morse, and Joyelle McSweeney, among others. Authors retain rights. Single copy: $10; subscription: $20 for 2 issues. Guidelines available online.

○ *Spinning Jenny* is 96 pages, digest-sized, perfect-bound, with heavy card cover. "We accept less than 5% of unsolicited submissions." Press run is 1,000.

MAGAZINES NEEDS "*Spinning Jenny* is an open forum for poetry. We are pleased to consider experimental writing and work by unpublished authors. However, writers are strongly encouraged to review a recent issue of the magazine before submitting their work. Please note that we are not currently accepting submissions. Please check our website for updates." Pays in contributor's copies.

SPITBALL

The Literary Baseball Magazine, 536 Lassing Way, Walton KY 41094. **E-mail:** spitball5@hotmail.com. **Website:** www.spitballmag.com. **Contact:** Mike Shannon, editor-in-chief. *Spitball: The Literary Baseball Magazine*, published semiannually, is a unique magazine devoted to poetry, fiction, and book reviews exclusively about baseball. Newcomers are very welcome, but they must know the subject. "Perhaps a good place to start for beginners is one's personal reactions to the game, a game, a player, etc., and take it from there." Writers submitting to *Spitball* for the first time must buy a sample copy (waived for subscribers). "This is a one-time-only fee, which we regret, but economic reality dictates that we insist those who wish to be published in *Spitball* help support it, at least at this minimum level." *Spitball* is 48 pages, digest-sized, computer-typeset, perfect-bound. Receives about 1,000 submissions/year, accepts about 40. Press run is 1,000. Sample copy: $6. Subscription: $12. Guidelines online.

MAGAZINES NEEDS Submit a "batch" of poems at a time ("we prefer to use several of same poet in an issue rather than a single poem"). Lines/poem: open. Cover letter is required. Include brief bio and SASE. "Many times we are able to publish accepted work almost immediately." All material published in *Spitball* will be automatically considered for inclusion in the next *Best of Spitball* anthology. Poems submitted to *Spitball* will be considered automatically for Poem of the Month, to appear on the website. "We sponsor the Casey Award (for best baseball book of the year) and hold the Casey Awards Banquet in late February or early March. Any chapbook of baseball poetry should be sent to us for consideration for the 'Casey' plaque that we award to the winner each year." Pays 2 contributor's copies.

TIPS "Take the subject seriously. We do. In other words, get a clue (if you don't already have one) about the subject and about the poetry that has already been done and published about baseball. Learn from it—think about what you can add to the canon that is original and fresh—and don't assume that just anybody with the feeblest of efforts can write a baseball poem worthy of publication. And most importantly, stick with it. Genius seldom happens on the first try."

SPOON RIVER POETRY REVIEW

4241 Department of English, Illinois State University, Normal IL 61790. **E-mail:** contact@srpr.org. **Website:** srpr.org. **Contact:** Kirstin Hotelling Zona, editor. *Spoon River Poetry Review*, published biannually, is "one of the nation's oldest continuously published poetry journals. We seek to publish the best of all poetic genres, experimental as well as mainstream, and are proud of our commitment to regional as well as international poets and readers. *SRPR* includes, alongside poems from emerging and established poets, a chapbook-length selection of poetry by our featured *SRPR* poet, a substantial interview with the featured poet, and a long review essay on books of recently published poetry written by established poet-critics. The Summer/Fall issue also spotlights the winner and runners-up of our highly competitive editor's prize contest." Accepts submissions from September 15-February 15 (postmarked). Acquires first North American serial rights. Responds in 2-6 months. Guidelines available in magazine or on website.

MAGAZINES NEEDS "At *SRPR*, both innovative and mainstream poems are welcome, though all poetry we publish must be as intellectually and emotionally ambitious as it is formally attentive." Submit 3-5 poems at a time via online submission form (with your full contact info at the top of each poem) or by postal mail with SASE. Pays 2 contributor's copies and a one-year subscription.

⑤ SPOTLIGHT ON RECOVERY MAGAZINE

R. Graham Publishing Company, 9602 Glenwood Rd., #140, Brooklyn NY 11236. (347)831-9373. **E-mail:** rgraham_100@msn.com. **Website:** www.spotlighton-recovery.com. **Contact:** Robin Graham, publisher and editor-in-chief. "This is the premiere outreach and resource magazine in New York. Its goal is to be the catalyst for which the human spirit could heal. Everybody knows somebody who has mental illness, substance abuse issues, parenting problems, educational issues, or someone who is homeless, unemployed, physically ill, or the victim of a crime. Many people suffer in silence. *Spotlight on Recovery* will provide a voice to those who suffer in silence and begin the dialogue of recovery." Buys second serial (reprint) rights, buys electronic rights. Pays on publication. Publishes ms an average of 6 months after acceptance. Responds in 2 weeks to queries; 1 month to mss. Editorial lead time 1 month. Sample copy and guidelines free.

MAGAZINES NEEDS open Pays 5 cents/word.

TIPS "Send a query and give a reason why you would choose the subject posted to write about."

SPRING

The Journal of the E.E. Cummings Society, 129 Lake Huron Hall, Grand Valley State University, Allendale MI 49401. **E-mail:** websterm@gvsu.edu. **Website:** faculty.gvsu.edu/websterm/cummings. **Contact:** Michael Webster, editor. *Spring: The Journal of the E.E. Cummings Society*, published annually (usually in the fall), is designed "to broaden the audience for E.E. Cummings and to explore various facets of his life and art." **Contributors are required to subscribe.** Reads May through August. Responds in 6 months.

MAGAZINES NEEDS Wants poems in the spirit of Cummings, primarily poems of 1 page or less. Submit as e-mail attachment. Include cover letter. Does not want "amateurish" work.

⌣ STAND MAGAZINE

School of English, University of Leeds, Leeds LS2 9JT, United Kingdom. (44)(113)343-4794. **E-mail:** editors@standmagazine.org. **Website:** www.stand-magazine.org. North American submissions: David Latané, *Stand Magazine*, Department of English, Virginia Commonwealth University, Richmond VA 23284.. **Contact:** Jon Glover, managing editor. *Stand Magazine* is concerned with what happens when cultures and literatures meet, with translation in its many guises, with the mechanics of language, with the processes by which the policy receives or disables its cultural makers. *Stand* promotes debate of issues that are of radical concern to the intellectual community worldwide. U.S. submissions can be made through the Virginia office (see separate listing). Does not accept e-mail submissions except from subscribers. Publishes ms an average of 1 year-18 months after acceptance. Guidelines online.

MAGAZINES NEEDS Submit 4-6 poems by mail. Include SASE.

⑤ STAR*LINE

Science Fiction and Fantasy Poetry Association, Languages and Literatures, University of Northern Iowa, Cedar Falls IA 50614-0502. **E-mail:** starlineeditor@gmail.com. **Website:** www.sfpoetry.com. **Contact:** Vince Gotera, editor. *Star*Line*, published quarterly in print and .pdf format by the Science Fiction and Fantasy Poetry Association, is a speculative poetry magazine. "Open to all forms as long as your poetry uses speculative motifs: science fiction, fantasy, or horror." Buys first North American serial rights. After publication. No more than 6 months. Responds in 1 month. Guidelines online.

MAGAZINES NEEDS Submit 3-5 poems at a time. Accepts e-mail submissions (preferred; pasted into body of message, no attachments). Pays 3¢/word rounded to the next dollar; minimum $3, maximum $25.

ALSO OFFERS The Association also publishes *The Rhysling Anthology*, a yearly collection of nominations from the membership "for the best long and short speculative poetry of the preceding year, and *Dwarf Stars*, an annual collection of micro-poetry (10 lines or fewer)."

STEPPING STONES MAGAZINE

P.O. Box 902, Norristown PA 19404-0902. **E-mail:** info@ssmalmia.com. **Website:** ssmalmia.com. **Contact:** Trinae Ross, publisher. "*Stepping Stones Magazine* is a not-for-profit organization dedicated to presenting awesome writing and art created by people from all lifestyles." Publishes fiction, nonfiction, and poetry." Acquires first electronic rights, one-time rights, reprint rights. Responds in 2 months. Guidelines available for SASE, by e-mail, or on website.

O Has published poetry by Richard Fenwick, Karlanna Lewis, and Stephanie Kaylor. Receives about 600 poems/year, accepts about 10-15%.

MAGAZINES NEEDS Send up to 5 poems via postal mail, e-mail (poetry@ssmalmia.com), or online submissions manager. Include brief bio. Length: up to 100 lines/poem.

THE WALLACE STEVENS JOURNAL

University of Antwerp, Prinsstraat 13, 2000 Antwerp, Belgium. **E-mail:** bart.eeckhout@uantwerp.be; jforjames@aol.com. **Website:** www.press.jhu.edu/journals/wallace_stevens_journal. **Contact:** Bart Eeckhout, editor; James Finnegan, poetry editor. *The Wallace Stevens Journal*, published semiannually by the Wallace Stevens Society, welcomes submissions on all aspects of Wallace Stevens's poetry and life. Subscription: $30 (includes membership in the Wallace Stevens Society).

O *The Wallace Stevens Journal* is 100-160 pages, digest-sized, typeset, flat-spined, with glossy cover with art. Receives 200 poems/year, accepts 15-20. Press run is 400+ institutional subscriptions through Project Muse (Johns Hopkins University Press).

MAGAZINES NEEDS Has published poetry by David Athey, Jacqueline Marcus, Charles Wright, X.J. Kennedy, A.M. Juster, and Robert Creeley.

STILL CRAZY

(614)746-0859. **E-mail:** editor@crazylitmag.com. **Website:** www.crazylitmag.com. **Contact:** Barbara Kussow, editor. *Still Crazy*, published biannually in January and July, features poetry, short stories, and essays written by or about people over age 50. The editor is particularly interested in material that challenges the stereotypes of older people and that por-

trays older people's inner lives as rich and rewarding. Wants writing by people over age 50 and writing by people of any age if the topic is about people over 50. Acquires one-time rights. Rights revert to author upon publication. Time between acceptance and publication is up to 1 year. Simultaneous submissions OK, but notify editor as soon as possible if work is accepted elsewhere. Previously published submissions are OK, but "author must make previous publication known at time of submission. We do not want materials that have appeared online elsewhere." Responds in 6 months to mss. Sometimes sends prepublication galleys. Sometimes comments on/critiques rejected mss. Single paper copy: $10. Subscriptions: $18 (2 issues per year). Downloads: $4. Sometimes publishes theme issues. Guidelines on website. Submit via submissions manager on website.

O Accepts 3-4 short stories per issue; 5-7 essays; 12-14 poems. Reads submissions year round.

MAGAZINES NEEDS Poems that convey a story; accessible, but with compelling images and language. The editor is particularly interested in material that challenges the stereotypes of older people and that portrays older people's inner lives as rich and rewarding. Seldom publish "rhyming poetry; do not want poetry that is too sentimental." Lines/poem: up to 50. Pays 1 contributor's copy.

TIPS Looking for interesting characters and interesting situations that might interest readers of all ages. Humor and lightness welcomed.

STIRRING

Sundress Publications, **E-mail:** stirring@sundresspublications.com. **E-mail:** stirring.nonfiction@gmail.com; reviews@sundresspublications.com; stirring.fiction@gmail.com; stirring.poetry@gmail.com; stirring.artphoto@gmail.com. **Website:** www.stirringlit.com. **Contact:** Luci Brown and Andrew Koch, managing editors and poetry editors; Shaun Turner, fiction editor; Donna Vorreyer, reviews writer; Katie Culligan, reviews editor; Gabe Montesanti, nonfiction editor. "*Stirring* is one of the oldest continually published literary journals on the Web. *Stirring* is a quarterly literary magazine that publishes poetry, short fiction, creative nonfiction, reviews and visual art by established and emerging writers and artists." Acquires first North American serial rights. Publishes ms 1-2 weeks after acceptance. Responds in 3-6 months. Visit our website for guidelines.

MAGAZINES NEEDS Has published poetry by Dorianne Laux, Sharon Olds, Patricia Smith, Chad Davidson. Receives about 2,500 poems/year, accepts 45-60. Submit up to 5 poems by e-mail to stirring.poetry@gmail.com. Doesn't want religious verse, children's verse, or previously published work. Length: 1-6 pages (most often accepts half- to full-page poems).

STONE SOUP

E-mail: editor@stonesoup.com. **Website:** https://stonesoup.com. **Contact:** Emma Wood, editor. *Stone Soup*, a digital magazine with a print annual, is the national magazine of writing and art by kids, founded in 1973. Receives 5,000 poetry submissions/year, accepts about 20. Subscription: $24.99/year (U.S.). "We have a preference for writing and art based on real-life experiences; no formula stories or poems. We only publish writing by children up to (and including) age 13. We do not publish writing by adults." Subscription includes downloadable PDFs of each issue as well as more than 15 years of back issues online. Buys all rights. Pays on publication. Publishes ms an average of 4 months after acceptance. View a PDF sample copy online. Guidelines online.

MAGAZINES NEEDS Prefers free verse but considers all kinds. Pays in a contributor copy of the print annual (a collection of the years' issues along with bonus content from the blogs), discounted subscription rates.

TIPS "All writing we publish is by young people ages 13 and under. We do not publish any writing by adults. We can't emphasize enough how important it is to read a couple of issues of the magazine. You can read stories and poems from past issues online. We have a strong preference for writing on subjects that mean a lot to the author. If you feel strongly about something that happened to you or something you observed, use that feeling as the basis for your story or poem. Stories should have good descriptions, realistic dialogue, and a point to make. In a poem, each word must be chosen carefully. Your poem should present a view of your subject, and a way of using words that are special and all your own."

STORYSOUTH

E-mail: terry@storysouth.com; fiction@storysouth.com; poetry@storysouth.com;. **Website:** www.storysouth.com. **Contact:** Terry Kennedy, editor; Cynthia Nearman, creative nonfiction editor; Drew Perry, fiction editor; Luke Johnson, poetry editor. *"storySouth* accepts unsolicited submissions of fiction, poetry, and creative nonfiction during 2 submis-sion periods annually: May 15-July 1 and November 15-January 1. Long pieces are encouraged. Please make only 1 submission in a single genre per reading period." Acquires first serial rights. Publishes ms 1 month after acceptance. Responds in 2-6 months to mss. Guidelines available online.

MAGAZINES NEEDS Submit 3-5 poems via online submissions manager. No word-count or line limit.

TIPS "What really makes a story stand out is a strong voice and a sense of urgency—a need for the reader to keep reading the story and not put it down until it is finished."

THE STORYTELLER

65 Highway 328 W., Maynard AR 72444. (870)647-2137. **E-mail:** storytelleranthology@gmail.com. **Website:** www.thestorytellermagazine.com. **Contact:** Regina Riney, editor. "We are here to help writers however we can and to help start them on their publishing career. Proofread! Make sure you know what we take and what we don't and also make sure you know the word count." Acquires first North American rights. Publishes ms an average of 1-12 months after acceptance. Responds in 1 week to queries; in 2 weeks to mss. Editorial lead time 6 months. Guidelines online.

MAGAZINES NEEDS Submit up to 3 poems with SASE. Does not want long rambling. Length: up to 40 lines/poem.

ALSO OFFERS Sponsors a quarterly contest. "Readers vote on their favorite poems. Winners receive a copy of the magazine and a certificate. We also nominate for the Pushcart Prize." See website for yearly contest announcements and winners.

TIPS "*The Storyteller* is one of the best places you will find to submit your work, especially new writers. Our best advice, be professional. You have one chance to make a good impression. Don't blow it by being unprofessional."

$ STRANGE HORIZONS

E-mail: management@strangehorizons.com; fiction@strangehorizons.com. **Website:** strangehorizons.com. **Contact:** Jane Crowley and Kate Dollarhyde, editors-in-chief. "*Strange Horizons* is a magazine of and about speculative fiction and related nonfiction. Speculative fiction includes science fiction, fantasy, horror, slipstream, and other flavors of fantastica." Work published in *Strange Horizons* has been shortlisted for or won Hugo, Nebula, Rhysling, Theodore Sturgeon, James Tiptree Jr., and World Fantasy

Awards. For nonfiction: buys exclusive online publication rights for 6 months and requests ongoing nonexclusive rights to display the work in archive. For fiction and poetry: buys first world exclusive English-language rights (including audio rights) for 2 months. Responds in 90 days.

MAGAZINES NEEDS "We're looking for high-quality SF, fantasy, horror, and slipstream poetry. We're looking for modern, exciting poems that explore the possible and impossible: stories about human and nonhuman experiences, dreams and reality, past and future, the here-and-now and otherwhere-and-elsewhen. We want poems from imaginative and unconventional writers; we want voices from diverse perspectives and backgrounds." Submit up to 6 poems within 2 calendar months via e-mail; 1 poem per e-mail. Include "POETRY SUB: Your Poem Title" in subject line. Pays $40 per poem.

STRAYLIGHT

UW-Parkside, English Department, University of Wisconsin-Parkside, 900 Wood Rd., Kenosha WI 53141. **E-mail:** submissions@straylightmag.com. **Website:** www.straylightmag.com. **Contact:** Dean Karpowicz. *Straylight*, published biannually, seeks fiction and poetry of almost any style "as long as it's inventive." Acquires first North American serial rights. Publication is copyrighted. Pays on publication. Publishes ms 6 months after acceptance. Responds in 3 weeks to queries; in 3 months to mss. Rarely comments on/critiques rejected mss. Sample copy: $10; subscription: $18. Guidelines online.

Literary magazine/journal: 6x9, 115 pages, quality paper, uncoated index stock cover. Contains illustrations, photographs.

MAGAZINES NEEDS Submit up to 6 poems at a time. Send poems with cover letter. Accepts submissions by online submission manager or mail (send either SASE or IRC for return of ms, or disposable copy of ms and #10 SASE for reply only). Include brief bio, list of publications. Pays 2 contributor's copies.

TIPS "We tend to publish character-based and inventive fiction with cutting-edge prose. We are unimpressed with works based on strict plot twists or novelties. Read a sample copy to get a feel for what we publish."

STRIDE MAGAZINE

Stride, 4b Tremayne Close, Devoran, Cornwall TR3 6QE, United Kingdom. **E-mail:** editor@stridemagazine.co.uk. **E-mail:** submissions@stridemagazine. co.uk. **Website:** stridemagazine.blogspot.co.uk. **Contact:** Rupert Loydell, editor. *Stride Magazine*, publishes new poetry, prose poetry and reviews. *Stride* is regularly updated with new contributions. You are invited to send 2-3 short poems or prose poems, in the body of an e-mail, to editor@stridemagazine.co.uk with your name. All copyright remains with authors. Please do not send biographical details or lists of previous publications. Please do not send rhyming doggerel or shaggy dog stories masquerading as poems. Please do not send previously published work. If you are interested in writing short, opinionated but informed reviews of poetry books (which will be sent to you) please use the same e-mail to contact me, Rupert Loydell, editor.

MAGAZINES NEEDS Submit 2-3 poems or prose poems at a time. Accepts e-mail submissions only (pasted into body of message; no attachments).

STRUGGLE

A Magazine of Proletarian Revolutionary Literature, P.O. Box 28536, Detroit MI 48228. (313)273-9039. **E-mail:** timhall11@yahoo.com. **Website:** www.strugglemagazine.net. **Contact:** Tim Hall, editor. "Irregularly published now after 30 years of existence funded solely by writers and activists, but planning to resume as a twice-yearly magazine featuring African American, Latino, and other writers of color; prisoners; disgruntled workers; activists in the anti-war, anti-racist, and other mass movements; and many writers discontented with the Democrats and with the Republicans, their joint austerity campaign against the workers and the poor, the racist police murders against people of color, the unending destruction of the environment, and their continuing aggressive wars and drone murders abroad. While we urge literature in the direction of revolutionary working-class politics and a vision of socialism as embodying a genuine workers' power, in distinction to the state-capitalist regimes of the former Soviet Union, present-day China, North Korea, Cuba, etc., we accept a broader range of rebellious viewpoints in order to encourage creativity and dialogue." No rights acquired. Responds in 3-4 months to queries. Sample copy: $5. Subscription: $10 for 2 issues; make checks payable to Tim Hall, Special Account, not to *Struggle*.

MAGAZINES NEEDS Submit up to 8 poems at a time. Accepts e-mail submissions (pasted into body of message, no attachments), but prefers postal mail. "Writers must include SASE. Name and address must appear on the opening page of each poem."

❧ STUDIO

A Journal of Christians Writing, 727 Peel St., Albury NSW 2640, Australia. (61)(2)6021-1135. **E-mail:** studio00@bigpond.net.au. **Contact:** Paul Grover, publisher. *Studio, A Journal of Christians Writing*, published three times a year, prints poetry and prose of literary merit, offering a venue for previously published, new, and aspiring writers and seeking to create a sense of community among Christians writing. Also publishes occasional articles as well as news and reviews of writing, writers, and events of interest to members. People who send material should be comfortable being published under this banner: *Studio, A Journal of Christians Writing. Studio* is 60-80 pages, digest-sized, professionally printed on high-quality paper, saddle-stapled, with matte card cover. Press run is 300 (all subscriptions). Rights remain with the author Time between acceptance and publication is 6-9 months. Responds in 1 month to poems; in 1 week to queries and mss. Editorial lead time is 1 month. Sample copy: $10 (AUD; airmail to U.S.). Subscription: $60 AUD for overseas subscribers. Guidelines available via e-mail.

MAGAZINES NEEDS Wants shorter pieces (of poetry) but with no specification as to form or length (necessarily less than 100 lines), subject matter, style, or purpose. Cover message with postal address is required in e-mail submission. E-mail submissions preferred. Include brief details of previous publishing history, if any. SAE with IRC required if sent via regular post: submissions via post must be typed and double-spaced on 1 side of A4 white paper. Name and address must appear on the reverse side of each page submitted via postal service. Has published poetry by John Foulcher, Andrew Lansdown, Geoff Page, Les Murray, and other Australian and American poets. Length: less than 100 lines/poem. Pays 1 contributor's copy.

ALSO OFFERS Reviews books of poetry in 250 words, single-book format. Send materials for review consideration. Conducts a biannual poetry and short story contest.

STUDIO ONE

Murray Hall 170, College of St. Benedict, 37 S. College Ave., St. Joseph MN 56374. **E-mail:** studio1@csbsju.edu. **Website:** digitalcommons.csbsju.edu/studio_one/. **Contact:** Lauren Berg and Mollee Girgen, editors-in-chief. *Studio One* is a literary and visual arts magazine published each spring by the College of Saint Benedict/Saint John's University. Its mission is to give new and established writers alike a forum in which to present their works. The magazine's focus is poetry, short fiction, essays, and all forms of reproducible visual art works. *Studio One* is student-run, and the student editors change yearly. Submissions are open to all students on either Saint John's or Saint Benedict's campuses and to the general public regardless of regional, national, or international location. Reading period: September through January. Sample copy can be obtained by sending a self-addressed, stamped manila envelope and $6.

MAGAZINES NEEDS Considers simultaneous submissions; no previously published poems. Accepts e-mail submissions (pasted into body of message); "clearly show page breaks and indentations." Seldom comments on rejected poems. Lines/poem: "poetry no more than 2 pages stands a better chance of publication."

❧❧ SUBTERRAIN

Strong Words for a Polite Nation, P.O. Box 3008, MPO, Vancouver BC V6B 3X5, Canada. (604)876-8710. **Fax:** (604)879-2667. **E-mail:** subter@portal.ca. **Website:** www.subterrain.ca. **Contact:** Brian Kaufman, editor-in-chief; Jessica Key, editorial and marketing assistant. *"subTerrain* magazine is published 3 times/year from modest offices just off of Main Street in Vancouver, BC. We strive to produce a stimulating fusion of fiction, poetry, photography, and graphic illustration from uprising Canadian, U.S., and international writers and artists." Pays on publication for first North American serial rights. Publishes ms 4-9 months after acceptance. Responds in 6-9 months to mss. Rarely comments on rejected mss. Sample copy: $5 (subterrain.ca/subscriptions). Guidelines online.

💬 Magazine: 8.5×11; 80 pages; colour matte stock paper; colour matte cover stock; illustrations; photos. "Strong words for a polite nation."

MAGAZINES NEEDS "We accept poetry, but we no longer accept unsolicited submissions, except when related to 1 of our theme issues." "We no longer accept unsolicited poetry submissions (unless specifically related to one of our theme issues)." Poems unrelated to any theme issues may be submitted to the annual "General" issue (usually the summer/fall issue). Pays $50/poem.

TIPS "Read the magazine first. Get to know what kind of work we publish."

SUBTROPICS

University of Florida, P.O. Box 112075, 4008 Turlington Hall, Gainesville FL 32611-2075. **E-mail:** subtropics@english.ufl.edu. **Website:** www.english.ufl.edu/subtropics. **Contact:** David Leavitt, editor. *Subtropics* seeks to publish the best literary fiction, essays, and poetry being written today, both by established and emerging authors. Will consider works of fiction of any length, from short shorts to novellas and self-contained novel excerpts. Gives the same latitude to essays. Appreciates work in translation and, from time to time, republishes important and compelling stories, essays, and poems that have lapsed out of print by writers no longer living. Member: CLMP. Buys first North American serial rights. Pays on acceptance for prose; pays on publication of the issue preceding the issue in which the author's work will appear for poetry. Publishes ms an average of 6 months after acceptance. Responds in 1 month to queries and mss. Rarely comments on/critiques rejected mss. Sample copy: $12.95. Guidelines online.

○ Literary magazine/journal: 9x6, 160 pages. Includes photographs. Submissions accepted from September 1-April 15.

MAGAZINES NEEDS Submit up to 4 poems via online submissions manager. Pays $100 per poem.

TIPS "We publish longer works of fiction, including novellas and excerpts from forthcoming novels. Each issue includes a short-short story of about 250 words on the back cover. We are also interested in publishing works in translation for the magazine's English-speaking audience."

THE SUN

107 N. Roberson St., Chapel Hill NC 27516. (919)942-5282. **Fax:** (919)932-3101. **Website:** www.thesunmagazine.org. **Contact:** Sy Safransky, editor. *The Sun* publishes essays, interviews, fiction, and poetry. "We are open to all kinds of writing, though we favor work of a personal nature." Buys first rights, buys one-time rights. Pays on publication. Publishes ms an average of 6-12 months after acceptance. Responds in 3-6 months. Sample copy online. Guidelines online.

MAGAZINES NEEDS Submit up to 6 poems at a time. Considers previously published poems but strongly prefers unpublished work. "Poems should be typed and accompanied by a cover letter and SASE." Recently published poems by Tony Hoagland, Ellen Bass, Steve Kowit, Brian Doyle, and Alison Luterman.

Rarely publishes poems that rhyme. Pays $100-200 and 1-year subscription.

TIPS "Do not send queries except for interviews. We're open to unusual work. Read the magazine to get a sense of what we're about. Our submission rate is extremely high. Please be patient after sending us your work and include return postage."

SUNSTONE

343 N. Third W., Salt Lake City UT 84103-1215. (801)355-5926. **E-mail:** info@sunstonemagazine.com. **Website:** www.sunstonemagazine.com. *Sunstone*, published 6 times/year, prints scholarly articles of interest to an open, Mormon audience; personal essays; fiction (selected only through contests), and poetry. Has published poetry by Susan Howe, Anita Tanner, Robert Parham, Ryan G. Van Cleave, Robert Rees, and Virgil Suárez. Acquires first North American serial rights. Publishes ms 2 years after acceptance. Responds in 3 months. Sample copy: $10 postpaid. Subscription: $45 for 6 issues. Guidelines available online.

○ *Sunstone* is 64 pages, magazine-sized, professionally printed, saddle-stapled, with semi-glossy paper cover. Receives more than 500 poems/year, accepts 40-50. Press run is 3,000.

MAGAZINES NEEDS Wants both lyric and narrative poetry that engages the reader with fresh, strong images; skillful use of language; and a strong sense of voice and/or place. Short poems, including haiku, limericks, couplets, and one liners, are welcome. Does not want didactic poetry, sing-song rhymes, or in-process work. Submit by mail or e-mail. Include name, address, and e-mail on each poem. Seldom comments on rejected poems. Length: up to 40 lines/poem. Pays 5 contributor's copies.

SYCAMORE REVIEW

Purdue University Department of English, 500 Oval Dr., West Lafayette IN 47907. (765) 494-3783. **Fax:** (765) 494-3780. **E-mail:** sycamore@purdue.edu. **Website:** www.sycamorereview.com. **Contact:** Anthony Sutton, editor in chief; Bess Cooley, managing editor. *Sycamore Review* is Purdue University's internationally acclaimed literary journal, affiliated with Purdue's College of Liberal Arts and the Dept. of English. Strives to publish the best writing by new and established writers. Looks for well-crafted and engaging work, works that illuminate our lives in the collective human search for meaning. Would like to publish more work that takes a reflective look at national identity and how we are perceived by the world. Looks for diversity of voice, pluralistic worldviews, and political and social context. Buys first North American serial rights.

○ Reading period: September 1-March 31.

MAGAZINES NEEDS Submi via online submissions manager. Does not publish creative work by any student currently attending Purdue University. Former students should wait 1 year before submitting. Pays $25/poem.

TIPS "We look for originality, brevity, significance, strong dialogue, and vivid detail. We sponsor the Wabash Prize for Poetry (deadline: December 1) and Fiction (deadline: April 17), $1,000 award for each. All contest submissions will be considered for regular inclusion in the *Sycamore Review*."

TAB

The Journal of Poetry & Poetics, Chapman University, Dept. of English, One University Dr., Orange CA 92866. (714)997-6750. **E-mail:** poetry@chapman.edu; leahy@chapman.edu. **Website:** www.chapman.edu/TAB-journal & https://anastamos.chapman.edu/. **Contact:** Anna Leahy, editor; Claudine Jaenichen, creative director. *TAB: A Journal of Poetry & Poetics* is a national and international journal of all things poetry. Through 2018, the journal published poems from established and emerging poets as well as critical essays, creative nonfiction, and interviews, and book reviews were written by Chapman University MFA students and others in both an innovative print issue and additional electronic issues. In 2019, *TAB* is transferring its electronic archive to the international, interdisciplinary journal *Anastamos*, and this new collaboration will allow poetry, poetry criticism, and related work to be published there. *TAB* will continue to publish a special print-issue-as-art-object each January and distribute it at the AWP Conference and elsewhere. *TAB* and its parent organization, Tabula Poetica, reaches audience of poets, poetry readers and appreciators, poetry scholars and critics, and students of poetry and is attentive to both print and electronic modes for reading experiences. Acquires first North American serial rights. All contributors receive a copy of the print issue. Publishes ms 2-6 months after acceptance. Response time varies. Contact us by e-mail. TAB is now collaborating with Anastamos. See the submission guidelines for Anastamos: https://anastamos.chapman.edu/.

○ TAB and Anastamos are now partners in poetry. Please see the Anastamos website for more information on submitting work there.

MAGAZINES NEEDS *TAB* is interested in all kinds of poetry—avant-garde, free verse, fixed form, prose poetry, and more. Do not submit any work that is not related to poetry or poetics. No greeting card poetry. No work by writers under 18 years of age unless solicited, and no work by students, faculty, or staff of Chapman University. No length restrictions.

TIPS "Read poetry and read it widely. Take a look at the wide range of work we publish—and listen to the audio. Revise before you submit. Starting in 2019, submissions should be made to *Anastamos*: https://anastamos.chapman.edu/. *TAB* will continue to publish one innovative print issue each year."

◔◉ TAKAHĒ

P.O. Box 13-335, Christchurch 8141, New Zealand. **E-mail:** admin@takahe.org.nz. **E-mail:** essays@takahe.org.nz; fiction@takahe.org.nz; poetry@takahe.org.nz. **Website:** www.takahe.org.nz. **Contact:** Jane Seaford and Rachel Smith, fiction editors. *Takahē* magazine is a New Zealand-based literary and arts magazine that appears 3 times/year with a mix of print and online issues. It publishes short stories, poetry, and art by established and emerging writers and artists as well as essays, interviews, and book reviews (by invitation) in these related areas. The Takahē Collective Trust is a nonprofit organization that aims to support emerging and published writers, poets, artists, and cultural commentators. Acquires worldwide first publication rights. Pays on publication. Responds in 4 months. Guidelines online.

MAGAZINES NEEDS Email submissions preferred (poetry@takahe.org.nz). Overseas submissions are only accepted by e-mail. Accepts up to 4 poems per submission and no more than 3 submissions a year. "Please be aware that we publish only a handful of overseas poets each year." Long work (multiple pages) is unlikely to be accepted. Pays small honorarium.

TIPS "Editorials, book reviews, artwork, and literary commentaries are by invitation only."

TALKING RIVER

Lewis-Clark State College, 500 Eighth Ave., Lewiston ID 83501. (208)792-2716. **E-mail:** talkingriver@lcmail.lcsc.edu. **Website:** www.lcsc.edu/talking-river. **Contact:** Kevin Goodan, editorial advisor. "*Talking River*, Lewis-Clark State College's literary journal, seeks examples of literary excellence and originality. Theme may and must be of your choosing. Send us your mss of poetry, fiction, and creative nonfiction. The journal is a national publication, featuring creative work by some of this country's best contemporary writers." Acquires one-time rights. Publishes ms 1-2 years after acceptance. Responds in 6 months to mss. Sample copy: $6. Guidelines available online.

○ Reads mss August 1-April 1 only.

MAGAZINES NEEDS Submit up to 5 poems via postal mail. Send SASE for reply and return of ms, or send disposable copy of ms. Pays contributor's copies; additional copies $6.

TIPS "We look for the strong, the unique; we reject clichéd images and predictable climaxes."

TAMPA REVIEW

University of Tampa Press, 401 W. Kennedy Blvd., Tampa FL 33606. (813)253-6266. **Fax:** (813)258-7593. **E-mail:** utpress@ut.edu. **Website:** www.ut.edu/tampareview. **Contact:** Richard Mathews, editor; Daniel Dooghan, nonfiction editor; Shane Hinton and Yuly Restrepo, fiction editors; Geoff Bouvier and Elizabeth Winston, poetry editors.. An international literary journal publishing art and literature from Florida and Tampa Bay as well as new work and translations from throughout the world. "We no longer accept paper submissions. Please submit all work via the online submission manager. You will find it on our website under the link titled 'How to Submit.'" Buys first North American serial rights. Pays on publication. Publishes ms an average of 10 months after acceptance. Responds in 3-4 months to mss. Editorial lead time 18 months. Sample copy: $12. Guidelines online.

MAGAZINES NEEDS No greeting card verse, hackneyed, sing-song, rhyme-for-the-sake-of-rhyme. Length: 2-225 lines. Pays $10/printed page, 1 contributor's copy, and offers 40% discount on additional copies.

HOW TO CONTACT Send complete ms via online submissions manager. We no longer accept submissions by mail.

TIPS "Send a clear cover letter stating previous experience or background. Our editorial staff considers submissions between September and December for publication in the following year."

TARPAULIN SKY

P.O. Box 189, Grafton VT 05146. **E-mail:** editors@tarpaulinsky.com. **Website:** www.tarpaulinsky.com. **Contact:** Resh Daily, managing editor. *Tarpaulin Sky*, published biannually in print and online, features the highest-quality poetry, prose, cross-genre work, art, photography, interviews, and reviews. Open to all styles and forms, providing the forms appear inevitable and/or inextricable from the poems. Especially fond of inventive/experimental and cross-/transgenre work. The best indication of aesthetic is found in the journal: Read it before submitting. Acquires first rights. Publishes ms 2-6 months after acceptance. Responds in 1-4 months.

MAGAZINES NEEDS Poetry is solicited from authors who send book mss during the press's reading period.

TAR RIVER POETRY

113 Erwin Hall, East Carolina University, E. Fifth St., Greenville NC 27858. **E-mail:** tarriverpoetry@gmail.com. **Website:** www.tarriverpoetry.com. **Contact:** Luke Whisnant, editor. *Tar River Poetry*, published twice/year, is an all-poetry magazine that publishes 40-50 poems/issue, providing the talented beginner and experienced writer with a forum that features all styles and forms of verse. Wants skillful use of figurative language and poems that appeal to the senses. Does not want sentimental, flat-statement poetry. Acquires first rights and reassigns reprint rights after publication. Responds in 6 weeks. Rarely comments on rejections due to volume of submissions. Sample copy: $7, postage paid. Subscription: $12 for 1 year; $20 for 2 years. Guidelines available for SASE or on website.

○ Only considers submissions 2 months of the year, usually September and February. Check website for reading periods before submitting. Work submitted at other times will not be considered. *Tar River Poetry* is 64 pages, 9x5, professionally printed with color cover. Receives 6,000-8,000 submissions/year, accepts 60-80. Press run is 900 (500 subscribers, 125 libraries).

MAGAZINES NEEDS Has published poetry by William Stafford, Sharon Olds, Carolyn Kizer, A.R. Ammons, and Claudia Emerson. Has also published many other well-known poets, as well as numerous new and emerging poets. Submit via online submissions manager. Pays 2 contributor's copies.

ALSO OFFERS Reviews books of poetry (up to 4,000 words), single- or multibook format. Query for reviews.

TIPS "We are usually not interested in obscure or abstract poetry, concrete poetry, or prose poems. We favor image-based narrative and lyric poetry that is accessible and meaningful without being simplistic, sophisticated without being pretentious. We publish both free verse and formal poems; for samples, see our website. Writers of poetry should first be readers of poetry. Subscribers receive expedited editorial decisions on their submissions."

⚫ TEARS IN THE FENCE

Portman Lodge, Durweston, Blandford Forum, Dorset DT11 0QA, United Kingdom. **E-mail:** tearsinthefence@gmail.com. **Website:** tearsinthefence.com. *Tears in the Fence*, published 3 times/year, is a "small-press magazine of poetry, prose poetry, creative nonfiction, fiction, interviews, essays, and reviews. We are open to a wide variety of poetic styles and work that shows social and poetic awareness whilst prompting close and divergent readings." *Tears in the Fence* is 184 pages, A5, digitally printed on 110-gms. paper, perfect-bound, with matte card cover. Press run is 600. Time between acceptance and publication is 3 months. Sample copy: $13. Subscription: $60/3 (£40/4) issues.

MAGAZINES NEEDS Send books for review to Ian Brinton, Brescia House, 2 Capel Road, Faversham, Kent, ME13 8RL, England. Submit poetry via e-mail as attachment. Has published Isobel Armstrong, Hannah Silva, Jennifer K. Dick, Basil King, Carrie Etter, Nathaniel Tarn, Chris McCabe, Sheila E. Murphy, Peter Riley, and Sarah Crewe. Length: open. Pays 1 contributor's copy.

ALSO OFFERS The magazine runs a regular series of readings in Dorset and an annual international literary Festival.

⚫ TEMPLAR POETRY & IOTA MAGAZINE

iOTA, **Templar Media Ltd**, Fenelon House, 58 Dale Rd., Matlock, Derbyshire DE4 3NB, England. (44)01629-582500. **E-mail:** info@templarpoetry.com. **Website:** www.templarpoetry.com. **Contact:** Alex McMillen. *iOTA* and Templar Poetry considers submissions throughout the year for publication in *iOTA Magazine* and Templar Poetry pamphlets, collections and other titles. *iOTA* is 94 or more pages, professionally printed, with full-color cover. Receives 6,000 poems/year, accepts about 300. Responds in 3 months (unless production of the next issue takes precedence).

MAGAZINES NEEDS Pays 1 contributor's copy.

ADDITIONAL INFORMATION The editors also publish Templar Poetry (www.templarpoetry.com), sponsor the annual Derwent Poetry Festival, and host an online poetry bookshop of their titles at www.templarpoetry.com. "Templar Poetry is a major UK poetry publisher and publishes poetry collections, nonfiction, and an annual anthology of poetry linked to

international pamphlet and collection awards. Details at www.templarpoetry.com

CONTEST/AWARD OFFERINGS Sponsors an annual poetry Pamphlet/Chapbook-Iota Shot Award, offering 2-3 awards of £100, plus publication of *ishot* chapbook. Submission fee: £15.50 online. Worldwide submissions in English welcome. **Deadline:** November 19.

TERRAIN.ORG: A JOURNAL OF THE BUILT + NATURAL ENVIROMENTS

Terrain.org, P.O. Box 19161, Tucson AZ 85731-9161. **E-mail:** contact2@terrain.org. **Website:** www.terrain.org. Reviews Editor address: P.O. Box 51332, Irvine CA 92619-1332.. **Contact:** Simmons B. Buntin, editor in chief. *Terrain.org* is based on, and thus welcomes quality submissions from, new and experienced authors and artists alike. Our online journal accepts only the finest poetry, essays, fiction, articles, artwork, and other contributions' material that reaches deep into the earth's fiery core, or humanity's incalculable core, and brings forth new insights and wisdom. *Terrain.org* is searching for that interface—the integration among the built and natural environments, that might be called the soul of place. The works contained within *Terrain.org* ultimately examine the physical realm around us and how those environments influence us and each other physically, mentally, emotionally, and spiritually." Acquires one-time rights. Sends galleys to author. Publication is copyrighted. Publishes mss 5 weeks-18 months after acceptance. Responds in 2 weeks to queries; in 4 months to mss. Sometimes comments on/critiques rejected mss. Guidelines available online.

⚫ Beginning March 2014, publication schedule is rolling; we will no longer be issue-based. Sends galleys to author. Publication is copyrighted. Sponsors *Terrain.org* Annual Contest in Poetry, Fiction, and Nonfiction. **Deadline:** August 1. Submit via online submissions manager.

MAGAZINES NEEDS Accepts submissions online at sub.terrain.org. Include brief bio. Send complete ms with cover letter. No erotica. Length: open.

TIPS "We have 3 primary criteria in reviewing fiction: (1) The story is compelling and well crafted. (2) The story provides some element of surprise; whether in content, form, or delivery we are unexpectedly delighted in what we've read. (3) The story meets an upcoming theme, even if only peripherally. Read fiction in the current issue and perhaps some archived work, and if you like what you read—and our overall enviromental slant—then send us your best work.

Make sure you follow our submission guidelines (including cover note with bio), and that your mss is as error-free as possible."

TEXAS POETRY CALENDAR

Kallisto Gaia Press, Kallisto Gaia Press, PO Box 220, Davilla TX 76523-0220. (254)654-7205. **E-mail:** tony@kallistogaiapress.org. **E-mail:** kallistogaiapress.submittable.com/submit. **Website:** www.kallistogaiapress.org. **Contact:** Tony Burnett, managing editor. *Texas Poetry Calendar,* published annually in July, features a "week-by-week calendar side-by-side with poems with a Texas connection." Wants "a wide variety of styles, voices, and forms, including rhyme, though a Texas connection is preferred. Humor is welcome! Poetry only!" Does not want "children's poetry, erotic poetry, profanity, obscure poems, previously published work, or poems over 35 lines." *Texas Poetry Calendar* is about 144 pages, digest-sized, offset-printed, spiral-bound, with full-color cardstock cover. Receives about 600 poems/year, accepts about 80-85. Press run is around 600. Accepted work receives monetary compensation. Reads submissions December 1-February 20. Buys first North American serial rights. Pays on publication. Publishes 3-6 months after acceptance. Sample copy: $14.95 plus $3 shipping. Make checks payable to Kallisto Gaia Press.

MAGAZINES NEEDS Poems related to the culture(s), geography, or iconography of Texas. Submit 3 poems through Submittable: kallistogaiapress.submittable.com/submit. No fax, e-mail, or snail mail submissions; only electronic submissions via Submittable. Cover letter is required. "Include a short bio (less than 100 words) and poem titles in cover letter. Also include e-mail address and phone number. Do not include poet's name on the poems themselves!" Never comments on rejected poems, but nominates poems for Pushcart Prizes each year. Deadline: January 15. Does not want children's, epic, erotica. Length: up to 35 lines/poem, including spaces and title. Pays $20 per acceptance.

THEMA

Thema Literary Society, P.O. Box 8747, Metairie LA 70011-8747. **E-mail:** thema@cox.net. **E-mail:** For writers living outside the U.S.. **Website:** themaliterarysociety.com. **Contact:** Virginia Howard, editor; Gail Howard, poetry editor. *"THEMA* is designed to stimulate creative thinking by challenging writers with unusual 'themes, such as "The Critter in the Attic' and 'Six before Eighty.' Appeals to writers, teachers of creative writing, artists, photographers, and general reading audience." *THEMA* is 100 pages, digest-sized professionally printed, with glossy card cover. Receives about 400 poems/year, accepts about 8%. Press run is 300 (180 subscribers, 30 libraries). Subscription: $30 U.S./$40 foreign. Has published poetry by Rosalie Calabrese, Deborah H. Doolittle, David Subacchi, and Wally Swist. Has published fiction/nonfiction by Virginia Butler, Madonna Dries Christensen, Tony Concannon, Diane Jackman, and Margaret Nelson. Has published photographs by Kathleen Gunton, Stanley Horowitz, and John McCluskey. Acquires one-time rights. Pays on acceptance. Publishes ms, on average, within 6 months after acceptance. Responds in 1 week to queries; 5 months to mss (after deadline for submission on given theme). Sample $15 U.S./$25 foreign. Upcoming themes and guidelines available in magazine, for SASE, by e-mail, or on website.

MAGAZINES NEEDS All poems must relate to one of *THEMA*'s upcoming themes (**indicate the target theme on submission of manuscript**). See website for themes. Submit up to 3 poems at a time. Include SASE. All submissions should be typewritten on standard $8\frac{1}{2}$x11 paper. Submissions are accepted all year, but evaluated after specified deadlines. **Specify target theme.** Editor comments on submissions. Each issue is based on an unusual premise. Please send SASE for guidelines before submitting poetry to find out the upcoming themes. Does not want scatologic language or explicit love poetry. Length: 1-3 pages. Payment: $10/poem and 1 contributor's copy.

THICK WITH CONVICTION

E-mail: twczine@gmail.com. **Website:** twczine.blogspot.com. **Contact:** Arielle LaBrea. *Thick with Conviction*, published online, is "looking for fresh and exciting voices in poetry. I don't want to take a nap while I'm reading, so grab my attention, make me sit up and catch my breath." Wants all genres of poetry, "poems that make me exhale a deep sigh after reading them. Basically, if I can't feel the words in front of me, I'm not going to be happy. I'd like to see new and cutting-edge poets who think outside the box but still know how to keep things from getting too strange and inaccessible." Does not want "teen angst poems, religious poems, or greeting-card tripe." Has published poetry by Kendall A. Bell, April Michelle Bratten, Kristina Marie Darling, James H. Duncan, Paul Hostovsky, and Kelsey Upward. Receives about 300 poems/year, accepts about 15%. Never comments on rejected poems. Acquires one-time rights. Rights revert to poet upon publication. Responds in 2-4 weeks. Guidelines available on website.

MAGAZINES NEEDS Submit up to 5 poems at a time in the body of an e-mail. Cover letter and bio is required. Reads submissions year round.

THINK JOURNAL

Taylor Hall 222B, Western State Colorado University, 600 N Adams St., Gunnison CO 81231. (970)943-2058. **E-mail:** drothman@western.edu; susandelaneyspear@msn.com. **Website:** www.western.edu/academics/graduate-programs/master-fine-arts-creative-writing/think-journal. **Contact:** Susan Spear, managing editor. *Think Journal*, established in 2008 by Christine Yurick, was acquired by the Graduate Program in Creative Writing at Western State Colorado University in 2013. *Think* publishes twice yearly and focuses metered, rhymed poems, in received or nonce forms, or free verse with a clear organizing principle. "The language we admire in poetry and in prose is both intellectually precise and emotionally rich. We welcome work from both established and emerging poets." Tries to respond to poems in 4 months. Editorial lead time 6 months. Yearly subscription: $15. Contact the webpage on Western's website.

MAGAZINES NEEDS Submit up to 5 poems on think-journal.submittable.com/submit. Pays 1 contributor's copy.

THIRD COAST

Western Michigan University, English Department, Kalamazoo MI 49008-5331. **E-mail:** editors@thirdcoastmagazine.com. **Website:** www.thirdcoastmagazine.com. David Greendonner. **Contact:** S.Marie LaFata-Clay, editor in chief. "*Third Coast* publishes poetry, fiction (including traditional and experimental fiction, shorts, and novel excerpts, but not genre fiction), creative nonfiction (including reportage, essay, memoir, and fragments), drama, and translations." Acquires first North American serial rights. Publishes ms an average of 6 months after acceptance. Responds in 4 months to queries and mss. Sample copy: $6 (back issue). Make checks payable to *Third Coast*. Guidelines available online.

○ *Third Coast* is 176 pages, digest-sized, professionally printed, perfect-bound, with 4-color cover with art. Reads mss from September through December of each year.

MAGAZINES NEEDS Has published poetry by Marianne Boruch, Terence Hayes, Alex Lemon, Philip Levine, David Shumate, Tomz Salamun, and Jean Valentine. Submit up to 5 poems via online submissions manager. No simple narratives or any simplistic poetry. Pays 2 contributor's copies and one-year subscription.

ALSO OFFERS Sponsors an annual poetry contest. First Prize: $1,000 and publication. Guidelines available on website. **Entry fee:** $16, includes 1-year subscription to *Third Coast*.

TIPS "We will consider many different types of fiction and favor those exhibiting a freshness of vision and approach."

⑤ THE THREEPENNY REVIEW

P.O. Box 9131, Berkeley CA 94709. (510)849-4545. **E-mail:** wlesser@threepennyreview.com. **Website:** www.threepennyreview.com. **Contact:** Wendy Lesser, editor. "We are a general-interest, national literary magazine with coverage of politics, the visual arts, and the performing arts." Reading period: January 1-June 30. Buys first North American serial rights. Pays on acceptance. Publishes ms an average of 1 year after acceptance. Responds in 2 days to 2 months Sample copy: $12, or online. Guidelines online.

MAGAZINES NEEDS No poems without capital letters or poems without a discernible subject. Length: up to 100 lines/poem. Pays $200.

TIPS "Nonfiction (political articles, memoirs, reviews) is most open to freelancers."

TIMBER JOURNAL

E-mail: timberjournal@gmail.com. **Website:** www.colorado.edu/timberjournal. **Contact:** Staff changes regularly; see website for current staff members. *Timber* is a literary journal run by students in the MFA program at the University of Colorado Boulder and dedicated to the promotion of innovative literature. Publishes work that explores the boundaries of poetry, fiction, creative nonfiction, and digital literatures. Produces both an online journal that explores the potentials of the digital medium and an annual print anthology. Responds in 2-3 months to mss. Guidelines available online.

○ Reading period: August-March (submit once during this time).

MAGAZINES NEEDS Submit up to 6 poems in single document via online submissions manager. Include 30- to 50-word bio. Pays 1 contributor's copy.

TIPS "We are looking for innovative poetry, fiction, creative nonfiction, and digital lit (screenwriting, digital poetry, multimedia lit, etc.)."

TIN HOUSE

McCormack Communications, P.O. Box 10500, Portland OR 97296. (503)219-0622. **E-mail:** info@tinhouse.com. **Website:** www.tinhouse.com. **Contact:** Cheston Knapp, managing editor; Holly MacArthur, founding editor. "We are a general-interest literary quarterly. Our watchword is quality. Our audience includes people interested in literature in all its aspects, from the mundane to the exalted." Buys first North American serial rights, anthology rights. Pays on publication. Publishes ms an average of 6 months after acceptance. Responds in 6 weeks to queries; in 4 months to mss. Editorial lead time 6 months. Sample copy: $15. Guidelines online.

Reading period: September 1-May 31.

MAGAZINES NEEDS Submit via online submissions manager or postal mail. Include cover letter. Pays $50-150.

TOASTED CHEESE

E-mail: editors@toasted-cheese.com. **E-mail:** submit@toasted-cheese.com. **Website:** www.toasted-cheese.com. *Toasted Cheese* accepts submissions of previously unpublished fiction, flash fiction, creative nonfiction, poetry, and book reviews. See site for book review requirements and guidelines. "Our focus is on quality of work, not quantity. Some issues will therefore contain fewer or more pieces than previous issues. We don't restrict publication based on subject matter. We encourage submissions from innovative writers in all genres and actively seek diverse voices." No simultaneous submissions. Be mindful that final notification of acceptance or rejection may take four months. No chapters or excerpts unless they read as a stand-alone story. No first drafts. Acquires electronic rights. Final acceptances are sent quarterly, approximately one month before each issue publishes. Responds in 4 months or less. Sample copy online. Follow submission guidelines at our website; see site for submission guidelines and samples of what Toasted Cheese publishes.

MAGAZINES NEEDS See site for submission guidelines and samples of what Toasted Cheese publishes. We don't publish poetry that is rhyming, sentimental, or non-specific. Toasted Cheese is a non-paying market.

TIPS "We are looking for clean, professional work from writers and poets of any experience level. Accepted stories and poems will be concise and compelling with a strong voice. We're looking for writers who are serious about the craft: tomorrow's literary stars before they're famous. See site for submission guidelines and samples of what Toasted Cheese publishes."

TRANSFERENCE

Department of World Languages and Literatures at Western Michigan University, 1903 West Michigan Ave., Kalamazoo MI 49008-5338. **E-mail:** lang-transference@wmich.edu. **E-mail:** molly.lynde-recchia@wmich.edu. **Website:** scholarworks.wmich.edu/transference. **Contact:** Molly Lynde-Recchia, editor-in-chief. Annual literary magazine. Publishes poetry from Arabic, Chinese, French and Old French, German, Japanese, Latin and Classical Greek into English, along with commentary on the art of translation and the choices and challenges involved with that process. Retains first North American serial rights and electronic rights. Does not offer payment. Publishes ms 4-8 months after acceptance. Response time to ms varies; 1 month to queries. Editorial lead time is approx. 6 months. Sample copy online, or send SASE and $10. Guidelines online.

MAGAZINES NEEDS Poetry must be a translation from another language into English. No self-translations. No minimum or maximum line length. Does not pay.

TIPS "Authors are responsible for obtaining permission to publish their translation from the original poem's author or copyright holder. Please see previous issues for an understanding of what we publish."

TRIQUARTERLY

School of Professional Studies, Northwestern University, 339 E. Chicago Ave., Chicago IL 60611. **E-mail:** triquarterly@northwestern.edu. **Website:** www.triquarterly.org. **Contact:** Carrie Muehle, managing editor. "*TriQuarterly*, the literary magazine of Northwestern University, welcomes submissions of fiction, creative nonfiction, poetry, short drama, and hybrid work. We also welcome short-short prose pieces." Reading period: November 15-May 1.

MAGAZINES NEEDS Submit up to 6 poems via online submissions manager. Pays honoraria.

TIPS "We are especially interested in work that embraces the world and continues, however subtly, the ongoing global conversation about culture and society that *TriQuarterly* pursued from its beginning in 1964."

TULANE REVIEW

Tulane University, Suite G08A Lavin-Bernick Center, Tulane University, New Orleans LA 70118. **E-mail:** litsoc@tulane.edu. **Website:** www.tulane.edu/~litsoc/index.html. *Tulane Review*, published biannually, is a national literary journal seeking quality submissions of prose, poetry, and art. Acquires first North American serial rights, second serial rights. Single copy: $8; subscription: $15. Make checks payable to *Tulane Review*. Guidelines available online.

○ *Tulane Review* is the recipient of an AWP Literary Magazine Design Award. *Tulane Review* is 70 pages, 7x9, perfect-bound, with 100# cover with full-color artwork.

MAGAZINES NEEDS Considers all types of poetry. Wants imaginative poems with bold, inventive images. Receives about 1,200 poems/year, accepts about 50 per issue. Has published poetry by Tom Chandler, Ace Boggess, Carol Hamilton, and Brady Rhoades. Submit up to 5 poems via online submissions manager. No longer accepts paper and e-mail submissions. Pays 2 contributor's copies.

TULE REVIEW

P.O. Box 160406, Sacramento CA 95816. (916)451-5569. **E-mail:** info@sacpoetrycenter@gmail.com. **Website:** www.tulereview.com. **Contact:** Frank Dixon Graham, editor in chief; Emily Wright, associate editor; Alex Russell, associate editor. *Tule Review*, published 1-2 times/year, uses "poetry, book reviews, and essays concerning contemporary poetry" Acquires first North American serial rights. Publishes ms 1-6 months after acceptance. Responds in 3-4 monts. Guidelines and upcoming themes available by e-mail or on website.

○ *Tule Review* accepts poetry and cover art submissions on a rolling basis, from May 1 to April 30. All material should be submitted through Submittable.com.

MAGAZINES NEEDS Submit up to 3 poems at a time using online submission form. Provide short, 5 line bio. Reads submissions year round. Wants "all styles and forms of poetry." Primarily publishes poets living in the greater Sacramento area, but accepts work from anywhere. Length: 96 lines maximum. Pays 1 contributor's copy.

⑤ UPSTREET

Ledgetop Publishing, P.O. Box 105, Richmond MA 01254-0105. (413)441-9702. **E-mail:** editor@upstreet-mag.org. **Website:** www.upstreet-mag.org. **Contact:** Vivian Dorsel, Founding Editor/Publisher. Buys first North American serial rights. Pays on publication. Publishes ms an average of 6 months after acceptance. Responds in 2 weeks to queries; 6 months to mss. Editorial lead time 6 months. Sample copy for $12.00, plus shipping. Guidelines online and in each issue.

MAGAZINES NEEDS Quality is only criterion. Does not consider unsolicited poetry. Pays $50-150.

TIPS "Get sample copy, submit electronically, and follow guidelines."

U.S. 1 WORKSHEETS

U.S. 1 Poets' Cooperative, U.S. 1 Worksheets, P.O. Box 127, Kingston NJ 08528. **E-mail:** us1poets@gmail.com. **Website:** www.us1poets.com. *"U.S. 1 Worksheets*, published annually, uses high-quality poetry and prose poems. We prefer complex, well-written work." Responds in 3 months to mss. Guidelines online.

MAGAZINES NEEDS Submit up to 5 poems at a time. "We rarely publish poems longer than 36 lines (1 page). Considers simultaneous submissions if indicated; no previously published poems. We are looking for well-crafted poetry with a focused point of view." Length: 36 lines or one page. No payment.

ADDITIONAL INFORMATION The U.S. 1 Poets' Cooperative co-sponsors (with the Delaware Valley Poets) a monthly poetry reading at the Princeton Public Library.

ALSO OFFERS Weekly critique sessions, Open to all. Free, e-mail for directions.

TIPS "Mss are accepted from May 1-June 15 and are read by rotating editors from the cooperative. Send us something unusual, something we haven't read before, but make sure it's poetry. Proofread carefully."

⑤ U.S. CATHOLIC

Claretian Publications, 205 W. Monroe St., Chicago IL 60606. (312)236-7782. **Fax:** (312)236-8207. **E-mail:** literaryeditor@uscatholic.org. **E-mail:** submissions@claretians.org. **Website:** www.uscatholic.org. *"U.S. Catholic* puts faith in the context of everyday life. With a strong focus on social justice, we offer a fresh and balanced take on the issues that matter most in our world, adding a faith perspective to such challenges as poverty, education, family life, the environment, and even pop culture." Buys all rights. Pays on acceptance. Publishes ms an average of 6 months after acceptance. Responds in 1 month to queries; in 2 months to mss. Editorial lead time 8 months. Guidelines on website.

○ Please include SASE with written ms.

MAGAZINES NEEDS Submit 3-5 poems at a time. Accepts e-mail submissions (pasted into body of message or as attachments). Cover letter is preferred. No light verse. Length: up to 50 lines/poem. Pays $75.

○$ VALLUM: CONTEMPORARY POETRY

5038 Sherbrooke West, P.O. Box 23077, CP Vendome, Montreal QC H4A 1T0, Canada. **E-mail:** info@vallummag.com; editors@vallummag.com. **Website:** www.vallummag.com. **Contact:** Joshua Auerbach and Eleni Zisimatos, editors. Poetry/fine arts magazine published twice/year. Publishes exciting interplay of poets and artists. Content for magazine is selected according to themes listed on website. Material is not filed but is returned upon request by SASE. E-mail response is preferred. Seeking exciting, unpublished, traditional or avant-garde poetry that reflects contemporary experience. *Vallum* is 100 pages, digest sized (7x8½), digitally printed, perfect-bound, with color images on coated stock cover. Includes ads. Single copy: $12 CDN; subscription: $20/year CDN; $24 U.S. (shipping included). Make checks payable to *Vallum*. Buys first North American serial rights. Copyright remains with the author. Pays on publication. Sample copy online. Guidelines online.

MAGAZINES NEEDS Pays honorarium for accepted poems.

ADDITIONAL INFORMATION "The Vallum Chapbook Series publishes 2-3 chapbooks by both well-known and emerging poets. Past editions include *Gospel of X* by George Elliott Clarke, *The Art of Fugue* by Jan Zwicky and *Address* by Franz Wright. *Vallum* does not currently accept unsolicited mss for this project."

CONTEST/AWARD OFFERINGS "Sponsors annual contest. First Prize: $750, Second Prize: $250 and publication in an issue of *Vallum*. Honourable mentions may be selected but are not eligible for cash prizes. Submit 3 poems. Entry fee: $25 U.S. / CAD (includes subscription to *Vallum*). Deadline: July 15. Guidelines available in magazine, by e-mail, and on website. Poems may be submitted in any style or on any subject; max. 3 poems, up to 60 lines per poem. Entries should be labelled 'Vallum Contest' and submitted online or by regular mail. Submissions are not returned. Winners will be notified via e-mail."

VALPARAISO POETRY REVIEW

Valparaiso Poetry Review, Department of English, Valparaiso University, Valparaiso IN 46383-6493. (219)464-5278. **Fax:** (219)464-5511. **E-mail:** vpr@valpo.edu. **Website:** www.valpo.edu/vpr. **Contact:** Edward Byrne, editor. *Valparaiso Poetry Review: Contemporary Poetry and Poetics*, published semiannually online, accepts "submissions of unpublished poetry, book reviews, author interviews, and essays on poetry or poetics that have not yet appeared online and for which the rights belong to the author. Query for anything else." Acquires one-time rights. "All rights remain with author." Publishes ms 6-12 months after acceptance. Responds in 6 weeks. Guidelines available online.

MAGAZINES NEEDS Wants poetry of any length or style, free verse, or traditional forms. Submit 3-5 poems at a time. Accepts e-mail submissions only Reads submissions year round. Seldom comments on rejected poems. Receives about 9,000 poems/year, accepts about 1%. Has published poetry by Charles Wright, Cornelius Eady, Dorianne Laux, Dave Smith, Claudia Emerson, Billy Collins, Brian Turner, Daisy Fried, Stanley Plumly, and Annie Finch.

ALSO OFFERS Reviews books of poetry in single- and multibook formats. Send materials for review consideration.

● VAN GOGH'S EAR

Best World Poetry & Prose, French Connection Press, 12 Rue Lamartine, Paris 75009, France. (33)(1)4016-1147. **E-mail:** tinafayeayres@gmail.com. **Website:** www.frenchcx.com/press; theoriginalvangoghsearanthology.com. *Van Gogh's Ear*, published annually in April, is an anthology series "devoted to publishing powerful poetry and prose in English and English translations by major voices and innovative new talents from around the globe." Acquires one-time rights. Time between acceptance and publication is 1 year. Responds in 9 months. Seldom comments on rejections. Always sends prepublication galleys. Single copy: $19; subscription: $36 for 2 years. Guidelines available in anthology or on website. "Every submission is closely read by all members of the editorial board and voted upon. Our continued existence, and continued ability to read your work, depends mainly on subscriptions/donations. Therefore, we must ask that you at least purchase a sample copy before submitting work."

○ *Van Gogh's Ear* is 280 pages, digest-sized, off-set-printed, perfect-bound, with 4-color matte cover with commissioned artwork. Poetry published in *Van Gogh's Ear* has appeared in *The Best American Poetry.*

MAGAZINES NEEDS Receives about 1,000 poems/year, accepts about 30%. Press run is 2,000 (105 subscribers, 25 libraries, 1,750 shelf/online sales); 120 distributed free to contributors and reviewers. Has published poetry by Tony Curtis, Yoko Ono, James Dean, Xaviera Hollander, and Charles Manson. Submit up to 6 poems by e-mail. Cover letter is preferred, along with a brief bio of up to 120 words. Length: up to 165 lines/poem. Pays 1 contributor's copy.

TIPS "As a 501(c)(3) nonprofit enterprise, *Van Gogh's Ear* needs the support of individual poets, writers, and readers to survive. Any donation, large or small, will help *Van Gogh's Ear* continue to publish the best cross-section of contemporary poetry and prose. Because of being an anglophone publication based in France, *Van Gogh's Ear* is unable to get any grants or funding. Your contribution will be tax-deductible. Make donation checks payable to Committee on Poetry-*VGE*, and mail them (donations **only**) to the Allen Ginsberg Trust, P.O. Box 582, Stuyvesant Station, New York NY 10009."

⑤ VANILLEROTICA LITERARY EZINE
Cleveland OH 44111. (216)203-4166. **E-mail:** talentdripseroticpublishing@yahoo.com. **Website:** eroticatalentdrips.wordpress.com. **Contact:** Kimberly Steele, founder. *Vanillerotica*, published bi-monthly online, focuses solely on showcasing new romantic erotic fiction. Acquires electronic rights only. Rights revert to authors and poets upon publication. Work archived on the site for 2 months. Time between acceptance and publication is 1 month. Responds to general and submission queries within a week. Guidelines online.

MAGAZINES NEEDS Submit poetry by e-mail to talentdripseroticpublishing@yahoo.com. Accepts e-mail pasted into body of message. Reads submissions during publication months only. Length: up to 30 lines/poem. Pays $10 for each accepted poem.

CONTEST/AWARD OFFERINGS *Vanillerotica Literary EZine* Poet of the Year Contest is held annually. **Prizes:** $75 1st place, $50 2nd place, and certificate. **Deadline:** November 25. Guidelines on website.

TIPS "Please read our take on the difference between *erotica* and *pornography* on the website. *Vanillerotica* does not accept pornography. And please keep poetry 30 lines or less."

VEGETARIAN JOURNAL
P.O. Box 1463, Baltimore MD 21203-1463. (410)366-8343. **E-mail:** vrg@vrg.org. **Website:** www.vrg.org. **Contact:** Debra Wasserman, editor. Quarterly nonprofit vegan magazine that examines the health, environmental and ethical aspects of veganism. "Highly-educated audience including health professionals." Sample copy: $4.

○ *Vegetarian Journal* is 36 pages, magazine-sized, professionally printed, saddle-stapled, with glossy card cover.

MAGAZINES NEEDS "Please, no submissions of poetry from adults; 18 and under only."

CONTEST/AWARD OFFERINGS The Vegetarian Resource Group offers an annual contest for ages 18 and under: $50 prize in 3 age categories for the best contribution on any aspect of vegetarianism. "Most entries are essay, but we would accept poetry with enthusiasm." **Deadline:** May 1 (postmark). Details available at website: http://www.vrg.org/essay/

TIPS Areas most open to freelancers are recipe section and feature articles. "Review magazine first to learn our style. Send query letter with photocopy sample of line drawings of food."

◐ VERANDAH LITERARY & ART JOURNAL
Faculty of Arts, Deakin University, 221 Burwood Hwy., Burwood VIC 3125, Australia. (614)2381-1048. **E-mail:** verandah@deakin.edu.au. **Website:** verandahjournal.wordpress.com. **Contact:** Verandah 34. *Verandah*, published annually, is a high-quality literary and art journal edited by professional writing students. It aims to give voice to new and innovative writers and artists. Acquires first Australian publishing rights. Sample: $20 AUD. Guidelines online.

○ Submission period: April 1 through June 30. Has published work by Margaret Atwood, Christos Tsiolka, Dorothy Porter, Seamus Heaney, Les Murray, Ed Burger, and John Muk Muk Burke. *Verandah* is a print journal roughly pages, professionally printed often on glossy stock, flat-spined, with full-color glossy card cover.

MAGAZINES NEEDS Submit via Submittable, see website for instructions. Reads submissions by June 30 deadline. Length: 100 lines maximum. Pays 1 contributor's copy, "with prizes awarded accordingly." Aims to pay ~$30 this year per piece.

TIPS "Check our website!"

VERSE

English Department, University of Richmond, Richmond VA 23173. **Website:** versemag.blogspot.com. **Contact:** Brian Henry, co-editor; Andrew Zawacki, co-editor. *Verse*, published 3 times/year, is an international poetry journal which also publishes interviews with poets, essays on poetry, and book reviews. Wants no specific kind; looks for high-quality, innovative poetry. Focus is not only on American poetry, but on all poetry written in English, as well as translations. Has published poetry by James Tate, John Ashbery, Barbara Guest, Gustaf Sobin, and Rae Armantrout. Guidelines available online.

- *Verse* is 128-416 pages, digest-sized, professionally printed, perfect-bound, with card cover. Receives about 5,000 poems/year, accepts 10%. Press run is 1,000. Single copy: $10; subscription: $15 for individuals, $39 for institutions. Sample: $6. *Verse* has a $10 reading fee for the print edition. Note that *Verse* will sometimes publish individual pieces on the website if they decide not to publish the entire body of work.

MAGAZINES NEEDS Submissions should be chapbook-length (20-40 pages). Pays $10/page, $250 minimum.

TIPS "Read widely and deeply. Avoid inundating a magazine with submissions; constant exposure will not increase your chances of getting accepted."

THE VIRGINIA QUARTERLY REVIEW

VQR, P.O. Box 400223, Charlottesville VA 22904. **E-mail:** editors@vqronline.org. **Website:** www.vqronline.org. **Contact:** Allison Wright, executive editor. "*VQR*'s primary mission has been to sustain and strengthen Jefferson's bulwark, long describing itself as 'A National Journal of Literature and Discussion.' And for good reason. From its inception in prohibition, through depression and war, in prosperity and peace, *The Virginia Quarterly Review* has been a haven—and home—for the best essayists, fiction writers, and poets, seeking contributors from every section of the United States and abroad. It has not limited itself to any special field. No topic has been alien: literary, public affairs, the arts, history, the economy. If it could be approached through essay or discussion, poetry or prose, *VQR* has covered it." Press run is 4,000. Buys first North American print and digital magazine rights, nonexclusive online rights, and other limited rights. Responds in 3 months to mss. Guidelines available on website.

MAGAZINES NEEDS Sponsors the Emily Clark Balch Prize for Poetry, an annual award of $1,000 given to the best poem or group of poems published in the *Review* during the year. *The Virginia Quarterly Review* prints approximately 12 pages of poetry in each issue. No length or subject restrictions. Issues have largely included lyric and narrative free verse, most of which features a strong message or powerful voice. Accepts online submissions only at virginiaquarterlyreview.submittable.com/submit. Pays $200/poem.

VISIONS-INTERNATIONAL

Black Buzzard Press, 309 Lakeside Dr., Garner NC 27529. (984)202-5559. **E-mail:** vias.poetry@gmail.com. **Website:** www.visionsi.com. **Contact:** Bradley R. Strahan. Buys first North American serial rights. Pays on publication. Publishes ms an average of 6 months after acceptance. Responds in 3 weeks to queries; 1 month to mss. Editorial lead time 1 month. Sample copy: $5.50. Guidelines online.

- "We publish well-crafted exciting poetry and translations from modern poets, everywhere. Particularly interested in translations from less well-known languages. For example, we've published work from Albanian, Armenian, Bulgarian, Faroese, Kurdish, Icelandic, and Urdu, just to name a few."

MAGAZINES NEEDS Send 3-5 unpublished poems not sent elsewhere. Please no self-centered workshop ramblings; no perfect form without meaningful content; no questionable language used purely for shock value. Length: 2-120 lines. Pays in copies.

TIPS "Know your craft. We are not a magazine for amateurs. We also are interested in translation from modern poets writing in any language into English."

VOICES ISRAEL

P.O. Box 21, Metulla 10292, Israel. **E-mail:** voicesisraelpoetryanthology@gmail.com; voicesisrael.webmaster@gmail.com. **Website:** www.voicesisrael.com. **Contact:** Dina Yehuda, editor. *Voices Israel*, published annually by The Voices Israel Group of Poets, is "an anthology of poetry in English, with worldwide contributions. We consider all kinds of poetry." Poems must be in English; translations must be accompanied by the original poem. Single copy: $25 for nonmembers. Sample: $15 (back issue). "Members receive the anthology with annual dues ($35)."

Voices Israel is about 300 pages, digest-sized, offset from laser output on ordinary paper, flat-spined, with varying cover. Press run is 350.

MAGAZINES NEEDS Submit up to 3 poems/year via online submissions manager. "We do not guarantee publication of any poem. In poems we publish, we reserve the right to correct obviously unintentional errors in spelling, punctuation, etc." Length: 40 lines or 400 words maximum.

ALSO OFFERS The annual International Reuben Rose Memorial Poetry Competition offers 1st Prize: $500; 2nd Prize $200; 3rd Prize: $100; and Honorable Mentions. Winning poems are published and distributed together with the *Voices Israel* anthology.

THE WAR CRY

The Salvation Army, 615 Slaters Lane, Alexandria VA 22314. (703)684-4128. **Fax:** (703)684-5539. **E-mail:** war_cry@usn.salvationarmy.org. **Website:** publications.salvationarmyusa.org. "Inspirational magazine with evangelical emphasis and portrayals that express the mission of the Salvation Army. Twelve issues published per year, including special Easter and Christmas issues." Buys first rights, buys one-time rights. Pays on acceptance. Publishes ms an average of 2 months to 1 year after acceptance. Responds in 3-4 weeks to mss. Editorial lead time 2 months before issue date; Christmas and Easter issues 6 months before issue date. Sample copy, theme list, and writer's guidelines free with #10 SASE or online.

Word limit for mss 800-1500 words.

MAGAZINES NEEDS Purchases limited poetry (10 per year maximum).

WATERWAYS

Poetry in the Mainstream, Ten Penny Players, Inc., 393 Saint Pauls Ave., Staten Island NY 10304-2127. (718)442-7429. **E-mail:** tenpennyplayers@si.rr.com. **Website:** www.tenpennyplayers.org/mags.html. **Contact:** Barbara Fisher and Richard Spiegel, poetry editors. *Waterways: Poetry in the Mainstream*, published 11 times/year, prints work by adult poets. "We publish theme issues and are trying to increase an audience for poetry and the printed and performed word. While we do 'themes,' sometimes an idea for a future magazine is inspired by a submission, so we try to remain open to poets' inspirations. Poets should be guided, however, by the fact that we are disability, children's, and animal rights advocates and are a NYC press. We are open to reading material from people we have never published, writing in traditional and experimental poetry forms." *Waterways* is 40 pages, 7x4.25, saddle-stapled. Back issues of *Waterways* are published online at www.tenpennyplayers.org and at scribd.com, in addition to being available in the limited printing paper edition. Accepts 40% of poems submitted. Press run is 150. Has published poetry by Kit Knight, James Penha, William Corner Clarke, Wayne Hogan, Sylvia Manning, and Monique Laforce. Acquires one-time rights. Responds in less than 1 month. Sometimes comments on rejected poems. Sample: $5. Subscription: $45. Guidelines available for SASE or on website.

MAGAZINES NEEDS Submit less than 10 poems at a time (for first submission). Accepts e-mail (pasted into body of message) and postal mail submissions (include SASE). Pays 1 contributor's copy.

TIPS "Send for our theme sheet and a sample issue, or view online. Mss that arrive without a return envelope are not sent back."

WEST BRANCH

Stadler Center for Poetry, Bucknell University, Lewisburg PA 17837-2029. (570)577-1853. **Fax:** (570)577-1885. **E-mail:** westbranch@bucknell.edu. **Website:** www.bucknell.edu/westbranch. **Contact:** G.C. Waldrep, editor. *West Branch* publishes poetry, fiction, and nonfiction in both traditional and innovative styles. Buys first North American serial rights. Pays on publication. Sample copy for $3. Guidelines available online.

Reading period: August 15 through April 1. No more than 3 submissions from a single contributor in a given reading period.

MAGAZINES NEEDS Pays $50/submission.

TIPS "All submissions must be sent via our online submission manager. Please see website for guidelines. We recommend that you acquaint yourself with the magazine before submitting."

WESTERN HUMANITIES REVIEW

University of Utah, 3528 LNCO / English Department, 255 S. Central Campus Dr., Salt Lake City UT 84112-0494. (801)581-6168. **Fax:** (801)585-5167. **E-mail:** managingeditor.whr@gmail.com. **Website:** www.westernhumanitiesreview.com. **Contact:** Michael Mejia, editor; Emily Dyer Barker, managing editor. *Western Humanities Review* is a journal of contemporary literature and culture housed in the University of Utah English Department. Publishes poetry, fiction, nonfiction essays, artwork, and work that resists categorization. Submissions are open year-round. All submissions must be sent through online submissions manager. Buys one-time rights. Pays in contributor copies. Publishes ms an average of 1 year after acceptance. Responds in 3-6 months. Sample copy: $10. Guidelines online.

MAGAZINES NEEDS Considers simultaneous submissions but no more than 5 poems or 25 pages per reading period. No fax or e-mail submissions. Reads submissions year-round. Wants quality poetry of any form, including translations. Has published poetry by Charles Simic, Olena Kalytiak Davis, Ravi Shankar, Karen Volkman, Dan Beachy-Quick, Lucie Brock-Broido, Christine Hume, and Dan Chiasson. Innovative prose poems may be submitted as fiction or nonfiction to the appropriate editor. Pays 2 contributor's copies.

CONTEST/AWARD OFFERINGS Sponsors an annual contest for writers in Utah, Colorado, Montana, Wyoming, Idaho, New Mexico, Nevada, and Arizona.

TIPS "Because of changes in our editorial staff, we urge familiarity with recent issues of the magazine. We do not publish writer's guidelines because we think that the magazine itself conveys an accurate picture of our requirements. Please, no e-mail submissions."

WESTVIEW

A Journal of Western Oklahoma, Southwestern Oklahoma State University, 100 Campus Dr., Weatherford OK 73096. **E-mail:** westview@swosu.edu. **Website:** dc.swosu.edu/westview/. **Contact:** Amanda Smith, editor. Westview, a literary journal published by Southwestern Oklahoma State university, is accepting short fiction, creative nonfiction, poetry, and artwork submissions (open theme/deadline/no fee). 5,000 word maximum for prose. Double-blind review. Submissions including identification information will be rejected. Simultaneous submissions allowed with notification of withdrawal if accepted elsewhere. Submit via http://dc.swosu.edu/westview/. Has published poetry by Carolynne Wright, Miller Williams, Walter McDonald, Robert Cooperman, Alicia Ostriker, and James Whitehead. Westview is 64 pages, magazine-sized, perfect-bound, with full-color glossy card cover. Receives about 500 poems/year; accepts 7%. Press run is 600 (250 subscribers; about 25 libraries). Subscription: $15/2 years; $25/2 years international. Sample: $6.

WESTWARD QUARTERLY

The Magazine of Family Reading, Laudemont Press, P.O. Box 369, Hamilton IL 62341. (800)440-4043. E-mail: editor@wwquarterly.com. **Website:** www.ww-quarterly.com. **Contact:** Shirley Anne Leonard, editor. WestWard Quarterly: The Magazine of Family Reading prints poetry. Every issue includes a "Featured Writer" and a piece on improving writing skills or writing different forms of poetry. WestWard Quarterly is 32 pages, digest-sized, laser-printed, saddle-stapled, with inkjet color cover with scenic photos, and includes ads. Receives about 1,500 poems/year, accepts about 12%. Press run is 150 (60 subscribers). Acquires one-time rights. Responds in weeks. Often comments on rejected poems. Single copy: $4 ($6 foreign); subscription: $15/year ($18 foreign). Contributors to an issue may order extra copies at a discounted price. Make checks payable to Laudemont Press. Guidelines available for SASE, by e-mail, or on website.

MAGAZINES NEEDS Wants "all forms, including rhyme—we welcome inspirational, positive, reflective, humorous material promoting nobility, compassion, and courage." Does not want "experimental or avant-garde forms, offensive language, depressing or negative poetry." Submit up to 5 poems at a time. Prefers e-mail submissions (pasted into body of message); no disk submissions. Reads submissions year round. Considers poetry by children and teens. Has published poetry by Esther Leiper-Estabrooks, Michael Keshigian, Richard Luftig, Jane Stuart, and Charles Waugaman. Length: up to 40 lines/poem. Pays 1 contributor's copy.

WHISKEY ISLAND MAGAZINE

English Dept., Cleveland State University, 2121 Euclid Ave., Cleveland OH 44115. (216)687-3951. **E-mail:** whiskeyisland@csuohio.edu. **Website:** whiskeyislandmagazine.com. **Contact:** Dan Dorman. Whiskey Island is a nonprofit literary magazine that has been published in one form or another by students of Cleveland State University for over 30 years. Responds in 3 months to mss. Sample copy: $6.

Reading periods: August 15 through November 15 and January 15 through April 15. Paper and e-mail submissions are not accepted. No multiple submissions.

MAGAZINES NEEDS Submit 3-5 poems via online submissions manager. Please combine all the poems you wish to submit into one document. Pays 2 contributor's copies.

WHITE WALL REVIEW

Department of English, Ryerson University, 10th Floor, Jorgenson Hall, 350 Victoria St., Toronto ON

M5B 2K3, Canada. **E-mail:** wwr@arts.ryerson.ca. **Website:** www.ryerson.ca/wwr/. *White Wall Review*, published annually in August, focuses on printing "clearly expressed, innovative poetry and prose. No style is unacceptable." Has published poetry by Vernon Mooers and David Sidjak. *White Wall Review* is 90-144 pages, digest-sized, professionally printed, perfect-bound, with glossy card cover. Press run is 500. Subscription: $10 plus GST.

MAGAZINES NEEDS Submit up to 5 poems at a time by mail only. Length: 5 pages/piece maximum. Cover letter is required. Include short bio. Guidelines available in magazine, for SASE. Responds "as soon as possible." Pays 1 contributor's copy.

TIPS "Innovative work is especially appreciated."

WICKED ALICE

E-mail: wickedalicepoetry@yahoo.com. **Website:** www.sundresspublications.com/wickedalice. **Contact:** Kristy Bowen, editor. "*Wicked Alice* is a women-centered online journal dedicated to publishing quality work by both sexes, depicting and exploring the female experience." Wants "work that has a strong sense of image and music. Work that is interesting and surprising, with innovative, sometimes unusual, use of language. We love humor when done well, strangeness, wackiness. Hybridity, collage, intertexuality." Acquires one-time rights. Responds in 1-6 months. Guidelines available online.

MAGAZINES NEEDS Submit 3-5 poems via e-mail. Has published poetry by Daniela Olszewska, Rebecca Loudon, Robyn Art, Simone Muench, Brandi Homan, and Karyna McGlynn. Receives about 500 poems/year, accepts about 8%. Does not want greeting card verse. Length: open.

WILD GOOSE POETRY REVIEW

Hickory NC 28235-5009. **E-mail:** asowens1@yahoo.com. **Website:** www.wildgoosepoetryreview.com. *Wild Goose Poetry Review* is "looking for good contemporary poetry. No particular biases. We enjoy humor, strong imagery, strong lines, narrative, lyric, etc. Not a fan of abstraction, cliché, form for the sake of form, shock for the sake of shock. As in any good poem, everything should be purposeful." Receives more than 1,000 poems/year, accepts less than 10%. Reviews books/chapbooks of poetry. Send materials for review consideration to Scott Owens. Has published poetry by Anthony Abbott, Karen Douglass, and Lisa Zaran. Author retains all rights. Time between acceptance and publication is up to 6 months. Usually responds to mss within 3 months.

MAGAZINES NEEDS Accepts e-mail submissions only, pasted into body of e-mail; no attachments; no disk submissions. Cover letter is preferred; include bio. Reads submissions year round.

WILD VIOLET

P.O. Box 39706, Philadelphia PA 19106. **E-mail:** wildvioletmagazine@yahoo.com. **Website:** www.wildviolet.net. **Contact:** Alyce Wilson, editor. *Wild Violet*, published monthly online, aims "to make the arts more accessible, to make a place for the arts in modern life, and to serve as a creative forum for writers and artists. Our audience includes English-speaking readers from all over the world who are interested in both 'high art' and pop culture." Requests limited electronic rights for online publication and archival only. Time between acceptance and publication is 6 months. "Decisions on acceptance or rejection are made by the editor." Responds in 1 week to queries; 3-6 months to mss. Guidelines online by e-mail or on website.

MAGAZINES NEEDS Wants "poetry that is well crafted, that engages thought, that challenges or uplifts the reader. We have published free verse, haiku, blank verse, and other forms. If the form suits the poem, we will consider any form." Does not want "abstract, self-involved poetry; poorly managed form; excessive rhyming; self-referential poems that do not show why the speaker is sad, happy, or in love." Has published poetry by Lyn Lifshin, Kimberly Gladman, Andrew H. Oerke, Simon Perchik, John Grey, Joanna Weston, and Amy Barone. Accepts about 15% of work submitted. Submit 3-5 poems at a time. Accepts e-mail submissions (pasted into body of message, or as text or Word attachment) and postal mail submissions; no disk submissions. Cover letter is preferred. Reads submissions year round. Seldom comments on rejected poems, unless requested. Occasionally publishes theme issues.

ALSO OFFERS Reviews books/chapbooks of poetry in 250 words, single-book format. Query for review consideration. Sponsors an annual poetry contest, offering 1st Prize: $100 and publication in *Wild Violet*; 2 Honorable Mentions will also be published. Guidelines available by e-mail or on website. **Entry fee:** $5/poem. Judged by independent judges.

TIPS "We look for stories that are well-paced and show character and plot development. Even short shorts should do more than simply paint a picture. Manuscripts stand out when the author's voice is fresh and engaging. Avoid muddying your story with too many characters, and don't attempt to shock the reader with an ending you have not earned. Experiment with styles and structures, but don't resort to experimentation for its own sake."

WILLOW REVIEW

College of Lake County Publications, College of Lake County, 19351 W. Washington St., Grayslake IL 60030-1198. (847)543-2956. **E-mail:** com426@clcillinois.edu. **Website:** www.clcillinois.edu/community/willowreview.asp. **Contact:** Michael Latza, editor. *Willow Review*, published annually, is interested in poetry, creative nonfiction, and fiction of high quality. "We have no preferences as to form, style, or subject, as long as each piece stands on its own as art and communicates ideas." The editors award prizes for best poetry and prose in the issue. Prize awards vary contingent on the current year's budget but normally range from $100-400. There is no reading fee or separate application for these prizes. All accepted mss are eligible."*Willow Review* can be found on EBSCOhost databases, assuring a broader targeted audience for our authors' work. *Willow Review* is a nonprofit journal partially supported by a grant from the Illinois Arts Council (a state agency), College of Lake County Publications, private contributions, and sales." All rights revert to author upon publication. Responds in 3-4 months to mss. Sample: $5 (back issue). Subscription: $18/3 issues, $30/6 issues. International: add $5 per issue. Guidelines available on website.

MAGAZINES NEEDS Considers simultaneous submissions "if indicated in the cover letter." No e-mail submissions; postal submissions only. Include SASE; mss will not be returned unless requested. Reads submissions September through May. Has published poetry by Lisel Mueller, Lucien Stryk, David Ray, Louis Rodriguez, John Dickson, and Patricia Smith. Pays 2 contributor's copies.

ALSO OFFERS Prizes totaling $400 are awarded to the best poetry and short fiction/creative nonfiction in each issue. The College of Lake County Reading Series (4-7 readings/academic year) has included Thomas Lux, Isabel Allende, Donald Justice, Galway Kinnell, Lisel Mueller, Amiri Baraka, and others. One reading is for contributors to *Willow Review*. Readings, usually held on Thursday evenings and widely publicized in Chicago and suburban newspapers, are presented to audiences of about 150 students and faculty of the College of Lake County and other area colleges, as well as residents of local communities.

⑤ WILLOW SPRINGS

668 N. Riverpoint Blvd. #259, Spokane WA 99202. (509)828-1486. **E-mail:** willowspringsewu@gmail.com. **Website:** willowsprings.ewu.edu. **Contact:** Samuel Ligon, editor. *Willow Springs* is a semiannual magazine covering poetry, fiction, literary nonfiction and interviews of notable writers. Published twice a year, in spring and fall. Reading period: September 1 through May 31 for fiction and poetry; year-round for nonfiction. Reading fee: $3/submission. Buys one-time rights. Publishes ms an average of 3 months after acceptance. Sample copy: $10. Guidelines online.

MAGAZINES NEEDS "Buy a sample copy to learn our tastes. Our aesthetic is very open." Submit only 3-5 poems at a time. Pays $20/poem and 2 contributor's copies.

TIPS "While we have no specific length restrictions, we generally publish fiction and nonfiction no longer than 10,000 words and poetry no longer than 120 lines, though those are not strict rules. *Willow Springs* values poems and essays that transcend the merely autobiographical and fiction that conveys a concern for language as well as story."

WITCHES AND PAGANS

BBI Media, Inc., P.O. Box 687, Forest Grove OR 97116. (503)430-8817. **E-mail:** editor2@bbimedia.com. **Website:** www.witchesandpagans.com. **Contact:** Anne Newkirk Niven. "Devoted exclusively to promoting and covering contemporary Pagan culture, *W&P* features exclusive interviews with the teachers, writers, and activists who create and lead our traditions, visits to the sacred places and people who inspire us, and in-depth discussions of our ever-evolving practices. You'll also find practical daily magic, ideas for solitary ritual and devotion, God/dess-friendly craft-projects, Pagan poetry and short fiction, reviews, and much more in every 88-page issue. *W&P* is available in either traditional paper copy sent by postal mail or as a digital PDF e-zine download that is compatible with most computers and readers." Buys first worldwide periodical and nonexclusive electronic rights. No cash payment, but 4 contributor's copies and one-year subscription given for published submissions. Publishes ms 3 months-2 years after acceptance. Responds in 1-2 weeks to queries; 1 month to mss. Editorial lead time is 3-4 months. Sample copy: $6. Guidelines online.

TIPS "Read the magazine, do your research, write the piece, send it in. That's really the only way to get started as a writer; everything else is window dressing."

⑤ WOODS READER

P.O. Box 46, Warren MN 56762. **E-mail:** editor@woodsreader.com. **Website:** www.woodsreader.com. **Contact:** S Sedgwick. A quarterly publication for those who love woodland areas: whether a public preserve, forest, tree farm, backyard woodlot or other patch of trees and wildlife. Will only consider articles based on woodlands. "We are looking for positive, whimsical, interesting articles. Our readers like to hear about others' experiences and insights. Please visit submissions page on website. We encourage stories of personal experience. We also buy forest ecology mss of general interest, DIY (photos must accompany), personal essays, book reviews (query first)." Buys first North American serial rights plus reprint rights, digital and print. Pays on acceptance or publication. Publishes ms 3-12 months after acceptance. Responds in 3 months or less. Sample copy available online for $8. Guidelines online or query.

MAGAZINES NEEDS Length: 2-16 lines. Pays $25.

THE WORCESTER REVIEW

P.O. Box 804, Worcester MA 01613. **E-mail:** editor.worcreview@gmail.com. **Website:** www.theworcesterreview.org. **Contact:** Diane Vanaskie Mulligan, managing editor. *The Worcester Review*, published annually by the Worcester County Poetry Association, encourages "critical work with a New England connection; no geographic limitation on poetry and fiction." Wants "work that is crafted, intuitively honest and empathetic. We like high-quality, creative poetry, artwork, and fiction. Critical articles should be connected to New England." *The Worcester Review* is 160 pages, digest-sized, professionally printed in dark type on quality stock, perfect-bound, with matte card cover. Press run is 600. Acquires one-time rights. Pays small honorarium upon publication. Publishes ms within 1 year of acceptance. Responds in 1-3 months to mss. Sometimes comments on rejected mss. Guidelines online.

MAGAZINES NEEDS Submit up to 5 poems at a time via online submission manager. Cover letter is optional. Has published poetry by Kurt Brown, Cleopatra Mathis, and Theodore Deppe. Pays 2 contributor's copies plus small honorarium.

TIPS "We generally look for creative work with a blend of craftsmanship, insight, and empathy. This does not exclude humor. We won't print work that is shoddy in any of these areas."

⑤ WORKERS WRITE!

Blue Cubicle Press, LLC, P.O. Box 250382, Plano TX 75025. **E-mail:** info@workerswritejournal.com. **Website:** www.workerswritejournal.com. **Contact:** David LaBounty, managing editor. "*Workers Write!* is an annual print journal published by Blue Cubicle Press, an independent publisher dedicated to giving voice to writers trapped in the daily grind. Each issue focuses on a particular workplace; check website for details. Submit your stories via e-mail or send a hard copy." Buys first North American serial rights, electronic rights, one-time rights, second serial (reprint) rights. Pays on acceptance. Publishes mss 4-6 months after acceptance. Responds in 1 week to queries; in 3 months to mss. Sample copy available on website. Writer's guidelines free for #10 SASE and on website.

MAGAZINES NEEDS Pays $5-10.

THE WRITE PLACE AT THE WRITE TIME

E-mail: questions@thewriteplaceatthewritetime.org. **E-mail:** submissions@thewriteplaceatthewritetime.org. **Website:** www.thewriteplaceatthewritetime.org. Assistant Editor: Denise Bouchard.. **Contact:** Nicole M. Bouchard, editor-in-chief. Online literary magazine, published 3 times/year. Publishes fiction, personal nonfiction, craft essays by professionals, and poetry that "speaks to the heart and mind. Our writers come from around the world and range from previously unpublished to having written for *The New York Times*, *Time* magazine, *The New Yorker*, *The Wall Street Journal*, *Glimmer Train*, *Newsweek*, *Business Week*, Random House, and Simon and Schuster. Interview subjects include *NYT* best-selling authors such as Tracy Chevalier, Dennis Lehane, Mona Simpson, Janet Fitch, Alice Hoffman, Joanne Harris, Arthur Golden, Jodi Picoult, and Frances Mayes." Acquires first electronic rights, archive rights, and one-time reprint rights. This varies depending on which issue the piece will appear in. Responds to queries in a few weeks or sooner. Responses regarding pieces slated for later issues may take a few months, depending on submission volume. Frequently comments on rejected mss. See current issue via website and view past issues in our online archives. Guidelines online.

MAGAZINES NEEDS Submit via e-mail—no attachments. Include cover letter with brief bio. Length: up to 30 lines/poem. "If we feel the strength of the submission merits added length, we are happy to consider exceptions."

TIPS "Through our highly personalized approach to content, feedback, and community, we aim to give a very human visage to the publishing process. We wish to speak deeply of the human condition through pieces that validate the entire spectrum of emotions and the real circumstances of life. Every piece has a unique power and presence that stands on its own; we've had writers write about surviving an illness, losing a child, embracing a foreign land, learning of their parent's suicide, discovering love, finding humor in dark hours, and healing from abuse. Our collective voice, from our aesthetic to our artwork to the words, looks at and highlights aspects of life through a storytelling lens that allows for or promotes a universal understanding."

WRITER'S BLOC

MSC 162, Fore Hall Rm. 110, 700 University Blvd., Texas A&M University-Kingsville, Kingsville TX 78363. (361)593-2516. **E-mail:** kfmrj00@tamuk.edu; connie.salgado@tamuk.edu. **E-mail.** WritersBloc-LitMag@hotmail.com. **Website:** www.tamuk.edu/artsci/langlit/writers_bloc.html. **Contact:** Dr. Michelle Johnson Vela. *Writer's Bloc*, published annually, prints poetry, short fiction, flash fiction, one-act plays, interviews, and essays. "About half of our pages are devoted to the works of Texas A&M University-Kingsville students and half to the works of writers and artists from all over the world." Wants quality poetry; no restrictions on content or form. Sample copy: $7. Guidelines online or in magazine.

○ *Writer's Bloc* is 96 pages, digest-sized. Press run is 300. Reading period: February through May.

MAGAZINES NEEDS Submit via e-mail or postal mail. Include cover letter with contact info, short bio. "Prose poems okay. Submissions should be typed, double-spaced; SASE required for reply. Mss are published upon recommendation by a staff of students and faculty." Seldom comments on rejected poems. Length: no more than 50 lines. Pays 1 contributor's copy.

THE WRITING DISORDER

A Literary Journal, P.O. Box 93613, Los Angeles CA 90093. **E-mail:** submit@thewritingdisorder.com. **Website:** www.writingdisorder.com. **Contact:** C.E. Lukather, editor; Paul Garson, managing editor; Ju-

lianna Woodhead, poetry editor. "*The Writing Disorder* is an online literary journal devoted to literature, art, and culture. Our mission is to showcase new and emerging writers—particularly those in writing programs—as well as established ones. We feature new fiction, poetry, nonfiction and art. Although we strive to publish original and experimental work, *The Writing Disorder* remains rooted in the classic art of storytelling. Send us your best work. Have someone proof your work before submitting. No limit on word count." Acquires first North American serial rights. Pays on publication. Publishes ms an average of 3-6 months after acceptance. Responds in 6-12 weeks to queries; 3-6 months to ms. Editorial lead time 3 months. Sample copy online. Guidelines online.

MAGAZINES NEEDS Query. Annual print anthology of best work published online. Pays a contributor's copy of anthology to writers whose work has been selected for inclusion.

TIPS "We are looking for work from new writers, writers in writing programs, and students and faculty of all ages."

❸ THE YALE REVIEW

The Yale Review, P.O. Box 208243, New Haven CT 06520-8243. (203)432-0499. **Fax:** (203)432-0510. **Website:** www.yale.edu/yalereview. **Contact:** J.D. McClatchy, editor. "Like Yale's schools of music, drama, and architecture, like its libraries and art galleries, *The Yale Review* has helped give the University its leading place in American education. In a land of quick fixes and short view and in a time of increasingly commercial publishing, the journal has an authority that derives from its commitment to bold established writers and promising newcomers, to both challenging literary work and a range of essays and reviews that can explore the connections between academic disciplines and the broader movements in American society, thought, and culture. With independence and boldness, with a concern for issues and ideas, with a respect for the mind's capacity to be surprised by speculation and delighted by elegance, *The Yale Review* proudly continues into its third century." Buys one-time rights. Pays prior to publication. Publishes ms an average of 6 months after acceptance. Responds in 1-3 months to mss. Sample copy online. Guidelines available online.

MAGAZINES NEEDS Submit with SASE. All submissions should be sent to the editorial office. Pays $100-250.

THE YALOBUSHA REVIEW

E-mail: yreditors@gmail.com. **Website:** yr.olemiss. edu. Acquires first North American serial rights. Responds in 2-4 months to mss.

MAGAZINES NEEDS Submit 3-5 poems via online submissions manager.

YEMASSEE

University of South Carolina, Department of English, Columbia SC 29208. **E-mail:** editor@yemasseejournal.com. **Website:** yemasseejournal.com. "*Yemassee* is the University of South Carolina's literary journal. Our readers are interested in exceptional fiction, poetry, creative nonfiction, and visual art. We publish in the fall and spring. We tend to solicit reviews and interviews but welcome unsolicited queries. We do not favor any particular aesthetic or school of writing." Buys first North American serial rights; buys electronic rights. Publishes ms an average of 4-6 months after acceptance. Responds in 1-4 months to queries and mss. Editorial lead time 3 months. Sample copy: $5. Guidelines online, as well as on our Submittable.

MAGAZINES NEEDS Submit 3-5 poems combined into a single document. Submissions for all genres should include a cover letter that lists the titles of the pieces included, along with your contact information (including author's name, address, e-mail address, and phone number). Does not want workshop poems, unpolished drafts, generic/unoriginal themes, or bad Hemingway. Does not want poems of such a highly personal nature that their primary relevance is to the author. Length: 1-120 lines. Pays 2 contributor's copies.

CONTEST/AWARD OFFERINGS Yemassee Poetry Contest: $750 award. Yemassee Poetry Chapbook Contest: $1000 award. Check website for deadline.

ZEEK

A Jewish Journal of Thought and Culture, 125 Maiden Ln., 8th Floor, New York NY 10038. (212)453-9435. **E-mail:** zeek@zeek.net. **Website:** www.zeek.net. **Contact:** Erica Brody, editor in chief. *ZEEK* "relaunched in late February 2013 as a hub for the domestic Jewish social justice movement, one that showcases the people, ideas, and conversations driving an inclusive and diverse progressive Jewish community. At the same time, we've reaffirmed our commitment to building on *ZEEK*'s reputation for original, ahead-of-the-curve Jewish writing and arts, culture and spirituality content, incubating emerging voices and artists, as well as established ones." *ZEEK* seeks "great writing in a variety of styles and voices, original thinking, and accessible content. That means we're interested in hearing your ideas for first-person essays, reflections and commentary, reporting, profiles, Q&As, analysis, infographics, and more. For the near future, *ZEEK* will focus on domestic issues. Our discourse will be civil." Responds in 6 weeks to queries.

MAGAZINES NEEDS "Pitches should be sent to zeek@zeek.net, with 'submission' or 'pitch' in the subject line. And please include a little bit about yourself and why you think your pitch is a good fit for *ZEEK*."

⑤ ZYZZYVA

57 Post St., Suite 604, San Francisco CA 94104. (415)757-0465. **E-mail:** editor@zyzzyva.org. **Website:** www.zyzzyva.org. **Contact:** Laura Cogan, editor; Oscar Villalon, managing editor. "Every issue is a vibrant mix of established talents and new voices, providing an elegantly curated overview of contemporary arts and letters with a distinctly San Francisco perspective." Buys first North American serial and one-time anthology rights. Pays on acceptance. Publishes ms an average of 3 months after acceptance. Responds in 1 week to queries; in 1 month to mss. Sample copy: $12. Guidelines available online.

Accepts submissions January 1-May 31 and August 1-November 30. Does not accept online submissions.

MAGAZINES NEEDS Submit by mail. Include SASE and contact information. Length: no limit. Pays $50.

TIPS "We are not currently seeking work about any particular theme or topic; that said, reading recent issues is perhaps the best way to develop a sense for the length and quality we are looking for in submissions."

BOOK/CHAPBOOK PUBLISHERS

//

Every poet dreams of publishing a collection of his or her work. However, it's surprising how many poets still envision putting out a thick, hardbound volume containing hundreds of poems. In reality, poetry books are usually slim, often paperback, with varying levels of production quality, depending on the publisher.

More common than full-length poetry books (i.e., 50-150 pages by modern standards) are poetry *chapbooks*, small editions of approximately 24-32 pages. They may be printed on quality paper with beautiful cover art on heavy stock; or they may be photocopied sheets of plain printer paper, folded and stapled or hand-sewn along the spine.

In this section you'll find a variety of presses and publishers of poetry books and chapbooks. However, it's a reflection of how poetry publishing works in the early 21st century that many book/chapbook publishing opportunities appear in the Contest & Awards section instead.

GETTING STARTED, FINDING A PUBLISHER

If you don't have a publisher in mind, read randomly through the listings, making notes as you go. (Don't hesitate to write in the margins, underline, use highlighters; it also helps to flag markets that interest you with Post-It Notes). Browsing the listings is an effective way to familiarize yourself with the kind of information presented and the publishing opportunities that are available at various skill levels. If you're thinking of a specific publisher by name, however, begin with the General Index. Here all *Poet's Market* listings are alphabetized.

ÉCRITS DES FORGES

992-A, rue Royale, Trois-Rivières QC G9A 4H9, Canada. (819)840-8492. **Website:** www.ecritsdesforges.com. **Contact:** Bernard Pozier, director. Pays royalties of 10-20%. Responds to queries in 6 months.

NEEDS Écrits des Forges publishes poetry only that is "authentic and original as a signature. We have published poetry from more than 1,000 poets coming from most of the francophone countries." Publishes 45-50 paperback books of poetry/year. Books are usually 80-88 pages, digest-sized, perfect-bound, with 2-color covers with art.

HOW TO CONTACT Query first with a few sample poems and a cover letter with brief bio and publication credits. Order sample books by writing or faxing.

AHSAHTA PRESS

MFA Program in Creative Writing, Boise State University, 1910 University Dr., MS 1525, Boise ID 83725. (208) 426-3414. **E-mail:** ahsahta@boisestate.edu. **Website:** ahsahtapress.org. **Contact:** Janet Holmes, director. A not-for-profit literary publisher, Ahsahta was founded in 1974 at Boise State University to preserve the best works by early poets of the American West. Its name, *ahsahta,* is the Mandan word meaning "Rocky Mountain bighorn sheep," and was first recorded by members of the Lewis and Clark expedition; the founding editors chose the word to honor the press's original mission to publish Western poetry. Peggy Pond Church, H.L. Davis, Hazel Hall, Gwendolen Haste, Haniel Long, and Norman Macleod are among the early Western writers Ahsahta Press restored to print. Soon after its inception, the press began publishing contemporary poetry by Western poets along with its reprint titles. Ahsahta editors discovered and initially published a number of widely popular poets from the West—among them David Baker, Katharine Coles, Wyn Cooper, Gretel Ehrlich, Cynthia Hogue, Leo Romero, and Carolyne Wright. With the inception of the M.F.A. Program in Creative Writing at Boise State University, Ahsahta Press expanded its scope, presenting the work of poets from across the nation whose work is selected through our national competitions or by general submission. These include Julie Carr, Anne Boyer, Kate Greenstreet, Brian Teare, James Meetze, and TC Tolbert. "Ahsahta Press champions and promotes surprising, relevant, and accessible experimental poetry that more commercially minded small presses avoid; in making it widely available, we aim to increase its readership." Publishes trade paperback originals. Pays 8% royalty on retail price for first 1,000 sold; 10% thereafter. Does not usually pay advance. Publishes ms 2 years after acceptance. Responds in 3 months to mss. Book catalog online. Guidelines online; submit through submissions manager.

NEEDS "We usually hold an open submissions period in May as well as the Sawtooth Poetry Prize competition in January and February, from which we publish 2-3 mss per year. We no longer publish chapbooks."

HOW TO CONTACT Submit complete ms. The press publishes runners-up as well as winners of the Sawtooth Poetry Prize. Forthcoming, new, and backlist titles available on website. Most backlist titles: $9.95; most current titles: $18.

TIPS "Ahsahta's motto is that poetry is art, so our readers tend to come to us for the unexpected—poetry that makes them think, reflect, question their preconceptions, and even do something they haven't done before."

ANHINGA PRESS

P.O. Box 3665, Tallahassee FL 32315. **E-mail:** info@anhinga.org. **Website:** www.anhingapress.org. **Contact:** Kristine Snodgrass, co-director. Publishes four full-length poetry collections and one chapbook per year. Also publishes anthologies, broadsides. Publishes hardcover and trade paperback originals. Pays 10% royalty on retail price. Does not pay advance. Responds in 3-5 months. Guidelines online.

NEEDS Not accepting any unsolicited submissions at this time. Enter Anhinga- Robert Dana for Poetry and Rick Campbell Chapbook Prize. Details on website.

ANVIL PRESS

P.O. Box 3008 MPO, Vancouver BC V6B 3X5, Canada. (604)876-8710. **Fax:** (604)879-2667. **E-mail:** info@anvilpress.com. **Website:** www.anvilpress.com. Anvil Press publishes contemporary adult fiction, poetry, and drama, giving voice to up-and-coming Canadian writers, exploring all literary genres, discovering, nurturing, and promoting new Canadian literary talent. Currently emphasizing urban/suburban themed fiction and poetry; de-emphasizing historical novels. Canadian authors only. No e-mail submissions. Publishes trade paperback originals. Pays advance. Average advance is $500-2,000, depending on the genre.

Publishes book 8 months after acceptance of ms. Responds in 2 months to queries; 6 months to mss. Book catalog for 9×12 SAE with 2 first-class stamps. Guidelines online.

NEEDS "Get our catalog, look at our poetry. We do very little poetry-maybe 1-2 titles per year."

HOW TO CONTACT Query with 8-12 poems and SASE.

TIPS "Audience is informed, educated, aware, with an opinion, culturally active (films, books, the performing arts). No U.S. authors. Research the appropriate publisher for your work."

⬤ ARC PUBLICATIONS

Nanholme Mill, Shaw Wood Rd., Todmorden, Lancashire OL14 6DA, United Kingdom. **E-mail:** info@arcpublications.co.uk. **E-mail:** international-editor@arcpublications.co.uk. **Website:** www.arcpublications.co.uk. **Contact:** John W. Clarke, domestic editor; James Byrne, international editor (outside Ireland/England). Responds in 6 weeks.

NEEDS Publishes "contemporary poetry from new and established writers from the UK and abroad, specializing in the work of world poets writing in English, and the work of overseas poets in translation."

HOW TO CONTACT Send 16-24 pages of poetry and short cover letter.

ARTE PUBLICO PRESS

University of Houston, 4902 Gulf Fwy, Bldg 19, Rm 100, Houston TX 77204-2004. **Fax:** (713)743-2847. **E-mail:** submapp@uh.edu. **Website:** artepublicopress.com. Arte Publico Press is the oldest and largest publisher of Hispanic literature for children and adults in the United States. "We are a showcase for Hispanic literary creativity, arts and culture. Our endeavor is to provide a national forum for U.S.-Hispanic literature." Publishes hardcover originals, trade paperback originals and reprints. Pays 10% royalty on wholesale price. Provides 20 author's copies; 40% discount on subsequent copies. Pays $1,000-3,000 advance. Publishes book 2 years after acceptance of ms. Responds in 1 month to queries and proposals; 4 months to mss. Book catalog available free. Guidelines online.

HOW TO CONTACT Submissions made through online submission form.

TIPS "Include cover letter in which you 'sell' your book—why should we publish the book, who will want to read it, why does it matter, etc. Use our ms submission online form. Format files accepted are: Word, plain/text, rich/text files. Other formats will not be accepted. Manuscript files cannot be larger than 5MB. Once editors review your ms, you will receive an e-mail with the decision. Revision process could take up to 4 months."

ASHLAND POETRY PRESS

401 College Ave., Ashland OH 44805. (419)289-5098. **E-mail:** app@ashland.edu. **Website:** www.ashlandpoetrypress.com. **Contact:** Cassandra Brown, managing editor. Publishes trade paperback originals. Makes outright purchase of $500-1,000. Publishes book 10 months after acceptance. Responds in 6 months to mss. Book catalog online. Guidelines online.

NEEDS "We accept unsolicited mss through the Snyder Prize competition each spring. The deadline is April 1." Judges are mindful of dedication to craftsmanship and thematic integrity.

HOW TO CONTACT E-mail.

CONTEST/AWARD OFFERINGS Snyder Prize.

TIPS "We rarely publish a title submitted off the transom outside of our Snyder Prize competition."

AUTUMN HOUSE PRESS

(412)362-2665. **E-mail:** info@autumnhouse.org. **Website:** www.autumnhouse.org. Managing Editor: Mike Good. Assistant Editor: Shelby Newsom. **Contact:** Christine Stroud, editor-in-chief. A nonprofit literary publisher, Autumn House Press was launched in 1998 when prominent American publishers, driven by economic concerns, dramatically reduced their poetry lists. Since our launch, Autumn House has expanded to publish fiction (2008) and nonfiction titles (2010). These books receive the same attention to design and manufacturing as our award-winning poetry titles. Autumn House publications have received a great deal of recognition and acclaim. In 2011, we earned a Certificate of Appreciation from the Pennsylvania legislature recognizing our contribution to the arts. Our books are regularly reviewed in *Ploughshares*, *Brevity*, *London Grip Review*, *The Women's Review of Books*, *The Jewish Review of Books*, and *Poets Quarterly*. Many of our poems have been featured in *The New York Times Magazine*, on *The Writer's Almanac*, and Ted Kooser's *American Life in Poetry*. Our titles also circulate within the local Pittsburgh community, with reviews in *The Pittsburgh City Paper* and *The Pittsburgh Post-Gazette*. Our books have won numerous awards over the years, such as *Love for Sale and Other Essays* by Clifford Thompson, which won the

2013 Whiting Award. Publishes trade paperback and electronic originals. Format: acid-free paper; offset printing. Pays 8% royalty on wholesale price. Pays $0-2,500 advance. Publishes twelve months after acceptance. Responds in 1-3 days on queries and proposals; 3 months on mss. Catalog online. Guidelines online.

HOW TO CONTACT Submit through our annual contest or open-call period. See guidelines online.

TIPS "Though we are open to all styles of poetry, fiction, and nonfiction, we suggest you familiarize yourself with previous Autumn House publications before submitting. We are committed not just to publishing the prominent voices of our age, but also to publishing first books and lesser-known authors who will become the important writers of their generation. Many of our past winners have been first-book authors. We encourage writers from all backgrounds to submit; it is our goal at Autumn House to develop a rich and varied literary tradition."

THE BACKWATERS PRESS

1124 Pacific St., #8392, Omaha NE 68108-3265. E-mail: thebackwaterspress@gmail.com. Website: www.thebackwaterspress.org. Editor Emeritus: Greg Kosmicki. Contact: Michael Catherwood, editor. The Backwaters Press is a 501-(C)-3 non-profit literary press that publishes poetry and poetry-related books, including anthologies. The press sponsors an annual book award prize, The Backwaters Prize, which includes a cash prize and publication. Publishes poetry in English; no children's poetry. Pays in copies, publication. Contest winner receives $2,500 and copies. Does not pay advance. Publishes ms 6-12 months after acceptance. Responds to contest: 2-3 months. All others, up to 6 months. Catalog online. Guidelines online.

NEEDS Only considers submissions to Backwaters Prize. More details on website. Open to all styles and forms.

HOW TO CONTACT Postal mail to above address; e-mail to the press. Complete book mss only.

CONTEST/AWARD OFFERINGS The Backwaters Prize. See contest guidelines online.

BEAR STAR PRESS

185 Hollow Oak Dr., Cohasset CA 95973. Website: www.bearstarpress.com. Contact: Beth Spencer, publisher/editor. "Bear Star is committed to publishing the best poetry it can attract. Each year it sponsors the Dorothy Brunsman contest, open to poets from Western and Pacific states. From time to time we add to our list

other poets from our target area whose work we admire." Publishes trade paperback originals. Pays $1,000, and 25 copies to winner of annual Dorothy Brunsman contest. Publishes book 9 months after acceptance. Responds in 2 weeks to queries. Guidelines online.

NEEDS Wants well-crafted poems. No restrictions as to form, subject matter, style, or purpose. "Poets should enter our annual book competition. Other books are occasionally solicited by publisher, sometimes from among contestants who didn't win."

HOW TO CONTACT Online submissions strongly preferred.

TIPS "Send your best work, consider its arrangement. A 'wow' poem early keeps me reading."

BILINGUAL REVIEW PRESS

Hispanic Research Center, Arizona State University, P.O. Box 875303, Tempe AZ 85287-5303. (480)965-3867. Fax: (480)965-0315. E-mail: brp@asu.edu. Website: www.asu.edu/brp. Contact: Gary Francisco Keller, publisher. "We are always on the lookout for Chicano, Puerto Rican, Cuban American, or other U.S. Hispanic themes with strong and serious literary qualities and distinctive and intellectually important topics." Responds in 3-4 weeks for queries; 3-4 months on requested mss.

HOW TO CONTACT Query with SASE. Query should describe book, TOC, sample poems, and any other information relevant to the rationale, content, audience, etc., for the book.

TIPS "Writers should take the utmost care in assuring that their manuscripts are clean, grammatically impeccable, and have perfect spelling. This is true not only of the English but the Spanish as well. All accent marks need to be in place as well as other diacritical marks. When these are missing it's an immediate first indication that the author does not really know Hispanic culture and is not equipped to write about it. We are interested in publishing creative literature that treats the U.S Hispanic experience in a distinctive, creative, revealing way. The kind of books that we publish we keep in print for a very long time irrespective of sales. We are busy establishing and preserving a U.S. Hispanic canon of creative literature."

BKMK PRESS

University of Missouri - Kansas City, 5101 Rockhill Rd., Kansas City MO 64110-2499. (816)235-2558. Fax: (816)235-2611. E-mail: bkmk@umkc.edu. Website: newletters.org/bkmk. "BkMk Press publishes fine literature. Reading period February-June." Publishes trade paperback originals. Responds in 4-6 months to queries. Guidelines online.

HOW TO CONTACT Submit 10 sample poems and SASE.

TIPS "We skew toward readers of literature, particularly contemporary writing. Because of our limited number of titles published per year, we discourage apprentice writers or 'scattershot' submissions."

BLACK LAWRENCE PRESS

E-mail: editors@blacklawrencepress.com. **Website:** www.blacklawrencepress.com. **Contact:** Diane Goettel, executive editor. Black Lawrence press seeks to publish intriguing books of literature—novels, short story collections, poetry collections, chapbooks, anthologies, and creative nonfiction. Will also publish the occasional translation from German. Publishes 22-24 books/year, mostly poetry and fiction. Mss are selected through open submission and competition. Books are 20-400 pages, offset-printed or high-quality POD, perfect-bound, with 4-color cover. Pays royalties. Responds in 6 months to mss. Catalog online.

HOW TO CONTACT Submit complete ms.

BLACK OCEAN

P.O. Box 52030, Boston MA 02205. **E-mail:** carrie@blackocean.org. **Website:** www.blackocean.org. **Contact:** Carrie Olivia Adams, poetry editor. Black Ocean is an award-winning independent publisher based out of Boston, with satellites in Detroit and Chicago. From early silent films to early punk rock, Black Ocean brings together a spectrum of influences to produce books of exceptional quality and content. In conjunction with our book releases we manifest our aesthetic in celebrations around the country. We believe in the fissures art can create in consciousness when, even if just for a moment, we experience a more vital way of operating in the world—and through that moment then seek out more extreme and enlightened modes of existence. We believe in the freedom we find through enlightened modes of existence, and we are committed to promoting artists we firmly believe in by sharing our enthusiasm for their work with a global audience. Publishes poetry, literary nonfiction, and translations. Catalog online. Guidelines online.

NEEDS Wants poetry that is well-considered, risks itself, and by its beauty and/or bravery disturbs a tiny corner of the universe. Mss are selected through open submission. Books are 60+ pages.

HOW TO CONTACT Book/chapbook mss may include previously published poems. We only accept unsolicited submissions during our open reading periods, and specific guidelines are updated and posted on our website.

TIPS "Before you submit, read our books."

BLAZEVOX [BOOKS]

131 Euclid Ave., Kenmore NY 14217. **E-mail:** editor@blazevox.org. **Website:** www.blazevox.org. **Contact:** Geoffrey Gatza, editor/publisher. "We are a major publishing presence specializing in innovative fictions and wide-ranging fields of innovative forms of poetry and prose. Our goal is to publish works that are challenging, creative, attractive, and yet affordable to individual readers. Articles of submission depend on many criteria, but overall items submitted must conform to one ethereal trait, your work must not suck. This put plainly, bad art should be punished; we will not promote it. However, all submissions will be reviewed and the author will receive feedback. We are human too." Pays 10% royalties on fiction and poetry books, based on net receipts. This amount may be split across multiple contributors. "We do not pay advances." Guidelines online.

HOW TO CONTACT Submit complete ms via e-mail.

TIPS "We actively contract and support authors who tour, read and perform their work, play an active part of the contemporary literary scene, and seek a readership."

BLUE LIGHT PRESS

P.O. Box 150300, San Rafael CA 94915. **E-mail:** bluelightpress@aol.com. **Website:** www.bluelightpress.com. **Contact:** Diane Frank, chief editor. "We like poems that are imagistic, emotionally honest, and push the edge—where the writer pushes through the imagery to a deeper level of insight and understanding. No rhymed poetry." Has published poetry by Stephen Dunn, Kim Addonizio, Jane Hirshfield, Rustin Larson, Mary Kay Rummel, Thomas Centolella,, Loretta Walker, Prartho Sereno, and K.B. Ballentine. "Books are elegantly designed and artistic. Our books are professionally printed, with original cover art, and we publish full-length books of poetry and chapbooks." Poetry books retail at 15.95. Authors receive a 30% royalty of profits (not of cover price). Author copies are available at close to a 50% discount, for sale at readings and book events. Does not pay advance. Publishes ms 2-8 months after acceptance. Catalog online. Guidelines by e-mail.

NEEDS Blue Light Press is dedicated to the publication of poetry that is imagistic, inventive, emotionally honest, and pushes the language to a deeper level of insight. "We are a collective of poets based in San Francisco, and our books are artistically designed. We also have an online poetry workshop with a wonderful group of American and international poets—open to new members 3 times/year. Send an e-mail for info — bluelightpress@aol.com." No rhymed poetry.

HOW TO CONTACT Send an e-mail for guidelines. bluelightpress@aol.com For guidelines, send an e-mail to bluelightpress@aol.com. "Let us know if you want guidelines for a chapbook or full-length ms."

CONTEST/AWARD OFFERINGS Blue Light Poetry Prize for a chapbook. Blue Light Book Award for a full-length ms. Send an email to bluelightpress@aol.com for guidelines.

ADDITIONAL INFORMATION We suggest reading our anthology, *River of Earth and Sky: Poems for the 21st Century*, selected by Diane Frank, for a generous helping of poems we love. More than 100 poets featured, mixing the best voices of our generation with the grass roots — poets who have won the Pulitzer Prize and the National Book Award, along with lesser known poets who also deserve to be read. Order at Amazon.com. Reviews: "Congratulations on this fantastic coming together of voices." Jane Hirshfield. "Anywhere I turn to read, masterly and compelling work." Robert Scotellaro.

TIPS "To see more than 100 poets we love, get a copy of *River of Earth and Sky: Poems for the Twenty-First Century*. It is full of examples of poems we like to publish. It's like a box of chocolates for poets."

BLUE MOUNTAIN PRESS

Blue Mountain Arts, Inc., P.O. Box 4219, Boulder CO 80306. (800)525-0642. **E-mail:** bmpbooks@sps.com. **Website:** www.sps.com. **Contact:** Patti Wayant, director. We are the book division of Blue Mountain Arts, a leading publisher of greeting cards, calendars, and gift books. The books we publish inspire hope, encourage confidence, bolster dreams, convey comfort, and/or express heartfelt feelings for friends, family, significant others, and other important people in life. They may be given as a gift to someone special or purchased for personal inspiration. Publishes hardcover originals, trade paperback originals, electronic origi-

nals. Pays royalty on wholesale price. Pays royalty advance. Publishes ms 12-16 months after acceptance. Responds in 2-4 months. E-mail to request submission guidelines.

○ We are open to receiving new book proposals that have a highly original and positive message. We publish in these categories: self-help, personal growth, inspirational but not religious, teen/tween, family, and relationships. We do not publish fiction, memoir/biographies, narrative nonfiction, chapbooks, literary poetry, or children's books, nor do we wish to receive poetry compilations or writings gathered from the public domain.

NEEDS We publish poetry appropriate for gift books, self-help books, and personal growth books. We do not publish chapbooks or literary poetry. We do not accept rhyming poetry.

HOW TO CONTACT Query. Submit 10+ sample poems.

BOA EDITIONS, LTD.

250 N. Goodman St., Suite 306, Rochester NY 14607. (585)546-3410. **Fax:** (585)546-3913. **E-mail:** contact@boaeditions.org. **Website:** www.boaeditions.org. Director of Development and Operations: Kelly Hatton. **Contact:** Ron Martin-Dent, director of publicity and production; Peter Conners, publisher. BOA Editions, Ltd., a not-for-profit publisher of poetry, short fiction, and poetry-in-translation, fosters readership and appreciation of contemporary literature. By identifying, cultivating, and publishing both new and established poets and selecting authors of unique literary talent, BOA brings high quality literature to the public. Publishes hardcover, trade paperback, and digital e-book originals. Negotiates royalties. Pays variable advance. Publishes ms 18-24 months after acceptance. Responds in 1 week to queries; 5 months to mss. Book catalog online. Guidelines online.

NEEDS Readers who, like Whitman, expect the poet to 'indicate more than the beauty and dignity which always attach to dumb real objects. They expect him to indicate the path between reality and their souls,' are the audience of BOA's books. BOA Editions, a Pulitzer Prize and National Book Award-winning not-for-profit publishing house, acclaimed for its work, reads poetry manuscripts for the American Poets Continuum Series (new poetry by distinguished poets in mid-to-late career), the New Poets of America Series (publication of a poet's first book, selected through the A. Poulin, Jr. Poetry Prize), and the America Reader Series (short fiction and prose on poetics).

HOW TO CONTACT Check BOA's website for reading periods for the American Poets Continuum Series and the A. Poulin, Jr. Poetry Prize. Please adhere to the general submission guidelines for each series. Guidelines online.

CONTEST/AWARD OFFERINGS The A. Poulin, Jr. Poetry Prize is awarded to honor a poet's first book, while also honoring the late founder of BOA Editions, Ltd., a not-for-profit publishing house of poetry and other literary works. Winners of the Poulin Prize receive a $1,000 honorarium and book publication by BOA Editions as part of the New Poets of America Series.

TIPS "Please adhere to the general submission guidelines on BOA's website for each series. BOA cannot accept unsolicited manuscript submissions outside of contests or open-reading periods."

BOTTOM DOG PRESS, INC.

P.O. Box 425, Huron OH 44839. (419)602-1556. E-mail: lsmithdog@smithdocs.net. **Website:** smithdocs.net. **Contact:** Larry Smith, director; Susanna Sharp-Schwacke, associate editor. Bottom Dog Press, Inc., "Is a nonprofit literary and educational organization dedicated to publishing the best writing and art from the Midwest and Appalachia. Query via e-mail first with 2 paragraphs on book and author." Publishes fiction, poetry, and memoirs. Pays 10 copies and 15% royalty. Does not pay advance. Publishes ms 4 months after acceptance.

BOYDS MILLS PRESS

Highlights for Children, Inc., 815 Church St., Honesdale PA 18431. (570)253-1164. **Website:** www.boydsmillspress.com. Boyds Mills Press publishes picture books, nonfiction, activity books, and paperback reprints. Their titles have been named notable books by the International Reading Association, the American Library Association, and the National Council of Teachers of English. They've earned numerous awards, including the National Jewish Book Award, the Christopher Medal, the NCTE Orbis Pictus Honor, and the Golden Kite Honor. Boyds Mills Press welcomes unsolicited submissions from published and unpublished writers and artists. Submit a ms with a cover letter of relevant information, including experience with writing and publishing. Label the package "Manuscript Submission" and include an SASE. For art samples, label the package "Art Sample Submission." All submissions will be evaluated for all imprints. Responds to mss within 3 months. Catalog online. Guidelines online.

HOW TO CONTACT Send a book-length collection of poems. Do not send an initial query. Keep in mind that the strongest collections demonstrate a facility with multiple poetic forms.

BRICK BOOKS

Box 20081, 431 Boler Rd., London ON N6K 4G6, Canada. (519)657-8579. **E-mail:** brick.books@sympatico.ca. **Website:** www.brickbooks.ca. **Contact:** Kitty Lewis, general manager. Brick Books has a reading period of January 1-April 30. Mss received outside that period will be returned. No multiple submissions. Pays 10% royalty in book copies only. "We publish only poetry by Canadian writers." Publishes trade paperback originals. Pays $300 advance against royalties. Publishes ms 2 years after acceptance. Responds in 3-4 months to queries. Book catalog free or online. Guidelines online.

HOW TO CONTACT Submit only poetry.

TIPS "Writers without previous publications in literary journals or magazines are rarely considered by Brick Books for publication."

BRICK ROAD POETRY PRESS, INC.

513 Broadway, Columbus GA 31901. (706)221-4370. **Fax:** (706)649-3094. **E-mail:** kbadowski@brickroadpoetrypress.com. **Website:** www.brickroadpoetrypress.com. **Contact:** Ron Self and Keith Badowski, co-editors/founders. The mission of Brick Road Poetry Press is to publish and promote poetry that entertains, amuses, edifies, and surprises a wide audience of appreciative readers. "We concentrate on publishing what we enjoy. Our preference is for poetry geared toward dramatizing the human experience in language rich with sensory image and metaphor, recognizing that poetry can be, at one and the same time, both familiar as the perspiration of daily labor and as outrageous as a carnival sideshow. We prefer poetry that offers a coherent human voice, a sense of humor, attentiveness to words and language, narratives with surprise twists, persona poems, and/or philosophical or spiritual themes explored through the concrete scenes and images." Does not want intentional obscurity or riddling, highfalutin vocabulary, greeting card verse, and/or abstractions. Publishes

poetry only: books (single author collections). Pays royalties and 15 author copies. Initial print run of 150, print-on-demand thereafter. Does not pay advance. Publishes 18 months after acceptance. Responds in 3-9 months. Guidelines online.

NEEDS "We prefer poetry that offers a coherent human voice, a sense of humor, attentiveness to words and language, narratives with surprise twists, persona poems, and/or philosophical or spiritual themes explored through the concrete scenes and images." Publishes poetry only: book-length, single author collections. Does not want intentional obscurity or riddling, highfalutin vocabulary, greeting card verse, and/or abstractions.

HOW TO CONTACT Contact us via our website. Open general submissions are accepted annually December 1-January 15. "We are moving toward blind reading of submissions. While there is always a chance we might recognize the work of a poet, we would like as much is humanly possible to read manuscripts without knowing the name of the author. To that end we request all submission documents omit the author's name from the cover page, the headings, and the content of the poetry. If you include a cover letter, omit your name there as well please. We accept .doc, .rtf, or .pdf file formats. We prefer electronic submissions via the submission manager on our website but will consider hard copy submissions by mail if USPS Flat Rate Mailing Envelope is used and with the stipulation that, should the author's work be chosen for publication, an electronic version (.doc or .rtf) must be prepared in a timely manner and at the poet's expense. Please omit the author's name from the cover letter and the manuscript. For hard copy submissions only, do include basic contact info on a separate sheet, including the name of the manuscript."

CONTEST/AWARD OFFERINGS Brick Road Poetry Press Book Contest, $1,000 prize and publication. Contest entries accepted annually August 1-November 1. Guidelines online.

TIPS "We want to publish poets who are engaged in the literary community, including regular submission of work to various publications and participation in poetry readings, workshops, and writers' groups. That said, we would never rule out an emerging poet who demonstrates ability and motivation to move in that direction. The best way to discover all that poetry can be and to expand the limits of your own craft is to ex-

pansively read poetry, both classic and contemporary . We recommend the following poets: Kim Addonizio, Ken Babstock, Coleman Barks, David Bottoms, Billy Collins, Morri Creech, Cynthia Cruz, Stephen Dunn, Alice Friman, Hannah Gamble, John Glenday, Beth A. Gylys, Jane Hirshfield, Jane Kenyon, Ted Kooser, Stanley Kunitz, Thomas Lux, Barry Marks, Michael Meyerhofer, Linda Pastan, Mark Strand, and Natasha D. Trethewey. Support your fellow poets and poetry in general by buying and reading lots of poetry books!"

BRONZE MAN BOOKS

Millikin University, 1184 W. Main, Decatur IL 62522. (217)424-6264. **E-mail:** sfrech@millikin.edu. **Website:** www.bronzemanbooks.com. **Contact:** Dr. Randy Brooks, publisher; Stephen Frech, editorial board, Edwin Walker, editorial board. A student-owned and operated press located on Millikin University's campus in Decatur, Ill., Bronze Man Books is dedicated to integrating quality design and meaningful content. The company exposes undergraduate students to the process of publishing by combining the theory of writing, publishing, editing and designing with the practice of running a book publishing company. This emphasis on performance learning is a hallmark of Millikin's brand of education. Publishes hardcover, trade paperback, literary chapbooks and mass market paperback originals. Outright purchase based on wholesale value of 10% of a press run. Publishes book 6-12 months after acceptance. Responds in 1-3 months.

HOW TO CONTACT Submit completed ms.

TIPS "The art books are intended for serious collectors and scholars of contemporary art, especially of artists from the Midwestern US. These books are published in conjunction with art exhibitions at Millikin University or the Decatur Area Arts Council. The children's books have our broadest audience, and the literary chapbooks are intended for readers of contemporary fiction, drama, and poetry."

⊘ CALAMARI PRESS

Via Titta Scarpetta #28, Rome 153, Italy. **E-mail:** derek@calamaripress.com. **Website:** www.calamaripress.com. **Contact:** Derek White. Calamari Press publishes books of literary text and art. Mss are selected by invitation. Occasionally has open submission period—check website. Helps to be published in *SleepingFish* first. Publishes paperback originals. Pays in author's copies. Ms published 2-6 months after acceptance. Responds to mss in 2 weeks. Guidelines online.

CARCANET PRESS

Alliance House, 4th Floor, 30 Cross St., Manchester England M2 7AQ, United Kingdom. 44(0)161-834-8730. **Fax:** 44(0)161-832-0084. **E-mail:** info@carcanet.co.uk. **Website:** www.carcanet.co.uk. **Contact:** Editorial manager. "Carcanet Press is one of Britain's leading poetry publishers. It provides a comprehensive and diverse list of modern and classic poetry in English and in translation. It now incorpprates Anvil Press Poetry and represents Northern House." Publishes trade paperback originals.

NEEDS Familiarize yourself with our books, and then submit between 6 and 10 pages or work (poetry or translations) and SASE. Replies are usually sent within 6 weeks. Writers wishing to propose other projects should send a full synopsis and cover letter, with sample pages, having first ascertained that the kind of book proposed is suitable for our programme. Do not call in person. The best way top understand Carcanet's editorial diversity is by reading the magazine PN Review, published by Carcanet (www.pnreview.co.uk).

HOW TO CONTACT Poetry submissions are welcome during our submission 'window'. See our website for information.

CARNEGIE MELLON UNIVERSITY PRESS

5032 Forbes Ave., Pittsburgh PA 15289. (412)268-2861. **Fax:** (412)268-8706. **E-mail:** carnegiemellonuniversitypress@gmail.com. **Website:** www.cmu.edu/universitypress/. **Contact:** Poetry Editor or Nonfiction Editor. Publishes hardcover and trade paperback originals. Book catalog and guidelines online.

NEEDS Holds annual reading period. "This reading period is only for poets who have not previously been published by CMP."

HOW TO CONTACT Submit complete ms. **Requires reading fee of $15.**

CAROLINA WREN PRESS

120 Morris St., Durham NC 27701. (919)560-2738. **E-mail:** carolinawrenpress@earthlink.net. **Website:** www.carolinawrenpress.org. **Contact:** Robin Miura, Editor & Director. "We publish poetry, fiction, and memoirs by or about people of color, women, gay/lesbian issues, and work by writers from, living in, or writing about the U.S. South." Accepts simultaneous submissions, but "let us know if work has been accepted elsewhere." We pay our authors an honorarium. Publishes ms 2 year after acceptance. Responds in 3 months to queries; 6 months to mss. Guidelines online.

NEEDS Publishes 2 poetry books/year, "usually through the Carolina Wren Press Poetry Series Contest. Otherwise we primarily publish women, minorities, and authors from, living in, or writing about the U.S. South." Not accepting unsolicited submissions except through Poetry Series Contest.

HOW TO CONTACT Accepts e-mail queries, but send only letter and description of work, no large files. Carolina Wren Press Poetry Contest for a First or Second Book takes submissions, electronically, from January to June of odd-numbered years.

TIPS "Best way to get read is to submit to a contest."

CHRONICLE BOOKS

680 Second St., San Francisco CA 94107. **E-mail:** submissions@chroniclebooks.com. **Website:** www.chroniclebooks.com. "We publish an exciting range of books, stationery, kits, calendars, and novelty formats. Our list includes children's books and interactive formats; young adult books; cookbooks; fine art, design, and photography; pop culture; craft, fashion, beauty, and home decor; relationships, mind-body-spirit; innovative formats such as interactive journals, kits, decks, and stationery; and much, much more." Generally pays authors in royalties based on retail price, "though we do occasionally work on a flat fee basis." Advance varies. Illustrators paid royalty based on retail price or flat fee. Publishes a book 1-3 years after acceptance. Responds to queries in 1 month. Book catalog for 9x12 SAE and 8 first-class stamps. Ms guidelines for #10 SASE.

HOW TO CONTACT Submit via mail only. Children's submissions only. Submit proposal (guidelines online) and allow up to 3 months for editors to review. If submitting by mail, do not include SASE since our staff will not return materials.

CITY LIGHTS BOOKS

261 Columbus Ave., San Francisco CA 94133. (415)362-8193. **Fax:** (415)362-4921. **Website:** www.citylights.com.

NEEDS City Lights Books is the legendary paperback house that achieved prominence with the publication of Allen Ginsberg's *Howl* and other poetry of the "Beat" school. Publishes "poetry, fiction, philosophy, political and social history."

HOW TO CONTACT Does not accept unsolicted mss. No inquiries or submissions by e-mail. "Before sending a book proposal, we urge you to look at our catalog to familiarize yourself with our publication.

If you feel certain that your work is appropriate to our list, then please send a query letter that includes your reésumeé (with a list of previous publications and a sample of no more than 10 pages." Include SASE for response. Responds in 3 months. Guidelines available on website.

CLEVELAND STATE UNIVERSITY POETRY CENTER

2121 Euclid Ave., RT 1841, Cleveland OH 44115. (216)687-3986. **Fax:** (216)687-6943. **E-mail:** poetrycenter@csuohio.edu. **Website:** www.csupoetrycenter. com. **Contact:** Dan Dorman, managing editor. The Cleveland State University Poetry Center was established in 1962 at the former Fenn College of Engineering to promote poetry through readings and community outreach. In 1971, it expanded its mission to become a national non-profit independent press under the auspices of the Cleveland State University Department of English, and has since published nearly 200 rangy, joyful, profound, astonishing, complicated, surprising, and aesthetically diverse collections of contemporary poetry and prose by established and emerging authors. The Cleveland State University Poetry Center publishes between three and five collections of contemporary poetry and prose a year, with a national distribution and reach. The Poetry Center currently acquires manuscripts through three annual contests (one dedicated to publishing and promoting first books of poetry, one to supporting an established poet's career, and one to publishing collections of literary essays). Pays $1,000 for competition winners. Publishes ms 1-2 years after acceptance. Responds in less than a year. Catalog online. Guidelines online.

HOW TO CONTACT Most mss are accepted through the competitions. All mss sent for competitions are considered for publication. Outside of competitions, mss are accepted by solicitation only.

✪ COACH HOUSE BOOKS

80 bpNichol Ln., Toronto ON M5S 3J4, Canada. (416)979-2217. **Fax:** (416)977-1158. **E-mail:** mail@chbooks.com. **E-mail:** editor@chbooks.com. **Website:** www.chbooks.com. **Contact:** Alana Wilcox, editorial director. Independent Canadian publisher of innovative poetry, literary fiction, nonfiction, and drama. Publishes trade paperback originals by Canadian authors. Pays 10% royalty on retail price. Publishes ms 1 year after acceptance. Responds in 6-8 months to queries. Guidelines online.

HOW TO CONTACT We much prefer to receive electronic submissions. Please put your cover letter and CV into one Word or PDF file along with the manuscript and e-mail it to editor@chbooks.com. We'd appreciate it if you would name your file following this convention: Last Name, First Name - MS Title. For fiction and poetry submissions, please send your complete manuscript, along with an introductory letter that describes your work and compares it to at least two current Coach House titles, explaining how your book would fit our list, and a literary CV listing your previous publications and relevant experience.

TIPS "We are not a general publisher, and publish only Canadian poetry, fiction, select nonfiction and drama. We are interested primarily in innovative or experimental writing."

COFFEE HOUSE PRESS

79 13th Ave. NE, Suite 110, Minneapolis MN 55413. (612)338-0125. **Fax:** (612)338-4004. **Website:** www. coffeehousepress.org. This successful nonprofit small press has received numerous grants from various organizations including the NEA, the McKnight Foundation and Target. Books published by Coffee House Press have won numerous honors and awards. Example: *The Book of Medicines*, by Linda Hogan won the Colorado Book Award for Poetry and the Lannan Foundation Literary Fellowship. Publishes hardcover and trade paperback originals. Responds in 4-6 weeks to queries; up to 6 months to mss. Book catalog and ms guidelines online.

HOW TO CONTACT Coffee House Press will not accept unsolicited poetry submissions. Please check our web page periodically for future updates to this policy.

TIPS "Look for our books at stores and libraries to get a feel for what we like to publish. No phone calls, e-mails, or faxes."

COPPER CANYON PRESS

P.O. Box 271, Port Townsend WA 98368. (360)385-4925. **Fax:** (360)385-4985. **E-mail:** poetry@coppercanyonpress.org. **Website:** www.coppercanyonpress. org. Managing Editor: Tonaya Craft. **Contact:** Joseph Bednarik and George Knotek, co-publishers. Copper Canyon Press is a nonprofit publisher that believes poetry is vital to language and living. Since 1972, the press has published poetry exclusively and has established an international reputation for its commitment to authors, editorial acumen, and dedication to the poetry audience. Catalog online. Guidelines online.

NEEDS Has open submission periods throughout the year; see website for details. Charges $35 fee for each submission, which entitles poets to select 2 Copper Canyon Press titles from a list.

HOW TO CONTACT Submit complete ms via Submittable.

TIPS "Please familiarize yourself with our mission, catalog, and submissions FAQ before submitting a manuscript."

☺ COTEAU BOOKS

Thunder Creek Publishing Co-operative Ltd., 2517 Victoria Ave., Regina SK S4P 0T2, Canada. (306)777-0170. **Fax:** (306)522-5152. **E-mail:** coteau@coteaubooks.com. **Website:** www.coteaubooks.com. **Contact:** Geoffrey Ursell, publisher. "Our mission is to publish the finest in Canadian fiction, nonfiction, poetry, drama, and children's literature, with an emphasis on Saskatchewan and prairie writers. De-emphasizing science fiction, picture books." Publishes chapter books for young readers aged 9-12 and novels for older kids ages 13-15 and for ages 15 and up. Publishes trade paperback originals and reprints. Pays 10% royalty on retail price. Publishes book 1 year after acceptance. Responds in 3 months. Book catalog available free. Guidelines online.

HOW TO CONTACT Submit 20-25 sample poems.

TIPS "Look at past publications to get an idea of our editorial program. We do not publish romance, horror, or picture books but are interested in juvenile and teen fiction from Canadian authors. Submissions, even queries, must be made in hard copy only. We do not accept simultaneous/multiple submissions. Check our website for new submission timing guidelines."

☻ CRESCENT MOON PUBLISHING

P.O. Box 1312, Maidstone Kent ME14 5XU, United Kingdom. (44)(162)272-9593. **E-mail:** cresmopub@yahoo.co.uk. **Website:** www.crmoon.com. **Contact:** Jeremy Robinson, director (arts, media, cinema, literature); Cassidy Hughes (visual arts). "Our mission is to publish the best in contemporary work, in poetry, fiction, and critical studies, and selections from the great writers. Currently emphasizing nonfiction (media, film, music, painting). De-emphasizing children's books." Publishes hardcover and trade paperback originals. Pays royalty. Pays negotiable advance. Publishes ms 18 months after acceptance. Responds in 2 months to queries; 4 months to proposals and mss. Book catalog and ms guidelines free.

NEEDS "We prefer a small selection of the poet's very best work at first. We prefer free verse or non-rhyming poetry. Do not send too much material."

HOW TO CONTACT Query and submit 6 sample poems.

TIPS "Our audience is interested in new contemporary writing."

CROSS-CULTURAL COMMUNICATIONS

Cross-Cultural Literary Editions, 239 Wynsum Ave., Merrick NY 11566-4725. (516)869-5635. **Fax:** (516)379-1901. **E-mail:** info@cross-culturalcommunications.com; cccpoetry@aol.com. **Website:** www.cross-culturalcommunications.com. **Contact:** Stanley H. Barkan; Bebe Barkan. Publishes hardcover and trade paperback originals. Publishes book 1 year after acceptance. Responds in 1 month to proposals; 2 months to mss. Book catalog (sample flyers) for #10 SASE. Inquire for specifics. Prefer submissions with a query letter including full contact data and brief bio. Focus on bilingual poetry: include original and translations, 3-6 samples.

☺ Focus on bilingual poetry.

HOW TO CONTACT For bilingual poetry submit 3-6 short poems in original language with English translation, a brief (3-5 lines) bio of the author and translator(s).

TIPS "Best chance: poetry from a translation."

DIAL BOOKS FOR YOUNG READERS

Imprint of Penguin Random House LLC, 1745 Broadway, New York NY 10019. (212)782-9000. **Website:** www.penguin.com/children. "Dial Books for Young Readers publishes quality picture books for ages 18 months-6 years; lively, believable novels for middle readers and young adults; and occasional nonfiction for middle readers and young adults." Publishes hardcover originals. Pays royalty. Pays varies advance. Responds in 4-6 months to queries. Book catalog and guidelines online.

TIPS "Our readers are anywhere from preschool age to teenage. Picture books must have strong plots, lots of action, unusual premises, or universal themes treated with freshness and originality. Humor works well in these books. A very well-thought-out and intelligently presented book has the best chance of being taken on. Genre isn't as much of a factor as presentation."

DUFOUR EDITIONS

P.O. Box 7, 124 Byers Rd., Chester Springs PA 19425. (610)458-5005. **Website:** www.dufoureditions.com.

Publishes hardcover originals, trade paperback originals and reprints. Pays $100-500 advance. Publishes ms 18 months after acceptance. Responds in 3-6 months. Book catalog available free.

HOW TO CONTACT Query.

⊘ THE ECCO PRESS

195 Broadway, New York NY 10007. (212)207-7000. **Fax:** (212)702-2460. **Website:** www.harpercollins. com. Publishes hardcover and trade paperback originals and reprints. Pays royalty. Pays negotiable advance. Publishes ms 1 year after acceptance.

TIPS "We are always interested in first novels and feel it's important that they be brought to the attention of the reading public."

● ÉDITIONS DU NOROÎT

4609 D'Iberville, Bureau 202, Montreal QC H2H 2L9, Canada. (514)727-0005. **Fax:** (514)723-6660. **E-mail:** lenoroit@lenoroit.com. **Website:** www.lenoroit.com. "Éditions du Noiroît publishes poetry and essays on poetry." Publishes trade paperback originals and reprints. Pays 10% royalty on retail price. Publishes ms 1 year after acceptance. Responds in 4 months to mss.

HOW TO CONTACT Submit 40 sample poems.

● EYEWEAR PUBLISHING

E-mail: info@eyewearpublishing.com. **Website:** store. eyewearpublishing.com. Managing Editor: Juliette van Wessem. **Contact:** Dr. Todd Swift, managing director and editor. Eyewear Publishing Ltd. is a small press founded in 2012 by Todd Swift, based in London, UK, with distribution in the USA. Our books have been recommended by such literary figures as Kaveh Akbar, Stephen Fry, Louis Theroux, Salman Rushdie, Clare Pollard, Vicki Feaver, Thomas Lux, Suhayl Saadi and The Rev. Jesse Jackson. We search for emerging talent, and neglected out-of-work authors, as well as well-established figures. We are welcoming, with a commitment to diversity. In 2019 we have acquired the famous Black Spring Press. Since 1985, Black Spring Press has produced work by Nick Cave, Anaïs Nin, Charles Baudelaire, Kyril Bonfiglioli, Carolyn Cassady and Leonard Cohen, among many impressive others. Firm publishes fiction, nonfiction, and poetry. Royalties vary from 10-20%. Pays variable advance. Response time varies. Guidelines online.

FARRAR, STRAUS & GIROUX

18 W. 18th St., New York NY 10011. (646)307-5151. **Website:** us.macmillan.com/fsg. **Contact:** Editorial

Department. "We publish original and well-written material for all ages." Publishes hardcover originals and trade paperback reprints. Pays 2-6% royalty on retail price for paperbacks, 3-10% for hardcovers. Pays $3,000-25,000 advance. Publishes ms 18 months after acceptance. Responds in 2-3 months. Catalog available by request. Guidelines online.

HOW TO CONTACT Send cover letter describing submission with 3-4 poems. By mail only.

FARRAR, STRAUS & GIROUX FOR YOUNG READERS

Macmillan Children's Publishing Group, 175 Fifth Ave., New York NY 10010. (212)741-6900. **Fax:** (212)633-2427. **E-mail:** childrens.editorial@fsgbooks. com. **Website:** www.fsgkidsbooks.com. Book catalog available by request. Ms guidelines online.

HOW TO CONTACT Submit cover letter, 3-4 poems by mail only.

TIPS "Study our catalog before submitting. We will see illustrators' portfolios by appointment. Don't ask for criticism and/or advice—due to the volume of submissions we receive, it's just not possible. Never send originals. Always enclose SASE."

FENCE BOOKS

Science Library 320, Univ. of Albany, 1400 Washington Ave., Albany NY 12222. (518)591-8162. **E-mail:** jessp.fence@gmail.com. **Website:** www.fenceportal. org. **Contact:** Submissions Manager. "Fence Books publishes poetry, fiction, and critical texts and anthologies, and prioritizes sustained support for its authors, many of whom come to us through our book contests and then go on to publish second, third, fourth books." Publishes hardcover originals. Guidelines online.

HOW TO CONTACT Submit via contests and occasional open reading periods.

FINISHING LINE PRESS

P.O. Box 1626, Georgetown KY 40324. **E-mail:** finishingbooks@aol.com. **E-mail:** http://finishinglinepress. submittable.com/submit. **Website:** www.finishinglinepress.com. **Contact:** Christen Kincaid, director. Finishing Line Press seeks to "discover new talent" and hopes to publish chapbooks by both men and women poets who have not previously published a book or chapbook of poetry. Has published *Parables and Revelations* by T. Crunk, *Family Business* by Paula Sergi, *Putting in a Window* by John Brantingham, and *Dusting the Piano* by Abigail Gramig. Publishes 100+ poetry chapbooks/year. Chapbooks are usually 16-35 pages, and perfect bound. Publishes 50+ full-length books per year. Submit poetry with cover letter, bio, acknowledgments, and **no reading fee in November**. Responds to queries and mss in up to 3 months. Pay varies; pays in author's copies. "Sales profits, if any, go to publish the next new poet." Sample chapbooks available by sending $6 to Finishing Line Press or through website. See The Finishing Line Press Open Chapbook Competition and the New Women's Voices Chapbook Competition. Member of CLMP. Pays in copies, or standard royalties contract. Pays advance against royalties for fiction and nonfiction. Responds in 3-6 months. Catalog online. Guidelines online.

NEEDS Finishing Line Press seeks to "discover new talent" and hopes to publish chapbooks by both men and women poets who have not previously published a book or chapbook of poetry. Has published *Parables and Revelations* by T. Crunk, *Family Business* by Paula Sergi, *Putting in a Window* by John Brantingham, and *Dusting the Piano* by Abigail Gramig. Publishes 50-60 poetry chapbooks/year. Chapbooks are usually 25-30 pages, digest-sized, laser-printed, saddle-stapled, with card covers with textured matte wrappers.

HOW TO CONTACT Submit poetry with cover letter, bio, acknowledgments, and **no reading fee in november**. Responds to queries and mss in up to 1 month. Pay varies; pays in author's copies. "Sales profits, if any, go to publish the next new poet." Sample chapbooks available by sending $6 to Finishing Line Press or through website. "We read manuscripts in November. There is no fee for manuscripts submitted via regular post during the month of November. If you would like to submit outside of the month of November, please see guidelines below: We read general submissions year round. Please include a $3 reading fee with your manuscript. Submit 16-35 pages of poetry, plus bio, acknowledgments, SASE and cover letter (you can pay by check or money order) or submit online using our online submissions manager."

CONTEST/AWARD OFFERINGS The Finishing Line Press Open Chapbook Competition and the New Women's Voices Chapbook Competition.

FLOATING BRIDGE PRESS

Pontoon Poetry, 909 NE 43rd St., #205, Seattle WA 98105. **E-mail:** editor@floatingbridgepress.org. **Website:** www.floatingbridgepress.org. **Contact:** John Pierce or Meghan McClure. Floating Bridge Press is a 501(c)(3) nonprofit literary arts organization, founded in 1994. Floating Bridge Press promotes the diverse voices of Washington State poets through an annual poetry chapbook competition, archival-quality books, online publishing, broadsides, and community readings. Floating Bridge Press publishes Washington State poets whose writing engages individuals, enriches communities, and enlivens the arts. "We believe that poets are leaders and poetry enriches the community; diverse voices enrich poetry; poetry deserves the highest editorial attention; poetry deserves promotion and increased attention in our community." Chapbooks of poetry and poems at our review, *Pontoon Poetry*. The winning poet receives a minimum of $500, 15 copies of a perfect-bound, archival-quality chapbook, local promotion, distribution of the chapbook, and a featured reading in the Seattle area. Three or four finalists receive $50 each and are also featured at the winner's reading. In 2015 and 2016 we published 2 finalist's chapbooks along with the winning chapbook. Publishes ms 6 months after acceptance. Responds in 3-6 months.

NEEDS Floating Bridge Press publishes chapbooks and anthologies by Washington State poets, selected through an annual competition.

HOW TO CONTACT Floating Bridge Press reads manuscripts for our Chapbook Competition from November 1st to March 15th. Submit through Submittable: https://floatingbridgepress.submittable.com/submit

The winning poet receives a minimum of $500, 15 copies of a perfect-bound, archival-quality chapbook, local promotion, distribution of the chapbook, and a featured reading in the Seattle area. Three or four finalists receive $50 each and are also featured at the winner's reading. In 2015 and 2016 we published 2 finalist's chapbooks along with the winning chapbook. Every poem will be considered for inclusion in our sister publication Pontoon Poetry and for the Paula Jones Gardiner Memorial Award.

CONTEST/AWARD OFFERINGS Floating Bridge Chapbook Competition, Paula Jones Gardiner Award

FOUR WAY BOOKS

Box 535, Village Station, New York NY 10014. (212)334-5430. **E-mail:** editors@fourwaybooks.com. **Website:** www.fourwaybooks.com. "Four Way Books is a not-for-profit literary press dedicated to publishing poetry and short fiction by emerging and established writers. Each year, Four Way Books publishes the winners of its national poetry competitions, as well as collections accepted through general submission, panel selection, and solicitation by the editors."

NEEDS Four Way Books publishes poetry and short fiction. Considers full-length poetry and story and novella mss only. Books are about 70-2-300 pages, digital printing, perfect-bound, with paperback binding, art/graphics on covers. Does not want individual poems or poetry intended for children/young readers.

HOW TO CONTACT See website for complete submission guidelines and open reading period in June. Book mss may include previously published poems. Responds to submissions in 4 months. Payment varies. Order sample books from Four Way Books online or through bookstores.

FUTURECYCLE PRESS

Lexington KY **Website:** www.futurecycle.org. **Contact:** Diane Kistner, director/editor-in-chief. Publishes English-language poetry books, chapbooks, and anthologies in print-on-demand and digital editions. Awards the FutureCycle Poetry Book Prize and honorarium for the best full-length book the press publishes each year. Pays in deeply discounted author copies (no purchase required). Responds in 3 months. Guidelines, sample contract, and detailed *Guide for Authors* online.

NEEDS Wants "poetry from imaginative, highly skilled poets, whether well known or emerging. We abhor the myopic, self-absorbed, and sloppy, but otherwise are eclectic in our tastes." Does not want concrete or visual poetry. Publishes 15+ poetry books/year and 5+ chapbooks/year. Ms. selected through open submission. Books average 62-110 pages; chapbooks 30-42 pages; anthologies 100+ pages.

HOW TO CONTACT Submit complete ms. No need to query.

GERTRUDE PRESS

P.O. Box 28281, Portland OR 97228. (503)515-8252. **E-mail:** editorgertrudepress@gmail.com. **Website:** www.gertrudepress.org. "Gertrude Press is a non-profit organization developing and showcasing the creative talents of lesbian, gay, bisexual, trans, queer-identified and allied individuals. We publish limited-edition fiction and poetry chapbooks plus the biannual literary journal, *Gertrude*." Reads chapbook mss only through contests.

TIPS Sponsors poetry and fiction chapbook contest. Prize is $175 and 50 contributor's copies. Submission guidelines and fee information on website. "Read the journal and sample published work. We are not impressed by pages of publications; your work should speak for itself."

GIVAL PRESS

Gival Press, LLC, P.O. Box 3812, Arlington VA 22203. (703)351-0079. **E-mail:** givalpress@yahoo.com. **Website:** www.givalpress.com. **Contact:** Robert L. Giron, editor-in-chief (area of interest: literary). "We publish literary works: fiction, nonfiction (essays, academic), and poetry in English, Spanish, and French." Publishes trade paperback, electronic originals, and reprints. Pays royalty. Per the contest prize, amount per the content. Outside of contests, yes. Publishes ms usually 1 to 2 years after acceptance, per contract. Responds in 3-5 months. If we get behind, it's okay to remind us. Prefer submissions via Submittable or e-mail (after query). Book catalog online. Guidelines online.

HOW TO CONTACT Query via e-mail; provide description, bio, etc.; submit 5-6 sample poems via e-mail.

TIPS "Our audience is those who read literary works with depth to the work. Visit our website—there is much to be read/learned from the numerous pages."

⊘ DAVID R. GODINE, PUBLISHER

15 Court Square, Suite 320, Boston MA 02108. (617)451-9600. **Fax:** (617)350-0250. **E-mail:** info@godine.com. **Website:** www.godine.com. "We publish books that matter for people who care." This publisher is no longer considering unsolicited mss of any type. Only interested in agented material.

GOLD WAKE PRESS

E-mail: gwakepress@gmail.com. **Website:** goldwake.com. Gold Wake Press is an independent literary house founded in the suburbs of Boston by Jared Michael Wahlgren, who ran the press until 2014. Guidelines online.

NEEDS Check website for open submission periods.

TIPS "The press seeks to bring voices to the spotlight who combine daring content with meticulous attention to form."

☺ GOOSE LANE EDITIONS

500 Beaverbrook Ct., Suite 330, Fredericton NB E3B 5X4, Canada. (506)450-4251. **Fax:** (506)459-4991. **E-mail:** info@gooselane.com. **Website:** www.gooselane.com. "Goose Lane publishes literary fiction and nonfiction from well-read and highly skilled Canadian authors." Publishes hardcover and paperback originals and occasional reprints. Pays 8-10% royalty on retail price. Pays $500-3,000, negotiable advance. Responds in 6 months to queries.

NEEDS Considers mss by Canadian poets only.

HOW TO CONTACT Submit cover letter, list of publications, synopsis, entire ms, SASE.

TIPS "Writers should send us outlines and samples of books that show a very well-read author with highly developed literary skills. Our books are almost all by Canadians living in Canada; we seldom consider submissions from outside Canada. We consider submissions from outside Canada only when the author is Canadian and the book is of extraordinary interest to Canadian readers. We do not publish books for children or for the young adult market."

⊘ GRAYWOLF PRESS

250 Third Ave. N., Suite 600, Minneapolis MN 55401. (651)641-0077. **Fax:** (651)641-0036. **Website:** www.graywolfpress.org. "Graywolf Press is an independent, nonprofit publisher dedicated to the creation and promotion of thoughtful and imaginative contemporary literature essential to a vital and diverse culture." Publishes trade cloth and paperback originals. Pays royalty on retail price. Pays $1,000-25,000 advance. Publishes 18 months after acceptance. Responds in 3 months to queries. Book catalog free. Guidelines online.

NEEDS "We are interested in linguistically challenging work."

HOW TO CONTACT Agented submissions only.

⊘ GROVE/ATLANTIC, INC.

154 W. 14th St., 12th Floor, New York NY 10011. **E-mail:** info@groveatlantic.com. **Website:** www.groveatlantic.com. "Due to limited resources of time and staffing, Grove/Atlantic cannot accept manuscripts that do not come through a literary agent. In today's publishing world, agents are more important than ever, helping writers shape their work and navigate the main publishing houses to find the most appropriate outlet for a project." Publishes hardcover and trade paperback originals, and reprints. Pays 7 ½-12 ½% royalty. Makes outright purchase of $5-500,000. Book published 9 months after acceptance of ms. Responds in 1 month to queries; 2 months to proposals; 4 months to mss. Book catalog available online.

HOW TO CONTACT Agented submissions only.

♻⊘ GUERNICA EDITIONS

1569 Heritage Way, Oakville ON L6M 2Z7, Canada. (905)599-5304. **E-mail:** michaelmirolla@guernicaeditions.com. **Website:** www.guernicaeditions.com. Associate Publisher/Publicist: Anna Geisler (annage-isler@guernicaeditions.com). **Contact:** Michael Mirolla, editor/publisher (poetry, nonfiction, short stories, novels). Guernica Editions is a literary press that produces works of poetry, fiction and nonfiction often by writers who are ignored by the mainstream. "We feature an imprint (MiroLand) which accepts memoirs, how-to books, graphic novels, genre fiction with the possibility of children's and cook books." A new imprint, Guernica World Editions, features writers who are non-Canadian. Publishes trade paperback originals and reprints. Pays 10% royalty on either cover or retail price. Pays $450-750 advance. Publishes 24-36 months after acceptance. Responds in 1 month to queries; 6 months to proposals; 1 year to mss. Book catalog online. Queries and submissions accepted via e-mail January 1-April 30.

NEEDS Feminist, gay/lesbian, literary, multicultural, poetry in translation. Full books only.

HOW TO CONTACT Query.

⊘ HARPERCOLLINS

195 Broadway, New York NY 10007. (212)207-7000. **Website:** www.harpercollins.com. HarperCollins, one of the largest English language publishers in the world, is a broad-based publisher with strengths in academic, business and professional, children's, educational, general interest, and religious and spiritual books, as well as multimedia titles. Publishes hardcover and paperback originals and paperback reprints. Pays royalty. Pays negotiable advance.

TIPS "We do not accept any unsolicited material."

HARPER PERENNIAL

10 E. 53rd St., New York NY 10022. **E-mail:** harperperennial@harpercollins.com. **Website:** harperperennial.tumblr.com. Harper Perennial is one of the paperback imprints of HarperCollins. "We publish paperback originals and reprints of authors like Ann Patchett, Justin Taylor, Barbara Kingsolver, and Blake Butler.

HIGH PLAINS PRESS

P.O. Box 123, 403 Cassa Rd., Glendo WY 82213. (307)735-4370. **Fax:** (307)735-4590. **E-mail:** editor@highplainspress.com. **Website:** www.highplainspress.com. **Contact:** Nancy Curtis, publisher. High Plains Press is a regional book publishing company specializing in books about the American West, with special interest in things relating to Wyoming. Publishes hardcover and trade paperback originals. Pays 10% royalty on wholesale price. Pays $200-2,000 advance.

Publishes book 2 years after acceptance of ms. Responds in 1 month to queries and proposals; 6 months on mss. Book catalog and guidelines online.

NEEDS "We publish 1 poetry volume a year. Sometimes we skip a year. Require connection to West. Consider poetry in August."

HOW TO CONTACT Submit 5 sample poems.

TIPS "Our audience comprises general readers interested in history and culture of the Rockies."

◐ HIPPOPOTAMUS PRESS

22 Whitewell Rd., Frome Somerset BA11 4EL, United Kingdom. (44)(173)466-6653. **E-mail:** mphippopress@aol.com. **Contact:** R. John, editor; M. Pargitter (poetry); Anna Martin (translation). "Hippopotamus Press publishes first, full collections of verse by those well represented in the mainstream poetry magazines of the English-speaking world." Publishes hardcover and trade paperback originals. Pays 7½-10% royalty on retail price. Pays advance. Publishes book 10 months after acceptance. Responds in 1 month to queries. Book catalog available free.

NEEDS "Read one of our authors—poets often make the mistake of submitting poetry without knowing the type of verse we publish."

HOW TO CONTACT Query and submit complete ms.

TIPS "We publish books for a literate audience. We have a strong link to the Modernist tradition. Read what we publish."

◐◯ HOUSE OF ANANSI PRESS

128 Sterling Rd., Lower Level, Toronto ON M6R 2B7, Canada. (416)363-4343. **Fax:** (416)363-1017. **Website:** www.anansi.ca. House of Anansi publishes literary fiction and poetry by Canadian and international writers. Pays 8-10% royalties. Pays $750 advance and 10 author's copies. Responds to queries within 1 year; to mss (if invited) within 4 months.

NEEDS "We seek to balance the list between well-known and emerging writers, with an interest in writing by Canadians of all backgrounds. We publish Canadian poetry only, and poets must have a substantial publication record—if not in books, then definitely in journals and magazines of repute." Does not want "children's poetry or poetry by previously unpublished poets."

HOW TO CONTACT Canadian poets should query first with 10 sample poems (typed double-spaced) and a cover letter with brief bio and publication cred-

its. Considers simultaneous submissions. Poems are circulated to an editorial board. Often comments on rejected poems.

IBEX PUBLISHERS

P.O. Box 30087, Bethesda MD 20824. (301)718-8188. **Fax:** (301)907-8707. **E-mail:** info@ibexpub.com. **Website:** www.ibexpublishers.com. "Ibex publishes books about Iran and the Middle East and about Persian culture and literature." Publishes hardcover and trade paperback originals and reprints. Payment varies. Book catalog available free.

NEEDS "Translations of Persian poets will be considered."

ILIUM PRESS

2407 S. Sonora Dr., Spokane WA 99037. (509)701-8866. **E-mail:** iliumpress@outlook.com. **Contact:** John Lemon, owner/editor. "Ilium Press is a small, 1-person press that I created to cultivate and promote the relevance of epic poetry in today's world. My focus is book-length narrative poems in blank (non-rhyming) metered verse, such as iambic parameter or sprung verse. I am very selective about my projects, but I provide extensive editorial care to those projects I take on." Publishes trade paperback originals and reprints, electronic originals and reprints. Pays 20-50% royalties on receipts. Does not pay advance. Publishes ms up to 1 year after acceptance. Responds in 6 months.

NEEDS Ilium Press specializes in original, book-length narrative epic poems written in blank (non-rhyming) metered verse (such as iambic pentameter or sprung verse) in contemporary language. "I'm looking for original work that shows how epic poetry is still relevant in today's world. Please query via e-mail if you have questions."

HOW TO CONTACT Submit via e-mail (preferred) or via mail with first 20 pages. Don't forget to include your contact information!

◐ INSOMNIAC PRESS

520 Princess Ave., London ON N6B 2B8, Canada. (416)504-6270. **Website:** www.insomniacpress.com. Publishes trade paperback originals and reprints, mass market paperback originals, and electronic originals and reprints. Pays 10-15% royalty on retail price. Pays $500-1,000 advance. Publishes ms 6 months after acceptance. Guidelines online.

NEEDS "Our poetry publishing is limited to 2-4 books per year and we are often booked up a year or two in advance."

HOW TO CONTACT Submit complete ms.

TIPS "We envision a mixed readership that appreciates up-and-coming literary fiction and poetry as well as solidly researched and provocative nonfiction. Peruse our website and familiarize yourself with what we've published in the past."

ITALICA PRESS

99 Wall St., Suite 650, New York NY 10005. (917)371-0563. **E-mail:** inquiries@italicapress.com. **Website:** www.italicapress.com. "Italica Press publishes English translations of modern Italian fiction and medieval and Renaissance nonfiction." Publishes hardcover and trade paperback originals. Pays 7-15% royalty on wholesale price; author's copies. Publishes ms 1 year after acceptance. Responds in 1 month to queries; 4 months to mss. Book catalog and guidelines online.

NEEDS Poetry titles are always translations and generally dual language.

HOW TO CONTACT Query with 10 sample translations of medieval and Renaissance Italian poets. Include cover letter, bio, and list of publications.

TIPS "We are interested in considering a wide variety of medieval and Renaissance topics (not historical fiction), and for modern works we are only interested in translations from Italian fiction by well-known Italian authors. Only fiction that has been previously published in Italian. A brief e-mail saves a lot of time. 90% of proposals we receive are completely off base—but we are very interested in things that are right on target."

ALICE JAMES BOOKS

114 Prescott St., Farmington ME 04938. (207)778-7071. **Fax:** (207)778-7766. **Website:** www.alicejamesbooks.org. "Alice James Books is a nonprofit cooperative poetry press. The founders' objectives were to give women access to publishing and to involve authors in the publishing process. The cooperative selects mss for publication through both regional and national competitions." Publishes trade paperback originals. Pays through competition awards. Publishes ms 1 year after acceptance. Responds promptly to queries; 4 months to mss. Book catalog online. Guidelines online.

NEEDS "Alice James Books is a nonprofit cooperative poetry press. The founders' objectives were to give women access to publishing and to involve authors in the publishing process. The cooperative selects mss for publication through both regional and national

competitions." Does not want children's poetry or light verse.

TIPS "Send SASE for contest guidelines or check website. Do not send work without consulting current guidelines."

THE JOHNS HOPKINS UNIVERSITY PRESS

2715 N. Charles St., Baltimore MD 21218. (410)516-6900. **Fax:** (410)516-6968. **Website:** www.press.jhu.edu. Publishes hardcover originals and reprints, and trade paperback reprints. Pays royalty. Publishes ms 1 year after acceptance.

NEEDS "One of the largest American university presses, Johns Hopkins publishes primarily scholarly books and journals. We do, however, publish short fiction and poetry in the series Johns Hopkins: Poetry and Fiction, edited by John Irwin."

KAYA PRESS

c/o USC ASE, 3620 S. Vermont Ave. KAP 462, Los Angeles CA 90089. (213) 740-2285. **E-mail:** info@kaya.com. **E-mail:** acquisitions@kaya.com. **Website:** www.kaya.com. Kaya is an independent literary press dedicated to the publication of innovative literature from the Asian Pacific diaspora. Publishes hardcover originals and trade paperback originals and reprints. Responds in 6 months to mss. Book catalog available free. Guidelines online.

HOW TO CONTACT Submit complete ms.

TIPS "Audience is people interested in a high standard of literature and who are interested in breaking down easy approaches to multicultural literature."

KELSEY STREET PRESS

Poetry by Women, 2824 Kelsey St., Berkeley CA 94705. **Website:** www.kelseyst.com. "A Berkeley, California press publishing collaborations between women poets and artists. Many of the press's collaborations focus on a central theme or conceit, like the sprawl and spectacle of New York in *Arcade* by Erica Hunt and Alison Saar." Hardcover and trade paperback originals and electronic originals.

HOW TO CONTACT Query.

KNOPF

Imprint of Random House, 1745 Broadway, New York NY 10019. **Fax:** (212)940-7390. **Website:** knopfdoubleday.com/imprint/knopf. Publishes hardcover and paperback originals. Royalties vary. Offers advance. Publishes ms 1 year after acceptance. Responds in 2-6 months to queries.

🌑 LANTANA PUBLISHING

London , United Kingdom. **E-mail:** info@lantanapublishing.com. **E-mail:** submissions@lantanapublishing.com. **Website:** www.lantanapublishing.com. Lantana Publishing is a young, independent publishing house producing inclusive picture books for children. "Our mission is to publish outstanding writing for young readers by giving new and aspiring BAME authors and illustrators a platform to publish in the UK and by working with much-loved authors and illustrators from around the world. Lantana's award-winning titles have so far received high praise, described as 'dazzling', 'delectable', 'enchanting' and 'exquisite' by bloggers and reviewers. They have been nominated for a Kate Greenaway Medal (three times), received starred Kirkus reviews (three times), been shortlisted for the Teach Early Years Awards, the North Somerset Teachers' Book Awards, and the Sheffield Children's Books Awards, and won the Children's Africana Best Book Award. Lantana's founder, Alice Curry, is the recipient of the 2017 Kim Scott Walwyn Prize for women in publishing." Pays royalty. Pays advance. Responds in 6 weeks. Guidelines online.

NEEDS "We are interested in receiving poetry submissions for young readers."

🌑⊘ LAPWING PUBLICATIONS

1 Ballysillan Dr., Belfast BT14 8HQ, Northern Ireland. (44)2890-500-796. **Fax:** (44)2890-295-800. **E-mail:** lapwing.poetry@ntlworld.com. **Website:** www.lapwingpoetry.com. **Contact:** Dennis Greig, editor. Pays 20 author's copies, no royalties. Responds to queries in 1 month; mss in 2 months.

🗨 Lapwing will produce work only if and when resources to do so are available.

NEEDS Lapwing publishes "emerging Irish poets and poets domiciled in Ireland, plus the new work of a suitable size by established Irish writers. Non-Irish poets are also published. Poets based in continental Europe have become a major feature. Emphasis on first collections preferably not larger than 80 pages.

HOW TO CONTACT "Submit 6 poems in the first instance; depending on these, an invitation to submit more may follow." Considers simultaneous submissions. Accepts e-mail submissions in body of message or in DOC format. Cover letter is required. "All submissions receive a first reading. If these poems have minor errors or faults, the writer is advised. Those which appeal at first reading are retained, and a con-

ditional offer is sent." Often comments on rejected poems. "After initial publication, irrespective of the quantity, the work will be permanently available using 'print-on-demand' production; such publications may not always be printed exactly as the original, although the content will remain the same."

TIPS "We are unable to accept new work from beyond mainland Europe and the British Isles due to delivery costs."

LEAPFROG PRESS

Box 505, Fredonia NY 14063. **E-mail:** leapfrog@leapfrogpress.com. **Website:** www.leapfrogpress.com. **Contact:** Nathan Carter, acquisitions editor; Lisa Graziano, publicity. Pays 10% royalty on net receipts. Average advance: negotiable. Publishes ms approximately 1 year after acceptance. Response time varies. One week to several months. Guidelines online. Submissions through Submittable only.

TIPS "We like anything that is superbly written and genuinely original. We like the idiosyncratic and the peculiar. We rarely publish nonfiction. Send only your best work, and send only completed work that is ready. That means the completed ms has already been through extensive editing and is ready to be judged. We consider submissions from both previously published and unpublished writers, and both agented and unagented submissions. We do not accept submissions through postal mail and cannot return physical letters or manuscripts."

LEE & LOW BOOKS

95 Madison Ave., #1205, New York NY 10016. (212)779-4400. **E-mail:** general@leeandlow.com. **Website:** www.leeandlow.com. "Our goals are to meet a growing need for books that address children of color, and to present literature that all children can identify with. We only consider multicultural children's books. Sponsors a yearly New Voices Award for first-time picture book authors of color. Contest rules online at website or for SASE." Publishes hardcover originals and trade paperback reprints. Pays net royalty. Pays authors advances against royalty. Pays illustrators advance against royalty. Photographers paid advance against royalty. Publishes book 2 years after acceptance. Responds in 6 months to mss if interested. Book catalog available online. Guidelines available online or by written request with SASE.

HOW TO CONTACT Submit complete ms.

TIPS "Check our website to see the kinds of books we publish. Do not send mss that don't fit our mission."

⊘ LES FIGUES PRESS

P.O. Box 7736, Los Angeles CA 90007. **E-mail:** info@lesfigues.com. **Website:** www.lesfigues.com. **Contact:** Teresa Carmody, director. Les Figues Press is an independent, nonprofit publisher of poetry, prose, visual art, conceptual writing, and translation. With amission is to create aesthetic conversations between readers, writers, and artists, Les Figues Press favors projects which push the boundaries of genre, form, and general acceptability. "We are currently closed to all submissions."

LETHE PRESS

118 Heritage Ave., Maple Shade NJ 8052. (609)410-7391. **Website:** www.lethepressbooks.com. "Welcomes submissions from authors of any sexual or gender identity." Guidelines online.

NEEDS "Lethe Press is a small press seeking gay and lesbian themed poetry collections." Lethe Books are distributed by Ingram Publications and Bookazine, and are available at all major bookstores, as well as the major online retailers.

HOW TO CONTACT Query with 7-10 poems, list of publications.

LOST HORSE PRESS

105 Lost Horse Lane, Sandpoint ID 83864, US. (208)255-4410. **E-mail:** losthorsepress@mindspring.com. **Website:** www.losthorsepress.org. **Contact:** Christine Holbert, publisher. Established in 1998, Lost Horse Press—a nonprofit independent press—publishes poetry titles by emerging as well as established poets, and makes available other fine contemporary literature through cultural, educational and publishing programs and activities. Lost Horse Press is dedicated to works—often ignored by conglomerate publishers—which are so much in danger of vanishing into obscurity in what has become the age of chain stores and mass appeal food, movies, art and books. Distributed by University of Washington Press. "*Does not accept unsolicited mss. However, we welcome submissions for the Idaho Prize for Poetry, a national competition offering $1,000 prize money plus publication for a book-length ms. Please check the submission guidelines for the Idaho Prize for Poetry on our website.*" Publishes hardcover and paperback poetry titles. 10% royalties Occasionally pays advance. Publishes ms 3-12 months after acceptance. Book catalog may be viewed online at www.losthorsepress.org, plus the University of Washington Press, our distributor, offers both online and print catalogs. Please check the Lost Horse Press website or the Submittable.com website for Submission Guidelines.

NEEDS Does not want language-based, rhyming, cowboy.

HOW TO CONTACT Submit poetry via Submittable.com.

CONTEST/AWARD OFFERINGS The Idaho Prize for Poetry.

LSU PRESS

338 Johnston Hall, Baton Rouge LA 70803. (225)578-6294. **Website:** lsupress.org. LSU Press has established itself as one of the nation's outstanding scholarly presses and garners national and international accolades, including 4 Pulitzer Prizes. Responds in 4-6 months. Catalog online. Guidelines online.

NEEDS Poetry proposals should include a cover letter, 4-5 sample pages from the ms, and a current resume.

⊘ LUNA BISONTE PRODS

137 Leland Ave., Columbus OH 43214-7505. **E-mail:** bennettjohnm@gmail.com. **Website:** www.johnmbennett.net. **Contact:** John M. Bennett, editor/publisher. Avant-garde literature and poetry only. Please look at our titles before querying Pays copy or copies of book; further copies at cost. Does not pay advance. Not considering unsolicited submissions at this time.

NEEDS "Interested in avant-garde and highly experimental work only." Has published poetry by Jim Leftwich, Sheila E. Murphy, Al Ackerman, Richard Kostelanetz, Carla Bertola, Olchar Lindsann, and many others. See http://www.lulu.com/spotlight/lunabisonteprods

HOW TO CONTACT Query first, with a few sample poems and cover letter with brief bio and publication credits. "Keep it brief. Chapbook publishing usually depends on grants or other subsidies, and is usually by solicitation. **Will also consider subsidy arrangements on negotiable terms.**" A sampling of various Luna Bisonte Prods products is available for $20.

MAGE PUBLISHERS, INC.

1780 Crossroads Dr., Odenton MD 21113. (202)342-1642. **Fax:** (202)342-9269. **E-mail:** as@mage.com. **Website:** www.mage.com. Mage publishes books relating to Persian/Iranian culture. Publishes hardcover originals and reprints, trade paperback originals.

Pays royalty. Responds in 1 month to queries. Book catalog available free. Guidelines online.

NEEDS Must relate to Persian/Iranian culture.

HOW TO CONTACT Query.

TIPS "Audience is the Iranian-American community in America and Americans interested in Persian culture."

✪ MANOR HOUSE PUBLISHING, INC.

452 Cottingham Crescent, Ancaster ON L9G 3V6, Canada. (905)648-2193. **E-mail:** mbdavie@manor-house.biz. **Website:** www.manor-house-publishing.com. **Contact:** Mike Davie, president (novels and nonfiction). Manor House is currently looking for new fully edited, ready-to-run titles to complete our spring-fall release lineup. This is a rare opportunity for authors, including self-published, to have existing or ready titles picked up by Manor House and made available to retailers throughout the world, while our network of rights agents provide more potential revenue streams via foreign language rights sales. We are currently looking for titles that are ready or nearly ready for publishing to be released this season. Such titles should be written by Canadian citizens residing in Canada and should be profitable or with strong market sales potential to allow full cost recovery and profit for publisher and author. Of primary interest are business and self-help titles along with other nonfiction, including new age. We will also consider non-Canadian writers provided the manuscript meets literary standards and profitability is a certainty. Publishes hardcover, trade paperback, and mass market paperback originals (and reprints if they meet specific criteria - best to inquire with publisher). Pays 10% royalty on retail price. Publishes book 6 mos to 1 year after acceptance. Queries and mss to be sent by e-mail only. "We will respond in 30 days if interested-if not, there is no response. Please do not follow up unless asked to do so." Book catalog online. Guidelines available.

NEEDS Poetry should engage, provoke, involve the reader (and be written by Canadian authors residing in Canada).

TIPS "Our audience includes everyone-the general public/mass audience. Self-edit your work first, make sure it is well written and well edited with strong Canadian content and/or content of universal appeal (preferably with a Canadian connection of some kind)." We will also consider non-Canadian writers provided the manuscript meets literary standards and profitability is a certainty.

MARINER BOOKS

222 Berkeley St., Boston MA 2116. (617)351-5000. **Website:** www.hmco.com.

Mariner Books' *Interpreter of Maladies*, by debut author Jhumpa Lahiri, won the 2000 Pulitzer Prize for fiction and *The Caprices*, by Sabina Murray, received the 2003 PEN/Faulkner Award. Mariner Books' *Interpreter of Maladies*, by debut author Jhumpa Lahiri, won the 2000 Pulitzer Prize for fiction and *The Caprices*, by Sabina Murray, received the 2003 PEN/Faulkner Award.

NEEDS Has published poetry by Thomas Lux, Linda Gregerson, and Keith Leonard.

HOW TO CONTACT Agented submissions only.

⊘ MAVERICK DUCK PRESS

E-mail: maverickduckpress@yahoo.com. **Website:** www.maverickduckpress.com. Assistant Editor: Brielle Kelton. **Contact:** Kendall A. Bell, editor. Maverick Duck Press is a "publisher of chapbooks from undiscovered talent. We are looking for fresh and powerful work that shows a sense of innovation or a new take on passion or emotion. Previous publication in print or online journals could increase your chances of us accepting your manuscript." Does not want "unedited work." Pays 20 author's copies.

HOW TO CONTACT Send ms in Microsoft Word format with a cover letter with brief bio and publication credits. Chapbook mss may include previously published poems. "Previous publication is always a plus, as we may be more familiar with your work. Chapbook mss should have 16-24 poems, but no more than 24 poems."

✪ MCCLELLAND & STEWART, LTD.

The Canadian Publishers, 320 Front St. W., Suite 1400, Toronto ON M5V 3B6, Canada. (416)364-4449. **Fax:** (416)598-7764. **Website:** www.mcclelland.com. Publishes hardcover, trade paperback, and mass market paperback originals and reprints. Pays 10-15% royalty on retail price (hardcover rates). Pays advance. Publishes ms 1 year after acceptance. Responds in 3 months to proposals.

NEEDS Only Canadian poets should apply. We publish only 4 titles each year. Query. *No unsolicited mss.*

MCSWEENEY'S POETRY SERIES

San Francisco CA **E-mail:** poetry@mcsweeneys.net. **Website:** mcsweeneys.net. McSweeney's regularly publishes poetry collections, as part of the McSweeney's Poetry Series. Catalog online. Guidelines online.

NEEDS The McSweeney's Poetry Series publishes new collections of poetry. "We are open to all styles.

HOW TO CONTACT Book-length mss should be sent as PDF to poetry@mcsweeneys.net. In the cover letter, include your name, phone number, and e-mail address.

TIPS "We're a very small operation, and we may not be able to get back to you about the manuscript. We will do our very best."

MERRIAM PRESS

489 South St., Hoosick Falls NY 12090. **E-mail:** ray@merriam-press.com. **Website:** www.merriam-press.com. **Contact:** Ray Merriam, owner. Merriam Press specializes in military history, particularly World War II history. We are also branching out into other genres, including fiction, historical fiction, poetry, children. Provide brief synopsis of ms. Never send any files in body of e-mail. Send manuscript as attachment to email. Publisher will ask for full ms for review. Publisher requires unformatted mss. Mss must be thoroughly edited and error-free. Publishes hardcover and softcover trade paperback original works and reprints. Titles are also made available in e-book editions. Pays 10% royalty for printed editions and 50% royalty for e-book editions. Royalty payment is based on the amount paid to the publisher, not the retail or list prices. Does not pay advance. Publishes ms 6 months or less after acceptance. Responds quickly (e-mail preferred) to queries. Book catalog available in print and PDF editions. Author guidelines and additional information are available on publisher's website.

NEEDS Especially but not limited to military topics.

HOW TO CONTACT Query with SASE or by e-mail first. Do not send ms (in whole or in part) unless requested to do so.

TIPS "Our military history books are geared for military historians, collectors, model kit builders, wargamers, veterans, general enthusiasts. We now publish some historical fiction and poetry and will consider well-written books on a variety of non-military topics."

⊘ MIAMI UNIVERSITY PRESS

301 S. Patterson Ave., 356 Bachelor Hall, Miami University, Oxford OH 45056. **E-mail:** mupress@miamioh.edu. **Website:** www.miamioh.edu/mupress. **Contact:** Keith Tuma, editor; Amy Toland, managing editor.

Publishes 1-2 books of poetry and/or poetry in translation per year and 1 novella, in paperback editions.

HOW TO CONTACT Miami University Press is unable to respond to unsolicited mss and queries.

MICHIGAN STATE UNIVERSITY PRESS

1405 S. Harrison Rd., Suite 25, East Lansing MI 48823. (517)355-9543. **Fax:** (517)432-2611. **E-mail:** msupress@msu.edu. **Website:** msupress.org. **Contact:** Alex Schwartz and Julie Loehr, acquisitions. Michigan State University Press has notably represented both scholarly publishing and the mission of Michigan State University with the publication of numerous award-winning books and scholarly journals. In addition, they publish nonfiction that addresses, in a more contemporary way, social concerns, such as diversity and civil rights. They also publish literary fiction and poetry. Publishes hardcover and softcover originals. Pays variable royalty. Book catalog and ms guidelines online.

NEEDS Publishes poetry collections.

HOW TO CONTACT Submit proposal with sample poems.

MILKWEED EDITIONS

1011 Washington Ave. S., Suite 300, Minneapolis MN 55415. (612)332-3192. **Fax:** (612)215-2550. **Website:** www.milkweed.org. "Milkweed Editions publishes with the intention of making a humane impact on society, in the belief that literature is a transformative art uniquely able to convey the essential experiences of the human heart and spirit. To that end, Milkweed Editions publishes distinctive voices of literary merit in handsomely designed, visually dynamic books, exploring the ethical, cultural, and esthetic issues that free societies need continually to address." Publishes hardcover, trade paperback, and electronic originals; trade paperback and electronic reprints. Pays authors variable royalty based on retail price. Offers advance against royalties. Pays varied advance from $500-10,000. Publishes book in 18 months. Responds in 6 months. Book catalog online. Only accepts submissions during open submission periods. See website for guidelines.

NEEDS Milkweed Editions is "looking for poetry manuscripts of high quality that embody humane values and contribute to cultural understanding." Not limited in subject matter. Open to writers with previously published books of poetry or a minimum of 6 poems published in nationally distributed commercial or literary journals. Considers translations and bilingual mss.

HOW TO CONTACT Query with SASE; submit completed ms.

TIPS "We are looking for excellent writing with the intent of making a humane impact on society. Please read submission guidelines before submitting and acquaint yourself with our books in terms of style and quality before submitting. Many factors influence our selection process, so don't get discouraged. Nonfiction is focused on literary writing about the natural world, including living well in urban environments."

⊘ MOVING PARTS PRESS

10699 Empire Grade, Santa Cruz CA 95060. (831)427-2271. **E-mail:** frice@movingpartspress.com. **Website:** www.movingpartspress.com. **Contact:** Felicia Rice, poetry editor. Moving Part Press publishes handsome, innovative books, broadsides, and prints that "explore the relationship of word and image, typography and the visual arts, the fine arts and popular culture."

HOW TO CONTACT *Does not accept unsolicited mss.*

NEW DIRECTIONS

80 Eighth Ave., New York NY 10011. **Fax:** (212)255-0231. **E-mail:** editorial@ndbooks.com. **Website:** www.ndbooks.com. **Contact:** Editorial Assistant. "Currently, New Directions focuses primarily on fiction in translation, avant garde American fiction, and experimental poetry by American and foreign authors. If your work does not fall into one of those categories, you would probably do best to submit your work elsewhere." Hardcover and trade paperback originals. Responds in 3-4 months to queries. Book catalog and guidelines online.

HOW TO CONTACT Query.

TIPS "Our books serve the academic community."

⊙ NEWEST PUBLISHERS LTD.

201, 8540-109 St., Edmonton AB T6G 1E6, Canada. (780)432-9427. **Fax:** (780)433-3179. **E-mail:** info@newestpress.com. **E-mail:** submissions@newestpress.com. **Website:** www.newestpress.com. NeWest publishes Western Canadian fiction, nonfiction, poetry, and drama. Publishes trade paperback originals. Pays 10% royalty. Publishes ms 2-3 years after acceptance. Responds in 6-8 months to queries. Book catalog for 9×12 SASE. Guidelines online.

NEW ISSUES POETRY & PROSE

Western Michigan University, 1903 W. Michigan Ave., Kalamazoo MI 49008-5463. (269)387-8185. **E-mail:** new-issues@wmich.edu. **Website:** newissuespress.com. **Contact:** Managing Editor. Publishes 18 months after acceptance. Guidelines online.

NEEDS New Issues Poetry & Prose offers two contests annually. The Green Rose Prize is awarded to an author who has previously published at least one full-length book of poems. The New Issues Poetry Prize, an award for a first book of poems, is chosen by a guest judge. Past judges have included Philip Levine, C.K. Williams, C.D. Wright, and Campbell McGrath. New Issues does not read mss outside our contests. Graduate students in the Ph.D. and M.F.A. programs of Western Michigan Univ. often volunteer their time reading mss. Finalists are chosen by the editors. New Issues often publishes 1-2 additional mss selected from the finalists.

NEW RIVERS PRESS

1104 Seventh Ave. S., Moorhead MN 56563. **Website:** www.newriverspress.com. **Contact:** Nayt Rundquist, managing editor. New Rivers Press publishes collections of poetry, novels, nonfiction, translations of contemporary literature, and collections of short fiction and nonfiction. "We continue to publish books regularly by new and emerging writers, but we also welcome the opportunity to read work of every character and to publish the best literature available nationwide. Each fall through the Many Voices Project competition, we choose 2 books: 1 poetry and 1 prose."

NEEDS The Many Voices Project awards $1,000, a standard book contract, publication of a book-length ms by New Rivers Press, and national distribution. All previously published poems must be acknowledged. "We will consider simultaneous submissions if noted as such. If your manuscript is accepted elsewhere during the judging, you must notify New Rivers Press immediately. If you do not give such notification and your manuscript is selected, your entry gives New Rivers Press permission to go ahead with publication."

HOW TO CONTACT Guidelines online.

NIGHTBOAT BOOKS

P.O. Box 10, Callicoon NY 12723. **Fax:** (603)448-9429. **Website:** nightboat.org. Nightboat Books, a nonprofit organization, seeks to develop audiences for writers whose work resists convention and transcends boundaries, by publishing books rich with poignancy, intelligence and risk. Catalog online. Guidelines online.

NEEDS Considers poetry submitted to its poetry prize. More information online.

TIPS "The name Nightboat signifies travel, passage, and possibility—of mind and body, and of language. The night boat maneuvers in darkness at the mercy of changing currents and weather, always immersed in forces beyond itself."

⊘ NINETY-SIX PRESS

Special Collections, James B. Duke Library, 3300 Poinsett Hwy., Greenville SC 29613. (864)294-2194. **Website:** library.furman.edu/specialcollections/96Press/index.htm. For a sample, send $10.

TIPS "Between 1991 and 2015, the Ninety-Six Press published only poetry by South Carolina authors. The Press is not considering new publishing projects at this time. Check our website for up-to-date information."

⊘ W.W. NORTON & COMPANY, INC.

500 Fifth Ave., New York NY 10110. (212)354-5500. **Fax:** (212)869-0856. **Website:** www.wwnorton.com. "W. W. Norton & Company, the oldest and largest publishing house owned wholly by its employees, strives to carry out the imperative of its founder to 'publish books not for a single season, but for the years' in fiction, nonfiction, poetry, college textbooks, cookbooks, art books and professional books. Due to the workload of our editorial staff and the large volume of materials we receive, *Norton is no longer able to accept unsolicited submissions.* If you are seeking publication, we suggest working with a literary agent who will represent you to the house."

OBERLIN COLLEGE PRESS

50 N. Professor St., Oberlin OH 44074. (440)775-8408. **Fax:** (440)775-8124. **E-mail:** oc.press@oberlin.edu. **Website:** www.oberlin.edu/ocpress. **Contact:** Marco Wilkinson, managing editor. Publishes hardcover and trade paperback originals. Pays 7½-10% royalty. Responds promptly to queries; 2 months to mss.

NEEDS *FIELD Magazine*—submit 2-6 poems through website "submissions" tab; FIELD Translation Series—query with SASE and sample poems; FIELD Poetry Series—*no unsolicited mss.* Enter mss in FIELD Poetry Prize ($1,000 and a standard royalty contract) held annually in May.

HOW TO CONTACT Submit complete ms.

TIPS "Queries for the FIELD Translation Series: send sample poems and letter describing project. Winner of the annual FIELD poetry prize determines publication. Do not send unsolicited manuscripts."

OHIO STATE UNIVERSITY PRESS

1070 Carmack Rd., 180 Pressey Hall, Columbus OH 43210-1002. (614)292-6930. **Fax:** (614)292-2065. **E-mail:** eugene@osupress.org. **E-mail:** lindsay@osupress.org. **Website:** www.ohiostatepress.org. **Contact:** Eugene O'Connor, acquisitions editor (medieval studies and classics); Lindsay Martin, acquisitions editor (literary studies). The Ohio State University Press publishes scholarly nonfiction, and offers short fiction and short poetry prizes. Currently emphasizing history, literary studies, political science, women's health, classics, Victoria studies. Pays royalty. Pays advance. Responds in 3 months to queries. Guidelines online.

NEEDS Offers poetry competition through *The Journal*.

OHIO UNIVERSITY PRESS

30 Park Place, Suite 101, Athens OH 45701. **Fax:** (740)593-4536. **E-mail:** huard@ohio.edu. **Website:** www.ohioswallow.com. **Contact:** Gillian Berchowitz, director. "In addition to scholarly works in African studies, Appalachian studies, US history, and other areas, Ohio University Press publishes a wide range of creative works as part of its Hollis Summers Poetry Prize (yearly deadline in December), its Modern African Writing series, and under its trade imprint, Swallow Press." Publishes hardcover and trade paperback originals and reprints. Sometimes pays advance. Publishes ms 1 year after acceptance. Responds in 1-3 months. Catalog online. Guidelines online.

CONTEST/AWARD OFFERINGS Named for the distinguished poet who taught for many years at Ohio University and made Athens, Ohio, the subject of many of his poems, the Hollis Summers Poetry Prize invites writers to submit unpublished collections of original poems. The competition is open to both those who have not published a book-length collection and those who have. $30 fee, Dec. 1 deadline. The general editor of the Hollis Summers Poetry Prize is David Sanders.

TIPS "Rather than trying to hook the editor on your work, let the material be compelling enough and well-presented enough to do it for you."

OMNIDAWN PUBLISHING

Website: www.omnidawn.com. Publishes ms 6-12 months after acceptance. Guidelines online.

TIPS "Check our website for latest information."

◯ OOLICHAN BOOKS

P.O. Box 2278, Lantzville BC V0B 1M0, Canada. (250)423-6113. **E-mail:** info@oolichan.com. **Web-**

site: www.oolichan.com. Publisher: Randal Macnair. Publishes hardcover and trade paperback originals and reprints. Pays royalty on retail price. Publishes ms 6-12 months after acceptance. Responds in 1-3 months. Book catalog online. Guidelines online.

🖵 Only publishes Canadian authors.

NEEDS "We are one of the few small literary presses in Canada that still publishes poetry. We try to include 2-3 poetry titles each year. We attempt to balance our list between emerging and established poets. Our poetry titles have won or been shortlisted for major national awards, including the Governor General's Award, the BC Book Prizes, and the Alberta Awards."

HOW TO CONTACT Submit 10 sample poems.

TIPS "Our audience is adult readers who love good books and good literature. Our audience is regional and national, as well as international. Follow our submission guidelines. Check out some of our titles at your local library or bookstore to get an idea of what we publish. Don't send us the only copy of your manuscript. Let us know if your submission is simultaneous, and inform us if it is accepted elsewhere. Above all, keep writing!"

OOLIGAN PRESS

369 Neuberger Hall, 724 SW Harrison St., Portland OR 97201. (503)725-9410. **E-mail:** acquisitions@ooliganpress.pdx.edu. **Website:** ooligan.pdx.edu. **Contact:** Acquisitions Co-Managers. "We seek to publish regionally significant works of literary, historical, and social value.

We define the Pacific Northwest as Northern California, Oregon, Idaho, Washington, British Columbia, and Alaska. We recognize the importance of diversity, particularly within the publishing industry, and are committed to building a literary community that includes traditionally underrepresented voices; therefore, we are interested in works originating from, or focusing on, marginalized communities of the Pacific Northwest." Publishes trade paperbacks, electronic originals, and reprints. Pays negotiable royalty on retail price. Publishes ms 12-18 months after acceptance. Responds in 3 weeks for queries; 3 months for proposals. Catalog online. Guidelines online.

NEEDS Ooligan is a not-for-profit general trade press that publishes books honoring the cultural and natural diversity of the Pacific Northwest. "We are limited in the number of poetry titles that we publish as poetry represents only a small percentage of our overall ac-

quisitions. We are open to all forms of style and verse; however, we give special preference to prose poetry and traditional verse. Although spoken word, slam, and rap poetry are of interest to the press, we will consider such work if it does not translate well to the written page. Ooligan does not publish chapbooks."

HOW TO CONTACT Query first through e-mail or Submittable.

TIPS "Search the blog for tips."

🚫 ORCHARD BOOKS (US)

557 Broadway, New York NY 10012. **Website:** www.scholastic.com. *Orchard is not accepting unsolicited mss.* Most commonly offers an advance against list royalties.

PALETTES & QUILLS

1935 Penfield Rd., Penfield NY 14526. (585)383-0812. **E-mail:** palettesnquills@gmail.com. **Website:** http://palettesandquills.simplesite.com/. **Contact:** Donna M. Marbach, publisher/owner. Palettes & Quills is devoted to the celebration and expansion of the literary and visual arts, offering both commissioned and consulting services. It works to support beginning and emerging writers and artists to expand their knowledge, improve their skills, and connect to other resources in the community. Further, Palettes & Quills seeks to increase the public's awareness and appreciation of these arts through education, advocacy, hands-on program assistance, and functioning as a small literary press. "We publish a chapbook every other year in a contest judged by a well-known poet. We also publish a monthly e-newsletter, and chapbooks/anthologies/ and broadsides on an irregular schedule. Reprints accepted only for our e-newsletter." Publishes chapbooks, broadsides, e-newsletter. Contest winner gets $200 and 50 books. Others are paid copies. Publishes ms 12 months after acceptance. Response time varies. "We try to respond as quick as we can." Guidelines online.

NEEDS Palettes & Quills "is at this point is only considering chapbooks that are poetry, creative nonfiction, or fiction, a poetry press only, and produces only a handful of publications each year, specializing in anthologies, individual chapbooks, and broadsides." Wants "work that should appeal to a wide audience." Does not want "poems that are sold blocks of text, long-lined and without stanza breaks. Wildly elaborate free-verse would be difficult and in all likelihood fight with art background, amateurish rhyming poem, overly sentimental poems, poems that use excessive profanity, or which denigrate other people, or political and religious diatribes."

HOW TO CONTACT Query first with 3-5 poems and a cover letter with brief bio and publication credits for individual unsolicited chapbooks. May include previously published poems. Chapbook poets would get 20 copies of a run; broadside poets and artists get 5-10 copies and occasionally paid $10 for reproduction rights. Anthology poets get 1 copy of the anthology. All poets and artists get a discount on purchases that include their work.

TIPS "We are very small and the best bet with us with our monthly e-newsletter Pencil Marks."

PAYCOCK PRESS

3819 N. 13th St., Arlington VA 22201. (703)525-9296. **E-mail:** rchrdpeabody9@gmail.com. **E-mail:** gargoyle@gargoylemagazine.com. **Website:** www.gargoylemagazine.com. **Contact:** Richard Peabody. "Too academic for the underground, too outlaw for the academic world. We tend to be edgy and look for ultra-literary work." Publishes paperback originals. Books: POD printing. Average print order: 500. Averages 1 total title/year. Member CLMP. Distributes through Amazon and website. Publishes ms 1 year after acceptance. Responds to queries in 1 month; mss in 4 months.

NEEDS Considers experimental, edgy poetry collections.

HOW TO CONTACT Accepts unsolicited mss. Accepts queries by e mail. Include brief bio. Send SASE for return of ms or send a disposable ms and SASE for reply only.

TIPS "Check out our website. Two of our favorite writers are Paul Bowles and Jeanette Winterson."

PELICAN PUBLISHING COMPANY

1000 Burmaster St., Gretna LA 70053. (504)368-1175. **Fax:** (504)368-1195. **E-mail:** editorial@pelicanpub.com. **Website:** www.pelicanpub.com. "We believe ideas have consequences. One of the consequences is that they lead to a best-selling book. We publish books to improve and uplift the reader. Currently emphasizing business and history titles." Publishes 20 young readers/year; 1 middle reader/year. "Our children's books (illustrated and otherwise) include history, biography, holiday, and regional. Pelican's mission is to publish books of quality and permanence that enrich the lives of those who read them." Publishes hardcover, trade paperback and mass market paperback originals and reprints. Pays authors in royalties; buys ms out-

right "rarely." Illustrators paid by "various arrangements." Advance considered. Publishes a book 9-18 months after acceptance. Responds in 1 month to queries; 3 months to mss. Requires exclusive submission. Book catalog and ms guidelines online.

NEEDS Considers poetry for "hardcover children's books only (1,100 words maximum), preferably with a regional focus. However, our needs for this are very limited; we publish 20 juvenile titles per year, and most of these are prose, not poetry." Books are 32 pages, magazine-sized, include illustrations.

TIPS "We do extremely well with cookbooks, popular histories, and business. We will continue to build in these areas. The writer must have a clear sense of the market and knowledge of the competition. A query letter should describe the project briefly, give the author's writing and professional credentials, and promotional ideas."

PENGUIN POETS

375 Hudson St., New York NY 10014. **Website:** www.penguinrandomhouse.com. Agented submissions only. Catalog online.

PERSEA BOOKS

277 Broadway, Suite 708, New York NY 10007. (212)260-9256. **Fax:** (212)267-3165. **E-mail:** info@perseabooks.com. **Website:** www.perseabooks.com. The aim of Persea is to publish works that endure by meeting high standards of literary merit and relevance. "We have often taken on important books other publishers have overlooked, or have made significant discoveries and rediscoveries, whether of a single work or writer's entire oeuvre. Our books cover a wide range of themes, styles, and genres. We have published poetry, fiction, essays, memoir, biography, titles of Jewish and Middle Eastern interest, women's studies, American Indian folklore, and revived classics, as well as a notable selection of works in translation." Responds in 8 weeks to proposals; 10 weeks to mss. Guidelines online.

NEEDS "We have a longstanding commitment to publishing extraordinary contemporary poetry and maintain an active poetry program. At this time, due to our commitment to the poets we already publish, we are limited in our ability to add new collections."

HOW TO CONTACT Send an e-mail to poetry@perseabooks.com describing current project and publication history, attaching a pdf or Word document with up to 12 sample pages of poetry. "If the timing is right and we are interested in seeing more work, we will contact you."

⊘ PERUGIA PRESS

P.O. Box 60364, Florence MA 01062. **E-mail:** editor@
perugiapress.com. **Website:** www.perugiapress.com.
Contact: Rebecca Olander, editor/director. Since 1997,
Perugia Press has been publishing first and second
books of poetry by women. "We publish one book a
year, the winner of the Perugia Press Prize. Our mission is to help right gender inequity in publishing by
launching women's voices into the world, one excellent book at a time." Publishes ms less than a year after
acceptance. See website.

CONTEST/AWARD OFFERINGS Perugia Press
Prize.

PIÑATA BOOKS

Imprint of Arte Publico Press, University of Houston, 4902 Gulf Fwy., Bldg. 19, Room 100, Houston
TX 77204-2004. (713)743-2845. **Fax:** (713)743-3080.
E-mail: submapp@uh.edu. **Website:** www.artepubli-
copress.com. "Piñata Books is dedicated to the publication of children's and young adult literature focusing on
U.S. Hispanic culture by U.S. Hispanic authors. Arte
Publico's mission is the publication, promotion and
dissemination of Latino literature for a variety of national and regional audiences, from early childhood to
adult, through the complete gamut of delivery systems,
including personal performance as well as print and
electronic media." Publishes hardcover and trade paperback originals. Pays 10% royalty on wholesale price.
Pays $1,000-3,000 advance. Publishes book 2 years af-
ter acceptance. Responds in 2-3 months to queries; 4-6
months to mss. Book catalog and guidelines online.

NEEDS Appropriate to Hispanic theme.

HOW TO CONTACT Submissions made through
online submission form.

TIPS "Include cover letter with submission explaining
why your manuscript is unique and important, why
we should publish it, who will buy it, etc."

⊘ PLAN B PRESS

2714 Jefferson Dr., Alexandria VA 22303. (215)732-
2663. **E-mail:** planbpress@gmail.com. **Website:** www.
planbpress.com. **Contact:** Steven Allen May, president. Plan B Press is a "small publishing company with
an international feel. Our intention is to have Plan B
Press be part of the conversation about the direction
and depth of literary movements and genres. Plan B
Press's new direction is to seek out authors rarely-to-
never published, sharing new voices that might not
otherwise be heard. Plan B Press is determined to

merge text with image, writing with art." Publishes
poetry and short fiction. Wants "experimental poetry,
concrete/visual work." Pays author's copies. Responds
to queries in 1 month; mss in 3 months.

NEEDS Wants to see: experimental, concrete, visual
poetry. Does not want "sonnets, political or religious
poems, work in the style of Ogden Nash."

PRESA PRESS

P.O. Box 792, Rockford MI 49341. **E-mail:** presapre-
ss@aol.com. **Website:** www.presapress.com. **Contact:**
Roseanne Ritzema, editor. Presa Press publishes perfect-
bound paperbacks of poetry. Wants "imagistic poetry
where form is an extension of content, surreal, experimental, and personal poetry." Does not want "overtly political or didactic material." Pays 5+ author/quotes copies.
Time between acceptance and publication is 8-12 weeks.
Responds to queries in 2-4 weeks; to mss in 8-12 weeks

NEEDS Acquires first North American serial rights
and the right to reprint in anthologies. Rights include
e-book publishing rights. Rights revert to poets upon
publication. Accepts postal submissions only. Cover
letter is preferred. Reads submissions year round. Poems are circulated to an editorial board. Send materials for review consideration to Roseanne Ritzema.

HOW TO CONTACT Query first, with a few sample
poems and a cover letter with brief bio and publication credits. Book/chapbook mss may include previously published poems.

PRESS 53

560 N. Trade St., Suite 103, Winston-Salem NC 27101.
(336)770-5353. **E-mail:** editor@press53.com. **Website:**
www.press53.com. **Contact:** Kevin Morgan Watson,
Publisher and Editor in Chief. "Press 53 was founded in October 2005 and quickly earned a reputation
for publishing quality short fiction and poetry collections." Poetry and short fiction collections only.
Pays 10% royalty on gross sales. Pays advance only
for contest winners. Publishes ms 1 year after acceptance. Catalog online. Guidelines online.

NEEDS "We love working with poets who have been
widely published and are active in the poetry community. We publish roughly 8-10 full-length poetry
collections of around 70 pages or more each year, plus
the winner of our Press 53 Award for Poetry." Does
not want experimental, overtly political or religious.

HOW TO CONTACT Finds mss through contests,
referrals, and scouting magazines, journals, and other
contests.

TIPS "We are looking for writers who are actively involved in the writing community, writers who are submitting their work to journals, magazines and contests, and who are getting published, building readership, and earning a reputation for their work."

PRESS HERE

22230 NE 28th Place, Sammamish WA 98074-6408. **Website:** www.gracecuts.com/press-here. **Contact:** Michael Dylan Welch, editor/publisher. Press Here publishes award-winning books of haiku, tanka, and related poetry by the leading poets of these genres, as well as essays, criticism, and interviews about these genres. "We publish work only by those poets who are already frequently published in the leading haiku and tanka journals." Publishes 1-2 poetry books/year, plus occasional books of essays or interviews. Mss are selected nearly always by invitation. Press Here publications have won the 1st-place Merit Book Award and other awards from the Haiku Society of America. Pays a negotiated percentage of author's copies (out of a press run of 200-1,000). Responds to queries in up to 1 month; to mss in up to 2 months. Catalog online.

NEEDS Does not want any poetry other than haiku, tanka, and related genres. Has published poetry by Lee Gurga, paul m., Paul O. Williams, Adele Kenny, Pat Shelley, Cor van den Heuvel, and William J. Higginson.

HOW TO CONTACT Query first, with a few sample poems and a cover letter with brief bio and publication credits. Book mss may include previously published poems ("previous publication strongly preferred"). "All proposals must be by well-established haiku or tanka poets, and must be for haiku or tanka poetry, or criticism/discussion of these genres. If the editor does not already know your work well from leading haiku and tanka publications, then he is not likely to be interested in your manuscript."

PRINCETON UNIVERSITY PRESS

41 William St., Princeton NJ 08540. (609)258-4900. **Fax:** (609)258-6305. **Website:** press.princeton.edu. **Contact:** Susan Stewart, editor. "The Lockert Library of Poetry in Translation embraces a wide geographic and temporal range, from Scandinavia to Latin America to the subcontinent of India, from the Tang Dynasty to Europe of the modern day. It especially emphasizes poets who are established in their native lands and who are being introduced to an English-speaking audience. Manuscripts are judged with several criteria in mind: the ability of the translation to stand on its own as poetry in English; fidelity to the tone and spirit of the original, rather than literal accuracy; and the importance of the translated poet to the literature of his or her time and country." Responds in 3-4 months. Guidelines online.

NEEDS Submit hard copy of proposal with sample poems or full ms. Cover letter is required. Reads submissions year round. Mss will not be returned. Comments on finalists only.

RAGGED SKY PRESS

270 Griggs Dr., Princeton NJ 08540. **E-mail:** raggedskyanthology@gmail.com. **Website:** www.raggedsky.com. **Contact:** Ellen Foos, publisher; Arlene Weiner, editor. Produces poetry anthologies and single-author poetry collections along with occasional inspired prose. Ragged Sky is a small, highly selective cooperative press. "We work with our authors closely." Individual poetry collections currently by invitation only. Learn more online. Publishes ms 1 year after acceptance. Responds in 3 weeks.

⊘ RATTAPALLAX PRESS

217 Thompson St., Suite 353, New York NY 10012. **Website:** www.rattapallax.com. **Contact:** Ram Devineni, founder/president; Flavia Rocha, editor-in-chief. Rattapallax Press publishes "contemporary poets and writers with unique, powerful voices." Publishes 5 paperbacks and 3 chapbooks/year. Books are usually 64 pages, digest-sized, offset-printed, perfect-bound, with 12-pt. CS1 covers.

HOW TO CONTACT Query first, with a few sample poems and cover letter with brief bio and publication credits. Include SASE. Requires authors to first be published in *Rattapallax*. Responds to queries in 1 month; to mss in 2 months. Pays royalties of 10-25%. Order sample books from website.

RED HEN PRESS

P.O. Box 40820, Pasadena CA 91114. (626)356-4760. **Fax:** (626)356-9974. **Website:** www.redhen.org. Managing Editor: Kate Gale. **Contact:** Mark E. Cull, publisher/executive director. "At this time, the best opportunity to be published by Red Hen is by entering one of our contests. Please find more information in our award submission guidelines." Publishes trade paperback originals. Publishes ms 1 year after acceptance. Responds in 1-2 months. Book catalog available free. Guidelines online.

HOW TO CONTACT Submit to Benjamin Saltman Poetry Award.

TIPS "Audience reads poetry, literary fiction, intelligent nonfiction. If you have an agent, we may be too small since we don't pay advances. Write well. Send queries first. Be willing to help promote your own book."

⊘ RED MOON PRESS

P.O. Box 2461, Winchester VA 22604. (540)722-2156. **E-mail:** jim.kacian@redmoonpress.com. **Website:** www.redmoonpress.com. **Contact:** Jim Kacian, editor/publisher. Red Moon Press "is the largest and most prestigious publisher of English-language haiku and related work in the world." Publishes 10-15 volumes/year, usually 2-3 anthologies, 8-12 individual collections of English-language haiku, and 1-3 books of essays, translations, or criticism of haiku. Under other imprints, the press also publishes chapbooks of various sizes and formats. English-language haiku, contemporary haiku in other languages in English translation, haiku anthologies, books of haiku theory and criticism, books on related genres (tanka, haibun, haiga, renga, renku, etc.). Every book is a separate consideration. Publishes 1-2 months after acceptance. Catalog online. Guidelines available.

HOW TO CONTACT Query first with book concept (not just "I've written a few haiku"); if interested we'll ask for samples. "Each contract separately negotiated."

✪ RONSDALE PRESS

3350 W. 21st Ave., Vancouver BC V6S 1G7, Canada. (604)738-4688. **Fax:** (604)731-4548. **E-mail:** ronsdale@shaw.ca. **Website:** ronsdalepress.com. **Contact:** Ronald B. Hatch (fiction, poetry, nonfiction, social commentary); Veronica Hatch (YA novels and short stories). "Ronsdale Press is a Canadian literary publishing house that publishes 12 books each year, four of which are young adult titles. Of particular interest are books involving children exploring and discovering new aspects of Canadian history or Canadian social issues." Publishes trade paperback originals. Pays 10% royalty on retail price. Publishes book 1 year after acceptance. Responds to queries in 2 weeks; mss in 2 months. Book catalog for #10 SASE. Guidelines online. Please, no first drafts or uneditited drafts.

NEEDS Poets should have published some poems in magazines/journals and should be well-read in contemporary masters.

HOW TO CONTACT Submit complete MS if you feel it is right for Ronsdale Press. If you want to save postage, send a sample.

TIPS "Ronsdale Press is a literary publishing house, based in Vancouver, and dedicated to publishing books from across Canada, books that give Canadians new insights into themselves and their country. We aim to publish the best Canadian writers."

ROSE ALLEY PRESS

4203 Brooklyn Ave. NE, #103A, Seattle WA 98105-5911. (206)633-2725. **E-mail:** rosealleypress@juno.com. **Website:** www.rosealleypress.com. **Contact:** David D. Horowitz. "Rose Alley Press primarily publishes books featuring rhymed metrical poetry and an annually updated booklet about writing and publication. We do not read or consider unsolicited manuscripts."

NEEDS Our focus is contemporary Pacific Northwest rhymed metrical poetry. We contact poets whose work we wish to publish. Please note we do not accept or consider unsolicited manuscripts. We wish all of our poet friends the very best, but given limitations of time and money, we can do only so much.

SAKURA PUBLISHING & TECHNOLOGIES

(330)360-5131. **E-mail:** skpublishing124@gmail.com. **Website:** www.sakura-publishing.com. **Contact:** Derek Vasconi, submissions coordinator. Visit our website for query guidelines. Mss that don't follow guidelines will not be considered. Sakura Publishing is a traditional, independent book publishing company that seeks to publish Asian-themed books, particularly Asian-Horror, or anything dealing with Japan, Japanese culture, and Japanese horror. Publishes trade paperback, mass market paperback and electronic originals and reprints. Currently accepts only the following genres: Asian fiction, Japanese fiction (in English), and Japanese non-fiction (stories about living in Japan in particular are of interest). Please do not send queries for any other genres. Royalty payments on paperback, e-book, wholesale, and merchandise Does not pay advance. Publishes ms 6 months after acceptance. Responds in 1 week. Book catalog available for #10 SASE. Guidelines online.

HOW TO CONTACT Follow guidelines online.

TIPS "When submitting, only include a short query letter, the first three chapters of your manuscript included in the body of the email (no attachments will be opened), and your marketing plan. If you do not include these things, your manuscript will not be considered for publication. Also, please note we are looking only for Asian themed horror, Asian themed fiction, Japanese nonfiction and in particular, anything that has to deal with Japan. If you have a Japanese horror manuscript, or you have a nonfiction book about living in Japan or dating in Japan, your manuscript will be given the highest preference and priority."

SALINA BOOKSHELF

1120 W. University Ave., Suite 102, Flagstaff AZ 86001. (877)527-0070. **Fax:** (928)526-0386. **Website:** www.salinabookshelf.com. Publishes trade paperback originals and reprints. Pays varying royalty. Pays advance. Publishes ms 1 year after acceptance. Responds in 3 months to queries.

NEEDS "We accept poetry in English/Southwest language for children."

HOW TO CONTACT Submit 3 sample poems.

SALMON POETRY

Knockeven, Cliffs of Moher, County Clare , Ireland. 353(0)852318909. **E-mail:** info@salmonpoetry.com. **E-mail:** jessie@salmonpoetry.com. **Website:** www.salmonpoetry.com. **Contact:** Jessie Lendennie, editor. Publishes contemporary poetry and literary nonfiction Pays advance. Publishes ms 2 years after acceptance. Responds in 3 months. Guidelines available.

NEEDS "Salmon Press is one of the most important publishers in the Irish literary world; specializing in the promotion of new poets, particularly women. Established in 1981 as an alternative voice in Irish literature, Salmon is known for its international list and over the years has developed a cross-cultural literary dialog, broadening Irish Literature and urging new perspectives on established traditions."

HOW TO CONTACT E-mail query with short biographical note and 5-10 sample poems.

TIPS "Read as much poetry as you can, and always research the publisher before submitting!"

SARABANDE BOOKS, INC.

822 E. Market St., Louisville KY 40206. (502)458-4028. **E-mail:** info@sarabandebooks.org. **Website:** www.sarabandebooks.org. **Contact:** Sarah Gorham, editor-in-chief. "Sarabande Books was founded to publish poetry, short fiction, and creative nonfiction. We look for works of lasting literary value. Please see our titles to get an idea of our taste. Accepts submissions through contests and open submissions." Publishes trade paperback originals. Pays royalty. 10% on actual income received. Also pays in author's copies. Pays $500-3,000

advance. Publishes ms 18 months after acceptance. Responds within 8 months. Book catalog available free. Contest guidelines for #10 SASE or on website.

NEEDS Poetry of superior artistic quality; otherwise no restraints or specifications. Sarabande Books publishes books of poetry of 48 pages minimum. Wants "poetry that offers originality of voice and subject matter, uniqueness of vision, and a language that startles because of the careful attention paid to it—language that goes beyond the merely competent or functional."

HOW TO CONTACT Mss selected through literary contests, invitation, and recommendation by a well-established writer.

TIPS "Sarabande publishes for a general literary audience. Know your market. Read-and buy-books of literature. Sponsors contests for poetry and fiction. Make sure you're not writing in a vacuum, that you've read and are conscious of contemporary literature. Have someone read your manuscript, checking it for ordering, coherence. Better a lean, consistently strong manuscript than one that is long and uneven. We like a story to have good narrative, and we like to be engaged by language."

SATURNALIA BOOKS

105 Woodside Rd., Ardmore PA 19003. (267)278-9541. **E-mail:** info@saturnaliabooks.com. **Website:** www.saturnaliabooks.org. **Contact:** Henry Israeli, publisher. "We do not accept unsolicited submissions. We hold a contest, the Saturnalia Books Poetry Prize, annually in which 1 anonymously submitted title is chosen by a poet with a national reputation for publication. The editors then select an Editors Prize for publication. Submissions are accepted during the month of March. The submission fee is $30, and the prize is $1,500 and 20 copies of the book for the Saturnalia Books Poetry Prize and $500 plus 20 free books for the Saturnalia Books Editors Award. See website for details." Publishes trade paperback originals and digital versions for e-readers. Pays authors 4-6% royalty on retail price. Pays $400-1,500 advance. Responds in 4 months on mss. Catalog online. No unsolicited submissions. Contest guidelines online.

HOW TO CONTACT "Saturnalia Books has no bias against any school of poetry, but we do tend to publish writers who take chances and push against convention in some way, whether it's in form, language, content, or musicality." Submit complete ms to contest only.

CONTEST/AWARD OFFERINGS Saturnalia Books Poetry Prize. Contest is open during the month of March.

TIPS "Our audience tend to be young avid readers of contemporary poetry. Read a few sample books first."

SHEARSMAN BOOKS, LTD

50 Westons Hills Dr., Emersons Green, Bristol BS16 7DF, United Kingdom. **E-mail:** editor@shearsman. com. **Website:** www.shearsman.com. **Contact:** Tony Frazer, editor. Publishes trade paperback originals. Pays 10% royalty on retail price after 150 copies have sold; authors also receive 10 free copies of their books. Does not pay advance. Publishes ms 9-18 months after acceptance. Responds in 3 months to mss. Book catalog online. Print copies available on request. Guidelines online.

NEEDS "Shearsman only publishes poetry, poetry collections, and poetry in translation (from any language but with an emphasis on work in Spanish & in German). Some critical work on poetry and also memoirs and essays by poets. Mainly poetry by British, Irish, North American, and Australian poets." No poetry by or for children. No devotional or religious verse.

TIPS "Book ms submission: most of the ms must have already appeared in the UK or USA magazines of some repute, and it has to fill 70-72 pages of half letter or A5 pages. You must have sufficient return postage, or permit email responses. Submissions can also be made by email. It is unlikely that a poet with no track record will be accepted for publication as there is no obvious audience for the work. Try to develop some exposure to UK and US magazines and try to assemble a MS only later."

SHIPWRECKT BOOKS PUBLISHING COMPANY LLC

309 W. Stevens Ave., Rushford MN 55971. **E-mail:** contact@shipwrecktbooks.com. **Website:** www.shipwrecktbooks.press. **Contact:** Tom Driscoll, managing editor. Publishes trade paperback originals, mass market paperback originals, and electronic originals. Authors receive 35% royalties unless otherwise negotiated. Average length of time between acceptance of a book-length ms and publication is 6-18 months. Responds to queries within 6 months. Catalog and guidelines online.

NEEDS Poetry bar is very high. High-quality contemporary poetry. No religious or holiday verse. We do not publish chapbooks.

HOW TO CONTACT Use submissions portal at www.shipwrecktbooks.press; follow guidelines. Paper submissions are no longer accepted.

CONTEST/AWARD OFFERINGS Midwest Independent Publishing Assn. Silver medal poetry 2015.

TIPS "Quality writing. Please follow our guidelines. Manuscript development and full editorial services available."

SIBLING RIVALRY PRESS

P.O. Box 26147, Little Rock AR 72221. **E-mail:** info@ siblingrivalrypress.com. **Website:** siblingrivalrypress. com. **Contact:** Bryan Borland, publisher; Seth Pennington, editor. While we champion our LGBTIQ authors and artists, and while we've been very fortunate in our successes in LGBTIQ publishing, we are an inclusive publishing house and welcome all authors, artists, and readers regardless of sexual orientation or identity. We publish work we love. Merit trumps category. SRP was the first press to ever win Lambda Literary Awards in both gay poetry and lesbian poetry. All SRP titles are housed permanently in the Library of Congress Rare Book and Special Collections Vault. Pays 30% royalties for print. Does not pay advance. Publishes ms 1.5 years after acceptance (on average). Catalog online. Guidelines online (changes each year).

NEEDS Opening reading period: March 1-June 1.

HOW TO CONTACT Submit complete ms.

TIPS "In lieu of a traditional cover letter, SRP asks authors to answer specific questions when submitting. Make sure you answer these questions."

SILVERFISH REVIEW PRESS

P.O. Box 3541, Eugene OR 97403. (541)344-5060. **E-mail:** sfrpress@earthlink.net. **Website:** www.silverfishreviewpress.com. "Sponsors the Gerald Cable Book Award. This prize is awarded annually to a book length manuscript of original poetry by an author who has not yet published a full-length collection. There are no restrictions on the kind of poetry or subject matter; translations are not acceptable. Winners will receive $1,000, publication, and 25 copies of the book. Entries must be postmarked by October 15. See website for instructions." Publishes trade paperback originals. Guidelines online.

TIPS "Read recent Silverfish titles."

SOUTHERN ILLINOIS UNIVERSITY PRESS

1915 University Press Dr., SIUC Mail Code 6806, Carbondale IL 62901. (618)453-2281. **Fax:** (618)453-1221.

E-mail: mkpriddy@siu.edu. **Website:** www.siupress. com. **Contact:** Kristine Priddy, Acquisitions Editor. Scholarly press specializes in theater studies, rhetoric and composition studies, American history, Civil War, regional and nonfiction trade, poetry. No fiction. Currently emphasizing theater and American history, especially Civil War. Publishes hardcover and trade paperback originals and reprints. Pays 5-10% royalty on wholesale price. Rarely offers advance. Publishes ms 1 year after acceptance. Responds in 2 months to queries. Book catalog and ms guidelines free.

NEEDS Crab Orchard Series in Poetry.

HOW TO CONTACT Guidelines online.

CONTEST/AWARD OFFERINGS Crab Orchard Series in Poetry Open Competition and First Book Award.

STEEL TOE BOOKS

Department of English, Western Kentucky University, 1906 College Heights Blvd. #11086, Bowling Green KY 42101. (270)745-5769. **E-mail:** tom.hunley@wku. edu. **Website:** www.steeltoebooks.com. **Contact:** Dr. Tom C. Hunley, director. Steel Toe Books publishes "full-length, single-author poetry collections. Our books are professionally designed and printed. We look for workmanship (economical use of language, high-energy verbs, precise literal descriptions, original figurative language, poems carefully arranged as a book); a unique style and/or a distinctive voice; clarity; emotional impact; humor (word plays, hyperbole, comic timing); performability (a Steel Toe poet is at home on the stage as well as on the page)." Does not want "dry verse, purposely obscure language, poetry by people who are so wary of being called 'sentimental' they steer away from any recognizable human emotions, poetry that takes itself so seriously that it's unintentionally funny." Has published poetry by Allison Joseph, Susan Browne, James Doyle, Martha Silano, Mary Biddinger, John Guzlowski, Jeannine Hall Gailey, and others. Publishes 1-3 poetry books/year. Mss are normally selected through open submission.

HOW TO CONTACT "Check the website for news about our next open reading period." Book mss may include previously published poems. Responds to mss in 3 months. Pays $500 advance on 10% royalties and 10 author's copies. Order sample books by sending $12 to Steel Toe Books. *Must purchase a ms in order to submit.* See website for submission guidelines.

SUBITO PRESS

University of Colorado at Boulder, Dept. of English, 226 UCB, Boulder CO 80309-0226. **E-mail:** subitopressucb@gmail.com. **Website:** www.subitopress. org. Subito Press is a non-profit publisher of literary works. Each year Subito publishes one work of fiction and one work of poetry through its contest. Publishes trade paperback originals. Guidelines online.

HOW TO CONTACT Submit complete ms to contest.

TIPS "We publish 2 books of innovative writing a year through our poetry and fiction contests. All entries are also considered for publication with the press."

SUNBURY PRESS, INC.

PO Box 548, Boiling Springs PA 17007. **E-mail:** info@ sunburypress.com. **E-mail:** proposals@sunburypress. com. **Website:** www.sunburypress.com. Sunbury Press, Inc., headquartered in Mechanicsburg, PA is a publisher of trade paperback, hard cover and digital books featuring established and emerging authors in many fiction and non-fiction categories. Sunbury's books are printed in the USA and sold through leading booksellers worldwide. "Please use our online submission form." Publishes trade paperback and hardcover originals and reprints; electronic originals and reprints. Pays 10% royalty on wholesale price. Publishes ms 6 months after acceptance. Responds in 3 months. Catalog and guidelines online. Online submission form.

HOW TO CONTACT Submit complete ms.

TIPS "We are a rapidly growing small press with six diverse imprints. We currently have over 250 authors and 500 works under management."

SWAN SCYTHE PRESS

1468 Mallard Way, Sunnyvale CA 94087. **E-mail:** robert.pesich@gmail.com. **Website:** www.swanscythepress.com. **Contact:** Robert Pesich, editor.

NEEDS "Swan Scythe Press, a publishing group located in Northern California, is committed to discovering and publishing the best new poets in America today. Its authors have won many national and local grants, awards and fellowships, and have distinguished themselves as artists and educators throughout the U.S. and in foreign countries. Founding Editor and Publisher Sandra McPherson, a widely-known and honored poet, along with the present Editor, James DenBoer, have now turned over the editorial functions of the press to Robert Pesich."

HOW TO CONTACT Query first before submitting a ms via e-mail or through website.

CONTEST/AWARD OFFERINGS Swan Scythe Press announces its 2019 poetry chapbook contest. Entry fee: $18. We are accepting submissions from March 1st to June 15th (postmark deadline). Winner receives $200 and 25 perfect-bound chapbooks. The 2018 winner is Rebecca Foust for *The Unexploded Ordnance Bin*. For full guidelines, visit www.swanscythepress.com and swanscythepress.submittable.com/submit.

TARPAULIN SKY PRESS

P.O. Box 189, Grafton VT 05146. **Website:** www.tarpaulinsky.com. Tarpaulin Sky Press publishes cross- and trans-genre works as well as innovative poetry and prose. Produces full-length books and chapbooks, hand-bound books and trade paperbacks, and offers both hand-bound and perfect-bound paperback editions of full-length books. "We're a small, author-centered press endeavoring to create books that, as objects, please our authors as much their texts please us."

HOW TO CONTACT Writers whose work has appeared in or been accepted for publication in *Tarpaulin Sky* may submit chapbook or full-length mss at any time, with no reading fee. Tarpaulin Sky Press also considers chapbook and full-length mss from writers whose work has not appeared in the journal, but **asks for a $20 reading fee**. Make checks/money orders to Tarpaulin Sky Press. Cover letter is preferred. Reading periods may be found on the website.

TEBOT BACH

P.O. Box 7887, Huntington Beach CA 92615. (714)968-0905. **Fax:** (714)968-0905. **E-mail:** info@tebotbach.org. **Website:** www.tebotbach.org. **Contact:** Mifanwy Kaiser, editor/publisher. Publishes mss 6 months-1 year after acceptance. Responds in 3 months.

NEEDS Offers 2 contests per year. The Patricia Bibby First Book Contest and The Clockwise Chapbook contest. Go online for more information.

HOW TO CONTACT Query first via e-mail, with a few sample poems and cover letter with brief bio.

TEXAS TECH UNIVERSITY PRESS

1120 Main St., Second Floor, Box 41037, Lubbock TX 79415. (806)742-2982. **Fax:** (806)742-2979. **E-mail:** ttup@ttu.edu. **Website:** www.ttupress.org. Texas Tech University Press, the book publishing office of the university since 1971 and an AAUP member since 1986, publishes nonfiction titles in the areas of natural history and the natural sciences; 18th century and Joseph Conrad studies; studies of modern Southeast Asia, particularly the Vietnam War; costume and textile history; Latin American literature and culture; and all aspects of the Great Plains and the American West, especially history, biography, memoir, sports history, and travel. In addition, the Press publishes several scholarly journals, acclaimed series for young readers, an annual invited poetry collection, and literary fiction of Texas and the West. Guidelines online.

NEEDS "TTUP publishes an annual invited first-book poetry manuscript (please note that we cannot entertain unsolicited poetry submissions)."

✪ THISTLEDOWN PRESS LTD.

410 2nd Ave., Saskatoon SK S7K 2C3, Canada. (306)244-1722. **Fax:** (306)244-1762. **E-mail:** editorial@thistledownpress.com. **Website:** www.thistledownpress.com. **Contact:** Allan Forrie, publisher. "Thistledown originates books by Canadian authors only, although we have co-published titles by authors outside Canada. We do not publish children's picture books." Pays authors royalty of 10-12% based on net dollar sales. Pays illustrators and photographers by the project (range: $250-750). Rarely pays advance. Publishes book 1 year after acceptance. Responds to queries in 6 months. Book catalog on website. Guidelines online.

NEEDS "We do not publish cowboy poetry, inspirational poetry, or poetry for children."

TIPS "Send cover letter including publishing history and SASE."

TIA CHUCHA PRESS

13197 Gladstone Ave., Unit A, Sylmar CA 91342. (818)939-3433. **Fax:** (818)367-5600. **E-mail:** info@tiachucha.com. **Website:** www.tiachucha.com. Interim Executive Director: Trini Rodriguez. Tia Chucha's Centro Cultural is a nonprofit learning and cultural arts center. "We support and promote the continued growth, development and holistic learning of our community through the many powerful means of the arts. Tia Centra provides a positive space for people to activate what we all share as humans: the capacity to create, to imagine and to express ourselves in an effort to improve the quality of life for our community." Publishes hardcover and trade paperback originals. Pays 10% royalty on wholesale price. Publishes ms 1 year after acceptance. Responds in 9 months to mss. Guidelines online.

NEEDS No restrictions as to style or content. "We only publish poetry at this time. We do cross-cultural and performance-oriented poetry. It has to work on the page, however."

HOW TO CONTACT Query and submit complete ms.

TIPS "We will cultivate the practice. Audience is those interested."

☺⊘ TIGHTROPE BOOKS

E-mail: tightropeasst@gmail.com. **Website:** www.tightropebooks.com. Publishes trade paperback originals.

☺ Press is going out of business and not accepting new manuscripts.

TITAN PRESS

E-mail: titan91416@yahoo.com. **Website:** https://www.facebook.com/RVClef. **Contact:** Romana Von Clef, editor. Little literary publisher. Publishes hardcover and paperback originals. Pays 20-40% royalty. Publishes ms 1 year after acceptance. Responds to queries in 3 months.

NEEDS Literary, not MFA banality.

TIPS "Look, act, sound, and *be* professional."

TORREY HOUSE PRESS

150 S. State St., Ste. 100 Ofc. 36, Salt Lake City UT 84111. **E-mail:** kirsten@torreyhouse.com. **Website:** www.torreyhouse.org. **Contact:** Kirsten Allen. Torrey House Press is an independent nonprofit publisher promoting environmental conservation through literature. Publishes hardcover, trade paperback, and electronic originals. Pays 5-15% royalty on retail price. Publishes ms 12-18 months after acceptance. Responds in 4-6 months. Catalog online. Guidelines online.

HOW TO CONTACT Query; submit complete ms.

TIPS Include writing experience (none okay).

☺ TRADEWIND BOOKS

202-1807 Maritime Mews, Granville Island, Vancouver BC V6H 3W7, Canada. (604)662-4405. **Website:** www.tradewindbooks.com. "Tradewind Books publishes juvenile picture books and young adult novels. Requires that submissions include evidence that author has read at least 3 titles published by Tradewind Books." Publishes hardcover and trade paperback originals. Pays 7% royalty on retail price. Pays variable advance. Publishes book 3 years after acceptance. Responds to mss in 2 months. Book catalog and ms guidelines online.

HOW TO CONTACT Please send a book-length collection only.

TRUMAN STATE UNIVERSITY PRESS

100 E. Normal Ave., Kirksville MO 63501. (660)785-7336. **E-mail:** tsup@truman.edu. **E-mail:** bsm@truman.edu. **Website:** tsup.truman.edu. **Contact:** Barbara Smith-Mandell, editor-in-chief.

TUPELO PRESS

P.O. Box 1767, North Adams MA 01247. (413)664-9611. **Website:** www.tupelopress.org. Publisher: Jeffrey Levine. **Contact:** Sarah Russell, administrative director. "We're an independent nonprofit literary press. We publish book-length poetry, poetry collections, translations, short story collections, novellas, literary nonfiction/memoirs and novels." Standard royalty contract. Pays advance in rare instances. Publishes ms 2 years after acceptance. Guidelines online.

NEEDS "Our mission is to publish riveting, smart, visually and "Emotionally and intellectually stimulating books of the highest quality. We want contemporary poetry, etc. by the most diverse list of emerging and established writers in the U.S. Keenly interested in poets of color"

HOW TO CONTACT Submit complete ms. **Charges $28 reading fee.**

CONTEST/AWARD OFFERINGS Four contests annually: Dorset Prize (open competition), Berkshire Prize for a first or second book of poetry, Snowbound Chapbook Award, Sunken Garden Chapbook Award.

TURNING POINT

WordTech Communications LLC, P.O. Box 541106, Cincinnati OH 45254. **E-mail:** connect@wordtechcommunications.com. **Website:** www.turningpointbooks.com. Pays in royalties. Catalog and guidelines online.

NEEDS "Dedicated to the art of story in poetry. We seek to publish collections of narrative poetry that tell the essential human stories of our times."

HOW TO CONTACT No e-mail submissions. No calls for book-length poetry right now.

☺ TURNSTONE PRESS

Artspace Building, 206-100 Arthur St., Winnipeg MB R3B 1H3, Canada. (204)947-1555. **Fax:** (204)942-1555. **Website:** www.turnstonepress.com. **Contact:** Submissions Assistant. "Turnstone Press is a literary publisher, not a general publisher, and therefore we are only interested in literary fiction, literary nonfiction—including literary criticism—and poetry. We do publish literary mysteries, thrillers, and noir under our Ravenstone imprint. We publish only Canadian authors or landed immigrants, we strive to publish a significant number of new writers, to publish in a variety of genres, and to have 50% of each year's list be Manitoba writers and/or books with Manitoba content." Publishes ms 2 years after acceptance. Responds in 4-7 months. Guidelines online.

HOW TO CONTACT Poetry mss should be a minimum 70 pages. Submit complete ms. Include cover letter.

TIPS "As a Canadian literary press, we have a mandate to publish Canadian writers only. Do some homework before submitting works to make sure your subject matter/genre/writing style falls within the publishers area of interest."

TWO SYLVIAS PRESS

P.O. Box 1524, Kingston WA 98346. **E-mail:** twosylviaspress@gmail.com. **Website:** twosylviaspress.com. **Contact:** Kelli Russell Agodon and Annette Spaulding-Convy. Two Sylvias Press is an independent press located in the Seattle area. "We publish poetry, memoir, essays, books on the craft of writing, and creativity tools, such as The Poet Tarot and The Daily Poet. The press draws its inspiration from the poetic literary talent of Sylvia Plath and the editorial business sense of Sylvia Beach." Two Sylvias Press values inclusiveness, diversity, respect, creativity, and freedom of expression. "We welcome all readers and writers." Publishes ms 12-18 months after acceptance. Catalog online. "We currently only have two calls for submissions of poetry books: our Poetry Chapbook Prize (in the spring & open to all poets) and our Wilder Full-Length Poetry Prize (in autumn & open to women over 50). Currently, we are not accepting any unsolicited work."

NEEDS Chapbook & Full Length Poetry Book Prizes. Occasional calls for submissions for specific poetry anthologies. Subscribe to the Two Sylvias Press newsletter (www.tinyletter.com/twosylviaspress) for updates on submission periods.

CONTEST/AWARD OFFERINGS Two Sylvias Press Chapbook Prize; Two Sylvias Press Wilder Poetry Book Series for Women over 50. All manuscripts received in these prizes are considered for publication.

TIPS "Created with the belief that great writing is good for the world, Two Sylvias Press mixes modern technology, classic style, and literary intellect with an eco-friendly heart. We are an indie press in the Seattle area that publishes books, offers online poetry writing retreats, writing prompts, and other creative tools for poets and writers. While we currently aren't accepting unsolicited manuscripts except for our poetry chapbook prize and a full-length poetry prize for women over 50, we recommend poets and writers interested in Two Sylvias Press subscribe to our newsletter to be the first to know when we are accepting new work. Many thanks to all the poets, writers, and readers who continue to support us and make art in challenging times."

THE UNIVERSITY OF AKRON PRESS

120 E. Mill St., Suite 415, Akron OH 44308. **E-mail:** uapress@uakron.edu. **Website:** www.uakron.edu/uapress. **Contact:** Dr. Jon Miller, director and acquisitions. The University of Akron Press is the publishing arm of The University of Akron and is dedicated to the dissemination of scholarly, professional, and regional books and other content. Publishes paperback and hardcover originals. Pays 7-15% royalty. Publishes book 9-12 months after acceptance. Responds in 4 weeks to queries/proposals; 3-4 months to solicited mss. Query prior to submitting. Guidelines online.

NEEDS Follow the guidelines and submit mss only for the contest: www.uakron.edu/uapress/poetry.html. The Akron Series in Poetry brings forth at least 2 new books of poetry every year, mainly through our prestigious and long-running Akron Poetry Prize. We also publish scholarship on poetics.

THE UNIVERSITY OF ARKANSAS PRESS

McIlroy House, 105 N. McIlroy Ave., Fayetteville AR 72701. (479)575-3246. **Fax:** (479)575-6044. **E-mail:** mbieker@uark.edu. **Website:** uapress.com. **Contact:** Mike Bieker, director. "The University of Arkansas Press publishes series on Ozark studies, the Civil War in the West, poetry and poetics, food studies, and sport and society." Publishes hardcover and trade paperback originals and reprints. Publishes book 1 year after acceptance. Responds in 3 months to proposals. Book catalog and ms guidelines online.

HOW TO CONTACT University of Arkansas Press publishes 4 poetry books per year through the Miller Williams Poetry Prize.

⊘ THE UNIVERSITY OF CHICAGO PRESS

1427 E. 60th St., Chicago IL 60637. (773)702-7700. **Fax:** (773)702-9756. **E-mail:** rpetilos@uchicago.edu.

Website: www.press.uchicago.edu. **Contact:** Randolph Petilos, Poetry and Medieval Studies Editor.

○ The University of Chicago Press, publisher of scholarly books and journals since 1891, on average publishes four books in our Phoenix Poets series annually, and two books of poetry in translation, also the occasional book of poems outside the series or as a paperback reprint from another publisher. Recently, our list of poets includes Ahmad Almallah, Charles Bernstein, Michael Collier, David Gewanter, Mark Halliday, Alan Shapiro, Bruce Smith, and Connie Voisine.

UNIVERSITY OF IOWA PRESS

100 Kuhl House, 119 W. Park Rd., Iowa City IA 52242. (319)335-2000. **Fax:** (319)335-2055. **E-mail:** james-mccoy@uiowa.edu. **Website:** www.uiowapress.org. **Contact:** James McCoy, director. The University of Iowa Press publishes both trade and academic work in a variety of fields. Publishes hardcover and paperback originals. Book catalog available free. Guidelines online.

NEEDS Currently publishes winners of the Iowa Poetry Prize Competition and Kuhl House Poets (by invitation only). Competition guidelines available on website.

UNIVERSITY OF NORTH TEXAS PRESS

1155 Union Circle, #311336, Denton TX 76203. (940)565-2142. **Fax:** (940)565-4590. **E-mail:** karen.devinney@unt.edu. **Website:** untpress.unt.edu. **Contact:** Ronald Chrisman, director; Karen De Vinney, assistant director. "We are dedicated to producing the highest quality scholarly, academic, and general interest books. We are committed to serving all peoples by publishing stories of their cultures and experiences that have been overlooked. Currently emphasizing military history, Texas history, music, Mexican-American studies." Publishes hardcover and trade paperback originals and reprints. Publishes ms 1-2 years after acceptance. Responds in 1 month to queries. Book catalog for 8 ½×11 SASE. Guidelines online.

NEEDS "The only poetry we publish is the winner of the Vassar Miller Prize in Poetry, an annual, national competition with a $1,000 prize and publication of the winning ms each Spring."

HOW TO CONTACT Query.

TIPS "We publish series called War and the Southwest; Texas Folklore Society Publications; the West-ern Life Series; Practical Guide Series; Al-Filo: Mexican-American studies; North Texas Crime and Criminal Justice; Katherine Anne Porter Prize in Short Fiction; and the North Texas Lives of Musicians Series."

UNIVERSITY OF PITTSBURGH PRESS

7500 Thomas Blvd., Pittsburgh PA 15260. (412)383-2456. **Fax:** (412)383-2466. **E-mail:** info@upress.pitt.edu. **Website:** www.upress.pitt.edu. **Contact:** Sandy Crooms, editorial director. The University of Pittsburgh Press is a scholarly publisher with distinguished books in several academic areas and in poetry and short fiction, as well as books about Pittsburgh and western Pennsylvania for general readers, scholars, and students. "Our mission is to extend the reach and reputation of the university through the publication of scholarly, artistic, and educational books that advance learning and knowledge and through the publication of regional books that contribute to an understanding of and are of special benefit to western Pennsylvania and the Upper Ohio Valley region. Book catalog online. Guidelines online.

NEEDS Publishes at least 4 books by poets who have previously published full-length collections of poetry.

HOW TO CONTACT Submit complete ms in September and October only.

TIPS "We pride ourselves on the eclectic nature of our list. We are not tied to any particular style or school of writing, but we do demand that any book we publish be of exceptional merit."

UNIVERSITY OF SOUTH CAROLINA PRESS

1600 Hampton St., 5th Floor, Columbia SC 29208. (803)777-5243. **Fax:** (803)777-0160. **E-mail:** batesvc@mailbox.sc.edu. **Website:** www.sc.edu/uscpress. **Contact:** Jonathan Haupt, director. "We focus on scholarly monographs and regional trade books of lasting merit." Publishes hardcover originals, trade paperback originals and reprints. Publishes ms 1 year after acceptance. Responds in 3 months to mss. Book catalog available free. Guidelines online.

NEEDS Palmetto Poetry Series, a South Carolina-based original poetry series edited by Nikky Finney. Director: Jonathan Haupt, director (jhaupt@mailbox.sc.edu).

UNIVERSITY OF TAMPA PRESS

The University of Tampa, 401 W. Kennedy Blvd., Tampa FL 33606. (813)253-6266. **E-mail:** utpress@ut.edu. **Website:** www.ut.edu/tampapress. **Contact:** Richard Mathews, editor. "We are a small university press publishing a limited number of titles each year, primarily in the areas of local and regional history, poetry, and printing history. We do not accept e-mail submissions." Publishes hardcover originals and reprints; trade paperback originals and reprints. Does not pay advance. Publishes ms 6 months-2 years after acceptance. Responds in 3-4 months to queries. Book catalog online.

NEEDS "We consider original poetry collections through the annual Tampa Review Prize for Poetry competition, with a deadline of December 31 each year."

HOW TO CONTACT Submit to the Tampa Review Prize for Poetry.

CONTEST/AWARD OFFERINGS Tampa Review Prize for Poetry: $2,000 plus book publication

UNIVERSITY OF WISCONSIN PRESS

1930 Monroe St., 3rd Floor, Madison WI 53711. **E-mail:** kadushin@wisc.edu; gcwalker@wisc.edu. **Website:** uwpress.wisc.edu. **Contact:** Gwen Walker, executive editor (gcwalker@wisc.edu); Dennis Lloyd, director (dlloyd2@wisc.edu). Pays royalty. Publishes 10-14 months after acceptance of final ms. Responds in 1-3 weeks to queries; 3-6 weeks to proposals. Rarely comments on rejected work. See submission guidelines on our website.

NEEDS The University of Wisconsin Press Awards the Brittingham Prize in Poetry and Felix Pollack Prize in Poetry. More details online.

TIPS "Make sure the query letter and sample text are well-written, and read guidelines carefully to make sure we accept the genre you are submitting."

⟳ VÉHICULE PRESS

P.O.B. 42094 BP Roy, Montreal QC H2W 2T3, Canada. (514)844-6073. **E-mail:** sd@vehiculepress.com. **E-mail:** admin@vehiculepress.com. **Website:** www.vehiculepress.com. **Contact:** Simon Dardick, nonfiction; Carmine Starnino, poetry; Dimitri Nasrallah, fiction. "Montreal's Véhicule Press has published the best of Canadian and Quebec literature-fiction, poetry, essays, translations, and social history." Publishes trade paperback originals by Canadian authors mostly. Pays 10-15% royalty on retail price. Pays $200-500 advance. Publishes ms 1 year after acceptance. Responds in 4 months to queries. Book catalog for 9 x 12 SAE with IRCs.

NEEDS Vehicle Press is a "literary press with a poetry series, Signal Editions, publishing the work of Canadian poets only." Publishes flat-spined paperbacks.

Publishes Canadian poetry that is "first-rate, original, content-conscious."

TIPS "Quality in almost any style is acceptable. We believe in the editing process."

⊘ WAKE FOREST UNIVERSITY PRESS

P.O. Box 7333, Winston-Salem NC 27109. (336)758-5448. **Fax:** (336)758-5636. **E-mail:** wfupress@wfu.edu. **Website:** wfupress.wfu.edu. **Contact:** Jefferson Holdridge, director/poetry editor; Dillon Johnston, advisory editor. "We publish only poetry from Ireland. I am able to consider only poetry written by native Irish poets. I must return, unread, poetry from American poets." Query with 4-5 samples and cover letter. Sometimes sends prepublication galleys. Buys North American or U.S. rights. Pays on 8% list royalty contract, plus 6-8 author's copies. Negotiable advance. Responds to queries in 1-2 weeks; to submissions (*if invited*) in 2-3 months.

WASHINGTON WRITERS' PUBLISHING HOUSE

P.O. Box 15271, Washington DC 20003. **Website:** www.washingtonwriters.org. Offers $1,000 and 50 copies of published book plus additional copies for publicity use. Guidelines online.

NEEDS Washington Writers' Publishing House considers book-length mss for publication by poets living within 75 driving miles of the U.S. Capitol (Baltimore area included) through competition only. Publishes 1-2 poetry books/year.

HOW TO CONTACT "No specific criteria, except literary excellence."

WAVE BOOKS

1938 Fairview Ave. E., Suite 201, Seattle WA 98102. (206)676-5337. **E-mail:** info@wavepoetry.com. **Website:** www.wavepoetry.com. "Wave Books is an independent poetry press based in Seattle, Washington, dedicated to publishing the best in contemporary American poetry, poetry in translation, and writing by poets. The Press was founded in 2005, merging with established publisher Verse Press. By publishing strong innovative work in finely crafted trade editions and handmade ephemera, we hope to continue to challenge the values and practices of readers and add to the collective sense of what's possible in contemporary poetry." Publishes hardcover and trade paperback originals. Catalog online.

HOW TO CONTACT "Please no unsolicited mss or queries. We will post calls for submissions on our website."

THE WAYWISER PRESS

P.O. Box 6205, Baltimore MD 21206. **E-mail:** info@waywiser-press.com. **Website:** waywiser-press.com. **Contact:** Philip Hoy. The Waywiser Press is a small independent company, with its main office in the UK, and a subsidiary in the USA. It publishes literary works of all kinds, but has a special interest in contemporary poetry in English. Royalties paid. Does not pay advance. Ms published 9-18 months after acceptance. Responds in 3-6 months. Catalog online. Guidelines online.

NEEDS Poets who've published one or no collections should submit to the Anthony Hecht Poetry Prize, open for submissions between August 1st and December 1st annually.

HOW TO CONTACT Submit complete ms by post (if prospective author has already published 2 or more collections).

TIPS "We are keen to promote the work of new as well as established authors, and would like to rescue still others from undeserved neglect."

⊘ WESLEYAN UNIVERSITY PRESS

215 Long Ln., Middletown CT 06459. (860)685-7711. **Fax:** (860)685-7712. **E-mail:** stamminen@wesleyan.edu. **Website:** www.wesleyan.edu/wespress. **Contact:** Suzanna Tamminen, director and editor-in-chief. "Wesleyan University Press is a scholarly press with a focus on poetry, music, dance and cultural studies." Wesleyan University Press is one of the major publishers of poetry in the nation. Poetry publications from Wesleyan tend to get widely (and respectfully) reviewed. **"We are accepting manuscripts by invitation only until further notice."** Publishes hardcover originals and paperbacks. Pays royalties, plus 10 author's copies. Responds to queries in 2 months; to mss in 4 months. Book catalog available free. Guidelines online.

NEEDS *Does not accept unsolicited mss.*

⊘ WHITE PINE PRESS

P.O. Box 236, Buffalo NY 14201. **E-mail:** wpine@whitepine.org. **Website:** www.whitepine.org. **Contact:** Dennis Maloney, editor. White Pine Press is a nonprofit literary publisher of literature in translation and poetry. Publishes trade paperback originals. Pays contributor's copies. Publishes ms 18 months after acceptance. Responds in 1 month to queries and proposals; 4 months to mss. Catalog online. Guidelines online.

○ Due to a large backlog we are not currently reading manuscripts outside of our annual poetry contest.

NEEDS "Only considering submissions for our annual poetry contest."

WORDSONG

815 Church St., Honesdale PA 18431. **Fax:** (570)253-0179. **Website:** www.wordsongpoetry.com. "We publish fresh voices in contemporary poetry." Pays authors royalty or work purchased outright. Responds to mss in 3 months.

HOW TO CONTACT *Agented submissions only.*

TIPS "Collections of original poetry, not anthologies, are our biggest need at this time. Keep in mind that the strongest collections demonstrate a facility with multiple poetic forms and offer fresh images and insights. Check to see what's already on the market and on our website before submitting."

WRITE BLOODY PUBLISHING

Austin TX **Website:** writebloody.com. **Contact:** Derrick Brown, president. We publish and promote great books of poetry every year. We are a small press with a snappy look, dedicated to quality literature that is proud to be printed in the USA. We are not a printer. We are a sweet publishing house located on the outskirts of Austin, Texas. Catalog online. Guidelines online.

NEEDS Reading period August 1-31. Check online for details.

TIPS "You must tour if you are part of our family. At least 20 shows a year. Just like a band."

YALE UNIVERSITY PRESS

P.O. Box 209040, New Haven CT 06520. (203)432-0960. **Fax:** (203)432-0948. **E-mail:** Contact specific editor (see website).. **Website:** yalebooks.com. "Yale University Press publishes scholarly and general interest books." Publishes hardcover and trade paperback originals. Book catalog and ms guidelines online.

NEEDS Submit to Yale Series of Younger Poets Competition.

HOW TO CONTACT Guidelines online.

TIPS "Audience is scholars, students and general readers."

CONTESTS & AWARDS

//

This section contains a wide array of poetry competitions and literary awards. These range from state poetry society contests (with a number of modest monetary prizes) to prestigious honors bestowed by private foundations, elite publishers and renowned university programs. Because these listings reflect such a variety of skill levels and degrees of competitiveness, it's important to read each carefully and note its unique requirements. *Never* enter a contest without consulting the guidelines and following directions to the letter (including manuscript formatting, number of lines or pages of poetry accepted, amount of entry fee, entry forms needed and other details).

IMPORTANT NOTE: As we gathered information for this edition of *Poet's Market*, we found that some competitions hadn't yet established their 2020 fees and deadlines. In such cases, we list the most recent information available as a general guide. Always consult current guidelines for updates before entering any competition.

WHAT ABOUT ENTRY FEES?

Most contests charge entry fees, and these are usually quite legitimate. The funds are used to cover expenses such as paying the judges, putting up prize monies, printing prize editions of magazines and journals, and promoting the contest through mailings and ads. If you're concerned about a poetry contest or other publishing opportunity, see "Is It a 'Con'?" for advice on some of the more questionable practices in the poetry world.

49TH PARALLEL AWARD FOR POETRY

Western Washington University, Mail Stop 9053, Bellingham WA 98225. (360)650-4863. **E-mail:** bellingham.review@wwu.edu. **Website:** www.bhreview.org. **Contact:** Susanne Paola Antonetta, Editor-in-Chief; Bailey Cunningham, Managing Editor. Annual poetry contest, supported by the *Bellingham Review*, given for a poem of any style or length. Deadline: March 15. Submissions period begins December 1 Prize: $1,000. Nickole Brown.

GIVAL PRESS OSCAR WILDE AWARD

Gival Press, LLC, Gival Press Oscar Wilde Award, Gival Press LLC, P.O. Box 3812, Arlington VA 22203. (703)351-0079. **E-mail:** givalpress@yahoo.com. **Website:** www.givalpress.com. **Contact:** Robert L. Giron, Editor. Award given to the best previously unpublished original poem—written in English, of any length, in any style, typed, double-spaced on 1 side only—that best relates gay/lesbian/bisexual/transgendered (GLBTQ) life, by a poet who is 18 years or older. Enter via portal: www.givalpress.submittable.com. Deadline: June 27 (postmarked). Prize: $100; the poem, along with information about the poet, will be published on the Gival Press website. Judged by the previous winner, who reads the poems anonymously.

✪ J.M. ABRAHAM POETRY AWARD

Writers' Federation of Nova Scotia, 1113 Marginal Rd., Halifax NS B3H 4P7, Canada. (902)423-8116. **Fax:** (902)422-0881. **E-mail:** director@writers.ns.ca. **Website:** www.writers.ns.ca. **Contact:** Marilyn Smulders, Executive Director.. The J.M. Abraham Poetry Award is an annual award designed to honor the best book of poetry by a resident of Atlantic Canada. Formerly known as the Atlantic Poetry Prize. Deadline: First Friday in December. Prize: Valued at $2,000 for the winning title.

AKRON POETRY PRIZE

E-mail: uapress@uakron.edu. **Website:** www.uakron.edu/uapress/akron-poetry-prize/. **Contact:** Mary Biddinger, Editor/Award Director.. Submissions must be unpublished. Considers simultaneous submissions (with notification of acceptance elsewhere). Submit at least 48 pages and no longer than 90 pages. See website for complete guidelines. Manuscripts will be accepted via Submittable.com between April 15 and June 15 each year. Competition receives 500+ entries. 2018 winner was Kimberly Quiogue Andrews for *A Brief History of Fruit* . Winner posted on website by September 30. Deadline: June 15. Open to submissions on April 15. Prize: $1,500, plus publication of a book-length ms.

○ Manuscripts must include a cover page (with author's name, mailing address, phone number, e-mail address, and manuscript title), a title page (with no identifying information), and an acknowledgments page listing poems previously published in periodicals (if applicable). Please do not submit manuscripts that have the author's name on each page. Manuscripts will go to the final judge blind.

MARIE ALEXANDER POETRY SERIES

English Department, 2801 S. University Ave., Little Rock AR 72204. **E-mail:** mariealexandereditor@gmail.com. **Website:** mariealexanderseries.com. **Contact:** Nickole Brown.. Annual contest for a collection of previously unpublished prose poems or flash fiction by a U.S. writer. Deadline: July 31. Open to submissions on July 1. Prize: $1,000, plus publication.

ALLIGATOR JUNIPER AWARD

Alligator Juniper/Prescott College, 220 Grove Ave., Prescott AZ 86301. (928)350-2012. **Fax:** (928)776-5102. **E-mail:** alligatorjuniper@prescott.edu. **Website:** www.prescott.edu/alligatorjuniper/national-contest/index.html. **Contact:** Skye Anicca, Managing Editor.. Annual contest for unpublished fiction, creative nonfiction, and poetry. Open to all age levels. Each entrant receives a personal letter from staff regarding the status of their submission, as well as minor feedback on the piece. Deadline: October 1. Prize: $1,000 plus publication in all three categories. Finalists in each genre are recognized as such, published, and paid in copies. Judged by distinguished writers in each genre and Prescott College writing students enrolled in the Literary Journal Practicum course.

AMERICAN LITERARY REVIEW CONTESTS

American Literary Review, P.O. Box 311307, University of North Texas, Denton TX 76203-1307. (940)565-2755. **E-mail:** americanliteraryreview@gmail.com. **Website:** www.americanliteraryreview.com. Contest to award excellence in short fiction, creative nonfiction, and poetry. Multiple entries are acceptable, but each entry must be accompanied with a reading fee. Do not put any identifying information in the file itself; include the author's name, title(s), address, e-mail address, and phone number in the boxes provided in the online submissions manager. Short fiction: Limit 8,000 words per work. Creative Nonfiction: Limit 6,500 words per work. Deadline: October 1. Submission period begins June 1. Prize: $1,000 prize for each category, along with publication in the Spring online issue of the *American Literary Review*.

THE AMERICAN POETRY REVIEW/ HONICKMAN FIRST BOOK PRIZE

320 S. Broad St., Hamilton 313, Philadelphia PA 19102. (215)717-6800. **E-mail:** escanlon@aprweb.org. **Website:** www.aprweb.org. **Contact:** Elizabeth Scanlon, editor. The prize is open to poets who have not published a book-length collection of poems with a registered ISBN. Translations are not eligible nor are works written by multiple authors. 2018 guest judge is Sharon Olds. Reading period: August 1-October 31. Prize: $3,000, plus publication

AMERICAN-SCANDINAVIAN FOUNDATION TRANSLATION PRIZE

The American-Scandinavian Foundation, 58 Park Ave., New York NY 10016. (212)779-3587. **E-mail:** grants@amscan.org; info@amscan.org. **Website:** www.amscan.org. **Contact:** Carl Fritscher, Fellowships & Grants Officer.. The annual ASF translation competition is awarded for the most outstanding translations of poetry, fiction, drama, or literary prose written by a Scandinavian author born after 1900. Deadline: June 15. Prize: The Nadia Christensen Prize includes a $2,500 award, publication of an excerpt in *Scandinavian Review*, and a commemorative bronze medallion. The Leif and Inger Sjöberg Award, given to an individual whose literature translations have not previously been published, includes a $2,000 award, publication of an excerpt in *Scandinavian Review*, and a commemorative bronze medallion.

THE ANHINGA-ROBERT DANA PRIZE FOR POETRY

Anhinga Press, P.O. Box 3665, Tallahassee FL 32315. **E-mail:** info@anhinga.org. **Website:** www.anhinga. org. **Contact:** Kristine Snodgrass, Co-director, Publisher. Offered annually for a book-length collection of poetry by an author writing in English. Guidelines on website. Past winners include Robin Beth Schaer, Hauntie. Deadline: Submissions will be accepted from February 15-May 31. Prize: $2,000, a reading tour of selected Florida colleges and universities, and the winning ms will be published. Past judges include Evie Shockley, Eduardo C. Corral, Jan Beatty, Richard Blanco, Denise Duhamel, Donald Hall, Joy Harjo.

ANNUAL WRITING CONTEST

E-mail: lumina@gm.slc.edu. **Website:** www.luminajournal.com/contest. Annual writing contest in poetry, fiction, or creative nonfiction (varies by year). Please visit website in August/September for complete and updated contest rules. Deadline varies by year. Usually in the early fall. Prize: Cash.

ARTS & LETTERS PRIZES

Arts & Letters Journal of Contemporary Culture, Campus Box 89, GC&SU, Milledgeville GA 31061. (478)445-1289. **E-mail:** al.journal@gcsu.edu. **Website:** al.gcsu.edu. **Contact:** The Editors.. Offered annually for unpublished work. Deadline: March 31. Prize: $1,000 prize for each of the four major genres. Fiction, poetry, and creative nonfiction winners are published in Fall or Spring issue. The prize-winning, one-act play is produced at the Georgia College campus (usually in March). Judged by the editors (initial screening); see website for final judges and further details about submitting work.

ATLANTIS AWARD

The Poet's Billow, 6135 Avon, Portage MI 49024. **E-mail:** thepoetsbillow@gmail.com. **Website:** thepoetsbillow.org. **Contact:** Robert Evory.. Annual award open to any writer to recognize one outstanding poem from its entries. Finalists with strong work will also be published. Submissions must be previously unpublished. Deadline: October 1. Submissions open July 1. Prize: $200 and winning poet will be featured in an interview on The Poet's Billow website. Poem will be published and displayed in The Poet's Billow Literary Art Gallery and nominated for a Pushcart Prize. If the poet qualifies, the poem will also be submitted to The Best New Poets anthology. Judged by the editors, and, occasionally, a guest judge.

AUTUMN HOUSE POETRY, FICTION, AND NONFICTION PRIZES

(412)362-2665. **E-mail:** info@autumnhouse.org. **Website:** autumnhouse.org. **Contact:** Christine Stroud, Editor-in-Chief. Offers annual prize and publication of book-length ms with national promotion. Submission must be unpublished as a collection, but individual poems, stories, and essays may have been previously published elsewhere. Considers simultaneous submissions. "Autumn House is a nonprofit corporation with the mission of publishing and promoting poetry and other fine literature. We have published books by Sherrie Flick, Ed Ochester, Gerald Stern, Sharma Shields, Clifford

Thompson, Danusha Lameris, Cameron Barnett, Dickson Lamb, Harrison Candelaria Fletcher, Ada Limon, and many others." Deadline: June 30. Prize: The winner (in each of 3 categories) will receive book publication, $1,000 advance against royalties, and a $1,500 travel/publicity grant to promote his or her book. Judged by Cornelius Eady (poetry), Aimee Bender (fiction), and Paul Lisicky (nonfiction).

AWP AWARD SERIES

Association of Writers & Writing Programs
5700 Rivertech Ct, Suite 225
, 20737-1250, 5700 Rivertech Ct, Suite 225, Riverdale Park MD 22030. **E-mail:** supriya@awpwriter.org. **Website:** www.awpwriter.org. **Contact:** Supriya Bhatnagar, Director of Publications.. AWP sponsors the Award Series, an annual competition for the publication of excellent new book-length works. The competition is open to all authors writing in English, regardless of nationality or residence, and is available to published and unpublished authors alike. Offered annually to foster new literary talent. Deadline: Postmarked between January 1 and February 28. Prize: AWP Prize for the Novel: $2,500 and publication by New Issues Press; Donald Hall Prize for Poetry: $5,500 and publication by the University of Pittsburgh Press; Grace Paley Prize in Short Fiction: $5,500 and publication by the University of Massachusetts Press; and AWP Prize for Creative Nonfiction: $2,500 and publication by the University of Georgia Press. Creative Nonfiction: Debra Monroe; Novel:Bonnie Jo Campbell; Poetry: Natasha D. Trethewey; Short Fiction: Dan Chaon.

THE MURIEL CRAFT BAILEY MEMORIAL AWARD

4956 St. John Dr., Syracuse NY 13215. (315)488-8077. **E-mail:** poetry@comstockreview.org. **Website:** www.comstockreview.org. **Contact:** Peggy Flanders, Associate Managing Editor (poetry@comstockreview.org); Betsy Anderson, Managing Editor (elanders2@yahoo.com).. Annual contest for best previously unpublished poem. Deadline: July 15. Prize: 1st place: $1,000; 2nd place: $250; 3rd place: $100; honorable mentions receive 1-year subscription to *Comstock Review*. Judged by David Kirby in 2019.

THE WILLIS BARNSTONE TRANSLATION PRIZE

The Evansville Review, Dept. of Creative Writing, University of Evansville, 1800 Lincoln Ave., Evansville IN 47722. (812)488-1042. **E-mail:** evansvillereview@evansville.edu. **Website:** https://www.evansville.edu/majors/creativewriting/evansvilleReview-Barnstone.cfm. The competition welcomes submissions of unpublished poetry translations from any language and time period (ancient to contemporary). The length limit for each translation is 200 lines. Deadline: December 1 Prize: $1000 for a translated poem. In the event that the judge selects multiple winners, the prize money will be divided equally among the winners. Final Judge: Willis Barnstone.

BARROW STREET PRESS BOOK CONTEST

P.O. Box 1558, Kingston RI 02881. **Website:** www.barrowstreet.org or wilde@my.uri.edu. The Barrow Street Press Book Contest award will be given for the best previously unpublished ms of poetry in English. Deadline: June 30 Prize: $1,000. 2019 Judge: Jericho Brown.

ELINOR BENEDICT POETRY PRIZE

Passages North, Northern Michigan University, 1401 Presque Isle Ave., Marquette MI 49855. **E-mail:** passages@nmu.edu. **Website:** passagesnorth.com/contests/. **Contact:** Jennifer A. Howard, Editor-in-Chief.. Prize given biennially for a poem or a group of poems. Deadline: April 15. Submission period begins February 15. Prize: $1,000 and publication for winner; 2 honorable mentions are also published; all entrants receive a copy of *Passages North*. Tarfia Faizullah.

GEORGE BENNETT FELLOWSHIP

Phillips Exeter Academy, 20 Main Street, Exeter NH 03833-2460. **E-mail:** teaching_opportunities@exeter.edu. **Website:** www.exeter.edu/bennettfellowship. Annual award for fellow and family to provide time and freedom from material considerations to a person seriously contemplating or pursuing a career as a writer. Applicants should have a ms in progress that they intend to complete during the fellowship period. Ms should be fiction, nonfiction, novel, short stories, or poetry. Duties: To be in residency at the Academy for the academic year; to make oneself available informally to students interested in writing. Committee favors writers who have not yet published a book with a major publisher. Deadline: November 30. A choice will be made, and all entrants notified in mid-April. Cash stipend (currently $15,260), room and board. Judged by committee of the English Department.

BERMUDA TRIANGLE PRIZE

The Poet's Billow, 6135 Avon St., Portage MI 49024. **E-mail:** thepoetsbillow@gmail.com. **Website:** http://thepoetsbillow.org. **Contact:** Robert Evory. Annual award open to any writer to recognize 3 poems that address a theme set by the editors. Finalists with strong work will also be published. Submissions must be previously unpublished. Please submit online. Deadline: April 30. Submission period begins November 15 Prize: $50 each to 3 poems. The winning poems will be published and displayed in The Poet's Billow Literary Art Gallery and nominated for a Pushcart Prize. If the poet qualifies, the poem will also be submitted to The Best New Poets anthology. Judge TBD.

THE PATRICIA BIBBY FIRST BOOK AWARD

Patricia Bibby Award, Tebot Bach, P.O. Box 7887, Huntington Beach CA 92615-7887. **E-mail:** mifanwy@tebotbach.org; info@tebotbach.org. **Website:** www.tebotbach.org. **Contact:** Mifanwy Kaiser. Annual competition open to all poets writing in English who have not committed to publishing collections of poetry of 36 poems or more in editions of over 400 copies. Offers award and publication of a book-length poetry ms by Tebot Bach. Deadline: November 1 Prize: $500 and book publication. Judges for each year's competition announced online.

BINGHAMTON UNIVERSITY MILT KESSLER POETRY BOOK AWARD

Binghamton University Creative Writing Program, Department of English, General Literature, and Rhetoric, Library North Room 1149, Vestal Parkway East, P.O. Box 6000, Binghamton NY 13902-6000. (607)777-2713. **Fax:** (607)777-2408. **E-mail:** cwpro@binghamton.edu. **Website:** www2.binghamton.edu/english/creative-writing/binghamton-center-for-writers. **Contact:** Maria Mazziotti Gillan, Creative Writing Program Director. Annual award for a book of poems written in English, 48 pages or more in length, selected by judges as the strongest collection of poems published in that year. Deadline: February 1 Prize: $1,000.

THE BITTER OLEANDER PRESS LIBRARY OF POETRY AWARD

BOPLOPA, The Bitter Oleander Press, 4983 Tall Oaks Dr., Fayetteville NY 13066-9776. (315)637-3047. **E-mail:** info@bitteroleander.com. **Website:** www.bitteroleander.com. **Contact:** Paul B. Roth. The Bitter Oleander Press Library of Poetry Award (BOPLOPA) is now in its 7th year after replacing the 15-year long run of the Frances Locke Memorial Poetry Award. Guidelines available on website. Deadline: June 15 (postmarked). Open to submissions on May 1. Early or late entries will be disqualified. Prize: $1,000, plus book publication of the winning ms. the following spring.

THE BLACK RIVER CHAPBOOK COMPETITION

E-mail: editors@blacklawrencepress.com. **Website:** www.blacklawrence.com. **Contact:** Kit Frick, senior editor. Twice each year Black Lawrence Press will run the Black River Chapbook Competition for an unpublished chapbook of poems or short fiction between 16-36 pages in length. Spring deadline: May 31. Fall deadline: October 31. Prize: $500, publication, and 10 copies. Judged by a revolving panel of judges, in addition to the Chapbook Editor and other members of the BLP editorial staff.

BLUE LIGHT POETRY PRIZE AND CHAPBOOK CONTEST

P.O. Box 150300, San Rafael CA 94915. **E-mail:** bluelightpress@aol.com. **Website:** www.bluelightpress.com. **Contact:** Diane Frank, chief editor. The Blue Light Poetry Prize and Chapbook Contest offers publication of your chapbook by Blue Light Press, 10 free copies of your book, and a 50% discount for additional books. (See separate listing in Book/Chapbook Publishers). Deadline: June 30. The winner will be published by Blue Light Press, with 10 free copies of the author's book. We offer a a 50% discount for additional books. We have a group of poets who read manuscripts. Some years, we publish more than one winner.

BLUE MOUNTAIN ARTS

SPS Studios, Inc., Blue Mountain Arts, Inc., P.O. Box 1007, Boulder CO 80306. (303)449-0536. **Fax:** (303)447-0939. **E-mail:** editorial@sps.com. **Website:** www.sps.com. **Contact:** Ingrid Heffner. Family owned and operated independent greeting card company thriving since its founding in 1971. Specializes in expressing feelings that may be difficult for buyer to express. With its own fine art department creating watercolor paintings and multimedia cards, hand-lettered, Blue Mountain Arts is sold worldwide and is unique with our poetry, artwork, handmade papers that make lifelong buyers. To put your best writing out there! No deadlines for every day poetry. Write editorial@sps.com for seasonal deadlines. If your poetry is accepted and tests well, you will get $300 and 24 copies of your card. Judged by the Blue Mountain Arts editorial staff.

✎ THE BOARDMAN TASKER PRIZE FOR MOUNTAIN LITERATURE

The Boardman Tasker Charitable Trust, 8 Bank View Rd., Darley Abbey Derby DE22 1EJ, UK. 01332 342246. **E-mail:** steve@people-matter.co.uk. **Website:** www.boardmantasker.com. **Contact:** Steve Dean.

Offered annually to reward a work with a mountain theme, whether fiction, nonfiction, drama, or poetry, written in the English language (initially or in translation). Subject must be concerned with a mountain environment. Previous winners have been books on expeditions, climbing experiences, a biography of a mountaineer, and novels. Guidelines available in January by e-mail or on website. Entries must be previously published. Open to any writer. The award is to honor Peter Boardman and Joe Tasker, who disappeared on Everest in 1982. Deadline: August 1 £3,000 Judged by a panel of 3 judges elected by trustees.

BOSTON GLOBE-HORN BOOK AWARDS

The Boston Globe, Horn Book, Inc., 300 The Fenway, Palace Road Building, Suite P-311, Boston MA 02115. (617)278-0225. **Fax:** (617)278-6062. **E-mail:** bghb@hbook.com; info@hbook.com. **Website:** www.hbook.com/bghb/. Offered annually for excellence in literature for children and young adults (published June 1-May 31). Categories: picture book, fiction and poetry, nonfiction. Judges may also name up to 2 honor books in each category. Books must be published in the US, but may be written or illustrated by citizens of any country. The Horn Book Magazine publishes speeches given at awards ceremonies. Guidelines for submitting books online. Deadline: May 15 Prize: $500 and an engraved silver bowl; honor-book recipients receive an engraved silver plate. Judged by a panel of 3 judges selected each year.

THE BOSTON REVIEW ANNUAL POETRY CONTEST

Poetry Contest, Boston Review, P.O. Box 425786, Cambridge MA 02142. (617)324-1360. **Fax:** (617)452-3356. **E-mail:** review@bostonreview.net. **Website:** www.bostonreview.net. Offers $1,500 and publication in *Boston Review* (see separate listing in Magazines/Journals). Deadline: June 1. Winner announced in early November on website. Prize: $1,500 and publication.

BOULEVARD POETRY CONTEST FOR EMERGING POETS

Boulevard, 4125 Juniata Street, #B, St. Louis MO 63116. **E-mail:** editors@boulevardmagazine.org. **Website:** www.boulevardmagazine.org. **Contact:** Jessica Rogen, Editor. Annual Emerging Poets Contest offers $1,000 and publication in *Boulevard* (see separate listing in Magazines/Journals) for the best group of 3 poems by a poet who has not yet published a book of poetry with a nationally distributed press. All entries will be considered for publication and payment at regular rates. Deadline: June 1. Prize: $1,000 and publication.

BARBARA BRADLEY PRIZE

New England Poetry Club, 376 School St., Watertown MA 02472. **E-mail:** contests@nepoetryclub.org. **Website:** www.nepoetryclub.org. **Contact:** Audrey Kalajin. For a lyric poem under 20 lines, written by a woman. Deadline: May 31 $200. Judged by well-known poets and sometimes winners of previous NEPC contests.

BRICK ROAD POETRY BOOK CONTEST

Brick Road Poetry Press, Inc., 513 Broadway, Columbus GA 31901-3117. (706)649-3080. **Fax:** (706)649-3094. **E-mail:** kbadowski@brickroadpoetrypress.com. **Website:** www.brickroadpoetrypress.com. **Contact:** Ron Self and Keith Badowski, Co-Editors/Founders. Annual competition for an original collection of 50-100 pages of poetry. Deadline: November 1st (Submission period begins August 1st) $1,000, publication in both print and e-book formats, and 25 copies of the book. May also offer publication contracts to the top finalists. Judged by Keith Badowski and Ron Self, Brick Road Poetry Editors.

TIPS "The best way to discover all that poetry can be, and to expand the limits of your own craft, is to expansively read poetry, both classic and contemporary."

THE BRIDPORT PRIZE

P.O. Box 6910, Bridport, Dorset DT6 9QB, United Kingdom. **E-mail:** info@bridportprize.org.uk; kate@bridportprize.org.uk. **Website:** www.bridportprize.org.uk. **Contact:** Kate Wilson, Bridport Prize Programme Manager. Award to promote literary excellence, discover new talent. Categories: Short stories, poetry, flash fiction, first novel. Deadline: May 31 each year. Prize: £5,000; £1,000; £500; various runners-up prizes and publication of approximately 13 best stories and 13 best poems in anthology; plus 6 best flash fiction stories. 1st Prize of £1,000 for the best short, short story of under 250 words. £1,000 plus up to a year's mentoring for winner of Peggy Chapman-Andrews Award for a first novel. A second anthology containing extracts of the twenty long-listed novels will be published for the first time in 2019. Judged by 1 judge for short stories (in 2019, Kirtsty Logan), 1 judge for poetry (in 2019, Holly McNish) and 1 judge for flash fiction (in 2019 Kirsty Logan). The Novel award is judged by a group comprising representatives from The Literary Consultancy, A.M. Heath Literary Agents, and (in 2019) judge Naomi Wood.

BRIGHT HILL PRESS ANNUAL FULL-LENGTH POETRY BOOK COMPETITION AND BRIGHT HILL PRESS ANNUAL POETRY CHAPBOOK COMPETITION

Bright Hill Press, Bright Hill Press Inc., 94 Church St., Treadwell NY 13846. Phone/**Fax:** (607)829-5055. **Fax:** (607)829-5054. **E-mail:** wordthur@stny.rr.com. **Web-site:** www.brighthillpress.org. **Contact:** Bertha Rogers, Editor; Beatrice Georgalidis, Executive Director. Bright Hill Press Annual Full-length Poetry Book Competition: Send 48-64 pages, bio, TOC, acknowledgments page, and 2 title pages (1 with name, address, etc.; 1 with title only). Poems can be published in journals or anthologies, but ms must not be published elsewhere, including self-published. Guidelines online for SASE or via e-mail. Simultaneous submissions welcome, but BHP must be notified if ms taken elsewhere. See website for deadline and other guidelines. Bright Hill Press Annual Poetry Chapbook Competition: Send 16-24 pages, bio, TOC, acknowledgments page, and 2 title pages (1 with name, address, etc.; 1 with title only). Poems can be published in journals or anthologies, but ms must not be published elsewhere, including self-published. Guidelines online for SASE, or via e-mail. Simultaneous submissions welcome, but BHP must be notified if ms taken elsewhere. See website for deadline and other guidelines. Bright Hill's purpose is to publish superior poetry. Deadline: December 31 (full-length poetry book competition); November 30 (chapbook competition). Book competition: $1,000, publication, and 30 copies of the winning book. Chapbook competition: $350, publication, and 30 copies of the winning chapbook.

💬 Read the guidelines. Follow the guidelines.

BRIGHT HILL PRESS POETRY CHAPBOOK COMPETITION

Bright Press Hill & Literary Center, 94 Church St., Treadwell NY 13846. (607)829-5055. **E-mail:** brighthillpress@stny.rr.com; wordthur@stny.rr.com. **Web-site:** www.brighthillpress.org. The annual Bright Hill Press Chapbook Award recognizes an outstanding collection of poetry. Guidelines available for SASE, by e-mail, or on website. Deadline: December 31. Prize: A publication contract with Bright Hill Press, $350, publication in print format, and 30 copies of the printed book. Judged by a nationally known poet.

BRITTINGHAM PRIZE IN POETRY

University of Wisconsin Press, 1930 Monroe St., 3rd Floor, Madison WI 5311-2059. (608)263-1110. **Fax:** (608)263-1132. **E-mail:** rwallace@wisc.edu. **E-mail:** uwiscpress@uwpress.wisc.edu. **Website:** www.wisc.edu/wisconsinpress/poetryguide.html. **Contact:** Ronald Wallace and Sean Bishop, Series Co-Editors. The annual Brittingham Prize in Poetry is 1 of 2 prizes awarded by The University of Wisconsin Press (see separate listing for the Felix Pollak Prize in Poetry in this section). The Press also publishes two or three additional books annually, drawn from the contest submissions. The Brittingham Prize in Poetry is awarded annually to the best book-length manuscript of original poetry submitted in an open competition. The award is administered by the University of Wisconsin–Madison English Department, and the winner is chosen by a nationally recognized poet. The resulting book is published by the University of Wisconsin Press. Deadline: Submit August 15-September 15. Prize: Offers $1,000, plus publication. Judged by a distinguished poet who changes annually.

BURNING BUSH POETRY PRIZE

P.O. Box 4658, Santa Rosa CA 95402. **Website:** www.bbbooks.com. Purpose of contest is to reward a poet whose writing inspires others to value human life and the natural world instead of values based on short-term economic advantage; speaks for community-centered values and democratic processes, and especially for those whose voices are seldom heard; demonstrates poetic excellence; and educates readers of the relevance of the past to the present and future. Deadline: June 1

BOB BUSH MEMORIAL AWARD FOR FIRST BOOK OF POETRY

E-mail: tilsecretary@yahoo.com. **Website:** www.texasinstituteofletters.org. Offered annually for best first book of poetry published in previous year. Writer must have been born in Texas, have lived in the state at least 2 consecutive years at some time, or the subject matter should be associated with the state. Deadline: See website for exact date. Prize: $1,000.

☯ CAA POETRY AWARD

Canadian Authors Association, 192 Spadina Avenue, Suite 107, Toronto ON M5T 2C2, Canada. **Website:** canadianauthors.org/national. Contest for full-length English-language book of poems for adults by a Canadian writer. Deadline: January

CALIFORNIA BOOK AWARDS

Commonwealth Club of California, 110 The Embarcadero, San Francisco CA 94105. (415)597-6700. **Fax:** (415)597-6729. **E-mail:** bookawards@commonwealthclub.org. **Website:** https://www.common-wealthclub.org/events/california-book-awards. **Contact:** Priscilla Vivio, bookawards@commonwealthclub.org, pvivio@commonwealthclub.org. Offered annually to recognize California's best writers and illuminate the wealth and diversity of California-based literature. Award is for published submissions appearing in print during the previous calendar year. Can be nominated by publisher or author. Open to California residents (or residents at time of publication). Deadline: December 22. Prize: Medals and cash prizes to be awarded at publicized event, annually in June for previous year submissions. Judged by 12-15 California professionals with a diverse range of views, backgrounds, and literary experience.

☺ CANADIAN AUTHORS ASSOCIATION AWARD FOR POETRY

192 Spadina Avenue, Suite 107, Toronto ON M5T 2C2, Canada. (416)975 1756. **E-mail:** admin@canadianauthors.org. **Website:** www.canadianauthors.org. **Contact:** Anita Purcell, Executive Director. Offered annually for a full-length English-language book of poems for adults, by a Canadian writer. Deadline: January 31. Prize: $1,000 and a silver medal. Judging: Each year a trustee for each award appointed by the Canadian Authors Association selects up to 3 judges. Identities of the trustee and judges are confidential.

CAROLINA WREN PRESS POETRY SERIES CONTEST

120 Morris St., Durham NC 27701. (919)560-2738. **Fax:** (919)560-2759. **E-mail:** carolinawrenpress@earthlink.net. **Website:** www.carolinawrenpress.org. **Contact:** Andrea Selch, Poetry Editor. Carolina Wren Press is a nonprofit organization whose mission is to publish quality writing, especially by writers historically neglected by mainstream publishing, and to develop diverse and vital audiences through publishing, outreach, and educational programs. Deadline: June 15 of odd-numbered years. Prize: $1,000 and publication.

CAVE CANEM POETRY PRIZE

Cave Canem Foundation, Inc., 20 Jay St., Suite 310-A, Brooklyn NY 11201-8301. (718)858-0000. **Website:** www.cavecanempoets.org. This 1st book award is dedicated to the discovery of exceptional mss by black poets of African descent. Deadline: March 31. 1st place: $1,000, plus publication by University of Georgia Press, 15 copies of the book, and a featured reading. Evie Shockley.

CIDER PRESS REVIEW BOOK AWARD

P.O. Box 33384, San Diego CA 92163. **E-mail:** editor@ciderpressreview.com. **Website:** http://ciderpressreview.com/. Annual award from *Cider Press Review*. Deadline: November 30. Open to submissions on September 1. Prize: $1,500, publication, and 25 author's copies of a book-length collection of poetry. Author receives a standard publishing contract. Initial print run is not less than 1,000 copies. CPR acquires first publication rights. Editors of Cider Press Review.

☺ THE CITY OF VANCOUVER BOOK AWARD

Cultural Services Dept., Woodward's Heritage Building, 111 W. Hastings St., Suite 501, Vancouver BC V6B 1H4, Canada. (604)871-6634. **Fax:** (604)871-6005. **E-mail:** marnie.rice@vancouver.ca; culture@vancouver.ca. **Website:** https://vancouver.ca/people-programs/city-of-vancouver-book-award.aspx. The annual City of Vancouver Book Award recognizes authors of excellence of any genre that reflect Vancouver's unique character, rich diversity and culture, history and residents. The book must exhibit excellence in one or more of the following areas: content, illustration, design, format. Deadline: May 22. Prize: $3,000. Judged by an independent jury.

CLEVELAND STATE UNIVERSITY POETRY CENTER BOOK COMPETITIONS

Cleveland State University Poetry Center, Cleveland State University Poetry Center, 2121 Euclid Avenue, Rhodes Tower, Room 1841, Cleveland OH 44115. (216)687-3986. **E-mail:** poetrycenter@csuohio.edu. **Website:** www.csupoetrycenter.com. **Contact:** Caryl Pagel. The Cleveland State University Poetry Center was established in 1962 at the former Fenn College of Engineering to promote poetry through readings and community outreach. In 1971, it expanded its mission to become a national non-profit independent press under the auspices of the Cleveland State University Department of English, and has since published nearly 200 rangy, joyful, profound, astonishing, complicated, surprising, and aesthetically diverse collections of contemporary poetry and prose by established and emerging authors. The Cleveland State University Poetry Center publishes between 3 and 5 collections of contemporary poetry and prose a year, with a national distribution and reach. The Poetry Center currently acquires manuscripts through 3 annual contests (1 dedicated to publishing and promoting first books of poetry, 1 to supporting an established poet's career, and 1 to publishing collections of literary essays). In addition to publishing, the Poetry Center actively promotes contemporary poetry and prose through an annual reading series, collaborative art events, participation in national writing conferences, and as an educational resource for Cleveland State University's undergraduate, M.A., and N.E.O.M.F.A. students by providing assistantship and internship opportunities, as well as involving students in the editorial and production aspects of literary publishing. Deadline: April 5. Prize: First Book and Open Book Competitions Awards: Publication and a $1,000 prize for an original manuscript of poetry in each category. 2018 Judges: CAConrad (First Book); Samuel Amadon, Leora Fridman, and Jane Lewty (Open Book); Brian Blanchfield (Essay).

CLOCKWISE CHAPBOOK COMPETITION

Tebot Bach, Tebot Bach, Clockwise, P.O. Box 7887, Huntington Beach CA 92615-7887. (714)968-0905. **Fax:** (714)968-4677. **E-mail:** mifanwy@tebotbach. org. **Website:** www.tebotbach.org/clockwise.html. Annual competition for a collection of poetry. Submit 24-32 pages of original poetry in English. Deadline: August 31. Prize: $500 and a book publication in Perfect Bound Editions. Winner announced in November with publication in May. Judged by Gail Wronsky.

CLOUDBANK BOOKS

Vern Rutsala Book Contest, Cloudbank Books, P.O. Box 610, Corvallis OR 97339. (541) 752-0075. **E-mail:** michael@cloudbankbooks.com. **Website:** www.cloudbankbooks.com. **Contact:** Michael Malan. *Cloudbank* is a 96-to-112 page print journal published annually. Included are poems, flash fiction, and book reviews. Regular submissions and contest submissions are accepted. The annual Vern Rutsala Book Contest results in a published book of poetry and/or flash fiction, plus monetary prize. Deadlines: Submissions for the journal's annual Cloudbank Contest are accepted from Nov. 1 through the last day in February. Non-contest submissions for the journal are accepted through April 30. Submissions for the Vern Rutsala Book Contest are accepted from July 1 through Oct. 31. The Cloudbank Contest prize is $200 and publication. Two contributors' copies are sent to all writers whose work appears in the magazine. The Vern Rutsala Book Contest winner receives $1,000 and publication of the manuscript. The Cloudbank Contest is judged by Editor Michael Malan and editorial staff. The Vern Rutsala Book Contest has an outside judge.

TOM COLLINS POETRY PRIZE

Fellowship of Australian Writers (WA), Fellowship of Australian Writers (WA), P.O. Box 6180, Swanbourne WA 6910, Australia. (61)(08)9384-4771. **Fax:** (61) (8)9384-4854 or. **E-mail:** fellowshipaustralianwriterswa@gmail.com. **Website:** www.fawwa.org. Annual contest for unpublished poems, maximum 60 lines. Reserves the right to publish entries in a FAWWA publication or on its website. Guidelines online or for SASE. Deadline: 15th December. Prize: 1st Place: $1,000; 2nd Place: $200; 3rd Place: $100.

THE COLORADO PRIZE FOR POETRY

Colorado Review,/ Center for Literary Publishing, Department of English, Colorado State University, 9105 Campus Delivery, Ft. Collins CO 80523. (970)491-5449. **E-mail:** creview@colostate.edu. **Website:** coloradoprize.colostate.edu. **Contact:** Stephanie G'Schwind, editor. Submission must be unpublished as a collection, but individual poems may have been published elsewhere. Submit mss of 48-100 pages of poetry on any subject, in any form, double- or single-spaced. Include 2 titles pages: 1 with ms title only, the other with ms title and poet's name, address, and phone number. Enclose SASE for notification of receipt and SASE for results; mss will not be returned. Guidelines available by SASE, e-mail, or online at website. Poets can also submit online via online submission manager through website. January 14. $2,000 and publication of a book-length ms. Judged by Kazim Ali.

CONCRETE WOLF POETRY CHAPBOOK/ LOUIS AWARD CONTEST

P.O. Box 445, Tillamook OR 97141. **E-mail:** concretewolfpress@gmail.com. **Website:** http://concretewolf. com. Prefers collections that have a theme, either obvious (i.e., chapbook about a divorce) or understated (i.e., all the poems mention the color blue). Likes a collection that feels more like a whole than a sampling of work. No preference as to formal or free verse. Slightly favors lyric and narrative poetry to language and concrete, but excellent examples of any style will grab their attention. Considers simultaneous submissions if notified of acceptance elsewhere. Deadline: November 30 and March 31. Prize: Publication and 100 author copies of a perfectly-bound collection distributed by the Ingram catalog and available on Amazon.

THE CONNECTICUT RIVER REVIEW POETRY CONTEST

P.O. Box 270554, W. Hartford CT 06127. **E-mail:** connpoetry@comcast.net. **Website:** ctpoetry.net. Deadline: September 30. Open to submissions on August 1. 1st Place: $400; 2nd Place: $100; 3rd Place: $50. Leslie McGarth

CRAB ORCHARD SERIES IN POETRY FIRST BOOK AWARD

First Book Award, Dept. of English, Mail Code 4503, Southern Illinois University Carbondale, 1000 Faner Dr., Carbondale IL 62901. (618)453-6833. **Fax:** (618)453-8224. **E-mail:** jtribble@siu.edu. **Website:** www.craborchardreview.siu.edu. **Contact:** Jon Tribble, series editor. Annual award that selects a first book of poems for publication from an open competition of manuscripts, in English, by a U.S. citizen, permanent resident, or person who has DACA/TPS status who has neither published, who has neither published, nor committed to publish, a volume of poetry 48 pages or more in length in an edition of over 500 copies (individual poems may have been previously published; for the purposes of the Crab Orchard Series in Poetry, a ms which was in whole or in part submitted as a thesis or dissertation as a requirement for the completion of a degree is considered unpublished and is eligible). Current or former students, colleagues, and close friends of the final judge, and current and former students and employees of Southern Illinois University Carbondale and authors who have published a book with Southern Illinois University Press or have a book under contract with Southern Illinois University Press are not eligible. Deadline: July 8. Submission period begins May 15. Prize: $2,500 and publication. Judged by a published poet. Check website for current judge.

CRAB ORCHARD SERIES IN POETRY OPEN COMPETITION AWARDS

Department of English, Mail Code 4503, Faner Hall 2380, Southern Illinois University Carbondale, Carbondale IL 62901. (618)453-6833. **Fax:** (618)453-8224. **E-mail:** jtribble@siu.edu. **Website:** www.craborchardreview.siu.edu. **Contact:** Jon Tribble, series editor. Annual competition to award unpublished, original collections of poems written in English by United States citizens, permanent residents, or persons who have DACA/TPS status (individual poems may have been previously published; for the purposes of the Crab Orchard Series in Poetry, a ms which was in whole or in part submitted as a thesis or disserta-

tion as a requirement for the completion of a degree is considered unpublished and is eligible). Two volumes of poems will be selected from the open competition of mss. Current or former students, colleagues, and close friends of the final judge, and current and former students and employees of Southern Illinois University Carbondale and authors who have published a book with Southern Illinois University Press or have a book under contract with Southern Illinois University Press are not eligible. Deadline: November 19. Submission period begins October 1. Prize: Both winners will be awarded a publication contract with Southern Illinois University Press, a $1,000 prize, and a $1,500 as an honorarium for a reading at Southern Illinois University Carbondale. Both readings will follow the publication of the poets' collections. Judged by a published poet. Check website for current judge.

THE CRAZYHORSE PRIZE IN POETRY

Crazyhorse, Department of English, College of Charleston, 66 George St., Charleston SC 29424. (843)953-4470. **E-mail:** crazyhorse@cofc.edu. **Website:** http://crazyhorse.cofc.edu. **Contact:** Prize Director. The *Crazyhorse* Prize in Poetry is for a single poem. All entries will be considered for publication. Submissions must be unpublished. Deadline: Crazyhorse welcomes general submissions of fiction, nonfiction, and poetry from September 1st through May 31st, with the exception of the month of January, during which we only accept entries for the Crazyhorse Prizes. Prize: $2,000 and publication in *Crazyhorse*. Judged by genre judges for first round, guest judge for second round. Judges change on a yearly basis.

DANCING POETRY CONTEST

Artists Embassy International, AEI Contest Chair, Judy Cheung, 704 Brigham Ave., Santa Rosa CA 95404-5245, USA. (707)528-0912. **E-mail:** jhcheung@comcast.net. **Website:** www.dancingpoetry.com. **Contact:** Judy Cheung, contest chair. Deadline: April 15. Prizes: Three Grand Prizes will receive $100 each, plus the poems will be danced and videotaped at this year's Dancing Poetry Festival; 6 First Prizes will receive $50 each; 12 Second Prizes will receive $25 each; and 30 Third Prizes will receive $10 each. Judged by members and associates of Artists Embassy International and the Poetic Dance Theater Company.

DER-HOVANESSIAN PRIZE

New England Poetry Club, 376 School St., Watertown MA 02472. **E-mail:** contests@nepoetryclub.

org. **Website:** www.nepoetryclub.org. **Contact:** Audrey Kalajin. For a translation from any language into English. Send a copy of the original. Funded by John Mahtesian. Deadline: May 31 Prize: $200. Judges are well-known poets and sometimes winners of previous NEPC contests.

DIAGRAM/NEW MICHIGAN PRESS CHAPBOOK CONTEST

New Michigan Press, P.O. Box 210067, English, ML 445, University of Arizona, Tucson AZ 85721. **E-mail:** nmp@thediagram.com. **Website:** www.thediagram. com. **Contact:** Ander Monson, editor. The annual *DIAGRAM*/New Michigan Press Chapbook Contest offers $1,000, plus publication and author's copies, with discount on additional copies. Deadline: April 26. Prize: $1,000, plus publication. Finalist chapbooks also considered for publication. Judged by editor Ander Monson.

DIAGRAM/NEW MICHIGAN PRESS CHAPBOOK CONTEST

Department of English, University of Arizona, New Michigan Press, P.O. Box 210067, Tucson AZ 85721-0067. **E-mail:** nmp@thediagram.com; editor@thediagram.com. **Website:** www.thediagram.com/contest.html. **Contact:** Ander Monson, editor. Contest for prose, poetry, or hybrid manuscript (images ok) between 18-44 pages. Deadline: April 28. Check website for more details. Prize: $1,000 and publication. Typically we also published 3-5 finalist chapbooks. Judged by editor Ander Monson.

JAMES DICKEY PRIZE FOR POETRY

Georgia State University, James Dickey Prize for Poetry, P.O. Box 3999, Atlanta GA 30302-3999. **Website:** fivepoints.gsu.edu. The James Dickey Prize for Poetry is for the best previously unpublished poem. Deadline: December 1. Open to submissions on September 1. Winner receives $1000 and publication in the Volume 16, number 1 issue.

DOBIE PAISANO WRITER'S FELLOWSHIP

The Graduate School, The University of Texas at Austin, Attn: Dobie Paisano Program, 110 Inner Campus Drive Stop G0400, Austin TX 78712-0531. (512)232-3612. **Fax:** (512)471-7620. **E-mail:** gbarton@austin.utexas.edu. **Website:** www.utexas.edu/ogs/Paisano. **Contact:** Gwen Barton. Sponsored by the Graduate School at The University of Texas at Austin and the Texas Institute of Letters, the Dobie Paisano Fellowship Program provides solitude, time, and a comfortable place for Texas writers or writers who have writ-

ten significantly about Texas through fiction, non-fiction, poetry, plays, or other mediums. The Dobie Paisano Ranch is a very rural and rustic setting, and applicants should read the guidelines closely to ensure their ability to reside in this secluded environment. Deadline: January 15. Applications are accepted beginning December 1 and must be post-marked no later than January 15. The Ralph A. Johnston memorial Fellowship is for a period of 4 months with a stipend of $6,250 per month. It is aimed at writers who have already demonstrated some publishing and critical success. The Jesse H. Jones Writing Fellowship is for a period of approximately 6 months with a stipend of $3,000 per month. It is aimed at, but not limited to, writers who are early in their careers.

☼ FAR HORIZONS AWARD FOR POETRY

The Malahat Review, University of Victoria, P.O. Box 1800, Stn CSC, Victoria BC V8W 3H5, Canada. (250)721-8524. **E-mail:** malahat@uvic.ca. **Website:** www.malahatreview.ca. **Contact:** L'Amour Lisik, Marketing and Circulation Manager. The biennial Far Horizons Award for Poetry offers $1,000 CAD and publication in *The Malahat Review* (see separate listing in Magazines/Journals). Winner and finalists contacted by e-mail. Winner published in fall in *The Malahat Review* and announced on website, Facebook page, and in quarterly e-newsletter *Malahat lite*. Open to "emerging poets from Canada, the United States, and elsewhere" who have not yet published a full-length book (48 pages or more). Deadline: May 1 (even-numbered years). Prize: $1,000.

JANICE FARRELL POETRY PRIZE CATEGORY

Soul-Making Keats Literary Competition, The Webhallow House, 1544 Sweetwood Dr., Broadmoor Vlg. CA 94015. **E-mail:** soulkeats@mail.com. **Website:** www.soulmakingcontest.us. **Contact:** Eileen Malone. Deadline: November 30. Prizes: First: $100, Second: $50, Third: $25. Judged by a local San Francisco Bay Area successfully published poet.

THE WILLIAM FAULKNER-WILLIAM WISDOM CREATIVE WRITING COMPETITION

Faulkner - Wisdom Competition, Pirate's Alley Faulkner Society, Inc., Faulkner – Wisdom Competition, 624 Pirate's Alley, New Orleans LA 70116. (504)586-1609. **E-mail:** faulkhouse@aol.com. **Website:** https://faulknersociety.org. **Contact:** Rosemary James, Award Director. general craft See guidelines posted at www.wordsandmusic.org. Deadline: May 31. Prizes:

$750-7,500 depending on category. Judged by established authors, literary agents, and acquiring editors.

THE JEAN FELDMAN POETRY PRIZE

E-mail: wwphpress@gmail.com. **Website:** www.washingtonwriters.org. **Contact:** Holly Karapetkova. Poets living within 75 miles of the Capitol are invited to submit a ms of either a novel or a collection of short stories. Ms should be 50-70 pages, single spaced. Deadline: November 15. Submission period begins July 1. Prize: $1,000 and 50 copies of the book.

FIELD POETRY PRIZE

Oberlin College Press/FIELD, 50 N. Professor St., Oberlin OH 44074-1095. (440)775-8408. **Fax:** (440)775-8124. **E-mail:** oc.press@oberlin.edu. **Website:** www.oberlin.edu/ocpress/prize.htm. **Contact:** Marco Wilkinson, Managing Editor. Offered annually for an unpublished book-length collection of poetry (mss of 50-80 pages). Contest seeks to encourage the finest in contemporary poetry writing. Open to any writer. Deadline: May 31. Opens to submissions on May 1. Prize: $1,000 and a standard royalty contract.

FINELINE COMPETITION FOR PROSE POEMS, SHORT SHORTS, AND ANYTHING IN BETWEEN

Mid-American Review, Dept. of English, Bowling Green State University, Bowling Green OH 43403. (419)372-2725. **E-mail:** mar@bgsu.edu. **Website:** www.bgsu.edu/midamericanreview. **Contact:** Abigail Cloud, Editor-in-Chief. Offered annually for previously unpublished submissions. Contest open to all writers not associated with current judge or *Mid-American Review*. Deadline: June 1. Prize: $1,000, plus publication in fall issue of *Mid-American Review*; 10 finalists receive notation plus possible publication. Judge will be a contemporary writer of note.

THE FINISHING LINE PRESS OPEN CHAPBOOK COMPETITION

Finishing Line Press, P.O. Box 1626, Georgetown KY 40324. **E-mail:** finishingbooks@aol.com. **Website:** www.finishinglinepress.com. **Contact:** Christen Kincaid, Director. Annual competition for poetry chapbook. $1,000

FIRST BOOK AWARD FOR POETRY

Zone 3, Austin Peay State University, Austin Peay State University, PO Box 4565, Clarksville TN 37044. (931)221-7031. **E-mail:** zone3@apsu.edu. **Website:** zone3press.com. **Contact:** Andrea Spofford, Poetry Editor; Aubrey Collins, Managing Editor. Biennial

poetry award for anyone who has not published a full-length collection of poems (48 pages or more). Jan.1-May 1, 2020. Prize: $1,000 and publication.

FISH POETRY PRIZE

Fish Poetry Contest, Fish Publishing, Dunbeacon, Durrus, Bantry Co. Cork P75 VK72, Ireland. **E-mail:** info@fishpublishing.com. **Website:** www.fishpublishing.com. **Contact:** Clem Cairns. For poems up to 300 words. Age Range: Adult. The best 10 will be published in the Fish Anthology, launched in July at the West Cork Literary Festival. Entries must not have been published before. Enter online or by post. See website for full details of competitions, and for information on the Fish Editorial and Critique Services and the Fish Online Writing Courses. The aim of the competition is to discover and publish new poets. Deadline: March 31. 1st Prize: $1,000. 2nd Prize: A week at Anam Cara Writers" Retreat in West Cork. Results announced May 15. Judged by Billy Collins in 2019.

FOLEY POETRY CONTEST

Foley Poetry Contest, America Magazine, 1212 Avenue of the Americas, New York NY 10019. (212)581-4640. **Fax:** (212)399-3596. **Website:** www.americamagazine.org. *America*, the national Catholic weekly by the Jesuits of North America, sponsors the annual Foley Poetry Contest. Offers $1,000 and 2 contributor's copies for the winning poem. Winner will be announced in the mid-June issue of America and on the website. Runners-up will have their poems printed in subsequent issues of *America*. Submissions must be unpublished and may not be entered in other contests. "Submit 1 poem per person, not to exceed 30 lines of verse, in any form. Name, address, telephone number, and e-mail address (if applicable) should be appended to the bottom of the page. Poems will not be returned, and e-mailed submissions are not accepted." Guidelines available in magazine, for SASE, or on website. Competition receives more than 1,000 entries/year. Deadline: March 31. Open to submissions on January 1. $1,000

THE FOUR WAY BOOKS LEVIS PRIZE IN POETRY

Four Way Books, POB 535, Village Station, New York NY 10014. (212)334-5430. **Fax:** (212)334-5435. **E-mail:** editors@fourwaybooks.com. **Website:** www.fourwaybooks.com. **Contact:** Ryan Murphy, Associate Director. The Four Way Books Levis Prize in Poetry offers publication by Four Way Books (see separate listing in Book Publishers), honorarium, and a reading at one or more participating series in New York City. Open to any poet writing in English who has not published a book-length collection of poetry. Entry form and guidelines available on website at www.fourwaybooks.com. Submission Dates: January 1 - April 7 (postmark) or online via our submission manager by April 8 at 3 AM EST. Winner announced by e-mail and on website. Prize: Publication and $1,000. Copies of winning books available through Four Way Books online and at bookstores (to the trade through University Press of New England). 2019 Judge: Gregory Pardlo

✪ FREEFALL SHORT PROSE AND POETRY CONTEST

Freefall Literary Society of Calgary, 922 9th Ave. SE, Calgary AB T2G 0S4, Canada. **E-mail:** editors@freeallmagazine.ca. **Website:** www.freefallmagazine.ca. **Contact:** Ryan Stromquist, Managing Editor. Offered annually for unpublished work in the categories of poetry (5 poems/entry) and prose (3,000 words or less). Recognizes writers and offers publication credits in a literary magazine format. Contest rules and entry form online. Acquires first Canadian serial rights; ownership reverts to author after one-time publication. Deadline: December 31. Prize: 1st Place: $500 (CAD); 2nd Place: $250 (CAD); 3rd Place: $75; Honorable Mention: $25. All prizes include publication in the spring edition of *FreeFall Magazine*. Winners will also be invited to read at the launch of that issue, if such a launch takes place. Honorable mentions in each category will be published and may be asked to read. Travel expenses not included. Judged by current guest editor for issue (who are also published authors in Canada).

GERTRUDE PRESS POETRY CHAPBOOK CONTEST

P.O. Box 28281, Portland OR 97228. **E-mail:** editor@gertrudepress.org; poetry@gertrudepress.org. **Website:** www.gertrudepress.org. Annual chapbook contest for 25-30 pages of poetry. Deadline: May 15. Submission period begins September 15. Prize: $200, publication, and 25 complimentary copies of the chapbook.

ALLEN GINSBERG POETRY AWARDS

The Poetry Center at Passaic County Community College, One College Blvd., Paterson NJ 07505-1179. (973)684-6555. **Fax:** (973)523-6085. **E-mail:** mgillan@pccc.edu. **Website:** www.poetrycenterpccc.com. **Contact:** Maria Mazziotti Gillan, Executive Director. All winning poems, honorable mentions, and editor's choice poems will be published in *The Paterson Literary Review*. Winners will be asked to participate in a reading that will be held in the Paterson Historic District. Submissions must be unpublished. February 1st, 2020 Prize: 1st Prize: $1,000; 2nd Prize: $200; 3rd Prize: $100.

GIVAL PRESS POETRY AWARD

Gival Press, LLC, P.O. Box 3812, Arlington VA 22203. (703)351-0079. **E-mail:** givalpress@yahoo.com. **Website:** www.givalpress.submittable.com. **Contact:** Robert L. Giron, editor. Offered every other year, with the next deadline of December 15, 2019, with book publication in 2020, for a previously unpublished poetry collection as a complete ms, which may include previously published poems; previously published poems must be acknowledged, and poet must hold rights. Guidelines for SASE, by e-mail, or online. Open to any writer, as long as the work is original, not a translation, and is written in English. The copyright remains in the author's name; certain rights fall to the publisher per the contract. Enter via portal: www.givalpress.submittable.com. The competition seeks to award well-written, origional poetry in English on any topic, in any style. Deadline: December 15 (postmarked). Prize: $1,000, publication, and 20 copies of the publication. The editor narrows entries to the top 10; previous winner selects top 5 and chooses the winner—all done anonymously.

✪ JOHN GLASSCO TRANSLATION PRIZE

Literary Translators' Association of Canada, ATTLC | LTAC; Concordia University, LB-601, 1455 de Maisonneuve Boulevard West, Montréal QC H3G 1M8, Canada. (514)848-2424, ext. 8702. **E-mail:** info@attlc-ltac.org. **Website:** attlc-ltac.org/john-glassco-translation-prize. **Contact:** Glassco Prize Committee. Offered annually for a translator's first book-length literary translation into French or English, published in Canada during the previous calendar year. The translator must be a Canadian citizen or permanent resident. Eligible genres include fiction, creative nonfiction, poetry, and children's books. Deadline: July 9. Prize: $1,000 and a 1-year membership to LTAC.

PATRICIA GOEDICKE PRIZE IN POETRY

CutBank Literary Magazine, *CutBank*, University of Montana, English Dept., LA 133, Missoula MT 59812. **E-mail:** editor.cutbank@gmail.com. **Website:** www.cutbankonline.org. **Contact:** Billy Wallace, Editor-in-Chief. The Patricia Goedicke Prize in Poetry seeks to highlight work that showcases an authentic voice, a boldness of form, and a rejection of functional fixedness. Deadline: January 15. Submissions period begins November 9. Prize: $500 and featured in the magazine. Judged by a guest judge each year.

GOLDEN ROSE AWARD

New England Poetry Club, 654 Green St., No. 2, Cambridge MA 02139. **E-mail:** contests@nepoetryclub.org; info@nepoetryclub.org. **Website:** www.nepoetryclub.org. **Contact:** NEPC contest coordinator. Given annually to the poet, who by their poetry, and inspiration to and encouragement of other writers, has made a significant mark on American poetry. Traditionally given to a poet with some ties to New England so that a public reading may take place. Judged by well-known poets and sometimes winners of previous NEPC contests.

✪ GOVERNOR GENERAL'S LITERARY AWARDS

Canada Council for the Arts, 150 Elgin St., P.O. Box 1047, Ottawa ON K1P 5V8, Canada. (800)263-5588, ext. 5573 or (613)566-4414, ext. 5573. **Website:** ggbooks.ca. The Canada Council for the Arts provides a wide range of grants and services to professional Canadian artists and art organizations in dance, media arts, music, theatre, writing, publishing, and the visual arts. The Governor General's Literary Awards are given annually for the best English-language and French-language work in each of 7 categories, including fiction, non-fiction, poetry, drama, young people's literature (text), young people's literature (illustrated books), and translation. Deadline: Depends on the book's publication date. See website for details. Prize: Each GG winner receives $25,000. Non-winning finalists receive $1,000. Publishers of the winning titles receive a $3,000 grant for promotional purposes. Evaluated by fellow authors, translators, and illustrators. For each category, a jury makes the final selection.

SUE GRANZELLA HUMOR PRIZE

Category in the Soul-Making Keats Literary Competition, The Webhallow House, 1544 Sweetwood Dr., Broadmoor Vlg. CA 94015-2029. **E-mail:** soulkeats@mail.com. **Website:** www.soulmakingcontest.us. **Contact:** Eileen Malone. Deadline: November 30. Prize: First Place: $100; Second Place: $50; Third Place: $25. Judged by Sue Granzella.

GREAT LAKES COLLEGES ASSOCIATION NEW WRITERS AWARD

The Great Lakes Colleges Association, 535 W. William St., Suite 301, Ann Arbor MI 48103. (734)661-2350. **Fax:** (734)661-2349. **E-mail:** wegner@glca.org. **Website:** https://glca.org/glcaprograms/new-writers-award. **Contact:** Gregory R. Wegner, Director of Program Development: wegner@glca.org.. The Great Lakes Colleges Association (GLCA) is a consortium of 13 independent liberal arts colleges in Ohio, Michigan, Indiana, and Pennsylvania. The Award's purpose is to celebrate literary achievement in a writer's first-published volume of fiction, poetry, or nonfiction. Deadline: June 25, 2019. Any work received with a postmark after this date will not be accepted. Prize: Honorarium of at least $500 from each member college that invites a winning to give a reading on its campus. Each award winner receives invitations from several of the 13 colleges of the GLCA to visit campus. At these campus events an author will give readings, meet students and faculty, and occasionally visit college classes. In addition to the $500 honorarium for each campus visit, travel costs to colleges are paid by the GLCA's member colleges. Judged by professors of literature and writers in residence at GLCA colleges.

GREEN PIECES PRESS ARIZONA LITERARY CONTEST BOOK AWARDS

Green Pieces Press, 6939 East Chaparral Rd., Paradise Valley AZ 85253-7000. (480)219-4559. **E-mail:** Director@AzLiteraryContest.com. **Website:** www.AzLiteraryContest.com. **Contact:** Lisa Aquilina, publisher. Green Pieces Press is honored to receive the baton from its contest predecessor and sponsor a refreshed, retooled 2019 annual literary competition for published books, unpublished novels, and Arizona Book of the Year. Cash prizes awarded ($1,000 Book of the Year) from Green Pieces Press. First Place in each of the nine categories ($200), Second Place $100, Third Place $50. All category finalists in 2019 have their literary works published in the *Arizona Literary Magazine 2020*. NEW PRIZE in 2019 for Unpublished Novel category. All Finalists have their completed manuscript submitted to Ingram Elliot Book Publishers for consideration and potential award of a standard, traditional publishing contract. All published work must have 2018 or 2019 copyright date at time of submission. Deadline: September 1, 2019. Begins accepting submissions January 1, 2019. Finalists notified by Labor Day weekend. Prizes: Grand Prize, Arizona Book of the Year Award: $1,000. All categories: 1st Prize: $200; 2nd Prize: $100; 3rd Prize: $50. Unpublished Novel finallists also have their manuscripts submitted to IngramElliott Book Publishers for consideration to be awarded traditional publishing contract. Features in *Arizona Literary Magazine 2020*. Judged by nationwide published authors, editors, literary agents, and reviewers. Winners announced prior to Thanksgiving 2019. International entries encouraged; only caveat, all entries must be written in English.

○ Competition receives approximately 1,000+ entries per year. Submissions welcome from authors worldwide. All entries must be published or written in English. The Contest Directors reserve the right not to award a prize in any or all categories if the entries received are insufficient for viable competition and/or entries received do not meet international literary standards.

THE GREEN ROSE PRIZE IN POETRY

New Issues Poetry & Prose, Deptartment of English, Western Michigan University, 1903 W. Michigan Ave., Kalamazoo MI 49008-5463. **E-mail:** new-issues@wmich.edu. **Website:** www.newissuespress.com. Offered annually for unpublished poetry. The university will publish a book of poems by a poet writing in English who has published 1 or more full-length collections of poetry. *New Issues* may publish as many as 2 additional mss from this competition. Guidelines for SASE or online. *New Issues Poetry & Prose* obtains rights for first publication. Book is copyrighted in the author's name. Deadline: Submit May 1-September 30. Winner is announced in January or February on website. Prize: $1,000, publication of a book of poems, and reading w/ $500 stipend + travel costs.

☁ THE GRIFFIN POETRY PRIZE

The Griffin Trust for Excellence in Poetry, The Griffin Trust For Excellence In Poetry, 363 Parkridge Crescent, Oakville ON L6M 1A8, Canada. (905)618-0420. **E-mail:** info@griffinpoetryprize.com. **Website:** www.griffinpoetryprize.com. **Contact:** Ruth Smith, Executive Director. The Griffin Poetry Prize is one of the world's most generous poetry awards. The awards go to one Canadian and one international poet for a first collection written in, or translated into, English. June 30, 201 for books published between January 1, 2019 and June 30, 2019; December 31, 2019 for books published between July 1, 2019 and December 31, 2019. Prize: Two $65,000 (CAD) prizes. An additional $10,000 (CAD) goes to each shortlisted poet for their participation in the Shortlist Readings. Judges are chosen annually by the Trustees of The Griffin Trust For Excellence in Poetry.

GUGGENHEIM FELLOWSHIPS

John Simon Guggenheim Memorial Foundation, John Simon Guggenheim Memorial Foundation, 90 Park Ave., New York NY 10016. (212)687-4470. **E-mail:** fellowships@gf.org. **Website:** www.gf.org. Often characterized as "midcareer" awards, Guggenheim Fellowships are intended for men and women who have already demonstrated exceptional capacity for productive scholarship or exceptional creative ability in the arts. Fellowships are awarded through two annual competitions: one open to citizens and permanent residents of the United States and Canada, and the other open to citizens and permanent residents of Latin America and the Caribbean. Candidates must apply to the Guggenheim Foundation in order to be considered in either of these competitions. The Foundation receives between 3,500 and 4,000 applications each year. Although no one who applies is guaranteed success in the competition, there is no prescreening: all applications are reviewed. Approximately 200 Fellowships are awarded each year. Deadline: September 17.

HACKNEY LITERARY AWARDS

Hackney Literary Awards, 4650 Old Looney Mill Rd., Birmingham AL 35243. **E-mail:** info@hackneyliteraryawards.org. **Website:** www.hackneyliteraryawards.org. **Contact:** Myra Crawford, PhD, Executive Director. Offered annually for unpublished novels, short stories (maximum 5,000 words), and poetry (50 line limit). Guidelines on website. Deadline: September 30 (novels), November 30 (short stories and poetry). Prize: $5,000 in annual prizes for poetry and short fiction ($2,500 national and $2,500 state level). 1st Place: $600; 2nd Place: $400; 3rd Place: $250; plus $5,000 for an unpublished novel. Competition winners will be announced on the website each March.

THE DONALD HALL PRIZE IN POETRY

Association of Writers & Writing Programs, 5700 Rivertech Ct., Suite 225, Riverdale Park MD 20737-1250. **E-mail:** chronicle@awpwriter.org. **Website:** www.awpwriter.org. The Donald Hall Prize for Poetry offers an award of $5,500, supported by Amazon.com, and publication by the University of Pittsburgh Press. Deadline: March 3. Opens to submissions January 1.

JAMES HEARST POETRY PRIZE

North American Review, University of Northern Iowa, 1222 W. 27th St., Cedar Falls IA 50614-0516. (319)273-3026. **Fax:** (319)273-4326. **E-mail:** nar@uni.edu. **Website:** www.northamericanreview.org. Contest to find the best previously unpublished poem. Deadline: October 31. Prize: 1st place: $1,000; 2nd place: $100; 3rd place: $50.

THE HILARY THAM CAPITAL COLLECTION

The Word Works, Nancy White, c/o SUNY Adiorndack, 640 Bay Rd., Queensbury NY 12804. **E-mail:** editor@wordworksbooks.org. **Website:** www.wordworksbooks.org. **Contact:** Nancy White, Editor. The Hilary Tham Capital Collection publishes only poets who volunteer for literary nonprofits. Every nominated poet is invited to submit; authors have until May 1 to send their ms via online submissions at website, or to Nancy White. Deadline: May 1. $25 reading fee Past judges include Denise Duhamel, Kimiko Hahn, Michael Klein, and Eduardo Corral.

ERIC HOFFER AWARD

Hopewell Publications, LLC, P.O. Box 11, Titusville NJ 08560-0011. **Fax:** (609)964-1718. **E-mail:** info@hopepubs.com. **Website:** www.hofferaward.com. **Contact:** Dawn Shows, EHA Coordinator. Annual contest for previously published books. Recognizes excellence in independent publishing in many unique categories: Art (titles capture the experience, execution, or demonstration of the arts); Poetry (all styles); Chapbook (40 pages or less, artistic assembly); General Fiction (non-genre-specific fiction); Commercial Fiction (genre-specific fiction); Science Fiction/Fantasy; Historical Fiction; Short Story/Anthology; Mystery/Crime; Children (titles for young children); Middle Reader; Young Adult (titles aimed at the juvenile and teen markets); Culture (titles demonstrating the human or world experience); Memoir (titles relating to personal experience); Business (titles with application to today's business environment and emerging trends); Reference (titles from traditional and emerging reference areas); Home (titles with practical applications to home or home-related issues, including family); Health (titles promoting physical, mental, and emotional well-being); Self-help (titles involving new and emerging topics in self-help); Spiritual (titles involving the mind and spirit, including religion); Legacy Fiction and Nonfiction (titles over 2 years of age that hold particular relevance to any subject matter or form); E-book Fiction; E-book Nonfiction. Open to any writer of published work within the last 2 years, including categories for older books. This contest recognizes excellence in independent publishing in many unique categories. Also awards the Montaigne Medal for most though-provoking book, the Da Vinci Eye

for best cover, and the First Horizon Award for best new authors. Results published in the US Review of Books. Deadline: January 21. Grand Prize: $2,500; honors (winner, runner-up, honorable mentions) in each category, including the Montaigne Medal (most thought-provoking), da Vinci Art (cover art), First Horizon (first book), and Best in Press (small, academic, micro, self-published).

THE BESS HOKIN PRIZE

Poetry, 61 W. Superior St., Chicago IL 60654. (312)787-7070. **Fax:** (312)787-6650. **E-mail:** editors@poetrymagazine.org. **Website:** www.poetrymagazine.org. Offered annually for poems published in *Poetry* during the preceding year (October-September). Upon acceptance, *Poetry* licenses exclusive worldwide first-serial rights, including electronic rights, for publication, as well as non-exclusive rights to reprint, reuse, and archive the work, in any format, in perpetuity. Copyright reverts to author upon first publication. "Established in 1948 through the generosity of our late friend and guarantor, Mrs. David Hokin, and is given annually in her memory." Prize: $1,000.

FIRMAN HOUGHTON PRIZE

New England Poetry Club, 53 Regent St., Cambridge MA 02140. **E-mail:** info@nepoetryclug.org. **Website:** www.nepoetryclub.org. **Contact:** Mary Buchinger, Co-President NEPC. For a lyric poem in honor of the former president of NEPC. Deadline: May 31. Prize: $200. Judged by well-known poets and sometimes winners of previous NEPC contests.

TOM HOWARD/MARGARET REID POETRY CONTEST

Winning Writers, 351 Pleasant St., PMB 222, Northampton MA 01060-3961. (866)946-9748. **Fax:** (413)280-0539. **E-mail:** adam@winningwriters.com. **Website:** www.winningwriters.com. **Contact:** Adam Cohen. Winning Writers provides expert literary contest information to the public. It is one of the "101 Best Websites for Writers" (*Writer's Digest*). Offers annual awards of Tom Howard Prize, for a poem in any style or genre, and Margaret Reid Prize, for a poem that rhymes or has a traditional style. See website for guidelines and to submit your poem. If you win a prize, requests nonexclusive rights to publish your submission online, in e-mail newsletters, in e-books, and in press releases. Deadline: September 30. Submission period begins April 15. Prizes: Two top awards of $1,500 each, with 10 Honorable Mentions of $100 each (any style). All entries that win cash prizes will be published on the Winning Writers website. The top two winners will also receive one-year gift certificates from the contest co-sponsor, Duotrope (a $50 value). Judged by Soma Mei Sheng Frazier, assisted by Jim DuBois.

THE JULIA WARD HOWE/BOSTON AUTHORS AWARD

The Boston Authors Club, The Boston Authors Club, Boston Authors Club, Attn. Mary Cronin, 2400 Beacon Street, Unit 208, Chestnut Hill MA 02467. E-mail: bostonauthors@aol.com. Website: www.bostonauthorsclub.org. Contact: Alan Lawson. This annual award honors Julia Ward Howe and her literary friends who founded the Boston Authors Club in 1900. It also honors the membership over 110 years; consisting of novelists, biographers, historians, governors, senators, philosophers, poets, playwrights, and other luminaries. Boston Authors Club has been awarding the Julia Ward Howe Prizes (named after the Club's first President) to outstanding adult and young-reader books for over 20 years. These awards recognize exceptional books by Boston-area authors in four separate categories: Fiction, Nonfiction, Poetry, and the Young Reader category. Deadline: January 31. Prize: $1,000. Judged by the members.

HENRY HOYNS & POE-FAULKNER FELLOWSHIPS

Creative Writing Program, 219 Bryan Hall, P.O. Box 400121, University of Virginia, Charlottesville VA 22904-4121. (434)924-6074. Fax: (434)924-1478. E-mail: creativewriting@virginia.edu. Website: creativewriting.virginia.edu. Contact: Barbara Moriarty, Administrative Assistant.. Two-year MFA program in poetry and fiction; all students receive fellowships and teaching stipends that total $20,000 in both years of study. Sample poems/prose required with application. Optional third year with partial funding. Deadline: December 15.

ILLINOIS STATE POETRY SOCIETY ANNUAL CONTEST

Illinois State Poetry Society, Alan Harris, 543 E. Squirrel Tail Dr., Tucson AZ 85704. E-mail: oasis@al-harris.com. Website: www.illinoispoets.org. Contact: Alan Harris. Annual contest to encourage the crafting of excellent poetry. Guidelines and entry forms available for SASE. Deadline: September 30. Cash prizes of $50, $30, and $10. 3 Honorable Mentions. Poet retains all rights. Judged by out-of-state professionals.

INDIANA REVIEW POETRY PRIZE

Indiana Review, Poetry Prize, Indiana Review, Ballantine Hall 529, 1020 E. Kirkwood Ave., Bloomington IN 47405-7103. E-mail: inreview@indiana.edu. Website: www.indianareview.org. Offered annually for unpublished work. Open to any writer. Guidelines available on website. All entries are considered for publication. Deadline: March 31. Submission period begins February 1. Prize: $1,000 and publication. Judged by Gabrielle Calvocoressi in 2018. Different judge every year.

IOWA POETRY PRIZE

University of Iowa Press, University of Iowa Press, 119 West Park Rd.,100 Kuhl House, Iowa City IA 52242-1000. (319)335-2000. Fax: (319)335-2055. E-mail: uipress@uiowa.edu. Website: www.uiowapress.org. Offered annually to encourage poets and their work. Submissions must be postmarked during the month of April; put name on title page only. This page will be removed before ms is judged. Open to writers of English (US citizens or not). Mss will not be returned. Previous winners are not eligible. Deadline: April 30. Prize: Publication under standard royalty agreement.

THE IOWA REVIEW AWARD IN POETRY, FICTION, AND NONFICTION

The Iowa Review, University of Iowa, 308 English-Philosophy Building, Iowa City IA 52242. E-mail: iowa-review@uiowa.edu. Website: www.iowareview.org. *The Iowa Review* Award in Poetry, Fiction, and Nonfiction presents $1,500 to each winner in each genre and $750 to runners-up. Winners and runners-up published in *The Iowa Review*. Deadline: January 31. Submission period begins January 1. Judges for the 2019 Awards are Kiki Petrosino (poetry), Rebecca Makkai (fiction), and Roxane Gay (nonfiction).

ALICE JAMES AWARD

Alice James Books, University of Maine at Farmington, 114 Prescott St., Farmington ME 04938. (207)778-7071. Fax: (207)778-7766. E-mail: ajb@alicejamesbooks.org; info@alice jamesbooks.org. Website: www.alicejamesbooks.org. Contact: Alyssa Neptune, managing editor. Offered annually for unpublished, full-length poetry collections. Emerging and established poets are welcome. Deadline: November 1. Prize: $2,000, publication, and distribution through Consortium.

ALICE JAMES AWARD

Alice James Books, Alice James Award, 114 Prescott St., Farmington ME 04938. (207)778-7071. Fax: (207)778-7766. E-mail: ajb@alicejamesbooks.org. Website:

www.alicejamesbooks.org. **Contact:** Alyssa Neptune, Managing Editor. For complete contest guidelines, visit website or send a SASE. Offered annually for unpublished, full-length, poetry collection. Deadline: November 1. Prize: $2,000 , book publication, and distribution through Consortium. Editorial Board.

JAPAN-U.S. FRIENDSHIP COMMISSION PRIZE FIR THE TRANSLATION OF JAPANESE LITERATURE

Website: http://www.keenecenter.org/. **Contact:** Yoshiko Niiya, Program Coordinator. The Donald Keene Center of Japanese Culture at Columbia University annually awards Japan-U.S. Friendship Commission Prizes for the Translation of Japanese Literature. A prize is given for the best translation of a modern work or a classical work, or the prize is divided between equally distinguished translations. Deadline: June 3. Prize: $6,000.

Translations must be book-length Japanese literary works: novels, collections of short stories, manga, literary essays, memoirs, drama, or poetry. Works may be unpublished manuscripts, works in press, or books published during the 2 years prior to the prize year.

RANDALL JARRELL POETRY COMPETITION

North Carolina Writers' Network, Terry L. Kennedy, MFA Writing Program, 3302 MHRA Building, UNC Greensboro, Greensboro NC 27402-6170. **E-mail:** tlkenned@uncg.edu. **Website:** www.ncwriters.org. **Contact:** Terry L. Kennedy, director. Offered annually for unpublished work to honor Randall Jarrell and his life at UNC Greensboro, by recognizing the best poetry submitted. Deadline: March 1. Prize: $200 and publication at *storySouth* (www.storysouth.com). Judged by Lauren Moseley in 2018.

JUNIPER PRIZE FOR POETRY

University of Massachusetts Press, 180 Infirmary Way, 4th Fl., Amherst MA 01003. (413)545-2217. **Fax:** (413)545-1226. **E-mail:** info@umpress.umass. edu; cjandree@umpress.umass.edu. **E-mail:** juniperprize@umpress.umass.edu. **Website:** www.umass. edu/umpress. **Contact:** Courtney Andree. The University of Massachusetts Press offers the annual Juniper Prize for Poetry, awarded in alternate years for the first and subsequent books. Deadline: September 30. Submission period begins August 1. Winners announced online in April on the press website. Prize: Publication and $1,000 in addition to royalties.

The Juniper Prize for Poetry is awarded annually to two original manuscripts of poems: one first book prize for a previously unpublished author and one prize for a previously published author. The University of Massachusetts Press publishes the winning manuscripts and the authors receive a $1,000 award upon publication.

BARBARA MANDIGO KELLY PEACE POETRY AWARDS

Nuclear Age Peace Foundation, Nuclear Age Peace Foundation, PMB 121, 1187 Coast Village Rd., Suite 1, Santa Barbara CA 93108-2794. (805)965-3443. **Fax:** (805)568-0466. **E-mail:** cwarner@napf.org. **Website:** www.wagingpeace.org; www.peacecontests.org. **Contact:** Carol Warner, Poetry Award Coordinator. The Barbara Mandigo Kelly Peace Poetry Contest was created to encourage poets to explore and illuminate positive visions of peace and the human spirit. The annual contest honors the late Barbara Kelly, a Santa Barbara poet and longtime supporter of peace issues. Awards are given in 3 categories: adult (over 18 years), youth (between 12 and 18 years), and youth under 12. All submitted poems should be unpublished. Deadline: July 1 (postmarked or e-mailed) Prize: Adult: $1,000; Youth (13-18): $200; Youth (12 and under): $200. Honorable Mentions may also be awarded. Judged by a committee of poets selected by the Nuclear Age Peace Foundation. The foundation reserves the right to publish and distribute the award-winning poems, including honorable mentions.

MILTON KESSLER MEMORIAL PRIZE FOR POETRY

Creative Writing Program, Binghamton University, Department of English, General Literature, and Rhetoric, Library North Room 1149, Vestal Parkway East, P.O. Box 6000, Binghamton NY 13902-6000. **Website:** www.binghamton.edu/english/creative-writing/binghamton-center-for-writers/binghamton-book-awards/kessler-poetry-awards.html. **Contact:** Maria Mazziotti Gillan, Director. Annual award for best previously published book (previous year). Deadline: March 1. 1st place: $1,000.

THE HAROLD MORTON LANDON TRANSLATION AWARD

Academy of American Poets, 75 Maiden Lane, Suite 901, New York NY 10038. (212)274-0343. **Fax:** (212)274-9427. **E-mail:** awards@poets.org. **Website:** www.poets.org. **Contact:** Programs Coordinator. This annual award recognizes a poetry collection translated from any language into English and published in the previous calendar year. A noted translator chooses the winning book. Deadline: February 15. Prize: $1,000.

THE JAMES LAUGHLIN AWARD

The James Laughlin Award, The Academy of American Poets, 75 Maiden Lane, Suite 901, New York NY 10038. **Website:** www.poets.org. Offered since 1954, the James Laughlin Award is given to recognize and support a second book of poetry forthcoming in the next calendar year. It is named for the poet and publisher James Laughlin, who founded New Directions in 1936. Deadline: May 15. $5,000; an all-expenses-paid weeklong residency at The Betsy Hotel in Miami Beach, Florida; and distribution of the winning book to approximately 1,000 Academy of American Poets members.

◉ THE STEPHEN LEACOCK MEMORIAL MEDAL FOR HUMOUR

Bette Walker, 149 Peter St. N., Orillia ON L3V 4Z4, Canada. (705)326-9286. **E-mail:** awardschair@leacock.ca. **Website:** www.leacock.ca. **Contact:** Bette Walker, Award Committee, Stephen Leacock Associates. The Leacock Associates awards the prestigious Leacock Medal for the best book of literary humor written by a Canadian and published in the current year. The winning author also receives a cash prize of $15,000, thanks to the generous support of the TD Financial Group. 2 runners-up are each awarded a cash prize of $3,000. Deadline: Postmarked before December 31. Prize: $15,000.

LEAGUE OF UTAH WRITERS WRITING CONTEST

The League of Utah Writers, The League of Utah Writers, P.O. Box 64, Lewiston UT 84320. (435)755-7609. **E-mail:** luwcontest@gmail.com; luwriters@gmail.com. **Website:** www.luwriters.org. Open to any writer, the LUW Contest provides authors an opportunity to get their work read and critiqued. Multiple categories are offered; see website for details. Entries must be the original and unpublished work of the author. Winners are announced at the Annual Writers Round-Up in September. Those not present will be notified by e-mail. Deadline: May 31. Submissions period begins March 1. Prize: Cash prizes are awarded. Judged by professional authors and editors from outside the League.

LES FIGUES PRESS NOS BOOK CONTEST

Les Figues Press, c/o Los Angeles Review of Books, 6671 Sunset Blvd., Suite 1521, Los Angeles CA 90028.

(323)734-4732. **E-mail:** info@lesfigues.com. **Website:** www.lesfigues.com. **Contact:** Teresa Carmody, Founding Editor. Les Figues Press creates aesthetic conversations between writers/artists and readers, especially those interested in innovative/experimental/avant-garde work. The Press intends in the most premeditated fashion to champion the trinity of Beauty, Belief, and Bawdry. Deadline: March 20 (submissions open until midnight PST) Prize: $1,000, plus publication by Les Figues Press.

LEVIS READING PRIZE

Virginia Commonwealth University, Department of English, Levis Reading Prize, VCU Department of English, 900 Park Avenue, Hibbs Hall, Room 306, Box 842005, Richmond VA 23284-2005. (804)828-1331. **Fax:** (804)828-8684. **E-mail:** bloomquistjmp@mymail.vcu.edu. **Website:** www.english.vcu.edu/mfa/levis. **Contact:** John-Michael Bloomquist. Offered annually for books of poetry published in the previous year to encourage poets early in their careers. The entry must be the writer's first or second published book of poetry. Previously published books in other genres, or previously published chapbooks or self-published material, do not count as books for this purpose. Deadline: February 1. Prize: $5,000 and an expense-paid trip to Richmond to present a public reading. Judges come from faculty of the VCU Department of English and MFA Program in Creative Writing.

THE RUTH LILLY POETRY PRIZE

Poetry, 61 W. Superior St., Chicago IL 60654. (312)787-7070. **Fax:** (312)787-6650. **E-mail:** editors@poetrymagazine.org; info@poetryfoundation.org. **Website:** www.poetrymagazine.org. Awarded annually, the $100,000 Ruth Lilly Poetry Prize honors a living U.S. poet whose lifetime accomplishments warrant extraordinary recognition. Established in 1986 by Ruth Lilly, the Prize is one of the most prestigious awards given to American poets and is one of the largest literary honors for work in the English language. Deadline: No submissions or nominations considered. Prize: $100,000.

LITERAL LATTÉ POETRY AWARD

Literal Latté, Literal Latté Awards, 200 E. 10th St., Suite 240, New York NY 10003. **E-mail:** LitLatte@aol.com. **Website:** www.literal-latte.com. **Contact:** Jenine Gordon Bockman, Editor. Offered annually to any writer for unpublished poetry (maximum 2,000 words per poem). All styles welcome. Winners published in *Literal Latté*. Deadline: Postmark by July 15.

Prizes: 1st Place: $1,000; 2nd Place: $300; 3rd Place: $200. Judged by the editors.

LITERAL LATTE FOOD VERSE CONTEST

Literal Latte, 200 E. 10th St., Suite 240, New York NY 10003. **E-mail:** litlatte@aol.com. **Website:** www. literal-latte.com. **Contact:** Jenine Gordon Bockman, editor. 25 years of stimulating the careers of writers and the minds of readers. Open to any writer. Poems should have food as an ingredient. Submissions required to be unpublished. Guidelines online at website. Submit poems, up to 10,000 words each. Literal Latté acquires first rights. Annual contest to give support and exposure to great writing. Deadline: March 15. Prize: $500. Judged by the editors.

THE HUGH J. LUKE AWARD

Prairie Schooner, 110 Andrews Hall, University of Nebraska-Lincoln, Lincoln NE 68588-0334. (402)472-0911. **Fax:** (402)472-1817. **E-mail:** prairieschooner@unl.edu. **Website:** www.prairieschooner.unl.edu. **Contact:** Kwame Dawes. Prize: $250. Judged by editorial staff of *Prairie Schooner*.

LUMINA POETRY CONTEST

Website: www.luminajournal.com. Poetry competition held once every 3 years by the Sarah Lawrence College's graduate literary journal. Rotates with a fiction and nonfiction contest. Deadline: October 15. Prize: 1st Place: $500 and publication; 2nd Place: $250 and publication; 3rd Place: $100 and online publication.

THE MACGUFFIN'S NATIONAL POET HUNT CONTEST

The MacGuffin, Poet Hunt Contest, Schoolcraft College, 18600 Haggerty Rd., Livonia MI 48152. (734)462-5327. **Fax:** (734)462-4679. **E-mail:** macguffin@schoolcraft.edu. **E-mail:** macguffin@schoolcraft.edu. **Website:** https://www.schoolcraft.edu/macguffin/contest-rules. **Contact:** Gordon Krupsky, Managing Editor. *The MacGuffin* is a national literary magazine from Schoolcraft College in Livonia, Michigan. The mission of *The MacGuffin* is to encourage, support, and enhance the literary arts in the Schoolcraft College community, the region, the state, and the nation. Deadline: June 15. Submissions period begins April 1. Prize: $500. Featuring guest judge Richard Tillinghast.

NAOMI LONG MADGETT POETRY AWARD

Broadside Lotus Press, Inc., Broadside Lotus Press, c/o Dr. Gloria House, 8300 East Jefferson Ave., Apt. #504, Detroit MI 48214. (313)736-5338. **E-mail:** broadsidelotus@gmail.com. **Website:** www.broadsidelotuspress.

org. **Contact:** Gloria House. Offered annually to recognize an unpublished book-length poetry ms by an African American. Guidelines available online. Deadline: March 1. Submission period begins January 2. Prize: $500 and publication by Lotus Press.

MAIN STREET RAG'S ANNUAL POETRY BOOK AWARD

Main Street Rag Publishing Company, P.O. Box 690100, Charlotte NC 28227-7001. (704)573-2516. **E-mail:** editor@mainstreetrag.com. **Website:** www. mainstreetrag.com. **Contact:** M. Scott Douglass, publisher/managing editor. The purpose of this contest is to select manuscripts for publication and offer prize money to the manuscript we feel best represents our label. Deadline: February 2. Prize: 1st Place: $1,200 and 50 copies of book; runners-up are also be offered publication. Judged by 1 panel that consists of *MSR* editors, associated editors and college level instructors, and previous contest winners.

✪ THE MALAHAT REVIEW LONG POEM PRIZE

The Malahat Review, Box 1800 STN CSC, Victoria BC V8W 3H5, Canada. **E-mail:** malahat@uvic.ca. **Website:** www.malahatreview.ca. **Contact:** L'Amour Lisik, Publicity Manager.. Long Poem Prize is offered in alternate years with the Novella Contest. Open to any writer. Offers 2 awards of $1,000 CAD each for a long poem or cycle (10-20 printed pages). Includes publication in *The Malahat Review* and a 1-year subscription. Open to entries from Canadian, American, and overseas authors. Obtains first world rights. Publication rights after revert to the author. Deadline: February 1 (odd-numbered years). Prize: Two $1,000 prizes. Winners published in the summer issue of *The Malahat Review*, announced in summer on website, Facebook page, and in quarterly e-newsletter *Malahat lite*. Judged by 3 recognized poets. Preliminary readings by editorial board.

THE MORTON MARR POETRY PRIZE

Southwest Review, Southern Methodist University, P.O. Box 750374, Dallas TX 75275-0374. (214)768-1037. **Fax:** (214)768-1408. **E-mail:** swr@mail.smu.edu. **Website:** www.smu.edu/southwestreview. **Contact:** Greg Brownderville, editor-in-chief. Annual award for poem(s) by a writer who has not yet published a book of poetry. Submit no more than 6 poems in a "traditional" form (e.g., sonnet, sestine, villanelle, rhymed stanzas, blank verse, et al.). Submissions will not be returned. Deadline: September 30. Prizes: $1,000 for 1st place; $500 for 2nd place; plus publication in the *Southwest Review*.

LENORE MARSHALL POETRY PRIZE

The Lenore Marshall Poetry Prize, The Academy of American Poets, 75 Maiden Lane, Suite 901, New York NY 10038. (212)274-0343, Ext. 13. **Fax:** (212)274-9427. **E-mail:** awards@poets.org. **Website:** www.poets.org. **Contact:** Programs Coordinator. Established in 1975, this $25,000 award recognizes the most outstanding book of poetry published in the United States in the previous calendar year. The prize includes distribution of the winning book to hundreds of Academy of American Poets members. Deadline: May 15. Prize: $25,000.

MARSH HAWK PRESS POETRY PRIZE

Marsh Hawk Press, Marsh Hawk Press, Inc., P.O. Box 206, East Rockaway NY 11518-0206. **E-mail:** marshhawkpress1@aol.com. **Website:** www.MarshHawkPress.org. **Contact:** Prize Director. The Marsh Hawk Press Poetry Prize offers $1,000, plus publication of a book-length ms. Additionally, The Robert Creeley Poetry Prize and The Rochelle Ratner Poetry Award, both cash prizes, go to the runners-up. Deadline: 11:59 PM EST on April 30 $1,000; book publication; and promotion, including a book launch in New York City. To be announced

MASS CULTURAL COUNCIL ARTIST FELLOWSHIP PROGRAM

Mass Cultural Council, Mass Cultural Council, 10 St. James Ave., #302, Boston MA 02116-3803. (617)727-3668. **Fax:** (617)727-0044. **E-mail:** mcc@art.state.ma.us. **Website:** www.massculturalcouncil.org; http://artsake.massculturalcouncil.org. **Contact:** Dan Blask, Program Officer. Awards in poetry, fiction/creative nonfiction, and dramatic writing (among other discipline categories) are given in recognition of exceptional original work (check website for award amount). Looking to award artistic excellence and creative ability, based on work submitted for review. Judged by independent peer panels composed of artists and arts professionals.

KATHLEEN MCCLUNG SONNET PRIZE CATEGORY

Soul-Making Keats Literary Competition, The Webhallow House, 1544 Sweetwood Dr., Broadmoor Village CA 94015-2029. **E-mail:** soulkeats@mail.com. **Website:** www.soulmakingcontest.us. **Contact:** Eileen Malone. Call for Shakespearean and Petrarchan

sonnets on the theme of the "beloved." Ongoing Deadline: November 30. Prize:1st Place: $100; 2nd Place: $50; 3rd Place: $25.

MCKNIGHT ARTIST FELLOWSHIPS FOR WRITERS, LOFT AWARD(S) IN CHILDREN'S LITERATURE/CREATIVE PROSE/POETRY

The Loft Literary Center, 1011 Washington Ave. S., Suite 200, Open Book, Minneapolis MN 55415. (612)215-2575. **Fax:** (612)215-2576. **E-mail:** loft@loft.org. **Website:** www.loft.org. **Contact:** Bao Phi. The Loft administers the McKnight Artists Fellowships for Writers. Five $25,000 awards are presented annually to accomplished Minnesota writers and spoken word artists. Four awards alternate annually between creative prose (fiction and creative nonfiction) and poetry/spoken word. The fifth award is presented in children's literature and alternates annually for writing for ages 8 and under and writing for children older than 8. The awards provide the writers the opportunity to focus on their craft for the course of the fellowship year. Prize: $25,000, plus up to $3,000 in reimbursement for a writer's retreat or conference. The judge is announced after selections are made.

MISSISSIPPI REVIEW PRIZE

Mississippi Review, Mississippi Review Prize, 118 College Dr., #5144, Hattiesburg MS 39406-0001. (601)266-4321. **Fax:** (601)266-5757. **E-mail:** msreview@usm.edu. **Website:** www.mississippireview.com. Annual contest starting August 1 and running until January 1. Winners and finalists will make up next spring's print issue of the national literary magazine *Mississippi Review*. Each entrant will receive a copy of the prize issue. Deadline: January 1. Prize: $1,000 in fiction and poetry. Judged by Andrew Malan Milward in fiction, and Angela Ball in poetry.

JENNY MCKEAN MOORE VISITING WRITER

Department of English, George Washington University, Phillips Hall, 801 22nd St. NW, Suite 643, Washington DC 20052. (202)994-6180. **Fax:** (202)994-7915. **E-mail:** engldept@gwu.edu; lpageinc@gwu.edu. **Website:** https://english.columbian.gwu.edu/activities-events. **Contact:** Lisa Page, Director of Creative Writing. The position is filled annually, bringing a visiting writer to The George Washington University. During each semester the Writer teaches 1 creative-writing course at the university as well as a community workshop. Seeks someone specializing in a different genre each year—fiction, poetry, creative nonfiction.

Annual stipend between $50,000 and $60,000, plus reduced-rent townhouse on campus (not guaranteed). Application deadline: December 12. Annual stipend varies, depending on endowment performance; most recently, stipend was $60,000, plus reduced-rent townhouse (not guaranteed).

THE KATHRYN A. MORTON PRIZE IN POETRY

Sarabande Books, Inc., Sarabande Books, Inc., 822 E. Market St., Louisville KY 40206. (502)458-4028. E-mail: info@sarabandebooks.org. Website: www.sarabandebooks.org. Contact: Sarah Gorham, Editor-in-Chief. The Kathryn A. Morton Prize in Poetry is awarded annually to a book-length ms (at least 48 pages). All finalists are considered for publication. Competition receives approximately 1,400 entries. Deadline: February 15. Submissions period begins January 1. Prize: $2,000, publication, and a standard royalty contract.

SHEILA MARGARET MOTTON PRIZE

New England Poetry Club, Mary Buchinger, NEPC President, 53 Regent Street, Cambridge MA 02140. (617)744-6034. E-mail: info@nepoetryclub.org. Website: www.nepoetryclub.org. Contact: Mary Buchinger, NEPC President. Awarded for a book of poems published in the last 2 years. Deadline: May 31. Prize: $250. Judged by well-known poets and sometimes winners of previous NEPC contests.

NATIONAL BOOK AWARDS

The National Book Foundation, 90 Broad St., Suite 604, New York NY 10004. (212)685-0261. E-mail: nationalbook@nationalbook.org. Website: www.nationalbook.org. The National Book Foundation and the National Book Awards celebrate the best of American literature, expand its audience, and enhance the cultural value of great writing in America. The contest offers prizes in 4 categories: fiction, nonfiction, poetry, and young people's literature. Books should be published between December 1 and November 30 of the previous year. Deadline: Submit entry form, payment, and a copy of the book by May 15. Prize: $10,000 in each category. Finalists will each receive a prize of $1,000. Judged by a category specific panel of 5 judges for each category.

🦢 NATIONAL POETRY COMPETITION

The Poetry Society, 22 Betterton St., London WC2H 9BX, United Kingdom. 020 7420 9880. E-mail: info@poetrysociety.org.uk. Website: www.poetrysociety.org.uk. Contact: Competition Organizer. The Poetry Society was founded in 1909 to promote "a more general recognition and appreciation of poetry." Since then, it has grown into one of Britain's most dynamic arts organizations, representing British poetry both nationally and internationally. Today it has nearly 4,000 members worldwide and publishes *The Poetry Review*. With innovative education and commissioning programs, and a packed calendar of performances, readings and competitions, The Poetry Society champions poetry for all ages. Deadline: October 31. 1st Prize: £5,000; 2nd Prize: £2,000; 3rd Prize: £1,000; plus 7 commendations of £200 each. Winners will be published in *The Poetry Review*, and on the Poetry Society website; the top 3 winners will receive a year's free membership of The Poetry Society. Mona Arshi, Helen Mort, and Maurice Riordan

NATIONAL WRITERS ASSOCIATION POETRY CONTEST

The National Writers Association, NWA Poetry Contest, 10940 S. Parker Rd. #508, Parker CO 80134. E-mail: natlwritersassn@hotmail.com. Website: www.nationalwriters.com. Contact: Sandy Whelchel, Director. Annual contest to encourage the writing of poetry, an important form of individual expression but with a limited commercial market. Deadline: October 1. Prize: 1st Place: $100; 2nd Place: $50; 3rd Place: $25.

THE PABLO NERUDA PRIZE FOR POETRY

Nimrod International Journal, 800 S. Tucker Dr., Tulsa OK 74104. (918)631-3080. Fax: (918)631-3033. E-mail: nimrod@utulsa.edu. Website: www.utulsa.edu/nimrod. Contact: Eilis O'Neal. Annual award to discover new writers of vigor and talent. Open to US residents only. Deadline: April 30. Prizes: 1st Place: $2,000 and publication; 2nd Place: $1,000 and publication. Judged by the *Nimrod* editors (finalists). A recognized author selects the winners.

THE NEUTRINO SHORT-SHORT CONTEST

Passages North, Passages North, Northern Michigan University, 1401 Presque Isle Ave., Marquette MI 49855. (906)227-1203. Fax: (906)227-1096. E-mail: passages@nmu.edu. Website: www.passagesnorth.com. Contact: Jennifer Howard. Offered every 2 years to publish new voices in literary fiction, nonfiction, hybrid-essays, and prose poems (maximum 1,000 words). Guidelines available for SASE or online. Deadline: April 15. Submission period begins February 15. Prize: $1,000, and publication for the winner; 2 honorable mentions also published; all entrants receive a copy of *Passages North*. 2019: Tarfia Faizullah

THE NEW ISSUES POETRY PRIZE

New Issues Poetry & Prose, New Issues Poetry & Prose, Department of English, Western Michigan University, 1903 W. Michigan Ave., Kalamazoo MI 49008-5463. **E-mail:** new-issues@wmich.edu. **Website:** www.new-issuespress.com. Offered annually for publication of a first book of poems by a poet writing in English who has not previously published a full-length collection of poems in an edition of 500 or more copies. *New Issues Poetry & Prose* obtains rights for first publication. Book is copyrighted in author's name. Guidelines for SASE or online. Additional mss will be considered from those submitted to the competition for publication. Considers simultaneous submissions, but *New Issues* must be notified of acceptance elsewhere. Deadline: December 30. Prize: $1,000, publication of a book of poems, reading w/ $500 stipend + travel costs. A national judge selects the prize winner and recommends other mss. The editors decide on the other books considering the judge's recommendation, but are not bound by it. 2018 judge: Cathy Park Hong.

NEW LETTERS LITERARY AWARDS

New Letters, University of Missouri-Kansas City, 5101 Rockhill Rd., Kansas City MO 64110-2499. (816)235-1168. **E-mail:** newletters@umkc.edu. **Website:** www.newletters.org/writers-wanted/writing-contests. **Contact:** Ashley Wann. Award has 3 categories (fiction, poetry, and creative nonfiction) with 1 winner in each. Offered annually for previously unpublished work. For guidelines, send an SASE to *New Letters*, or visit http://www.newletters.org/writers-wanted/writing-contests. Deadline: May 18. 1st place: $1,500, plus publication in poetry and fiction category; 1st place: $2,500, plus publication in essay category. Judged by regional writers of prominence and experience. Final judging by someone of national repute. Previous judges include Maxine Kumin, Albert Goldbarth, Charles Simic, and Janet Burroway.

NEW LETTERS PRIZE FOR POETRY

New Letters Awards for Writers, UMKC, University House, 5101 Rockhill Rd., Kansas City MO 64110-2499. (816)235-1168. **E-mail:** newletters@umkc.edu. **Website:** www.newletters.org. **Contact:** Ashley Wann. The annual *New Letters* Poetry Prize awards $1,500 and publication in *New Letters* (see separate listing in Magazines/Journals) to the best group of 3-6 poems. All entries will be considered for publication in *New Letters*. Deadline: May 20 (postmarked). $1,500 and publication.

NEW MILLENNIUM AWARDS FOR FICTION, POETRY, AND NONFICTION

New Millennium Writings, New Millennium Writings, 340 S Lemon Ave #6906, Walnut CA 91789. (865)254-4880. **Website:** www.newmillenniumwritings.org. **Contact:** Alexis Williams, Editor and Publisher. No restrictions as to style, content, or number of submissions. Previously published pieces acceptable if online or under 5,000 print circulation. Simultaneous and multiple submissions welcome. Deadline: Postmarked on or before January 31 for the Winter Awards and June 23 for the Summer Awards. Prize: $1,000 for Best Poem; $1,000 for Best Fiction; $1,000 for Best Nonfiction; $1,000 for Best Flash Fiction (Short-Short Fiction).

NEW SOUTH WRITING CONTEST

English Department, Georgia State University, P.O. Box 3970, Atlanta GA 30302-3970. **E-mail:** newsoutheditors@gmail.com. **Website:** newsouthjournal.com/contest. **Contact:** Anna Sandy, editor-in-chief. Offered annually to publish the most promising work of up-and-coming writers of poetry (up to 3 poems) and fiction (9,000-word limit). Rights revert to writer upon publication. Guidelines online. Deadline: April 15. Prize: 1st Place: $1,000 in each category; 2nd Place: $250 Judged by Natalie Eilbert in poetry and SJ Sindu in prose.

NFSPS POETRY CONVENTION MADNESS CONTEST

Peter Stein, PO Box 17344, Minneapolis MN 55417. **E-mail:** pwilliamstein@yahoo.com; schambersmediator@yahoo.com. **Website:** www.mnpoets.com. **Contact:** Peter Stein; Sue Chambers. Enter to win your way to the NFSPS National Poetry Convention in Chaska, MN, June 9th-13th. For more details about the event, visit www.nfspsconvention.com. Deadline: January 31. Prizes: 1st Place: Hotel Lodging at Oak Ridge Convention Center for 4 nights, June 9th-12th. 2nd Place: Meals payed for during the course of the convention. 3rd Place: Registration to the Convention. 1st-3rd Honorable Mentions: Subscription to Poem by Post for one year.

THE NIGHTBOAT POETRY PRIZE

Nightboat Books, 310 Nassau Avenue, Brooklyn NY 11222. **E-mail:** info@nightboat.org. **Website:** www.nightboat.org. **Contact:** Stephen Motika. Annual contest for previously unpublished collection of poetry (48-90 pages). Deadline: November 15. 1st place: $1,000, plus publication and 25 copies of published book.

NORTH CAROLINA WRITERS' FELLOWSHIPS

North Carolina Arts Council, NC Department of Natural and Cultural Resources, North Carolina Arts Council, Mail Service Center #4632, Raleigh NC 27699-4632. (919)814-6512. **E-mail:** david.potorti@ncdcr.gov. **Website:** www.ncarts.org. **Contact:** David Potorti, literature and theater director. The North Carolina Arts Council offers fellowship grants to support writers of fiction, creative non-fiction, poetry, spoken word, playwrighting, screenwriting and literary translation. Offered every even-numbered year to support writers of fiction, creative non-fiction, poetry, spoken word, playwriting, screenwriting and literary translation. See website for guidelines and other eligibility requirements. Deadline: November 1 of even-numbered years. Next deadline is Nov. 1, 2020. Prize: $10,000 grant. Reviewed by a panel of literature professionals (writers and editors).

NORTHERN CALIFORNIA BOOK AWARDS

Northern California Book Reviewers Association, Northern California Book Awards, c/o Poetry Flash, 1450 Fourth St. #4, Att'n: NCBR, Berkeley CA 94710. (510)525-5476. **E-mail:** ncbr@poetryflash.org; editor@poetryflash.org. **Website:** www.poetryflash.org. **Contact:** Joyce Jenkins, Executive Director. Annual Northern California Book Award for outstanding book in literature; open to books published in the current calendar year by Northern California authors. NCBR presents annual awards to Bay Area (northern California) authors annually in fiction, nonfiction, poetry, and children's literature. Encourages writers and stimulates interest in books and reading. Deadline: January 18. Prize: $100 honorarium and award certificate. Judging by voting members of the Northern California Book Reviewers.

◑ NOVA WRITES COMPETITION FOR UNPUBLISHED MANUSCRIPTS

Writers' Federation of Nova Scotia, 1113 Marginal Rd., Halifax NS B3H 4P7. (902)423-8116. **Fax:** (902)422-0881. **E-mail:** programs@writers.ns.ca. **Website:** www.writers.ns.ca. **Contact:** Robin Spittal, Communications and Development Officer. Annual program designed to honor work by unpublished writers in all 4 Atlantic Provinces. Entry is open to writers unpublished in the category of writing they wish to enter. Prizes are presented in the fall of each year. Categories include: short form creative nonfiction, long form creative nonfiction, novel, poetry, short story, and writing for children/young adult novel. Judges return written comments when competition is concluded. Deadline: January 3. Prizes vary based on categories. See website for details.

OHIO POETRY DAY CONTESTS

Dept. of English, Heidelberg College, 310 East Market, Tiffin OH 44883. **Website:** ohiopoetryday.blogspot.com. **Contact:** Bill Reyer, Contest Chair. Several poetry categories open to poets from Ohio and out-of-state. Deadline: May 15. Prizes range $5-100.

OKLAHOMA BOOK AWARDS

200 NE 18th St., Oklahoma City OK 73105. (405)521-2502. **Fax:** (405)525-7804. **E-mail:** connie.armstrong@libraries.ok.gov. **Website:** www.odl.state.ok.us/ocb. **Contact:** Connie Armstrong, executive director. This award honors Oklahoma writers and books about Oklahoma. Awards are presented to best books in fiction, nonfiction, children's, design and illustration, and poetry books about Oklahoma or books written by an author who was born, is living or has lived in Oklahoma. SASE for award rules and entry forms. Winner will be announced at banquet in Oklahoma City. The Arrell Gibson Lifetime Achievement Award is also presented each year for a body of work. Deadline: January 10. Prize: Awards a medal. Judging by a panel of 5 people for each category, generally a librarian, a working writer in the genre, booksellers, editors, etc.

◑ OPEN SEASON AWARDS

The Malahat Review, University of Victoria, P.O. Box 1700, Stn CSC, Victoria BC V8V 2Y2, Canada. (250)721-8524. **Fax:** (250)472-5051. **E-mail:** malahat@uvic.ca. **Website:** www.malahatreview.ca. **Contact:** L'Amour Lisik, publicity manager. The Open Season Awards accepts entries of poetry, fiction, and creative nonfiction. Winners published in the spring issue of *The Malahat Review*, announced in the winter on our website, social media pages, and in our monthly e-newsletter, *Malahat lite*. Deadline: November 1. Prize: $6,000 over three categories (poetry, fiction, creative nonfiction) and publication in *The Malahat Review*.

OREGON BOOK AWARDS

925 SW Washington St., Portland OR 97205. (503)227-2583. **Fax:** (503)241-4256. **E-mail:** la@literary-arts.org. **Website:** www.literary-arts.org. **Contact:** Susan Denning, director of programs and events. The annual Oregon Book Awards celebrate Oregon authors in the areas of poetry, fiction, nonfiction, drama and young readers'

literature published between August 1 and July 31 of the previous calendar year. Awards are available for every category. See website for details. Deadline: August 26. Prize: Grant of $2,500. (Grant money could vary.) Judged by writers who are selected from outside Oregon for their expertise in a genre. Past judges include Mark Doty, Colson Whitehead and Kim Barnes.

OREGON LITERARY FELLOWSHIPS

925 S.W. Washington, Portland OR 97205. (503)227-2583. **E-mail:** susan@literary-arts.org. **Website:** www.literary-arts.org. **Contact:** Susan Moore, Director of programs and events. Oregon Literary Fellowships are intended to help Oregon writers initiate, develop, or complete literary projects in poetry, fiction, literary nonfiction, drama, and young readers literature. Writers in the early stages of their career are encouraged to apply. The awards are merit-based. Deadline: Last Friday in June. Prize: $3,000 minimum award, for approximately 8 writers and 2 publishers. Judged by out-of-state writers

GUY OWEN AWARD

Southern Poetry Review, Department of Languages, Literature, and Philosophy, Armstrong Atlantic State University, 11935 Abercorn St., Savannah GA 31419-1997. (912)344-3196. **E-mail:** editor@southernpoetryreview.org. **Website:** www.southernpoetryreview.org. **Contact:** Tony Morris, associate editor. The annual Guy Owen Prize offers $1,000 and publication in *Southern Poetry Review* to the winning poem selected by a distinguished poet. All entries will be considered for publication. Deadline: May 31 (postmarked). Open to submissions March 1.

PANGAEA PRIZE

The Poet's Billow, 6135 Avon St, Portage MI 49024. **E-mail:** thepoetsbillow@gmail.com. **Website:** http://thepoetsbillow.org. **Contact:** Robert Evory. Annual award open to any writer to recognize the best series of poems, ranging between two and up to seven poems in a group. Finalists with strong work will also be published. Submissions must be previously unpublished. Please submit online. Deadline: May 1. Prize: $100. The winning poem will be published and displayed in The Poet's Billow Literary Art Gallery and nominated for a Pushcart Prize. If the poet qualifies, the poem will also be submitted to The Best New Poets anthology. Judged by the editors, and, occasionally, a guest judge.

THE PATERSON POETRY PRIZE

The Poetry Center at Passaic County Community College, One College Blvd., Paterson NJ 07505. (973)684-

6555. **Fax:** (973)523-6085. **E-mail:** mgillan@pccc.edu. **Website:** www.pccc.edu/poetry. **Contact:** Maria Mazziotti Gillan, executive director. The Paterson Poetry Prize offers an annual award for the strongest book of poems (48 or more pages) published in the previous year. The winner will be asked to participate in an awards ceremony and to give a reading at The Poetry Center. Minimum press run: 500 copies. Publishers may submit more than 1 title for prize consideration; 3 copies of each book must be submitted. Include SASE for results; books will not be returned (all entries will be donated to The Poetry Center Library). Guidelines and application form (required) available for SASE or on website. Deadline: February 1. Prize: $1,000.

PAVEMENT SAW PRESS CHAPBOOK AWARD

321 Empire St., Montpelier OH 43543-1301. **E-mail:** info@pavementsaw.org. **E-mail:** editor@pavementsaw.org. **Website:** www.pavementsaw.org. **Contact:** David Baratier, editor. Pavement Saw Press has been publishing steadily since the fall of 1993. Each year since 1999, they have published at least 4 full-length paperback poetry collections, with some printed in library edition hard covers, 1 chapbook, and a yearly literary journal anthology. They specialize in finding authors who have been widely published in literary journals but have not published a chapbook or full-length book. Deadline: December 31 (postmark). Prize: Chapbook Award offers $500, publication, and 40 author copies.

JUDITH SIEGEL PEARSON AWARD

E-mail: fm8146@wayne.edu. **Website:** https://wsuwritingawards.submittable.com/submit. **Contact:** Donovan Hohn. Offers an annual award for the best creative or scholarly work on a subject concerning women. The type of work accepted rotates each year: nonfiction in 2018; fiction in 2019; drama in 2020, poetry in 2021. Open to all interested writers and scholars. Only submit the appropriate genre in each year. Deadline: February 22. Prize: $500. Judged by members of the writing faculty of the Wayne State University English Department.

JEAN PEDRICK PRIZE

New England Poetry Club, 2 Farrar St., Cambridge MA 02138. **E-mail:** contests@nepoetryclub.org. **Website:** www.nepoetryclub.org. **Contact:** Audrey Kalajin. Prize for a chapbook of poems published in the last two years. Deadline: May 31. Prize: $100. Judged by well-known poets and sometimes winners of previous NEPC contests.

PEN AWARD FOR POETRY IN TRANSLATION

PEN America, 588 Broadway, Suite 303, New York NY 10012. **E-mail:** awards@pen.org. **Website:** www.pen.org/awards. **Contact:** Arielle Anema. This award recognizes book-length translations of poetry from any language into English, published during the current calendar year. All books must have been published in the US. Translators may be of any nationality. US residency/citizenship not required. Deadline: Submissions are accepted during the summer of each year. Visit PEN.org/awards for updated on deadline dates. Prize: $3,000. Judged by a single translator of poetry appointed by the PEN Translation Committee.

PEN CENTER USA LITERARY AWARDS

(323)424-4939. **E-mail:** awards@penusa.org. **E-mail:** awards@penusa.org. **Website:** www.penusa.org. Offered for work published or produced in the previous calendar year. Open to writers living west of the Mississippi River. Award categories: fiction, poetry, research nonfiction, creative nonfiction, translation, young adult, graphic literature, drama, screenplay, teleplay, journalism. Deadline: See website for details. Prize: $1,000.

PEN/JOYCE OSTERWEIL AWARD FOR POETRY

E-mail: awards@pen.org. **Website:** www.pen.org/awards. **Contact:** Arielle Anema, Literary Awards Coordinator. *Candidates may only be nominated by members of PEN.* This award recognizes the high literary character of the published work to date of a new and emerging American poet of any age, and the promise of further literary achievement. Nominated writer may not have published more than 1 book of poetry. Offered in odd-numbered years and alternates with the PEN/Voelcker Award for Poetry. Submissions will be accepted during the summer of even-numbered year. Visit PEN.org/awards for up-to-date information on deadlines. Prize: $5,000. Judged by a panel of 3 judges selected by the PEN Awards Committee.

PENNSYLVANIA POETRY SOCIETY ANNUAL CONTESTS

5 Coachmans Court, Norwalk CT 06850. **Website:** nfsps.com/pa. **Contact:** Colleen Yarusavage. Pennsylvania Poetry Society offers several categories of poetry contests with a range of prizes from $10-100. Deadline: January 15.

PEN/VOELCKER AWARD FOR POETRY

E-mail: awards@pen.org. **Website:** www.pen.org/awards. **Contact:** Arielle Anema, Literary Awards Coordinator. The PEN/Voelcker Award for Poetry, established by a bequest from Hunce Voelcker, this award is given to a poet whose distinguished and growing body of work to date represents a notable and accomplished presence in American literature. The poet honored by the award is one for whom the exceptional promise seen in earlier work has been fulfilled, and who continues to mature with each successive volume of poetry. The award is given in even-numbered years and carries a stipend of $5,000. Deadline: Nominations from PEN Members will be accepted during the summer of each odd-numbered year. Visit PEN.org/awards for up-to-date information on deadlines. Prize: $5,000. Judged by a panel of 3 poets or other writers chosen by the PEN Literary Awards Committee.

PERUGIA PRESS PRIZE

Perugia Press, P.O. Box 60364, Florence MA 01062. **Website:** www.perugiapress.com. **Contact:** Susan Kan. The Perugia Press Prize is for a first or second poetry book by a woman. Poet must have no more than 1 previously published book of poems (chapbooks don't count). Deadline: November 15. Open to submissions on August 1. Prize: $1,000 and publication. Judged by panel of Perugia authors, booksellers, scholars, etc.

THE PINCH LITERARY AWARDS

Literary Awards, The Pinch, Department of English, The University of Memphis, Memphis TN 38152-6176. (901)678-4591. **Website:** www.pinchjournal.com. Offered annually for unpublished short stories and prose of up to 5,000 words and 1-3 poems. Deadline: March 15. Open to submissions on December 15. Prizes: $1,000 for 1st place in each category.

THE PLEIADES PRESS EDITORS PRIZE FOR POETRY

Pleiades Press, Pleiades Press, Dept of English, Martin 336, University of Central Missouri, Warrensburg MO 64093. (660)543-8106. **E-mail:** pleiades@ucmo.edu. **Website:** www.ucmo.edu/pleiades/. The annual Pleiades Press Editors Prize for Poetry is open to all American writers, regardless of previous publication. Submission must be unpublished as a collection, but individual poems may have been previously published elsewhere. Submit at least 48 pages of poetry (one copy). Include 2 cover sheets: one with ms title, poet's name, address, and phone number; the second with ms title only. Also include acknowledgments page for previously published poems. Guidelines online. Deadline: May 11. Prize: $2,000 and the winning collection will be published in paperback and nationally distributed.

PNWA LITERARY CONTEST

Pacifc Northwest Writers Association, PMB 2717, 1420 NW Gilman Blvd., Suite 2, Issaquah WA 98027. (452)673-2665. **Fax:** (452)961-0768. **E-mail:** pnwa@pnwa.org. **Website:** www.pnwa.org. Annual literary contest with 12 different categories. See website for details and specific guidelines. Each entry receives 2 critiques. Winners announced at the PNWA Summer Conference, held annually in mid-July. Deadline: February 20. Prize: 1st Place: $600; 2nd Place: $300; 3rd Place: $100. Judged by an agent or editor attending the conference.

THE POETRY CENTER BOOK AWARD

The Poetry Center, San Francisco State University, 1600 Holloway Ave., San Francisco CA 94132. (415)338-2227. **Fax:** (415)338-0966. **E-mail:** poetry@sfsu.edu. **Website:** www.sfsu.edu/~poetry. Offered annually for books of poetry and chapbooks, published in year of the prize. "Prize given for an extraordinary book of American poetry written in English." Please include a cover letter noting author name, book title(s), name of person issuing check, and check number. Will not consider anthologies or translations. Deadline: January 31 for books published and copywrited in the previous year. 1st place: $500 and an invitation to read in the Poetry Center Reading Series.

POETRY SOCIETY OF AMERICA AWARDS

15 Gramercy Park, New York NY 10003. **E-mail:** psa@poetrysociety.org. **Website:** www.poetrysociety.org. Offers 7 categories of poetry prizes between $250-2,500. 5 categories are open to PSA members only. Free entry for members; $15 for non-members. Submit between October 1-December 22.

POETS & PATRONS ANNUAL CHICAGOLAND POETRY CONTEST

Sponsored by Poets & Patrons of Chicago, 416 Gierz St., Downers Grove IL 60515. **E-mail:** eatonb1016@aol.com. **Website:** www.poetsandpatrons.net. **Contact:** Barbara Eaton, director. Annual contest for unpublished poetry. Guidelines available for self-addressed, stamped envelope. The purpose of the contest is to encourage the crafting of poetry. Deadline: September 1. Prize: 1st Place: $45; 2nd Place: $20; 3rd Place: $10 cash. Poet retains rights. Judged by out-of-state professionals.

POETS OUT LOUD PRIZE

Poets Out Loud, Fordham University at Lincoln Center, 113 W. 60th St., Room 924-I, New York NY 10023. (212)636-6792. **Fax:** (212)636-7153. **E-mail:** pol@fordham.edu. **Website:** www.fordham.edu/pol. Annual competition for an unpublished, full-length poetry ms (50-80 pages). Deadline: November 1. Prize: $1,000, book publication, and book launch in POL reading series.

FELIX POLLAK PRIZE IN POETRY

University of Wisconsin Press, 1930 Monroe St., 3rd Floor, Madison WI 53711. (608)263-1110. **Fax:** (608)263-1120. **E-mail:** uwiscpress@wisc.edu. **Website:** uwpress.wisc.edu. The Felix Pollak Prize in Poetry is awarded annually to the best book-length ms of original poetry submitted in an open competition. The award is administered by the University of Wisconsin–Madison English department, and the winner is chosen by a nationally recognized poet. The resulting book is published by the University of Wisconsin Press. Deadline: September 15. Prize: $1,000 cash prize, plus publication.

A. POULIN, JR. POETRY PRIZE

BOA Editions, Ltd., 250 Goodman St. N., Suite 306, Rochester NY 14607. **E-mail:** contact@boaeditions.org. **Website:** www.boaeditions.org. The A. Poulin, Jr. Poetry Prize is awarded to honor a poet's first book, while also honoring the late founder of BOA Editions, Ltd., a not-for-profit publishing house of poetry, poetry in translation, and short fiction. Published books in other genres do not disqualify contestants from entering this contest. Deadline: November 30. Open to submissions on August 1. Prize: Awards $1,000 honorarium and book publication in the A. Poulin, Jr. New Poets of America Series.

PRAIRIE SCHOONER BOOK PRIZE

Prairie Schooner and the University of Nebraska Press, Prairie Schooner Prize Series, 123 Andrews Hall, Lincoln NE 68588-0334. (402)472-0911. **E-mail:** PSBookPrize@unl.edu. **Website:** prairieschooner.unl.edu. **Contact:** Kwame Dawes, editor. Annual competition/award for poetry and short story collections. Deadline: March 15. Prize: $3,000 and publication through the University of Nebraska Press.

PRESS 53 AWARD FOR POETRY

Press 53, 560 N. Trade St., Suite 103, Winston-Salem NC 27101. (336)770-5353. **E-mail:** kevin@press53.com. **Website:** www.press53.com. **Contact:** Kevin

Morgan Watson, publisher. Awarded to an outstanding, unpublished collection of poetry. Deadline: July 31. Submission period begins April 1. Winner and finalists announced on by November 1. Publication in April. Prize: Publication of winning poetry collection as a Tom Lombardo Poetry Selection, $1,000 cash advance and 50 copies of the book. Judged by Press 53 poetry series editor Tom Lombardo.

PRIME NUMBER MAGAZINE AWARDS

Press 53, 560 N. Trade St., Suite 103, Winston-Salem NC 27101. (336)770-5353. **E-mail:** kevin@press53.com. **Website:** www.press53.com. **Contact:** Kevin Morgan Watson, publisher. Awards $1,000 each for poetry and short fiction. Deadline: April 15. Submission period begins January 1. Finalists and winners announced by August 1. Winners published in Prime Number Magazine in October. Prize: $1,000 cash. All winners receive publication in Prime Number Magazine online. Judged by industry professionals to be named when the contest begins.

✪ PRISM INTERNATIONAL ANNUAL SHORT FICTION, POETRY, AND CREATIVE NONFICTION CONTESTS

PRISM International, Creative Writing Program, UBC, Buch. E462, 1866 Main Mall, Vancouver BC V6T 1Z1, Canada. **E-mail:** promotions@prismmagazine.ca. **Website:** www.prismmagazine.ca. **Contact:** Claire Matthews. Offered annually for unpublished work to award the best in contemporary fiction, poetry, drama, translation, and nonfiction. Works of translation are eligible. Guidelines are available on website. Acquires first North American serial rights upon publication, and limited web rights for pieces selected for website. Open to any writer except students and faculty in the Creative Writing Department at UBC, or people who have taken a creative writing course at UBC within 2 years of the contest deadline. Entry includes subscription. Deadlines: Creative Nonfiction: July 15; Fiction: January 15; Poetry: October 15. Prize: All grand prizes are $1,500, $600 for first runner up, and $400 for second runner up. Winners are published.

THE PSA NATIONAL CHAPBOOK FELLOWSHIPS

Poetry Society of America, 15 Gramercy Park, New York NY 10003. (212)254-9628. **Fax:** (212)673-2352. **Website:** www.poetrysociety.org. Open to any US citizen or anyone currently living within the US who has not published a full-length poetry collection. Charges

$12 entry fee. Winner receives $1,000 and welcomed as guest for a month-long artist's residency at PLAYA and invited to teach a single class at Purchase College for $1,000 under the sponsorshp of the Royal and Shirley Durst Chair in Literature. Deadline: December 22.

PUSHCART PRIZE

Pushcart Press, P.O. Box 380, Wainscott NY 11975. (631)324-9300. **Website:** www.pushcartprize.com. **Contact:** Bill Henderson. Published every year since 1976, The Pushcart Prize - Best of the Small Presses series "is the most honored literary project in America. Hundreds of presses and thousands of writers of short stories, poetry and essays have been represented in the pages of our annual collections." Little magazine and small book press editors (print or online) may make up to six nominations from their year's publicatoins by the deadline. The nominations may be any combination of poetry, short fiction, essays or literary whatnot. Editors may nominate self-contained portions of books — for instance, a chapter from a novel. Deadline: December 1.

RATTLE POETRY PRIZE

Rattle, 12411 Ventura Blvd., Studio City CA 91604. (818)505-6777. **E-mail:** tim@rattle.com. **Website:** www.rattle.com. **Contact:** Timothy Green, Editor.. *Rattle's* mission is to promote the practice of poetry. "More than anything, our goal is to promote a community of active poets." Deadline: July 15. Prize: One $10,000 winner and ten $200 finalists will be selected in a blind review by the editors of *Rattle* and printed in the Winter issue; one $1,000 Readers' Choice Award will then be chosen from among the finalists by subscriber and entrant vote. Judged by the editors of *Rattle*.

✪ THE RBC BRONWEN WALLACE AWARD FOR EMERGING WRITERS

The Writers' Trust of Canada, 460 Richmond St. W., Suite 600, Toronto ON M5C 1P1, Canada. (416)504-8222. **Fax:** (416)504-9090. **E-mail:** djackson@writerstrust.com. **Website:** www.writerstrust.com. **Contact:** Devon Jackson. Presented annually to a Canadian writer under the age of 35 who is not yet published in book form. The award, which alternates each year between poetry and short fiction, was established in memory of Bronwen Wallace and honours her wish to help more writers achieve success at a young age. Prize: $10,000. Two finalists receive $2,500 each.

RHINO FOUNDERS' PRIZE

RHINO, The Poetry Forum, P.O. Box 591, Evanston IL 60204. **E-mail:** editors@rhinopoetry.org. **Website:**

rhinopoetry.org. **Contact:** Editors. Send best unpublished poetry (3-5 pages). Visit website for previous winners and more information. Deadline: October 31. Open to submissions on September 1. Prize: $500, publication, featured on website, and nominated for a Pushcart Prize. Two runners-ups will receive $50, publication, and will be featured on website. Occasionally nominates runner-up for a Pushcart Prize.

RHODE ISLAND ARTIST FELLOWSHIPS AND INDIVIDUAL PROJECT GRANTS

Rhode Island State Council on the Arts, State of Rhode Island, One Capitol Hill, 3rd Floor, Providence RI 02908. (401)222-3880. **Fax:** (401)222-3018. **E-mail:** Cristina.DiChiera@arts.ri.gov. **Website:** www.arts.ri.gov. **Contact:** Cristina DiChiera, director of individual artist programs. Annual fellowship competition is based upon panel review of poetry, fiction, and playwriting/screenwriting manuscripts. Project grants provide funds for community-based arts projects. Rhode Island artists who have lived in the state for at least 12 consecutive months may apply without a nonprofit sponsor. Applicants for all RSCA grant and award programs must be at least 18 years old and not currently enrolled in an arts-related degree program. Online application and guidelines can be found at www.arts.ri.gov/grants/guidelines/. Deadline: April 1 and October 1. Fellowship awards: $5,000 and $1,000. Grants range from $500-5,000, with an average of around $1,500. Judged by a rotating panel of artists.

ROANOKE-CHOWAN POETRY AWARD

The North Carolina Literary & Historical Assoc., 4610 Mail Service Center, Raleigh NC 27699-4610. (919)807-7290. **Fax:** (919)733-8807. **E-mail:** michael.hill@ncdcr.gov. **Website:** litandhist.ncdcr.gov. **Contact:** Michael Hill, awards coordinator. Offers annual award for an original volume of poetry published during the 12 months ending June 30 of the year for which the award is given. Deadline: July 15.

LORI RUDNITSKY FIRST BOOK PRIZE

Persea Books, P.O. Box 1388, Columbia MO 65205. **Website:** www.perseabooks.com. "This annual competition sponsors the publication of a poetry collection (at least 40 pages) by an American woman poet who has yet to publish a full-length book of poems." Deadline: October 31. Prize: $1,000, plus publication of book. In addition, the winner receives the option of an all-expenses-paid residency at the Civitella Ranieri Center, a renowned artists retreat housed in a 15th-century castle in Umbertide, Italy.

BENJAMIN SALTMAN POETRY AWARD

Red Hen Press, P.O. Box 40820, Pasadena CA 91114. (818)831-0649. **Fax:** (818)831-6659. **E-mail:** productioncoordinator@redhen.org. **Website:** www.redhen.org. Offered annually for unpublished work to publish a winning book of poetry. Open to any writer. Deadline: August 31. 1st place: $3,000 and publication.

ERNEST SANDEEN PRIZE IN POETRY AND THE RICHARD SULLIVAN PRIZE IN SHORT FICTION

University of Notre Dame, Dept. of English, 356 O'Shaughnessy Hall, Notre Dame IN 46556-5639. (574)631-7526. **Fax:** (574)631-4795. **E-mail:** creativewriting@nd.edu. **Website:** http://english.nd.edu/creative-writing/publications/sandeen-sullivan-prizes. **Contact:** Director of Creative Writing. The Sandeen & Sullivan Prizes in Poetry and Short Fiction is awarded to the author who has published at least one volume of short fiction or one volume of poetry. Awarded biannually, but judged quadrennially. Submissions Period: May 1 - September 1. Prize: $1,000, a $500 award and a $500 advance against royalties from the Notre Dame Press.

MAY SARTON AWARD

New England Poetry Club, 654 Green St., No. 2, Cambridge MA 02139. (617)744-6034. **E-mail:** contests@nepoetryclub.org. **Website:** www.nepoetryclub.org. **Contact:** NEPC contest coordinator. "Given intermittently to a poet whose work is an inspiration to other poets. Recipients are chosen by the board." To recognize emerging poets of exceptional promise and distinguished achievement. Established to honor the memory of longtime Academy Fellow May Sarton, a poet, novelist, and teacher who during her career encouraged the work of young poets. Deadline: May 31. Prize: $250. Judges are well-known poets and sometimes winners of previous NEPC contests.

☺ SASKATCHEWAN BOOK AWARDS

315-1102 8th Ave., Regina SK S4R 1C9, Canada. (306)569-1585. **E-mail:** director@bookawards.sk.ca. **Website:** www.bookawards.sk.ca. **Contact:** Courtney Bates-Hardy, executive director. Saskatchewan Book Awards celebrates, promotes, and rewards Saskatchewan authors and publishers worthy of recognition through 14 awards, granted on an annual or semiannual basis. Awards: Fiction, Nonfiction, Poetry, Scholarly, First Book, Prix du Livre Français, Regina, Saskatoon, Indigenous Peoples' Writing, Indigenous Peoples' Publishing, Publishing in Education, Publishing, Children's Literature/Young Adult Literature, Book of the Year. November 1. Prize: $2,000 (CAD) for all awards except Book of the Year, which is $3,000 (CAD). Juries are made up of writing and publishing professionals from outside of Saskatchewan.

THE SCARS EDITOR'S CHOICE AWARDS

E-mail: editor@scars.tv. **Website:** http://scars.tv (contest direct link http://scars.tv/contests.htm). **Contact:** Janet Kuypers, editor/publisher (whom all reading fee checks need to be made out to). Award to showcase good writing in an annual book. Prize: Publication of story/essay and 1 copy of the book.

THE MONA SCHREIBER PRIZE FOR HUMOROUS FICTION AND NONFICTION

3940 Laurel Canyon Blvd., #566, Studio City CA 91604, USA. **E-mail:** brad.schreiber@att.net. **Website:** www.bradschreiber.com. **Contact:** Brad Schreiber.. Established in 2000 to honor Mona Schreiber, a writer and teacher. Entry fees are the same as in 2000 and money from entries helps pay for prizes. The purpose of the contest is to award the most creative humor writing, in any form, under than 750 words, in either fiction or nonfiction, including but not limited to stories, articles, essays, speeches, shopping lists, diary entries, or anything else writers dream up. Complete rules and previous winning entries on website. Deadline: December 1. Prize: 1st Place: $500; 2nd Place: $250; 3rd Place: $100. Judged by Brad Schreiber, journalist, consultant, instructor, author of, among other books, the humor-writing, how-to *What Are You Laughing At?*

SCREAMINMAMAS MOTHER'S DAY POETRY CONTEST

1911 Cleveland St., Hollywood FL 33020. **E-mail:** screaminmamas@gmail.com. **Website:** www.screaminmamas.com/contests. **Contact:** Darlene Pistocchi, editor/managing director. "What does it mean to be a mom? There is so much to being a mom—get deep, get creative! We challenge you to explore different types of poetry: descriptive, reflective, narrative, lyric, sonnet, ballad, limerick.. you can even go epic!" Open only to moms. Deadline: December 31. Prize: Publication.

☯ SHORT GRAIN CONTEST

P.O. Box 3986, Regina SK S4P 3R9, Canada. (306)791-7749. **E-mail:** grainmag@skwriter.com. **Website:** www.grainmagazine.ca/short-grain-contest. **Contact:** Jordan Morris, business administrator (inquiries only). The annual Short Grain Contest includes a category for poetry of any style up to 100 lines and

fiction of any style up to 2,500 words, offering 3 prizes. Deadline: April 1. Prize: $1,000, plus publication in *Grain Magazine*; 2nd Place: $750; 3rd Place: $500.

SKIPPING STONES HONOR (BOOK) AWARDS

P.O. Box 3939, Eugene OR 97403, USA. (541)342-4956. **Fax:** (541)342-4956. **E-mail:** editor@skippingstones.org. **Website:** www.skippingstones.org. **Contact:** Arun N. Toké. *Skipping Stones* is a well respected, multicultural literary magazine now in its 29th year. Annual award to promote multicultural and/or nature awareness through creative writings for children and teens and their educators. Seeks authentic, exceptional, child/youth friendly books that promote intercultural, international, intergenerational harmony, or understanding through creative ways. Deadline: February 29. Prize: Honor certificates; gold seals; reviews; press release/publicity. Judged by a multicultural committee of teachers, librarians, parents, students and editors.

SKIPPING STONES YOUTH AWARDS

P.O. Box 3939, Eugene OR 97403-0939. (541)342-4956. **Fax:** (541)342-4956. **E-mail:** editor@skippingstones.org. **Website:** www.skippingstones.org. **Contact:** Arun N. Toké. Annual awards to promote creativity as well as multicultural and nature awareness in youth. Deadline: June 25. Prize: Publication in the autumn issue of *Skipping Stones*, honor certificate, subscription to magazine, plus 5 multicultural and/or nature books. Judged by editors and reviewers at *Skipping Stones* magazine.

SLAPERING HOL PRESS CHAPBOOK COMPETITION

The Hudson Valley Writers' Center, 300 Riverside Dr., Sleepy Hollow NY 10591. (914)332-5953. **E-mail:** info@writerscenter.org. **Website:** www.writerscenter.org. **Contact:** Margo Stever, editor. The annual competition is open to poets who have not published a book or chapbook, though individual poems may have already appeared. Purpose is to provide publishing opportunities for emerging poets. Deadline: June 15. The winner receives a $500 cash award, publication, ten copies, a reading at the Hudson Valley Writers Center, plus travel expenses up to $500 if needed. Winning poets are also offered editorial and marketing advice.

SLIPSTREAM ANNUAL POETRY CHAPBOOK CONTEST

Slipstream, Slipstream Poetry Contest, Dept. W-1, P.O. Box 2071, Niagara Falls NY 14301. **E-mail:** editors@slipstreampress.org. **Website:** www.slipstreampress.org. **Contact:** Dan Sicoli, co-editor. *Slipstream Magazine* is a yearly anthology of some of the best poetry you'll find today in the American small press. Offered annually to help promote a poet whose work is often overlooked or ignored. Open to any writer. Deadline: December 1. Prize: $1,000, plus 50 professionally-printed copies of your book.

THE BERNICE SLOTE AWARD

Prairie Schooner, 110 Andrews Hall, PO Box 880334, Lincoln NE 68588-0334. (402)472-0911. **Fax:** (402)472-1817. **E-mail:** PrairieSchooner@unl.edu. **Website:** www.prairieschooner.unl.edu. **Contact:** Kwame Dawes. Offered annually for the best work by a beginning writer published in *Prairie Schooner* in the previous year. Celebrates the best and finest writing that they have published for the year. Prize: $500. Judged by editorial staff of *Prairie Schooner*.

JEFFREY E. SMITH EDITORS' PRIZE IN FICTION, NONFICTION AND POETRY

The Missouri Review, 357 McReynolds Hall, UMC, Columbia MO 65201. (573)882-4474. **Fax:** (573)884-4671. **E-mail:** contest_question@moreview.com. **Website:** www.missourireview.com. **Contact:** Editor. Offered annually for unpublished work in 3 categories: fiction, essay, and poetry. Guidelines online or for SASE. Deadline: October 16. Prize: $5,000 and publication for each category winner.

HELEN C. SMITH MEMORIAL AWARD FOR BEST BOOK OF POETRY

E-mail: tilsecretary@yahoo.com. **Website:** http://texasinstituteofletters.org/. Offered annually for the best book of poems published January 1-December 31 of previous year. Poet must have been born in Texas, have lived in the state at some time for at least 2 consecutive years, or the subject matter must be associated with the state. Deadline: January 10. Prize: $1,200.

KAY SNOW WRITING CONTEST

Willamette Writers, Willamette Writers, 2108 Buck St., West Linn OR 97068. (503)305-6729. **Fax:** (503)344-6174. **E-mail:** reg@willamettewriters.com. **Website:** www.willamettewriters.org. Willamette Writers is the largest writers' organization in Oregon and one of the largest writers' organizations in the United States. It is a non-profit, tax-exempt Oregon corporation led by volunteers. Elected officials and directors administer an active program of monthly meetings, special seminars, workshops, and an annual writing conference. Continuing with established programs and starting new ones is only made possible by strong volunteer support. The purpose of this annual writing contest, named in honor of Willamette Writer's founder, Kay Snow, is to help writers reach professional goals in writing in a broad array of categories and to encourage student writers. Deadline: April 23. Submission deadline begins January 15. Prize: One first prize of $300, one second place prize of $150, and a third place prize of $50 per winning entry in each of the six categories. Student first prize is $50, $20 for second place, $10 for third.

THE RICHARD SNYDER MEMORIAL PUBLICATION PRIZE

Ashland Poetry Press, 401 College Ave., Ashland University, Ashland OH 44805. **E-mail:** app@ashland.edu. **Website:** www.ashlandpoetrypress.com. **Contact:** Cassandra Brown, managing editor. Submissions must be unpublished in book form. Considers simultaneous submissions. Submit 50-96 pages of poetry. Competition receives 400+ entries/year. Winners will be announced in *Writer's Chronicle* and *Poets & Writers*. Copies of winning books available from Small Press Distribution and directly from the Ashland University Bookstore online. The Ashland Poetry Press publishes 2-4 books of poetry/year. Deadline: April 1. Prize: $1,000 plus book publication. Judged by Elizabeth Spires in 2016.

SOCIETY OF CLASSICAL POETS POETRY COMPETITION

The Society of Classical Poets, 11 Heather Ln., Mount Hope NY 10940. **E-mail:** submissions@classicalpoets.org. **Website:** www.classicalpoets.org. **Contact:** Evan Mantyk, president. Annual competition for a group of poems that address one or more of the following themes: exposing the negative effects of socialism and communism on the West, raising awareness about human rights abuses in China, or celebrating the beauty of classical arts. Poems must incorporate meter and rhyme. All entries are considered for publication. Deadline: December 31. Prize: $1,000. Judged by Evan Mantyk, the society's president.

There are minor modifications to themes and the amount of money awarded from year to year, check website for details.

SOCIETY OF MIDLAND AUTHORS AWARD

Society of Midland Authors, P.O. Box 10419, Chicago IL 60610-0419. **E-mail:** marlenetbrill@comcast.net. **Website:** www.midlandauthors.com. **Contact:** Marlene Targ Brill, awards chair. Since 1957, the Society has presented annual awards for the best books written by Midwestern authors. The Society began in 1915. The Society of Midland Authors (SMA) Award is presented to one title in each of 6 categories: adult nonfiction, adult fiction, adult biography and memoir, children's nonfiction, children's fiction, and poetry. There may be honor book winners as well. Books and entry forms must be mailed to the 3 judges in each category; for a list of judges and the entry and payment forms, visit the SMA website. Do not mail books to the society's P.O. box. The fee can be sent to the SMA P.O. box or paid via Paypal. Deadline: The first Saturday in January for books from the previous year. Prize: $500 and a plaque that is awarded at the SMA banquet in May in Chicago. Honorary winners receive a plaque. Check the SMA website for each year's judges at the end of October.

SOUL-MAKING KEATS LITERARY COMPETITION

The Webhallow House, 1544 Sweetwood Dr., Broadmoor Vlg. CA 94015-2029. **E-mail:** soulkeats@mail.com. **Website:** www.soulmakingcontest.us. **Contact:** Eileen Malone, contest founder/director. Annual open contest offers cash prizes in each of 12 literary categories. Competition receives 600 entries/year. Names of winners and judges are posted on website. Winners announced in January by SASE and on website. Winners are invited to read at the Koret Auditorium, San Francisco. Event is televised. Ongoing Deadline: November 30. Prizes: 1st Prize: $100; 2nd Prize: $50; 3rd Prize: $25.

THE SOW'S EAR CHAPBOOK COMPETITION

The Sow's Ear Review, 1748 Cave Ridge Rd., Mount Jackson VA 22842. **E-mail:** sepoetryreview@gmail.com. **Website:** www.sowsearpoetry.org. **Contact:** Sarah Kohrs, managing editor. The Sow's Ear Poetry Review sponsors an annual chapbook competition. Open to adults. Deadline: May 1 (postmark). Prize: Offers $1,000, publication as the spring issue of the magazine, 25 author's copies, and distribution to subscribers.

THE SOW'S EAR POETRY COMPETITION

The Sow's Ear Poetry Review, 1748 Cave Ridge Rd., Mount Jackson VA 22842. **E-mail:** sepoetryreview@gmail.com. **Website:** www.sowsearpoetry.org. **Contact:** Sarah Kohrs, managing editor. Deadline: November 1. Prize: $1,000, publication, and the option of publication for approximately 20 finalists.

THE EDWARD STANLEY AWARD

Prairie Schooner, 110 Andrews Hall, P.O. Box 880334, Lincoln NE 68588-0334. (402)472-0911. **Fax:** (402)472-9771. **E-mail:** prairieschooner@unl.edu. **Website:** www.prairieschooner.unl.edu. **Contact:** Ashley Strosnider.. Prize: $1,000. Editorial staff

WALLACE E. STEGNER FELLOWSHIPS

Creative Writing Program, Stanford University, Stanford CA 94305-2087. (650)723-0011. **E-mail:** stegnerfellowship@stanford.edu. **Website:** https://creativewriting.stanford.edu/stegner-fellowship/overview. Offers 5 fellowships in poetry and 5 in fiction for promising writers who can benefit from 2 years of instruction and participation in the program. Online application preferred. Deadline: December 1. Open to submissions on September 1. Prize: Fellowships of $37,500, plus tuition and health insurance.
Competition receives about 1,500 entries/year.

STEVENS POETRY MANUSCRIPT CONTEST

NFSPS Stevens Poetry Manuscript Competition, 4 Bowie Pt, Sherwood AR 72120. **E-mail:** stevens.nfsps@gmail.com. **Website:** www.nfsps.org. **Contact:** Amanda Partridge, chair. National Federation of State Poetry Societies (NFSPS) offers annual award of $1,000, publication of ms, and 50 author's copies for the winning poetry manuscript by a single author. Deadline: Fall, varies from year to year. For 2018, probably September 15; Submissions open August 15. Prize: $1,000, publication and 50 copies of the book.

THE RUTH STONE POETRY PRIZE

Vermont College of Fine Arts, 36 College St., Montpelier VT 05602. (802)828-8517. **E-mail:** hungermtn@vcfa.edu. **Website:** www.hungermtn.org. **Contact:** Cameron Finch, managing editor. The Ruth Stone Poetry Prize is an annual poetry contest. Deadline: March 1. Prize: One first place winner receives $1,000 and publication on Hunger Mountain online. One runner-up receives $100 and online publication. Other finalists considered for print publication.

THE ELIZABETH MATCHETT STOVER MEMORIAL AWARD

Southwest Review, Southern Methodist University, P.O. Box 750374, Dallas TX 75275-0374. (214)768-1037. **Fax:** (214)768-1408. **E-mail:** swr@mail.smu.edu. **Website:** www.smu.edu/southwestreview. **Contact:** Greg Brownderville, editor-in-chief. Offered annually to the best works of poetry that have appeared in the magazine in the previous year. Please note that mss are submitted for publication, not for the prizes themselves. Guidelines for SASE and online. Prize: $300. Judged by Greg Brownderville.

⬤ STROKESTOWN INTERNATIONAL POETRY COMPETITION

Strokestown International Poetry Festival, Strokestown Poetry Festival Office, Strokestown, County Roscommon , Ireland. (+353) 71 9633759. E-mail: director@strokestownpoetry.org. Website: www.strokestownpoetry.org. Contact: Martin Dyar, Director. This annual competition was established to promote excellence in poetry and participation in the reading and writing of it. Acquires first publication rights. Deadline: January. Prize: 1st Place: €1,500; 2nd Place: €500; 3rd Place: €300; 3 shortlisted prizes of €100 each.

◎ SUBTERRAIN MAGAZINE'S LUSH TRIUMPHANT LITERARY AWARDS COMPETITION

P.O. Box 3008 MPO, Vancouver BC V6B 3X5, Canada. (604)876-8710. Fax: (604)879-2667. E-mail: subter@portal.ca. Website: www.subterrain.ca. Entrants may submit as many entries in as many categories as they like. Fiction: Max of 3,000 words. Poetry: A suite of 5 related poems (max of 15 pages). Creative Nonfiction (based on fact, adorned with fiction): Max of 4,000 words. Deadline: May 15. Prize: Winners in each category will receive $1,000 cash (plus payment for publication) and publication in the Winter issue. First runner-up in each category will be published in the Spring issue of *subTerrain*.

THE TAMPA REVIEW PRIZE FOR POETRY

University of Tampa, 401 W. Kennedy Blvd., Tampa FL 33606. 813-253-6266. E-mail: utpress@ut.edu. Website: www.ut.edu/tampareview. Annual award for the best previously unpublished collection of poetry (at least 48 pages, though preferably 60-100). Deadline: December 31. Prize: $2,000, plus publication.

THE TENTH GATE PRIZE

The Word Works, P. O. Box 42164, Washington D.C. 20015, USA. E-mail: editor@wordworksbooks.org. Website: www.wordworksbooks.org. Contact: Leslie McGrath, Series Editor; Nancy White, Editor. Publication and $1000 cash prize awarded annually by The Word Works to a full-length ms by a poet who has already published at least 2 full-length poetry collections. Founded in honor of Jane Hirshfield, The Tenth Gate Prize supports the work of mid-career po-

ets. Deadline: July 15. Open to submissions on June 1. Prize: $1,000 and publication. Judged by the editors.

◗ Submission through online submissions manager, only. Reading is "blind," and all styles and voices are welcome.

THE TEXAS INSTITUTE OF LETTERS LITERARY AWARDS

E-mail: Betwx@aol.com. Website: www.texasinstituteofletters.org. The Texas Institute of Letters gives annual awards for books by Texas authors and writers who have produced books about Texas, including Best Books of Poetry, Fiction, and Nonfiction. Awards are also given for best Short Story, Magazine or Newspaper Article, Essay, and best Books for Children and Young Adults. Work submitted must have been published in the year stipulated, and entries may be made by authors or by their publishers. Complete guidelines and award information is available on the Texas Institute of Letters website.

TOR HOUSE PRIZE FOR POETRY

Robinson Jeffers Tor House Foundation, Poetry Prize Coordinator, Tor House Foundation, Box 223240, Carmel CA 93922. (831)624-1813. Fax: (831)624-3696. E-mail: thf@torhouse.org. Website: www.torhouse.org. Contact: Eliot Ruchowitz-Roberts, Poetry Prize Coordinator. The annual Prize for Poetry is a living memorial to American poet Robinson Jeffers (1887-1962). Open to well-crafted poetry in all styles, ranging from experimental work to traditional forms, including short narrative poems. Poems must be original and unpublished. Deadline: March 15. Prize: $1,000 honorarium for award-winning poem; $200 Honorable Mention.

KINGSLEY & KATE TUFTS POETRY AWARDS

Claremont Graduate University, Claremont Graduate University, 160 E. Tenth St., Harper East B7, Claremont CA 91711-6165. (909)621-8974. E-mail: tufts@cgu.edu. Website: https://arts.cgu.edu/tufts-poetry-awards/. The annual $100,000 Kingsley Tufts Poetry Award is presented for book published by a mid-career poet; the Award was created to honor the poet and provide the resources to allow the writer to continue working towards the pinnacle of their craft. The $10,000 Kate Tufts Award is presented annually for a first book by a poet of genuine promise. "Any poet will tell you that the only thing more rare than meaningful recognition is a meaningful payday. For two outstanding poets each year, the Kingsley and Kate Tufts awards represent both." Deadline: July 1, for books published in the preceding year. Prize: $100,000 for the Kingsley Tufts Poetry Award and $10,000 for the Kate Tufts Discovery Award. Please see website for current judges.

☼ UTMOST CHRISTIAN POETRY CONTEST

Utmost Christian Writers Foundation, 121 Morin Maze NW, Edmonton AB T6K 1V1, Canada. (780)265-4650. **E-mail:** nnharms@telusplanet.net. **Website:** www.utmostchristianwriters.com. **Contact:** Nathan Harms, executive director. Utmost is founded on—and supported by—the dreams, interests and aspirations of individual people. Deadline: February 28. Prizes: 1st Place: $1,000; 2nd Place: $500; 10 prizes of $100 are offered for honorable mention; $300 for best rhyming poem; and $200 for an honorable mention rhyming poem. Judged by a committee of the Directors of Utmost Christian Writers Foundation (who work under the direction of Barbara Mitchell, chief judge).

DANIEL VAROUJAN AWARD

New England Poetry Club, 376 School St., Watertown MA 02472. **E-mail:** contests@nepoetryclub.org. **Website:** www.nepoetryclub.org. **Contact:** Audrey Kalajin. For an unpublished poem (not a translation) worthy of Daniel Varoujan, a poet killed by the Turks in the genocide which destroyed three-fourths of the Armenian population. Deadline: May 31. Prize: $1,000. Judged by well-known poets and sometimes winners of previous NEPC contests.

VASSAR MILLER PRIZE IN POETRY

University of North Texas Press, 1155 Union Circle, #311336, Denton TX 76203. (940)565-2142. **Fax:** (940)565-4590. **Website:** http://untpress.unt.edu. **Contact:** John Poch. Annual prize awarded to a collection of poetry. Deadline: Mss may be submitted between 9 A.M. on September 1 and 5 P.M. on October 31, through online submissions manager only. Prize: $1,000 and publication by University of North Texas Press. Judged by a different eminent writer selected each year. Some prefer to remain anonymous until the end of the contest.

ANNUAL VENTURA COUNTY WRITERS CLUB SHORT STORY CONTEST

Ventura County Writers Club Short Story Contest, P.O. Box 3373, Thousand Oaks CA 91362. **E-mail:** vcwc.contestchair@gmail.com. **Website:** www.venturacountywriters.com. **Contact:** Contest Chair. Annual short story contest for youth and adult writers.

High school division for writers still in school. Adult division for those 18 and older. Club membership not required to enter and entries accepted worldwide as long as fees are paid, story is unpublished and in English. Enter through website. Winners get cash prizes and are published in club anthology. Deadline: November 15. Adult Prizes: 1st Place: $500; 2nd Place: $250; 3rd Place: $125. High School Prizes: 1st Place: $100; 2nd Place: $75; 3rd Place: $50.

MARICA AND JAN VILCEK PRIZE FOR POETRY

Bellevue Literary Review, New York University School of Medicine, OBV-A612, 550 First Ave., New York NY 10016. (212)263-3973. **E-mail:** info@blreview.org. **Website:** www.blreview.org. **Contact:** Stacy Bodziak. The annual Marica and Jan Vilcek Prize for Poetry recognizes outstanding writing related to themes of health, healing, illness, the mind, and the body. All entries will be considered for publication. No previously published poems (including Internet publication). Submit up to 3 poems (5 pages maximum). Electronic (online) submissions only; combine all poems into 1 document and use first poem as document title. See guidelines for additional submission details. Guidelines available for SASE or on website. Deadline: July 1. Prize: $1,000 for best poem and publication in *Bellevue Literary Review*. Previous judges include Mark Doty, Cornelius Eady, Naomi Shihab Nye, Tony Hoagland, Kazim Ali, and Ada Limon.

WABASH PRIZE FOR POETRY

Sycamore Review, Department of English, 500 Oval Dr., Purdue University, West Lafayette IN 47907. **E-mail:** sycamore@purdue.edu; sycamorepoetry@purdue.edu. **Website:** www.sycamorereview.com/contest/. **Contact:** Anthony Sutton, editor-in-chief. Annual contest for unpublished poetry. Deadline: December 1. Prize: $1,000 and publication.

THE WASHINGTON PRIZE

The Word Works, Dearlove Hall, SUNY Adirondack, 640 Bay Rd., Queensbury NY 12804. **E-mail:** editor@wordworksbooks.org. **Website:** www.wordworksbooks.org. **Contact:** Rebecca Kutzer-Rice, Washington Prize administrator. In addition to its general poetry book publications, The Word Works runs four imprints: The Washington Prize, The Tenth Gate Prize, International Editions, and the Hilary Tham Capital Collection. Selections announced in late summer. Book publication planned for spring of the following year. The Washington Prize allows poets from all stages of their careers to compete on a level playing field for publication and national recognition. Deadline: Submit January 15-March 15 (postmark). Prize: $1,500 and publication of a book-length ms of original poetry in English by a living US or Canadian citizen. Judged by two tiers of readers, followed by five final judges working as a panel.

○ The Washington Prize is open to all American and Canadian poets with a full-length collection ready to publish. Submissions are read blind, so the poets' past publication history is not known by the readers or judges.

THE ROBERT WATSON LITERARY PRIZE IN FICTION AND POETRY

The Robert Watson Literary Prizes, *The Greensboro Review*, MFA Writing Program, 3302 MHRA Building, Greensboro NC 27402-6170. (336)334-5459. **E-mail:** tgr@uncg.edu. **Website:** www.greensbororeview.org. **Contact:** Terry Kennedy, editor. Offered annually for fiction (up to 25 double-spaced pages) and poetry (up to 10 pages). Entries must be unpublished. Open to any writer. Deadline: September 15. Prize: $1,000 each for best short story and poem. Judged by editors of *The Greensboro Review*.

WERGLE FLOMP HUMOR POETRY CONTEST

Winning Writers, 351 Pleasant St., PMB 222, Northampton MA 01060. (866)946-9748. **Fax:** (413)280-0539. **E-mail:** adam@winningwriters.com. **Website:** www.winningwriters.com. **Contact:** Adam Cohen. Winning Writers provides expert literary contest information to the public. It is one of the "101 Best Websites for Writers" (*Writer's Digest*). Deadline: April 1. Prize: 1st prize of $1,000; 2nd prize of $250; 10 honorable mentions of $100 each. All winners of cash prizes published on website. The winner will also receive a one-year gift certificate from the contest co-sponsor, Duotrope (a $50 value). Judged by Jendi Reiter, assisted by Lauren Singer Ledoux.

◐ WESTERN AUSTRALIAN PREMIER'S BOOK AWARDS

State Library of Western Australia, Perth Cultural Centre, 25 Francis St., Perth WA 6000, Australia. (61)(8)9427-3151. **E-mail:** premiersbookawards@slwa.wa.gov.au. **Website:** pba.slwa.wa.gov.au. **Contact:** Karen de San Miguel. Annual competition for Australian citizens or permanent residents of Australia, or writers whose work has Australia as its primary focus. Categories: children's books, digital narrative, fiction, nonfiction, poetry, scripts, writing for young adults, West Australian history, and Western Australian emerging writers. Deadline: January 31. Prize: Awards $25,000 for Premier's Prize; awards $15,000 each for the Children's Books, Digital Narrative, Fiction, and Nonfiction categories; awards $10,000 each for the Poetry, Scripts, Western Australian History, Western Australian Emerging Writers, and Writing for Young Adults; awards $5,000 for People's Choice Award.

WESTERN HERITAGE AWARDS

National Cowboy & Western Heritage Museum, 1700 NE 63rd St., Oklahoma City OK 73111-7997. (405)478-2250. **Fax:** (405)478-4714. **Website:** www.nationalcowboymuseum.org. **Contact:** Jessica Limestall. The National Cowboy & Western Heritage Museum Western Heritage Awards were established to honor and encourage the legacy of those whose works in literature, music, film, and television reflect the significant stories of the American West. Accepted categories for literary entries: western novel, nonfiction book, art book, photography book, juvenile book, magazine article, or poetry book. The WHA are presented annually to encourage the accurate and artistic telling of great stories of the West through 16 categories of western literature, television, film and music; including fiction, nonfiction, children's books and poetry. See website for details and category definitions. Deadline: November 30. Prize: Awards a Wrangler bronze sculpture designed by famed western artist, John Free. Judged by a panel of judges selected each year with distinction in various fields of western art and heritage.

WESTMORELAND POETRY & SHORT STORY CONTEST

Westmoreland Arts & Heritage Festival, 252 Twin Lakes Road, Latrobe PA 15650-9415. (724)834-7474. **Fax:** (724)850-7474. **E-mail:** info@artsandheritage.com. **Website:** www.artsandheritage.com. **Contact:** Diane Shrader. Offered annually for unpublished work. Two categories: Poem and Short Story. Short story entries no longer than 4,000 words. Family-oriented festival and contest. Deadline: February 17. Prizes: Award: $200; 1st Place: $125; 2nd Place: $100; 3rd Place: $75.

WHITE PINE PRESS POETRY PRIZE

White Pine Press, P.O. Box 236, Buffalo NY 14201. **E-mail:** wpine@whitepine.org. **Website:** www.whitepine.org. **Contact:** Dennis Maloney, editor. Offered annually for previously published or unpublished poets. Manuscript: 60-80 pages of original work; translations are not eligible. Poems may have appeared in magazines or limited-edition chapbooks. Open to any US citizen. Deadline: November 30 (postmarked). Prize: $1,000 and publication. Final judge is a poet of national reputation. All entries are screened by the editorial staff of White Pine Press.

STAN AND TOM WICK POETRY PRIZE

Wick Poetry Center, P.O. Box 5190, Kent OH 44240. (330)672-2067. **E-mail:** wickpoetry@kent.edu. **Website:** www.kent.edu/wick/stan-and-tom-wick-poetry-prize. **Contact:** David Hassler, director. Offered annually to a poet who has not previously published a full-length collection of poetry (a volume of 50 or more pages published in an edition of 500 or more copies). Deadline: May 1. Submissions period begins February 1. Prize: $2,500 and publication of full-length book of poetry by Kent State University Press.

WILLA LITERARY AWARD

E-mail: 2019willachair@gmail.com. **Website:** www.womenwritingthewest.org. **Contact:** Carmen Peone. The WILLA Literary Award honors the year's best in published literature featuring women's or girls' stories set in the West. Women Writing the West (WWW), a nonprofit association of writers and other professionals writing and promoting the Women's West, underwrites and presents the nationally recognized award annually (for work published between January 1 and December 31). The award is named in honor of Pulitzer Prize winner Willa Cather, one of the country's foremost novelists. The award is given in 8 categories: historical fiction, contemporary fiction, original softcover fiction, creative nonfiction, scholarly nonfiction, poetry, children's fiction and nonfiction and young adult fiction/nonfiction. Entry forms available on the website. Deadline: November 1–February 1. Prize: $150 and a trophy. Finalist receives a plaque. Both receive digital and sticker award emblems for book covers. Notice of Winning and Finalist titles mailed to more than 4,000 booksellers, libraries, and others. Award announcement is in early August, and awards are presented to the winners and finalists at the annual WWW Fall Conference. Also, the eight winners will participate in a drawing for 2 two week all expenses paid residencies donated by Playa at Summer Lake in Oregon. Judged by professional librarians not affiliated with WWW.

TENNESSEE WILLIAMS/NEW ORLEANS LITERARY FESTIVAL CONTESTS

Tennessee Williams/New Orleans Literary Festival, 938 Lafayette St., Suite 514, New Orleans LA 70113. (504)581-1144. **E-mail:** info@tennesseewilliams.net. **Website:** www.tennesseewilliams.net/contests. **Contact:** Paul J. Willis. Annual contests for: Unpublished One Act, Unpublished Short Fiction, Unpublished Flash Fiction, and Unpublished Poem. "Our competitions provide writers a large audience during one of the largest literary festivals in the nation." Deadline: October 1 (One Act, Fiction); October 15 (Poetry, Very Short Fiction) Prize: One Act: $1,500, staged read at the next festival, VIP All-Access Festival pass, and publication in Bayou. Poetry: $1,000, public reading at next festival, VIP all-access pass, publication in Louisiana Cultural Vistas Magazine. Fiction: $1,500, public reading at next festival, publication in Louisiana Literature, VIP all-access pass. Very Short Fiction: $500, publication in the New Orleans Review, VIP all-access past. Judged by special guest judges, who change every year.

○ See website for full details.

MILLER WILLIAMS POETRY PRIZE

University of Arkansas Press, McIlroy House, 105 N. McIlroy Ave., Fayetteville AR 72701. (479)575-7258. **E-mail:** cmoss@uark.edu, mbieker@uark.edu. **Website:** https://www.uapress.com/millerwilliamspoetryseries/. **Contact:** Billy Collins, judge and series editor; Mike Bieker, director. Each year, the University of Arkansas Press accepts submissions for the Miller Williams Poetry Series and from the books selected awards the Miller Williams Poetry Prize in the following summer. Deadline: September 30. Accepts submissions all year long. Prize: $5,000 and publication. One finalist will also receive publication. Judged by Billy Collins, series editor.

WISCONSIN INSTITUTE FOR CREATIVE WRITING FELLOWSHIP

6195B H.C. White Hall, 600 N. Park St., Madison WI 53706. **E-mail:** sbbishop@wisc.edu. **Website:** creativewriting.wisc.edu/fellowships.html. **Contact:** Sean Bishop, graduate coordinator. Fellowship provides time, space and an intellectual community for writers working on first books.Since 2012, we have also considered applicants who have published only one full-length collection of creative writing prior to the application deadline, although unpublished authors remain eligible, and quality of writing remains the near-exclusive criterion for selection. Receives approximately 300 applicants a year for each genre. Judged by English Department faculty and current fellows. Candidates can have up to one published book in the genre for which they are applying. Open to any writer with either an M.F.A. or Ph.D. in creative writing. Results announced on website by May 1. Deadline: Last day of February. Open to submissions on February 1. Prize: $38,000 for a 9-month appointment.

THE J. HOWARD AND BARBARA M.J. WOOD PRIZE

Poetry, 61 W. Superior St., Chicago IL 60654. (312)787-7070. **Fax:** (312)787-6650. **E-mail:** editors@poetrymagazine.org. **Website:** www.poetrymagazine.org. Offered annually for poems published in *Poetry* during the preceding year (October-September). Upon acceptance, *Poetry* licenses exclusive worldwide first serial rights, including electronic rights, for publication, as well as non-exclusive rights to reprint, reuse, and archive the work, in any format, in perpetuity. Copyright reverts to author upon first publication. Prize: $5,000.

⚙ THE WORD AWARDS

The Word Guild, The Word Guild, Suite # 226, 245 King George Rd, Brantford ON N3R 7N7, Canada. 800-969-9010 x 1. **E-mail:** info@thewordguild.com. **E-mail:** info@thewordguild.com. **Website:** www.thewordguild.com. **Contact:** Karen deBlieck. The Word Guild is an organization of Canadian writers and editors who are Christian, and who are committed to encouraging one another and to fostering standards of excellence in the art, craft, practice and ministry of writing. Memberships available for various experience levels. Yearly conference Write Canada (please see website for information) and features keynote speakers, continuing classes and workshops. Editors and agents on site. The Word Awards is for work published in the past year, in almost 30 categories including books, articles, essays, fiction, nonfiction, novels, short stories, songs, and poetry. Please see website for more information. Deadline: January 15. Prize $50 CAD for article and short pieces; $100 CAD for book entries. Finalists book entries are eligible for the $5,000 Grace Irwin prize. Judged by industry leaders and professionals.

WORKING PEOPLE'S POETRY COMPETITION

Partisan Press, Blue Collar Review, P.O. Box 11417, Norfolk VA 23517. **E-mail:** red-ink@earthlink.net. **Website:** www.partisanpress.org. Deadline: May 15.

Prize: $100, 1-year subscription to *Blue Collar Review* and 1-year posting of winning poem to website. Judged by editorial committee.

WORLD'S BEST SHORT-SHORT STORY CONTEST, NARRATIVE NONFICTION CONTEST & SOUTHEAST REVIEW POETRY CONTEST

The Southeast Review, Florida State University, English Department, Tallahassee FL 32306. **E-mail:** southeastreview@gmail.com. **Website:** www.southeastreview.org. **Contact:** Erin Hoover, editor. Annual award for unpublished short-short stories (500 words or less), poetry, and narrative nonfiction (6,000 words or less). Visit website for details. Deadline: March 15. Prize: $500 per category. Winners and finalists will be published in *The Southeast Review*.

JAMES WRIGHT POETRY AWARD

Mid-American Review, Dept. of English, Bowling Green State University, Bowling Green OH 43403. (419)372-2725. **Fax:** (419)372-4642. **E-mail:** clouda@bgsu.edu. **Website:** www.bgsu.edu/midamericanreview. **Contact:** Abigail Cloud, poetry editor. Offered annually for unpublished poetry. Open to all writers not associated with *Mid-American Review* or judge. Deadline: November 1. Prize: $1,000 and publication in spring issue of *Mid-American Review*. Judged by editors and a well known poet, i.e., Kathy Fagan, Bob Hicok, Michelle Boisseau. Judged by Maggie Smith in 2016.

WRITER'S DIGEST ANNUAL WRITING COMPETITION

Writer's Digest, a publication of Active Interest Media, Inc., 5720 Flatiron Pwky., Boulder CO 80301. **E-mail:** writersdigestwritingcompetition@aimmedia.com. **Website:** www.writersdigest.com. Writing contest with 9 categories: Inspirational Writing (spiritual/religious, maximum 2,500 words); Memoir/Personal Essay (maximum 2,000 words); Magazine Feature Article (maximum 2,000 words);Children's/Young Adult Fiction (maximum 2,000 words) Short Story (genre, maximum 4,000 words); Short Story (mainstream/literary, maximum 4,000 words); Rhyming Poetry (maximum 32 lines); Nonrhyming Poetry (maximum 32 lines); Stage Play/TV/Movie Script (first 15 pages and 1-page synopsis). Entries must be original, in English, unpublished/unproduced (except for Magazine Feature Articles), and not accepted by another publisher/producer at the time of submission. Writer's Digest retains one-time publication rights to the winning entries in each category. Deadline: May (early bird); June. Grand Prize: $5,000 and a trip to the Writer's Digest Conference to meet with editors and agents; 1st Place: $1,000; 2nd Place: $500; 3rd Place: $250; 4th Place: $100; 5th Place:$50; Sixth through Tenth place winners in each category:$25; and more.

WRITER'S DIGEST SELF-PUBLISHED BOOK AWARDS

Writer's Digest, a publication of Active Interest Media, Inc., 5720 Flatiron Pwky., Boulder CO 80301. **E-mail:** writersdigestselfpublishingcompetition@aimmedia. com. **Website:** www.writersdigest.com. **Contact:** Nicole Howard. Contest open to all English-language, self-published books for which the authors have paid the full cost of publication, or the cost of printing has been paid for by a grant or as part of a prize. Categories include: Mainstream/Literary Fiction, Genre Fiction, Nonfiction, Inspirational (spiritual/new age), Life Stories (biographies/autobiographies/family histories/memoirs), Children's Books, Reference Books (directories/encyclopedias/guide books), Poetry, and Middle-Grade/Young Adult Books. Judges reserve the right to re-categorize entries. Judges reserve the right to withhold prizes in any category. All winners will be notified in October. Early bird deadline: April 2. Prizes: Grand Prize: $8,000, a trip to the Writer's Digest Conference, promotion in *Writer's Digest*, 10 copies of the book will be sent to major review houses, and a guaranteed review in *Midwest Book Review*; 1st Place (9 winners): $1,000 and promotion in *Writer's Digest*; Honorable Mentions: promotion on writersdigest.com. All entrants will receive a brief commentary from one of the judges.

WRITER'S DIGEST SELF-PUBLISHED E-BOOK AWARDS

Writer's Digest, a publication of Active Interest Media, Inc., 5720 Flatiron Pwky., Boulder CO 80301. **E-mail:** writersdigestselfpublishingcompetition@aimmedia. com. **Website:** www.writersdigest.com. **Contact:** Nicole Howard. Contest open to all English-language, self-published e-books for which the authors have paid the full cost of publication, or the cost of publication has been paid for by a grant or as part of a prize. Categories include: Mainstream/Literary Fiction, Genre Fiction, Nonfiction (includes reference books), Inspirational (spiritual/new age), Life Stories (biographies/autobiographies/family histories/memoirs), Children's Books, Poetry, and Middle-Grade/

Young Adult Books. Judges reserve the right to re-categorize entries. Judges reserve the right to withhold prizes in any category. All winners will be notified by December 31. Early bird deadline: August 1; Deadline: September 4. Prizes: Grand Prize: $5,000, promotion in *Writer's Digest* and more; 1st Place (9 winners): $1,000 and promotion in *Writer's Digest*; Honorable Mentions: promotion on writersdigest. com. All entrants will receive a brief commentary from one of the judges.

WRITERS-EDITORS NETWORK INTERNATIONAL WRITING COMPETITION

CNW Publishing, P.O. Box A, North Stratford NH 03590-0167. **E-mail:** contestentry@writers-editors. com. **E-mail:** info@writers-editors.com. **Website:** www.writers-editors.com. **Contact:** Dana K. Cassell, executive director. Annual award to recognize publishable talent. New categories and awards for 2018: Nonfiction (unpublished or self-published; may be an article, blog post, essay/opinion piece, column, nonfiction book chapter, children's article or book chapter); fiction (unpublished or self-published; may be a short story, novel chapter, Young Adult [YA] or children's story or book chapter); poetry (unpublished or self-published; may be traditional or free verse poetry or children's verse). Guidelines available online. Deadline: March 15. Prize: 1st Place: $150 plus one year Writers-Editors membership; 2nd Place: $100; 3rd Place: $75. All winners and Honorable Mentions will receive certificates as warranted. Most Promising entry in each category will receive a free critique by a contest judge. Judged by editors, librarians, and writers.

♻ WRITERS' GUILD OF ALBERTA AWARDS

Writers' Guild of Alberta, Percy Page Centre, 11759 Groat Rd., Edmonton AB T5M 3K6, Canada. (780)422-8174. **Fax:** (780)422-2663. **E-mail:** mail@ writersguild.ca. **Website:** writersguild.ca. **Contact:** Executive Director. Offers the following awards: Wilfrid Eggleston Award for Nonfiction; Georges Bugnet Award for Fiction; Howard O'Hagan Award for Short Story; Stephan G. Stephansson Award for Poetry; R. Ross Annett Award for Children's Literature; Gwen Pharis Ringwood Award for Drama; Jon Whyte Memorial Essay Award; James H. Gray Award for Short Nonfiction. Deadline: December 31. Prize: Winning authors receive $1,500; short piece prize winners receive $700.

WRITERS' LEAGUE OF TEXAS BOOK AWARDS

Writers' League of Texas, 611 S. Congress Ave., Suite 200A-3, Austin TX 78704. (512)499-8914. **Fax:** (512)499-0441. **E-mail:** sara@writersleague.org. **Website:** www.writersleague.org. **Contact:** Sara Kocek. Open to Texas authors of books published the previous year. To enter this contest, you must be a Texas author. "Texas author" is defined as anyone who (whether currently a resident or not) has lived in Texas for a period of 3 or more years. This contest is open to indie or self-published authors as well as traditionally-published authors. Deadline: February 28. Open to submissions October 7. Prize: $1,000 and a commemorative award.

THE YALE SERIES OF YOUNGER POETS

Yale University Press, P.O. Box 209040, New Haven CT 06520-9040. **Website:** youngerpoets.yupnet.org. The Yale Series of Younger Poets champions the most promising new American poets. The Yale Younger Poets prize is the oldest annual literary award in the United States. Deadline: November 15. Submissions period begins October 1.

ZONE 3 FIRST BOOK AWARD FOR POETRY

Zone 3, Austin Peay State University, Austin Peay State University, PO Box 4565, Clarksville TN 37044. (931)221-7031. **Fax:** (931)221-7149. **E-mail:** spofforda@aspu.edu; wallacess@apsu.edu. **Website:** www.apsu.edu/zone3/. **Contact:** Andrea Spofford, poetry editor; Susan Wallace, managing editor. Offered annually for anyone who has not published a full-length collection of poems (48 pages or more). Submit a ms of 48-80 pages. Deadline: May 1. Prize: $1,000 and publication.

GRANTS

State & Provincial

//

Arts councils provide assistance to artists (including poets) in the form of fellowships or grants. These grants can be substantial and confer prestige upon recipients; however, only state or province residents are eligible. Check websites for guidelines.

UNITED STATES ARTS AGENCIES

ALABAMA STATE COUNCIL ON THE ARTS, 201 Monroe St., Montgomery AL 36130-1800. (334)242-4076. E mail: staff@arts.alabama.gov. Website: www.arts.state.al.us.

ALASKA STATE COUNCIL ON THE ARTS, 411 W. Fourth Ave., Suite 1-E, Anchorage AK 99501-2343. E-mail: aksca_info@eed.state.ak.us. Website: www.eed.state.ak.us/aksca.

ARIZONA COMMISSION ON THE ARTS, 417 W. Roosevelt St., Phoenix AZ 85003-1326. (602)771-6501. E-mail: info@azarts.gov. Website: www.azarts.gov.

ARKANSAS ARTS COUNCIL, 1500 Tower Bldg., 323 Center St., Little Rock AR 72201. (501)324-9766. E-mail: info@arkansasarts.com. Website: www.arkansasarts.com.

CALIFORNIA ARTS COUNCIL, 1300 I St., Suite 930, Sacramento CA 95814. (916)322-6555. E-mail: info@caartscouncil.com. Website: www.cac.ca.gov.

COLORADO COUNCIL ON THE ARTS, 1625 Broadway, Suite 2700, Denver CO 80202. (303)892-3802. E-mail: online form. Website: www.coloarts.state.co.us.

COMMONWEALTH COUNCIL FOR ARTS AND CULTURE, P.O. Box 5553, CHRB, Saipan MP 96950. E-mail: galaidi@vzpacifica.net. Website: www.geocities.com/ccacarts/ccacwebsite. html.

CONNECTICUT COMMISSION ON CULTURE & TOURISM, Arts Division, One Financial Plaza, 755 Main St., Hartford CT 06103. (860)256-2800. Website: www.cultureandtourism.org.

DELAWARE DIVISION OF THE ARTS, Carvel State Office Bldg., 4th Floor, 820 N. French St., Wilmington DE 19801. E-mail: delarts@state.de.us. Website: www.artsdel.org.

DISTRICT OF COLUMBIA COMMISSION ON THE ARTS & HUMANITIES, 410 Eighth St. NW, 5th Floor, Washington DC 20004. E-mail: cah@dc.gov. Website: http://dcarts.dc.gov.

FLORIDA ARTS COUNCIL, Division of Cultural Affairs, R.A. Gray Building, Third Floor, 500 S. Bronough St., Tallahassee FL 32399-0250. (850)245-6470. E-mail: info@florida-arts.org. Website: http://dcarts.dc.gov.

GEORGIA COUNCIL FOR THE ARTS, 260 14th St., Suite 401, Atlanta GA 30318. (404)685-2787. E-mail: gaarts@gaarts.org. Website: www.gaarts.org.

GUAM COUNCIL ON THE ARTS & HUMANITIES AGENCY, P.O. Box 2950, Hagatna GU 96932. (671)646-2781. Website: www.guam.net.

HAWAII STATE FOUNDATION ON CULTURE & THE ARTS, 2500 S. Hotel St., 2nd Floor, Honolulu HI 96813. (808)586-0300. E-mail: ken.hamilton@hawaii.gov. Website: http.state.hi.us/sfca.

IDAHO COMMISSION ON THE ARTS, 2410 N. Old Penitentiary Rd., Boise ID 83712. (208)334-2119 or (800)278-3863. E-mail: info@arts.idaho.gov. Website: www.arts.idaho.gov.

ILLINOIS ARTS COUNCIL, James R. Thompson Center, 100 W. Randolph, Suite 10-500, Chicago IL 60601. (312)814-6750. E-mail: iac.info@illinois.gov. Website: www.state.il.us/agency/iac.

INDIANA ARTS COMMISSION, 150 W. Market St., Suite 618, Indianapolis IN 46204. (317)232-1268. E-mail: IndianaArtsCommission@iac.in.gov. Website: www.in.gov/arts.

INSTITUTE OF PUERTO RICAN CULTURE, P.O. Box 9024184, San Juan PR 00902-4184. (787)724-0700. E-mail: www@icp.gobierno.pr. Website: www.icp.gobierno.pr.

IOWA ARTS COUNCIL, 600 E. Locust, Des Moines IA 50319-0290. (515)281-6412. Website: www.iowaartscouncil.org.

KANSAS ARTS COMMISSION, 700 SW Jackson, Suite 1004, Topeka KS 66603-3761. (785)296-3335. E-mail: KAC@arts.state.ks.us. Website: http://arts.state.ks.us.

KENTUCKY ARTS COUNCIL, 21st Floor, Capital Plaza Tower, 500 Mero St., Frankfort KY 40601-1987. E-mail: kyarts@ky.gov. Website: http://artscouncil.ky.gov.

LOUISIANA DIVISION OF THE ARTS, Capitol Annex Bldg., 1051 N. 3rd St., 4th Floor, Room #420, Baton Rouge LA 70804. (225)342-8180. Website: www.crt.state.la.us/arts.

MAINE ARTS COMMISSION, 193 State St., 25 State House Station, Augusta ME 04333-0025. (207)287-2724. E-mail: MaineArts.info@maine.gov. Website: www.mainearts.com.

MARYLAND STATE ARTS COUNCIL, 175 W. Ostend St., Suite E, Baltimore MD 21230. (410)767-6555. E-mail: msac@msac.org. Website: www.msac.org.

MASSACHUSETTS CULTURAL COUNCIL, 10 St. James Ave., 3rd Floor, Boston MA 02116-3803. (617)727-3668. E-mail: mcc@art.state.ma.us. Website: www.massculturalcouncil.org.

MICHIGAN COUNCIL OF HISTORY, ARTS, AND LIBRARIES, 702 W. Kalamazoo St., P.O. Box 30705, Lansing MI 48909-8205. (517)241-4011. E-mail: artsinfo@michigan.gov. Website: www.michigan.gov/hal/0,1607,7-160-17445_19272---,00.html.

MINNESOTA STATE ARTS BOARD, Park Square Court, 400 Sibley St., Suite 200, St. Paul MN 55101-1928. (651)215-1600 or (800)866-2787. E-mail: msab@arts.state.mn.us. Website: www.arts.state.mn.us.

MISSISSIPPI ARTS COMMISSION, 501 N. West St., Suite 701B, Woolfolk Bldg., Jackson MS 39201. (601)359-6030. Website: www.arts.state.ms.us.

MISSOURI ARTS COUNCIL, 815 Olive St., Suite 16, St. Louis MO 63101-1503. (314)340-6845 or (866)407-4752. E-mail: moarts@ded.mo.gov. Website: www.missouriartscouncil.org.

MONTANA ARTS COUNCIL, 316 N. Park Ave., Suite 252, Helena MT 59620-2201. (406)444-6430. E-mail: mac@mt.gov. Website: www.art.state.mt.us.

NATIONAL ASSEMBLY OF STATE ARTS AGENCIES, 1029 Vermont Ave. NW, 2nd Floor, Washington DC 20005. E-mail: nasaa@nasaa-arts.org. Website: www.nasaa-arts.org.

NEBRASKA ARTS COUNCIL, 1004 Farnam St., Plaza Level, Omaha NE 68102. (402)595-2122 or (800)341-4067. Website: www.nebraskaartscouncil.org.

NEVADA ARTS COUNCIL, 716 N. Carson St., Suite A, Carson City NV 89701. (775)687-6680. E-mail: online form. Website: http://dmla.clan.lib.nv.us/docs/arts.

NEW HAMPSHIRE STATE COUNCIL ON THE ARTS, 21/2 Beacon St., 2nd Floor, Concord NH 03301-4974. (603)271-2789. Website: www.nh.gov/nharts.

NEW JERSEY STATE COUNCIL ON THE ARTS, 225 W. State St., P.O. Box 306, Trenton NJ 08625. (609)292-6130. Website: www.njartscouncil.org.

NEW MEXICO ARTS, DEPT. OF CULTURAL AFFAIRS, P.O. Box 1450, Santa Fe NM 87504-1450. (505)827-6490 or (800)879-4278. Website: www.nmarts.org.

NEW YORK STATE COUNCIL ON THE ARTS, 175 Varick St., New York NY 10014. (212)627-4455. Website: www.nysca.org.

NORTH CAROLINA ARTS COUNCIL, 109 East Jones St., Cultural Resources Building, Raleigh NC 27601. (919)807-6500. E-mail: ncarts@ncmail.net. Website: www.ncarts.org.

NORTH DAKOTA COUNCIL ON THE ARTS, 1600 E. Century Ave., Suite 6, Bismarck ND 58503. (701)328-7590. E-mail: comserv@state.nd.us. Website: www.state.nd.us/arts.

OHIO ARTS COUNCIL, 727 E. Main St., Columbus OH 43205-1796. (614)466-2613. Website: www.oac.state.oh.us.

OKLAHOMA ARTS COUNCIL, Jim Thorpe Building, 2101 N. Lincoln Blvd., Suite 640, Oklahoma City OK 73105. (405)521-2931. E-mail: okarts@arts.ok.gov. Website: www.arts.state.ok.us.

OREGON ARTS COMMISSION, 775 Summer St. NE, Suite 200, Salem OR 97301-1280. E-mail: oregon.artscomm@state.or.us. Website: www.oregonartscommission.org.

PENNSYLVANIA COUNCIL ON THE ARTS, 216 Finance Bldg., Harrisburg PA 17120. (717)787-6883. Website: www.pacouncilonthearts.org.

RHODE ISLAND STATE COUNCIL ON THE ARTS, One Capitol Hill, Third Floor, Providence RI 02908. (401)222-3880. E-mail: info@arts.ri.gov. Website: www.arts.ri.gov.

SOUTH CAROLINA ARTS COMMISSION, 1800 Gervais St., Columbia SC 29201. (803)734-8696. E-mail: info@arts.state.sc.us. Website: www.southcarolinaarts.com.

SOUTH DAKOTA ARTS COUNCIL, 711 E. Wells Ave., Pierre SD 57501-3369. (605)773-3301. E-mail: sdac@state.sd.us. Website: www.artscouncil.sd.gov.

TENNESSEE ARTS COMMISSION, 401 Charlotte Ave., Nashville TN 37243-0780. (615)741-1701. Website: www.arts.state.tn.us.

TEXAS COMMISSION ON THE ARTS, E.O. Thompson Office Building, 920 Colorado, Suite 501, Austin TX 78701. (512)463-5535. E-mail: front.desk@arts.state.tx.us. Website: www.arts.state.tx.us.

UTAH ARTS COUNCIL, 617 E. South Temple, Salt Lake City UT 84102-1177. (801)236-7555. Website: http://arts.utah.gov.

VERMONT ARTS COUNCIL, 136 State St., Drawer 33, Montpelier VT 05633-6001. (802)828-3291. E-mail: online form. Website: www.vermontartscouncil.org.

VIRGIN ISLANDS COUNCIL ON THE ARTS, 5070 Norre Gade, St. Thomas VI 00802-6872. (340)774-5984. Website: http://vicouncilonarts.org.

VIRGINIA COMMISSION FOR THE ARTS, Lewis House, 223 Governor St., 2nd Floor, Richmond VA 23219. (804)225-3132. E-mail: arts@arts.virginia.gov. Website: www.arts.state.va.us.

WASHINGTON STATE ARTS COMMISSION, 711 Capitol Way S., Suite 600, P.O. Box 42675, Olympia WA 98504-2675. (360)753-3860. E-mail: info@arts.wa.gov. Website: www.arts.wa.gov.

WEST VIRGINIA COMMISSION ON THE ARTS, The Cultural Center, Capitol Complex, 1900 Kanawha Blvd. E., Charleston WV 25305-0300. (304)558-0220. Website: www.wvculture.org/arts.

WISCONSIN ARTS BOARD, 101 E. Wilson St., 1st Floor, Madison WI 53702. (608)266-0190. E-mail: artsboard@arts.state.wi.us. Website: www.arts.state.wi.us.

WYOMING ARTS COUNCIL, 2320 Capitol Ave., Cheyenne WY 82002. (307)777-7742. E-mail: ebratt@state.wy.us. Website: http://wyoarts.state.wy.us.

CANADIAN PROVINCES ARTS AGENCIES

ALBERTA FOUNDATION FOR THE ARTS, 10708-105 Ave., Edmonton AB T5H 0A1. (780)427-9968. Website: www.affta.ab.ca/index.shtml.

BRITISH COLUMBIA ARTS COUNCIL, P.O. Box 9819, Stn. Prov. Govt., Victoria BC V8W 9W3. (250)356-1718. E-mail: BCArtsCouncil@gov.bc.ca. Website: www.bcartscouncil.ca.

THE CANADA COUNCIL FOR THE ARTS, 350 Albert St., P.O. Box 1047, Ottawa ON K1P 5V8. (613)566-4414 or (800)263-5588 (within Canada). Website: www.canadacouncil.ca.

MANITOBA ARTS COUNCIL, 525-93 Lombard Ave., Winnipeg MB R3B 3B1. (204)945-2237 or (866)994-2787 (in Manitoba). E-mail: info@artscouncil.mb.ca. Website: www.artscouncil.mb.ca.

NEW BRUNSWICK ARTS BOARD (NBAB), 634 Queen St., Suite 300, Fredericton NB E3B 1C2. (506)444-4444 or (866)460-2787. Website: www.artsnb.ca.

NEWFOUNDLAND & LABRADOR ARTS COUNCIL, P.O. Box 98, St. John's NL A1C 5H5. (709)726-2212 or (866)726-2212. E-mail: nlacmail@nfld.net. Website: www.nlac.nf.ca.

NOVA SCOTIA DEPARTMENT OF TOURISM, CULTURE, AND HERITAGE, Culture Division, 1800 Argyle St., Suite 601, P.O. Box 456, Halifax NS B3J 2R5. (902)424-4510. E-mail: cultaffs@gov.ns.ca. Website: www.gov.ns.ca/dtc/culture.

ONTARIO ARTS COUNCIL, 151 Bloor St. W., 5th Floor, Toronto ON M5S 1T6. (416)961-1660 or (800)387-0058 (in Ontario). E-mail: info@arts.on.ca. Website: www.arts.on.ca.

PRINCE EDWARD ISLAND COUNCIL OF THE ARTS, 115 Richmond St., Charlottetown PE C1A 1H7. (902)368-4410 or (888)734-2784. E-mail: info@peiartscouncil.com. Website: www.peiartscouncil.com.

QUÉBEC COUNCIL FOR ARTS & LITERATURE, 79 boul. René-Lévesque Est, 3e étage, Quebec QC G1R 5N5. (418)643-1707 or (800)897-1707. E-mail: info@calq.gouv.qc.ca. Website: www.calq.gouv.qc.ca.

THE SASKATCHEWAN ARTS BOARD, 2135 Broad St., Regina SK S4P 1Y6. (306)787-4056 or (800)667-7526 (Saskatchewan only). E-mail: sab@artsboard.sk.ca. Website: www.artsboard.sk.ca.

YUKON ARTS FUNDING PROGRAM, Cultural Services Branch, Dept. of Tourism & Culture, Government of Yukon, Box 2703 (L-3), Whitehorse YT Y1A 2C6. (867)667-8589 or (800)661-0408 (in Yukon). E-mail: arts@gov.yk.ca. Website: www.tc.gov.yk.ca/216.html.

CONFERENCES & WORKSHOPS

///

There are times when we want to immerse ourselves in learning. Or perhaps we crave a change of scenery, the creative stimulation of being around other artists, or the uninterrupted productivity of time alone to work.

That's what this section of *Poet's Market* is all about, providing a selection of writing conferences and workshops, artist colonies and retreats, poetry festivals, and even a few opportunities to go traveling with your muse. These listings give the basics: contact information, a brief description of the event, lists of past presenters, and offerings of special interest to poets. Contact an event that interests you for additional information, including up-to-date costs and housing details. (Please note that most directors had not finalized their 2020 plans when we contacted them for this edition of *Poet's Market*. However, where possible, they provided us with their 2020 dates, costs, faculty names or themes to give you a better idea of what each event has to offer.)

Before you seriously consider a conference, workshop or other event, determine what you hope to get out of the experience. Would a general conference with one or two poetry workshops among many other types of sessions be acceptable? Or are you looking for something exclusively focused on poetry? Do you want to hear poets speak about poetry writing, or are you looking for a more participatory experience, such as a one-on-one critiquing session or a group workshop? Do you mind being one of hundreds of attendees, or do you prefer a more intimate setting? Are you willing to invest in the expense of traveling to a conference, or would something local better suit your budget? Keep these questions and others in mind as you read these listings, view websites and study conference brochures.

AMERICAN CHRISTIAN WRITERS CONFERENCES

P.O. Box 110390, Nashville TN 37222. (800)219-7483 or (615)331-8668. **E-mail:** acwriters@aol.com. **Website:** www.acwriters.com. **Contact:** Reg Forder, director. ACW hosts a dozen annual two-day writers conferences and mentoring retreats across America taught by editors and professional freelance writers. These events provide excellent instruction, networking opportunities, and valuable one-on-one time with editors. Open to all forms of Christian writing (fiction, nonfiction, and scriptwriting). Conferences are held between March and November during each year.

COSTS/ACCOMMODATIONS Special rates are available at the host hotel (usually a major chain like Holiday Inn). Costs vary and may depend on type of event (conference or mentoring retreat).

ADDITIONAL INFORMATION E-mail or call for conference brochures.

✎ ANAM CARA WRITER'S AND ARTIST'S RETREAT

Eyeries, Beara, Co. Cork , Ireland. +353 (0)27 74441. **Fax:** +353 (0)27 74448. **E-mail:** anamcararetreat@gmail.com. **Website:** www.anamcararetreat.com. **Contact:** Sue Booth-Forbes, Director. general craft, mixed media art "High on a hillside between Coulagh Bay and Mishkish on the Kealincha River awaits Anam Cara, a tranquil spot set apart to nurture and to provide sanctuary for novice as well as experienced people working in the creative arts. Whether you retreat to work on your own project or as part of a workshop group, you will find support, creature comforts, and peace—all you need to do your best work. An all-inclusive residential retreat, Anam Cara offers private and common working rooms and 5 acres of walking paths, quiet nooks and crannies, gardens and meadows, a river island, and the Kealincha River cascades."

💬 "Hands down, the best part of being Anam Cara's director is getting to know the writers and artists-in-residence (now over a thousand) and their work. They have taught me and each other much about the creative process. Their genre/medium may be similar to someone else's, but their approach is always unique and inspirational. One intention for naming the retreat Anam Cara was to provide a space for people who, as they worked with their creative gifts, would recognize the 'soul friend' in themselves, in their work, and in others."

COSTS/ACCOMMODATIONS Costs for all-inclusive individual and workshop retreats are available upon request. See website for details about the 5 working bedrooms at Anam Cara designated for individual retreats. Participants in workshop retreats stay either at Anam Cara or at nearby bed-and-breakfasts in ensuite rooms. Requests for specific information about rates and availability for both individual and workshop retreats are made by sending an email to anamcararetreat@gmail.com.

ADDITIONAL INFORMATION Requests for specific information about rates and availability for both individual and workshop retreats are made by contacting Sue at anamcararetreat@gmail.com.

ANNUAL SPRING POETRY FESTIVAL

City College, 160 Convent Ave., New York NY 10031. (212)650-6356. **Website:** www.ccny.cuny.edu/poetry/festival. **Contact:** Pamela Laskin. Friday, May 3, 2019, (9 a.m.-5 p.m.) Workshops geared to all levels. Open to students. Write for more information. Site: Theater B of Aaron Davis Hall.

✎ ART WORKSHOPS IN GUATEMALA

4758 Lyndale Ave. S., Minneapolis MN 55419. (612)825-0747. **E-mail:** info@artguat.org. **Website:** www.artguat.org. **Contact:** Liza Fourre, director. Ten day workshops, with a focus on the arts and Mayan culture, held year-round. Maximum class size: 12 students.

COSTS/ACCOMMODATIONS See website. Includes tuition, lodging, breakfast, and ground transportation.

ADDITIONAL INFORMATION For brochure/guidelines, visit website, e-mail, or call.

ASPEN SUMMER WORDS WRITERS CONFERENCE & LITERARY FESTIVAL

Aspen Words, 110 E. Hallam St., Suite 116, Aspen CO 81611. (970)925-3122. **Fax:** (970)925-5700. **E-mail:** aspenwords@aspeninstitute.org. **Website:** www.aspenwords.org. **Contact:** Caroline Tory. Annual conference held each summer. June 16-21, 2019. Offers workshops in fiction, memoir, novel editing, and playwriting. Past years' faculty have included fiction writers Ann Hood, Richard Russo, Akhil Sharma, and Hannah Tinti; memoir writers Andre Dubus III and Dani Shapiro; and playwright Sharr White. Aspen Summer Words features lectures, readings, panel discussions, and the opportunity to meet with agents and editors.

COSTS/ACCOMMODATIONS Non-Juried 5-Day Writing Workshop: $1525.00. 3-Day Readers Retreat: $425. Financial aid is available on a limited basis.

ADDITIONAL INFORMATION To apply for a juried workshop, see website for an application and complete guidelines.

ASSOCIATION OF WRITERS & WRITING PROGRAMS CONFERENCE & BOOKFAIR

Association of Writers & Writing Programs, University of Maryland, 5700 Rivertech Court, Suite 225, Riverdale Park MD 20737-1250. (301)226-9711. **Fax:** (301)226.9797. **E-mail:** conference@awpwriter.org; events@awpwriter.org. **Website:** www.awpwriter.org/awp_conference. Each year, AWP holds its annual conference and bookfair in a different city to celebrate the authors, teachers, writing programs, literary centers, and publishers of that region. The conference features more than 500 readings, lectures, and panel discussions; 800 presses, publishers, and other literary organizations in the bookfair; and hundreds of book signings, receptions, dances, and informal gatherings. It is the largest literary conference in North America.

ADDITIONAL INFORMATION Upcoming conference locations include San Antonio (March 4-7, 2020), Kansas City (March 3-6, 2021) and Philadelphia (March 23-26, 2022).

ATLANTIC CENTER FOR THE ARTS

1414 Art Center Ave., New Smyrna Beach FL 32168. (386)427-6975. **Fax:** (386)427-5669. **E-mail:** program@atlanticcenterforthearts.org. **Website:** www.atlanticcenterforthearts.org. Internship and residency programs. A Florida artist-in-residence program in which artists of all disciplines work with current prominent artists in a supportive and creative environment. See website for application schedule and materials.

COSTS/ACCOMMODATIONS Accommodations available on site. $900; $25 non-refundable application fee. Financial aid is available. Participants are responsible for all materials, transportation, and weekend meals.

AUSTIN INTERNATIONAL POETRY FESTIVAL

E-mail: aipfest@outlook.com. **E-mail:** editor@aipf.org. **Website:** www.aipf.org. **Contact:** Director. Annual poetry festival held every spring. Registration is required for all poets. This four-day citywide, all-inclusive celebration of poetry and poets has grown to become "the largest non-juried poetry festival in the United States." The festival includes assigned readings and workshops, open mics, music and poetry presentations, anthology competitions, poetry slams, an all-night open mic, and special events.

COSTS/ACCOMMODATIONS See website for host hotel. Anthology submission fee $30 USD (half supports youth literacy initiative). Attendance registration $55 USD includes, program bio, scheduled reading and workshop assignment, admission to special events (discount registration available for retired, college, and military poets).

ADDITIONAL INFORMATION Offers multiple poetry contests as part of festival. Guidelines available on website. Registration form available on website.

BREAD LOAF WRITERS' CONFERENCE

Middlebury College, Middlebury College, Middlebury VT 05753. (802)443-5286. **Fax:** (802)443-2087. **E-mail:** blwc@middlebury.edu. **Website:** www.middlebury.edu/bread-loaf-conferences/bl_writers. Annual conference held in late August. 2019 dates: August 14-24. Duration: 10 days. Average attendance: 230. Offers workshops for fiction, nonfiction, and poetry. Agents and editors attend.

COSTS/ACCOMMODATIONS Bread Loaf campus of Middlebury College in Ripton, Vermont. $3,525 for general contributors and $3,380 for auditors. Both options include room and board.

ADDITIONAL INFORMATION The application deadline for the 2019 conference: October 15, 2018-February 15, 2019; there is a $20 application fee.

CAPE COD WRITERS CENTER ANNUAL CONFERENCE

P.O. Box 408, Osterville MA 02655. (508)420-0200. **E-mail:** writers@capecodwriterscenter.org. **Website:** www.capecodwriterscenter.org. **Contact:** Nancy Rubin Stuart, executive director. Announcing the 57th broad-based literary conference August 1-4, 2019 at the Resort and Conference Center at Hyannis, MA. Workshops in fiction, nonfiction, poetry, memoir, mystery, thrillers, writing for children, social media, screenwriting, promotion, pitches and queries, agent meetings and ms mentorship with agents, editors, and faculty.

COSTS/ACCOMMODATIONS Resort and Conference Center of Hyannis, Massachusetts. Costs vary, depending on the number of courses selected, beginning at $125. Several scholarships are available.

CAVE CANEM

20 Jay St., Suite 310-A, Brooklyn NY 11201. (718)858-0000. **Fax:** (718)858-0002. **E-mail:** alisonmeyers@ccpoets.org; info@ccpoets.org. **Website:** www.cavecanempoets.org. **Contact:** Alison Meyers, executive director. Focuses on African-American writers, particularly poets. Offers workshops and an annual retreat.

🔈 "Since 1999, nearly 900 emerging poets have participated in Cave Canem's community-based workshops, rare opportunities to work with accomplished poets for free or low-cost fees. Limited to an enrollment of 12-15, eight-session workshops offer rigorous instruction, careful critique and an introduction to the work of established poets—all within the welcoming environment of our Brooklyn loft."

COSTS/ACCOMMODATIONS Costs vary by workshop. Check website for updated information.

CELEBRATION OF SOUTHERN LITERATURE

Southern Lit Alliance, 301 E. 11th St., Suite 301, Chattanooga TN 37403. (423)267-1218. **Fax:** (866)483-6831. **Website:** www.southernlitalliance.org. Biennial conference held in odd-numbered years. "The Celebration of Southern Literature stands out because of its unique collaboration with the Fellowship of Southern Writers, an organization founded by towering literary figures like Eudora Welty, Cleanth Brooks, Walker Percy, and Robert Penn Warren to recognize and encourage literature in the South. The Fellowship awards 11 literary prizes and inducts new members, making this event the place to discover up-and-coming voices in Southern literature. The Southern Lit Alliance's Celebration of Southern Literature attracts more than 1,000 readers and writers from all over the United States. It strives to maintain an informal atmosphere where conversations will thrive, inspired by a common passion for the written word. The Southern Lit Alliance (formerly the Arts & Education Council) started as one of 12 pilot agencies founded by a Ford Foundation grant in 1952. The Alliance is the only organization of the 12 still in existence. The Southern Lit Alliance celebrates Southern writers and readers through community education and innovative literary arts experiences."

CHAUTAUQUA WRITERS' CENTER

P.O. Box 28, 1 Ames Ave., Chautauqua NY 14722. **Website:** https://chq.org/season/literary-arts/writers/writers-center.

COSTS/ACCOMMODATIONS See website for accommodation options, ranging from the Athenaeum Hotel to local rooming houses and condos. Check website for costs. Register online at chqtickets.com.

COLGATE WRITERS' CONFERENCE

Office of Summer Programs, Colgate University, 13 Oak Dr., Hamilton NY 13346. (315)228-7771. **E-mail:** writersconference@colgate.edu. **Website:** www.colgate.edu/community/summerprograms/adult-programs/colgate-writers-conference. Annual conference held in June. 2019 dates: June 16-22. Application deadline: April 21.

COSTS/ACCOMMODATIONS Available on site. See website for details. Meal plan available for day students.

ADDITIONAL INFORMATION Each applicant must submit a ms with application. Brochure and registration form available for SASE or on website.

THE COLRAIN POETRY MANUSCRIPT CONFERENCE

E-mail: conferences@colrainpoetry.com. **Website:** www.colrainpoetry.com. "Colrain is the original, one-of-a-kind manuscript conference. Faculty includes nationally renowned poet-editors and publishers. Work with the best for the best results. Our unique, realistic method of manuscript evaluation sets poets with a manuscript in progress on a path toward publication. Poets also get a look into the publication world and make important contacts with leading editors, teachers, and publishers."

ADDITIONAL INFORMATION Details, application, and registration form available on website.

GERALDINE R. DODGE POETRY FESTIVAL

Website: www.dodgepoetryfestival.org. Biennial festival held in even numbered years. "The Geraldine R. Dodge Poetry Festival, an initiative of the Geraldine R. Dodge Foundation, is a celebration of poetry that immerses participants in 4 days of readings, performances, and conversations. In its 30-year history, the Dodge Poetry Festival has involved nearly 600 poets, including Nobel Laureates and U.S. Poet Laureates; Pulitzer Prize and National Book Award winners; Guggenheim, Fulbright, MacArthur, and NEA fellows; and an unparalleled array of much-published and award-winning poets."

COSTS/ACCOMMODATIONS Audience members responsible for own lodging and meals. Information on overnight accommodations available on website. Check website for latest information. Passes can be purchased at a discount for multiple days.

ADDITIONAL INFORMATION Sign up online for mailing list.

THE FROST PLACE CONFERENCE ON POETRY

(603)823-5510. **E-mail:** frost@frostplace.org. **Website:** www.frostplace.org. Annual poetry conference held in July. 2019 dates: July 6-12. "Spend a week at 'intensive poetry camp' with writers who are deeply committed to learning more about the craft of writing poetry." Offers daily workshops, classes, lectures, and writing and revising time in a supportive and dynamic environment.

COSTS/ACCOMMODATIONS Application fee: $25. Conference Package Rate: $1,750. Commuter Rate: $1,400 Day Rate: $350. See website for discount options.

THE FROST PLACE POETRY CONFERENCES

The Frost Place, P.O. Box 74, 158 Ridge Road, Franconia NH 03580. (603)823-5510. **E-mail:** frost@frostplace.org. **Website:** www.frostplace.org. **Contact:** Paige Roberts, Assistant to the Director - proberts@frostplace.org.. Each year The Frost Place hosts three annual summer poetry conferences: the Conference on Poetry and Teaching, the Conference on Poetry, and the Poetry Seminar. See website for details, www.frostplace.org. 2019 dates: Conference on Poetry and Teaching June 22-26; Writing Intensive June 26-27; Conference on Poetry July 6-12. Poetry Seminar August 4-10.

COSTS/ACCOMMODATIONS Varies.

ADDITIONAL INFORMATION The Frost Place Conference on Poetry (July 6-12, 2019); Conference on Poetry and Teaching (June 22-26, 2019).

HAIKU NORTH AMERICA CONFERENCE

Website: www.haikunorthamerica.com. **Contact:** Michael Dylan Welch. Biennial conference held in odd numbered years. 2019 dates: August 7-11, in Winston-Salem, North Carolina. Haiku North America (HNA) is the largest and oldest gathering of haiku poets in the United States and Canada. There are no membership fees, and HNA provides news and interaction on the HNA website/blog. All haiku poets and interested parties are welcome. HNA is a long weekend of papers, panels, workshops, readings, performances, book sales, and much socialization with many of the continent's leading poets, translators, scholars, editors, and publishers. Both established and aspiring haiku poets are welcome.

COSTS/ACCOMMODATIONS Official conference hotel offers discounted rates. See HNA website for more information. Typically around $200, including a banquet and a conference anthology. Visit website for full details.

HIGHLAND SUMMER CONFERENCE

P.O. Box 7014, Radford University, Radford VA 24142. **E-mail:** tburriss@radford.edu. **Website:** tinyurl.com/q8z8ej9. **Contact:** Dr. Theresa Burriss. The Highland Summer Writers' Conference is a 4-day lecture-seminar workshop combination conducted by well known guest writers. 2019 details: "The 42nd annual HSC will be held at Radford University's beautiful Selu Conservancy the entire week of July 8-12. Multi-genre Affrilachian author Crystal Wilkinson will serve as guest writer/facilitator. Interested individuals can enroll in the conference to obtain traditional three-hour course credit at the graduate or undergraduate level, or register through the Appalachian Regional & Rural Studies Center at a reduced rate for continuing education credits or to simply participate. For more information, please contact Theresa Burriss." It offers the opportunity to study and practice creative and expository writing within the context of regional culture. The evening readings are free and open to the public. Services at a reduced rate for continuing education credits or to simply participate.

INDIANA UNIVERSITY WRITERS' CONFERENCE

Lindley Hall 215, 150 South Woodlawn Avenue, Bloomington IN 47405. (812)855-1877. **E-mail:** writecon@indiana.edu. **Website:** https://www.pw.org/content/indiana_university_writers_conference. **Contact:** Bob Bledsoe, Director. Annual conference/workshops held in June. 2019 dates: June 1-5. Average attendance: 100. The Indiana University Writers' Conference believes in a craft-based teaching of creative writing. We emphasize an exploration of creativity through a variety of approaches, offering workshop-based craft discussions, classes focusing on technique, and talks about the careers and concerns of a writing life.

COSTS/ACCOMMODATIONS Information on accommodations available on website. The cost for the Poetry, Fiction Workshops is $385-670, depending on workshop. Lodging and meals are not included;

lodging is available in campus dormitories for $50 per night or in the campus hotel for $134 per night. The registration fee is $30; general registration is first come, first served. To apply for a workshop, submit 8-10 pages of poetry or 15-20 pages of prose; admissions are made on a rolling basis. Visit the website for more information.

ADDITIONAL INFORMATION Follow the conference on Twitter at @iuwritecon.

IOWA SUMMER WRITING FESTIVAL

The University of Iowa, 250 Continuing Education Facility, University of Iowa, Iowa City IA 52242. (319)335-4160. **Fax:** (319)335-4039. **E-mail:** iswfestival@uiowa.edu. **Website:** https://iowasummerwritingfestival.org/. Annual festival held in June and July. More than 100 workshops and more than 50 instructors. Workshops are 1 week or a weekend. Attendance is limited to 12 people per class, with more than 1,500 participants throughout the summer. Offers courses across the genres: novel, short story, poetry, essay, memoir, humor, travel, playwriting, screenwriting, writing for children, and women's writing. Held at the University of Iowa campus. Speakers have included Marvin Bell, Lan Samantha Chang, John Dalton, Hope Edelman, Katie Ford, Patricia Foster, Bret Anthony Johnston, and Barbara Robinette Moss.

COSTS/ACCOMMODATIONS Accommodations available at area hotels. Information on overnight accommodations available by phone or on website. See website for registration and conference fees.

ADDITIONAL INFORMATION Brochures are available in February. Inquire via e-mail or on website. "Register early. Classes fill quickly."

IWWG SPRING BIG APPLE CONFERENCE

(917)720-6959. **E-mail:** iwwgquestions@iwwg.org. **Website:** www.iwwg.org. One or 2-day annual conference held from in New days York in spring and includes writing workshops, new-authors panel discussing publishing trends, fairs agents panel, and open one-on-one pitch sessions.

JACKSON HOLE WRITERS CONFERENCE

P.O. Box 1974, Jackson WY 83001. (307)413-3332. **E-mail:** jhwritersconf@gmail.com. **Website:** jacksonholewritersconference.com. general craft Annual conference held in June. 2019 dates: June 27-29. Conference duration: 3-4 days. Average attendance: 110. Covers fiction, creative nonfiction, poetry and KidsLit, and offers ms critiques from authors, agents, and editors. Agents in attendance will take pitches from writers. Paid ms critique programs are available.

COSTS/ACCOMMODATIONS Accommodations not included. $375 thru May 12, 2019; critiques additional.

ADDITIONAL INFORMATION Held at the Center for the Arts in Jackson, Wyoming, and online.

JENTEL ARTIST RESIDENCY PROGRAM

Jentel Foundation, 130 Lower Piney Creek Rd., Banner WY 82832. (307)737-2311. **Fax:** (307)737-2305. **E-mail:** jentel@jentelarts.org. **Website:** www.jentelarts.org. "The Jentel Artist Residency Program offers dedicated individuals a supportive environment in which to further their creative development. Here artists and writers experience unfettered time to allow for thoughtful reflection and meditation on the creative process in a setting that preserves the agricultural and historical integrity of the land."

COSTS/ACCOMMODATIONS Residents are responsible for travel expenses and personal items. Jentel provides a private accommodation in a large house with common living and dining areas; fully equipped kitchen; library with computer, printer, and internet access; media room with television, DVD/video player, and CD player; spacious private bedroom; and separate private studio. Staff takes residents grocery shopping weekly after the stipend is distributed. Staff will pick up and drop off residents at the airport and bus station in Sheridan, 20 miles from the ranch setting of Jentel.

ADDITIONAL INFORMATION Brochure and application form online.

KENTUCKY WOMEN WRITERS CONFERENCE

University of Kentucky College of Arts & Sciences, 232 E. Maxwell St., Lexington KY 40506. (859)257-2874. **E-mail:** kentuckywomenwriters@gmail.com. **Website:** kentuckywomenwriters.org. **Contact:** Julie Wrinn, director. Conference held in second or third weekend of September. September 19-22, 2019. Duration: 2 days. Site: Carnegie Center for Literacy in Lexington, Kentucky. Average attendance: 150-200. Conference covers poetry, fiction, creative nonfiction, and playwriting. Includes writing workshops, panels, and readings featuring contemporary women writers.

COSTS/ACCOMMODATIONS $200 for general admission and a workshop and $125 for admission with no workshop.

ADDITIONAL INFORMATION Sponsors prizes in poetry ($300), fiction ($300), nonfiction ($300), playwriting ($500), and spoken word ($500). Winners are also invited to read during the conference. Pre-registration opens May 1.

KENYON REVIEW WRITERS WORKSHOP

Kenyon Review, Kenyon College, Gambier OH 43022. (740)427-5208. **Fax:** (740)427-5417. **E-mail:** kenyonreview@kenyon.edu; writers@kenyonreview.org. **Website:** www.kenyonreview.org/workshops. **Contact:** Anna Duke Reach, director. Annual 8-day workshops held in June and July. Participants apply in poetry, fiction, literary nonfiction, nature writing, translation, or the workshop for teachers, and then participate in intensive daily workshops that focus on the generation and revision of significant new work. Held on the campus of Kenyon College in the rural village of Gambier, Ohio. Workshop leaders include Lee K. Abbot, David Baker, Katherine M. Hedeen, Joanna Klink, E.J. Levy, Elizabeth Lowe, Rebecca McClanahan, Dinty W. Moore, Carl Phillips, Natalie Shapero, and Nancy Zafris. 2019 dates: June 16-22 and July 7-13.

COSTS/ACCOMMODATIONS The workshop operates a shuttle to and from Gambier and the airport in Columbus, Ohio. Offers overnight accommodations. Participants are housed in Kenyon College student housing. Fiction, literary nonfiction, poetry, nature writing, translation: $2,295. Teachers: $1,795. All rates include tuition and room and board.

ADDITIONAL INFORMATION Application includes a writing sample. Admission decisions are made on a rolling basis. Starting in November, workshop information is available online. For a brochure, send e-mail, visit website, call, or fax. Accepts inquiries by SASE, e-mail, phone, and fax.

KUNDIMAN POETRY AND FICTION RETREAT

113 West 60th Street, Room 924, New York NY 10023. **E-mail:** info@kundiman.org. **Website:** kundiman.org/retreat. **Contact:** Mindy Wong, manager. Annual retreat held at Fordham University's Rose Hill campus. 2019 dates: June 19-23. "During the Retreat, nationally renowned Asian-American poets and writers conduct workshops with fellows. Readings, writing circles, and informal social gatherings are also scheduled. Through this Retreat, Kundiman hopes to provide a safe and instructive environment that identifies and addresses the unique challenges faced by emerging Asian-American writers." Submit a cover letter and brief writing sample (5-7 pages of poetry or 5 pages of prose, 1250 words maximum). Visit website for more information.

COSTS/ACCOMMODATIONS Room and board is free to accepted fellows. Tuition is $375. Application Fee: $25.

ADDITIONAL INFORMATION For more information, guidelines, and online application, visit website.

MENDOCINO COAST WRITERS' CONFERENCE

P.O. Box 2087, Fort Bragg CA 95437. **E-mail:** info@mcwc.org. **Website:** www.mcwc.org. **Contact:** Lisa Locascio, Executive Director. Situated where summers are temperate and the seascape spectacular, this friendly conference emphasizes craft and community. Visiting faculty—top authors who are also outstanding teachers—will challenge you to find and express your own voice. MCWC 2019 faculty include: Myriam Gurba, Ingrid Rojas Contreras, Shobha Rao, Mitali Perkins, Jeannie Vanasco, Scott Sigler, Ismail Muhammad, Victoria Chang, and Charlotte Gullick with keynote speaker Sharon Olds. You will work closely with authors, editors, literary agents, and writers of many levels of experience, interests, ages, and backgrounds. Participants meet for three mornings with their intensive workshop group. Afternoons and evenings include craft seminars, pitch sessions, open-mics, literary readings, publishing panels, and social events. Optional manuscript consultations are available with the instructor, editor, or agent of your choice, on a limited first-come, first-served basis. All registrants may enter conference contests with cash prizes and possible publication in Noyo River Review. 2019 conference dates are August 1-3 with an optional Publishing Bootcamp taught by Philip Marino (senior editor at Little, Brown) on August 4.

COSTS/ACCOMMODATIONS Many lodging options in the scenic coastal area. $575 registration includes morning intensives, afternoon panels and seminars, social events, and most meals. Scholarships available. Opt-in for consultations and Publishing Boot Camp. Early application advised.

ADDITIONAL INFORMATION "Take your writing to the next level with encouragement, expertise, and inspiration in a literary community where authors are also fantastic teachers." General registration opens March 1.

MONTEVALLO LITERARY FESTIVAL

Comer Hall, Station 6420, University of Montevallo, Montevallo AL 35115. (205)665-6420. **Fax:** (205)665-6420. **E-mail:** murphyj@montevallo.edu. **Website:** www.montevallo.edu/arts-sciences/college-of-arts-sciences/departments/english-foreign-languages/student-organizations/montevallo-literary-festival. **Contact:** Dr. Jim Murphy, director. "Each April, the University of Montevallo's Department of English and Foreign Languages hosts the annual Montevallo Literary Festival, a celebration of creative writing dedicated to bringing literary writers and readers together on a personal scale. Our friendly, relaxed festival runs all day into the evening, featuring readings by all invited writers, book signings, a question-and-answer panel, social gatherings, and dinner with live music."

JENNY MCKEAN MOORE COMMUNITY WORKSHOPS

English Department, George Washington University, Phillips Hall, 801 22nd St. NW, Suite 643, Washington DC 20052. (202)994-6180. **Fax:** (202)994-6637. **E-mail:** engldept@gwu.edu; lpageinc@aol.com. **Website:** www.gwu.edu/~english/creative_jennymckeanmoore.html. **Contact:** Lisa Page, director of creative writing. Workshop held each semester at the university. Average attendance: 15. Concentration varies depending on professor—usually fiction or poetry. The creative writing department brings an established poet or novelist to campus each year to teach a writing workshop for GW students and a free community workshop for adults in the larger Washington community. Details posted on website in June, with an application deadline at the end of August or in early September.

ADDITIONAL INFORMATION Admission is competitive and by decided by the quality of a submitted ms.

MOUNT HERMON CHRISTIAN WRITERS CONFERENCE

P.O. Box 413, Mount Hermon CA 95041. **E-mail:** info@mounthermon.org. **Website:** writers.mounthermon.org. **Contact:** Kathy Ide, director. Annual professional conference held over Palm Sunday weekend. Friday lunch through Tuesday breakfast. Pre-conference mentoring clinics run from Wednesday dinner till Friday lunch. Average attendance: 350-400. Sponsored by and held at the 440-acre Mount Hermon Christian Conference Center near San Jose, California, in the heart of the coastal redwoods. We are a broad-ranging conference for all areas of Christian writing, including fiction, nonfiction, sci-fi/fantasy, children's, teen, young adult, poetry, magazines, and devotional writing. This is a working, how-to conference, with Major Morning Tracks in several genres (including tracks for teen writers and professional authors), Morning Mentoring Clinics, and 40 or more afternoon workshops. Faculty-to-student ratio is about 1 to 6. Many of our more than 70 faculty members are literary agents, acquisitions editors, and representatives from major Christian publishing houses nationwide. Attendees can submit up to two manuscript samples to faculty members for review or critique for no additional charge. Ample opportunities for one-on-one appointments.

COSTS/ACCOMMODATIONS Options include modern cabins (with full kitchens) or lodges (similar to hotel rooms), available in economy, standard, and deluxe. See website for pricing.

NAPA VALLEY WRITERS' CONFERENCE

Napa Valley College, 1088 College Ave., St. Helena CA 94574. (707)967-2900 ext. 4. **E-mail:** info@napawritersconference.og. **Website:** www.napawritersconference.org. **Contact:** Catherine Thorpe, managing director. Established 1981. Annual weeklong event. 2019 dates: July 28-August 2. Location: Upper Valley Campus in the historic town of St. Helena, 25 miles north of Napa in the heart of the valley's wine growing community. Average attendance: 48 in poetry and 48 in fiction. "Serious writers of all backgrounds and experience are welcome to apply." Offers poets and fiction writers workshops, lectures, faculty readings at Napa Valley wineries, and one-on-one faculty counseling. "Poetry session provides the opportunity to work both on generating new poems and on revising previously written ones."

On Twitter as @napawriters and on Facebook as facebook.com/napawriters.

COSTS/ACCOMMODATIONS Applications for admission to the 2019 conference are now closed as of April 30, 2019. The total participation fee for the 2019 program is $1,025, and includes daily breakfast and lunch, two dinners, wine tastings, and attendance at all conference events. $25 reading fee–Pay with your application. $1,025 participation fee–due on acceptance, non-refundable after June 5. Financial Assistance: A limited number of grants are available to cover all or part of the conference participation fee, with awards made on the basis of merit and need.

PALM BEACH POETRY FESTIVAL

3199 B-3 Lake Worth Rd., Lake Worth FL (561)868-2063. **E-mail:** news@palmbeachpoetryfestival.org. **Website:** www.palmbeachpoetryfestival.org. **Contact:** Susan R. Williamson, Festival Director.

COSTS/ACCOMMODATIONS Area hotels may offer discounted rates. Participants responsible for all meals except Gala Dinner. Participant tuition is $950, and auditor tuition is $550. Applications require a $25 non-refundable application fee plus a $250 tuition deposit. Cost for the optional One-On-One Conference is $99.

ADDITIONAL INFORMATION Guidelines available by e-mail. Brochure and registration forms available by fax, e-mail, and on website. Application deadline in November.

SAN DIEGO STATE UNIVERSITY WRITERS' CONFERENCE

SDSU College of Extended Studies, 5250 Campanile Dr., San Diego State University, San Diego CA 92182. (619)594-2099. **Fax:** (619)594-8566. **E-mail:** sdsuwritersconference@mail.sdsu.edu. **Website:** ces.sdsu.edu/writers. Just as all good literary works must come to an end, so must we. The San Diego State Writers' Conference bids you farewell, and wishes you every success in your writing endeavors. Use your conference memories, epiphanies, and connections as fuel to maintain your momentum in pursuing your goals.

SANTA BARBARA WRITERS CONFERENCE

27 W. Anapamu St., Suite 305, Santa Barbara CA 93101. (805)568-1516. **E-mail:** info@sbwriters.com. **Website:** www.sbwriters.com. Annual conference held in June. 2019 dates: June 16-21 at Santa Barbara Hyatt for 47th anniversary. Average attendance: 200. 30+ writing workshops, panels, speakers, agents, and fellow word crafters. Covers fiction, nonfiction, journalism, memoir, poetry, playwriting, screenwriting, travel writing, young adult, children's literature, humor, and marketing. Speakers have included Ray Bradbury, William Styron, Eudora Welty, James Michener, Sue Grafton, Charles M. Schulz, Clive Cussler, Fannie Flagg, Elmore Leonard, and T.C. Boyle. Agents will appear on a panel; in addition, there will be an agents and editors day that allows writers to pitch their projects in one-on-one meetings.

COSTS/ACCOMMODATIONS Hyatt Santa Barbara. $150 for single-day; $699 for full conference.

ADDITIONAL INFORMATION Register online or contact for brochure and registration forms.

✪ SASKATCHEWAN FESTIVAL OF WORDS

217 Main St. N., Moose Jaw Saskatchewan S6H 0W1, Canada. (306)691-0557. **E-mail:** amanda@festivalofwords.com. **Website:** www.festivalofwords.com. The Saskatchewan Festival of Words (established in 1996) is a registered charity and nonprofit organization that holds an annual literary festival the third weekend in July with over 50 events over 4 days in and around historic downtown Moose Jaw. This year our Festival will be held on July 18-21, 2019.

COSTS/ACCOMMODATIONS Passes are available for $175 ($200 after June 1) for a full pass, $100 for a flex pass, and $55 for a student pass. Learn more about passes on our website. We also have tickets available for events from $10-30 and free events too!

SEWANEE WRITERS' CONFERENCE

735 University Ave., 119 Gailor Hall, Stamler Center, Sewanee TN 37383. (931)598-1654. **E-mail:** swc@sewanee.edu. **Website:** www.sewaneewriters.org. **Contact:** Adam Latham. Annual conference. 2019 dates: July 16-28. Average attendance: 150. Accepting applications January 5-March 20. The University of the South will host the 30th session of the Sewanee Writers' Conference. Thanks to the generosity of the Walter E. Dakin Memorial Fund, supported by the estate of the late Tennessee Williams, the Conference will gather a distinguished faculty to provide instruction and criticism through workshops and craft lectures in poetry, fiction, and playwriting. During a 12-day period, participants will read and critique workshop manuscripts under the leadership of some of our faculty. Faculty members give scheduled readings and craft lectures; open mic readings accommodate many others. Additional writers, along with a host of writing professionals, visit to give readings, participate in panel discussions, and answer questions from the audience. Receptions and mealtimes offer ample social opportunities. 2019 faculty includes fiction writers Jeffery Renard Allen, Tony Earley, Adrianne Harun, Randall Kenan, Michael Knight, Bobbie Ann Mason, Jill McCorkle, Tim O'Brien, Christine Schutt, and Steve Yarbrough; poets B.H. Fairchild, Robert Hass, Mark Jarman, Maurice Manning, Marilyn Nelson, Mary Jo Salter, A.E. Stallings, and Sidney Wade; and

playwrights Dan O'Brien and Naomi Iizuka. Charles Martin, A.E. Stallings, and N.S. Thompson will offer a supplemental poetry translation workshop, and Charles Martin, Alice McDermott, and Wyatt Prunty will read from their work.

COSTS/ACCOMMODATIONS Participants are housed in single rooms in university dormitories. Bathrooms are shared by small groups. $1,100 for tuition, and $700 for room, board, and activity costs.

THE SOUTHAMPTON WRITERS CONFERENCE

Stony Brook Southampton MFA in Creative Writing Program, 239 Montauk Hwy., Southampton NY 11968. (631)632-5007. **E-mail:** christian.mclean@stonybrook.edu. **Website:** www.stonybrook.edu/writers. **Contact:** Christian McLean. Annual conference held in summer. 2019 dates: July 10-21. Since 1976, the Southampton Writers Conference has brought together writers at all stages of their careers with world-class novelists, essayists, editors, poets, and children's book authors for lectures, readings, panels, and workshops. All writers are welcome to apply to the conference. 5-day and 12-day writing workshops and 12-day residency program. Workshops and Faculty include Jericho Brown, Billy Collins, Karen E. Bender, Ursula Hegi, Melissa Bank, Frederic Tuten, Lucas Hnath, Alan Kingsberg, and more. Also special guests include Meg Wolitzer, Katherine Faw, Megan Lynch, Julie Langsdorf, Tony Tulathimutte, Nora Decter, Daniel Menaker, Richard Panek, Tom Dyja and more.

COSTS/ACCOMMODATIONS Participants can stay on campus in air-conditioned dorms. 5-day workshop only: $1,495. 5-day workshop plus residency: $1,995 (12 days total). 12-day workshop: $1,995. 12-day residency: $500. 12-day lecture series: $500 (does not include afternoon faculty-led workshop).

SOUTH CAROLINA WRITERS WORKSHOP

4711 Forest Dr., Suite 3, P.M.B. 189, Columbia SC 29206. **E-mail:** scwwliaison@gmail.com. **Website:** www.myscwa.org. Conference held in October at the Metropolitan Conference Center in Columbia. Held almost every year. Conference duration: 3 days. Features critique sessions, open mic readings, and presentations from agents and editors. More than 50 different workshops for writers to choose from, dealing with all subjects of writing craft, writing business, getting an agent, and more. Agents will be in attendance.

STEAMBOAT SPRINGS WRITERS CONFERENCE

A Day For Writers, Steamboat Springs Arts Council, Eleanor Bliss Center for the Arts at the Depot, P.O. Box 774284, Steamboat Springs CO 80477. (970)879-9008. **E-mail:** info@steamboatwriters.com. **Website:** www.steamboatwriters.com. **Contact:** Barbara Sparks. Annual event will be Saturday July 27, 2019. Instructors Juan Morales, poet, and Emily Sinclair, essayist. Workshops geared toward intermediate levels. Open to professionals and amateurs alike. Average attendance: 35-40 (registration limited, conference fills quickly). Optional pre-conference gathering Friday night. Meet-and-greet buffet social followed by Five Minutes of Fame session for conference participants to share their work.

🗨 "A Day for Writers" emphasizes instruction within the seminar format. Novices and polished professionals benefit from a unique feature that offers one workshop at a time. All participants engage together, adding to the informal and intimate community feeling. It's perfect for nonfiction writers seeking a combination of inspiration, craft techniques and camaraderie.

COSTS/ACCOMMODATIONS $60 early registration; $75 after May 31. Registration fee includes continental breakfast and luncheon.

SUMMER WRITING PROGRAM

Naropa University, 2130 Arapahoe Ave., Boulder CO 80302. (303)245-4862. **Fax:** (303)546-5287. **E-mail:** swp@naropa.edu. **Website:** www.naropa.edu/swp. **Contact:** Kyle Pivarnik, special projects manager. Annual event in summer. 2019 dates: 9-29. Workshop duration: 4 weeks. Average attendance: 250. Offers college credit. Accepts inquiries by e-mail, phone. With 13 workshops to choose from each of the 4 weeks of the program, students may study poetry, prose, hybrid/cross-genre writing, small press printing, or book arts. Site: All workshops, panels, lectures, and readings are hosted on the Naropa University main campus. Located in downtown Boulder, the campus is within easy walking distance of restaurants, shopping, and the scenic Pearl Street Mall.

COSTS/ACCOMMODATIONS See website for pricing information.

ADDITIONAL INFORMATION Writers can elect to take the Summer Writing Program for noncredit, graduate credit, or undergraduate credit. The registration procedure varies, so participants should consider which option they are choosing. All participants can elect to take any combination of the first, second, third, and fourth weeks. To request a catalog of upcoming programs or to find additional information, visit the website. Naropa University welcomes participants with disabilities.

TAOS SUMMER WRITERS' CONFERENCE

Department of English Language and Literature, MSC 03 2170, 1 University of New Mexico, Albuquerque NM 87131. (505)277-5572. **E-mail:** nmwriter@unm.edu. **Website:** taosconf.unm.edu. **Contact:** Sharon Oard Warner, founding director. Annual conference held in July. Offers workshops and master classes in the novel, short story, poetry, creative nonfiction, memoir, prose style, screenwriting, humor writing, yoga and writing, literary translation, book proposal, the query letter, and revision. Participants may also schedule a consultation with a visiting agent/editor.

COSTS/ACCOMMODATIONS Week-long workshop registration: $700. Weekend workshop registration: $400. Master classes: $1,350-1,625. Publishing consultations: $175.

UNIVERSITY OF NORTH DAKOTA WRITERS CONFERENCE

Department of English, Merrifield Hall, Room 110, 276 Centennial Dr., Stop 7209, Grand Forks ND 58202. (701)777-2393. **Fax:** (701)777-2373. **E-mail:** crystal.alberts@und.edu. **Website:** und.edu/orgs/writers-conference. **Contact:** Crystal Alberts, director. Annual event. 2019 dates: March 20-22. Duration: 3 days. Offers panels, readings, and films focused around a specific theme. Almost all events take place in the University of North Dakota Memorial Union, which has a variety of small rooms and a 600-seat main hall. Past speakers have included Art Spiegelman, Truman Capote, Colson Whitehead, Gwendolyn Brooks, Allen Ginsberg, Roxane Gay, Viet Thanh Nguyen, and Louise Erdrich.

COSTS/ACCOMMODATIONS Information on overnight lodging & ADA accommodations available on website. All events are free and open to the public. Donations accepted.

ADDITIONAL INFORMATION Schedule and other information available on website.

VERMONT STUDIO CENTER

P.O. Box 613, 80 Pearl Street, Johnson VT 05656. (802)635-2727. **Fax:** (802)635-2730. **E-mail:** info@vermontstudiocenter.org. **Website:** www.vermontstu-diocenter.org. **Contact:** Gary Clark, President. 2019: 35th anniversary. Founded by artists in 1984, the Vermont Studio Center is the largest international artists' and writers' residency program in the United States, hosting 50 visual artists and writers each month from across the country and around the world. The Studio Center provides 4- to 12-week studio residencies on a historic 30-building campus along the Gihon River in Johnson, Vermont, a village in the heart of the northern Green Mountains.

COSTS/ACCOMMODATIONS Accommodations available on site. "Residents live in single rooms in 10 modest, comfortable houses adjacent to the Red Mill Building. Rooms are simply furnished and have shared baths. Complete linen service is provided. The Studio Center is unable to accommodate guests at meals, overnight guests, spouses, children, or pets." The total cost of supporting an artist or writer for 4 weeks at VSC is $4,950, which includes a private bedroom, 24-hour access to a private studio space, access to our Visiting Artists and Writers program, 20 hot meals per week, and round-the-clock fresh fruit, hot and cold beverages, and breakfast cereal. No VSC resident is required to pay this cost in full. All successful applicants' residency fees are subsidized thanks to the generous support of our donors and foundation partners. The current full (subsidized) fee is $4,250* for a 4-week residency and ranges down to $0 for those who are awarded a fellowship. Financial support is available to 100% of admitted residents who request it. *We are very grateful to any residents who opt to pay this fee in full, as it allows us to offer more financial assistance to talented artists and writers who would otherwise be unable to attend our program. Generous fellowship and grant assistance is available.

ADDITIONAL INFORMATION Fellowships application deadlines are February 15, June 15, and October 1. Writers are encouraged to visit website for more information. May also e-mail, call, fax.

WESLEYAN WRITERS CONFERENCE

Wesleyan University, 294 High St., Room 207, Middletown CT 06459. (860)685-3604. **Fax:** (860)685-2441. **E-mail:** agreene@wesleyan.edu. **Website:** www.wesleyan.edu/writing/conference. **Contact:** Anne Greene, director. Annual conference held in June. 2018 dates: June 12-16. Average attendance: 100. Focuses on the novel, fiction techniques, short stories, poetry, screenwriting, nonfiction, literary journalism, memoir, mixed media work, and publishing. The conference is held on the campus of Wesleyan University, in the hills overlooking the Connecticut River. Features a faculty of award-winning writers, seminars, and readings of new fiction, poetry, nonfiction, and mixed media forms—as well as guest lectures on a range of topics including publishing. Both new and experienced writers are welcome. Participants may attend seminars in all genres. Speakers have included Esmond Harmsworth (Zachary Shuster Harmsworth), Daniel Mandel (Sanford J. Greenburger Associates), Amy Williams (ICM and Collins McCormick), and many others. Agents will be speaking and available for meetings with attendees. Participants are often successful in finding agents and publishers for their mss. Wesleyan participants are also frequently featured in the anthology *Best New American Voices*.

COSTS/ACCOMMODATIONS Meals are provided on campus. Lodging is available on campus or in town.

ADDITIONAL INFORMATION Ms critiques are available but not required.

WILDACRES WRITERS WORKSHOP

233 S. Elm St., Greensboro NC 27401. (336)255-8210. **E-mail:** judihill@aol.com. **Website:** www.wildacreswriters.com. **Contact:** Judi Hill, director. 2019 dates: Retreat: June 30-July 6; Writing workshop: July 6-July 13. Join us this summer in the beautiful Blue Ridge Mountains of North Carolina! For over 25 years, our residential summer writing workshop has ranked among the finest in the country. Almost half of our attendees have been to Wildacres before. Published, unpublished, and talented beginning writers are welcome at Wildacres Writing Workshop, but you must be a serious writer to attend. These are residential "working" workshops where your manuscript is critiqued and given the attention it deserves. Class sizes are 10 or less and leadership is at the Master Class level. All faculty members must meet strict requirements in terms of their education and teaching experience. Workshop focuses on novel, short story, flash fiction, poetry, and nonfiction. Faculty have included Ron Rash, Carrie Brown, Dr. Janice Fuller, Phillip Gerard, Luke Whisnant, Dr. Joe Clark, John Gregory Brown, Dr. Phebe Davidson, Lee Zacharias, and Vicki Lane. This group also has a weeklong writing retreat that is different from the workshop.

COSTS/ACCOMMODATIONS $850 for Workshop only; $1,300 for Workshop & Retreat. Prices include room (double)/no private rooms, meals, workshop, and all evening programs. Balance is due June 1. No exceptions. Check the website for more info.

ADDITIONAL INFORMATION Include a one-page writing sample with registration.

WINTER POETRY & PROSE GETAWAY

Murphy Writing of Stockton University, 30 Front Street, Hammonton NJ 08037, USA. (609)626-3594. **E-mail:** info@wintergetaway.com. **Website:** www.stockton.edu/wintergetaway; stockton.edu/murphywriting. **Contact:** Amanda Murphy, Director. 2020 dates: January 17-20. Annual January conference at the Jersey Shore. Join us at the historic Seaview Hotel near Atlantic City. Enjoy challenging and supportive workshops, insightful feedback and an encouraging community. Choose from workshops in poetry, fiction, nonfiction, memoir, and more.

"At most conferences, writers listen to talks and panels and sit in sessions where previously written work is discussed. At the Getaway, they write. Most workshops are limited to 10 or fewer participants. By spending the entire weekend in one workshop, participants will venture deeper into their writing, making more progress than they thought possible."

COSTS/ACCOMMODATIONS Room packages at the historic Stockton Seaview Hotel are available. See website or call for past fee information. Scholarships available.

ADDITIONAL INFORMATION Previous faculty has included Julianna Baggott, Christian Bauman, Laure-Anne Bosselaar, Kurt Brown, Mark Doty (National Book Award winner), Stephen Dunn (Pulitzer Prize winner), Dorianne Laux, Carol Plum-Ucci, James Richardson, Mimi Schwartz, Terese Svoboda, and more.

WRITEAWAYS

E-mail: writeawaysinfo@gmail.com. **Website:** https://www.writeaways.com. **Contact:** Mimi Herman. "We created Writeaways—writing getaways—to help you find the time you need to write. We provide writing instruction, fabulous food and company in beautiful places, and an inspiring place for you to take a writing vacation with your muse. We pamper you while providing rigorous, supportive assistance to help you become the best writer possible. We have week-long workshops in France and Italy, and weekend-plus-optional-retreat programs in North Carolina."

For 2019, consider these dates: Workshop by the River (NC): May 17-19; Retreat by the River (NC): May 19-21; France (Chateau du Pin): September 26-October 3; Italy (Villas Cini and Casanova): October 5-12; The Grand Tour (France and Italy back to back): September 26 -October 12.

COSTS/ACCOMMODATIONS North Carolina: The Whitehall, Camden, North Carolina. France: Chateau du Pin, near Champtocé-sur Loire (18 miles west of Angers). Italy: Villas Cini and Casanova, near Bucine, between Siena and Arezzo. North Carolina workshop: Price TBA (check web site for the latest information). France and Italy: $2,350 single room, $2,100 shared rooms. The Grand Tour (France and Italy): $4,200 each single room, $4,000 each shared room.

☻ WRITE IT OUT

P.O. Box 704, Sarasota FL 34230. (941)359-3824. **E-mail:** rmillerwio@gmaill.com. **Website:** www.writeitout.com. **Contact:** Ronni Miller, director. Workshops of various lengths held throughout the year, some in the United States and some abroad. The workshops cover expressive writing and painting, fiction, poetry, and memoir. Offers "small groups, option to spend time writing and not attend classes, and personal appointments with instructors." Facilitators have included novelist Arturo Vivante.

COSTS/ACCOMMODATIONS Costs vary.

ADDITIONAL INFORMATION Conference information available year round. For brochures/guidelines e-mail, call, or visit website. Accepts inquiries by phone, e-mail.

WRITER'S DIGEST ANNUAL CONFERENCE

Active Interset Media, Inc., 5720 Flatiron Pkwy., Boulder CO 80301. **E-mail:** writersdigestconference@aimmedia.com. **Website:** www.writersdigestconference.com. **Contact:** Taylor Sferra. The Writer's Digest conferences feature an amazing lineup of speakers to help writers with the craft and business of writing. Each calendar year typically features multiple conferences around the country. In 2020, the New York conference will be August 13-16 at the New York Hilton Midtown. The most popular feature of the east coast conference is the agent pitch slam in which potential authors are given the ability to pitch their books directly to agents. For more details, see the website.

COSTS/ACCOMMODATIONS A block of rooms at the event hotel is reserved for guests. See the travel page on the website for more information. Cost varies by location and year. There are typically different pricing options for those who wish attend the pitch slam and those who just want to attend the conference education.

WRITERS OMI AT LEDIG HOUSE

55 Fifth Ave., 15th Floor, New York NY 10003. (212)206-6114. **E-mail:** writers@artomi.org. **Website:** www.artomi.org. Residency duration: 2 weeks to 2 months. Average attendance and site: "Up to 20 writers per session—10 at a given time—live and write on the stunning 300 acre grounds and sculpture park that overlooks the Catskill Mountains." Application deadline: October 20.

COSTS/ACCOMMODATIONS Residents provide their own transportation. Offers overnight accommodations.

ADDITIONAL INFORMATION "Agents and editors from the New York publishing community are invited for dinner and discussion. Bicycles, a swimming pool, and nearby tennis court are available for use."

WRITING WORKSHOPS AT CASTLE HILL

10 Meetinghouse Rd., P.O. Box 756, Truro MA 02666. (508)349-7511. **Fax:** (508)349-7513. **E-mail:** info@castlehill.org. **Website:** www.castlehill.org/writing. Workshops on poetry, fiction, narrative nonfiction, memoir, and more, geared toward intermediate and advanced levels. Open to students. The dates, courses, and instructors change each year, so check the website for details of individual upcoming events. Site: Truro Center for the Arts at Castle Hill in Massachusetts.

THE HELENE WURLITZER FOUNDATION

P.O. Box 1891, Taos NM 87571. (575)758-2413. **Fax:** (575)758-2559. **E-mail:** hwf@taosnet.com. **Website:** www.wurlitzerfoundation.org. **Contact:** Nic Knight, executive director. Foundation offers 10- and 12-week residencies. Request application by e-mail or visit website to download.

COSTS/ACCOMMODATIONS Provides individual housing in fully furnished studios/houses (casitas), rent- and utility-free. Artists are responsible for transportation to and from Taos, their meals, and materials for their work. Bicycles are provided upon request.

ORGANIZATIONS

There are many organizations of value to poets. These groups may sponsor workshops and contests, stage readings, publish anthologies and chapbooks or spread the word about publishing opportunities. A few provide economic assistance or legal advice. The best thing organizations offer, though, is a support system to which poets can turn for a pep talk, a hard-nosed (but sympathetic) critique of a manuscript or simply the comfort of talking and sharing with others who understand the challenges, and joys, of writing poetry.

Whether national, regional or as local as your library or community center, each organization has something special to offer. The listings in this section reflect the membership opportunities available to poets with a variety of organizations. Some groups provide certain services to both members and nonmembers.

To find out more about groups in your area (including those that may not be listed in *Poet's Market*), contact your YMCA, community center, local colleges and universities, public library and bookstores (and don't forget newspapers and the Internet). If you can't find a group that suits your needs, consider starting one yourself. You might be surprised to discover there are others in your locality who would welcome the encouragement, feedback and moral support of a writer's group.

92ND STREET Y UNTERBERG POETRY CENTER

1395 Lexington Ave., New York NY 10128. (212)415-5500. **Website:** www.92y.org/poetry. The Unterberg Poetry Center offers "students of all ages the opportunity to hone their skills as writers and deepen their appreciation as readers." Offers annual series of readings by major literary figures (weekly readings late September through May), writing workshops, master classes in fiction and poetry, and lectures and literary seminars. Also co-sponsors the "Discovery"/Boston Review Poetry Contest.

THE ACADEMY OF AMERICAN POETS

75 Maiden Ln., Suite 901, New York NY 10038. (212)274-0343. **Fax:** (212)274-9427. **E-mail:** academy@poets.org. **Website:** www.poets.org. Founded in 1934, the Academy of American Poets is the nation's largest member-supported cultural organization championing poets and poetry in the U.S. Our mission is to foster the appreciation of contemporary poetry and to support poets at all stages of their careers. To accomplish this, we bring attention to poets by showcasing their poems, essays and interviews in our digital and print publications, namely Poets.org, Poem-a-Day series, *American Poets* magazine, as well as on our active social media channels. During National Poetry Month, which we founded and continue to organize, we promote readers' engagement with poetry and offer a special project for students that invites them to learn more about contemporary poets. We create opportunities for poets and readers to interact at live readings and convenings, both in New York City where we are headquartered, and in other cities across the U.S., such as Boston and Miami, with partner organizations. We honor outstanding artistic achievement by American poets with a collection of prestigious annual prizes. And, we inspire educators and students to respectively teach and pursue poetry by offering resources in an Educator Newsletter and on Poets.org. We aim to represent the best and breadth of American Poetry, recognizing that poets' work today exists contemporaneously with that of historical American poets. Taken together, our programs aim to fuel national interest in and conversation about great American poetry.

AMERICAN HAIKU ARCHIVES

California State Library, Library & Courts II Bldg, 900 N St., Sacramento CA 95814. **E-mail:** welchm@aol.com.

Website: www.americanhaikuarchives.org. **Contact:** Michael Dylan Welch. The American Haiku Archives is "the world's largest public collection of haiku and related poetry books and papers outside Japan." This repository is housed at the California State Library in Sacramento, California, and is dedicated to preserving the history of North American haiku. Materials are publicly available for research purposes through the library's California History Room. The American Haiku Archives actively seeks donations of books, journals, recordings, letters, ephemera, and personal papers relating to haiku and related poetry in all languages, but especially North American languages. The American Haiku Archives also appoints an honorary curator every July for a one-year term. The intent of this appointment is to honor leading haiku poets, translators, or scholars for their accomplishments or service in support of haiku poetry as a literary art. Past honorary curators have been John Stevenson, Patricia Donegan, Haruo Shirane, Ruth Yarrow, Marlene Mountain, Charles Trumbull, LeRoy Gorman, Jerry Ball, Gary Snyder, Stephen Addiss, George Swede, H. F. Noyes, Hiroaki Sato, Francine Porad, Makoto Ueda, William J. Higginson, Leroy Kanterman, Lorraine Ellis Harr, Robert Spiess, Cor van den Heuvel, Jerry Kilbride, and Elizabeth Searle Lamb. Additional information online.

ARIZONA AUTHORS' ASSOCIATION

6939 East Chaparral Rd., Paradise Valley AZ 85253. (602)510-8076. **E-mail:** azauthors@gmail.com. **E-mail:** lisa@greenpiccestoons.com. **Website:** www.azauthors.com. **Contact:** Lisa Aquilina, President. Since 1978, Arizona Authors' Association has served to offer professional, educational and social opportunities to writers and authors and serves as an informational and referral network for the literary community. Members must be authors, writers working toward publication, agents, publishers, publicists, printers, illustrators, etc. Az Authors' publishes a bimonthly newsletter and the renown annual *Arizona Literary Magazine*. The Association sponsors the international Arizona Literary Contest including poetry, essays, short stories, new drama writing, novels, and published books with cash prizes and awards bestowed at a Fall ceremony. Winning entries are published or advertised in the *Arizona Literary Magazine*. First and second place winners in poetry, essay and short story categories are entered in the annual Pushcart Prize. Learn more online.

THE AUTHORS GUILD, INC.

31 E. 32nd St., 7th Floor, New York NY 10016. (212)563-5904. **Fax:** (212)564-5363. **E-mail:** staff@ authorsguild.org. **Website:** www.authorsguild.org. **Contact:** Mary Rasenberger, executive director. Purpose of organization: to offer services and materials intended to help authors with the business and legal aspects of their work, including contract problems, copyright matters, freedom of expression and taxation. Guild has 8,000 members. Qualifications for membership: Must be book author published by an established American publisher within 7 years or any author who has had 3 works (fiction or nonfiction) published by a magazine or magazines of general circulation in the last 18 months. Associate membership also available. Different levels of membership include: associate membership with all rights except voting available to an author who has a firm contract offer or is currently negotiating a royalty contract from an established American publisher. "The Guild offers free contract reviews to its members. The Guild conducts several symposia each year at which experts provide information, offer advice and answer questions on subjects of interest and concern to authors. Typical subjects have been the rights of privacy and publicity, libel, wills and estates, taxation, copyright, editors and editing, the art of interviewing, standards of criticism and book reviewing. Transcripts of these symposia are published and circulated to members. The *Authors Guild Bulletin*, a quarterly journal, contains articles on matters of interest to writers, reports of Guild activities, contract surveys, advice on problem clauses in contracts, transcripts of Guild and League symposia and information on a variety of professional topics. Subscription included in the cost of the annual dues.

BOWERY POETRY CLUB

308 Bowery St., New York NY 10012. **Website:** bowerypoetry.com. The Bowery Poetry Club and Cafe hosts regional open mic and poetry events. "Hosting between 20 and 30 shows a week, the Bowery Poetry Club (BPC) is proud of our place in the lineage of populist art: The Yiddish theater, burlesque, vaudeville, beat poetry, jazz, and punk that gave the Bowery its name." Offers workshops for adults and young poets. "Each Tuesday night at 6:30 pm touring Slam poets give a craft talk as part of our WordShop series." Nationally known writers give readings that are open to the public. Sponsors open mic readings for the public each Tuesday night at 7 pm as part of the Urbana Poetry Slam; format: open mic, featured poet, poetry slam. See website for more information and schedule.

BRIGHT HILL LITERARY CENTER

94 Church St., Treadwell NY 13846. (607)829-5055. **E-mail:** wordthur@stny.rr.com. **E-mail:** brighthillpress@stny.rr.com. **Website:** www.brighthillpress. org. Bright Hill Literary Center serves residents in the Catskill Mountain region, greater New York, and throughout the U.S. Includes the Bright Hill Library and Internet Center, with "thousands of volumes of literary journals, literary prose and poetry, literary criticism and biography, theater, reference, art, and children's books available for reading and research (noncirculating, for the time being). Wireless Internet access is available." Sponsors workshops for children and adults. Learn more online.

☻ BURNABY WRITERS' SOCIETY

6584 Deer Lake Ave., Burnaby BC V5G 3T7, Canada. **E-mail:** info@bws.ca. **Website:** burnabywritersnews. blogspot.com. **Contact:** Lara Varesi. Corresponding membership in the society, including a newsletter subscription, is open to anyone, anywhere. Currently has 40 members. Society stages monthly writing workshops. Sponsors open mic readings for the public. Sponsors a contest open to British Columbia residents. Competition receives about 100 entries/ year. Past contest winners include Mildred Tremblay, Irene Livingston, and Kate Braid. Additional information online.

COLUMBINE POETS OF COLORADO

National Federation of State Poetry Societies, P.O. Box 6245, Broomfield CO 80021. (303)431-6774. **Website:** columbinepoetsofcolorado.com. **Contact:** Anita Jepson-Gilbert, president. Statewide organization open to anyone interested in poetry. Currently has around 100 members in 3 Chapters, now in Denver, Salida, and Loveland, CO. An affiliate of the National Federation of State Poetry Societies (NFSPS). Offerings for the Denver Foothills Chapter include weekly workshops and monthly critiques. Sponsors contests, awards for students and adults, an Annual Poetry Fest and some publications. Additional information available with SASE, by phone or e-mail.

☻ Columbine Poets Inc. is a state society of Colorado poet. We hold contests for our members only and we are not a publisher of magazines or books.

COMMUNITY OF LITERARY MAGAZINES AND PRESSES (CLMP)

154 Christopher St., Suite 3C, New York NY 10014. (212)741-9110. **E-mail:** info@clmp.org. **Website:** www.clmp.org. Dedicated to supporting and actively promoting the field of independent literary publishing. Open to publishers who are primarily literary in nature, have published at least 1 issue/title prior to applying for membership, publish at least 1 issue/title annually on an ongoing basis, have a minimum print run of 500 per issue or title, do not charge authors a fee, are not primarily self-publishing, and do not primarily publish children's/students' work. Currently has over 500 members. Levels of membership/dues: based on publishing organization's annual budget. See website for complete member application process. Benefits include free and discounted monographs, subscription to e-mail listserves and online databases, plus many valuable services. Additional information online.

CONNECTICUT POETRY SOCIETY

P.O. Box 702, Manchester CT 06040. **E-mail:** connpoetry@comcast.net. **Website:** ctpoetry.net. **Contact:** Tony Fusco, president. The Connecticut Poetry Society is a nonprofit organization dedicated to the promotion and enjoyment of poetry through chapter meetings, contests, and poetry-related events. Statewide organization open to non-Connecticut residents. Currently has about 175 members. Membership benefits include automatic membership in The National Federation of State Poetry Societies (NFSPS); a free copy of *The Connecticut River Review*, a national poetry journal published by CPS; opportunity to publish in *Long River Run II*, a members-only poetry journal; quarterly CPS and NFSPS newsletters; annual April poetry celebration; and membership in any of 10 state chapters. Sponsors conferences and workshops. Sponsors The Connecticut River Review Annual Poetry Contest, The Brodinsky-Brodine Contest, The Winchell Contest, and The Lynn Decaro High School Competition. Members and nationally known writers give readings that are open to the public. Members meet monthly. Additional information online.

FURIOUS FLOWER POETRY CENTER

500 Cardinal Dr., MSC3802, James Madison University, Harrisonburg VA 22807. (540)568-8883. **E-mail:** furiousflower@jmu.edu. **Website:** www.jmu.edu/furiousflower. **Contact:** Joanne V. Gabbin, executive director. The mission of the Furious Flower Poetry Center is to advance the genre of African American Poetry by providing opportunities for education, research, and publication. Furious Flower Poetry Center serves as a resource for the campus and local Harrisonburg community. The Center hosts visiting poets, sponsors poetry workshops for emerging poets, holds an annual poetry camp for children in the community, and produces scholarly texts, videos and DVDs on African American poetry. Furious Flower has sponsored two decade-defining conferences celebrating the African American poetic tradition.

GEORGIA POETRY SOCIETY

740 Emily Place NW, Atlanta GA 30318. **E-mail:** gps@georgiapoetrysociety.org. **Website:** www.georgiapoetrysociety.org. Statewide organization open to any person who is in accord with the objectives to secure fuller public recognition of the art of poetry, stimulate an appreciation of poetry, and enhance the writing and reading of poetry. Currently has 200 members. Membership includes affiliation with NFSPS. Holds at least 1 workshop annually. Contests are sponsored throughout the year, some for members only. "Our contests have specific general rules, which should be followed to avoid the disappointment of disqualification. See the website for details." Publishes The Reach of Song, an annual anthology devoted to contest-winning poems and member works. Each quarterly meeting (open to the public) features at least 1 poet of regional prominence. Also sponsors monthly local poetry groups listed on our website. Sponsors Poetry in the Schools project. Additional information online.

GREATER CINCINNATI WRITERS' LEAGUE

E-mail: j.patrick.venturella@gmail.com. **Website:** www.cincinnatiwritersleague.org. **Contact:** Patrick Venturella, president. Purpose is to "support those who write poetry in the Cincinnati area and to promote excellence in poetry writing. We believe in creative freedom, with open, constructive critique as a learning tool." Offerings include monthly meetings with critique or a workshop on a subject of interest to poets. Poems submitted by members are critiqued by guest critics (published poets who are also teachers or professors of poetry and/or creative writing). Group discussion of critiqued poems follows. Sponsors fall poetry contest with cash prizes; also sponsors a category of the annual Ohio Poetry Day contest with cash prizes. Occasionally publishes an anthology. Members occasionally give readings that are open to the public (see website for meeting time and place). Additional information online.

HAIKU SOCIETY OF AMERICA

930 Pine St. #105, San Francisco CA 94108. **E-mail:** fay.hsa.president@gmail.com. **Website:** www.hsa-haiku.org. The Haiku Society of America is composed of haiku poets, editors, critics, publishers, and enthusiasts dedicated to "promoting the creation and appreciation of haiku and related forms (haibun, haiga, renku, senryu, sequences, and tanka) among its members and the public." Currently has over 800 members. Membership benefits include a year's subscription to the Society's journal, *Frogpond*, and to the quarterly HSA newsletter *Ripples*; the annual information sheet; an annual address/e-mail list of HSA members; and eligibility to submit work to the members' anthology. Administers the following annual awards: The Harold G. Henderson Awards for haiku, The Gerald Brady Awards for senryu, The Bernard Lionel Einbond Awards for renku, The Merit Book Awards, and The Nicholas Virgilio Haiku Awards for youth. Additional information online.

THE HUDSON VALLEY WRITERS' CENTER

300 Riverside Dr., Sleepy Hollow NY 10591. (914)332-5953. **Fax:** (914)332-4825. **E-mail:** info@writerscenter.org. **Website:** www.writerscenter.org. **Contact:** Jennifer Franklin, program director. The Hudson Valley Writers' Center is a nonprofit organization devoted to furthering the literary arts in our region. Its mission is to promote the appreciation of literary excellence, to stimulate and nurture the creation of literary works in all sectors of the population, and to bring the diverse works of gifted poets and prose artists to the attention of the public. Open to all. Currently has 350 members. Offerings include public readings by established and emerging poets/writers, workshops and classes, monthly open mic nights, paid and volunteer outreach opportunities, and an annual chapbook competition with Slapering Hol Press. Additional information online.

INTERNATIONAL READING ASSOCIATION

P.O. Box 8139, Newark DE 19714. (302)731-1600. **E-mail:** councils@reading.org. **E-mail:** mpost@reading.org. **Website:** www.reading.org. The International Reading Association seeks to promote high levels of literacy for all by improving the quality of reading instruction through studying the reading process and teaching techniques; serving as a clearinghouse for the dissemination of reading research through conferences, journals, and other publications; and actively encouraging the lifetime reading habit. Its goals include professional development, advocacy, partnerships, research, and global literacy development. Sponsors annual convention. Publishes a newsletter called "Reading Today." Sponsors a number of awards and fellowships. More information online.

INTERNATIONAL WOMEN'S WRITING GUILD

International Women's Writing Guild, 5 Penn Plaza, 19th Floor, PMB# 19059, New York NY 10001. (917)720-6959. **E-mail:** iwwgquestions@gmail.com. **Website:** www.iwwg.wildapricot.org. **Contact:** Marj Hahne, Interim Director of Operations. IWWG is a network for the personal and professional empowerment of women through writing. Open to any woman connected to the written word regardless of professional portfolio. IWWG sponsors several annual conferences in all areas of the U.S. The major event, held in the summer, is a week-long conference attracting hundreds of women writers from around the globe.

IOWA POETRY ASSOCIATION

16096 320th Way, Earlham IA 50072. **E-mail:** ipa@iowapoetry.com. **Website:** www.iowapoetry.com. **Contact:** Marilyn J Baszczynski, Editor. Statewide organization open to "anyone interested in poetry, with a residence or valid address in the state of Iowa." Offerings include "semiannual workshops to which a poem may be sent in advance for critique; annual contest—also open to nonmembers—with no entry fee; IPA Newsletter, published 4 times/year, including a quarterly national publication listing of contest opportunities; and an annual poetry anthology, *Lyrical Iowa*, containing prize-winning and high-ranking poems from contest entries. No requirement for purchase to ensure publication." Semiannual workshops "are the only 'meetings' of the association." Additional information online.

THE KENTUCKY STATE POETRY SOCIETY

Website: www.kystatepoetrysociety.org. Regional organization open to all. Member of The National Federation of State Poetry Societies (NFSPS). Currently has about 230 members. Offerings include association with other poets; information on contests and poetry happenings across the state and nation; annual state and national contests; national and state annual conventions with workshops, selected speakers, and open poetry readings. Sponsors workshops, contests, awards. Membership includes the quarterly KSPS Newsletter. Also includes a quarterly newsletter, *Strophes*, of the NFSPS; and the KSPS journal, *Pegasus*, published 3 times/year: a Spring/ Summer and Fall/ Winter issue which solicits good poetry for publication (need not be a member to submit), and a Prize Poems issue of 1st Place contest winners in over 30 categories. Members or nationally known writers give readings that are open to the public. Members meet annually. More information online.

☺ THE LEAGUE OF CANADIAN POETS

312-192 Spadina Ave., Toronto ON M5T 2C2, Canada. (416)504-1657. **E-mail:** info@poets.ca. **Website:** www.poets.ca. **Contact:** Joanna Poblocka, executive director. A nonprofit national association of professional publishing and performing poets in Canada. Its purpose is "to enhance the status of poets and nurture a professional poetic community to facilitate the teaching of Canadian poetry at all levels of education and to develop the audience for poetry by encouraging publication, performance, and recognition of Canadian poetry nationally and internationally. As well as providing members and the public with many benefits and services, the League speaks for poets on many issues such as freedom of expression, Public Lending Right, CanCopy, contract advice, and grievance." Open to all Canadian citizens and landed immigrants; applications are assessed by a membership committee. Currently has 600 members. Membership benefits include a 1-year subscription to monthly e-newsletter, discount on Gift Shop purchases, listing in online members' catalog, and more (benefits increase with membership level). Sponsors The Pat Lowther Memorial Award (for a book of poetry by a Canadian woman published in the preceding year; $1,000 CAD prize) and The Gerald Lampert Memorial Award (recognizes the best first book of poetry published by a Canadian in the preceding year; $1,000 CAD). Additional information online.

THE LOFT LITERARY CENTER

Suite 200, Open Book, 1011 Washington Ave. S., Minneapolis MN 55415. (612)215-2575. **E-mail:** loft@loft.org. **Website:** www.loft.org. Founded in 1974, The Loft Literary Center is one of the nation's leading literary arts centers. The Loft advances the artistic development of writers, fosters a thriving literary community, and inspires a passion for literature.

MASSACHUSETTS STATE POETRY SOCIETY

64 Harrison Ave., Lynn MA 01905. **E-mail:** msps.jcmaes@comcast.net. **Website:** mastatepoetrysociety.tripod.com. **Contact:** Jeanette C. Maes, president. Dedicated to the writing and appreciation of poetry and promoting the art form. Statewide organization open to anyone with an interest in poetry. Currently has 200 members. Member benefits include subscription to *Bay State Echo*, published 5 times/year with members' news and announcements; members-only contests; round-robin critique groups; members-only annual anthology; workshops at society meetings; and automatic membership in National Federation of State Poetry Societies (NFSPS). Sponsors contests open to all poets. Guidelines online. Members or nationally known writers give readings that are open to the public. Sponsors open mic readings for members and the public for National Poetry Day. Members meet 5 times/year. Additional information online.

MOUNTAIN WRITERS SERIES

Mountain Writers Center, 2804 S.E. 27th Ave., #2, Portland OR 97202. **E-mail:** programs@mountainwriters.org. **Website:** www.mountainwriters.org. Mountain Writers Series is an independent nonprofit organization dedicated to supporting writers, audiences, and other sponsors by promoting literature and literacy through artistic and educational literary arts events in the Pacific Northwest. Currently has about 150 members. Mountain Writers Series offers intensive one-day and 2-day workshops, weekend master classes, 5-week, 8-week, and 10-week courses about writing. Sponsors readings that are open to the public. Nationally and internationally known writers are sponsored by the Mountain Writers Series Northwest Regional Residencies Program (reading tours) and the campus readings program (Pulitzer Prize winners, Nobel Prize winners, MacArthur Fellows, etc.). Additional information online.

NATIONAL FEDERATION OF STATE POETRY SOCIETIES (NFSPS)

E-mail: jbob214@yahoo.com. **Website:** www.nfsps.com. "NFSPS is a nonprofit organization exclusively educational and literary. Its purpose is to recognize the importance of poetry with respect to national cultural heritage. It is dedicated solely to the furtherance of poetry on the national level and serves to unite poets in the bonds of fellowship and understanding." Currently has 7,000 members. Any poetry group located in a state not already affiliated, but interested in affiliating with NFSPS, may contact the membership chairman (see website). In a state where no valid group exists, help may also be obtained by individuals interested in organizing a poetry group for affiliation. Most reputable state poetry societies are members of the National Federation and advertise their various poetry contests through the NFSPS quarterly newsletter *Strophes*. NFSPS holds an annual 3-day convention in a different state each year with workshops, an awards banquet, and addresses by nationally known poets. Sponsors an annual 50-category national contest. Additional information online.

NATIONAL WRITERS ASSOCIATION

10940 S. Parker Rd., #508, Parker CO 80138. **E-mail:** natlwritersassn@hotmail.com. **Website:** www.nationalwriters.com. Association for freelance writers. Qualifications for membership: associate membership—must be serious about writing; professional membership—must be published and paid writer (cite credentials). Sponsors workshops/conferences: TV/screenwriting workshops, NWAF Annual Conferences, Literary Clearinghouse, editing and critiquing services, local chapters, National Writer's School. Open to non-members. Publishes industry news of interest to freelance writers; how-to articles; market information; member news and networking opportunities. Sponsors poetry contest; short story contest; article contest; novel contest. Awards cash for top 3 winners; books and/or certificates for other winners; honorable mention certificate places 5-10. Contests open to nonmembers.

NATIONAL WRITERS UNION

256 W. 38th St., Suite 703, New York NY 10018. (212)254-0279. **Fax:** (212)254-0673. **E-mail:** nwu@nwu.org. **Website:** www.nwu.org. Advocacy for freelance writers. Qualifications for membership: "Membership in the NWU is open to all qualified writers, and no one shall be barred or in any manner prejudiced within the Union on account of race, age, sex, sexual orientation, disability, national origin, religion or ideology. You are eligible for membership if you have published a book, a play, three articles, five poems, one short story or an equivalent amount of newsletter, publicity, technical, commer-

cial, government or institutional copy. You are also eligible for membership if you have written an equal amount of unpublished material and you are actively writing and attempting to publish your work." Holds workshops throughout the country. Members only section on website offers rich resources for freelance writers. Skilled contract advice and grievance help for members.

NEW HAMPSHIRE WRITERS' PROJECT

2500 North River Rd., Manchester NH 03106. (603)314-7980. **E-mail:** info@nhwritersproject.org. **Website:** www.nhwritersproject.org. Statewide organization open to writers at all levels in all genres. Currently has 600+ members. Offerings include workshops, seminars, an annual conference, and a literary calendar. Sponsors day-long workshops and 4- to 6-week intensive courses. Also sponsors the biennial New Hampshire Literary Awards for outstanding literary achievement (including The Jane Kenyon Award for Outstanding Book of Poetry). Publishes *NH Writer*, a quarterly newsletter for and about New Hampshire writers. Members and nationally known writers give readings that are open to the public. Additional information online.

THE NORTH CAROLINA POETRY SOCIETY

E-mail: calnordt@aol.com. **Website:** www.ncpoetrysociety.org. **Contact:** Cal Nordt, Vice President of Communications. The North Carolina Poetry Society holds poetry-related contests and gives away several awards each year, for both Adults and Students (which includes 3rd Graders all the way to University Undergraduates). Statewide organization open to non-NC residents. Purpose: to encourage the reading, writing, study, and publication of poetry. NCPS brings poets together in meetings that feature workshops, presentations by noted poets and publishers, book and contest awards, and an annual anthology of award-winning poems. Currently has 350 members from NC and beyond. Sponsors annual Poetry Contest with categories for adults and students. Contests are open to anyone, with small fee for nonmembers. Winning poems are published in *Pinesong*, NCPS's annual anthology. A free copy is given to all winners, who are also invited to read at Awards Day. NCPS also sponsors the annual Brockman-Campbell Book Award for a book of poetry over 20 pages by a North Carolina poet (native-born or current resident for 3 years. NCPS also cosponsors the Gilbert-Chappell Distinguished Poet

Series with The North Carolina Center for the Book, for the purpose of mentoring young poets across the state. Additional information online.

NORTH CAROLINA WRITERS' NETWORK

P.O. Box 21591, Winston-Salem NC 27120. (336)293-8844. **E-mail:** mail@ncwriters.org. **Website:** www.ncwriters.org. Supports the work of writers, writers' organizations, independent bookstores, little magazines and small presses, and literary programming statewide. Currently has 1,400 members. Membership benefits include *The Writers' Network News*, a twice-yearly newsletter containing organizational news, trends in writing and publishing, and other literary material of interest to writers; and access to the NCWN online resources, other writers, workshops, conferences, readings and competitions, and NCWN's critiquing and editing service. Annual Fall Conference features nationally known writers, publishers, and editors, held in a different North Carolina location each November. Sponsors competitions in short fiction, nonfiction, and poetry. Guidelines online.

OHIO POETRY ASSOCIATION

E-mail: charles@ohiopoetryassn.org. **Website:** www.ohiopoetryassn.org. Promotes the art of poetry, and furthers the support of poets and others who support poetry. Statewide membership with additional members in several other states, Japan, and England. Affiliated with the National Federation of State Poetry Societies (NFSPS). Open to poets and writers of all ages and ability, as well as to non-writing lovers of poetry. Currently has about 215 members. Member benefits include regular contests; meeting/workshop participation; assistance with writing projects; networking; twice-yearly magazine, *Common Threads*, publishing only poems by members; quarterly Ohio Poetry Association Newsletter ; quarterly NFSPS newsletters (*Strophes*); automatic NFSPS membership; and contest information and lower entry fees for NFSPS contests. Members are automatically on the mailing list for Ohio Poetry Day contest guidelines (OPA financially supports Ohio Poetry Day). Individual chapters regularly host workshops and seminars. Members and nationally known writers give readings that are open to the public (at quarterly meetings; public is invited). Sponsors open mic readings for members and the public. Members meet quarterly (September, December, March, May). Additional information available online. "In short, OPA provides poets with opportunities to share info, critique, publish, sponsor contests, and just socialize.

PEN AMERICAN CENTER

588 Broadway, Suite 303, New York NY 10012. (212)334-1660. **E-mail:** info@pen.org. **Website:** www.pen.org. An association of writers working to advance literature, to defend free expression, and to foster international literary fellowship. PEN welcomes to its membership all writers and those belonging to the larger literary community. We ask that writers have at least one book published or be writers with proven records as professional writers; playwrights and screenwriters should have at least one work produced in a professional setting. Others should have achieved recognition in the literary field. Editors, literary agents, literary scouts, publicists, journalists, bloggers, and other literary professionals are all invited to join as Professional Members. If you feel you do not meet these guidelines, please consider joining as an Advocate Member. Candidates for membership may be nominated by a PEN member or they may nominate themselves with the support of two references from the literary community or from a current PEN member. PEN members receive a subscription to the PEN journal, the PEN Annual Report, and have access to medical insurance at group rates. Members living in the New York metropolitan and tri-state area, or near the Branches, are invited to PEN events throughout the year. Membership in PEN American Center includes reciprocal privileges in PEN American Center branches and in foreign PEN Centers for those traveling abroad. Application forms are available online. PEN American Center is the largest of the 141 centers of PEN International, the world's oldest human rights organization and the oldest international literary organization. PEN International was founded in 1921 to dispel national, ethnic, and racial hatreds and to promote understanding among all countries. PEN American Center, founded a year later, works to advance literature, to defend free expression, and to foster international literary fellowship. The Center has a membership of 3,400 distinguished writers, editors, and translators. In addition to defending writers in prison or in danger of imprisonment for their work, PEN American Center sponsors public literary programs and forums on current issues, sends prominent authors to inner-city schools to encourage reading and writing, administers literary prizes, promotes in-

ternational literature that might otherwise go unread in the United States, and offers grants and loans to writers facing financial or medical emergencies.

PITTSBURGH POETRY EXCHANGE

P.O. Box 4279, Pittsburgh PA 15203. (412)481-POEM. **E-mail:** ppepoets@yahoo.com. **Website:** pghpoetry-exchange.pghfree.net. **Contact:** Michael Wurster, co-ordinator. A community-based volunteer organization for local poets, it functions as a service organization and information exchange, conducting ongoing workshops, readings, and discussions to promote poets and poetry. No dues or fees. "Any monetary contributions are voluntary, often from outside. Currently has about 30 members (with a mailing list of 400). Sponsors a monthly workshop (first Monday, 7 pm, Brentwood Public Library) a discussion of a poetry book (fourth Wed., Coffee Tree, Walnut St., 7:30 pm). Poets from out of town may contact the Exchange for assistance in setting up readings at bookstores to help sell their books. "We have been partnering with Autumn House Press in co-sponsoring events and bringing some of its authors to town." Additional information online. "Pittsburgh is a very exciting literary town."

⚫ POETRY BOOK SOCIETY

12 Mosley St., Newcastle upon Tyne NE1 1DE, United Kingdom. (44)(191)230-8100. **E-mail:** pbs@inpress-books.co.uk. **Website:** www.poetrybooks.co.uk. A book club that promotes "the best newly published contemporary poetry to as wide an audience as possible." Membership: 2,200. All members receive a subscription to the quarterly *PBS Bulletin*, 25% discount on almost all poetry books published in the UK, and advance notice of poetry events; Full Members also receive 4 PBS Choice selections free. New members receive a welcome gift. The PBS selectors also recommend other books of special merit each quarter. Sponsors the T.S. Eliot Prize for the best new single author collection published in the UK and Ireland in the calendar year. The Poetry Book Society is subsidized by the Arts Council of England. Additional information online.

THE POETRY FOUNDATION

61 W. Superior St., Chicago IL 60654. (312)787-7070. **Fax:** (312)787-6650. **E-mail:** info@poetryfoundation.org. **Website:** poetryfoundation.org. The Poetry Foundation is an independent literary organization committed to a vigorous presence for poetry in our culture. It exists to discover and celebrate the best poetry and to place it before the largest possible audience. Initiatives include publishing *Poetry* magazine; distributing Ted Kooser's *American Life in Poetry* newspaper project; funding and promotion of Poetry Out Loud: National Recitation Contest (in partnership with the National Endowment for the Arts and state arts associations); *Poetry Everywhere*, a series of short poetry films airing on public television and on transportation systems across the country; *The Essential American Poets* podcast series featuring seminal recordings of major American Poets reading from their work, as selected by former Poet Laureate Donald Hall; and www.poetryfoundation.org, an award-winning comprehensive online resource for poetry featuring an archive of more than 6,500 poems by more than 600 classic and contemporary poets. The site also includes the poetry blog Harriet," poetry-related articles, a bestseller list, video programming, a series of poetry podcasts, and reading guides about poets and poetry. The Poetry Foundation annually awards the Ruth Lilly Poetry Prize, of $100,000, and the Ruth Lilly Poetry Fellowships, 5 annual awards of $15,000 to young poets to support their further studies in poetry." More information online.

⚫ THE POETRY LIBRARY

The Poetry Library, Level 5, Royal Festival Hall, London SE1 8XX, United Kingdom. (44)(207)921-0943/0664. **Fax:** (44)(207)921-0607. **E-mail:** info@poetrylibrary.org.uk. **Website:** www.poetrylibrary.org.uk. **Contact:** Chris McCabe, Poetry Librarian. A "free public library of modern poetry. It contains a comprehensive collection of all British poetry published since 1912 and an international collection of poetry from all over the world, either written in or translated into English. As the United Kingdom's national library for poetry, it offers loan and information services and a large collection of poetry magazines, cassettes, compact discs, videos, records, poem posters, and cards; also press cuttings and photographs of poets. The library also offers an e-loans service for those who can't make it into the library in person."

⚫ THE POETRY SOCIETY

22 Betterton St., London WC2H 9BX, United Kingdom. (44)(207)420-9880. **E-mail:** info@poetrysociety.org.uk. **Website:** www.poetrysociety.org.uk. One of Britain's most dynamic arts organizations, with membership open to all. "The Poetry Society exists to help

poets and poetry thrive in Britain today. Our members come from all over the world, and their support enables us to promote poetry on a global scale." Publishes *Poetry Review*, Britain's most prominent poetry magazine, and *Poetry News*, the Society's newsletter, as well as books and posters to support poetry in the classroom. Runs the National Poetry Competition and The Foyle Young Poets of the Year Award (for poets aged 11-17), as well as many other competitions, services, and education projects for readers and writers of poetry. More information online.

POETRY SOCIETY OF AMERICA

15 Gramercy Park, New York NY 10003. (212)254-9628. **Website:** www.poetrysociety.org. The Poetry Society of America is a national nonprofit organization for poets and lovers of poetry. All paid members receive *Crossroads: The Journal of the Poetry Society of America*; additional benefits available as membership levels increase. Sponsors readings and lectures as well as the Poetry in Motion program. Provides free-to-join PSA electronic mailing list for news of upcoming events. PSA also sponsors a number of competitions for members and nonmembers.

POETRY SOCIETY OF NEW HAMPSHIRE

170 Browns Ridge Rd., Ossipee NH 03864. **E-mail:** info@poetrysocietyofnewhampshire.org. **Website:** www.poetrysocietyofnewhampshire.org. A statewide organization for anyone interested in poetry. Currently has 200 members. Offerings include annual subscription to quarterly magazine, *The Poet's Touchstone*; critiques, contests, and workshops; public readings; and quarterly meetings with featured poets. Members and nationally known writers give readings that are open to the public. Sponsors open mic readings for members and the public. Additional information available for SASE or by e-mail. "We do sponsor a national contest four times a year. People from all over the country enter and win."

THE POETRY SOCIETY OF SOUTH CAROLINA

P.O. Box 1090, Charleston SC 29402. **E-mail:** president@poetrysocietysc.org. **Website:** www.poetrysocietysc.org. The Poetry Society of South Carolina supports "the reading, writing, study, and enjoyment of poetry." Statewide organization open to anyone interested in poetry. Offers programs in Charleston that are free and open to the public September-May (except for members-only holiday party in Decem-

ber). Currently has 150 members. Membership benefits include discounts to PSSC-sponsored seminars and workshops held in various SC locations; a copy of the annual Yearbook of contest-winning poems; eligibility to read at the open mic and to enter contests without a fee; and an invitation to the annual holiday party. Sponsors a monthly Writers' Group, a January open mic reading featuring PSSC members, a Charleston Poetry Walk during Piccolo Spoleto in June, and a May Forum leading to an audience-selected poetry prize. Sponsors two yearly contests, totaling 20-25 contest categories, some with themes; some are open to all poets, others open only to SC residents or PSSC members. Guidelines available online. Also offers the Skylark Prize, a competition for SC high school students. Sometimes offers a chapbook competition. Members and nationally known writers give readings that are open to the public. Additional information online.

POETRY SOCIETY OF TENNESSEE

18 S. Rembert, Memphis TN 38104. **Website:** poetrysocietytn.org. Purpose is "to promote writing, reading, and appreciation of poetry among members of the society and the community; to improve poetry writing skills of members and local students." State poetry society, with some out-of-state members. Affiliate of National Federation of State Poetry Societies (NFSPS). Current membership about 70. Yearbook contains names, addresses, e-mail addresses of officers and members; winning poems by members and student members; and more. Society activities include programs with speakers; poetry contests, readings, and workshops; one meeting a year dedicated to students; plus Mid-South Poetry Festival first Saturday in October with workshop and prizes. Poetry readings about four times a year in local restaurants and bookstores.

POETRY SOCIETY OF TEXAS

8117 Alderwood Place, Plano TX 75025. **E-mail:** bta1955@hotmail.com. **Website:** www.poetrysocietyoftexas.org. The purpose of the society shall be to secure fuller public recognition of the art of poetry, to encourage the writing of poetry by Texans, and to kindle a finer and more intelligent appreciation of poetry, especially the work of living poets who interpret the spirit and heritage of Texas. Poetry Society of Texas is a member of the National Federation of State Poetry Societies (NFSPS). Has 18 chapters in cities throughout the state. Currently has 300 members. Offerings include annual contests with prizes in excess of $6,000 as well as monthly contests (general and humorous); 8 monthly meetings; annual awards banquet; annual summer conference in a different location each year; and Poetry in Schools with contests at state and local chapter levels. "Our monthly state meetings are held at the Preston Royal Branch of the Dallas Public Library. Our annual awards banquet is held at a nice hotel in Dallas. Our summer conference is held at a site chosen by the hosting chapter. Chapters determine their meeting sites." PST publishes *A Book of the Year*, which presents annual and monthly award-winning poems, coming contest descriptions, minutes of meetings, by-laws of the society, history, and information. Also publishes the *The Bulletin*, a monthly newsletter that features statewide news documenting contest winners, state meeting information, chapter and individual information, news from the NFSPS, and announcements of coming activities and offerings for poets. Members and nationally known writers give readings. "All of our meetings are open to the public." Additional information online.

POETS & WRITERS, INC.

90 Broad St, Suite 2100, New York NY 10004. (212)226-3586. **Website:** www.pw.org. Poets & Writers' mission is "to foster the professional development of poets and writers, to promote communication throughout the U.S. literary community, and to help create an environment in which literature can be appreciated by the widest possible public." The largest nonprofit literary organization in the nation, P&W offers information, support, resources, and exposure to poets, fiction writers, and nonfiction writers at all stages in their careers. Sponsors the Readings/Workshops Program, through which P&W sponsors more than 1,700 literary events in New York, California, and other cities in the U.S. Sponsors the Writers Exchange Contest; the Jacobson Poetry Prize; and the Amy Award. Additional information online.

POETS HOUSE

10 River Terrace, New York NY 10282. (212)431-7920. **Fax:** (212)431-8131. **E-mail:** info@poetshouse.org. **Website:** www.poetshouse.org. Poets House, a national poetry library and literary center, is a "home for all who read and write poetry." Resources include the 70,000-volume poetry collection, conference room, exhibition space, a programming hall, and a Children's Room. Over 200 annual public pro-

grams include panel discussions and lectures, readings, seminars and workshops, and children's events. In addition, Poets House continues its collaboration with public library systems, Poetry in The Branches, a multi-faceted program model to help libraries nationwide create a complete environment for poetry locally (see website for information). Finally, each year Poets House hosts the Poets House Showcase, a comprehensive exhibit of the year's new poetry releases from commercial, university, and independent presses across the country. "Poets House depends, in part, on tax-deductible contributions of its nationwide members." Additional information online.

SCIENCE FICTION POETRY ASSOCIATION

P.O. Box 2472, Dublin CA 94568. **E-mail:** sfpapres@gmail.com. **Website:** www.sfpoetry.com. The Science Fiction Poetry Association was founded "to bring together poets and readers interested in science fiction poetry (poetry with some element of speculation, usually science fiction, fantasy, or horror)." Membership benefits include 6 issues/year of *Star*Line*, a journal filled with poetry, reviews, articles, and more; one issue of the annual Rhysling Anthology of the best science fiction poetry of the previous year; opportunity to nominate one short poem and one long poem to be printed in the anthology, and to vote for which poems should receive that year's Rhysling award; half-priced advertising on the SFPA website, with greater subject matter leeway than non-members; eligibility to vote for SFPA officers (or run for officer); mailings with the latest news. Additional information online.

● SCOTTISH POETRY LIBRARY

5 Crichton's Close, Canongate, Edinburgh EH8 8DT, Scotland. (44)(131)557-2876. **Website:** www.scottishpoetrylibrary.org.uk. A reference information source and free lending library; also lends by post. Arranges poetry-writing workshops throughout Scotland, mainly for young people. The library has a web-based catalog available that allows searches of all the library's resources, including books, magazines, and audio material—over 30,000 items of Scottish and international poetry. Need not be a member to borrow material; memberships available strictly to support the library's work. Benefits include semiannual newsletter, annual report, new publications listings, and book offers. The School of Poets is open to anyone; "at meetings, members divide into small groups in which each participatn reads a poem, which is then analyzed and discussed."

Also offers a Critical Service in which groups of up to 6 poems, not exceeding 200 lines in all, are given critical comment by members of the School: 15 for each critique (with SAE). Additional information online.

TANKA SOCIETY OF AMERICA

439 S. Catalina Ave., #306, Pasadena CA 91106. **Website:** www.tankasocietyofamerica.org. **Contact:** Kathabela Wilson, secretary. The Tanka Society of America, a nonprofit volunteer organization, aims to further the writing, reading, study, and appreciation of tanka poetry in English. Open to anyone interested in tanka. Membership dues for USA, Canada, and International are available online. Membership offerings include the quarterly *Ribbons: Tanka Society of America Journal* and eligibility to submit poems to annual members' anthology. The Tanka Society of American also conducts an annual international tanka competition with cash awards and publication of winning poems. Additional information online.

WISCONSIN FELLOWSHIP OF POETS

Website: www.wfop.org. Statewide organization open to residents and former residents of Wisconsin who are interested in the aims and endeavors of the organization. Currently has 485 members. Sponsors biannual conferences, workshops, contests and awards. Publishes *Wisconsin Poets' Calendar*, poems of Wisconsin (resident) poets. Also publishes *Museletter*, a quarterly newsletter. Members or nationally known writers give readings that are open to the public. Sponsors open mic readings. Additional information online.

WORCESTER COUNTY POETRY ASSOCIATION

P.O. Box 804, Worcester MA 01613. (508)797-4770. **E-mail:** wcpaboard@yahoo.com. **E-mail:** Submissions via Submittable only.. **Website:** worcestercountypoetry.org. **Contact:** Membership Chair. The Worcester County Poetry Association is "open to all who appreciate poetry and wish to support the vibrant Worcester poetry community." Membership benefits include annual subscription to *The Worcester Review*; all WCPA mailings, including broadsides, calendars, and *The Issue*; and fee-free submission to the WCPA Annual Poetry Contest. Additional information online.

WORDS WITHOUT BORDERS

154 Christopher St., Suite 3C, New York NY 10014. **E-mail:** info@wordswithoutborders.org. **Website:** www. wordswithoutborders.org. Words Without Borders opens doors to international exchange through translation, publications, and promotion of the world's best writing. Our ultimate aim is to introduce exciting international writing to the general public—travelers, teachers, students, publishers, and a new generation of eclectic readers— by presenting international literature as a portal through which to explore the world. The heart of WWB's work is its online magazine. Monthly issues feature new selections of contemporary world literature, most of which would never have been accessible to English-speaking readers without WWB. Members and international writers give readings that are open to the public. Finally, our education program WWB Campus, introduces students at both the high school and college levels to a broad spectrum of contemporary international literature. Our goal is to provide content and resources that help educators incorporate contemporary literature in their curricula.

THE WORD WORKS

P.O. Box 42164, Washington DC 20015. **E-mail:** editor@wordworksdc.com. **Website:** www.wordworksdc.com. Word Works is "a nonprofit literary organization publishing contemporary poetry in single-author editions." Membership benefits at the basic level include choice of 2 books from The Word Works book list, newsletter, and 20% discount on additional book orders; in addition to these benefits, sustaining members are eligible for online critique of several poems via e-mail. Sponsors an ongoing poetry reading series, educational programs, and the Hilary Tham Capital Collection. Sponsors The Washington Prize, one of the older ms publishing prizes, and The Jacklyn Potter Young Poets Competition. Additional information online.

THE WRITER'S CENTER

4508 Walsh St., Bethesda MD 20815. (301)654-8664. **Website:** www.writer.org. **Contact:** Ed Spitzberg, executive director. The Writer's Center is a nonprofit community of writers supporting each other in the creation and marketing of literary texts. Annually conducts over 300 workshops; hosts literary events, readings, and conferences; publishes *The Workshop & Event Guide*, a quarterly magazine of articles and writing news for members. Also publishes *Poet Lore*, America's oldest poetry journal. Additional information online.

☁ WRITERS' FEDERATION OF NOVA SCOTIA

1113 Marginal Rd., Halifax NS B3H 4P7, Canada. (902)423-8116. **Fax:** (902)422-0881. **E-mail:** director@ writers.ns.ca. **Website:** www.writers.ns.ca. **Contact:** Marilyn Smulders, executive director. Purpose of organization: "to foster creative writing and the profession of writing in Nova Scotia; to provide advice and assistance to writers at all stages of their careers; and to encourage greater public recognition of Nova Scotian writers and their achievements." Regional organization open to anybody who writes. Currently has 800+ members. Offerings include resource library with over 2,500 titles, promotional services, workshop series, annual festivals, mentorship program. Publishes *Eastword*, a bimonthly newsletter containing "a plethora of information on who's doing what; markets and contests; and current writing events and issues." Members and nationally known writers give readings that are open to the public. Additional information online.

☁ WRITERS' GUILD OF ALBERTA

11759 Groat Rd. NW, Edmonton AB T5M 3K6, Canada. (780)422-8174. **E-mail:** mail@writersguild.ca. **Website:** writersguild.ca. **Contact:** Carol Holmes. Purpose of organization: to support, encourage and promote writers and writing, to safeguard the freedom to write and to read, and to advocate for the well-being of writers in Alberta. Currently has over 1,000 members. Offerings include retreats/conferences; monthly events; bimonthly magazine that includes articles on writing and a market section; weekly electronic bulletin with markets and event listings; and the Stephan G. Stephansson Award for Poetry (Alberta residents only). Holds workshops/conferences. Publishes a newsletter focusing on markets, competitions, contemporary issues related to the literary arts (writing, publishing, censorship, royalties etc.). Sponsors annual literary awards in 5 categories (novel, non-fiction, children's literature, poetry, drama). Awards include $1,500. Open to nonmembers.

THE WRITERS ROOM

740 Broadway at Astor Place, 12th Floor, New York NY 10003. (212)254-6995. **E-mail:** writersroom@ writersroom.org. **Website:** www.writersroom.org. Provides a "home away from home" for any writer who needs space to work. Currently has about 350 members. Emerging and established writers may ap-

ply. Large loft provides desk space, Internet access, storage, and more. Call for application or download from website.

WB YEATS SOCIETY OF NY

National Arts Club, 15 Gramercy Park S., New York NY 10003. **E-mail:** info@yeatssociety.org. **Website:** www.yeatssociety.org. **Contact:** Andrew McGowan, president. Founded "to promote the legacy of Irish poet and Nobel Laureate William Butler Yeats through an annual program of lectures, readings, poetry competition, and special events." National organization open to anyone. Currently has 450 members. Sponsors The Yeats Poetry Prize, annual poetry competition. Also sponsors conferences/workshops. Each April, presents an all-day Saturday program, "A Taste of Yeats Summer School in Ireland." Nationally known writers give readings that are open to the public. Members meet approximately monthly, September to June. Additional information online.

POETS IN EDUCATION

Whether known as PITS (Poets in the Schools), WITS (Writers in the Schools), or similar names, programs exist nationwide that coordinate residencies, classroom visits and other opportunities for experienced poets to share their craft with students. Many state arts agencies include such "arts in education" programs in their activities. Another good source is the National Assembly of State Arts Agencies, which offers an online directory of contact names and addresses for arts education programs state-by-state. The following list is a mere sampling of programs and organizations that link poets with schools.

THE ACADEMY OF AMERICAN POETS, 584 Broadway, Suite 604, New York NY 10012-5243. (212)274-0343. E-mail: academy@poets.org. Website: www.poets.org.

ARKANSAS WRITERS IN THE SCHOOLS, WITS Director, 333 Kimpel Hall, University of Arkansas, Fayetteville AR 72701. (479)575-5991. E-mail: wits@cavern.uark.edu. Website: www.uark.edu/~wits.

CALIFORNIA POETS IN THE SCHOOLS, 1333 Balboa St. #3, San Francisco CA 94118. (415)221-4201. E-mail: info@cpits.org. Website: www.cpits.org.

E-POETS.NETWORK, a collective online cultural center that promotes education through videoconferencing (i.e., "distance learning"); also includes the *Voces y Lugares* project. Website: http://learning.e-poets.net (includes online contact form).

IDAHO WRITERS IN THE SCHOOLS, Log Cabin Literary Center, 801 S. Capitol Blvd., Boise ID 83702. (208)331-8000. E-mail: info@thecabinidaho.org. Website: www.thecabin idaho.org.

INDIANA WRITERS IN THE SCHOOLS, University of Evansville, Dept. of English, 1800 Lincoln Ave., Evansville IN 47722. (812)488-2962. E-mail: rg37@evansville.edu. Website: http://english.evansville.edu/WritersintheSchools.htm.

MICHIGAN CREATIVE WRITERS IN THE SCHOOLS, ArtServe Michigan, 17515 W. Nine Mile Rd., Suite 1025, Southfield MI 48075. (248)557-8288. Website: www.artservemichigan.org.

NATIONAL ASSEMBLY OF STATE ARTS AGENCIES, 1029 Vermont Ave. NW, 2nd Floor, Washington DC 20005. (202)347-6352. E-mail: nasaa@nasaa-arts.org. Website: www.nasaa-arts.org.

NATIONAL ASSOCIATION OF WRITERS IN EDUCATION (NAWE), P.O. Box 1, Sheriff Hutton, York YO60 7YU England. (44)(1653)618429. Website: www.nawe.co.uk.

OREGON WRITERS IN THE SCHOOLS, Literary Arts, 224 NW 13th Ave., Suite 306, Portland OR 97209. (503)227-2583. E-mail: john@literary-arts.org. Website: www.literary-arts.org/wits.

PEN IN THE CLASSROOM (PITC), Pen Center USA, Þco Antioch University, 400 Corporate Pointe, Culver City CA 90230. (310)862-1555. E-mail: pitc@penusa.org. Website: www.penusa.org/go/classroom.

"PICK-A-POET," The Humanities Project, Arlington Public Schools, 1439 N. Quincy St., Arlington VA 22207. (703)228-6299. E-mail: online form. Website: www.humanitiesproject.org.

POTATO HILL POETRY, 6 Pleasant St., Suite 2, South Natick MA 01760. (888)5-POETRY. E-mail: info@potatohill.com. Website: www.potatohill.com (includes online contact form).

SEATTLE WRITERS IN THE SCHOOLS (WITS), Seattle Arts & Lectures, 105 S. Main St., Suite 201, Seattle WA 98104. (206)621-2230. Website: www.lectures.org/wits.html.

TEACHERS & WRITERS COLLABORATIVE, 520 Eighth Ave., Suite 2020, New York NY 10018. (212)691-6590 or (888)BOOKS-TW (book orders). E-mail: info@twc.org. Website: www.twc.org. "A catalog of T&W books is available online, or call toll-free to request a print copy.

TEXAS WRITERS IN THE SCHOOLS, 1523 W. Main, Houston TX 77006. (713)523-3877. E-mail: mail@witshouston.org. Website: www.writersintheschools.org.

WRITERS & ARTISTS IN THE SCHOOLS (WAITS), COMPAS, Landmark Center, Suite 304, 75 Fifth St. West, St. Paul MN 55102-1496. (651)292-3254. E-mail: daniel@compas.org. Website: www.compas.org.

YOUTH VOICES IN INK, Badgerdog Literary Publishing, Inc., P.O. Box 301209, Austin TX 78703-0021. (512)538-1305. E-mail: info@badgerdog.org. Website: www.badgerdog.org

GLOSSARY

//

This glossary is provided as a quick-reference only, briefly covering poetic styles and terms that may turn up in articles and listings in *Poet's Market*.

A3, A4, A5. Metric equivalents of 11¾×16½, 8¼×11¾, and 5⅞×8¼ respectively.

ABSTRACT POEM. Conveys emotion through sound, textures, rhythm and rhyme rather than through the meanings of words.

ACKNOWLEDGMENTS PAGE. A page in a poetry book or chapbook that lists the publications where the poems in the collection were originally published; may be presented as part of the copyright page or as a separate page on its own.

ACROSTIC. Initial letters of each line, read downward, form a word, phrase, or sentence.

ALLITERATION. Close repetition of consonant sounds, especially initial consonant sounds.

ALPHABET POEM. Arranges lines alphabetically according to initial letter.

AMERICAN CINQUAIN. Derived from Japanese haiku and tanka by Adelaide Crapsey; counted syllabic poem of 5 lines of 2-4-6-8-2 syllables, frequently in iambic feet.

ANAPEST. Foot consisting of 2 unstressed syllables followed by a stress.

ANTHOLOGY. A collection of selected writings by various authors.

ASSONANCE. Close repetition of vowel sounds.

AVANT-GARDE. Work at the forefront—cutting edge, unconventional, risk-taking.

ATTACHMENT. A computer file electronically "attached" to an e-mail message.

AUD. Abbreviation for Australian Dollar.

B&W. Black & white (photo or illustration).

BALLAD. Narrative poem often in ballad stanza (4-line stanza with 4 stresses in lines 1 and 3, 3 stresses in lines 2 and 4, which also rhyme).

BALLADE. 3 stanzas rhymed *ababbcbC* (*C* indicates a refrain) with envoi rhymed *bcbC*.

BEAT POETRY. Anti-academic school of poetry born in '50s San Francisco; fast-paced free verse resembling jazz.

BIO. A short biographical statement often requested with a submission.

BLANK VERSE. Unrhymed iambic pentameter.

CAD. Abbreviation for Canadian Dollar.

CAESURA. A deliberate rhetorical, grammatical, or rhythmic pause, break, cut, turn, division, or pivot in poetry.

CAMERA-READY. Poems ready for copy camera platemaking; camera-ready poems usually appear in print exactly as submitted.

CHANT. Poem in which one or more lines are repeated over and over.

CHAPBOOK. A small book of about 24-50 pages.

CIRCULATION. The number of subscribers to a magazine/journal.

CINQUAIN. Any 5-line poem or stanza; also called "quintain" or "quintet." (See also *American cinquain*.)

CLMP. Council of Literary Magazines and Presses; service organization for independent publishers of fiction, poetry, and prose.

CONCRETE POETRY. See *emblematic poem*.

CONFESSIONAL POETRY. Work that uses personal and private details from the poet's own life.

CONSONANCE. See *alliteration*.

CONTRIBUTOR'S COPY. Copy of book or magazine containing a poet's work, sometimes given as payment.

COUPLET. Stanza of 2 lines; pair of rhymed lines.

COVER LETTER. Brief introductory letter accompanying a poetry submission.

COVERSTOCK. Heavier paper used as the cover for a publication.

DACTYL. Foot consisting of a stress followed by 2 unstressed syllables.

DIDACTIC POETRY. Poetry written with the intention to instruct.

DIGEST-SIZED. About 5½×8½, the size of a folded sheet of conventional printer paper.

DOWNLOAD. To "copy" a file, such as a registration form, from a website.

ECLECTIC. Open to a variety of poetic styles (as in "eclectic taste").

EKPHRASTIC POEM. Verbally presents something originally represented in visual art, though more than mere description.

ELECTRONIC MAGAZINE. See *online magazine*.

ELEGY. Lament in verse for someone who has died, or a reflection on the tragic nature of life.

EMBLEMATIC POEM. Words or letters arranged to imitate a shape, often the subject of the poem.

ENJAMBMENT. Continuation of sense and rhythmic movement from one line to the next; also called a "run-on" line.

ENVOI. A brief ending (usually to a ballade or sestina) no more than 4 lines long; summary.

EPIC POETRY. Long narrative poem telling a story central to a society, culture, or nation.

EPIGRAM. Short, satirical poem or saying written to be remembered easily, like a punch-line.

EPIGRAPH. A short verse, note, or quotation that appears at the beginning of a poem or section; usually presents an idea or theme on which the poem elaborates, or contributes background information not reflected in the poem itself.

EPITAPH. Brief verse commemorating a person/group of people who died.

EURO. Currency unit for the 27 member countries of the European Union.

EXPERIMENTAL POETRY. Work that challenges conventional ideas of poetry by exploring new techniques, form, language, and visual presentation.

FAQ. Frequently Asked Questions.

FIBS. Short form based on the mathematical progression known as the Fibonacci sequence; syllable counts for each line are 1/1/2/3/5/8/13 (count for each line is derived by adding the counts for the previous two lines).

FLARF. A malleable term that may refer to 1) poetic and creative text pieces by the Flarflist Collective; any poetry created from search engine (such as Google) results; any intentionally bad, zany, or trivial poetry.

FONT. The style/design of type used in a publication; typeface.

FOOT. Unit of measure in a metrical line of poetry.

FOUND POEM. Text lifted from a non-poetic source such as an ad and presented as a poem.

FREE VERSE. Unmetrical verse (lines not counted for accents, syllables, etc.).

GALLEYS. First typeset version of a poem, magazine, or book/chapbook.

GHAZAL. Persian poetic form of 5-15 unconnected, independent couplets; associative jumps may be made from couplet to couplet.

GLBT. Gay/lesbian/bisexual/transgender (as in "GLBT themes").

GREETING CARD POETRY. Resembles verses in greeting cards; sing-song meter and rhyme.

HAIBUN. Originally, a Japanese form in which elliptical, often autobiographical prose is interspersed with haiku.

HAIKAI NO RENGA. See *renku*.

HAY(NA)KU. A 3-line form, with 1 word in line 1, 2 words in line 2, and 3 words in line 3.

HAIKU. Originally, a Japanese form of a single vertical line with 17 sound symbols in a 5-7-5 pattern. In English, typically a 3-line poem with fewer than 17 syllables in no set pattern, but exhibiting a 2-part juxtapositional structure, seasonal reference, imagistic immediacy, and a moment of keen perception of nature or human nature.

HOKKU. The starting verse of a renga or renku, in 5, 7, and then 5 sound symbols in Japanese; or in three lines, usually totaling fewer than 17 syllables, in English; the precursor for what is now called haiku. (See also *haiku*.)

HONORARIUM. A token payment for published work.

IAMB. Foot consisting of an unstressed syllable followed by a stress.

IAMBIC PENTAMETER. Consists of 5 iambic feet per line.

IMAGIST POETRY. Short, free verse lines that present images without comment or explanation; strongly influenced by haiku and other Oriental forms.

IRC. International Reply Coupon; a publisher can exchange IRCs for postage to return a manuscript to another country.

JPEG. Short for *Joint Photographic Experts Group*; an image compression format that allows digital images to be stored in relatively small files for electronic mailing and viewing on the Internet.

KYRIELLE. French form; 4-line stanza with 8-syllable lines, the final line a refrain.

LANGUAGE POETRY. Attempts to detach words from traditional meanings to produce something new and unprecedented.

LIMERICK. 5-line stanza rhyming *aabba*; pattern of stresses/line is traditionally 3-3-2-2-3; often bawdy or scatalogical.

LINE. Basic compositional unit of a poem; measured in feet if metrical.

LINKED POETRY. Written through the collaboration of 2 or more poets creating a single poetic work.

LONG POEM. Exceeds length and scope of short lyric or narrative poem; defined arbitrarily, often as more than 2 pages or 100 lines.

LYRIC POETRY. Expresses personal emotion; music predominates over narrative or drama.

MAGAZINE-SIZED. About 8½×11, the size of an unfolded sheet of conventional printer paper.

METAPHOR. 2 different things are likened by identifying one as the other (A=B).

METER. The rhythmic measure of a line.

MINUTE. 12-line poem consisting of 60 syllables, with a syllabic line count of 8,4,4,4,8,4,4,4, 8,4,4,4; often consists of rhyming couplets.

MODERNIST POETRY. Work of the early 20th century literary movement that sought to break with the past, rejecting outmoded literary traditions, diction, and form while encouraging innovation and reinvention.

MS. Manuscript.

MSS. Manuscripts.

MULTI-BOOK REVIEW. Several books by the same author or by several authors reviewed in one piece.

NARRATIVE POETRY. Poem that tells a story.

NEW FORMALISM. Contemporary literary movement to revive formal verse.

NONSENSE VERSE. Playful, with language and/or logic that defies ordinary understanding.

OCTAVE. Stanza of 8 lines.

ODE. A songlike, or lyric, poem; can be passionate, rhapsodic, and mystical, or a formal address to a person on a public or state occasion.

OFFSET-PRINTED. Printing method in which ink is transferred from an image-bearing plate to a "blanket" and then from blanket to paper.

ONLINE MAGAZINE. Publication circulated through the Internet or e-mail.

P&H. Postage & handling.

P&P. Postage & packing.

PANTOUM. Malayan poetic form of any length; consists of 4-line stanzas, with lines 2 and 4 of one quatrain repeated as lines 1 and 3 of the next; final stanza reverses lines 1 and 3 of the previous quatrain and uses them as lines 2 and 4; traditionally each stanza rhymes *abab*.

"PAYS IN COPIES." See *contributor's copy*.

PDF. Short for *Portable Document Format*, developed by Adobe Systems, that captures all elements of a printed document as an electronic image, allowing it to be sent by e-mail, viewed online, and printed in its original format.

PERFECT-BOUND. Publication with glued, flat spine; also called "flat-spined."

PETRARCHAN SONNET. Octave rhymes *abbaabba*; sestet may rhyme *cdcdcd*, *cdedce*, *ccdccd*, *cddcdd*, *edecde*, or *cddcee*.

POD. See *print-on-demand*.

PRESS RUN. The total number of copies of a publication printed at one time.

PREVIOUSLY PUBLISHED. Work that has appeared before in print, in any form, for public consumption.

PRINT-ON-DEMAND. Publishing method that allows copies of books to be published as they're requested, rather than all at once in a single press run.

PROSE POEM. Brief prose work with intensity, condensed language, poetic devices, and other poetic elements.

PUBLISHING CREDITS. A poet's magazine publications and book/chapbook titles.

QUATRAIN. Stanza of 4 lines.

QUERY LETTER. Letter written to an editor to raise interest in a proposed project.

READING FEE. A monetary amount charged by an editor or publisher to consider a poetry submission without any obligation to accept the work.

REFRAIN. A repeated line within a poem, similar to the chorus of a song.

REGIONAL POETRY. Work set in a particular locale, imbued with the look, feel, and culture of that place.

RENGA. Originally, a Japanese collaborative form in which 2 or more poets alternate writing 3 lines, then 2 lines for a set number of verses (such as 12, 18, 36, 100, and 1,000). There are specific rules for seasonal progression, placement of moon and flower verses, and other requirements. (See also *linked poetry*.)

RENGAY. An American collaborative 6-verse, thematic linked poetry form, with 3-line and 2-line verses in the following set pattern for 2 or 3 writers (letters represent poets, numbers indicate the lines in each verse): A3-B2-A3-B3-A2-B3 or A3-B2-C3-A2-B3-C2. All verses, unlike renga or renku, must develop at least one common theme.

RENKU. The modern term for renga, and a more popular version of the traditionally more aristocratic renga. (See also *linked poetry*.)

RHYME. Words that sound alike, especially words that end in the same sound.

RHYTHM. The beat and movement of language (rise and fall, repetition and variation, change of pitch, mix of syllables, melody of words).

RICH TEXT FORMAT. Carries the .rtf filename extension. A file format that allows an exchange of text files between different word processor operating systems with most of the formatting preserved.

RIGHTS. A poet's legal property interest in his/her literary work; an editor or publisher may acquire certain rights from the poet to reproduce that work.

RONDEAU. French form of usually 15 lines in 3 parts, rhyming *aabba aabR aabbaR* (*R* indicates a refrain repeating the first word or phrase of the opening line).

ROW. "Rest of world."

ROYALTIES. A percentage of the retail price paid to the author for each copy of a book sold.

SADDLE-STAPLED. A publication folded, then stapled along that fold; also called "saddle-stitched."

SAE. Self-addressed envelope.

SASE. Self-addressed, stamped envelope.

SASP. Self-addressed, stamped postcard.

SENRYU. Originally, a Japanese form, like haiku in form, but chiefly humorous, satirical, or ironic, and typically aimed at human foibles. (See also *haiku* and *zappai*.)

SEQUENCE. A group or progression of poems, often numbered as a series.

SESTET. Stanza of 6 lines.

SESTINA. Fixed form of 39 lines (6 unrhymed stanzas of 6 lines each, then an ending 3-line stanza), each stanza repeating the same 6 non-rhyming end-words in a different order; all 6 end-words appear in the final 3-line stanza.

SHAKESPEAREAN SONNET. Rhymes *abab cdcd efef gg*.

SIJO. Originally a Korean narrative or thematic lyric form. The first line introduces a situation or problem that is countered or developed in line 2, and concluded with a twist in line 3. Lines average 14-16 syllables in length.

SIMILE. Comparison that uses a linking word (*like*, *as*, *such as*, *how*) to clarify the similarities.

SIMULTANEOUS SUBMISSION. Submission of the same manuscript to more than one publisher at the same time.

SONNET. 14-line poem (traditionally an octave and sestet) rhymed in iambic pentameter; often presents an argument but may also present a description, story, or meditation.

SPONDEE. Foot consisting of 2 stressed syllables.

STANZA. Group of lines making up a single unit; like a paragraph in prose.

STROPHE. Often used to mean "stanza"; also a stanza of irregular line lengths.

SUBSIDY PRESS. Publisher who requires the poet to pay all costs, including typesetting, production, and printing; sometimes called a "vanity publisher."

SURREALISTIC POETRY. Of the artistic movement stressing the importance of dreams and the subconscious, nonrational thought, free associations, and startling imagery/juxtapositions.

TABLOID-SIZED. 11×15 or larger, the size of an ordinary newspaper folded and turned sideways.

TANKA. Originally, a Japanese form in one or 2 vertical lines with 31 sound symbols in a 5-7-5-7-7 pattern. In English, typically a 5-line lyrical poem with fewer than 31 syllables in no set syllable pattern, but exhibiting a caesura, turn, or pivot, and often more emotional and conversational than haiku.

TERCET. Stanza or poem of 3 lines.

TERZA RIMA. Series of 3-line stanzas with interwoven rhyme scheme (*aba*, *bcb*, *cdc* . . .).

TEXT FILE. A file containing only textual characters (i.e., no graphics or special formats).

TROCHEE. Foot consisting of a stress followed by an unstressed syllable.

UNSOLICITED MANUSCRIPT. A manuscript an editor did not ask specifically to receive.

URL. Stands for "Uniform Resource Locator," the address of an Internet resource (i.e., file).

USD. Abbreviation for United States Dollar.

VILLANELLE. French form of 19 lines (5 tercets and a quatrain); line 1 serves as one refrain (repeated in lines 6, 12, 18), line 3 as a second refrain (repeated in lines 9, 15, 19); traditionally, refrains rhyme with each other and with the opening line of each stanza.

VISUAL POEM. See *emblematic poem*.

WAKA. Literally, "Japanese poem," the precursor for what is now called tanka. (See also *tanka*.)

WAR POETRY. Poems written about warfare and military life; often written by past and current soldiers; may glorify war, recount exploits, or demonstrate the horrors of war.

ZAPPAI. Originally Japanese; an unliterary, often superficial witticism masquerading as haiku or senryu; formal term for joke haiku or other pseudo-haiko.

ZEUGMA. A figure of speech in which a single word (or, occasionally, a phrase) is related in one way to words that precede it, and in another way to words that follow it.

GENERAL INDEX

SUBJECT INDEX

Gothic/Horror/Dark Poetry

Hispanic/Latino

Humor/Satire

Poetry for Children

Poetry for Teens

Political

Regional

Specialized various

Spirituality/Inspirational

Writing